# BIZ~JET '83

*HS 125-700B 7T-VCW photo:*                                              *British Aerospace*

## BRIAN GATES

This edition ©1983    Brian Gates


Published by Aviation Data Centre Ltd.
Unit Four, Browells Lane,
Feltham, Middlesex, England.

and

Aviation Data Centre
41B Luke Drive, H.I.A., Middletown
PA 17057. USA.




ISBN No. 0 946141 04 5

Library of Congress Card No. 82 72627

All rights reserved, no part of this book may be reproduced or transmitted in any form or
by any means, electronic or mechanical including photocopy, recording or by any
information retrieval system, without permission in writing from the publisher.

Printed in Great Britain by
Intergraphic Print (UK) Ltd,. Unit Four, Browells Lane,
Feltham, Middlesex. England.

# INTRODUCTION

1982 can only be described as a very difficult year for everyone associated with business aviation. Companies flew less hours, new aircraft sales decreased, manufacturers cut work forces and closed plants. However, the recent lowering of interests rates should stimulate world economies out of recession, and benefit corporate aviation in the coming year.

Cessna Aircraft Co. rolled-out the first production Citation III from its Wichita plant on September 15th 1982. Orders for this model stand at 140 with deliveries commencing early next year. Citations now total 1100 worldwide. Gates Learjet Corp. have announced the delivery of three 'Special Mission' sea patrol 35As to the Finnish Air Force. In 1983 they plan to expand the SM role by introducing an ECM trainer and early warning demonstrator. Also planned are three longer range versions of the series 55. Competing with the Dee Howard XR Learjets is the Robertson TF-25, which has aerodynamic mods plus JT15D-5 turbofans, and claims an estimated 40% increased range. Deliveries of Canadair's 'transcontinental widebody' CL-600 Challengers are well underway. The wingletted GE turbofanned, intercontinental longer range CL-601 made its first flight on April 10th 1982, and is continuing its certification programme at Mojave, Ca Gulfstream-American is maintaining a steady delivery rate of its G-3 including three multi-mission platforms with cargo doors and other systems for the Royal Danish Air Force. Their G-2B programme now has 34 orders. Dassault's Falcon 200 was certified by the FAA on July 6th 1982 and exceeded its performance guarantee with a range of 2600nm with NBAA reserves, and a significant reduction in take-off runway requirements. The first delivery of the fuel efficient, high cruising speed, Electronic Flight Instrument System equipped Falcon 100 is expected soon. Falcon 50 deliveries now exceed 100. FEDEX have converted one of their cargo Falcons (N22FE) to a 6 passenger business jet with original windows replaced, with plans for further conversions as orders dictate. Following extensive flight testing and FAA certification Mitsubishi Diamond deliveries have now begun. Israel Aircraft Industries' Astra is expected to be rolled-out during September 1983 with an anticipated first flight date of early 1984. Deliveries of the British Aerospace HS 125 are steady. Worldwide sales now stand at 540, with 314 going to North America. As well as continuing to service and support the existing Sabreliner fleet, Rockwell is proceeding with its 40R life extension programme. However the go-ahead for the 60TF (Series 65 wing on customer aircraft and 731 powerplant) has for the moment been withheld. Demand for Boeing airliners remains good. Customers appreciating that it can often be less expensive to purchase, convert and operate an airliner than a top of the line business jet.

Presenting an accurate list of Mexican activity is still difficult, and any information, sightings or photographs of Mexican aircraft would be appreciated .

This 15th edition maintains the same format as previous issues. Several more brief-format production lists have been added. Cessna pre-delivery data is from official sources and may differ from previous listings. Some strange s/ns amongst the 551 series may be noted. This is a complicated move by Cessna to eventually match up Unit No. and s/n. Also note that some Citations may have changed from SP to Standard and v-v with a consequent change in s/n. Correspondence concerning the contents of Biz-Jet is welcomed. Write to: Brian Gates, 11 Oaklands Drive, Wokingham, RG11 2SA, England.

01 November 1982

# CONTENTS

# ACKNOWLEDGEMENTS

My sincere thanks are due to the following for their invaluable help: Falcon Jet Corp., Dassault International, Omni International, Cessna Aircraft Company, Rockwell International Corp., Gulfstream American Corp., Atlantic Aviation Corp., IATS Inc., Aviation Research, American Register Quarterly, Aviation Letter, A. Heumann for Swiss allocations, Nelson de Barros Pereira Jr. for Brasilian allocations, D. Daw and W. Bigsworth for Australian data, F. Lovenvig for Scandinavian information, N. Hartoch, Alex Kvassay, A. Mawman, P. Longley, J. Birch and to many other enthusiasts who provided a little but essential data. The cover photographs were provided by British Aerospace Inc. and British Aerospace Aircraft Group, Hatfield.

# FIRST FLIGHT DATES

| | | | |
|---|---|---|---|
| MS 760 Paris | 29/JUL/54 | JetStar-731 | 10/JUL/74 |
| JetStar | 04/SEP/57 | Beech 200 | 12/MAR/75 |
| Sabreliner | 16/SEP/58 | Westwind-1124 | 21/JUL/75 |
| DH 125 | 13/AUG/62 | JetStar 2 | 18/AUG/76 |
| Jet Commander | 27/JAN/63 | Falcon 50 | 07/NOV/76 |
| Mystere 20 | 04/MAY/63 | Citation 2 | 31/JAN/77 |
| Learjet | 07/OCT/63 | Sabre-65 | 29/JUN/77 |
| HFB 320 | 21/APR/64 | Learjet 28 | 24/AUG/77 |
| PD 808 | 29/AUG/64 | Falcon 20G | 28/NOV/77 |
| Gulfstream 2 | 02/OCT/66 | HS 125/731 | 07/SEP/78 |
| Citation | 15/SEP/69 | Sabre-60A | 08/SEP/78 |
| Sabre-75 | 04/DEC/69 | MU-300 | 29/AUG/78 |
| Corvette | 16/JUL/70 | Challenger | 08/NOV/78 |
| Westwind-1123 | 28/SEP/70 | Learjet 55 | 19/APR/79 |
| Falcon 10 | 01/DEC/70 | Citation 3 | 30/MAY/79 |
| Sabre-75A | 18/OCT/72 | Westwind 2 | |
| Learjet 35/36 | 04/JAN/73 | Gulfstream 3 | 02/DEC/79 |
| | | Challenger 601 | 10/APR/82 |

The following is a list of civilian and military 'Executive Jets' operating and registered throughout the world. Each aircraft is listed by registration, type, serial/constructors number, owner/operator and previous identity.

## CIVIL OPERATED

### SWAZILAND

| | | | | |
|---|---|---|---|---|
| 3D-AAC | Gulfstream 2 | 136 | Timber Sales (Pty) Ltd. Piggs Peak. | ZS-JIS/N65M/N874GA |
| 3D-ABZ | HS 125/403B | 25242 | Anglo Vaal, Lanseria, RSA. | G-BDKF/VH-TOM/G-5-20 |
| 3D-ACB | Falcon 10 | 21 | Rembrandt Tobacco, Capetown, RSA. | (HB-VDT)/F-WJMK |
| 3D-ACQ | Citation | 550-0165 | DIAMCOR Ltd. | N98871 |
| 3D-ACR | Citation | 500-0268 | Premier Milling, Lanseria, RSA. | ZS-JKR/N5268J |
| 3D-ACT | Citation | 550-0237 | Peak Timber Sales (Pty) Ltd. Piggs Peak. | N6804M |
| 3D-ART | Falcon 10 | 61 | Rembrandt Tobacco, ⸴h   wn, RSA. F-BFDG/F-BIPF/F-WZGD/D-CBMB/F-WPUV |
| 3D-AVH | Citation | 550-0308 | Atair, Lanseria, RSA. | N68891 |
| 3D-AVL | HS 125/F400B | 25254 | Anglo Vaal, Lanseria, RSA. | G-AYLG |

### YEMEN

| | | | |
|---|---|---|---|
| 4W-ACM | HS 125/700B | 7178 | Shaher Traders, Sana'a. |

### ISRAEL

| | | | | |
|---|---|---|---|---|
| 4X-CJA | Westwind-Sea Scan | 154 | Israel Aircraft Industries, Tel Aviv. | |
| 4X-CJP | Westwind 1124 | 376 | Israel Aircraft Industries, Tel Aviv. | 4X-CUN |
| 4X-COA | Jet Commander | 71 | IAI Avionics Development Aircraft. | N721GB/N150HR/N150CT/N150CM /N1500M |
| 4X-CTJ | Westwind Two | 342 | Israel Aircraft Industries, Tel Aviv. | |
| 4X-CTQ | Westwind 1124 | 349 | Israel Aircraft Industries, Tel Aviv. | |

### LIBYA

| | | | | |
|---|---|---|---|---|
| 5A-DAF | Mystere 20C | 128 | Libyan Arab Airlines, Benghazi. | F-WMKJ |
| 5A-DAG | Mystere 20C | 143 | Libyan Arab Airlines, Benghazi. | F-WMKH |
| 5A-DAJ | JetStar-8 | 5136 | LAA/Government of Libya, Tripoli. | LAAF001/N5500L |
| 5A-DAK | B 707-3L5C | 21228 | Government of Libya, Tripoli. | |
| 5A-DAR | JetStar 2 | 5221 | Government of Libya, Tripoli. | N5547L |
| 5A-DCK | Corvette | 38 | Government of Libya, Tripoli. | |
| 5A-DCM | Falcon 50 | 68 | Govt. of Libya, Tripoli. | |
| 5A-DCO | Mystere 20 | 190 | Libyan Arab Airlines, Benghazi. | 5A-DAH/LAAF002/F-WNGN |
| 5A-DDR | Gulfstream 2 | 240 | Govt. of Libya, Tripoli. | |
| 5A-DDS | Gulfstream 2 | 242 | Govt. of Libya, Tripoli. | |

### TANZANIA

| | | | | |
|---|---|---|---|---|
| 5H-CCM | F-28-3000 | 11137 | Government of Tanzania, Dar es Salaam. | PH-ZBS/PH-EXS |
| 5H-SMZ | HS 125/700B | 7172 | Government of Zanzibar. | G-BKFS/5H-SMZ |

### NIGERIA

| | | | | |
|---|---|---|---|---|
| 5N-AGN | F-28-1000 | 11049 | Federal Military Government, Lagos. | PH-EXG/PH-EXD |
| 5N-AGV | Gulfstream 2 | 177 | Federal Military Government, Lagos. | N17587 |
| 5N-AGY | B 727-2N5 | 22825 | Federal Military Government, Lagos. | |
| 5N-ALH | HS 125/1B | 25089 | Aero Contractors (Nigeria) Ltd. | OO-SKJ/G-ATPB |
| 5N-ALX | HS 125/600B | 6012 | Aero Contractors (Nigeria) Ltd. | G-BAYT/G-5-17 |
| 5N-ALY | HS 125/1B-522 | 25106 | Aero Contractors (Nigeria) Ltd. | G-AWUF/HZ-BIN |
| 5N-AMK | HS 125/1-522 | 25010 | RCN, Lagos. | G-ASSM |
| 5N-AML | Gulfstream 2 | 186 | Al Hadji Deribe, Lagos. | D-AFKG/(D-ACVG)/N17582 |
| 5N-AMR | Citation | 550-0045 | I Rabiu & Sons. Kano. | N4CR/N4CH/N3284M |
| 5N-ANG | HS 125/600B | 6050 | Federal Military Government, Lagos. | G-5-12 |
| 5N-AOC | Learjet | 25D-322 | AIC Co. Ltd. Lagos. | |
| 5N-APN | Citation | 500-0286 | Nigerian Police Force, Lagos. | N286CC/N5286J |
| 5N-AQY | HS 125/403B | 25231 | Edok-Eter-Mandilas, Lagos. | G-BEME/D-CBVW |
| 5N-ASQ | Learjet | 25D-344 | Imani and Sons. | N37943/N3798L |

| Regis-tration | Type | C/N | Owner/Operator | Previous Identities |
|---|---|---|---|---|
| 5N-AVJ | HS 125/700B | 7118 | Nigerian National Petroleum Co. Lagos. | (G-BIHZ) |
| 5N-AVK | HS 125/700B | 7160 | Federal Ministry of Aviation (CAFU), Lagos. | G-5-19 |
| 5N-AVL | Citation | 500-0417 | Civil Aviation Flying Unit. | |
| 5N-AVM | Citation | 500-0654 | Civil Aviation Flying Unit. | N2626Z |
| 5N-AVV | HS 125/3B | 25138 | Intercontinental Airlines, Lagos. | I-BOGI/HB-VBN/G-AVVA/G-5-16 |
| 5N-AWC | HS 125/1B | 25025 | C and C Construction. | F-BOHU/HB-VAR/D-COME |
| 5N-AYK | HS 125/600B | 6060 | Yakamata Air Services, Kano. | G-BFIC/HZ-MF1/G-5-12 |
| 5N-AYM | Mystere 20F | 427 | Imani & Sons. | F-WROV |
| 5N- | HS 125/700B | 7181 | | |
| 5N- | Falcon 50 | 110 | | F-WPXG |
| G-ASNU | HS 125/1 | 25005 | Flintgrange Ltd/FANZ Organisation. | D-COMA/(D-CFKG)/G-ASNU |
| G-ASSI | HS 125/1 | 25008 | Panatrade Ltd, Lagos. | |
| G-AVRF | HS 125/3B | 25133 | Flintgrange Ltd/FANZ Organisation. | |
| G-AVXK | HS 125/3B-RA | 25143 | OGI Cargo Co. | D-CHTH/G-AVXK/G-5-18 |
| G-BART | HS 125/600B | 6005 | Cross Oceans Ltd/Chief H. O. Lawson. | |
| G-GGAE | HS 125/3B-RA | 25157 | Afrotek. | VR-BGD/D-CAMB |
| G-MKOA | HS 125/F403B | 25227 | Chief M K O Abiola/RCN, Lagos. | G-AYFM |
| N310AD | JetStar-6 | 5051 | Indimi Enterprises. | N31S/N44MF/N400KC/N9217R |
| N727UD | B 727-30 | 18367 | United Air Services Dantata Group, Kano. | N2703J/D-ABIL |
| N1039 | Gulfstream 2 | 40 | Dantata, Kano. | (N5040)/N1040 |

MAURITANIA

| | | | | |
|---|---|---|---|---|
| 5T-RIM | Caravelle 6R | 91 | Government of Islamic Republic of Mauritania. | 5T-MAL/5T-CJW/OY-SBV /PH-TVZ/OY-SBV/N1006U |

TOGO

| | | | | |
|---|---|---|---|---|
| 5V-TAD | B 720-047B | 19523 | Government of Togo, Lome. | N3167 |
| 5V-TAE | Falcon 10 | 167 | Government of Togo, Lome. | N39K/N233FJ/F-WZGT |

UGANDA

| | | | | |
|---|---|---|---|---|
| 5X-UPF | Gulfstream 2TT | 133 | Government of Uganda, Kampala. | N17583/N88906 |

KENYA

| | | | | |
|---|---|---|---|---|
| N101PG | Learjet | 35A-228 | Geosurvey International Inc. Nairobi. | |
| N930GL | Learjet | 35A-330 | Boscovic Aviation Charter Ltd. Nairobi. | |

SENEGAL

| | | | | |
|---|---|---|---|---|
| 6V-AAR | Caravelle 3 | 5 | Government of Senegal Dakar. | 6V-ACP/F-BHRC |
| 6V-AEA | Corvette | 8 | ASECNA/Africair, Dakar. | F-WPTT |
| 6V-AEF | B 727-2M1 | 21091 | Government of Senegal, Dakar. | N40104/(PK-PJP)/N8284V |

MALAWI

| | | | | |
|---|---|---|---|---|
| 7Q- | Citation | 501-0200 | Limbe Leaf Tobacco Co. | N6783L |

ALGERIA

| | | | | |
|---|---|---|---|---|
| 7T-VCW | HS 125/700B | 7163 | Etablissement National pour l'Exploitation Meteorlogique et Aeronautique | G-5-12 |
| 7T-VRP | Mystere 20E | 271 | Government of Algeria, Boufarik. | F-WNGN |

BARBADOS

| | | | | |
|---|---|---|---|---|
| 8P-BAR | Citation | 550-0239 | Barclays Bank International ltd, Bridgetown. | N6803L |

ZAMBIA

| | | | | |
|---|---|---|---|---|
| 9J-ADU | Citation | 500-0153 | Nchanga Consolidated Copper Mines. Lusaka. | |
| 9J-AEJ | Citation | 500-0353 | Mines Air Service Ltd Lusaka. | (N5359J) |
| 9J-SAS | HS 125/1B | 25067 | Safari Air Services. | ZS-MAN/9J-RAN |

| Regis-tration | Type | C/N | Owner/Operator | Previous Identities |
|---|---|---|---|---|

**KUWAIT**

| | | | | |
|---|---|---|---|---|
| 9K-AEB | Gulfstream 2 | 244 | Govt of Kuwait. | N17584 |
| 9K-AEC | Gulfstream 2 | 248 | Govt of Kuwait. | N17589 |
| 9K-AEF | Falcon 50 | 40 | Gulf International Group. | F-WZHG |
| 9K-AGA | HS 125/700B | 7184 | Kuwait Airways | G-5-12 |
| 9K-AGB | HS 125/700B | 7187 | Kuwait Airways | |
| VR-BAT | B 727-76 | 20371 | Kirby Leasing Inc. Houston,Tx. | VH-TJF |
| VR-BOX | B 737-269 | 21206 | Alghanim/Constance Leasing/Star Jet Corp. Kuwait. | 9K-ACV |
| VR-CBA | B 727-30 | 18935 | Muburak Al Hassawi. | N833N/N90557/D-ABIT |

**MALAYSIA**

| | | | | |
|---|---|---|---|---|
| 9M-SSB | HS 125/403B | 25215 | Bristows-Malaysia. | G-BHFT/HB-VBZ |
| 9M-WAN | Citation | 550-0272 | Hornbill Skyways | N68633 |

**ZAIRE**

| | | | | |
|---|---|---|---|---|
| 9Q-CCF | HS 125/403B | 25247 | K.D.L. Railways. | G-AYRR |
| 9Q-CFW | HS 125/600B | 6031 | SOZACOM. | G-5-14 |
| 9Q-CHD | HS 125/403B | 25217 | Government of Republic of Zaire, Kinshasa. | G-AXYJ |
| 9Q-CKZ | Mystere 20CC | 73 | Government of Republic of Zaire, Kinshasa. | VH-BIZ/(F-BHRB)/VH-BIZ /F-WJML |
| 9Q-CLY | B 707-336C | 20517 | GKN-EMZ Enterprises Minieres du Zaire. | G-AYLT |

**SINGAPORE**

| | | | | |
|---|---|---|---|---|
| N78MD | Falcon 10 | 18 | J Ray McDermott & Co Inc. Singapore. | N111FJ/F-WJMJ |
| N482U | Learjet | 35A-482 | Upali (USA) Inc/ARMCO Pacific Ltd. Singapore. | |
| N750CS | Sabre-65 | 465-37 | Coastal Petroleum (Far East) Ltd. Singapore. | |
| N1728E | Citation | 501-0147 | Heli-Orient/Asian Aviation Services Inc. | |
| N2649E | Citation | 550-0144 | Heli-Orient/Asian Aviation Services Inc. | |
| N26178 | Citation | 550-0160 | Upali-USA Inc. NYC. | (9V-PUW) |
| N26507 | Citation | 501-0142 | Heli-Orient/Asian Aviation Services Inc. | |
| N68615 | Citation | 550-0251 | Heli-Orient/Asian Aviation Services Inc. | |

**RWANDA**

| | | | | |
|---|---|---|---|---|
| 9XR-CH | Caravelle 3 | 209 | Government of Rwanda, Kigali. | F-BUFM/YU-AJE/F-BRUJ/LN-KLN |

**OMAN**

| | | | | |
|---|---|---|---|---|
| A40-AA | Gulfstream 2TT | 183 | Sultan H.M. Qaboos bin Said, Seeb. | N17581 |
| A40-AB | VC 10/1103 | 820 | Sultan H.M. Oaboos bin Said, Seeb. | G-ASIX |
| A40-CA | Learjet | 35A-165 | Inspector General of Police, Oman. | N40144 |
| A40-CF | B 727-30 | 18369 | Inspector General of Police, Oman. | D-ABIN |
| A40-GA | Mystere 20E | 285 | C-in-C, Sultan of Oman Air Force. | A40-AA/F-WRQT |
| A40-HMQ | DC-8-73 | 46149 | Sultan H.M. Oaboos bin Said, Seeb. | A40-HM/N803WA/(N6167A) |

**UNITED ARAB EMIRATES**

| | | | | |
|---|---|---|---|---|
| A6-AAA | B 737-2P6 | 21613 | Abu Dhabi Development Co. | (A6-HHK)/(A40-BI) |
| A6-CKZ | Gulfstream 3 | 317 | Government of UAE. | N344GA/C-GKRL |
| A6-DPA | B 707-330B | 20123 | Government of UAE. | D-ABUJ |
| A6-HEM | Mystere 20F | 344 | Dubai Air Wing, UAE. | F-WRQP |
| A6-HHM | B 727-264 | 22982 | Government of Dubai, UAE. | N4554N |
| A6-HHR | B 720-023B | 18016 | Government of Abu Dhabi. (To 70-ACP Alyemda JUN/82) | N7530A |
| A6-HHZ | Gulfstream 2 | 164 | Sheikh Zayed, Abu Dhabi. | 9K-ACX/N17582 |
| A6-HPZ | B 707-3L6B | 21049 | Sheikh Zayed, Abu Dhabi. | (A6-HHP)/N62393/9M-TDM/N62393 |
| A6-HRM | B 707-3L6C | 21096 | Ruler of Dubai (r/c Falcon One). | G-CDHW/9M-TMS/N48055 |
| A6-HRR | B 727-2M7 | 21951 | Dubai Air Wing, UAE. | N741RW |
| A6-RAK | HS 125/600B | 6063 | Government of Ras Al Khaimah. | G-5-13 |
| A6-UAE | B 707-330B | 18931 | Government of UAE. | D-ABUK |
| A6- | Gulfstream 3 | 356 | Government of Dubai, UAE. | |

| Registration | Type | C/N | Owner/Operator | Previous Identities |
|---|---|---|---|---|
| G-ARVF | VC 10/1101 | 808 | Sheikh Zayed, Abu Dhabi. (WFU ?) | |
| N82MD | Falcon 10 | 77 | J Ray McDermott & Co. Inc. Dubai | N158FJ/F-WNGN |
| N829GA | Gulfstream 2 | 245 | Texas Commerce Bank, Houston, Tx./Emirates Air Service. | |

**QATAR**

| Registration | Type | C/N | Owner/Operator | Previous Identities |
|---|---|---|---|---|
| A7-AAA | B 707-3P1C | 21334 | Ruler of Qatar, Doha. (r/c Amiri One). | |
| A7-AAB | B 727-2P1 | 21595 | Qatari Government, Doha. (r/c Amiri Two). | |
| A7- | B 707-336C | 20375 | Ruler of Qatar, Doha (r/c Amiri Three). | G-AXGX |

**BAHRAIN**

| Registration | Type | C/N | Owner/Operator | Previous Identities |
|---|---|---|---|---|
| A9C-BA | B 727-2M7 | 21824 | Government of Bahrain. (r/c Bahraini One) | N740RW |
| A9C-BG | Gulfstream 2TT | 202 | Government of Bahrain. (r/c Bahraini Two) | |

**BAHAMAS**

| Registration | Type | C/N | Owner/Operator | Previous Identities |
|---|---|---|---|---|
| C6-BEJ | Gulfstream 2 | 194 | Chartair/Count Agusta. | HB-IMW |
| C6-BEN | Falcon 10 | 109 | Petrocolor Services Inc. New York. | N77NR/N183FJ/F-WNGD |
| C6-BER | Falcon 50 | 20 | Petrocolor Services Inc. New York. | N50FR/F-WZHK |
| C6-BET | HS 125/700B | 7054 | Norwest S.A. Ltd. Nassau. | |
| C6-BEV | MS 760 Paris-2 | 111 | | I-FINR |
| C6-BPC | DH 125/1A | 25016 | Causba Corp. | C-FOPC/CF-RWA/G-ASSL |

**MOZAMBIQUE**

| Registration | Type | C/N | Owner/Operator | Previous Identities |
|---|---|---|---|---|
| C9-TAC | HS 125/700B | 7175 | Empresa Nacional de Transporte e Trabalho Aereo. | (C9-TTA) |

**CHILE**

| Registration | Type | C/N | Owner/Operator | Previous Identities |
|---|---|---|---|---|
| CC-ECN | Citation | 550-0104 | Aeroservicios Ltd. | N2633N |
| CC-ECO | Learjet | 35-050 | CORFO=Corporacion de Fomento, Santiago. | |
| CC-ECP | Learjet | 35-066 | CORFO=Corporacion de Fomento, Santiago. operated by Grupo 6 (Transport & Survey), Punta Arenas. | |

**CANADA**

| Registration | Type | C/N | Owner/Operator | Previous Identities |
|---|---|---|---|---|
| C-FALC | DH 125/731 | 25087 | Aluminium Co. of Canada, Montreal. | G-ATOX |
| C-FANL | DH 125/731 | 25042 | The Molson Companies Ltd. Toronto. | |
| C-FAOS | BH 125/400A | NA771 | Algoma Steel Corp. Sault-Ste-Marie. | N68BH |
| C-FBAX | Citation | 500-0020 | Fraser Co. Ltd Edmundston, N.B. | N520CC |
| C-FBCL | Citation | 500-0042 | Government of British Columbia, Victoria. | N542CC |
| C-FBCM | Citation | 500-0071 | Government of British Columbia, Victoria. | N571CC |
| C-FBFP | Learjet | 35-038 | Business Flights Ltd. Calgary. | VH-ELJ/(VH-UDC) |
| C-FBNK | BH-125/731 | NA746 | Bank of Montreal/Execaire Aviation. | N42BH |
| C-FCFP | Citation | 500-0125 | Renaissance Resources Ltd, Calgary. | |
| C-FCPW | Citation Eagle | 500-0002 | Flexi-Coil Ltd. Saskatoon. | N82020 |
| C-FCSS | Learjet | 24B-197 | Interflite Aviation Services, Mount Hope. | N953GA |
| C-FDAC | Learjet | 25B-091 | Kingston Air Service, Norman Rogers Airport. | N96MJ/D-CBPD/N500MJ /N500CD/N500CA |
| C-FDOM | DH 125/731 | 25018 | Execaire Aviation, Montreal. | |
| C-FDTF | JetStar-6 | 5088 | Canadian MOT, Ottawa. | N9244R |
| C-FDTM | JetStar-6 | 5052 | Canadian MOT, Ottawa. | N66CR/N300P/N9218R |
| C-FDTX | JetStar-6 | 5018 | Canadian MOT, Ottawa. | N9287R |
| C-FENJ | Citation Eagle | 500-0122 | Canadian International Paper Co. Montreal. | N122CC |
| C-FETN | JetStar-6 | 5021 | Canadian MOT, Ottawa. | |
| C-FFBC | Jet Commander | 119 | Futura Airlines Ltd, Vancouver. | |
| C-FFNM | Gulfstream 2 | 52 | Falconbridge Nickel Mines, Toronto. | |
| C-FHLL | DH 125/1A | 25034 | Labrador Mining & Exploration Co. Toronto. | |
| C-FHSS | BH 125/600A | 6003 | Simpsons-Sears Ltd. Toronto. | N80BH |
| C-FIOT | Gulfstream 2 | 78 | Imperial Oil Ltd. Toronto. | PH-FJP/N17585 |
| C-FIPG | HS 125/700A | NA0294 | Interprovincial Pipeline, Edmonton. | G-BIMY |
| C-FIPJ | DH 125/1A | 25053 | Sceptre Resources Ltd. Calgary. | CF-IPG |
| C-FJES | Falcon 20F | 236 | Seagrams/Execaire Aviation, Montreal. | (N4416F)/F-WPXK |
| C-FMDB | DH 125/731 | 25075 | Quebec North Shore & Labrador Railway, Montreal. | N666M/G-ATLJ |
| C-FNCG | Sabre-40 | 282-90 | NORCEN Energy Resources Ltd. Toronto. | N928R |
| C-FNER | DH 125/731 | NA714 | Toronto Dominion Bank/Execaire Aviation. | G-AWPD |
| C-FNOR | Gulfstream 2 | 54 | Noranda Mines Ltd. Toronto. | N123H |
| C-FOIL | Westwind 1124 | 336 | Ocelot Industries, Calgary. | N245S/4X-CTD |

| Registration | Type | C/N | Owner/Operator | Previous Identities |
|---|---|---|---|---|
| C-FPPN | BH 125/731 | NA773 | West Coast Transmission, Vancouver. | N70BH |
| C-FPQG | DH 125/1A | 25036 | Government of Quebec , Quebec City. | |
| C-FPXD | B 727-171C | 19859 | Panarctic Oils Ltd. Calgary. | N1727T |
| C-FRBC | JetStar-8 | 5160 | Royal Bank of Canada, Montreal. | N5524L |
| C-FROC | Gulfstream 2 | 134 | Ranger Oil (Canada) Ltd. Calgary. | N806CC |
| C-FROX | Learjet | 25C-070 | Ranger Oil (Canada) Ltd. Calgary. | N255GL |
| C-FSDH | DH 125/731 | NA724 | Ledair Ltd. Montreal. | |
| C-FSEN | DH 125/1A | 25027 | Government of Quebec (Air Ambulance) | |
| C-FSIM | DH 125/1A | 25039 | Capital 111 Control Corp. Winnipeg. | |
| C-FSUN | Citation Eagle | 500-0292 | Suncor Inc. Calgary. | N255LJ/N10FM/N5292J |
| C-FTXT | Learjet | 25-057 | Business Flights Ltd. Calgary. | |
| C-FWEC | Jet Commander | 115 | International Nickel Ltd. Toronto. | |
| C-FWOA | Jet Commander | 21 | Canadian Intercity Airspeed, Winnipeg. | N252R |
| C-FWOS | DH 125/731 | 25159 | Camflo Mines Ltd. Toronto. | G-AVZL |
| C-FWRA | Falcon 20C | 110 | Argus Corp. Toronto. | N989F/F-WMKG |
| C-FYPB | Falcon 20F | 254 | Tele-Direct/Execaire Aviation, Montreal. | N4423F/F-WNGO |
| C-GABX | HS 125/700A | NA0233 | Nova An Alberta Corp. Calgary. | G-BFZI |
| C-GATU | JetStar-8 | 5143 | Cathton Holdings Ltd. Edmonton. | N5878D/N5070L/N31UT/N100UA/N5507L |
| C-GAZU | JetStar-731 | 49/5083 | Allarco Developments, Edmonton. | N257HA/N257H/N161LM/N141LM/N208L |
| C-GBCB | Citation | 550-0051 | Government of British Columbia, Victoria. | C-GJAP/N1958E |
| C-GBCK | Citation | 500-0204 | Dept. of Transportation & Communications, Victoria, B.C. | |
| C-GBEY | Challenger | 1008 | Canadian MOT, Ottawa | |
| C-GBFA | Learjet | 35A-248 | Business Flights Ltd. Calgary. | N3811G |
| C-GBFL | Falcon 20F | 239 | British Columbia Forest Products, Vancouver. | N1OMT/N4417F/F-WPXM |
| C-GBFP | Learjet | 25B-167 | Burmac Corp. Toronto. | |
| C-GBFY | Challenger | 1009 | Canadair Ltd. Montreal. (Prototype Winglets FF 13/NOV/81). | |
| C-GBKC | Challenger | 1007 | Canadian MOT, Ottawa. | HZ-TAG/C-GBKC |
| C-GBLF | Learjet | 35A-091 | Loram International Ltd. Calgary. | VH-TLJ |
| C-GBNE | Citation | 500-0378 | Province of Manitoba, Winnipeg. | N3156M |
| C-GBRM | HS 125/700A | NA0266 | Gulf Canada Ltd. Toronto. | G-BHMP/G-5-11 |
| C-GBTB | Citation | 501-0138 | Beach Industries Ltd, Smith Falls, Ont. | 8P-BAB/8P-BAR/(N26509) |
| C-GBWA | Learjet | 24D-261 | Brooker-Wheaton Aviation, Edmonton. | D-COOL/D-IDAT |
| C-GBWB | Learjet | 24-168 | Brooker-Wheaton Aviation, Edmonton. | N51CH/N700ST/N695ST |
| C-GBWL | Learjet | 35-049 | Brooker-Wheaton Aviation, Edmonton. | N3759C/JY-AEV |
| C-GCFB | Gulfstream 2 | 28 | Canadian MOT, Ottawa. | N7004T/N700ST/N695ST |
| C-GCGS | Challenger | 1002 | Canadair Ltd. Montreal. (-X suffix for test flights). | |
| C-GCGT | Challenger 601 | 3991 | Canadair Ltd. Montreal. (-X suffix for test flights). | |
| C-GCIB | Challenger | 1010 | Canadian Imperial Bank, Toronto. | |
| C-GCTD | Citation Eagle | 500-0056 | Alberta Northern Airlines, Calgary. | N500DB/N556CC/N777JM |
| C-GDAO | HS 125/700A | NA0270 | Noranda Mines Ltd, Toronto. | G-BHSK/G-5-16 |
| C-GDCC | Sabre-60 | 306-51 | Campeau Corp. Ottawa. | N928R/N7531N |
| C-GDDB | Learjet | 23-041 | Northwest Charters, Calgary. | N666MP/N205RJ |
| C-GDDC | Citation | 551-0046 | Pal Air Ltd. Calgary. | N6804Y |
| C-GDDM | Citation | 501-0101 | Tonto Drilling, Vancouver. | N3170M |
| C-GDJH | Learjet | 35A-353 | Canada Learjet Ltd. Vancouver. | N3819G |
| C-GDJW | Jet Commander | 111 | Business Air Services (Toronto) Ltd. | N999CA/N344PS |
| C-GDKS | Learjet | 24B-217 | Dreco Energy Services, Edmonton. | N8536Y/C-GPDB/N777MQ/N777MC |
| C-GDLR | Citation | 550-0062 | Woodward Stores (BC) Ltd. Vancouver. | (N77SF)/N26615) |
| C-GDOC | Westwind-1123 | 166 | Dupont of Canada, Montreal. | |
| C-GDPA | B 737-2T2C | 22056 | Dome Petroleum. Calgary. | |
| C-GDPB | Gulfstream 2 | 232 | Dome Petroleum. Calgary. | N806GA |
| C-GDPD | Citation | 550-0071 | Dome Petroleum. Calgary. | N4308G |
| C-GDPF | Citation | 550-0112 | Dome Petroleum. Calgary. | (N26656) |
| C-G | B 727-2T2 | 22793 | Dome Petroleum. Calgary. | N1779B |
| C-GDUC | Westwind Two | 357 | Dupont of Canada, Montreal. | N357W/4X-CUK |
| C-GDWN | Citation | 500-0029 | Air Niagara (1978) Ltd. Toronto. | N31ST/N529CC |
| C-GDWS | Citation Eagle | 500-0303 | Dowell of Canada, Calgary. | N19U/N19M/(N5303J) |
| C-GEEN | Learjet | 24-087 | Highline Airways, Saskatoon. | D-IKAB/N7VS/CF-UYT/N407V |
| C-GENJ | Citation | 500-0196 | Skycharter Ltd. Mississauga. | N74FC |
| C-GENL | B 737-2S5C | 22148 | Eldorado Aviation Ltd. Saskatoon. | |
| C-GESZ | Citation | 500-0022 | Air Niagara Ltd. St Catherines, Ont. | N800JD/N522JD/N522CC |
| C-GFAN | Westwind-1124 | 218 | Triona Investments Ltd/Futura, Vancouver. | N100AK/N218WW/4X-CLP |
| C-GFCD | HS 125/731 | NA756 | First City Developments, Vancouver. | N100MT/N7NP/N701Z/N51BH |
| C-GFCL | DH 125/1A | 25107 | Fiberglas Canada Ltd. Toronto. | N2426/N7125J/G-ATUX |
| C-GFCS | Falcon 10 | 37 | Canadian Superior Oil, Calgary. | F-WJML |
| C-GFEE | Citation | 501-0169 | Austin Airways, Timmins, Ont. | D-IBWG/N2617U |
| C-GFJB | Learjet | 24D-260 | Northwood Pulp & Timber Ltd. Vancouver. | N60GL |
| C-GFRK | Learjet | 35A-093 | Execaire Aviation Ltd, Montreal. | N804CC |

9

| Registration | Type | C/N | Owner/Operator | Previous Identities |
|---|---|---|---|---|
| C-GGFW | Citation | 550-0276 | B.C. Hydro & Power, Vancouver. | N68649 |
| C-GGYV | Learjet | 35-040 | Oxford Development Group, Edmonton. | |
| C-GHBQ | Westwind-1124 | 220 | Trizec Corp. Calgary. | N1124G/4X-CLR |
| C-GHDP | Learjet | 24D-257 | Hayes-Dana Ltd. St. Catherines, Ontario. | N427JX |
| C-GHEC | Citation | 500-0161 | British Columbia Telephone Co. Vancouver. | |
| C-GHMH | Learjet | 25-011 | Provincial Aviation Inc. Montreal. | N49BA/N167LJ |
| C-GHOL | Citation | 550-0012 | Husky Oil, Calgary. | N513CC/N3208M |
| C-GHOO | Learjet | 35-057 | Home Oil Ltd. Calgary, Alb. | N57GL/N551MD |
| C-GHOS | Citation | 501-0016 | Husky Oil Operations, Calgary. | N517A/N36864 |
| C-GHPR | Jet Commander | 83 | Alberta Northern Airlines, Calgary. | N83AL/N23FF/N4550E |
| C-GHYD | Citation | 550-0063 | B.C. Hydro & Power, Vancouver. | (N26616) |
| C-GIAC | Citation | 500-0076 | Great West Steel, Vancouver. | N810SG/N810SC/N576CC |
| C-GIAD | Citation | 500-0185 | Innotech Aviation, Montreal. | N500AZ/N500WP/N500JP/N22FE/N22FH |
| C-GIRE | Learjet | 35-004 | Central Trust Co. Moncton. | N74MJ/N74MB/N74MP |
| C-GJAP | Citation | 550-0341 | Air Niagara (1978) Ltd. Toronto. | N68032 |
| C-GJLK | Westwind-1124 | 278 | MacMillan Bloedel Ltd. Vancouver. | N505BC/4X-CNX |
| C-GJLL | Westwind-1123 | 171 | J L Levesque, Montreal. | 4X-CJU |
| C-GKCI | HS 125/700A | NA0248 | Irving Oil Transport Ltd. Saint John. | G-BGSR/G-5-13 |
| C-GKFS | Jet Commander | 62 | Kelowna Flightcraft Ltd. B.C. | N1777T/N5415 |
| C-GKFT | Jet Commander | 5 | Kelowna Flightcraft Ltd. Kelowna, BC. | N18CA/N334RK/N364G |
| C-GLBD | HS 125/600A | 6032 | Power Corp. Montreal. | G-DBOW/N4BR/N38BH |
| C-GLBT | Learjet | 25B-182 | John Labbatt Ltd/Execaire Aviation. | |
| C-GLEO | HS 125/1A-522 | 25080 | Ledair (Canada) Ltd. Montreal. | EI-BGW/G-BDYE/3D-AAB/VQ-ZIL |
| C-GLMK | Learjet | 36A-019 | Intergrated Building Supply Corp. Edmonton. | N89MJ/N300CC |
| C-GMBH | Westwind-1124 | 286 | Hudson's Bay Mining, Calgary. | N1124U/4X-CQF |
| C-GMGA | Learjet | 35A-346 | Sefel & Assoc. Calgary. | N3803G |
| C-GMLC | Citation | 500-0305 | M Loeb Ltd. Ottawa. | N805BB/N305BB/(N5305J) |
| C-GMMO | Citation Eagle | 500-0227 | Colonial Oil & Gas, Calgary. | N423RD/G-BCRM/(N227CC) |
| C-GMTT | Westwind-1124 | 288 | Alberta Energy Corp. Edmonton. | N1124Q/4X-CQH |
| C-GNTL | Falcon 20F | 257 | Northern Telecom, Toronto. | N300CC/N781W/N4425F/F-WMKH |
| C-GNTZ | Falcon 20F | 256 | Northern Telecom, Toronto. | N3RC/N4416F/F-WNGL |
| C-GOCM | Citation | 500-0154 | Millardair, Toronto. | |
| C-GOGO | Challenger | 1022 | Ontario Ministry of National Resources. | C-GLWZ |
| C-GOIL | Citation | 500-0361 | Ocelot Industries, Calgary. | N5361J/D-IKPW/N5361J |
| C-GPAW | Citation | 550-0004 | Pratt & Whitney Aircraft of Canada Ltd. Longueuil, P.Q. | N98786 |
| C-GPCC | HS 125/700A | NA0242 | Pancanadian Petroleum Ltd. Calgary. | N60HJ/N700UR/G-5-14 |
| C-GPCO | Citation | 500-0317 | Aviair Aviation Ltd. Kamloops, BC. | N37489/D-ICCA/N5317J |
| C-GPDH | Jet Commander | 82 | Burns Food, Calgary. | N927S/N82JC/N4NK/N9932 |
| C-GPFC | Learjet | 35A-092 | Pocklington Financial Corp. Edmonton. | N424JR/N722GL |
| C-GPPS | HS 125/700A | NA0220 | Petro-Canada Explorations, Calgary. | G-BFMP |
| C-GPTC | Citation | 500-0377 | Bradley Air Services Ltd. Carp. Ont. | N98749 |
| C-GPUN | Learjet | 35-058 | Worldways Airlines, Vancouver. | |
| C-GQBE | B727-25 | 18970 | Westbourne Industrial Enterprises, Calgary. | N8146N |
| C-GRCO | Learjet | 25B-095 | Interflite Aviation Services, Mount Hope. | N303SQ/N303SC/N200BC |
| C-GRDP | Westwind-1124 | 188 | McCain Foods, Florenceville, N.B. | N1124G/4X-CKL |
| C-GRDR | Learjet | 25B-145 | Dominion Road Machinery, Goderich, Ontario. | N131GL |
| C-GRHC | Citation | 550-0046 | Standard Developments, Calgary. | (N3292M) |
| C-GRIO | Citation | 550-0133 | Air Niagara (1978) Ltd. Toronto. | G-BHBH/N2634Y |
| C-GRIS | Falcon 10 | 2 | Skycharter, Toronto. | N103JM/N1OFJ/F-WJMM |
| C-GRQA | Citation | 500-0374 | Austin Airways, Timmins, Ont. | N3141M |
| C-GRRS | Sabre-60 | 306-78 | Campeau Corp. Ottawa. | N65752 |
| C-GRSD | Falcon 20C | 157 | Innotech Aviation Ltd/Dept. of Minés & Technical Surveys. Ottawa. | |
| | | | C-GRSD-X/117508/N166RS/N4363F/F-WJMM | |
| C-GSAS | Learjet | 25B-109 | Skycharter Ltd. Toronto. | N333HP/N888DH |
| C-GSAX | Learjet | 24-129 | Saxon Industial Management,Edmonton. | N44GA/D-IFUM/N656LJ |
| C-GSBR | Gulfstream 3 | 307 | Denison Mines Ltd. Toronto. | N17584 |
| C-GSCL | HS 125/700A | NA0222 | Shell Canada Ltd. Toronto. | G-BFSI |
| C-GSIV | Learjet | 24-108 | Grelling Investments. | N661SS/N661BS/N661CP/N745W/N1966L |
| C-GSKL | Learjet | 25B-179 | Skycharter Ltd. Toronto. | N659HX |
| C-GSLL | Citation Eagle | 501-0030 | Luscar Ltd. Edmonton. | N100CJ/N301MG/N301MC/N36890 |
| C-GSRN | Learjet | 36A-039 | Petro-Canada Explorations, Calgary. | N217CS |
| C-GSTT | HS 125/600B | 6021 | GenStar, Montreal. | HB-VDL/G-5-11 |
| C-GSWS | Westwind-1124 | 259 | Vanco Flightcraft Ltd. Vancouver. | N1124N/4X-CNE |
| C-GTBR | Citation | 550-0087 | Canadian Forest Products Ltd. Vancouver. | (C-FCFP)/N2663J |
| C-GTCB | Gulfstream 2 | 162 | Trans Canada Pipelines, Toronto. | N74RV/N530SW/(C-GANE) |
| C-GTCP | JetStar-8 | 5158 | Trans Canada Pipelines, Toronto. | N516DM/N5522L |

| Registration | Type | C/N | Owner/Operator | Previous Identities |
|---|---|---|---|---|
| C-GTEP | Gulfstream 2 | 247 | Tele Direct Ltd, Montreal. | N888MC/N828GA |
| C-GTJT | Learjet | 24-160 | Baltic Drilling (1979) Ltd, Edmonton. | N111WJ/N645G |
| C-GTLU | Falcon 20F | 262 | Tele-Direct/Al Hickman Aviation. | N501AS/VH-WLH/N750ME/N720ML/N4427F |
| | | | | /F-WJMK |
| C-GTPC | BH 125/600A | 6025 | Price Company/Execaire Aviation, Montreal. | N36BH |
| C-GTWO | Gulfstream 2 | 140 | Inco Ltd. & Alcan Ltd. Toronto. | N881GA |
| C-GTXV | Challenger | 1046 | Petro-Canada Exploration, Calgary. | |
| C-GVCA | Learjet | 35-043 | Peter Bawden/Business Flights Ltd. Calgary. | |
| C-GVCB | Learjet | 35-012 | Peter Bawden/Business Flights Ltd. Calgary. | N71LA/N711 |
| C-GVER | Citation | 500-0369 | North Canada Air Ltd. Prince Albert. | N3132M |
| C-GVQR | DH 125/731 | NA754 | Hudson's Bay Co. Calgary. | C-FTEC |
| C-GVVA | Learjet | 35-002 | Sulaero Ltd. Calgary. | N355C/N352GL |
| C-GVVB | Learjet | 36A-025 | Sulaero Ltd. Calgary. | OE-GLP/N730GL/N774AB |
| C-GVVT | Citation | 501-0087 | Creighton Holding Ltd. Calgary. | N501SE/(N3183M) |
| C-GWCR | Citation | 550-0191 | Weldwood Canada Ltd. Vancouver. | N88707 |
| C-GWFG | Learjet | 24D-256 | West Fraser Air Ltd. Vancouver. | N703J/HB-VCW |
| C-GWPV | Jet Commander | 105 | Skalbania Ltd, Jasper, Edmonton. | N230RC/F-BPIB/N618JC |
| C-GWRT | Challenger | 1016 | Sugra Ltd. Toronto. | |
| C-GWSH | Westwind-1123 | 165 | Burns Food Ltd. Calgary. | N1123R |
| C-GXFZ | Citation | 500-0032 | Air Niagara (1978) Ltd. Toronto. | N536V/N532CC |
| C-GXKQ | Challenger | 1004 | Canadair Ltd. Montreal. (-X Suffix for test flights) | |
| C-GYYZ | HS 125/700A | NA0205 | Nova, An Alberta Corp. Calgary. | (G-BEWV)/G-5-11 |
| C-GZIM | Learjet | 25D-208 | Noranda Mines Ltd. Toronto. | N54YP/N54YR |
| C-GZVV | Learjet | 35A-153 | Perimeter Aviation Ltd. Winnipeg. | |
| C-GZZX | HS 125/700A | NA0323 | Canadian Superior Oil, Calgary. | N700RR/G-5-17 |
| C-G | Gulfstream 3 | 353 | Noranda Mines Ltd. Toronto. | |
| N65ST | Gulfstream 2 | 5 | GenStar Montreal. | N100PJ/N100P |

URUGUAY

| | | | | |
|---|---|---|---|---|
| CX-CMJ | Westwind-1124 | 251 | Construction Mendes Jr. | N6MJ/4X-CMW |

FEDERAL GERMAN REPUBLIC

| | | | | |
|---|---|---|---|---|
| D-BBWK | Falcon 50 | 23 | Korf Transport GmbH. Baden-Baden. | (D-BBAD)/F-WZHG |
| D-BIRD | Falcon 50 | 16 | Dornier Reparaturwerft/Deutsche BVV, Munich. | (N50FM)/F-WZHH |
| D-B | Falcon 50 | 57 | Giesecke & Devrient, Munich. | HB-IER/F-WZHC |
| D-CALL | Mystere 20F | 392 | F. Flick GmbH. Dusseldorf. | F-WRQT |
| D-CARA | HFB 320 | 1021 | DFVLR Research Centre, Braunschweig. | |
| D-CARD | Learjet | 35A-426 | Aero Dienst GmbH. Nuremberg. | |
| D-CARG | Learjet | 35A-433 | Aero Dienst GmbH. Nuremberg. | |
| D-CARH | Learjet | 35A-444 | Aero Dienst GmbH. Nuremberg. | N3818G |
| D-CARL | Learjet | 35A-387 | Aero Dienst GmbH. Nuremberg. | |
| D-CARO | Learjet | 35A-325 | Michael Roth, Ruekersdorf. | |
| D-CART | Learjet | 35A-354 | Bavaria Flug, Munich. | N1450B |
| D-CARX | Learjet | 55-034 | Aero Dienst GmbH. Nuremberg | N3795Y |
| D-CAVI | Learjet | 35A-174 | Avia Luftreederei GmbH. Neustadt. | N65DH/TR-LYC |
| D-CBAG | Falcon 10 | 91 | Bertelsmann AG. Paderborn. | F-WJMJ |
| D-CBAT | Citation | 550-0289 | Peter Dreidoppel, Dusseldorf. | N68629 |
| D-CBBA | Westwind-1124 | 294 | Genavia-RFB, Lubeck. | 4X-CON |
| D-CBBB | Westwind-1124 | 296 | Genavia-RFB, Lubeck. | 4X-COP |
| D-CBBC | Westwind-1124 | 297 | Genavia-RFB, Lubeck. | 4X-COQ |
| D-CBBD | Westwind-1124 | 310 | Genavia-RFB, Lubeck. | 4X-CRD |
| D-CBRK | Learjet | 35-026 | Bayerisches Rotes Kreuz, Munich. | D-CDHS |
| D-CBUR | Falcon 10 | 98 | Burda GmbH. Offenburg. | F-WPXG |
| D-CCAD | Learjet | 35A-263 | Minitrans GmbH. Munich. | |
| D-CCAX | Learjet | 35A-284 | Joachim Bohl, Freudenstadt. | (D-CEFL) |
| D-CCAY | Learjet | 35A-112 | Gustav Schickendanz Kg. Nuremberg. | N3810G |
| D-CCCA | Learjet | 35A-160 | Maschinenfabrik E Mollers GmbH. Paderborn. (800th Learjet). | |
| D-CCDB | Falcon 20F | 381 | Daimler Benz AG. Stuttgart. | (I-LAFA)/F-WROS |
| D-CCHB | Learjet | 35A-089 | Bauhaus GmbH. Mannheim. | N3547F |
| D-CCHS | Learjet | 55-049 | Bochumer Mineralol GmbH. Dusseldorf. | |
| D-CCMB | Falcon 20F | 377 | Daimler Benz AG. Stuttgart. | F-WRQP |
| D-CCPD | Learjet | 36-004 | Minitrans, Munich. | (D-CCAC)/N1918W |
| D-CDAX | Learjet | 35A-135 | Blendax-Werke R Schneider GmbH. Dusseldorf. | N22MJ/(OO-LFX) |
| D-CDHS | Learjet | 35A-311 | Bochumer Mineralol GmbH. Dusseldorf. | |
| D-CDPD | Learjet | 25B-177 | Peter Dreidoppel, Dusseldorf. | N745W/N11PH |
| D-CDWN | Learjet | 35A-175 | Diehl Werke Kg. Nuremberg. | |

| Regis-tration | Type | C/N | Owner/Operator | Previous Identities |
|---|---|---|---|---|
| D-CELA | Learjet | 36-002 | Dee Howard Aircraft Sales Inc. San Antonio, Tx. | N18AT/YV-89CP /YV-161P/YV-TASG/D-CMAR/N362GL |
| D-CELL | Mystere 20D | 201 | Transalpina Flugzeughalter GmbH. Munich. | F-WLCY |
| D-CFCF | HS 125/F400B | 25248 | Conti-Flug, Cologne. | |
| D-CFSK | HS 125/600B | 6053 | Gemeinsame Flugvermessungsstelle, Lechfeld. | |
| D-CGSO | Mystere 20E | 306 | Giesecke & Devrient/Union Air, Munich. | (HB-VDO)/(HB-VDY)/F-WRQS |
| D-CHEF | Learjet | 25D-260 | PJC GmbH. Dusseldorf. | (D-CHBM)/N39413 |
| D-CIEL | Falcon 10 | 155 | Hertie Waren & Kaufhaus GmbH. Frankfurt. | (N220FJ)/F-WZGC |
| D-CITA | Learjet | 35A-070 | ACV GmbH. Munich. | |
| D-CJET | HS 125/600B | 6027 | Haeger & Schmidt GmbH. Dusseldorf. | |
| D-CLVW | HS 125/700B | 7100 | Volkswagenwerke AG. Wolfsburg. | (G-5-19) |
| D-CMAN | Falcon 10 | 71 | Mobel Mann, Karlsruhe. | F-WJMM |
| D-CMAX | Mystere 20C | 158 | Grundigwerke GmbH. Nuremberg. | F-WMKJ |
| D-CMET | Mystere 20E | 329 | DFVLR, Oberpfapfenhofen. | F-WRQV |
| D-CMMM | Learjet | 24D/A-328 | DAL Mobilien-Vermietungs GmbH. Mainz. | D-IMMM |
| D-CMVW | HS 125/700B | 7112 | Volkswagenwerke AG.Wolfsburg. | |
| D-CNCI | Citation | 550-0415 | Nixdorf Computer AG. Paderborn. | |
| D-CNCP | Citation | 550-0105 | Nixdorf Computer AG. Paderborn. | N116CC/N26649 |
| D-COGA | Learjet | 24B-223 | H Korner GmbH. Frankfurt. | D-IOGA |
| D-COME | Falcon 10 | 67 | H Bauer Verlag, Hamburg. | N151FJ/F-WLCU |
| D-CONA | Learjet | 35A-114 | Gunter Eheim-Contact Air, Stuttgart. | N3807G |
| D-CONO | Learjet | 35-055 | Gunter Eheim-Contact Air, Stuttgart. | |
| D-CONU | Mystere 20F | 383 | Gunter Eheim-Contact Air, Stuttgart. (500th Falcon). | F-WROR |
| D-CONY | Learjet | 35A-195 | Gunter Eheim-Contact Air, Stuttgart. | N1471B |
| D-COSA | HFB 320 | 1056 | M-B-B GmbH. Munich. | |
| D-COTT | Mystere 20E | 314 | Dornier GmbH. | F-WNGL |
| D-IABC | Citation | 500-0182 | Eisenlegieren Handelsges MbH. Duisberg. | |
| D-IAEC | Citation | 501-0203 | Metimex Metall GmbH, Dusseldorf. | N67830 |
| D-IAEV | Citation | 500-0355 | Intraha Vermogenslagen GmbH. Duisberg. | G-DJBB/N36846 |
| D-IANO | Citation | 501-0121 | Viktor Bondarenko, Munich. | N26506 |
| D-IATC | Citation | 500-0116 | CFG - Centurion Flugzeug Handels GmbH, Cologne. | EC-CJH/N116CC |
| D-IBPF | Citation | 551-0038 | Pfleuger Flug/Inge Nanz, Stuttgart. | N6801Z |
| D-ICCC | Citation | 500-0269 | Synchron Air, Saarbrucken. | (D-IKUC)/N5269J |
| D-ICTA | Citation | 551-0051 | Wiking Helikopters Service GmbH. Wilhelmshaven. | N6863C |
| D-IDFD | Citation | 500-0225 | DFD Flugdienst GmbH Dusseldorf. | OO-GPN/PH-SAW/N5B/(N5225J) |
| D-IGGK | Citation | 501-0143 | Eisenlegieren Handelsges MbH. Duisberg. | N26523 |
| D-IGLU | Citation | 501-0159 | Joachim Bohl, Freudenstadt. | N2652Y |
| D-IGMB | Citation | 501-0067 | Erwin Gruber Munich. | SE-DEO/N2959A |
| D-IKFJ | Citation | 500-0178 | ALN-Vermogensverwaltungs GmbH, Munich. | |
| D-IMLN | Citation | 500-0129 | Paul Leisitz Maschinenfabrik, Nuremberg. | |
| D-IMTM | Citation | 551-0009 | Heinrich Then, Gemuenda. | N1959E |
| D-INCC | Citation | 500-0128 | Metimex Metall GmbH. Dusseldorf. | |
| HB-VFA | HS 125/700B | 7007 | Knorr-Bremsen AG. Munich. | |
| HB-VGF | HS 125/700B | 7062 | Robert Bosch GmbH. Stuttgart. | G-5-16 |
| HB-VGG | HS 125/700B | 7070 | Robert Bosch GmbH. Stuttgart. | |
| N61 | Sabre-75A | 380-29 | FAA, Frankfurt. | |
| N64 | Sabre-75A | 380-35 | FAA, Frankfurt. | |

## SPAIN

| | | | | |
|---|---|---|---|---|
| EC-CKR | Learjet | 25B-184 | Olarra S.A. Bilbao. | |
| EC-DEB | Learjet | 35A-137 | Gestair, Madrid. | HB-VFL/N3819G |
| EC-DJC | Learjet | 35A-278 | Gestair, Madrid. | ECT-028/HB-VGL/N1476B |
| EC-DOH | Citation | 551-0039 | Jose Uriarte/Terrain Iberica SA, Vitoria. | ECT-023/N6860Y |
| EC-DQC | Corvette | 24 | Euroflot, Madrid. | F-BVPI |
| EC-DQE | Corvette | 26 | Teire S.A. Madrid. | F-GDAY/PH-JSB/F-ODFQ/N618AC/F-WNGV |
| EC-DQG | Corvette | 27 | Dominguez, Toledo. | F-BVPH |

## IRELAND

| | | | | |
|---|---|---|---|---|
| EI-BJL | Citation | 550-0039 | Helicopter Maintenance/Carrow More Ltd. Castlebar. | G-BJHH/(N3273M) |
| EI-BJN | Citation | 501-0175 | Tool & Mould Steel (Ireland) Ltd. Cologne. | N2072A |

## IRAN

| | | | | |
|---|---|---|---|---|
| EP-AGA | B 737-286 | 21317 | Islamic Republic of Iran, Teheran. | |
| EP-AGY | Mystere 20E | 286 | Government of Iran, Teheran. | F-WRQU |

| Regis-tration | Type | C/N | Owner/Operator | Previous Identities |
|---|---|---|---|---|
| EP-AKC | Mystere 20E | 301 | National Iranian Oil Co. Teheran. | F-WNGL |
| EP-FIC | Mystere 20E | 334 | Civil Aviation Organization, Teheran. | F-WRQU |
| EP-FID | Mystere 20E | 338 | Civil Aviation Organization, Teheran. | F-WMKG |
| EP-FIE | Mystere 20E | 251 | Civil Aviation Organization, Teheran. | EP-VAP/F-WRQR |
| EP-FIF | Mystere 20E | 320 | Civil Aviation Organization, Teheran. | EP-AHV/F-WRQS |
| EP-FIG | Mystere 20E | 318 | Civil Aviation Organisation. Teheran. | EP-VSP/(EP-VAS)/F-WRQT |
| EP-PLN | B 727-30 | 18363 | Islamic Republic of Iran, Teheran. | EP-SHP/(N44CR)/N16768/D-ABIF |
| EP-SEA | Mystere 20F | 367 | Atomic Energy Organization, Teheran. | F-WRQR |

### FRANCE

| Regis-tration | Type | C/N | Owner/Operator | Previous Identities |
|---|---|---|---|---|
| F-BIHY | Mystere 20C | 141 | Ste Jas Hennessey, Cognac. | F-BPIO/F-WMKF |
| F-BINR | Falcon 50 | 2 | AMD, Bordeaux. | F-WINR |
| F-BJET | MS 760 Paris-1A | 39 | R.F. (D.G.A.C.), Paris. | F-WJAA |
| F-BJLH | Falcon 10 | 1 | Leadair, Paris. | F-WJLH/PH-ILT/F-BSQU/F-WSQU |
| F-BJLV | MS 760 Paris-1A | 72 | Centre Ecole de St. Yan. | |
| F-BJLX | MS 760 Paris-1A | 86 | Centre Ecole de St. Yan. | |
| F-BJLY | MS 760 Paris-2 | 89 | Centre Ecole de St. Yan. | |
| F-BKFB | Learjet | 36A-046 | Groupement International de Commerce, Paris. | |
| F-BLKL | MS 760 Paris-3 | 01 | S.N.I.A.S., Marseilles. | F-WLKL |
| F-BMSS | Mystere 20F | 2 | IGN=Institut Geographique National, Creil. | F-WMSS |
| F-BNDB | Falcon 50 | 1 | Dassault-Breguet Aviation, Bordeaux. | F-WAMD |
| F-BNRG | MS 760 Paris-2 | 101 | C.N. de St. Yan. | F-ZJNH |
| F-BOJO | MS 760 Paris-2 | 2 | C.N. de St. Yan. | EP-HIM |
| F-BOXV | Mystere 20C | 104 | EFS/Euralair International, Paris. | (OT-JFA)/F-WJMK |
| F-BRGF | Learjet | 24D-289 | Euralair International, Paris. | (HB-VDO) |
| F-BRNL | Learjet | 24B-183 | Euralair International, Paris. | OY-AGZ/N676LJ |
| F-BRNZ | Corvette | 2 | S.N.I.A.S. Paris. | F-WRNZ |
| F-BRPK | Mystere 20C | 188 | Europe Falcon Service, Paris. | (F-BRPF)/F-WJMK |
| F-BSBU | Mystere 20E | 263 | Europe Falcon Service, Paris. | HB-VCR/F-WMKJ |
| F-BSIM | HS 125/3B | 25130 | Productions Claude Carrere, Paris. | TR-LXO/F-BSIM/HB-VAZ/G-AVRD /G-5-14 |
| F-BSQN | Falcon 10 | 03 | Dassault-Breguet Aviation, Istres. | F-WSQN |
| F-BSRL | Learjet | 24B-210 | Euralair International, Paris. | ZS-LLG |
| F-BSTM | AC680-VTU | 1540-6 | Ste Turbomeca, Pau. | F-WSTM/G-AWXK/N6300 |
| F-BSTR | Mystere 20F | 246 | Europe Falcon Service, Paris. | F-WJMK |
| F-BSUX | Learjet | 23-045A | Ste General Aviation, Nantes. | HB-VBB/N803LJ |
| F-BSYF | Mystere 20C | 25 | Institut Geographique National, Creil. | HB-VCO/F-BOON/F-WNGN |
| F-BTCY | Mystere 20C | 13 | Europe Falcon Service, Paris. | D-CILL/F-BOEF/TR-LOL/F-BOEF/F-WMKH |
| F-BTDA | Jet Commander | 145 | Ste Civile Jet Stream, Paris. | (N17DW)/HB-VCC/N9045N |
| F-BTEL | Citation | 550-0190 | Euralair International, Paris. | N98715 |
| F-BTML | Mystere 20C | 67 | Ste Martell, Cognac. | F-BOOA/F-WJMN |
| F-BTTL | Corvette | 28 | Uni-Air, Toulouse. | F-WNGX |
| F-BTTU | Corvette | 37 | S.F.A., St. Yan | |
| F-BTTV | Corvette | 11 | S.N.I.A.S,. Paris. | F-ODKS/TR-LWY/F-BTTS/N613AC/(F-BIFU) |
| F-BTYV | Learjet | 24B-206 | Ste Uni-Air/Buzzichelli/Cie Integra/St Pierre Fabre, Toulouse. | HB-VBY |
| F-BUQN | Corvette | 3 | S.N.I.A.S,. St. Nazaire. | F-WUQN |
| F-BUQP | Corvette | 4 | Air Entreprise, Paris. | F-WUQP |
| F-BUUL | Citation | 500-0136 | Entreprise Guiraudee et Affeve, Toulouse. | |
| F-BUUV | Learjet | 24B-195 | Ste Uni-Air International, Toulouse. | N272GL/N202BT |
| F-BUYE | Mystere 20E | 288 | Europe Falcon Service, Paris. | F-WRQZ |
| F-BVEC | Learjet | 24D-271 | Ste. Air Provence International, Lyon. | HB-VDK/N3818G |
| F-BVPA | Corvette | 5 | Ste Regourd/Leadair, Paris. | |
| F-BVPB | Corvette | 6 | SNIAS, Paris. | F-OGJL/F-BVPB/F-WUQR |
| F-BVPG | Corvette | 25 | Ste Uni-Air, Toulouse. | F-OBXV/F-BVPG/F-WNGU |
| F-BVPK | Corvette | 7 | S.F.A., St. Yan. | N611AC/F-OBZR |
| F-BVPN | Mystere 20E | 311 | Ste Michelin, Clermont Ferrand. | F-WRQS |
| F-BVPR | Falcon 10 | 5 | Europe Falcon Service, Paris. | F-WLCT |
| F-BVPS | Corvette | 14 | Ste Uni-Air, Toulouse. | |
| F-BVPT | Corvette | 16 | SFACT, St.Yan. | |
| F-BXAG | Falcon 10 | 7 | Ste Eurofer, Paris. | VR-BFF/F-WJMN |
| F-BXAS | AC690A-TU | 11240 | Ste Turbomeca, Pau. | F-WXAS |
| F-BXPT | Learjet | 23-014 | Ste Air Entreprise/Ste Commerciale des Resines, Nantes. | (HB-VEL)/JY-AEG/N426EJ/N814L |
| F-BXQL | MS 760 Paris 2B | 105 | Euralair International, Paris. | N760Q/PH-MSU/F-BJZT |
| F-BYAL | Learjet | 25C-084 | Euralair International. Paris. | N200SF/N200QM/(C-GWUZ)/N2000M |

13

| Registration | Type | C/N | Owner/Operator | Previous Identities |
|---|---|---|---|---|
| F-BYCC | Falcon 10 | 76 | Leadair, Paris. | F-WPUU |
| F-BYCV | Falcon 10 | 93 | Natio Equipment, Bordeaux. | F-WNGN |
| F-BYFB | HS 125/700B | 7166 | Groupement International de Commerce, Paris. | G-5-18 |
| F-GAMA | Learjet | 23-023 | Aero Stock, Paris. | HB-VEL/JY-AEH/N429EJ |
| F-GAPC | Mystere 20C | 184 | Air Gefco, Paris. | D-COMF/F-BTMF/F-WRQQ |
| F-GAPY | Learjet | 23-027 | (See N108TW) | |
| F-GASL | HS 125/700B | 7022 | Ste Schlumberger, Paris. | (G-5-11) |
| F-GBGD | Learjet | 36-016 | Euralair International, Paris | JY-AET/HB-VEE |
| F-GBMB | Learjet | 35-018 | Ste Natio Location, Toulouse. | D-CORA |
| F-GBMD | Mystere 20F | 375 | Europe Falcon Service, Paris. | F-WRQR |
| F-GBMH | Falcon 10 | 103 | Lyon Air, Lyons. | F-WPXL |
| F-GBRF | Falcon 10 | 38 | Roquette Brothers, Paris. | N2OEE/N2OET/N2OES/N127FJ/F-WJMM |
| F-GBTC | Falcon 10 | 124 | Thomson-CSF, Paris. | F-WPUY |
| F-GBTI | Falcon 10 | 24 | Ste Technal International, Toulouse. | N1924V/N116FJ/F-WJML |
| F-GBTL | Citation | 550-0073 | Euralair International, Paris. | N4621G |
| F-GBTM | Falcon 20F | 397 | Europe Falcon Service, Paris. | F-WRQP |
| F-GCMS | Learjet | 35A-257 | Air Affaires International, Paris. | |
| F-GCSZ | Citation | 550-0182 | Groupement International de Commerce, Paris. | (F-BKFB)/N88830 |
| F-GCTT | Falcon 10 | 127 | EFS-Unijet, Paris. | F-WNGN |
| F-GDAE | Learjet | 24-105 | Air Entreprise, Paris. | TR-LYB/N111EJ/N111EK/N425NJ |
| F-GDAV | Learjet | 23-017 | Air Entreprise, Paris. | F-GBTA/N3OBP/N32SD/N658L/N233R |
| F-GDAZ | Corvette | 35 | SNIAS, St.Nazaire. | PH-JSC |
| F-GDCN | Learjet | 35A-432 | Uni-Air, Toulouse. | |
| F-GDCP | Learjet | 35A-071 | Uni-Air, Toulouse. | F-WDCP/JY-AFD |
| F-GDFE | Falcon 50 | 56 | AMD-BA, Paris. | F-WZHR |
| F-GDHK | Gulfstream 3 | 340 | H.R.H. Prince Karim Aga Khan, Paris. | |
| F-GDLR | Falcon 10 | 121 | Soc. Locafrance-Natio Equipment/Leadair, Paris. | HB-VFT/(HB-VFS)/F-WPUU |
| F-ODOK | Mystere 20C | 162 | | HB-VED/D-CBBT/OO-WTB/F-WNGO |
| F-OGJL | Corvette | 6 | S.N.I.A.S. Paris. | F-BVPB/F-WUQR |
| F-WATF | Mystere 20G | 362 | AMD, Bordeaux. 20G Prototype. | |
| F-WRQP | Falcon 20 | 434 | AMD-BA, Bordeaux. | |
| F-WRQR | Falcon 20 | 451 | | |
| F-WRQS | Falcon 20 | 455 | | |
| F-WUAS | Corvette | 1 | S.N.I.A.S., St. Nazaire. | F-BUAS/F-WUAS |
| F- | Mystere 20E | 309 | | TR-LUW/F-WROT |
| N121AM | Falcon 20E | 310 | IBM World Trade Asia Corp. Paris. | (N37OME)/N4450F/F-WMKH |
| N121EU | Falcon 20E | 297 | IBM World Trade Asia Corp. | (N37OEU)/N4443F/F-WMKF |
| N131WT | Falcon 50 | 28 | IBM World Trade Asia Corp. | N53FJ/F-WZHE |
| VR-BTT | Falcon 50 | 32 | Inter Insurance/Castolin Eutectic Institute. | F-WZHJ |

GREAT BRITAIN

| Registration | Type | C/N | Owner/Operator | Previous Identities |
|---|---|---|---|---|
| G-APRU | MS 760 Paris 1A | 8 | Cranfield Institute of Technology . | G-36-2/F-WJAC |
| G-ARVF | VC 10/1101 | 808 | Sheikh Zayed, Abu Dhabi, United Arab Emirates. | |
| G-ASNU | HS 125/1 | 25005 | Flintgrange Ltd/Chief F A Nzerebi, Nigeria. | D-COMA/(D-CFKG)/G-ASNU |
| G-ASSI | HS 125/1 | 25008 | Panatrade Ltd. Lagos. | |
| G-ATPD | HS 125/1B-522 | 25085 | McAlpine Aviation Ltd. Luton. | 5N-AGU/G-ATPD |
| G-ATPE | HS 125/1B | 25092 | Moseley Group (P.S.V.) Ltd. East Midlands. | |
| G-ATPK | BAC 1-11/301 | 034 | Chemco Equipment Finance Ltd. London/Bryan Aviation. | VP-BCP/G-ATPK |
| G-AVAI | HS 125/3B | 25125 | Aravco Ltd. London. | LN-NPA/G-AVAI |
| G-AVDX | HS 125/3B-RA | 25113 | CAA=Civil Aviation Authority, Stansted. | (G-5-13) |
| G-AVOI | HS 125/3B | 25128 | MarstApoll Aviation Ltd. | |
| G-AVPE | HS 125/3B | 25127 | British Aerospace Aircraft Group, Filton. | |
| G-AVRF | HS 125/3B | 25133 | Flintgrange Ltd/Chief F A Nzerebi, Nigeria. | |
| G-AVRG | HS 125/3B-RA | 25144 | Rogers Aviation, Cranfield. | G-5-12 |
| G-AVVB | HS 125/3B-RA | 25140 | Brown & Root (UK) Ltd. London. | G-5-17 |
| G-AVXK | HS 125/3B-RA | 25143 | Overseas Business Services Charter/OGI Cargo Co. Nigeria. | D-CHTH/G-AVXK/G-5-18 |
| G-AWXO | HS 125/400B | 25178 | Al-Kharafi Aviation Ltd/McAlpine Aviation, Luton. | |
| G-AWYE | HS 125/1B-S522 | 25090 | Rolls Royce Ltd. East Midlands. | HB-VAT |
| G-AXDM | HS 125/400B | 25194 | Ferranti Ltd. Edinburgh. | |
| G-AXPU | HS 125/3B-RA | 25171 | McAlpine Aviation Ltd. Luton. | G-IBIS/G-AXPU/HB-VBT/G-5-19 |
| G-AYER | HS 125/403B | 25238 | MAM Aviation Ltd, London. | 9K-ACR/G-AYER |
| G-AYOJ | HS 125/403B | 25246 | Bakerloo Investments Co. Hamilton, Bermuda. | 9O-COH/G-AYOJ/(G-5-16) |
| G-AZCH | HS 125/3B-RA | 25154 | Leopard Aviation Ltd. Milton Keynes/Sheikh Gabri Gabel, Saudi Arabia. | EP-AHK |
| G-AZVS | HS 125/3B | 25132 | Merlin-Air Executive Air Travel, Manchester. | OY-DKP |

| Registration | Type | C/N | Owner/Operator | Previous Identities |
|---|---|---|---|---|
| G-BARR | HS 125/600B | 6019 | Rolls Royce Ltd. East Midlands. | |
| G-BART | HS 125/600B | 6005 | Cross Oceans Ltd. London/Chief H O Lawson, Nigeria. | |
| G-BATA | HS 125/400B | 25257 | Beecham- Imperial Aviation Ltd London. | G-5-19 |
| G-BAXL | HS 125/3B | 25069 | Dennis Vanguard International (Switchgear) Ltd. Air Commuter, Coventry. | VH-ECF |
| G-BAZA | HS 125/F400B | 25272 | Northern Industries Ltd. Newcastle. | G-5-15 |
| G-BAZB | HS 125/400B | 25252 | Short Brothers Harland Ltd. Belfast, N.I. | XX505/G-5-17 |
| G-BBCL | HS 125/600B | 6015 | British Aerospace, Weybridge. | G-5-20/IAC239/G-BBCL/9K-ACZ/G-BBCL/G-BJCB/G-BBCL/G-5-19 |
| G-BBEP | HS 125/600B | 6030 | H. Goodman-Air Europe, Gatwick. | G-BJOY/G-BBEP |
| G-BCKM | Citation | 500-0198 | Comet Radiovision Services Ltd. Humberside. | |
| G-BCXF | HS 125/600B | 6054 | Montaguis Ltd. Luton. | 9K-AED/G-BCXF/G-5-17 |
| G-BCYF | Mystere 20E | 304 | Nidiva Services (UK) Ltd. | F-WRQP |
| G-BEFZ | HS 125/700B | 7001 | McAlpine Aviation Ltd. Luton. | VR-HIM/G-BEFZ |
| G-BEIZ | Citation | 500-0354 | Casair & Co Ltd, Teesside. | (N5363J) |
| G-BEJM | BAC 1-11/423 | 118 | Ford Motor Co. Stansted. | VC92-2111 |
| G-BEJW | BAC 1-11/423 | 154 | Ford Motor Co. Stansted. | VC92-2110 |
| G-BETV | HS 125/600B | 6035 | Tenneco, London. | F-BKMC |
| G-BEWW | HS 125/600B | 6001 | McAlpine Aviation Ltd/Truzone Ltd. Luton. | N711AG/N82BH/G-AZUF |
| G-BFAN | HS 125/600F | 25258 | British Aerospace Aircraft Group, Hatfield. | G-AZHS/(G-5-14) |
| G-BFAR | Citation | 500-0368 | Fairflight Ltd. Biggin Hill. | N36912 |
| G-BFMC | BAC 1-11/414 | 160 | Ford Motor Co. Stansted. | D-ANNO |
| G-BFPI | HS 125/700B | 7025 | McAlpine Aviation Ltd. Luton. | VR-HIN/G-BFPI/(G-5-12) |
| G-BFRM | Citation | 550-0027 | Marshalls of Cambridge. | N527CC/N3245M |
| G-BFSO | HS 125/700B | 7028 | Dravidian Air Services Ltd. London. | |
| G-BFSP | HS 125/700B | 7031 | Dravidian Air Services Ltd. London. | |
| G-BFVI | HS 125/700B | 7037 | Bristows Helicopters Ltd. Redhill. | G-5-18 |
| G-BFXT | HS 125/700B | 7034 | Coca Cola Exporting Co. London. | G-5-14 |
| G-BGOP | Falcon 20F | 406 | Datsun (UK) Ltd. London. | F-WMKF |
| G-BGTD | HS 125/700B | 7073 | Rank Xerox (UK) Ltd. London. | G-5-12 |
| G-BGTU | BAC 1-11/409 | 108 | Turbo Union Ltd. Filton. | YS-01C/TI-1056C |
| G-BGYR | HS 125/600B | 6045 | British Areospace Aircraft Group, Warton. | G-5-11/EC-CQT/G-5-18 |
| G-BHBH | Citation | 550-0133 | Rio Tinto Zinc/R. Armfield, Biggin Hill. | N2634Y |
| G-BHLF | HS 125/700B | 7091 | GEC-Marconi/McAlpine Aviation Ltd Luton. | |
| G-BHSU | HS 125/700B | 7103 | Shell Aircraft Ltd. London. | G-5-12 |
| G-BHSV | HS 125/700B | 7107 | Shell Aircraft Ltd. London. | |
| G-BHSW | HS 125/700B | 7109 | Shell Aircraft Ltd. London. | |
| G-BHTT | Citation | 500-0404 | Lucas Industries Ltd. Birmingham. | N2614H |
| G-BIRU | HS 125/700B | 7136 | Barclay Mercantile/MAM Aviation, London. | |
| G-BIZZ | Citation | 500-0411 | Vickers Ltd. | |
| G-BJDJ | HS 125/700B | 7142 | Consolidated Contractors Co. | G-5-12 |
| G-BJIL | Citation | 550-0328 | RTZ Services Ltd. London. | N67988 |
| G-BJIR | Citation | 550-0296 | Royco Homes Ltd. Marlow, Oxford. | N6888C |
| G-BJVP | Citation | 550-0342 | Fairflight Ltd. Biggin Hill. | N6804L |
| G-BJWB | HS 125/700B | 7158 | Opencity Ltd/McAlpine/Artoc, Kuwait. | G-5-14 |
| G-BKAA | HS 125/700B | 7139 | Saudi Catering & Contracting/Albert Abela, London. | (G-GAIL)/G-5-18 |
| G-BKAJ | HS 125/400B | 25235 | D A J Gibson/MAM Aviation Ltd. London. | G-AYNR/HB-VCE/G-5-18 |
| G-BKBA | HS 125/F403B | 25270 | McAlpine Aviation Ltd. Luton. | G-BBGU/G-5-13 |
| G-BKBH | HS 125/600B | 6052 | McAlpine Aviation Ltd. Luton. | G-BDJE/G-5-11 |
| G-BKBM | HS 125/600B | 6039 | McAlpine Aviation Ltd. Luton. | G-BCCL |
| G-BKBU | HS 125/600B | 6042 | McAlpine Aviation Ltd. Luton. | G-BBRO |
| G-BKCD | HS 125/600B | 6056 | McAlpine Aviation Ltd. Luton. | G-BDOA/G-5-13 |
| G-BKHK | HS 125/700B | 7189 | Scorpio Aviation & Marine (Has G-OBSM reserved). | |
| G-BJKV | HS 125/700B | 7046 | British Aerospace Aircraft Group, Hatfield. | 4W-ACE |
| G-BMCL | Citation | 550-0082 | Yewlands Executive Transport, Stansted. | N26627 |
| G-BSAA | HS 125/3B | 25117 | ARAVCO London. | 5N-AKT/5N-AET |
| G-BSAL | Gulfstream 2 | 214 | Shell Aviation Ltd. Heathrow. | N17582 |
| G-BSAN | Gulfstream 3 | 345 | Shell Aviation Ltd. Heathrow. | |
| G-BSHL | HS 125/600B | 6024 | S H Services Ltd/McAlpine, Luton. | G-BBMD/N50GD/G-BBMD |
| G-CXMF | Gulfstream 2 | 204 | Gulfstream Investments Ltd. Jersey, C.I. | N17588 |
| G-DBBI | HS 125/700B | 7130 | Barclays Bank International, London. | |
| G-DJBE | Citation | 550-0154 | D J B Engineering Ltd. Teeside. | (N8887N) |
| G-DJHH | Citation | 550-0262 | Humber Kitchens Ltd. Humberside. | N6862C |
| G-DMAN | HS 125/600B | 6033 | McAlpine/E D & F Mann. | F-BUYP |
| G-FERY | Citation | 550-0030 | European Ferries, Luton. | G-DJBI/(N3249M) |
| G-FIVE | HS 125/1 | 25004 | British Air Ferries, Southend. | G-ASEC |
| G-FOUR | HS 125/3B | 25131 | British Air Ferries, Southend. | F-BPMC/G-AVRE |

| Registration | Type | C/N | Owner/Operator | Previous Identities |
|---|---|---|---|---|
| G-GAIL | Citation | 550-0353 | Heron Aviation Ltd. Leavesden. (For USA OCT/82) | |
| G-GAYL | Learjet | 35A-429 | Heron Aviation Ltd. Leavesden. | G-ZING |
| G-GENE | Citation | 501-0170 | Falmer Aircraft, Leavesden. | N501HP/(N6778Y) |
| G-GGAE | HS 125/3B-RA | 25157 | Expotech (UK) Ltd/Afrotek, Nigeria. | VR-BGD/D-CAMB |
| G-HADI | Gulfstream 2TT | 235 | Arab Express Ltd. London. | N17581 |
| G-HHOI | HS 125/700B | 7097 | Trust House Forte Ltd. London. | (G-BHTJ) |
| G-JETA | Citation | 550-0094 | IDS Aircraft Ltd. London. | (N26630) |
| G-JETB | Citation | 550-0288 | IDS Aircraft Ltd. London. | N6865C |
| G-JETC | Citation | 550-0282 | IDS Aircraft Ltd. London. | N68644 |
| G-JETD | Citation | 550-0419 | IDS Aircraft Ltd. London. | |
| G-JJSG | Learjet | 35A-324 | John Jefferson Smurfit Group, Dublin. | |
| G-JRCT | Citation | 550-0088 | IDS Aircraft Ltd. London. | N2663N |
| G-LEAR | Learjet | 35A-265 | Northern Executive Aviation, Manchester. | (G-ZEST)/N1462B |
| G-MFEU | HS 125/600B | 6062 | Clartacrest Ltd. London. | G-5-15 |
| G-MKOA | HS 125/F403B | 25227 | Chief M K O Abiola/RCN, Lagos, Nigeria. | G-AYFM |
| G-MINE | Citation | 550-0343 | Mining Supplies Ltd. | (N1214D) |
| G-OBAE | HS 125/700B | 7094 | British Aerospace Ltd. Chester. | |
| G-OJOY | HS 125/700B | 7061 | H. Goodman-Air Europe, Gatwick. | G-BGGS/G-5-19 |
| G-OMCL | Citation | 550-0413 | Micro Consultants Ltd. London. | |
| G-ONPN | HS 125/1B | 25063 | Shirlstar Container Ltd. Luton. | G-BAXG/HB-VAN |
| G-OTKI | Citation | 550-0230 | (Never G- Regd. but where ?). | (N6804N) |
| G-TACE | HS 125/403B | 25223 | MAM/BSM, London. | G-AYIZ/F-BSSL/PJ-SLB/G-AYIZ |
| G-TEFH | Citation | 500-0176 | TBT Transport Ltd. East Midlands. | G-BCII |
| G-TJCB | HS 125/700B | 7127 | J C Bamford (Excavators) Ltd. East Midlands. | |
| G-UESS | Citation | 500-0326 | Osiwel Ltd. London. | N45LC/N5326J |
| G-ZEAL | Learjet | 35A-275 | Fairflight Charter/Jointair, Stansted. | N10872 |
| G-ZEIZ | Learjet | 36A-047 | Royco Homes Ltd. Marlow, Oxford. | |
| G-ZONE | Learjet | 35A-365 | Jointair Ltd. Stansted. | |
| N12ME | Citation | 500-0137 | Lotus Cars, Norwich. | N12MB/N137CC |
| N15AW | Citation | 500-0139 | A W Alloys, Stansted. | N3771U/OE-FDP/(N5353J) |
| N15SC | Learjet | 35A-139 | Sea Containers Associates, Luton. | |
| N110KS | Challenger | 1006 | Kalair USA Corp. | C-GCSN |
| N26178 | Citation | 550-0160 | A W Alloys, Stansted. | (9V-PUW) |
| VR-CBE | B 727-46 | 19282 | Resebury Corp, Panama. | N4245S/D-AHLQ/JA8325 |
| VR-CBL | Falcon 50 | 95 | ARAVCO, London. | F-WPXD |
| VR-CBM | Gulfstream 2 | 34 | ARAVCO, London. | N11SX/N130A/N230E |

## SWITZERLAND AND LIECHSTENSTEIN

| Registration | Type | C/N | Owner/Operator | Previous Identities |
|---|---|---|---|---|
| HB-IEH | B 737-2V6 | 22431 | Petrolair Systems, Athens. | N57008 |
| HB-IER | Falcon 50 | 57 | Socavia/Giesecke & Devrient, Munich. | F-WZHC |
| HB-IES | Falcon 50 | 61 | Logarcheo Anstalt Vaduz, Geneva. | F-WZHI |
| HB-IET | Falcon 50 | 48 | El Azem Co. | F-WZHK |
| HB-IEU | Falcon 50 | 27 | Gatair SA, Geneva. | F-WZHN |
| HB-IEV | Falcon 50 | 34 | Ilair AG. Zurich/EJA SA. Geneva. | F-WZHH |
| HB-IEX | Gulfstream 2 | 169 | Interjet AG/Private Jet Services. Basle. | N17584 |
| HB-IEY | Gulfstream 2 | 210 | Petrolair, Athens, Greece. | |
| HB-IEZ | Gulfstream 2TT | 246 | Sit Set AG. Geneva. | N17587 |
| HB-IMX | Gulfstream 2 | 335 | Sit Set AG/Jet Aviation Geneva. S.A. | |
| HB-IMZ | Gulfstream 2 | 88 | Natascha Estab. Vaduz. | N2637M/N2600/N881GA |
| HB-ITR | Gulfstream 2 | 144 | Lonrho/Lonair S.A. Lausanne. | N17585 |
| HB- | Gulfstream 3 | 352 | Lonrho/Lonair S.A. Lausanne. | N17586 |
| HB-PAA | MS 760 Paris | 69 | Dr. Alfred Gerber, Zurich. | J-4117/HB-PAA |
| HB-VBM | Mystere 20C | 136 | Ilair AG/Alag, Zurich. | F-GCGU/9K-ACQ/HB-VBM/F-WMKJ |
| HB-VBS | Mystere 20C | 55 | Aeroleasing/Fred-Air, Zug. | VR-BCJ/F-WNGO |
| HB-VDC | Citation | 500-0100 | Southern Consultants, Lugano. | OE-FNL/D-ICPW/HB-VDC/N695R6 |
| HB-VDD | Falcon 10A | 36 | Air Charter/Kraus & Naimer, Vienna. | F-WJMJ |
| HB-VDM | Citation | 500-0126 | Sirius AG. Zurich. | (N626CC) |
| HB-VDX | Falcon 10 | 56 | ALAG, Zurich. | F-WPUY |
| HB-VDY | Mystere 20E | 245 | Schweizerische Kreditanstalt, Zurich. | HB-VDP/F-BUIX/SX-ABA/F-WLCS |
| HB-VDZ | Mystere 20E | 255 | Omar Yehia/Mission Permanente d'Oman, Geneva. | RJAF122/F-WROP |
| HB-VEG | Falcon 10 | 70 | Starjet Establishment for Aviation, Vaduz. | F-WJMM |
| HB-VEH | Citation | 500-0230 | Fidinam S.A. Lugano. | N230CC/N5230J |
| HB-VEM | Learjet | 35A-068 | Swiss Air Ambulance, Zurich. | |
| HB-VEP | MS 760 Paris 2 | 98 | Regis Fraissinet, Geneva. | F-BOHN/D-INGA |
| HB-VEW | Learjet | 35A-088 | Jet Air Services AG. Zurich. | N3545F |
| HB-VEZ | Mystere 20D | 228 | Private Jet Services, Basle/Jet Flug. | C-GWSA/3D-LLG/ZS-LLG/ZS-LAL /F-WNGL |

| Regis-tration | Type | C/N | Owner/Operator | Previous Identities |
|---|---|---|---|---|
| HB-VFA | HS 125/700B | 7007 | Chartag GmbH. Zurich. | |
| HB-VFB | Learjet | 35A-145 | Swiss Air Ambulance, Zurich. | N39394 |
| HB-VFD | Learjet | 36A-029 | John von Neumann, Geneva. | (N79JS) |
| HB-VFK | Learjet | 35A-118 | Koci S.A. Geneva. | N39391 |
| HB-VFO | Learjet | 35A-184 | Citicorp International/Transair SA. Geneva. | N1462B |
| HB-VFS | Learjet | 36A-042 | Executive Jet Aviation, Geneva. | N39391 |
| HB-VFV | Learjet | 36A-040 | Protea Anstalt, Vaduz, Liechstenstein. | |
| HB-VFW | Challenger | 1049 | Swiss Air Ambulance, Zurich. | N2720B/C-GLXM |
| HB-VFX | Learjet | 35A-191 | Petrolair Systems SA. Geneva. | (YV-15CP)/N3810G |
| HB-VFZ | Learjet | 35A-222 | EJA, Geneva. | |
| HB-VGA | Challenger | 1029 | Air Charter/Kraus & Naimer, Vienna. | |
| HB-VGC | Learjet | 35A-259 | Fidinam S.A. Lugano. | N39413 |
| HB-VGD | Citation | 500-0082 | Private Jet Services, Basle. | EC-CCY/N582CC |
| HB-VGF | HS 125/700B | 7062 | Scintilla-Bosch, Stuttgart. | G-5-16 |
| HB-VGG | HS 125/700B | 7070 | Scintilla-Bosch, Stuttgart. | |
| HB-VGH | Learjet | 35A-206 | Executive Jet Aviation, Geneva. | (N66HM)/N760GL |
| HB-VGK | Citation | 551-0008 | Age of Enlightenment Travel AG, Seelisberg. | N108WG/(N3261M) |
| HB-VGM | Learjet | 35A-288 | Minitair S.A. Geneva. | N1476B |
| HB-VGP | Citation | 550-0189 | Private Jet Services. AG. Zurich. | D-CAAT/N98601 |
| HB-VGR | Citation | 550-0080 | Private Jet Services. Basle. | G-BFLY/(N26624) |
| HB-VGS | Citation | 550-0183 | Private Jet Services. Basle. | (XC-DUF)/N98630 |
| HB-VGT | Learjet | 35A-309 | Skyjet AG. Zurich | |
| HB-VGU | Learjet | 35A-331 | John von Neumann, Geneva. | N10870 |
| HB-VGV | Learjet | 55-015 | John von Neumann, Geneva. | |
| HB-VGX | Learjet | 35A-372 | Zakair SA. Fribourg. | |
| HB-VGY | Learjet | 35A-370 | Alair AG. Zurich/Sonco Hotel AG. Appenzell. | |
| HB-VGZ | Learjet | 55-024 | Aeroleasing SA. Geneva | |
| HB-VHA | Citation | 501-0142 | Alair AG. Zurich/Gerh-Schleiftechnik AG. Naefels. | N26507 |
| HB-VHB | Learjet | 35A-359 | Glorenade Anstalt, Vaduz, Liechstenstein. | (N127RM) |
| HB-VHC | Challenger | 1028 | Kontinair AG. | C-GLXM |
| HB-VHD | Learjet | 35A-395 | Transair (Suisse) SA. Geneva. | |
| HB-VHF | Learjet | 36A-048 | Executive Jet Aviation SA. Geneva. | |
| HB-VHG | Learjet | 35A-445 | Transair (Suisse) S.A. Geneva. | N3802G |
| HB-VHI | Citation | 500-0344 | Stauffer Chemical (Europe) SA. Geneva. | N632SQ/N632SC/(N5344J) |
| HB-VHK | Learjet | 55-045 | Transair (Suisse) SA. Geneva. | |
| HB-VHL | Learjet | 55-054 | | |
| N18RN | Gulfstream 2 | 231 | NOGA/Chemco International Leasing Inc. NY. | VR-BHD/VR-CAG/N1102 /N808GA |
| N180RN | B 737-2W8 | 22628 | NOGA/Chemco International Leasing Inc. NY. | |
| VR-BHC | Learjet | 24XR-267 | John von Neumann, Geneva. | N124GA/N78AE/N46023/HB-VCY |

COLOMBIA

| | | | | |
|---|---|---|---|---|
| HK-2150 | Westwind-1124 | 181 | Helicol-Avianca, Bogota. | HK-2150X/4X-CKE |
| HK-2485X | Westwind Two | 239 | Helicol-Avianca, Bogota. | 4X-CMK |
| HK-2624X | Learjet | 25D-339 | | N3798D |

SOUTH KOREA

| | | | | |
|---|---|---|---|---|
| HL7226 | Citation | 500-0294 | Korean Air Lines, Seoul. | N5294J |
| HL7234 | Falcon 20F | 370 | Korean Air Lines, Seoul. | N1038F/F-WMKG |
| HL7277 | Citation | 500-0327 | Korean Ministry of Transport, Seoul. | N5327J |

SAUDI ARABIA

| | | | | |
|---|---|---|---|---|
| HZ-AAA | Citation | 550-0116 | Arabian International Services Co. Jeddah. | N2745M |
| HZ-AB1 | BAC 1-11/414 | 158 | Abdul Aziz Al-Ibrahim. | HZ-AMH/HZ-MF1/D-AISY |
| HZ-ABM | Learjet | 35A-243 | Sheikh Ali bin Hussein Al Musallam. | N3812G |
| HZ-ADC | Gulfstream 2 | 187 | Raytheon Middle East Systems, Bedford, Ma. | N804GA/N17583 |
| HZ-AFG | Gulfstream 2 | 175 | Saudia, Jeddah. | N17585 |
| HZ-AFH | Gulfstream 2 | 171 | Saudia, Jeddah. | N17586 |
| HZ-AFI | Gulfstream 2TT | 201 | Saudia, Jeddah. | N17585 |
| HZ-AFJ | Gulfstream 2TT | 203 | Saudia, Jeddah. | N17587 |
| HZ-AFK | Gulfstream 2TT | 239 | Saudia, Jeddah. | N17582 |
| HZ-AFL | Gulfstream 3 | 311 | Saudia, Jeddah. | N17585 |
| HZ-AFM | Gulfstream 3 | 324 | Saudia, Jeddah. | |
| HZ-ALJ | Citation | 550-0069 | Abdul Latis Jameer Est. Jeddah. | HZ-AAA/3A-MWA/F-GBPL/N2069A |

| Regis-tration | Type | C/N | Owner/Operator | Previous Identities |
|---|---|---|---|---|
| HZ-AM2 | Learjet | 55-040 | National Commercial Bank, Jeddah. | HZ-AMII/N3802G |
| HZ-AMB | NAL 1-11/401 | 9/069 | Sheikh A M Baroom. | VR-CAM/3D-LLG/N5029 |
| HZ-AMK | BAC 1-11/410 | 054 | Sheikh Abdul Maksoud Khotah. | N770S/N77CS/N3939V/G-ASYE/N4111X |
| HZ-A01 | Mystere 20F | 359 | Akram Ojjeh/TAG International. | HZ-TAG/(N64769)/F-WRQR |
| HZ-A02 | Falcon 10 | 118 | Akram Ojjeh/TAG International. | HZ-NOT/HZ-AMA/F-WPXI |
| HZ-AZP | Learjet | 25B-081 | Beta Co. | HZ-MOA/N110GL/N111GL |
| HZ-BL1 | BAC 1-11/401 | 080 | Sheikh bin Laden. | HZ-MFA/N90TF/N22RB/N10HM/N5038 |
| HZ-B01 | HS 125/1B | 25094 | Sheikh Salem bin Laden. | G-ATWH |
| HZ-CA1 | Sabre-75A | 380-55 | Dallah AVCO Transarabia, Jeddah. | N33KA/N2139J |
| HZ-DAT | B 707-123B | 17644 | Dallah AVCO. | N7517A |
| HZ-DA2 | HS 125/700B | 7088 | Dallah AVCO. | |
| HZ-DA3 | HS 125/700B | 7115 | Dallah AVCO. | |
| HZ-DA4 | HS 125/700B | 7124 | Dallah AVCO. | |
| HZ-DA5 | B 727-212 | 21460 | Dallah AVCO. | 9V-SGF |
| HZ-DC2 | Mystere 20F | 363 | Sheikh Al Khereiji. | F-WROV |
| HZ-FBT | JetStar-731 | 44/5086 | Saud Special Services. | N60UJ/N600J/N27RL/N27R |
| HZ-FMA | HS 125/1B | 25105 | Saudi Arabian Carpets. | G-AYRY/D-CKCF/(D-CKOW) |
| HZ-GRP | B 727-76 | 20228 | REDEC. | HZ-GP2/N8043E/VH-TJE |
| HZ-HE4 | B 727-29C | 19987 | Sheikh Hassan Enany. | N444SA/N696WA/OO-STE |
| HZ-HM1 | B 747SP-68 | 21652 | Saudi Royal Family, | N1780B |
| HZ-HM2 | B 707-368C | 21081 | King Fahd, Riyadh. | HZ-HM1 |
| HZ-HM3 | B 707-368C | 21368 | Saudi Royal Family. | HZ-ACK |
| HZ-HM4 | B 737-268 | 22050 | Saudi Royal Family. | HZ-AGT |
| HZ-JAM | BAC 1-11/412 | 111 | Sheikh Abdul Momenah. | N90AM/N767RV/N221CN/AN-BBI |
| HZ-KA1 | B 720-047B | 18451 | Sheikh Kamal Adham, Jeddah. | HZ-NAA/N93145 |
| HZ-KA2 | HS 125/600B | 6057 | Sheikh Kamal Adham, Jeddah. | G-5-17 |
| HZ-KA3 | Mystere 20C | 174 | Sheikh Kamal Adham, Jeddah. | F-WSHT/HB-VER/TL-KAZ/TL-AAY/F-WNGL |
| HZ-KA4 | B 720-047B | 18453 | Sheikh Kamal Adham, Jeddah. | N93147 |
| HZ-KA5 | HS 125/600B | 6049 | Sheikh Kamal Adham, Jeddah. | G-BCXL/ZS-JHL/G-BCXL |
| HZ-MA1 | Sabre-60 | 306-110 | Sheikh Ashmawi Associates-Saudi Arabian Markets. | N60RS/N2103J |
| HZ-MAA | NAL 1-11/401 | 10/060 | National Commercial Bank, Jeddah. | HZ-NB3/HZ-GP2/HZ-GRP/N102GP /N111NA/N5020 |
| HZ-MAM | BAC 1-11/475 | 259 | Sheikh M Al Midani. | |
| HZ-MMM | HS 125/700B | 7010 | Sheikh M Al Midani | (G-5-16) |
| HZ-M01 | BAC 1-11/204 | 135 | Mohammed Othman/Saudi Wings. | N1125J |
| HZ-MPM | Gulfstream 2 | 4 | Mobil Oil/Petromin. | VR-CAS/9K-ACY/N680RZ/N680RW/N832GA |
| HZ-MS1 | Learjet | 35A-467 | Whittaker Corp/Armed Forces Medical Services. | N37960 |
| HZ-MSD | Gulfstream 2 | 256 | Whittaker Corp/Armed Forces Medical Services. | N17581 |
| HZ-NAD | HS 125/700B | 7064 | NADCO. | |
| HZ-NB2 | NAL 1-11/401 | 12/064 | National Commercial Bank of Saudia Arabia. | N5024 |
| HZ-NCB | Sabre-60 | 306-94 | REDEC. | HZ-MA1/N65778 |
| HZ-NIR | NAL 1-11/401 | 7/088 | Rashid Engineering. | N5042 |
| HZ-NR1 | Sabre-75A | 380-71 | Rashid Engineering. | |
| HZ-NR2 | Gulfstream 3 | 304 | Rashid Engineering. | N17583 |
| HZ-PCA | Gulfstream 2 | 179 | Directorate Of Civil Aviation. | HZ-CAD/N17588 |
| HZ-PET | Gulfstream 2 | 139 | Mobil Oil/Petromin. | N18N/N880GA |
| HZ-PL1 | Falcon 20E | 293 | Mobil Oil/Petromin. | N2613/N2615/N4442F/F-WMKJ |
| HZ-PL7 | Falcon 20E | 241 | Mobil Oil/Petromin. | HZ-HE4/N48AD/SE-DCO/F-WROP |
| HZ-RBH | Sabre-75A | 380-57 | Civil Construction Establishment. | N75A/N80RS/N2147J |
| HZ-RC1 | HS 125/700B | 7040 | Saudi Parsons/Royal Commission. | |
| HZ-RC2 | HS 125/700B | 7055 | Saudi Parsons/Royal Commission. | G-5-16 |
| HZ-RC3 | Gulfstream 3 | 331 | Royal Commission for Jubail & Yuambu. | N17LB/N307GA |
| HZ-RH1 | NAL 1-11/401 | 13/081 | Civil Construction Establishment | N5039 |
| HZ-RH2 | Gulfstream 3 | 346 | Saudi Oger Ltd. | |
| HZ-SH4 | JetStar-8 | 5148 | Shobokshi Group, Jeddah. | N21SH/N964M/N5512L |
| HZ-SJW | HS 125/600B | 6059 | Jouanou & Parskevaides Saudi Arabia Ltd. | HZ-DAC/G-5-19 |
| HZ-SMB | Learjet | 25XR-073 | Sheikh Salem bin Laden. | N3JX/N3JL/I-TAKY/HB-VCM |
| HZ-SOG | Sabre-75A | 380-72 | Saudi Oger Ltd. | |
| HZ-TAG | Challenger | 1014 | TAG International. | N97941 |
| HZ-TA1 | B 727-30 | 18365 | Prince Talud bin Abdul Aziz, Jeddah. | N16767/D-ABIH |
| HZ-THZ | JetStar-731 | 34/5050 | Harb Al Zuhair, Riyadh. | N141TC/N208L/N207L |
| HZ-WBT | JetStar 8 | 5133 | Prince Waleed. | VR-CAW/C-GPGD/N322K/N329K/N7978S |
| HZ-ZTC | Citation | 550-0134 | | HZ-AAI/N2635D |
| HZ- | Falcon 50 | 73 | | F-WPXE |
| HZ- | Gulfstream 3 | 358 | | |
| N27MJ | Learjet | 25-050 | MJI/Sheikh bin Laden. | D-CONE/N44EE/N44EL |
| N51DB | Learjet | 25XR-246 | James Bath/Sheikh bin Laden. | N40162 |
| N74G | Learjet | 25B-174 | MJI/Northrop. | |

18

| Regis-tration | Type | C/N | Owner/Operator | Previous Identities |
|---|---|---|---|---|
| N80BT | Learjet | 25D-248 | MJI/Northrop/RSAF 015, Dhahran. | |
| N107A | Gulfstream 2 | 53 | ARAMCO, Jeddah. | |
| N108BN | B 707-138B | 18740 | TAG International. | VH-EBM |
| N300AG | JetStar-6 | 5056 | HRH Prince Fahd Bin Nasser Bin Abdul Aziz Al Saud. | N105GH/N105G /N9223R |
| N308A | Gulfstream 2 | 155 | ARAMCO, Jeddah. | |
| N332LS | Learjet | 25B-122 | Lockheed Aircraft Corp. Ontario, Ca. | N23TA |
| N499AS | JetStar-8 | 5146 | Abdul Aziz Al Sulaiman/ROLACO | N4990D/C-GWSA/N80GM/N5510L |
| N777XX | Challenger | 1017 | TAG International/Aviation Methods, SFO. | N4247C/C-GBPX |
| N800LS | Falcon 20C | 144 | National Medical Enterprises, Riyadh. | N888JR/N888L/N4356F/F-WJMJ |
| N919G | Gulfstream 2 | 29 | Western Electric International. | N930BS/N869GA |
| N2615 | Gulfstream 2 | 148 | Mobil Saudi Arabia Inc. Jeddah. | N710MP/N710MR |
| N3794B | Learjet | 55-021 | James Bath, League City, Tx./Bin Laden Aviation. | |
| N5034 | NAL 1-11/401 | 15/076 | TAG Aircraft Services Ltd. | |
| N58937 | B 707-138B | 18334 | TAG Aviation Ltd. Wilmington, De. | 9Y-TDB/VH-EBK |
| C-GTLU | Falcon 20F | 262 | Al Hickman Aviation. | N501AS/VH-WLH/N750ME/N720ML/N4427F/F-WJMK |
| VR-BGT | Gulfstream 2 | 211 | Ditco Air Ltd/Sheikh El Khereiji. | N17581 |

ITALY

| Regis-tration | Type | C/N | Owner/Operator | Previous Identities |
|---|---|---|---|---|
| I-ARIB | Citation | 550-0284 | Soc. Aer-Marche, Falconara. | N6801R |
| I-ATMO | Mystere 20C | 94 | Soc. Nicomede S.R.L Milan. | F-WNGO |
| I-AUNY | Citation | 501-0213 | SPEI Leasing/Soc. Unifly, Rome. | N6785D |
| I-CAIC | Falcon 10 | 89 | Soc. C A I, Rome. | F-WZGF/D-CADB/F-WPXM |
| I-CHIC | Falcon 10 | 126 | Soc. VIP-Air, Milan. | F-WNGM |
| I-CHOC | Falcon 10 | 113 | Soc. VIP-Air, Milan. | (I-SHOP)/F-WPXE |
| I-CIGB | Citation | 501-0163 | CIGA Hotels, Venice. | (I-AGIK)/N1354G |
| I-CMUT | Mystere 20F | 389 | Soc. Locafit, Milan. | F-WROV |
| I-DEAF | Citation | 550-0255 | Soc. Ital-Avio SPRL. | N6861L |
| I-DEAN | Learjet | 25D-314 | Soc. De Angelis, Rome. | |
| I-DECI | Citation | 501-0118 | Soc. SPEI Leasing, Rome. | N2649Z |
| I-DJMA | Falcon 10 | 179 | Soc. CAI, Rome. | F-WZGL |
| I-DKET | Mystere 20C | 160 | Soc. Fiat, Turin. | F-WMKG |
| I-EDIF | Mystere 20E | 300 | Soc. Locatrice Italiana, Rome. | F-WROP |
| I-EDIM | Mystere 20E | 295 | Soc. VIP-Air, Milan. | F-WRQO |
| I-EDIS | Mystere 20E | 280 | Soc. VIP-Air, Milan. | F-WPXK |
| I-EKET | Mystere 20C | 170 | Soc. Fiat, Turin. | F-WPUV |
| I-FBCT | Citation | 550-0081 | Consorzio Fabocart S.p.a. Milan. | N26626 |
| I-FIMI | Learjet | 35A-090 | Soc. Air Fimi, Milan. | HB-VEY |
| I-FKET | Mystere 20E | 279 | Soc. Fiat, Turin. | F-WMKJ |
| I-FLYA | Citation | 501-0099 | Eurofly Service S.p.a. Turin/Olivetti Leasing. | N3170A |
| I-FLYB | Citation | 500-0392 | Eurofly Service S.p.a. Turin/Locafit S.p.a. | N26461 |
| I-FLYC | Learjet | 35A-298 | Eurofly Service S.p.a. Turin/Olivetti Leasing. | |
| I-GIAZ | Mystere 20E | 252 | Soc. Indunstrie Zanussi, Pordenone (Treviso). | F-WROP |
| I-GJBO | HS 125/400B | 25240 | Soc. Alba Serv. Aerotrasporti,Milan. | G-AYLI/G-5-11 |
| I-ITAL | HFB 320 | 1040 | Soc. Aliserio, Milan. | D-CESU |
| I-KIDO | Falcon 50 | 31 | Soc. Gitanair, Milan. | (N54FJ)/F-WZHC |
| I-KISS | Learjet | 25B-193 | Soc. Cama Sud, Turin. | HB-VEF |
| I-KODE | Citation | 501-0218 | Soc. Locafit, Rome. | N1958E |
| I-KUNA | Citation | 500-0053 | Soc. ASSILEASING, Rome. | N90WJ/I-CITY/N553CC |
| I-LEAR | Learjet | 25D-207 | Soc. Prelloyd, Milan. | (I-GIAN)/N3513F |
| I-LIAB | Mystere 20C | 172 | ALI=Aeroleasing Italiana. | F-BRHB/F-WNGM |
| I-LIAC | Mystere 20D | 234 | ALI=Aeroleasing Italiana. | D-COLL/(D-CIBM)/F-WLCU |
| I-LIAD | Learjet | 35A-111 | ALI=Aeroleasing Italiana. | OE-GMA/(I-SIDU)/(HB-VFE)/N3815G |
| I-MMAE | Learjet | 35A-116 | Soc. Locatelli Estramed S.p.a. Rome. | |
| I-MUDE | Falcon 10 | 136 | Soc. CAI, Rome. | F-WZGH |
| I-OTEL | Citation | 501-0048 | CIGA Hotels, Venice. | (I-DAEP)/N414CC/N87510 |
| I-PEGA | Citation | 500-0081 | Soc. Gambogi, Pisa. | HB-VDA/N5B/N581CC |
| I-PIAL | PD 808 | 504 | Soc. Rinaldo Piaggio, Genoa. | |
| I-RACE | HS 125/1 | 25006 | Soc. Delta Pedano, Milan. | HB-VAG |
| I-REAL | Mystere 20E | 267 | Soc. SARAS, Saroch (Cagliari). | F-WROZ |
| I-RELT | Sabre-40A | 282-133 | Soc. Elettronica, Rome. | N41NR/N65740 |
| I-RIED | Mystere 20C | 77 | Soc. Rizzoli Editore, Milan. | F-WNGO |
| I-ROST | Citation | 500-0381 | Soc. Fabocart, Milan. | N445CC/N3104M |
| I-SAFR | Falcon 50 | 29 | Soc. FIAT, Turin. | F-WZHB |
| I-SAME | Falcon 50 | 37 | Soc. CAI, Rome. | (I-CAIK)/F-WZHM |
| I-SFRA | Falcon 10 | 130 | Soc. Feruzzi, Forli. | F-WZGB |

| Regis-tration | Type | C/N | Owner/Operator | Previous Identities |
|---|---|---|---|---|
| I-SNAC | Falcon 50 | 30 | Soc. Naz. Metanodotti, Rome-Ciampino. | F-WZHD |
| I-SNAF | HS 125/3B | 25145 | Soc. Air-SIFO, Milan. | G-AVXL/LN-NPC/G-AVXL/(G-5-20) |
| I-SNAG | Mystere 20E | 240 | Soc. Naz. Metanodotti, Milan. | F-WLCX |
| I-SNAM | Mystere 20C | 176 | Soc. Naz. Metanodotti, Milan. | F-WMKG |
| I-SNAV | Mystere 20C | 119 | Soc. Naz. Metanodotti, Milan. | F-WJMK |
| I-UUNY | Citation | 500-0358 | Soc. Unifly, Rome. | SE-DEP/N82MJ/(EP-PAQ)/N36870 |
| I-VIKI | Citation | 550-0348 | Soc. Italiana Constr. Elettriche, Perugia. | N381CC |

## DJIBOUTI

| | | | | |
|---|---|---|---|---|
| J2-KAC | Mystere 20F | 342 | Government of Djibouti. | YI-AHI/F-WROP |

## GUINEA-BISSAU

| | | | | |
|---|---|---|---|---|
| J5-GAS | Mystere 20F | 296 | Government of Guinea-Bissau. | D2-EBB/HB-VDB/F-WROP |

## JAPAN

| | | | | |
|---|---|---|---|---|
| JA8431 | Gulfstream 2 | 141 | JCAB=Japanese Civil Aviation Board, Tokyo. | N17584 |
| JA8438 | Citation | 500-0321 | Asahi Shimbun Publishing Co. Tokyo. | N5321J |
| JA8463 | Falcon 10 | 152 | Sony Corp. Tokyo. | N8463/N216FJ/F-WZGY |
| JA8474 | Citation | 500-0415 | Asahi Shimbun Publishing Co. Tokyo. | N2072A |
| JQ8005 | Diamond One | | | |

## JORDAN

| | | | | |
|---|---|---|---|---|
| JY-AFE | Learjet | 35A-075 | Arab Wings, Amman. | HB-VEV/N3503F |
| JY-AFF | Learjet | 35A-081 | Arab Wings, Amman. | N3523F |
| JY-AFL | Sabre-75A | 380-56 | Arab Wings, Amman. | N2146J |
| JY-AFO | Sabre-75A | 380-61 | Arab Wings, Amman. | N2522E |
| JY-AFP | Sabre-75A | 380-62 | Arab Wings, Amman. | |
| JY-AHS | B 727-30 | 18934 | Arab Wings, Amman. | JY-HMH/N62119/D-ABIS |
| JY-HNH | B 727-2U5 | 22362 | H.R.H. King Hussein of Jordan, Amman. | |

## NORWAY

| | | | | |
|---|---|---|---|---|
| LN-AFC | Citation | 501-0262 | K/S A/S Flyfinas, Lysaker. | N9712T/YV-79CP/(YV-O-SID-3)/N36898 |
| LN-HOT | Citation | 550-0076 | Helikopter Service A/S. Oslo. | (N2663X) |
| LN-VIP | Citation | 550-0124 | Helikopter Service A/S. Oslo. | N2746U |

## ARGENTINA

| | | | | |
|---|---|---|---|---|
| LQ-JRH | HFB 320 | 1050 | Gas del Estado, Buenos Aires. | LV-POP/D-CISU |
| LQ-MRM | Citation | 500-0386 | Argentine Federal Police, Buenos Aires. | LV-PAX/N3173M |
| LV-ALF | Learjet | 35A-371 | Cia Loma Negra, SA. | |
| LV-ALW | HS 125/700B | 7133 | YPF, Buenos Aires. | LV-PMM/G-5-14 |
| LV-APL | Citation | | | |
| LV-JTZ | Learjet | 24D-234 | Sr. Wm. Reynal, Buenos Aires. | |
| LV-JXA | Learjet | 24D-240 | Aeromaster S.R.L., Buenos Aires. | |
| LV-LOG | Learjet | 36-005 | Bunge y Born, Buenos Aires. | |
| LV-LRC | Learjet | 24D-316 | Province of Tierra del Fuego. | |
| LV-LZR | Citation | | Cessna Aircraft Co. Wichita, Ks. | |
| LV-MBP | Learjet | 25D-229 | Banco de Intercambio Regional S.A. Buenos Aires. | N39415 |
| LV-MGB | Citation | 500-0372 | Ceramica San Lorenzo, Buenos Aires. | LV-PZI/N36943 |
| LV-MMR | Citation | 500-0375 | Automotores Y Servicios SA. Buenos Aires. | LV-PAT/N3147M |
| LV-MMV | Learjet | 25D-259 | Banco d'Italia y Rio Plata. | LV-PAW |
| LV-MST | Learjet | 25D-245 | SALTA Gobernacion Provinciade. Buenos Aires. | LV-PAF/N39398 |
| LV-MZG | Citation | 501-0117 | Lineas Aereas Surenas SA. Buenos Aires. | LV-PDW/N26493 |
| LV-MYN | Citation | 500-0393 | | LV-PDZ/N26497 |
| LV-OAS | Learjet | 35A-271 | Ledesma, Buenos Aires. | N1088A |
| LV-OEL | Learjet | 25D-307 | Sarmiento Newspapers. | LV-PEU |
| LV-OFV | Learjet | 35A-312 | Estab. Modelo Terrabusi SACI, Buenos Aires. | LV-PHX |
| LV-ONN | Learjet | 35A-355 | Dahm Automotores SA. C.I.I.F., Buenos Aires. | LV-PJZ/N1468B |
| LV-PNB | Citation | 551-0361 | Citibank NA, Buenos Aires. | N6799C |
| LV-PUY | Citation | 500-0332 | Cygnus S.A.C.I., Buenos Aires. | N5332J |
| LV- | Citation | 501-0197 | | N6781Z |

| Regis-<br>tration | Type | C/N | Owner/Operator | Previous<br>Identities |
|---|---|---|---|---|
| PERU | | | | |
| OB-M-1171 | Citation | 550-0047 | Southern Peru Copper Corp. | (NboVM)/N3313M |
| LEBANON | | | | |
| OD-PAL | Mystere 20F | 395 | Government of Lebanon, Beirut. | (HZ-AKI)/F-WROX |
| AUSTRIA | | | | |
| OE-FAP | Citation | 500-0300 | Grondmet Handels GmbH. Vienna. | (N5300J) |
| OE-FPH | Citation | 501-0173 | Porsche Konstruktionen, Salzburg. | (N6778V) |
| OE-FYF | Citation | 501-0106 | Veit GmbH. Puch bei Hallein. | (N123YF)/(N2649J) |
| OE-GAG | Falcon 10 | 151 | Nikki Lauda, Vienna. | N26CP/N217FJ/F-WZGX |
| OE-GCP | Citation | 550-0323 | Automobilvertriebs AG. Salzburg. | (N5703C) |
| OE-GLF | Mystere 20E | 323 | Luftfahrzeug Service/Lauda Air. Vienna. | I-FCIM/HB-VEB/F-WRQS |
| OE-GLG | Falcon 10 | 96 | Montana Flug. | XA-SAR/N174FJ/F-WNGD |
| OE-GLL | Mystere 20E | 307 | Luftfahrzeug Service, Vienna. | I-GCAL/HB-VDV/F-WRQT |
| OE-GLS | Citation | 550-0270 | Tyrolean Airways, Innsbruck. | N6863B |
| OE-GMP | Learjet | 35A-122 | Air Charter Austria, Vienna. | D-CCHS |
| OE-GNK | Learjet | 55-013 | Air Charter Austria, Vienna. | (D-CCHS) |
| OE-GNP | Learjet | 35A-347 | Viennair Luftfahrt GmbH. Vienna. | |
| OE-IEB | B707-321B | 18339 | Plyglobe Handels GmbH. Vienna. | N764SE/N764PA |
| HB-VDD | Falcon 10A | 36 | Kraus & Naimer, Vienna. | F-WJMJ |
| FINLAND | | | | |
| OH-CIT | Citation | 500-0397 | Jet Flite OY. Helsinki. | N6563C/(N1958E) |
| OH-FFA | Mystere 20C | 178 | Finnaviation. Helsinki. | F-WPXF |
| OH-GLB | Learjet | 24D-262 | Kone OY. Helsinki. | N2GR |
| BELGIUM | | | | |
| OO-LFA | Learjet | 24D-248 | Abelag Aviation, Brussels. | |
| OO-LFY | Learjet | 35A-200 | Abelag Aviation, Brussels. | D-CCAR/N3818G |
| OO-MRC | Corvette | 30 | Hessenatie-Sotramat Aviation NV. Antwerp. | TR-LAH/OO-MRC/F-BTTP<br>/F-WNGQ |
| OO-MRE | Corvette | 15 | Hessenatie-Sotramat Aviation NV. Antwerp. | OO-MRA/SE-DEN/F-WIFA |
| OO-SEL | Citation | 500-0133 | Air Select, Antwerp. | F-BUYL/N133CC |
| OO-VPQ | Mystere 20E | 315 | Benelux Falcon Service, Brussels. | F-BVPQ/F-WRQP |
| DENMARK | | | | |
| OY-AJV | Citation | 500-0279 | Kali A/S, Copenhagen. | D-IMEN/(N5279J) |
| OY-APM | HS 125/400B | 25253 | Maerskair/A P Moller, Copenhagen. | G-5-18 |
| OY-ARA | Corvette | 32 | Corvette K/S vid Scan Fly A/S, Copenhagen. | SE-DED/OY-ARA/F-BTTQ<br>/F-WNGR |
| OY-ARB | Corvette | 34 | Sterling Airways, Copenhagen. | SE-DEE/OY-ARB/F-BYCR/F-WNGS |
| OY-ARP | Citation | 500-0040 | Lilly Asmin Hansen, Arhus. | D-IKAN/N714US/JA8422/N540CC |
| OY-ASO | Learjet | 35A-119 | Kali A/S, Copenhagen. | N93MJ/D-CHER/HB-VFG |
| OY-BDS | Mystere 20C | 180 | Danfoss Aviation, Sonderborg. | F-WMKF |
| OY-BLG | Learjet | 35-022 | Grundfos A/S, Bjorringsbro. | |
| OY-GKC | Citation | 550-0085 | Lego Systems, Billund. | (N2663Y) |
| OY-SBR | Corvette | 23 | Sterling Airways, Copenhagen. | F-BVPF |
| OY-SBT | Corvette | 33 | Sterling Airways, Copenhagen. | F-BTTT |
| PAPUA NEW GUINEA | | | | |
| P2-BCM | Westwind-1124 | 317 | Bougainville Copper Mines, Kieta. | VH-AYI/4X-CRK |
| P2-PNG | Gulfstream 2 | 103 | Government of Papua New Guinea. | P2-PNF/N833GA/G-BDMF/N801GA/N855GA |
| HOLLAND | | | | |
| PH-CTA | Citation | 500-0088 | RLS=Rijksluchtvaartschool, Eelde. | N588CC |
| PH-CTB | Citation | 500-0093 | RLS, Eelde. | N593CC |
| PH-CTC | Citation | 500-0098 | RLS, Eelde. | N598CC |
| PH-CTD | Citation | 500-0157 | RLS, Eelde. | |

| Regis-tration | Type | C/N | Owner/Operator | Previous Identities |
|---|---|---|---|---|
| PH-CTE | Citation | 500-0167 | RLS, Eelde. | |
| PH-CTF | Citation | 500-0177 | RLS, Eelde. | |
| PH-CTG | Citation | 500-0234 | RLS, Eelde. | (N5234J) |
| PH-HES | Citation | 550-0020 | Heerema Engineering Service, The Hague. | N3236M |
| PH-HET | Citation | 550-0294 | Heerema Engineering Service, The Hague. | N68872 |
| PH-HFC | HFB 320 | 1035 | RLS, Eelde. | D-CERU |
| PH-ILF | Mystere 20C | 147 | N V Philips, Eindhoven. | F-WLCU |
| PH-ILR | Falcon 50 | 15 | N V Philips, Eindhoven. | F-WZHM |
| PH-ILX | Mystere 20E | 266 | N V Philips, Eindhoven. | F-WROR |
| PH-ILY | Mystere 20E | 326 | N V Philips, Eindhoven. | F-WROQ |
| PH-LPS | Mystere 20C | 63 | N V Philips, Eindhoven. | F-WMKI |
| PH-MBX | Citation | 550-0166 | Martinair Holland N V. Amsterdam. | N88731 |
| PH-PBX | F 28-1000 | 11045 | Dutch Royal Flight, Amsterdam. | |
| PH-SDL | Falcon 50 | 66 | Film Air, Dino de Laurentis. | F-WZHF |
| N26498 | Citation | 500-0398 | Ster Disposables Group. | (PH-JOB) |

## INDONESIA

| | | | | |
|---|---|---|---|---|
| PK-CAG | Mystere 20F | 408 | Directorate of Civil Aviation, Jakarta. | F-WROS |
| PK-PJD | HS-125/600B | 6017 | Pertamina Oil, Jakarta. | G-BBAS/G-5-18 |
| PK-PJE | HS 125/F600B | 6029 | Pertamina Oil, Jakarta. | (G-BBRT) |
| PK-PJM | F 28-4000 | 11178 | Pertamina Oil, Jakarta. | PH-EXW |
| PK-PJQ | B 707-3M1C | 21092 | Govt. of Republik Indonesia, Jakarta. | |
| PK-PJR | HS-125/3B-RA | 25147 | Pertamina Oil, Jakarta. | G-5-14 |
| PK-PJS | F 28-1000 | 11030 | Pertamina Oil, Jakarta. | D-ABAM |
| PK-PJT | F 28-1000 | 11042 | Pertamina Oil, Jakarta. | (PK-PJX) |
| PK-PJU | F 28-1000 | 11029 | Pertamina Oil, Jakarta. | D-ABAN/PH-ZBD |
| PK-PJV | F 28-1000 | 11073 | Pertamina Oil, Jakarta. | PH-EXT |
| PK-PJW | F 28-4000 | 11148 | Pertamina Oil, Jakarta. | PH-EXT |
| PK-PJY | F 28-4000 | 11146 | Pertamina Oil, Jakarta. | PH-EXN |

## BRAZIL

| | | | | |
|---|---|---|---|---|
| PP-EEM | HS 125/400B | 25197 | Governor of Sao Paulo State. | G-5-11 |
| PP-SED | Sabre-40A | 282-121 | Banco de Investimentos BCN SA. Belo Horizonte. | N8349N |
| PT-ASJ | Falcon 10 | 95 | Servair/VW-Mercedes, Sao Paulo. | N173FJ/F-WPXD |
| PT-CMY | Learjet | 25C-108 | Cruzeiro Aerofoto, Rio de Janeiro. | |
| PT-CXJ | Learjet | 24-176 | Taxi Aereo Lider Ltda, Belo Horizonte. | |
| PT-DTY | HS 125/F400B | 25243 | Banco do Brazil, Brasilia. | G-AYOI/G-5-13 |
| PT-FAF | Learjet | 25C-099 | Banco de Habitacao, Brasilia. | PT-IKR |
| PT-FAT | Learjet | 35A-361 | Banco Central do Brasil, Brasilia. | PT-LBS/N924GL |
| PT-FOH | Falcon 20C | 113 | Brazilian Coffee Institute, Rio. | PP-FOH/N993F/F-WNGL |
| PT-IDW | HFB 320 | 1052 | Quimica Industrial Paulista SA. Sao Paulo. | D-CORI |
| PT-IIQ | Learjet | 25C-089 | Taxi Aereo Marilia S.A. Sao Paulo. | |
| PT-ILJ | Citation | 500-0057 | Brasil Warrant, Admin. de Bens e Empresas Ltda. Rio. | N557CC |
| PT-IOB | HFB 320 | 1053 | Industria Villares, Sao Paulo. | D-CORO |
| PT-IQL | Citation | 500-0069 | Cia Mineira de Matais, Belo Horizonte. | N569CC |
| PT-ISN | Learjet | 25C-113 | Jose Afonso Assupcao, Belo Horizonte. | |
| PT-ISO | Learjet | 25C-115 | Carbonifera Metropolitana S.A. Porto Alegre. | |
| PT-JGU | Learjet | 24D-276 | Bradesco Financiadora S.A. Sao Paulo. | |
| PT-JKQ | Learjet | 24D-284 | Iochpe-Arrendamento Mercantil SA. Porto Alegre. | |
| PT-JKR | Learjet | 24D-278 | Taxi Aereo Lider Ltda. Belo Horizonte. | |
| PT-JMJ | Citation | 500-0134 | Construtora Mendes Junior S.A. Belo Horizonte. | N134CC |
| PT-JNJ | Sabre-40A | 282-118 | Grupo Votorantim, Sao Paulo. | N8339N |
| PT-KAP | Learjet | 25C-156 | Bandeirantes Participacoes Admin. Sao Paulo. | |
| PT-KBC | Learjet | 25C-165 | Banco Bozzano Simonsen Leasing SA. Rio | |
| PT-KBD | Learjet | 25B-166 | Leasing Sul SA. Porto Alegre. | |
| PT-KBR | Citation | 500-0156 | Frigorifico Mouran S.A. Sao Paulo. | |
| PT-KIR | Citation | 500-0103 | Construcoes e Comercio Camargo Correa SA. Sao Paulo. | N103CC/(N603CC) |
| PT-KKV | Learjet | 25C-172 | Cia Comercio e Navegacao. | |
| PT-KOT | Sabre-60 | 306-80 | Atlantica Cia Nacional de Seguros, Rio. | N65756 |
| PT-KPA | Citation | 500-0181 | Weston Taxi Aereo SA. Recife. | |
| PT-KPB | Citation | 500-0188 | SOCILA/Cosorcio Bonfiglioli, Sao Paulo. | N5223J |
| PT-KPE | Learjet | 24D-315 | Cimento Caue S.A. Belo Horizonte. | |
| PT-KQT | Learjet | 36- 011 | Banco Real S.A. Sao Paulo. | |
| PT-KTO | Falcon 10 | 63 | Participacoes Morre Vermelho Ltda. Sao Paulo. | N147FJ/F-WLCX |

| Regis-tration | Type | C/N | Owner/Operator | Previous Identities |
|---|---|---|---|---|
| PT-KTU | Learjet | 36A-018 | Hidroservice, Sao Paulo. | |
| PT-KXZ | Citation | 500-0043 | Taxi Aereo Lider Ltda. Belo Horizonte. | N5072E/N5072L/N34UT/N104UA /N543CC |
| PT-KYR | Learjet | 25D-266 | Taxi Aereo Marilia SA. Sao Carlos. | |
| PT-KZR | Learjet | 35A-252 | Banco Bamerindus SA, Curitiba. | N28CR |
| PT-LAA | Learjet | 35A-295 | Cimento Nassau/Lider Nordeste Taxi Aereo Ltda. Recife. | |
| PT-LAS | Learjet | 35A-326 | Taxi Aereo Lider Ltda. Belo Horizonte. | |
| PT-LAU | Learjet | 24D-239 | Taxi Aereo Lider Ltda. Belo Horizonte. | N83MJ/F-GBLZ/D-ILHM/D-ILVW |
| PT-LAX | Citation | 500-0194 | Taxi Aereo Lider Ltda. Belo Horizonte. | N310U/OY-ASR/D-IMSM /I-AMBR/N180CC |
| PT-LBN | Citation | 500-0079 | Soc. Terraplenagem Civil e. Agropecuaria, Sao Paulo. | N40JF/N31088 /D-INHH/N579CC |
| PT-LBW | Learjet | 25XR-056 | ALCOA Aluminio S.A. Sao Paulo. | N780A |
| PT-LBY | Learjet | 35A-411 | Confeccoes Guararapes SA. Natal. | |
| PT-LCC | Citation | 500-0413 | Banco do Comercio & Industria SA. Sao Paulo. | (PT-LBZ)/N6783X |
| PT-LCD | Learjet | 35A-103 | Taxi Aereo Lider S.A. Sao Paulo. | N50MJ/N96RE |
| PT-LCN | Learjet | 24D-287 | Taxi Aereo Lider Ltda. Belo Horizonte. | N92565/I-MABU/HB-VDN/EC-CJA /HB-VDN |
| PT-LCO | Falcon 10 | 154 | Omnium Transportation Co/Frota Oceanica Brasileira, Rio. | N219FJ /F-WZGA |
| PT-LCR | Citation | 550-0142 | Taxi Aereo Marilia, Sao Paulo. | N2648Z |
| PT-LCV | Learjet | 24D-254 | Yellow Express Services Inc. Miami, Fl. | N13606/D-CCAT/D-ICAY |
| PT-LCW | Citation | 550-0333 | Itamarati SA/Taxi Aereo Marilia, Sao Paulo. | N67990 |
| PT- | Learjet | 35A-436 | | N37988 |
| PT-LDH | Citation | 500-0049 | Banco Nacional de Credito Co-operative, Sao Paulo. | PT-FXB/PP-FXB /N549CC |
| PT-LDI | Citation | 500-0335 | Veloz Taxi Aereo Ltda. Aracatuba. | N2937L/ZP-PUP/ZP-PNB/N5335J |

PHILIPPINES

| | | | | |
|---|---|---|---|---|
| RP-C1 | BAC 1-11/408 | 128 | Government of Philippines, Manila. | G-BIII/G-AWKJ |
| RP-57 | Learjet | 35A-244 | Philippines National Oil Co. Manila. | N1451B |
| RP-C102 | Citation Eagle | 500-0123 | Air Manila. | RP-C7777/N523CC/(PI-C7777)/N123CC |
| RP-C550 | Citation | 550-0031 | Ayala Corp. Makati, Rizal. | N3250M |
| RP-C581 | Citation | 550-0152 | Manila Electric. | (N107)/N88840 |
| RP-C911 | B 707-321 | 17606 | Government of Philippines, Manila. | N728PA/N99WT/N11RV/N728PA |
| RP-C1177 | F-28-3000 | 11153 | Government of Philippines, Manila. | PH-ZBV/PH-EXV |
| RP-C1714 | HS 125/700B | 7085 | San Miguel Corp. | G-BHIO/G-5-15 |
| RP-C1747 | Learjet | 24XR-264 | Menzi Agricultural Corp. Manila. | PI-C1747 |
| RP-C1964 | Citation | 500-0242 | Meralco Securities Corp. Pasig, Rizal. | N5242J |
| RP-C1980 | Mystere 20F | 400 | Central Bank of Philippines. | F-WRQR |
| RP-C4121 | Learjet | 25D-287 | Hamix International Co. | N39416 |
| RP-C5128 | Learjet | 36A-037 | Construction & Development Corp. Manila. | |
| RP-C6610 | Learjet | 25D-289 | Northern Cement, Manila. | N1087T |
| RP-C | Citation | 550-0145 | Tagum Agricultural Development Co. Manila. | N2653R |
| RP-C | Citation | 550-0181 | Tagum Agricultural Development Co. Manila. | N88826 |

SWEDEN

| | | | | |
|---|---|---|---|---|
| SE-DCU | Learjet | 24-124 | Swedair, Stockholm. | OY-EGE/N462LJ |
| SE-DCW | Learjet | 24-109 | Swedair, Stockholm. | OY-RYA/HB-VAS |
| SE-DDE | Citation | 500-0063 | Kungsair AB. Goteborg/Blidberg & Metcalfe Shipping AB. | N563CC |
| SE-DDF | Falcon 10 | 27 | Volvo AB. Goteburg. | F-WLCX |
| SE-DDG | Learjet | 35A-172 | Swedair, Stockholm. | N748GL |
| SE-DEA | Learjet | 35-051 | Basair, Vasteras. | |
| SE-DEL | Falcon 10 | 14 | SAAB-Scania AB. Linkoping. | F-WJMK |
| SE-DEM | Learjet | 35A-317 | Beijerinvest AB/Basair Vasteras. | N10871 |
| SE-DES | Citation | 500-0405 | Bofors, Sweden. | (N6782T) |
| SE-DET | Citation | 500-0406 | Bofors, Sweden. | N67289 |
| SE-DEU | Citation | 500-0036 | Jan Drews/Travelair. | OY-DVL/N536CC |
| SE-DEV | Citation | 550-0123 | Kungsair AB. Gothenburg/Blidberg & Metcalfe Shipping AB. | N81TF /N36CJ/(CC-CGX)/N2746F |
| SE-DEY | Citation | 500-0370 | Stockholm Air Service. | N36897 |
| SE-DEZ | Citation | 500-0371 | Kungsair AB. Norkoping/AB Bohman & Johansson. | N36919 |

SUDAN

| | | | | |
|---|---|---|---|---|
| ST-PRS | Mystere 20F | 372 | Government of Sudan, Khartoum. | F-WRQV |

| Regis-tration | Type | C/N | Owner/Operator | Previous Identities |
|---|---|---|---|---|
| **EGYPT** | | | | |
| SU-AXJ | B 707-366C | 20919 | Egyptian Government, Cairo. (r/c Egyptian 01). | |
| SU-AXN | Mystere 20E | 294 | Egyptian Government, Cairo. | F-BVPM/F-WROT |
| SU-AYD | Mystere 20F | 361 | Government/Air Force, Cairo. | F-WMKF |
| SU-AYN | B 707-351C | 21226 | Egyptian Government, Cairo. (r/c Egyptian 02) | |
| SU-AZJ | Mystere 20F | 358 | Arab Organization for Industrialization, Cairo. | F-WRQY/SU-AZJ/F-WRQS |
| SU-BAO | B 707-351C | 19775 | Arab Organization for Industrialization, Cairo. | N384US |
| 4W-ACM | HS 125/700B | 7178 | Shaher Traders, Sana'a. (based Cairo). | |
| **GREECE** | | | | |
| N9FB | Falcon 20E | 275 | Frank Basil Aviation Ltd. Washington DC. | N661JB/N4434F/F-WMKH |
| HB-IEH | B 737-2V6 | 22431 | Petrolair Systems, Athens. | |
| HB-IEY | Gulfstream 2 | 210 | Petrolair Systems, Athens. | |
| HB-VFX | Learjet | 35A-191 | Petrolair Systems, Athens. | YV-15CP/N3810G |
| **CAMEROUN** | | | | |
| TJ-AAK | Gulfstream 2 | 93 | Government of Cameroun, Yaounde. | N8785R/N885GA |
| TJ-AAM | B 727-2R1 | 21636 | Government of Cameroun, Yaounde. | |
| **CENTRAL AFRICAN REPUBLIC** | | | | |
| TL-AAI | Caravelle 3 | 10 | noted Orly 5/79-AUG 82, no titles. | F-BNGE/XV-NJA/PP-VJC/F-WJAP |
| TL-KAB | Caravelle | 42 | Republique Centrafrique, Bangui. | F-BLKF/F-BJAO/N420GE/F-WJAM |
| TL-RCA | Corvette | 39 | Government of Central African Republic, Bangui. | TL-SMI/F-OBYG/F-WNGY |
| **CONGO REPUBLIC** | | | | |
| TN-ACP | F 28-1000 | 11072 | Government of Congo Republic, Brazzaville. (Transferred to Lina Congo AUG/82). | PH-EXS |
| TN-ADI | Corvette | 9 | Government of Congo Republic, Brazzaville. | F-OCRN/F-BTTR/N612AC /F-BRQK/F-WRQK |
| **GABON** | | | | |
| TR-KHC | Gulfstream 3 | 326 | Government of Gabon, Libreville. | N17582 |
| TR-LAH | Corvette | 30 | Air Inter Gabon, Port Gentil. | OO-MRC/F-BTTP/F-WNGQ |
| TR-LAI | Falcon 50 | 78 | Ministry of Cooperation, Libreville. | F-ODEO/F-WPXF |
| TR-LTR | F 28-1000 | 11104 | Government of Gabon, Libreville. | PH-EXU |
| TR-LTZ | DC-8-73CF | 46053 | Government of Gabon, Libreville. | N8638 |
| TR-LYM | Corvette | 12 | Air Inter Gabon, Port Gentil. | F-BVPC |
| TR-LZI | Learjet | 35A-313 | Air Affaires, Libreville. | (F-GCLT)/N39413 |
| TR-LZT | Corvette | 20 | Air Inter Gabon, Port Gentil. | F-BTTN/N616AC/F-WNGS |
| **TCHAD** | | | | |
| TT-AAM | Caravelle 6R | 100 | Conseil Superieur Militaire, N, Djamena. | (TT-AAD)/PH-TRS/N1015U |
| **BENIN** | | | | |
| TY-BBM | Falcon 50 | 17 | Government of Benin | 5A-DGI/F-WZHI |
| **MALI** | | | | |
| TZ-PBF | Corvette | 19 | Government of Mali, Bamako. | F-BVPL/F-OCJL/F-BVPL |
| **AUSTRALIA** | | | | |
| VH-AJK | Westwind-1124 | 256 | Wings Australia, Sydney. | 4X-CNB |
| VH-AJP | Westwind-1124 | 238 | Wings Australia, Sydney. | 4X-CMJ |
| VH-AJQ | Westwind-1124 | 281 | Wings Australia, Sydney. | 4X-CQA |
| VH-AJS | Learjet | 35A-188 | Wings Australia, Sydney. | |

| Registration | Type | C/N | Owner/Operator | Previous Identities |
|---|---|---|---|---|
| VH-AJV | Learjet | 35A-189 | Wings Australia, Sydney. | N3811G |
| VH-ANI | Learjet | 35A-468 | Australian National Industries/Capitol Jet, Sydney. | |
| VH-ASG | Gulfstream 2 | 95 | Mines Transportation/Associated Airlines Pty. Ltd. Melbourne. | N887GA |
| VH-ASM | Gulfstream 2 | 91 | Mines Transportation/Associated Airlines Pty. Ltd. Melbourne. | G-AYMI /N17586 |
| VH-ASR | Westwind-1124 | 316 | Mines Transportation, Melbourne. | 4X-CRJ |
| VH-BNK | Citation | 501-0171 | North Broken Hill Co. Pty. Ltd. | N67780 |
| VH-BQR | Learjet | 35A-471 | Rivkin & Co. Sydney. | |
| VH-BRX | Citation | 551-0064 | Bruck (Australia) Pty Ltd. | N6889T |
| VH-BSJ | Learjet | 24D-266 | Capitol Motors Ltd. Auburn, NSW. | N266BS |
| VH-CAO | HS 125/3B | 25015 | Capitol Motors Ltd. Auburn, NSW. | |
| VH-CPH | Learjet | 35A-400 | Publishing & Broadcasting Ltd/Consolidated Press Holdings, Sydney. | |
| VH-DJT | Falcon 10 | 169 | Drayton Investments, Brisbane. | N235FJ/F-WZGV |
| VH-ELC | Learjet | 35A-428 | Utah Development Corp. Brisbane, Qd. | |
| VH-FJZ | Falcon 20F | 442 | Bond Corp. Perth. | N446F/F-WJML |
| VH-FOX | Learjet | 35A-427 | P. Fox/Adelaide Holdings Ltd. Sydney. | N1087Z |
| VH-HSS | HS 125/700B | 7169 | Shell Australia Ltd. Melbourne. | (VH-SOA)/G-5-21 |
| VH-ING | Citation | 550-0141 | Inghams Enterprises Pty Ltd. Bankstown. | N26461 |
| VH-IWJ | Westwind-1124 | 371 | Jet Corp. of Australia, Melbourne. | 4X-CUH |
| VH-IWW | Westwind-1124 | 314 | Canberra Jet Charter/Schutt Aviation, Melbourne. | 4X-CRH |
| VH-KDI | Citation | 550-0135 | Southern Pacific Petroleum, Bankstown, NSW. | N6800J |
| VH-KDP | Citation | 550-0259 | Aviation Centre Charter, Bankstown. | N68617 |
| VH-KNJ | Westwind-1124 | 381 | Jet Corp. of Australia, Melbourne. | 4X-CUW |
| VH-KNS | Westwind 1124 | 323 | Wings Australia, Sydney. | N816H/4X-CRQ |
| VH-KTI | Learjet | 35A-239 | Katies Pty Ltd. Sydney. | (HB-VGC)/N847GL |
| VH-LGH | Learjet | 55-048 | Executive Air West/Hancock Prospecting Pty. Ltd. Perth.N3796Z/(N734) |
| VH-MAY | Citation | 550-0017 | Australian Jet Charter, Sydney. | N3230M |
| VH-MEI | Falcon 10 | 50 | Mount Enid Iron, Perth. | F-WLCS |
| VH-MIE | Learjet | 35A-459 | Mimair Pty. Ltd. Brisbane. | |
| VH-SDN | Learjet | 35A-342 | Stillwell/Sydney Doctors Nominees/Esso Australia. | N37931/N1088D |
| VH-SLJ | Learjet | 35-046 | Stillwell Aviation, Melbourne. | |
| VH-SQH | Westwind-1124 | 366 | Jet Corp. of Australia, Melbourne. | 4X-CUT |
| VH-SWC | Citation | 500-0394 | Presidential Jet Services, Perth. | (N2648Y) |
| VH-SWL | Citation | 550-0188 | Sea World/Surfer's Paradise, Queensland. | N98765 |
| VH-TNN | Learjet | 25C-181 | Stillwell/Smithfield Mall, Sydney. | |
| VH-TNP | Citation | 550-0168 | Skywest Airlines, Perth. | (VH-ICT)/N88740 |
| VH-ULT | Learjet | 35A-463 | Trak Investment Pty Ltd. Melbourne. | |
| VH-WFE | Learjet | 35A-221 | Wards Express, Melbourne. | N845GL |
| VH-WFJ | Learjet | 35A-242 | Wards Express, Melbourne. | N846GL |
| VH-WFP | Learjet | 35A-466 | Westfield Holdings, Sydney. | |
| VH-WGJ | Citation | 550-0054 | Flightways Air Services, Perth. | N501AA/(N3301M) |
| VH-WNP | Citation | 550-0102 | Skywest Airlines, Perth. | N2664Y |
| VH-WNZ | Citation | 550-0057 | Skywest Airlines, Perth. | (N2661N) |
| VH-WWY | Westwind-1124 | 325 | Barclay Jet Charter, Brisbane. | 4X-CRS |
| VH- | Citation | 550-0339 | | N6802Y |

## ZIMBABWE

| | | | | |
|---|---|---|---|---|
| VP-WKY | Learjet | 25B-160 | Messina Management Services. | ZS-MTD |

## BERMUDA

| | | | | |
|---|---|---|---|---|
| VR-BAT | B 727-76 | 20371 | Alghanim/Constance Leasing, Kuwait. | VH-TJF |
| VR-BEG | B 737-2S9 | 21957 | Maritime Investment & Shipping/Niarchos. | N57008 |
| VR-BFX | Learjet | 35-054 | Olympic Maritime/Springfield Shipping Corp. | |
| VR-BGT | Gulfstream 2 | 211 | Ditco Air Ltd/Sheikh El Khereiji. | N17581 |
| VR-BGW | B 727-30 | 18366 | Sigair Ltd/Ditco Air Ltd. | (N44RO)/N44R/N9233Z/D-ABIK |
| VR-BHB | Learjet | 36-007 | Burgess Co. Ltd. | SX-AHF/N226CC/N138GL |
| VR-BHC | Learjet | 24XR-267 | John von Neumann, Geneva. | N124GA/N78AE/N46023/HB-VCY |
| VR-BHE | HS 125/700A | 7020 | Air St. George Ltd. Hamilton. | G-EFPT/(G-BFVN)/(G-BEFT) |
| VR-BHF | JetStar-731 | 12/5062 | Louis Luyt Group, Lanseria, RSA. | N111G/RP-57/N2200M/N679RW |
| VR-BHH | HS 125/700A | NA0299 | Air St. George Ltd. Hamilton. | N125BE/G-5-19 |
| VR-BHJ | Falcon 10 | 104 | Guildford Ltd. Hamilton. | N90DM/N179FJ/F-WPUU |
| VR-BHK | B 727-30 | 18933 | Ahmad S M Al-Mohanna/Gulf Trading Co. Ltd. Hamilton. | N727CH/D-ABIR |
| VR-BHL | Falcon 20F | 429 | Sioux Co. Ltd. Hamilton. | F-WMKF |
| VR-BHM | DC-8-62 | 46111 | Sigair Ltd. | N8054U |
| VR-BHN | B 727-30 | 18370 | Brithin Co. Ltd. Hamilton. | N26565/D-ABIP |

| Regis-tration | Type | C/N | Owner/Operator | Previous Identities |
|---|---|---|---|---|
| VR-BHO | B 727-95 | 19251 | Sirtair Ltd. Hamilton. | N29895/G-BFGN/N1635 |
| VR-BHP | B 727-30 | 18371 | Jet Aviation (Bermuda) Ltd. | N727CH/D-ABIO |
| VR-BJD | Gulfstream 2 | 219 | Transworld Oil,Bergendal, Holland. | N84V |
| VR-BOX | B 737-269 | 21206 | Constance Leasing/Star Jet Corp. Kuwait. | 9K-ACV |
| VR-BTT | Falcon 50 | 32 | Inter Insurance/Castolin Eutectic Institute. | F-WZHJ |
| VR- | HS 125/700A | NA0304 | Air St. George Ltd. Hamilton. | N700BB/G-5-17 |
| VR- | Gulfstream 3 | 347 | Transworld Oil, Bergendal, Holland. | |

## CAYMAN ISLANDS

| | | | | |
|---|---|---|---|---|
| VR-CAN | B 707-138B | 18067 | 46 pax exec. | 9Y-TDC/VH-EBH |
| VR-CAU | Jet Commander | 72 | Executive Transport Corp. Grand Cayman. | N2WU/I-LECO/N7KR/N777WJ |
| | | | | /N757AL |
| VR-CBA | B 727-30 | 18935 | Muburak Al Hassawi, Kuwait. | N833N/N90557/D-ABIT |
| VR-CBD | HS 125/600B | 6041 | Hector Rebaque/RTS Ltd. Grand Cayman. | G-BCJU/G-5-13 |
| VR-CBE | B 727-46 | 19282 | Resebury Corp. Panama. | N4245S/D-AHLO/JA8325 |
| VR-CBL | Falcon 50 | 95 | ARAVCO Ltd./Flight Path Ltd. Grand Cayman. | F-WPXD |
| VR-CBM | Gulfstream 2 | 34 | Al-Mojil/ARAVCO Ltd. | N11SX/N130A/N230E |
| VR-CBO | Falcon 50 | 98 | ARAVCO Ltd. | F-WPXF |
| VR-CBG | B 727-193 | 19620 | ARAVCO, Ltd/Flight Path Ltd. Grand Cayman. | G-BEGZ/XY-ADR/N878PC |
| VR-CYR | HFB 320 | 1057 | RGWY (Cayman) Ltd. | (N107TW)/D-COSE |

## MEXICO

| | | | | |
|---|---|---|---|---|
| XA-ABB | Learjet | 24D-299 | Intervuelo S.A. Mexico City. | N299EJ |
| XA-ABC | Sabre-60 | 306-63 | Aviones Banco Comercio S.A. de C.V. Mexico City. | XA-CIS/XB-BIP |
| | | | | /N978R |
| XA-ACC | Learjet | 35A-176 | Intervuelo S.A. Mexico City. | N317MR |
| XA-ADD | Learjet | 24D-298 | Intervuelo S.A. Mexico City. | N298EJ |
| XA-AGA | Citation | 501-0095 | Puerto Vallarte Aerotaxi. | N612DS/N3172M |
| XA-APD | Sabre-40A | 282-123 | Commander Mexicana S.A. de C.V. Mexico City. | N8350N |
| XA-ATA | Learjet | 35A-264 | Minera Autlan S.A. de C.V. | |
| XA-AVE | Westwind-1123 | 160 | Hernandez Jose & Associates. | N221RJ/N221MJ/N1123W/4X-CJJ/USCG160 |
| * XA-AVR | Sabre-65 | 465-27 | Abel Vasquez Rana, Mexico City. | XA-ARE |
| XA-BAF | Sabre-40 | 282-39 | Transportes Ejecutivos S.A. Mexico City. | N333B/N947R/N442A/N6394C |
| XA-BQA | Westwind-1124 | 276 | SARSA, Mexico City. | VR-CAD/4X-CNV |
| XA-BRE | Learjet | 35A-373 | Aerolineas Ejecutivas SA. | SE-DER |
| XA-BUR | Citation | 500-0245 | Guanos y Fertilzantes de Mexico S.A. | TI-AHH/(TI-AHE)/N5245J |
| XA-BUX | Learjet | 35-020 | Aerotaxis de Mexico, Mexico City. | |
| XA-BUY | Learjet | 24D-270 | Servicios Ejecutivos Nacionales S.A. | XB-NAG |
| XA-CAP | Learjet | 24F-349 | Corp. Aerea Nortena SA. | N349BS/VH-FLJ |
| XA-COC | Learjet | 25B-194 | Aero Ventas S.A. Monterrey. | |
| XA-DAK | Learjet | 25B-190 | Aerotaxis de Mexico, Mexico City. | |
| XA-DET | Learjet | 24F-337 | Aero Empresa Mexicana/Domecq Wine. | XA-GEO |
| XA-DIJ | Learjet | 24D-269 | Leopoldo Silva/Jet Rent S.A. | |
| XA-DIN | BH-125/400A | NA768 | Servicios Aereos del Centro. | N69KA/N125BH/N65BH/G-5-20 |
| XA-EGC | Sabre-40 | 282-61 | Transportes Ejecutivos S.A. | XA-RGC/N231A/N550LL/N550L |
| XA-EKO | Citation | 500-0140 | Herfe Constructors. | N977EE/(N777SC)/N111AT/N300PX/N140CC |
| XA-ELR | Learjet | 25D-290 | | N221AP |
| XA-ELU | Learjet | 35A-261 | Aviacion Ejecutiva Mexicana S.A.=AVEMEX. | N900RD |
| XA-ESR | Sabre-40 | 282-59 | SENSA, Mexico City. | N17LT/N2SN/N48WP/N48WS/N7509V |
| XA-ESS | Learjet | 23-037 | Aero Servicios Ejecutivos, Sinaloa. | N50AJ/N13LJ/N41AJ/N65LJ/N51AJ |
| | | | | /N988SA/N266JP |
| XA-FIU | Falcon 10 | 83 | Aeropersonal S.A. | N5GD/N163FJ/F-WPXG |
| XA-FOU | Gulfstream 2 | 152 | Aviones Televisa/Jet Ejecutivos S.A. | N17587 |
| XA-FTN | Sabre-40 | 282-80 | Aerotaxi Mexicana S.A. | N40WH/N40JF/N360E/N36050/N2249B |
| XA-GAP | Sabre-65 | 465-8 | Sr. Gabriel Alarcon , Mecico City. | N10581 |
| XA-GRB | Learjet | 25D-309 | Aero Lineas Romero. | |
| XA-GUB | DH 125/400A | NA720 | Aero Astra, Mexico City. | N7LG/N4PN/N140C/G-AWXE |
| XA-GZA | JetStar-731 | 41/5100 | Servicios Aereos Regiomontanos, Monterrey. | N35JJ/XA-FIU/N207L |
| | | | | /N9256R |
| XA-HEV | Citation | 500-0363 | Taxis Aereos del Pacifico, Mexico City. | (I-CCCB)/N36881 |
| XA-HEW | Falcon 20F | 250 | Commercial Aerea S.A. Chihuahua. | N111AM/N4422F/F-WMKF |
| XA-HIR | DH 125/1A-522 | 25068 | T A Virba S.A. | XB-VUI/XA-BEM/XB-BEA |

26

| Regis-tration | Type | C/N | Owner/Operator | Previous Identities |
|---|---|---|---|---|
| XA-HOK | Sabre-40 | 282-17 | Travel Air S.A. | N900CS/N392F/N382RF/N9110/N6371C |
| XA-HOS | Learjet | 35A-341 | Aerotaxis de Mexico S.A. | D-CARE/N3802G |
| XA-HOU | DH 125/1A-522 | 25060 | Grupo Insa. | XA-BOJ/XB-EAL/XB-FIS/N22DE/N22DL/N2728/N26011/N2601 |
| | | | | /G-ATIM |
| XA-HRM | JetStar-731 | 46/5066 | HERMES. | N7782/N228Y/N9230R |
| XA-IEM | Citation | 501-0021 | Transporto Integral. | YV-166CP/(YV-135CP)/N36883 |
| XA-IIX | Citation | 500-0274 | AYT Aerea S.A. | (N140H)/N111TH/(N5274J) |
| XA-JEQ | BH 125/600A | 6047 | GAMESA. | N600TT/N400NE/N400NW/N4203Y/(C-GBNS)/N44BH/G-5-16 |
| XA-JEX | Citation | 500-0395 | Arrendamiento de Aviones Jet. | N2651S |
| XA-JEZ | Citation | 550-0103 | Aerotaxi Villa Rica S.A. | N2747U |
| XA-JIN | Learjet | 25D-210 | Aerotaxis de Mexico. | N133MR |
| XA-JIQ | Learjet | 24D-317 | Servicios Especiales del Pacifico Jalisco S.A. Leon, Gto. | N45AJ |
| | | | | /ZS-JJO/N133GL |
| XA-JIX | HS 125/700A | NA0268 | SARSA, Mexico City. | G-5-16 |
| XA-JOC | Learjet | 25D-303 | Jet Rent S.A. | |
| XA-JUA | Citation | 500-0247 | Aeroservicio Monterrey S.A. de C.V. | N9065J/N4110S/(N5347J) |
| XA-JUD | Sabre-40R | 282-43 | Commander Mexicana S.A. Mexico City. | N730R/N6398C |
| XA-JUE | Sabre-40R | 282-48 | Commander Mexicana S.A. | N153G/N90GM/N747R/N6555C |
| XA-JUZ | HS 125/1A | 25014 | Governor of Campeche. | N621ST/N734AK/N125G/G-ASSK |
| XA-KAC | HS 125/700A | NA0271 | SARSA, Mexico City. | G-5-15 |
| XA-KAH | Citation | 500-0289 | Aeroejecutivo S.A. | N5591A/YV-50CP/N5289J |
| XA-KAJ | Learjet | 28-004 | Provendora de Servicios S.A. | HB-VGB/N125NE/N39394 |
| XA-KAS | Learjet | | | |
| XA-KCM | Learjet | 35A-418 | Aerotaxis de Mexico/Kimberly-Clark. | |
| XA-KIF | HS 125 | | | |
| XA-KIQ | Citation | 550-0161 | Aero Gisa S.A. | N999AU/N88732 |
| XA-KIS | HS 125/700A | NA0280 | SARSA, Mexico City. | G-5-18 |
| XA-KOF | DH 125/1A | 25065 | Astro Q S.A. | N1YE/N631SO/N631SC/G-ATKL |
| XA-KON | HS 125/700A | NA0278 | SARSA, Mexico City. | G-5-14 |
| XA-KUG | Westwind | | | |
| XA-KUJ | Citation Eagle | 500-0313 | Salinas Y Roche. | N76GT/(N5313J) |
| XA-KUT | HS 125/600A | 6028 | Aeroastra S.A. Monterrey. | C-GDHW/C6-BDH/VP-BDH/G-5-12 |
| XA-LAN | Learjet | 35A-267 | AVEMEX=Aviacion Ejecutiva Mexicana S.A. | N39418 |
| XA-LAP | Learjet | 25D-336 | Taxi Aereo de Vera Cruz SA. | |
| XA-LEI | Sabre- | | | |
| XA-LEL | Sabre-40R | 282-68 | Commander Mexicana S.A. | N60RB/N22MV/N22MY/N801NC/N788R/N2235B |
| XA-LEO | Citation | 500-0273 | Servicio Aereo Leo Lopez S.A. Chihuahua. | N273RC/N5273J |
| XA-LET | Learjet | 25D-244 | Aero Chumbo. | N7LA |
| XA-LIJ | Westwind-1124 | 285 | Aerolineas Marcos S.A. | VR-CAC/4X-CPS |
| XA-LIM | Citation | 501-0193 | Aeroejecutivo S.A. | N164CB/N6778T |
| XA-LIO | Falcon 10 | 40 | Construcciones Protexa. | N15SJ/N10XX/N128FJ/F-WJMN |
| XA-LIX | Sabre-40A | 282-128 | Travel Air SA. Mexico City. | N99AP |
| XA-LOB | Falcon 20C | 39 | Construcciones Protexa. | N910U/N50MM/N6565A/N5555U/N843F/F-WNGM |
| XA-LOF | Learjet | 25D-338 | Avia Centro Taxi. | |
| XA-LOH | Falcon 50 | 9 | Aero Personal S.A. de C.V. | I-SAFP/F-WZHD |
| XA-LOK | Falcon 10 | 175 | Aero Personal S.A. de C.V. | N241FJ/F-WZGF |
| XA-LOQ | Sabre-60 | 306-145 | Aero Campeche SA. | N730CA/N60SL |
| XA-LOT | Citation | 550-0211 | Aeropyc S.A. | N6801T |
| XA-LOV | HS 125/403B | NA776 | Heliservicios Campeche. | G-BACI/N73BH |
| XA-LUC | Sabre-65 | 465-55 | Commander.Mexicana S.A/Servitam. | N2574E |
| XA-LUD | Citation | 500-0408 | Construcciones Protexa. | N67805 |
| XA-LUN | Citation | 501-0002 | | N165CB/OE-FPO/N5253J |
| XA-LUV | Citation | 500-0412 | Aerolineas Ejecutivos S.A. de C.V. | N67R2F |
| XA-MAH | HS 125/600A | 6065 | Constructora Gengreto del Norte, Mexico City. | G-BJCB/G-5-16 |
| XA-MAL | Citation | 501-0015 | Aeroservicios Monterrey SA. de CV. | N1832R/N1823B/N36862 |
| XA-MEY | Gulfstream 3 | 252 | Aviones B C, Mexico City. | (N777SL)/N17582/(N301GA) |
| XA-MHA | Learjet | 25XR-222 | Constructora Midas. | XA-KEY/N4MR/N726GL/N1476R |
| XA-MIC | Gulfstream 3 | 323 | Aviones Televisa/Jet Ejecutivas S.A. | |
| XA-MIX | Gulfstream 2 | 237 | Cerveceria Moctezuma SA/Aerolineas Ejecutivas SA. | N25BH/N816GA |
| XA-MLG | Sabre-65 | 465-48 | ATILA=Aerotaxis Inmediatos de la Laguna S.A. de C.V. Torreon, Coahuila. | N2539F |
| XA-OVR | Sabre-65 | 465-12 | Sr. Olegario Vasquez Rana, Mexico City. | |
| XA-PAZ | Citation | 500-0060 | | XA-SEN/N712G/N712J/N560CC |
| XA-RGB | JetStar-731 | 33/5079 | | N923RR |
| XA-RGC | Sabre-60 | 306-125 | Transportes Ejecutivos SA. Mexico City. | N32PC/N2134J |
| XA-RMF | Learjet | 25D-308 | Aerotaxis de Mexico. | N23AM |

| Registration | Type | C/N | Owner/Operator | Previous Identities |
|---|---|---|---|---|
| XA-SAI | BH 125/600A | 6016 | Servicios Aereos Integrades, Mexico City. | N99SC/N27BH |
| XA-SEN | Sabre-40 | 282-7 | Servicios Ejecutivos Nacionales S.A. Mexico City. | N122RP/N43NR /N101US/N42NR/N1102D/N576R/N360J/N6361C |
| XA-SFS | Jet Commander | | | |
| XA-SIN | JetStar-8 | 5005 | Governor of Sinaloa. | N70TP/N712RD/N716RD/N12121/N161LM |
| XA-TEL | Citation | 550-0254 | Alquiladora do Casas. | N171CB/N6860S |
| XA-TIP | Learjet | 24D-293 | Aerotaxi de Mexico/Cerveceria Moctezuma S.A. | |
| XA-VIT | Sabre-60 | 306-50 | Aero Vitro SA. Monterey. | N100Y/N948R/N7529N |
| XA-ZAI | JetStar | | | |
| XA-ZAP | Learjet | 35A-129 | Aerotaxis de Mexico. | N229X/N22BX |
| XA-ZOM | Sabre-60A | 306-47 | Axel Rent S.A. Mexico City. | XA-ZUM/XB-ZUM/N927R/N4765N |
| XA-ZUM | Sabre-65 | 465-15 | Axel Rent S.A. Mexico City. | N2513E |
| XA- | Sabre-60 | 306-125 | Transportes Ejecutivos S.A. Mexico City. | N32PC/N2134J |
| XA- | JetStar-8 | 5105 | Constructora Midas. | N17005/N7005/N2277T/N277T |
| XA- | Citation | 500-0414 | Aero Ejecutivo. | N6887M |
| XA- | Westwind Two | 350 | Aerolineas Marcos S.A. | VR-CBB/4X-CTR |
| XB-AER | Westwind-1123 | 172 | Grupo Cydsa, Monterrey. | N1123H/4X-CJV |
| XB-AKW | DH 125/1A | 25102 | Casa Guajardo. | N756M/N756/G-ATUU |
| XB-ALO | Falcon 20E | 287 | Protexa Monterrey. | YV-38CP/YV-TAVA/N4438F/F-WMKF |
| XB-AMO | Citation | 500-0152 | International Ceramic Sales Inc. Monterrey. | N152CC/N53J/I-FERN /N152CC |
| XB-AXP | BH 125/400A | NA755 | Fabricas del Calzado, Mexico City. | N5MW/N755GW/N711SD/N50BH |
| XB-BAK | Falcon 10 | 65 | Protexa, Monterey. | N149FJ/F-WJMJ |
| XB-BBL | Sabre-40A | 282-116 | Altos Hornos de Mexico. | N4PH |
| XB-CCM | BH 125/400A | NA750 | Mexican Coca-Cola Export Co. | XA-DIW/N304P/N300P/N46BH/G-AXYI |
| XB-CCO | Citation | 500-0175 | Aerogisa S.A. Coah. | (XA-HOO)/N175CC |
| XB-CUX | BH 125/400A | NA764 | Cementos Guadalajara S.A. | N59BH |
| XB-CXF | Citation | 500-0143 | Solv. Y P Quimic. | XC-GUO/N143CC |
| XB-CXK | HS 125/700A | NA0313 | Novedades Editores. | G-BJOW/G-5-14 |
| XB-CXO | JetStar-8 | 5141 | Sindicato Petrolero. | N4493S/HZ-SH1/N4436S/N244/N12241/N7967S/N711Z /N5505L |
| XB-CYA | Corvette | 36 | Grupo Madeiro, Tampico. | F-OCDE/PH-JSD/F-BTTS |
| XB-CYI | Corvette | 40 | Grupo Madeiro, Tampico. | F-ODJS/F-WNGZ |
| XB-DBJ | JetStar-8 | 5145 | Compania El Universal S.A. | N46K/N5509L |
| XB-DLM | B 737- | | | |
| XB-DUH | JetStar-8 | 5157 | Mexicana de Cobre S.A. | N29WP/N9WP/N5521L |
| XB-DUS | Sabre-40A | 282-106 | Sociedad Industrial S.A. Tampico Tamps. | N7595N |
| XB-EFR | Citation | 500-0090 | Tracto Partes S.A. | N590RB/N590CC |
| XB-ELU | Citation | 500-0402 | Ealy Ortiz J.F. | XA-JFE/(G-BHIW)/(N1779E) |
| XB-JFE | JetStar | | Compania El Universal S.A. | |
| XB-JMM | Sabre-60 | 306-130 | Partido Revolucionario Institucional. | XA-JIK/XA-OVR/N2145J |
| XB-JMR | Sabre-60 | 306-35 | Cia J M Romo S.A., Aquascalientes. | N3456R/N4748N |
| XB-KOG | Westwind-1124 | 224 | Grupo Cydsa, Monterrey. | N898SR/4X-CLV |
| XB-LCR | B 737- | | | |
| XB-MBW | JetStar | | | |
| XB-NIB | Sabre-40A | 282-125 | Vidriera-Monterrey S.A. Monterrey./Aero Vitro. | N8356N |
| XB-OEM | Falcon 50 | 80 | Organization Editorial Mexicana. | N87FJ/F-WZHN |
| XB-PUE | DH 125/3A-RA | 25158 | Novedadeso Editores S.A. | G-AVZK |
| XB-RGS | Sabre 40A | 282-114 | Banpais SA. Monterey. (N7SL)/XA-ATC/XC-SUB/XA-ATC/N64MG/N64MC | |
| XB-SII | Falcon 10 | 4 | Cementos Azteca SA. Mariano Escobedo. | N101FJ/F-WJMK |
| XB-VIW | JetStar-8 | 5140 | Cerveceria Moctezuma SA. | N5504L |
| XB-VRM | Falcon 20E | 248 | Organization Editorial Mexicana. | XB-OEM/XB-AOU/N37JJ/OH-FFV/F-WROV |
| XB-ZRB | Falcon 10 | 107 | Zeferino Romero Bringas, Tehuacan. | N182FJ/F-WPUY |
| XC-ASA | Citation | 500-0061 | Aeropuertos y Servicios Auxiliares, Mexico City. | XC-GAD/N561CC |
| XC-ASB | Citation | 500-0251 | | XC-ORO/N500LP/(HB-VGI)/I-COKE/N5251J |
| XC-AZU | Learjet | 24XR-285 | Comision Nacional de la Industria Azucarea. | |
| XC-BCA | Westwind | | | |
| XC-BCO | DC-9-15RC | 47087 | Bank of Mexico, Mexico City. | N9358/N8917 |
| XC-BDC | Citation | | | |
| XC-BDM | DC-9-15RC | 47154 | Bank of Mexico, Mexico City. | N9353/N8912 |
| XC-BEN | Citation | 500-0243 | PEMEX, Mexico City. | XC-GOY/N5243J |
| XC-BEZ | Citation | 500-0072 | Transportes de la Procuraduria de la Republica, Mexico City. | M491 /N49R/N572CC |
| XC-BIN | Falcon 20D | 198 | PEMEX, Mexico City. | N74196/FEC14/VR-BDK/F-WNGO |
| XC-BJA | Citation | | | |
| XC-BOC | Citation | 500-0169 | Comision Federal de Electricidad, Mexico City. | XC-CON/N19CM/N20FL |

| Regis-tration | Type | C/N | Owner/Operator | Previous Identities |
|---|---|---|---|---|
| XC-CFE | Gulfstream 2 | 161 | Comision Federal de Electricidad, Mexico City. | XC-FEZ/XA-ABC |
| XC-CFM | Learjet | 25D-284 | Comision de Fomento Minero. | |
| XC-CIR | Citation | 501-0090 | Gobierno del Estado Guererro. | N3165M |
| XC-CUZ | Learjet | 35A-213 | Procurad General. | N935NA/N800RD |
| XC-DAA | Learjet | 25D-283 | Procurad General. | N40144 |
| XC-DAD | Learjet | 25D-223 | CONASUPO, Mexico City. | N23AM |
| XC-DFS | Learjet | 29-002 | Dir General de Seguridad. | N723LL |
| XC-DIP | Falcon 20E | 282 | Banco Nacional do Credito Rural. | N282C/N282JJ/N131JA/N4436F/F-WMKG |
| XC-DOK | Citation | 550-0198 | PEMEX. Mexico City. | N67980 |
| XC-DOP | Learjet | | | |
| XC-DUF | Citation | 550-0206 | PEMEX, Mexico City. | N679CC |
| XC-FIA | Sabre-75A | 380-53 | Instituto Mexicano del Seguro Social. | N75HZ/N8526A/HZ-THZ/JY-AFN N75NR/N2137J |
| XC-FIF | Learjet | 25D-332 | Aseguradora Nacional Agricola S.A. | |
| XC-FIU | Citation | 500-0012 | Secretariat of Communications & Transport. | N512CC/N6563C |
| XC-FIV | Citation | 500-0013 | Secretariat of Communications & Transport. | N513CC |
| XC-FIZ | Citation | 500-0409 | Secretariat of Communications & Transport. | N67815 |
| XC-FOO | Citation | 550-0193 | Governor of Quintana Roo. | (N47RP)/N6802T |
| XC-GAW | Citation | 500-0410 | Estado de Tamaulipas. | N6780Z |
| XC-GII | Learjet | | | |
| XC-GNL | Learjet | 25D-329 | Governor of Nuevo Leon. | N3799B |
| XC-GOV | Citation | 500-0189 | Comision Federal de Electricidad. | |
| XC-GOW | Citation | 500-0193 | PEMEX=Petroleos Mexicanos SA. | |
| XC-GOX | Citation | 500-0197 | PEMEX, Mexico City. | |
| XC-GTO | Citation | 500-0396 | Gobierno del Estado de Guanajuato. | (XA-JEW)/N26514 |
| XC-GUB | Learjet | 25D-306 | Dept. of Transportes Aereos Sarh. | XA-DUB |
| XC-GUH | Citation | 500-0221 | Comision Federal de Electricidad. | N221CC |
| XC-GUO | Citation | 500-0201 | ANAG, Mexico City. | |
| XC-HAD | Jet Commander | 85 | | N201S/N4554E |
| XC-HDA | Westwind | | Bank of Mexico, Mexico City. | |
| XC-HIS | Learjet | 25D-312 | Governor of Chiapas. | N94MJ |
| XC-IPP | Learjet | 35-028 | Productores Pesquenos. | N20BG/N135GL |
| XC-IST | Learjet | 29-001 | Institute of Security and Social Services. | N929GL/HB-VFY |
| XC-MEX | Gulfstream 2 | 96 | Bank of Mexico, Mexico City. | N75SR/N75WC/N100WC/N100KS/N888GA |
| XC-PET | Gulfstream 2TT | 173 | PEMEX, Mexico City. | N801GA |
| XC-PGR | Learjet | 35A-460 | | |
| XC-PMX | Citation | 500-0376 | PEMEX, Mexico City. | N36949 |
| XC-PPM | Citation | 500-0329 | Productores Pesquenos. | XC-IPP/N5329J/ZS-JOK/N5329J |
| XC-RPP | Learjet | 25D-236 | Tesoreria de la Federacion. | N1466B |
| XC-SAG | Learjet | 24D-255 | Secretariat of Agriculture, Mexico City. | |
| XC-SCT | Citation | 500-0010 | Secretariat of Communications & Transport.(For Rereg). | XC-FIT /N510CC |
| XC-SCT | Citation | 550-0138 | Secretariat of Communications & Transport. | N2646X |
| XC-SEY | Falcon 20C | 169 | Ministry of Public Education. | N4370F/F-WNGN |
| XC-SUP | Learjet | 24XR-319 | CONASUPO, Mexico City. | |
| XC-TIJ | HFB 320 | 1049 | Governor of Baja California. | XC-DGA/D-CISO |
| XC-VSA | Learjet | 28-002 | Governor of Tabasco. | N511DB/N39404 |

IRAQ

| | | | | |
|---|---|---|---|---|
| YI-AHH | Mystere 20F | 337 | Government/Iraqi Airways, Baghdad. | F-WROR |
| YI-AHJ | Mystere 20F | 343 | Government/Iraqi Airways, Baghdad. | F-WROR |
| YI-AKA | JetStar 2 | 5233 | Government/Iraqi Airways, Baghdad. | N4048M |
| YI-AKB | JetStar 2 | 5235 | Government/Iraqi Airways, Baghdad. | N4055M |
| YI-AKC | JetStar 2 | 5237 | Government/Iraqi Airways, Baghdad. | N4058M |
| YI-AKD | JetStar 2 | 5238 | Government/Iraqi Airways, Baghdad. | N4062M |
| YI-AKE | JetStar 2 | 5239 | Government/Iraqi Airways, Baghdad. | N4063M |
| YI-AKF | JetStar 2 | 5240 | Government/Iraqi Airways, Baghdad. | N4065M |
| YI-ALB | Falcon 50 | 71 | Government/Iraqi Airways, Baghdad. | F-WZHF |
| YI-ALC | Falcon 50 | 101 | Government/Iraqi Airways, Baghdad. | F-WPHX |

NICARAGUA

| | | | | |
|---|---|---|---|---|
| YN-BPR | HS 125/600B | 6037 | Junta de Reconstruction Nacional Nicaragua. | AN-BPR |
| YN-BVO | Learjet | 35A-280 | Aerotaxi Ejecutivo S.A. Managua. | HP-912/N8OMJ |

YUGOSLAVIA

| Regis-tration | Type | C/N | Owner/Operator | Previous Identities |
|---|---|---|---|---|
| YU-BIA | Citation | 500-0031 | Social Republic of Croatia, Zagreb/Gorenje. | N531CC |
| YU-BIH | Learjet | 24D-320 | Government of Slovenia, Ljubljana. | N3802G |
| YU-BJG | Learjet | 25B-187 | Government of Yugoslavia, Belgrade. | |
| YU-BKJ | Learjet | 25B-205 | Government of Macedonia, Skopje. | N1468B |
| YU-BKR | Learjet | 25D-221 | Government of Yugoslavia, Belgrade. | N3819G |
| YU-BKZ | Citation | 500-0373 | Government of Bosnia & Herzogovina. | N98449 |
| YU-BLY | Sabre-75A | 380-65 | Government of Croatia, Zagreb. | |
| YU-BME | HS 125/600B | 6048 | INA-Yugoslav Oil Corp. Belgrade. | G-BHIE/HB-VDS |
| YU-BML | Citation | 500-0399 | Sour Fero-Elektro. | N2069A |
| YU-BNA | Falcon 50 | 43 | Government of Yugoslavia, Belgrade. | 72102/F-WZHO |

VENEZUELA

| | | | | |
|---|---|---|---|---|
| YV-01CP | Learjet | 35A-157 | Transporte Transilac S.A. Maracaibo. | N746GL |
| YV-06CP | Citation | 551-0006 | Siderurgica del Orinoco, Caracas. | N3227A |
| YV-07P | Citation | 500-0253 | S.A. Petrolera Las Mercedes, Caracas. | YV-T-MMM/N5253J |
| YV-12CP | Learjet | 55-031 | | |
| YV-19CP | Citation | 551-0004 | Dr. Alfonso Riverol, Caracas. | N553CJ/N98784 |
| YV-21CP | Citation | 550-0115 | Delpre C.A. Caracas. | YV-TAFA |
| YV-36CP | Citation | 550-0064 | Servicios Tecnicos Maracaibo C.A. Caracas. | N26617 |
| YV-41CP | Learjet | 55-019 | Construcciones CADE. | |
| YV-52CP | Citation | 500-0367 | Construcciones CADE. | N36906 |
| YV-55CP | Citation | 500-0215 | Bank of Maracaibo, Caracas. | YV-TOOO/N215CC |
| YV-62CP | Citation | 500-0297 | SACCO=Sociedad Anonima de Credito y Comercio, Caracas. | (N818CD)/N5297J |
| YV-99CP | Falcon 10 | 172 | Fabrica Nacional/FANAS. Caracas. | N238FJ/F-WZGZ |
| YV-101CP | Falcon 10 | 47 | Gustavos Zingg, Caracas. YV-221CP/PJ-AYA/YV-07CP/N132FJ/F-WLCY | |
| YV-123CP | Jet Commander | 16 | Bermudaz Motors C.A., Caracas. | N177A/N217PM/N96B |
| YV-132CP | Learjet | 25C-071 | Aero Ejecutivos | YV-130P/YV-T-DTT |
| YV-137CP | Citation | 551-0010 | Charter Ejecutivo S.R.L. | N3291M |
| YV-140CP | Citation | 551-0002 | SAECA, Caracas. | N3210M |
| YV-65CP | Learjet | 35A-161 | C.A de Edificaciones - Resid D Paulo. | |
| YV-17CP | Falcon 10 | 100 | Banco de la Construccion y de Oriente C.A. | N10FJ/N177FJ/F-WPXI |
| YV-147CP | Citation | 551-0020 | Inversiones Menil S.A. Chua, Caracas. | N26638 |
| YV-151CP | Citation | 551-0005 | Dayco C.A., Caracas. | N3216M |
| YV-159CP | Citation | 500-0362 | Pavimentadora Life C.A., Chuao, Caracas. | N36893 |
| YV-160CP | Westwind-1124 | 211 | Transpolar, Caracas. | 4X-CLI |
| YV-162CP | Citation | 550-0300 | Aeroservicios Alas C.A. | N68881 |
| YV-169CP | Citation | 551-0007 | Pavimentadora Life C.A. Chuao, Caracas. | N3223M |
| YV-190CP | Westwind-1124 | 219 | Transpolar, Caracas. | 4X-CLO |
| YV-203CP | Learjet | 25C-061 | Tranarg C.A. Caracas. | N9CN/PT-DUO/N251GL |
| YV-205CP | Citation | 551-0003 | Inmueble/Fernando Zubillaga, Caracas. | N3237M |
| YV-210CP | Westwind-Two | 308 | Maraven S.A. Maquetia. | 4X-CRB |
| YV-213CP | Citation | 551-0015 | Fundo Agropecuario el Retiro, Caracas. | (N26613) |
| YV-265CP | Learjet | 35A-247 | Paicosa Co. | |
| YV-276CP | Citation | 550-0405 | Consolid-Air SA. | |
| YV-286CP | Learjet | 35A-268 | J V Persand & Co. | N10870 |
| YV-292CP | Learjet | 55-052 | | |
| YV-298CP | Citation | 550-0155 | Servicios Tecnicos Maracaibo C.A. | (YV-209CP)/N6566C |
| YV-299CP | Citation | 551-0025 | Fabrica National de Ascensores. | N2746B |
| YV-300CP | Citation | 551-0032 | Aero Charter Aviation C.A. | (N98715) |
| YV-301CP | Citation | 551-0031 | Inversiones Finalven C.A. | N6565C/(N98749) |
| YV-326CP | Learjet | 35A-352 | Servicios Aero Facility. | |
| YV-327CP | Learjet | 35A-344 | Oficina Central Asesoria y Ayuda Tencia C.A. Caracas. | N40149 |
| YV-370CP | Citation | | | |
| YV-387CP | Westwind-1124 | 306 | Aerospace C.A. | 4X-COZ |
| YV-393CP | Westwind-1124 | 262 | Venezuela TV Corp. Caracas. | N40DG/N262WW/4X-CNH |
| YV-432CP | Learjet | 35A-437 | Transporte Transilaca CA. Maracaibo. | N3803G |
| YV-433CP | Learjet | 35A-431 | "El Correcaminos" - The Roadrunner. | |
| YV-434CP | Learjet | 35A-422 | TAECA. | |
| YV-451CP | Westwind Two | 343 | Maraven SA. Maquetia. | 4X-CTK |
| YV-452CP | Falcon 50 | 4 | Maraven SA. Caracas. | N50FJ/N110FJ/F-WZHA |
| YV-572CP | Corvette | 17 | Hydrowell. | F-BTTM/N614AC/F-WNGO |
| YV-O-MRI -1 | Learjet | 35A-270 | Ministery of Interior Relations. | N10871 |
| YV-O-MTC -2 | Citation | 500-0383 | Ministry of Communications, Caracas. | N3180M |

| Regis-tration | Type | C/N | Owner/Operator | Previous Identities |
|---|---|---|---|---|
| YV-O-MTC -20 | Citation | 550-0224 | Ministry of Communications, Caracas. | YV-O-MTC/N6802Y |
| YV- | Citation | 500-0171 | | N171CC |
| YV- | Citation | 500-0095 | | N2200R/(N578WB)/N595CC |

## SOUTH AFRICA

| Regis-tration | Type | C/N | Owner/Operator | Previous Identities |
|---|---|---|---|---|
| ZS-BMB | Falcon 50 | 91 | Government of the Republic of S. Africa. | F-WZHY |
| ZS-CAL | HS 125/3B-RA | 25172 | Directorate of Civil Aviation, Pretoria. | G-AXEG |
| ZS-INS | Learjet | 35A-238 | Aaron Searl, Lanseria. | 3D-ACZ/ZS-INS/N80HK/N844GL |
| ZS-JOO | Citation | 500-0291 | Industrial Development Corp. Jo'burg. | N5291J |
| ZS-JWC | Learjet | 23-030 | Cansas International Corp. Nelspruit. | N431CA/ZS-JWC/N431CA/N431EJ |
| ZS-KOO | Citation | 550-0139 | Natal Ammonium. Lanseria. | N2646Y |
| ZS-KPA | Citation | 501-0183 | Grinaker Holdings Pty. Ltd. | N6777V |
| ZS-KJY | Learjet | 24-165 | S.K.K. Pty Ltd. Lanseria. | N469J/N844GA |
| ZS-LDK | Citation | 550-0274 | African Explosives & Chemical Industries, Lanseria. | N6864C |
| ZS-LDV | Citation | 500-0418 | Industrial Development Corp. Jo'burg. | N262RB |
| ZS-LEE | Citation | 550-0347 | | N6826U |
| ZS-LHW | Citation | | Mmabatho Air Services/Boputhatswana Government. | |
| ZS-LTK | Learjet | 24-103 | Cansas International Corp. Nelspruit. | N72442/ZS-LTK/N714X |
| ZS-RCC | Citation | 500-0106 | Roberts Construction Co. Jo'burg. | N606CC |
| ZS-SBL | B 737-244 | 19707 | Dept. of Transport Services. | |
| ZS- | Learjet | 35A-475 | National Airways Corp, Rand Airport. | N3797K/N10873 |
| VR-BHF | JetStar-731 | 12/5062 | Louis Luyt Group. Lanseria. | N111G/RP-57/N2200M/N679RW |

## PARAGUAY

| Regis-tration | Type | C/N | Owner/Operator | Previous Identities |
|---|---|---|---|---|
| ZP-PNB | Citation | 550-0291 | Nicolas Santiago Bo, Jr. Asuncion. | N6887T |

## UNITED STATES OF AMERICA

| Regis-tration | Type | C/N | Owner/Operator | Previous Identities |
|---|---|---|---|---|
| N1 | JetStar 731 | 53/5001 | FAA, Dept. of Transportation, Washington DC. | N21/N1/N9201R |
| N1AH | Learjet | 25D-316 | AGH Aviation, Dallas, Tx. | N3793X |
| N1AP | Citation | 550-0049 | Arnold Palmer, Latrobe, Pa. | N3296M |
| N1BG | BH 125/731 | NA774 | Brown Group Inc. N.Y. | N71BH |
| N1BX | Falcon 20F | 380 | Travenol Laboratories Inc., Deerfield. Il. | N8BX/N136F/F-WMKI |
| N1C | DH 125/400A | NA729 | Sears Roebuck & Co., Atlanta, Ga. | N702S/G-AXJE |
| N1CC | B 727-21 | 18998 | Luqa Inc. Jacksonville, Fl. | N320AS/N320PA |
| N1DA | Learjet | 35-013 | Donald Anderson, Roswell, NM. | |
| N1DC | Learjet | 35A-464 | Cotton Petroleum Corp. Tulsa, Ok. | |
| N1ED | Learjet | 35A-392 | Edward J DeBartolo Corp. Youngstown, Oh. | N931GL |
| N1FE | Falcon 20DC | 84 | 'Karen', Federal Express Corp. | N530L/N975F/F-WJMK |
| N1GY | Sabre-40 | 282-81 | G Yobe Electric Inc. Sharon, Pa. | N416CS/N99CR/N360N/N36065/N2250B |
| N1H | Gulfstream 2 | 129 | Harrah's, Reno, Nv. | N871GA |
| N1HA | Citation | 501-0072 | Canron Corp. West Columbia, SC. | N3110M |
| N1HP | Learjet | 35-039 | Helmerich & Payne Inc. Tulsa, Ok. | |
| N1JB | Citation | 501-0188 | Park Avenue Leasing & Rental Inc. Winter Park, Fl. | N6778C |
| N1JR | Learjet | 25B-188 | Jartran Inc. Coral Gables, Fl. | A40-AJ/G-BCSE |
| N1JS | Westwind-1124 | 249 | John Scantlin, Klamath Falls, Or. | 4X-CMU |
| N1JU | Jet Commander | 13 | Bassett & Tesini, Fort Lauderdale, Fl. | (N404PC)/N1JU/N12CJ/N5OVF /N450RA |
| N1KT | Jet Commander-B | 135 | KT Air Inc/Simpson Electric Building Co. Elgin, Il. | N2DB/N700HB /N5043E |
| N1LO | Citation | 501-0139 | La Quinta Motor Inns Inc. Muscatine, Ia. | N526CC/N2651B |
| N1MN | Sabre-60 | 306-58 | Douglas Oil Purchasing Inc. Mobile, Al. | N80ER/N80E/N7578N |
| N1MY | DH 125/1A-522 | 25082 | Marshall R. Young Oil Co. Fort Worth, Tx. | N125CA/N2125/N909B /G-ATNM |
| N1MX | Citation | 501-0158 | Manitowoc Company Inc. Wi. | N2611Y |
| N1PB | Falcon 10 | 92 | Palm Beach Inc. Cincinnati, Oh. | (N61BP)/N172FJ/F-WNGM |
| N1PG | Gulfstream 3 | 334 | Procter & Gamble Co. Cincinnati, Oh. | |
| N1QC | Sabre-40 | 282-44 | Gateway Corporate Jet Sales, Alton, Il. | N1DC/N4567/N6399C |
| N1SV | Citation | 550-0150 | Vierson & Cochran Drilling Co. Medford, Or. | N266RA |
| N1R | B720-023B | 18022 | Los Angeles Dodgers Inc. Ca. | N7536A |
| N1TC | Falcon 10 | 144 | Toro. Co. Minneapolis, Mn./V.A Deverian | N208FJ/F-WZGP |
| N1U | Falcon 20C | 65 | UCO Aviation Inc. Big Timber, Mt. | N777WL/N777WJ/N393F/N393RF /N383RF/N890F/F-WNGN |
| N1UH | Citation | 551-0017 | Aviation Equipment Leasing, Rockville, Md. | N2052A |

| Registration | Type | C/N | Owner/Operator | Previous Identities |
|---|---|---|---|---|
| N1UL | Citation | 501-0107 | O E Company, Cleveland, Oh. | (N33VV)/(N333BG)/N3204M |
| N1UP | Sabre-60 | 306-40 | The Upjohn Co. Kalamazoo, Mi. | N711WK/N907R/N4753N |
| N1WS | Westwind-1124 | 252 | Western Preferred Corp. Fort Worth, Tx. | 4X-CMX |
| N1WZ | Sabre-40A | 282-117 | Oxford Development Corp. Monroeville, Pa. | I-MORA/(HB-VCZ)/N8338N |
| N1ZC | Learjet | 25XR-022 | H B Zachary Co. San Antonio, Tx. | N925WP/N943GA |
| N2 | Citation | 550-0006 | FAA, Dept. of Transportation, Washington DC. | N98820 |
| N2AJ | Westwind-1124 | 277 | Urban Investment Development Co. Chicago, Il. | N288WW/4X-CNW |
| N2AV | Westwind Two | 322 | Aviex Jet Inc. Houston, Tx. | 4X-CRP |
| N2BT | Citation | 501-0054 | Big Three Industries Inc. Houston, Tx. | N98563 |
| N2CA | Citation | 551-0024 | Coin Acceptors Inc. St. Louis, Mo. | N26628 |
| N2CC | B 727-21 | 19006 | Luqa Inc. Jacksonville, Fl. | N324AS/N324PA |
| N2FE | Falcon 20DC | 132 | 'Cheryl', Federal Express Corp. | N560L/N4348F/F-WMKG |
| N2G | DH 125/3A-RA | NA703 | General Tire & Rubber Co. Akron, Oh. | N612G/G-AVOJ/G-5-11 |
| N2H | Falcon 20F | 327 | Harrah's, Reno, Nv. | N3H/N4458F/F-WMKI |
| N2HW | Sabre-60 | 306-68 | Howmet Airplane Co. Inc. Greenwich, Ct. | N8000 |
| N2JZ | Citation | 550-0055 | U.S. Department of Energy, Las Vegas, Nv. | (N1466K)/N55CC/(N3308M) |
| N2KW | DH 125-731 | 25020 | Tri W Corp. St. Louis, Mo. | N959KW/N167J/G-ASZM |
| N2LN | Citation | 500-0391 | Liberty National Life Insurance Co. Birmingham, Al. | N3205M |
| N2MK | JetStar 2 | 5226 | Morrison-Knudsen Co. Boise, Id. | N4026M |
| N2MP | Falcon 10 | 31 | Missouri Improvement Co. St. Louis. | N122FJ/F-WLCU |
| N2N | Sabre-65 | 465-63 | Natural Gas Pipeline Co. Chicago. Il. | |
| N2PK | Gulfstream 2 | 206 | EAF/Listowel Corp. | |
| N2SN | Learjet | 23-072 | Calforina Overseas Bank, Ca. | N31S/N4VS/N33IJR/N331WR |
| N2SP | Gulfstream 3 | 364 | | |
| N2TE | MS 760 Paris | 5 | Genav Corp/Tom Edwards, Rockledge, Fl. | N2NC/N760H |
| N2TN | Citation | 500-0231 | VP Leasing Corp/Cannon Aviation Co. Hickory, NC. | N99TD/(N5231J) |
| N2UP | Sabre-60 | 306-17 | The Upjohn Co. Kalamazoo, Mi. | N988R/(D-COUP)/N4727N |
| N2WL | Learjet | 35A-245 | Cardinal Associates, Lexington, Ma. | |
| N2ZC | Citation | 501-0049 | H B Zachary Co. San Antonio, Tx. | N98586 |
| N3BL | Learjet | 23-003 | Bassett & Tesini Inc. Ft Lauderdale, Fl. | (N1OMC)/N2008/N2OOY/N803L |
| N3BM | Sabre-65 | 465-51 | Morris Communications Corp. Augusta, Ga. | |
| N3DZ | Learjet | 24D-279 | Dan Urschel-Tradewind Airport, Canadian, Tx. | N3DU/N849GL/VH-SBC |
| N3E | Gulfstream 2 | 185 | Cameron Iron Works Inc. Houston, Tx. | N372GM/N372CM |
| N3EK | JetStar-731 | 17/5076 | Cameron Iron Works Inc. Houston, Tx. | N3E/N100C/N9235R |
| N3FE | Falcon 20DC | 151 | 'Shannon', Federal Express Corp. Memphis, Tn. | N810PA/N810F /N4360F/F-WMKI |
| N3GL | Learjet | 24-173 | Gary Laughlin, Dallas, Tx. | N102GP/N33ST/N110SO/N872JR/N852GA |
| N3HB | Learjet | 35A-182 | Sale, Tucson, Az. | N33HB/N1450B |
| N3JJ | Citation Eagle | 500-0299 | Farley Aviation Corp. Durham, NC. | HB-VEO/(D-IVVV)/N5299J |
| N3JL | Learjet | 35A-289 | J Guy Beatty, Chattanooga, Tn. | |
| N3PC | Citation | 550-0210 | Paccar Inc. Wilmington, De. | N762PF/(N177CM)/N68018 |
| N | Citation | 500-0067 | | N3PC/N567CC |
| N3PG | Gulfstream 3 | 336 | Procter & Gamble Co. Cincinnati, Oh. | |
| N3Q | Citation | 650-0007 | Pioneer Corp. Amarillo, Tx. | |
| N3QM | Sabre-40A | 282-131 | Rebel Oil Co. Oklahoma City, Ok. | N3BM/N9251N |
| N3QZ | Citation Eagle | 500-0238 | Nielson Enterprises Inc. Cody, Wy. | N3Q/(N5238J) |
| N3R | Citation | 550-0111 | Weyerhauser Co. Tacoma, Wa. | N26652 |
| N3RA | Learjet | 35A-138 | NCRA Sales, McPherson, Ks. | N31FB/N7735A |
| N3RC | Falcon 10 | 69 | Lamda International Inc. Little Rock, Ar. | N43CC/N153FJ/F-WJML |
| N3RN | Sabre-75A | 380-38 | Unitrust Inc. Houston, Tx. | N85031/D-CAVW/N2102J |
| N3TE | Sabre-75 | 370-8 | Howell Petroleum Corp. Houston, Tx. | N7591N |
| N3VF | Westwind Two | 324 | V F Corp. Reading, Pa. | 4X-CRR |
| N3VG | Learjet | 35A-305 | V A Deverian, San Marino, Ca. | |
| N3WZ | Falcon 10 | 30 | Masco Corp. Taylor, Mi. | N156X/N30FJ/N294W/N121FJ/F-WLCT |
| N3ZA | Learjet | 23-024 | White Industries Inc. Bates City, Mo. | (N702RK)/N803JA/N488J/N21U /N202Y |
| N3ZD | Citation | 500-0224 | Cosden Pipeline Co. Big Spring, Tx. | N77RE/(N224CC) |
| N4AC | Falcon 50 | 96 | AMCA International, Hannover, NH. | F-WPXE |
| N4CP | Learjet | 55-029 | Chas. Pfizer Inc. Trenton, NJ. | |
| N4CR | DH 125/1A-522 | 25109 | Pendleton Truck & Trailer Leasing, Or. | N201H/G-ATUZ |
| N4F | Learjet | 24D-294 | Bruno Ferrari, Latrobe, Pa. | |
| N4FE | Falcon 20DC | 108 | 'Miss Chi', Federal Express Corp. Memphis, Tn. | N5CA/D-CBAT/F-WNGO |
| N4J | Learjet | 35A-110 | Interstate Constructors Inc. Wilmington. | (N12EP) |
| N4KH | Citation | 500-0062 | Oerke Enterprises Inc. Texline, Tx. | N4CH/N562CC |
| N4LG | Citation | 500-0130 | Raleigh Durham Aviation Inc. Morrisville, NC. | OY-ARW/N4LG/VH-CRM |
| N4M | Sabre-65 | 465-18 | Natural Gas Pipeline Co. of America, Chicago, Il. | |
| N4PG | Sabre-80A | 380-49 | Procter & Gamble Co. Cincinnati, Oh. | N4PO/(N41B)/N4PG/N2128J |
| N4PN | Learjet | 25-003 | Precision National Corp. Mount Vernon. | N11JC/N594GA |

| Registration | Type | C/N | Owner/Operator | Previous Identities |
|---|---|---|---|---|
| N4RU | Learjet | 24F-348 | Stevens Beechcraft, Greer, SC. | N4RT/N725GL |
| N4SE | Sabre-60 | 306-37 | Weyerhauser Co. Gig Harbor, Wa. | N4S/N4750N |
| N4SP | Jetstar-8 | 5081 | Saral Publications Inc. Virginia Gardens, Fl. | N200AL/N200A |
| N4TE | Citation | 500-0149 | R J Gallagher Co. Houston, Tx. | (N43TC)/N4TL |
| N4TL | Citation | 550-0108 | Amory Garment Co. Ms. | (N2665F) |
| N4VC | Learjet | 25B-161 | Valeron Corp.Oak Park, Mi. | |
| N4VF | Citation | 550-0053 | H D Lee Inc. Shawnee Mission, Ks. | (N3300M) |
| N4WG | Westwind-1124 | 200 | Wyman Gordon Co. Worcester, Ma. | N1124X/4X-CKX |
| N5C | Falcon 20C | 17 | Champlin Petroleum Co. Fort Worth, Tx. | N5450/N545C/N802F/F-WMKF |
| N5D | Learjet | 23-095 | The Dee Howard Co. San Antonio, Tx. | N974D/N366EJ |
| N5DL | HS 125/600A | 6051 | RELCO/Thriftway Inc. Cincinnati, Oh. | N22DL/C-GRNS/(N45BH) |
| N5DM | Learjet | 23-028 | Donald McCoy, Dallas, Tx. | N818LJ |
| N5ES | Falcon 10 | 174 | E Systems Inc. Greenville, Tx. | N240FJ/F-WZGE |
| N5FE | Falcon 20DC | 20 | 'Traci', Federal Express Corp. Memphis, In. | N367GA/N367G/N842F /F-WMKJ |
| N5JR | Jet Commander | 49 | Norman Lively, Port Chester, N.Y. | N430C |
| N5LC | BAC 1-11/401 | 073 | James Stewart, Minneapolis, Mn. | N111FL/N5031 |
| N5LL | Learjet | 25B-183 | Lars Linden, N. Wilkesboro, NC. | N66JD |
| N5NE | DC-9-14 | 45706 | Northwest Pipeline Co. Wilmington, De. | I-SARV/N3311L |
| N5PG | Sabre-80A | 380-50 | Procter & Gamble Co. Cincinnati, Oh. | N5E0/N5PG/N2129J |
| N5Q | Citation | 550-0036 | Pioneer Corp. Amarillo, Tx. | N5BAN/(N3262M) |
| N5RD | Gulfstream 2 | 142 | RDC Marine Inc. Houston, Tx. | N60CC/N882GA |
| N5RT | Falcon 20C | 96 | Richmond Tank Car Co. Houston, Tx. | N511S/N981F/F-WNGM |
| N5SJ | BH 125/600A | 6014 | MJI, Lincoln, Ne. | N922GR/N922CR/N26BH |
| N5TC | Citation | 501-0044 | First Southeast Risk Management Inc. Marietta, Ga. | N98675 |
| N5TK | Citation | 500-0266 | U.S. Customs Service, Washington DC. | N5266J |
| N5TR | Citation | 500-0288 | Five Oaks Ltd/Boyce and Sons, Ashland, Or. | N9013S/0Y-ASD/D-IDWN /N288CC/(N5288J) |
| N5UE | Diamond One | A026SA | | |
| N5VP | Citation | 501-0046 | Jetaire, Las Vegas, Nv. | N405CC/N36916 |
| N5YP | Citation | 501-0083 | Flint Engineering & Construction Co. Billings, Mt. | N462CC/N3159M |
| N5ZZ | Citation | 500-0155 | Robert Zeff, Detroit, Mi. | N920W/(N655CC) |
| N6CD | Citation | 500-0151 | A G & H Enterprises Inc. Portland, Or. | N151CC |
| N6FE | Falcon 20DC | 50 | 'Michelle', Federal Express Corp. Memphis, Tn. | N6565A/N804F /N879F/F-WNG0 |
| N6GC | Learjet | 25-034 | Jet Courier Service, Oh. | N242WT/N954FA/N954GA |
| N6GJ | Learjet | 23-069 | Executive Jets Intl. Ft. Lauderdale, Fl. | N9AJ/N814LJ |
| N6HT | Citation | 501-0008 | Hilliard Oil & Gas Inc. Menlo Park, Ca. | N362CC/N5362J |
| N6JW | Gulfstream 2 | 138 | Jim Walter Corp. Tampa, Fl. | |
| N6K | Sabre-65 | 465-3 | NL Industries Inc. Stratford, Ct. | N65RS |
| N6LL | Learjet | 25D-256 | Modern Globe Leasing Inc. N. Wilkesboro, NC. | |
| N6MK | Sabre-60 | 306-98 | Mallinkrodt Inc. St. Louis, Mo. | N65786 |
| N6NP | Sabre-65 | 465-9 | Northwest Pipeline Corp. Salt Lake City, Ut. | |
| N6NR | Sabre-65 | 465-29 | Rockwell International Corp. Pittsburgh, Pa. | |
| N6PG | Sabre-75A | 380-66 | Procter & Gamble Co. Cincinnati, Oh. | N6VL/N6PG/N2536E |
| N6Q | Citation | 550-0043 | Pioneer Corp. Amarillo, Tx. | N3285M |
| N6SS | DH 125/1A-522 | 25100 | Accident Narssarssuag, Greenland 19 JUN/81. Dismantled and transported to USA for reassembly and retrofit. | N44T0/N44TG/N104 /N7SZ/N952B/N125J/G-ATNT |
| N6TM | Sabre-60 | 306-72 | Liberty National Life Insurance Co. Brimingham, Al. | N550SL/N231A /N231CA |
| N6VF | Citation | 500-0045 | H D Lee Co. Shawnee Mission, Ks. | N44VF/N545CC |
| N6VG | Falcon 10 | 62 | V A Deverian, Beaverton, Or. | N12LB/N146FJ/F-WJMM |
| N7AB | Learjet | 24E-355 | American Building Inc. Eufala, Al. | |
| N7CJ | Citation | 501-0116 | C James McCormick, Vincennes, In. | N500XX/(N26496) |
| N7ES | HFB 320 | 1045 | Consolidated Equipment Corp. Wilmington, De. | N4ZA/N894HJ/N5602 /D-CIRU (N6890E) |
| N7FD | Citation | 550-0322 | Amdahl Corp. Sunnyvale, Ca. | |
| N7FE | Falcon 20DC | 46 | 'Lisa', Federal Express Corp. | N23555/CF-ESO/F-WMKG |
| N7FJ | Learjet | 23-058 | Chipola Aviation Inc. Marianna, Fl. | N66MP/N363EJ |
| N7GF | Learjet | 23-016 | Lewis Industries Inc. Baton Rouge, La. | N7CF/N500K |
| N7HF | Sabre-65 | 465-13 | Hershey Foods Corp. Pa. | |
| N7HV | BH 125/731 | NA775 | The Hoover Co. North Canton, Oh. | N5V/N72BH |
| N7LA | Learjet | 35A-308 | Aero Center Inc. Laredo, Tx. | N747GM/N99MJ |
| N7LC | Learjet | 25D-328 | Lavay Air Services Inc. Georgetown, De. | |
| N7NE | Citation | 501-0261 | Northern Engraving Co. Inc. Sparta, Wi. | |
| N7NF | Sabre-60 | 306-126 | NECO Ltd. | N7NR/N60SL/N2141J |

33

| Registration | Type | C/N | Owner/Operator | Previous Identities |
|---|---|---|---|---|
| N7NP | JetStar 2 | 5229 | Northwest Pipeline Corp. Salt Lake City. | N4038M |
| N7NR | Sabre-65 | 465-44 | Rockwell International Corp. Pittsburgh, Pa. | |
| N7PG | Gulfstream 2 | 62 | Procter & Gamble Co. Cincinnati, Oh. | N3ZQ/N1PG/N372GM/N372CM/N834GA |
| N7TJ | Learjet | 25-007 | Jordan Aviation Inc. Denver, Co. | N551MB/N551MD |
| N7US | Learjet | 35A-291 | U.S. Aviation Underwriters N.Y.C. | |
| N7WF | Citation | 501-0010 | WMS Famco, Oregon City, Or. | (N500MD)/N7WF/EP-PBC/N7WF/N36859 |
| N7YP | Citation | 550-0164 | State of Alabama Transportation Dept. | N164CC |
| N8AF | Sabre-40 | 282-24 | Universal Tank/Royal Air Fleet, Indianapolis, In. | N40DW/N360Q/N720J N6378 |
| N8BX | Citation | 550-0319 | Baxter/Travenol Aircraft Inc. Deerfield, Il. | N6890G |
| N8FD | Citation | 550-0349 | Federal Data Corp. Chevy Chase, Md. | |
| N8FE | Falcon 20DC | 199 | 'Wendy', Federal Express Corp. | N4388F/F-WMKH |
| N8GA | Westwind Two | 356 | Galaxy Aviation Corp. Oklahoma City, Ok. | N356WW/4X-CUJ |
| N8GE | Jet Commander | 63 | Galaxy Aviation Corp. Oklahoma City, Ok. | N8GA/N9DM/N15G/N7784/N6546V |
| N8JG | Citation | 500-0074 | Semco Instruments Inc. Hollywood, Ca. | N574W/N574CC |
| N8JL | Westwind Two | 359 | Petroleum Equipment Tools Co. Houston, Tx. | 4X-CUM |
| N8LC | Sabre-60 | 306-21 | Xcel Products Co. Houston, Tx. | N60HC/N442A/N948R/N4731N |
| N8LL | Learjet | 28-005 | Lars Linden, Wilkesboro, NC. | (N31WT) |
| N8MA | Learjet | 35A-229 | ARO Corp. Bryan, Oh. | |
| N8MQ | Learjet | 25B-085 | Banc One Financial Corp. Cincinnati, Oh. | N8MA |
| N8NR | Sabre-60 | 306-141 | Rockwell International Corp. Pittsburgh, Pa. | (N89N) |
| N8PG | Gulfstream 2 | 21 | Procter & Gamble Co. Cincinnati, Oh. | N7ZX/N3PG/N4PG |
| N8QP | Westwind-1124 | 217 | American Quasar Petroleum Co. Ft. Worth, Tx. | 4X-CLO |
| N8RA | Jet Commander | 104 | Roger Larson, Bellaire Bluffs, Fl. | N87B/N4674E |
| N8RF | Citation | 500-0293 | J R F Inc. Greenville, Ms. | (N5293J) |
| N8SC | JetStar-731 | 9/5106 | Singer Co. N.Y. | CF-GWI/N288U/N238U |
| N9AT | Learjet | 25B-125 | Asplundh Aviation, Philadelphia, Pa. | (N85AT)/N4MR |
| N9CN | Learjet | 35-016 | State Development Board, Columbia, SC. | N5867/N136GL |
| N9CZ | Learjet | 25-040 | TigerAir Inc. Atlanta, Ga. | N41AJ/C-GOSL/(N2273G)/F-BSUR/HB-VBI /N687LJ |
| N9DM | Falcon 20C | 18 | Dynamark Corp. Bedford, Tx. | N777JF/D-COLO/N803LC/N803F /N840F/F-WNGM |
| N9FB | Falcon 20E | 275 | Basil Aviation Ltd. Washington DC | N661JB/N4434F/F-WMKH |
| N9FE | Falcon 20DC | 216 | 'Laurie', Federal Express Corp. | N4402F/F-WLCT |
| N9GT | Citation | 501-0068 | General Telephone Co. Bloomington, Il. | N438CC/N2841A |
| N9HM | Learjet | 35A-199 | Holt Machinery Co. San Antonio, Tx. | N40144 |
| N9HN | Learjet | 25C-146 | Capital Air Surveys, Pittsburgh, Pa. | C-GRQX/N9HN/N9HM/N146LJ |
| N9JJ | Learjet | 23-039 | Les Jones, Houston, Tx. | N30SC/N15SC/N800JA/N43B |
| N9KH | Learjet | 28-001 | Oxford International, Corpus Christi, Tx. | N9RS |
| N9LD | Learjet | 24F-336 | Leeson Electric Corp. W Bend. | N162J/I-DDAE/N3818G |
| N9LR | Citation | 550-0250 | Jetstream Corp. Wilmington, NC. | N68599 |
| N9NP | Sabre-60 | 306-133 | Northwest Pipeline Corp. Salt Lake City, Ut. | N6NE/N2151J |
| N9NT | Sabre-60 | 306-135 | Natsomas N. America Inc. Houston, Tx. | N9NR/N2535E |
| N9TK | Citation | 501-0064 | Howard W Meister, Irvine, Ca. | (N33KW)/N2768A |
| N9VC | Westwind-1123 | 162 | Summit Corp. Dallas, Tx. | N234RC/N78LB/N1123S/4X-CJL |
| N9WP | NAL 1-11/401 | 4/078 | Walter Probst, Incline, Nv. | N5036 |
| N10AG | Falcon 20 | 6 | AMAX Inc. Stapleton-Denver, Co. | (N110FJ)/N600BT/N102FJ /F-WJML |
| N10AH | Falcon 10 | 139 | American Hospital Supply Corp. Evanston, Il. | N204FJ/F-WZGK |
| N10AZ | Learjet | 35A-080 | Anschutz Corp. Denver, Co. | N23HB/N109GL |
| N10BD | Learjet | 25B-120 | Bill Daniels & Associates, Denver, Co. | N278LE/N744MC/N111AF |
| N10C | HS 125/700A | NA0235 | Dennis O'Connor, Victoria, Tx. | N700GB/G-5-18 |
| N10CN | Sabre-75A | 380-54 | Consolidated Natural Gas, Bridgeport, WV/Rockwell. | N62NR/N6NR/N2138J |
| N10CP | Learjet | 24-112 | Commerce Service Corp. Dallas, Tx. | N2200T/CF-ECB |
| N10CR | Learjet | 55-057 | National Cash Register. | |
| N10CX | JetStar-8 | 5162 | Clorox Co. Oakland, Ca. | N5526L |
| N10CZ | HS 125/700A | NA0227 | Congoleum Inc. Milwaukee, Wi. | G-5-19 |
| N10DG | Citation | 500-0120 | Anderson- Greenwood & Co. Bellaire, Tx. | N120CC/(N620CC) |
| N10EH | Citation | 501-0027 | Sinclair Marketing Inc. W. Yellowstone, Mt. | N350CC/N5350J |
| N10FE | Falcon 20DC | 16 | 'Audrey', Federal Express Corp. | N354H/N807F/F-WNGL |
| N10FJ | Falcon 10 | 106 | Falcon Jet Corp. Teterboro, NJ. | N1JN/N181FJ/F-WPUX |
| N10FN | Citation | 550-0241 | First National Bank, St. Louis, Mo. | N6804Z |
| N10FU | Learjet | 24E-340 | Andusan Farms, Emeryville, Ca. | |
| N10GE | Citation | 501-0022 | ACME AIR Corp. Ft. Smith, Ar. | (N995AU)/N110H/N11DH/N385CC /N36884 |
| N10J | Citation | 501-0037 | Carpenter Tech Corp. Reading, Pa. | N36922 |
| N10JK | Citation | 550-0175 | Lee Bangerter, Portland, Or. | |
| N10JP | Jet Commander | 96 | Paco Aire Inc. Louisville, Ky. | N1QH/N1QL/N7EC/N59CT/N56WH/N56S |

| Registration | Type | C/N | Owner/Operator | Previous Identities |
|---|---|---|---|---|
| N10JZ | Falcon 10 | 13 | Telemedia/John Zenko, Chicago, Il. | N72EU/N210FJ/N734S/N108FJ/F-WLCS |
| N10LB | Gulfstream 2 | 168 | Lind-Air Inc. Cincinnati, Oh. | N812GA |
| N10LN | DH 125/3A-RA | 25156 | L B Nelson Corp. Portland, Or. | N522M/G-AVZJ |
| N10LR | Citation | 550-0059 | Rinco Avn, Inc. El Paso, Tx. | (N2662F) |
| N10M | Sabre-75 | 370-2 | Mid-Continent Systems, W. Memphis, Ar. | N80K/N8NR/N75NR/N7585N |
| N10MB | Westwind-1123 | 157 | Martin Seretean, Dalton, Ga. | N11230 |
| N10MR | Westwind-1124 | 258 | Minnesota Rubber, Minneapolis. | 4X-CND |
| N10NL | Citation | 501-0043 | O'Neal Steel Inc. Birmingham, Al | N98510 |
| N10PW | HS 125/700A | NA0273 | Pennwalt Corp. Philadelphia, Pa. | G-5-20 |
| N10QD | Falcon 10 | 178 | Quarles Drilling, Tulsa, Ok. | N244FJ/F-WZGK |
| N10RE | Learjet | 35A-345 | Reliable Electric Co. Franklin Park, Il. | N3818G |
| N10SN | Jet Commander | 69 | Sky Sales & Service Inc. Oklahoma City. Ok. | N89B |
| N10TB | Falcon 10 | 72 | Tom Brown, Midland, Tx. | N154FJ/F-WLCX |
| N10TJ | Falcon 10 | 99 | Thoroughbred Jet Aviation Inc. Waterford, Va. | N176FJ/F-WPXH |
| N10TX | Falcon 10 | 9 | Texas Industries Inc. Dallas, Tx. | N103FJ/F-WJMM |
| N10UC | Citation Eagle | 500-0283 | Utah International Inc. San Francisco, Ca. | N5283J |
| N10WF | Learjet | 35A-377 | Wm. Fuller, Lenoir, Tx. | N933GL/(N711EV) |
| N10XY | B727-76 | 19254 | Occidental Petroleum Corp. Los Angeles, Ca. | N8043B/VH-TJD |
| N11A | Citation | 500-0111 | Southtrust Corp. Birmingham, Al. | N111CC |
| N11AK | Learjet | 25B-082 | Jetaway Inc. Sevierville, Tn. | N15AK/N427RD/N30P/HB-VCK |
| N11AL | Gulfstream 2 | 97 | Emra Corp. San Anselmo, Ca. | N66TF/I-SMEG/N889GA |
| N11AM | Learjet | 35A-340 | International Association of Machinists, Washington D.C. | |
| N11DH | Falcon 10 | 142 | ACME Air Corp. Fort Smith, Ar. | N10HK/N207FJ/F-WZGN |
| N11FH | Learjet | 24-131 | Frederick Harcourt, Whittier, Ca. | N282R/N232R/N659LJ |
| N11KA | Citation | 500-0119 | Southern Packaging & Storage Co. Greenville, Tn. | N111SU/N619CC |
| N11MC | Jet Commander | 55 | Halliburton Co. Tomball, Tx. | 4X-CON/D-CEAS/(D-CHAS) |
| N11QC | Citation | 500-0008 | G S Cortazar, Brownsville, Tx. | N11TC/N502CC/HB-VCX/N508CC |
| N11QM | Learjet | 23-091 | Great Gibraltar Corp. Cleveland, Oh. | N110M/N430J/N430JA |
| N11TC | Falcon 20C | 146 | Teledyne Industries Inc. Mobile, Al. | N777EG/N964M/N4357F/F-WJMN |
| N11UE | JetStar-6 | 5038 | Aircraft Trading Centre, Palm Beach, Fl. | N11UF/N22CH/N341N/N341NS /N9212R |
| N11UL | Sabre-60 | 306-103 | Universal Leaf Tobacco Inc. Richmond, Va. | N65794 |
| N11WP | Jet Commander | 100 | Paul Broadhead, Meridian, Ms. | N16GR/N605V/N4663E |
| N11WQ | Citation | 500-0058 | R J B Development Co. Reno, Nv. | N11WC/N558CC |
| N12AM | Citation | 500-0235 | Gutman & Co. Chicago, Il. | N235CC/N5235J |
| N12BN | HS 125/731 | 25214 | International Harvester Co. Chicago, Il. | N731HS/G-5-20/G-AXTU/N600A /N60PC/N40PC/G-AXTU |
| N12DE | Citation | 501-0081 | Copeland Corp. Sidney, Oh. | N3146M |
| N12FC | Citation | 550-0326 | Federal Intermediate Credit Bank, Spokane, Wa. | N6802T |
| N12GK | Citation | 551-0054 | Omni Inc. Franklin, NC. | N6862D |
| N12HJ | Learjet | 23-040 | Harris Jet Service, Orlando, Fl. | N98386/YV-01CP/N673WM/N433EJ |
| N12JA | Citation | 550-0203 | J A Jones Construction Co. Charlotte, NC. | N67990 |
| N12MB | Falcon 10 | 112 | Wing Corp. Houston, Tx. | N12XX/N186FJ/F-WPXD |
| N12ME | Citation | 500-0137 | Lotus Cars, Norwich, UK. | N12MB/N137CC |
| N12MF | Falcon 20D | 179 | Marathon Manufacturing Co. Houston, Tx. | N12LB/N10LB/N4375F/F-WNGO |
| N12MJ | Learjet | 24E-331 | MJI. Lincoln, Nb. | |
| N12TX | Falcon 10 | 147 | Texas Industries Inc. Dallas, Tx. | N212FJ/F-WZGS |
| N12U | Falcon 10 | 75 | Mountain States Tel & Tel Co. Denver. | N157FJ/F-WNGM |
| N13AD | Jet Commander | 103 | Sandia Drilling Co. Edmond, Ok. | N10HV/N487G/N136K/N1121S |
| N13BT | Citation | 501-0078 | C & A Aviation Inc. Los Angeles, Ca. | (N777BT)/(N3127M) |
| N13GW | Gulfstream 2 | 775 | Gulf & Western Industries Inc. N.Y. | N804GA |
| N13KL | Learjet | 24F-332 | Northeast Aviation Inc. NY. | |
| N13MJ | Learjet | 24D-314 | MJI Lincoln, Nb. | N501MH |
| N13SN | Learjet | 23-009 | ECE Corp. State College, Pa. | N5BL/N425EJ |
| N13UR | Citation Eagle | 500-0011 | UNR Air Inc. Falls Church, Va. | N227H/N511CC |
| N13VG | Learjet | 35A-386 | V A Deverian, Pasadena, Ca. | |
| N14BC | Learjet | 24B-209 | Jet Services Inc. Greensboro, N.C. | N16MT/N970GA |
| N14BN | Westwind-1124 | 337 | Burlington Northern. | 4X-CTE |
| N14CF | Learjet | 36-015 | CF Sales Inc. Chicago, Il. | |
| N14CQ | Sabre-60 | 306-83 | Continental Grain, N.Y. | N14CG |
| N14DM | Diamond One | A017SA | | |
| N14FE | Falcon 20DC | 227 | 'Ann-Marie'. Federal Express Corp. | N4410F/F-WMKG |
| N14GD | DH 125/3A-RA | NA704 | Gordon Gund, Princeton, NJ. | N208H/N55G/N75C/G-AVOK/G-5-12 |
| N14JA | HS 125/700A | NA0236 | J A Jones Construction Co. Charlotte, NC. | N700UK/G-5-11 |
| N14LJ | Learjet | 25-014 | Avia Jet Management Corp. Dallas, Tx. | N8CL/N127AJ/N316M/N204A /N914SB/N857GA |
| N14M | Sabre-65 | 465-4 | Mellon National Bank, W. Mifflin, Pa. | N1058X |
| N14PC | Gulfstream 2 | 170 | Pepsico Inc. Charlotte, NC. | N991GA |

35

| Regis-tration | Type | C/N | Owner/Operator | Previous Identities |
|---|---|---|---|---|
| N14TT | Citation | 500-0237 | John Stiteler/Arizona Jet Charter, Phoenix, Az. | (N5237J) |
| N14TX | Learjet | 35A-321 | Fidelity Union Life Insurance Co. Dallas, Tx. | |
| N14U | Falcon 10 | 90 | Mountain States Telephone & Telegraph, Denver, Co. | N170FJ/F-WNGD |
| N14VC | Learjet | 25D-263 | Gates Learjet Corp. Wichita, Ks. | N40162 |
| N15AG | HS 125/700A | NA0309 | Liggett Group/Amstar Corp. NY. | G-5-17 |
| N15AK | Sabre-65 | 465-70 | Alaska Interstate/AKI Finance Corp. Houston, Tx. | |
| N15AT | Falcon 20F | 403 | Figgie International, Willoughby, Oh. | N189F/F-WJMK |
| N15AW | Citation | 500-0139 | A W Alloys, Stansted, UK. | N3771U/OE-FDP/(N5353J) |
| N15BN | Westwind-1124 | 352 | Burlington Northern Inc. Seattle, Wa. | 4X-CTT |
| N15CC | Citation | 500-0101 | Hudson International Inc. Rockhill, SC. | N6JU/N6JL/N1HM/N101CD /N12MB/N601CC |
| N15EH | Learjet | 35A-126 | Sinclair Marketing Inc. W. Yellowstone, Mt. | N744GL |
| N15ER | Learjet | 25D-267 | E W Richardson, Albuquerque, NM. | |
| N15FE | Falcon 20DC | 229 | 'Donna', Federal Express Corp. Tn. | N4411F/F-WJMJ |
| N15M | Learjet | 25TF-036 | Charles Oliver, Chapel Hill, NC. (Also carries N25TF) | N15CC/N741ED /N741E/N956J/N956GA |
| N15MJ | Learjet | 25-018 | MJI, Lincoln, Ne. | N117CH/N99ES/N32PC/N77SA/N323WA/N861GA |
| N15NP | DC-9-14 | 45702 | Northwest Pipeline Co. Wilmington, De. | I-SARJ/N3307L |
| N15PN | Sabre-75A | 380-15 | Pneumo Corp. Boston, Ma. | N1841F/N1841D/N80NR/(N338K)/N67566 |
| N15PR | Citation | 501-0077 | Fournet, Guidry & Henderson Jets, Lafayette. | (N3124M) |
| N15SC | Learjet | 35A-139 | Sea Containers Associates, New York. | |
| N15TG | Gulfstream 2 | 253 | Texas Gas Transmission Co Houston, Tx. | |
| N15TS | Sabre-40 | 282-18 | Ecology Chemical & Refining Co. Manor, Pa. | N113SC/N1072/N107G/N6372C |
| N15TW | Diamond One | A014SA | | |
| N15WH | Learjet | 35A-085 | F & D Enterprises Inc. Las Vegas, Nv. | |
| N16CP | Learjet | 24-147 | National Jets Inc. Fort Lauderdale, Fl. | N595GA/N673LJ |
| N16FE | Falcon 20DC | 230 | 'Laura Jane', Federal Express Corp. | N4412F/F-WJML |
| N16GH | Jet Commander | 110 | Lomex Ltd. Oklahoma City, Ok. | N181SV/N101SV/4X-CPA/N4716E |
| N16GT | Learjet | 25D-230 | General Telephone Co., San Angelo, Tx. | |
| N16HC | Learjet | 24-126 | Caesars World Inc. Los Angeles, Ca. | (N345SF)/N332FP/N332WR/N653LJ |
| N16MK | Jet Commander | 84 | Peninsular Jets, Ft. Lauderdale, Fl. | N600ER/N600TP/N600TD/N312S |
| N16NK | Gulfstream 2 | 156 | Castor Trading Co. Coral Gables, Fl. | N7000G/N400SJ/N806GA |
| N16PN | Sabre-60 | 306-99 | Rockwell International. | N905R/N657R9 |
| N16R | Falcon 20F | 305 | R J R Aircraft Inc. Winston Salem, NC. | N444 6F/F-WMKJ |
| N16SK | Jet Commander | 101 | Milton Koy, Houston, Tx. | N16MA/N16A/N5JC/N45JF/N100KY/N899S |
| N16VG | Citation | 501-0157 | Gordon Rosenburg, San Ardo, Ca. | (N88BR)/N2052A |
| N16WG | DH 125/731 | NA718 | WKG Inc/Star Aviation Inc. Houston, Tx. | (N7WG)/N900DS/N600JA/N600LP /N600L/G-AWXC |
| N17EM | Learjet | 35A-287 | Citicorp Multilease (Sec) Int. Wilmington, De. | |
| N17FE | Falcon 20DC | 232 | 'Sonya', Federal Express Corp. Tn. | N4413F/F-WJMN |
| N17ND | Learjet | 35A-438 | Jetaway Air Service, Muskegon, Mi. | |
| N17RG | Citation | 550-0222 | Ryan Group Aviation Inc. Chicago, Il. | N6800Z |
| N17S | Citation | 550-0098 | Sperry Flight Systems, Phoenix, Az. | (N26635) |
| N18BG | Citation | 501-0018 | Konfara Co. Phoenix, Az. | N378CC/N36871 |
| N18CC | Citation | 550-0424 | | |
| N18FE | Falcon 20DC | 233 | 'Polly', Federal Express Corp. Tn. | N4414F/F-WLCV |
| N18GW | Westwind-1124 | 187 | Gulf & Western Industries Inc. N.Y. | N1124N/4X-CKK |
| N18HC | Citation | 501-0223 | L & M Radiator Co. Hibbing, Mn. | N1959E |
| N18HH | NAL 1-11/401 | 11/068 | Helmsley Spear Inc. West Palm Beach, Fl. | N200CC/N5028/N3E/N5028 |
| N18JL | Jet Commander | 51 | T Smith & Son Inc. Metairie, La. | N93JR/N21BC/N69WW /N303LA/SE-DCK/N618JC |
| N18LB | Gulfstream 3 | 309 | ACSC/United Dairy Farmers Inc. | |
| N18MJ | Learjet | 25D-218 | Z & W Ltd. Chicago, Il. | |
| N18RN | Gulfstream 2 | 231 | Chemco International Leasing Inc. NY. | VR-BHD/VR-CAG/N1102/N808GA |
| N18SF | Westwind Two | 374 | | 4X-CUL |
| N18TA | Learjet | 25D-280 | LKA Aviation Inc/Thunderbird Airways, Houston, Tx. | N280LA |
| N18X | Falcon 10 | 42 | Joy Manufacturing Co. Pittsburgh, Pa. | N126FJ/F-WLCU |
| N19BD | Falcon 20C | 161 | Black & Decker Manufacturing Co. Towson, Md. | N93CD/N4365F/F-WMKF |
| N19ES | JetStar 2 | 5204 | Esmark Inc. Chicago, Il. | N5530L |
| N19FM | Learjet | 24D-311 | Holt Machinery Co. San Antonio, Tx. | N19HM/N5TD/N5TR/N66LW |
| N19HH | BH 125/600A | 6004 | The Halter Co. New Orleans, La. | N94BB/N94BD/N81BH |
| N19HM | | | Holt Machinery Co. San Antonio, Tx. | |
| N19LH | Learjet | 35A-279 | Hillair Inc. San Diego, Ca. | |
| N19MQ | Citation | 500-0165 | Riblet Products Inc. Elkhart, In. | N19M |
| N19MS | Sabre-40 | 282-82 | A M Leasing Inc. Minneapolis, Mn. | (N777ST)/N713MR/N736R/N574R |
| N19PC | Sabre-75A | 380-2 | Paccar Inc. Cleveland, Oh. | N2440C/N2440G/N8445N |
| N19UC | Westwind-1124 | 232 | Sale, Blountville, Tx. | N1124D/4X-CMD |

| Regis-tration | Type | C/N | Owner/Operator | Previous Identities |
|---|---|---|---|---|
| N19M | Sabre-60 | 306-56 | Mellonbank, Pittsburgh, Pa. | N14M/N935R/N7576N |
| N20BE | Falcon 20D | 203 | County Line Cheese/Beatrice Foods, In. | N1875B/N4378F/F-WPXH |
| N20CG | Falcon 20F | 281 | Washington Jet/Garber Bros. | D-CORF/F-WROR |
| N20CN | Citation | 550-0285 | Consolidated Natural Gas Corp. Bridgeport, WV. | N6863T |
| N20CR | Learjet | 35A-098 | NCR Corp. Dayton, Oh. | |
| N20CX | Challenger | 1051 | Clorox Co. Oakland, Ca. | N27341/C-GLXO |
| N20DK | Learjet | 25B-198 | Fred Shaulis, Friedens, Pa. | |
| N20EP | Learjet | 23-008 | Philip Schofield, La Jolla, Ca. | N20BD/N20S/N1203/N825LJ |
| N20FE | Falcon 20DC | 235 | 'Tal', Federal Express Corp. Tn. | N4415F/F-WPXJ |
| N20FX | HS 125/700A | NA0286 | Twentieth Century Fox Films Corp. SFO, Ca. | N125AU/G-5-14 |
| N20G | Sabre-60 | 306-59 | Goodyear Tire & Rubber Co. Akron, Oh. | N945R |
| N20GT | Citation | 501-0174 | Global Truck & Equipment Inc. Houston, Tx. | N6779Y |
| N20MJ | Learjet | 25D-277 | Tem-Cole Jet Aviation Inc. McClure, Oh. | |
| N20PY | Learjet | 25D-249 | Amstar Financial Corp. Dallas, Tx. | |
| N20RD | Learjet | 25D-334 | Sunny South Aircraft Service Inc. Ft. Lauderdale, Fl. | |
| N20RG | DH 125/1A | 25091 | Richard Socha, Clearwater, Fl. | N1230G/G-ATNP |
| N20RT | Citation | 500-0033 | Richard Beauchamp/Refrigerated Transport Co. Inc. Forest Park, Ga. | N58PL/N65MA/N533BF/N533CC |
| N20S | HS 125/700A | NA0243 | Storer Broadcasting Co. Miami, Fl. | N130BH/G-5-17 |
| N20SM | Citation | 500-0001 | State of Mississippi, Jackson, Mi. | N502CC/(N510CC) |
| N20SR | Falcon 20F | 369 | Shelton Ranch Corp. Portland, Or. | N1037F/F-WROP |
| N20TA | Learjet | 23-062 | T D K Leasing Inc. Dover, De. | N670MF |
| N20UC | Sabre 65 | 465-46 | Utah International Inc. San Francisco, Ca. | |
| N20UG | Learjet | 36A-031 | Bowlen Holdings Inc. Portland, Or. | N20UC |
| N21AK | Jet Commander | 59 | Kroblin Refrigerated Xpress Inc. Waterloo, La. | N59JC/N6538V |
| N21AM | Gulfstream 2 | 110 | Airmark Corp. Malibu, Ca. | N200PB/N200GN/N5000G/N814GA |
| N21AR | DH 125/3A-RA | NA706 | Agency Records Control Inc. York, Nb. | N114PC/(N711SW)/N214TC /N214JR/N77617/G-AVRH |
| N21BS | Citation | 501-0025 | RLLK Inc. Eunice, La. | N389CC/N36888 |
| N21CC | Citation | 500-0099 | International Paper Co. N.Y. | N599CC |
| N | Citation | 551-0431 | Ernest Hahn Inc. El Segundo, Ca. | N1218V |
| N21FE | Falcon 20DC | 226 | 'Angela', Federal Express Corp. Memphis, Tn. | N4409F/F-WSOK/F-WPXI |
| N21MF | DH 125/1A-522 | 25097 | Taylor's Gin Co. Friars Point, Ms. | N12KW/N125V/LN-NPE/G-ATSP |
| N22BM | Learjet | 36A-032 | B J McAdams Inc. Wooster, Oh. | N745GL/N40146 |
| N22BX | Sabre-60 | 306-138 | Bendix Corp. Southfield, Mi. | N2508E |
| N22CH | Sabre-40A | 282-99 | C H Heist, Clearwater, Fl. | N78TC/N7594N |
| N22CP | Learjet | 35A-178 | Pfizer Inc. Trenton, NJ. | N40146 |
| N22DN | Citation | 500-0127 | Delavan Manufacturing Co. W. Des Moines, Ia. | N701AT/N701AS |
| N22EH | DH 125/731 | NA715 | HKA Associates, El Segundo, Ca. | N8000B/N800CB/N400CC/N200CC/N77RS /G-AWPE |
| N22ES | Falcon 10 | 122 | Esmark Inc. Chicago, Il. | N193FJ/F-WPUV |
| N22FE | Falcon 20DC | 223 | 'Holly', Federal Express Corp. Tn. | N4407F/F-WPUX |
| N22FM | Citation | 500-0229 | Federal-Mogul Corp. Detroit, Mi. | |
| N22HC | Falcon 20C | 14 | Floyd Hardesty, Tulsa, Ok. | N22DL/CF-DML/N804F/F-WMKJ |
| N22JG | Citation | 500-0208 | Comexagro Corp. Houston, Tx. | N82JT |
| N22LH | Citation | 500-0319 | Lewis Hyman, Beverly Hills, Ca. | N5319J/HZ-NCI/N5319J |
| N22MH | Learjet | 24D-259 | Malone & Hyde Inc. Memphis, Tn. | N200JR |
| N22MJ | Learjet | 24E-329 | MJI,Lincoln, Nb. | N21AG/N102GL |
| N22MY | Sabre-60 | 306-117 | Murray Ohio Manufacturing Co. Brentwood, Tn. | N2120J |
| N22NJ | Learjet | 25C-097 | WER Aviation Corp. Charlotte, NC. | I-SFER/(OY-ASK)/HB-VCS |
| N22NM | Learjet | 24E-341 | UCO Aviation Inc. Whittier, Ca. | N22BM |
| N22RB | JetStar-6 | 5093 | Rogers Brothers, Beaumont, Tx. | N76EB/N5000C/N711Z/N9249R |
| N22RD | Jet Commander | 99 | Perry Aviation Inc. Odessa, Tx. | N22RT/N922CP/N922CR/N4661E |
| N22SD | Citation | 501-0177 | Equus Aviation Inc. Houston, Tx. | (N999RB)/N6779P |
| N22SF | Learjet | 35A-168 | State Farm Mutual Auto Insurance Co. Bloomington. | |
| N22T | Citation | 550-0409 | Texas-American Bank Services Inc. Ft. Worth, Tx. | N1216J |
| N22TP | Citation | 501-0014 | James C Ray, Phoenix, Az. | N36860 |
| N23 | B 720-061 | 18066 | FAA,Oklahoma City, Ok. (WFU ?) | N113 |
| N23A | Gulfstream 2 | 153 | Superior Oil Co. Midland, Tx. | N881GA |
| N23AC | Westwind-1124 | 341 | John A Frye Shoe Co. Wilmington, De. | N1124P/4X-CUR |
| N23AM | Learjet | 24D-247 | Alex Matway/Interair Services Inc. Clearwater, Fl. | D-ICAP/HB-VCN |
| N23AJ | Learjet | 23-053 | Gulfstream-American Corp. Van Nuys, Ca. | F-BTOK/HB-VBC/N361EJ |
| N23BX | Sabre-65 | 465-61 | Bendix Corp. Detroit, Mi. | |
| N23DB | Learjet | 25B-086 | A D Bowen Corp. Abilene, Tx. | N28RP/N123DM |
| N23EH | Citation | 501-0187 | E Hahn Inc. El Segundo, Ca. | N21EH/(N414CB)/N576CC/N6779D |
| N23ES | Falcon 10 | 123 | Esmark Inc. Chicago, Il. | N194FJ/F-WPUX |

37

| Regis-<br>tration | Type | C/N | Owner/Operator | Previous<br>Identities |
|---|---|---|---|---|
| N23ET | Falcon 10 | 11 | Falcon Jet Corp. Teterboro, NJ. | N23ES/N106FJ/F-WJMK |
| N23FE | Falcon 20DC | 224 | 'Kristene', Federal Express Corp. Tn. | N4408F/F-WPUY |
| N23G | Learjet | 3GA-026 | Goodyear Tire & Rubber Co. Akron, Oh. | N726GL |
| N23HB | Learjet | 55-046 | Hamilton Bros/Delaware Air Jet Inc. Denver, Co. | |
| N23HM | Learjet | 25D-262 | Southeastern Jet Corp. Charlotte, NC. | |
| N23M | Gulfstream 2 | 105 | 3M Co. St. Paul, Mn. (r/c Mining Two). | N807GA |
| N23ND | Citation | 550-0253 | Noble Drilling Corp. Tulsa, Ok. | N68621 |
| N23SB | JetStar Two | 5227 | U S Tobacco Co. Greenwich, Ct. | N211PA/N4033M |
| N23SG | Learjet | 24XR-233 | Union Planters National Leasing, Memphis, Tn. | N78AF/D-IGSO/N253GL |
| N23TJ | Learjet | 23-033 | Precision Flite Inc. Wilmington, De. | N60DH/XA-GAM/XA-LGM/N453JT<br>/N453LJ/N158MJ |
| N23VG | Learjet | 35A-379 | F B N Ltd. Pasadena, Ca. | |
| N23W | Gulfstream 2 | 116 | First Security Bank, Salt Lake City, Ut. | N20XY/9M-ARR/N821GA |
| N23Y | Westwind-1123 | 155 | Triad Aviation Corp. Corpus Christi, Tx. | |
| N24AJ | Learjet | 24-151 | Howard Olsen, Oklahoma City, Ok. | N50JF/N664GL/N664CL/N111HJ/N153H |
| N24BA | Learjet | 24A-100 | Bass Aviation Inc. Hattiesburg, Ms. | N361AA/N424NJ/N989SA/N144X<br>/CF-BCJ/N427LJ |
| N24CH | Citation | 501-0247 | | N2627U |
| N24FE | Falcon 20DC | 220 | 'Tammy-Elaine', Federal Express Corp. | N4404F/F-WPUU |
| N24FF | Learjet | 23-034 | Century West Inc. Cheyenne, Wy. | N241BN/N242WT |
| N24G | Sabre-65 | 465-5 | Goodyear Tire & Rubber Co. Akron, Oh. | |
| N24GB | Sabre-60 | 306-14 | J D Allen & Co. Oklahoma City, Ok. | (N60AG)/N24G/N4724N |
| N24JK | Learjet | 35A-339 | MDFC Equipment Leasing, Long Beach, Ca. | |
| N24KF | Learjet | 24-161 | H H Rainer, Charlotte, NC. | N24KT/N224KT/N649G |
| N24KT | Westwind-1124 | 266 | Jostens Inc. Minneapolis, Mn. | 4X-CNL |
| N24RH | Westwind-1124 | 214 | Huber Hunt & Nichols Inc. Indianapolis, In. | N214WW/N1124N/4X-CLL |
| N24SB | Westwind-Two | 369 | U.S. Tobacco Co. Greenwich, Ct. | 4X-CUF |
| N24SR | Westwind-Two | 332 | Southland Royalty Co. Fort Worth, Tx. | 4X-CRZ |
| N24TA | Learjet | 25B-155 | Richard Kucel, Houston, Tx. | |
| N24UG | JetStar-8 | 5108 | United Gas Pipeline Co. Houston, Tx. | N1207Z/N7953S |
| N24XR | Learjet | 24XR-150 | Dee Howard 'Extra Range', San Antonio, Tx. | N211BL/N211HJ/N596HF<br>/N596GA/N3807G |
| N25 | Citation Eagle | 500-0084 | FAA, Washington DC. | N2/N10/N584CC |
| N25AM | Learjet | 25D-321 | Alex Matway, Clearwater, Fl. | |
| N25BX | Sabre-75A | 380-47 | HCW Inc. Chicago, Il. | N25BH/N2126J |
| N25CP | Falcon 20C | 121 | Cotton Petroleum Corp. Tulsa, Ok. | N1199M/N813P/N813PA/N242LB<br>/N4341F/F-WJMJ |
| N25DD | Citation | 501-0085 | I D T Corp. Summerville, SC. | N34AA/N475CC/N3189M |
| N25EL | Learjet | 35A-419 | Enterprise Leasing Co. St. Louis, Mo. | N935GL |
| N25FS | Learjet | 35A-198 | Great Western Management & Realty Corp. Houston, Tx. | |
| N25GL | Learjet | 25D-362 | | |
| N25HS | Citation | 501-0222 | Space City Aviation Inc. Spring, Tx. | N6781R |
| N25JD | Learjet | 25B-114 | Robinson Bros. Drilling Co. Woodward, Ok. | N77PK/N45HB/(C-GLRE)<br>/N47HC |
| N25NP | Learjet | 25B-107 | Geo J. Priester, Wheeling, Il. | N57DM/N225CC |
| N25NY | Learjet | 25D-304 | Poten Leasing Corp. NY. | |
| N25PL | Learjet | 25B-130 | Jet Airways Inc. Eugene, Or. | N111BL |
| N25PM | DH 125/3A | 25114 | Falcon Products, St. Louis, Mo. | N78RZ/N44KG/N44K/N425K/G-ATYJ |
| N25RE | Westwind-1124 | 248 | Aviation Equipment Leasing Inc. Washington DC. | 4X-CMT |
| N25RF | Learjet | 35A-227 | Combs Gates Denver Inc. Co. | N211BY |
| N25UG | Gulfstream 2 | 205 | United Gas Pipeline Co. Houston, Tx. | |
| N25ZC | Sabre-65 | 465-30 | Ziegler Inc. Minneapolis, Mn. | |
| N26FE | Falcon 20DC | 204 | 'Hope' Federal Express Corp. Tn. | N4392F/F-WMKI |
| N26GB | Learjet | 35A-131 | HIBOS Co. Houston, Tx. | N3812G |
| N26GL | Learjet | 36-001 | Gates Learjet Corp. Wichita, Ks. | |
| N26GW | Westwind-1124 | 272 | Cumberland Life Insurance Co. Dallas, Tx. | 4X-CNR |
| N26H | HS 125/700A | NA0325 | Halliburton Co. Dallas, Tx. | N700HA/G-5-20 |
| N26L | Gulfstream 2 | 193 | Square D Co. Park Ridge, Il. | N808GA |
| N26LB | Falcon 50 | 7 | Great American Life Insurance Co. Cincinnati, Oh. | N8516Z/HZ-A03<br>HZ-AKI/F-WZHA |
| N26MW | Citation | 501-0100 | Wyman Kinzua Corp. Hepner, Or. | N41ST/N485CC/(N3207M) |
| N26S | JetStar-731 | 16/5128 | Sun Co. Philadelphia, Pa. | N7973S |
| N26T | Westwind-1124 | 293 | Baggett Transportation Co. Inc. Birmingham, Al. | N26TV/4X-COM |
| N26TL | DH 125/1A | 25037 | J A Kent, Houston, Tx. | N26T/N787X/D-CAFI/G-ATFO |
| N26VM | Learjet | 24D-236 | Gates Learjet Corp. Tucson, Az. | |
| N26WD | Citation | 500-0282 | Antos, Ruckel & Sheppard, Seminole, Fl. | N282CC/(N5282J) |
| N27 | B 727-61 | 19176 | FAA, Oklahoma City, Ok. | N127 |
| N27AC | Falcon 20F | 355 | AMCA International Corp. Hanover, NH. | N20FJ/N4467F/F-WMKF |

38

| Registration | Type | C/N | Owner/Operator | Previous Identities |
|---|---|---|---|---|
| N27BD | Jet Commander | 53 | Bon-Del Inc. Mesa, Az. | N925HB/N103F/N10MF/N1230D/N1230 |
| N27BL | Learjet | 35A-163 | B L Jet Sales Inc. Dover, De. | YV-173CP |
| N27DA | Falcon 10 | 17 | SAAHS, Orlando, Fl. | N29966/VH-FFB/OH-FFB/F-WLCS |
| N27FE | Falcon 20DC | 207 | 'Jennifer Jay' Federal Express Corp. | N4395F/F-WMKF |
| N27KG | Learjet | 25D-335 | Keith Graham, Great Falls, Mt. | |
| N27MD | Jet Commander | 102 | Mason Dixon Lines Inc. Kingsport, Tn. | |
| N27MJ | Learjet | 25-050 | Corporate Air Inc. Hartford, Ct. | D-CONE/N44EE/N44EL |
| N27NB | Learjet | 35A-251 | Nolan K Bushnell, Cupertino, Ca. | |
| N27R | Falcon 20F | 356 | R J Reynolds Tobacco Co. Winston Salem, NC. | N4468F/F-WMKG |
| N27SF | Citation | 500-0064 | Horizon Lease Corp/Seneca Foods Corp. NY. | N564CC |
| N27W | F 28-1000 | 11016 | Temple Eastex Corp. Diboll, Tx. | N281FH/PH-ZAL |
| N28AA | Learjet | 25-037 | Alpha Aviation Inc. Dallas, Tx. | N18JF/N737EF |
| N28BG | Learjet | 35A-258 | Konfara Co. Phoenix, Az. | (N1700) |
| N28BK | Learjet | 24-175 | Aviation Associates, Salt Lake City, Ut. | N288K/N859L/N859GM |
| N28BP | Learjet | 25D-302 | Impala Electronics Inc. Tampa, Fl. | XA-KOV/N521JP |
| N28C | Falcon 20F | 404 | Edwin Cox, Athens, Tx. | N404F/F-WJMK |
| N28FE | Falcon 20DC | 209 | 'Janet' Federal Express Corp. Tn. | N4396F/F-WLCX |
| N28GP | BH 125/400A | NA767 | Genuine Parts Co. Atlanta, Ga. | N92BH/N64BH |
| N28JG | Citation | 501-0194 | Geupel Construction Co. Columbus, Oh. | N6781L |
| N28LA | Learjet | 25XR-029 | Loyal American Insurance Co. | N28OLC |
| N28MJ | Learjet | 25D-286 | Gates Learjet Corp. Wichita, Ks. | |
| N28ST | Learjet | 23-013 | Standard-Taylor Industries Inc. Montgomery, Al. | N37BL/N888DS /N201BA/N613W |
| N28TP | Sabre-40A | 282-132 | Tom's Food Ltd. Columbus, Ga. | N9252N |
| N28WW | Westwind-1124 | 368 | M K D G Inc. Denver, Co. | 4X-CUE |
| N29 | DC-9-15 | 45732 | FAA, Oklahoma City, Ok. | N119/HB-IFB |
| N29AC | Citation | 501-0226 | AMCA International Corp. Hanover, NH. | (N2615D) |
| N29FE | Falcon 20DC | 210 | 'Adina' Federal Express Corp. Tn. | N4397F/F-WNGL |
| N29GH | Westwind-1124 | 197 | Galveston-Houston Co. Houston, Tx. | N214CC/4X-CKU |
| N29GP | HS 125/700A | NA0250 | Genuine Parts Co. Atlanta, Ga. | N130BE/G-5-15 |
| N29LP | Westwind-1124 | 280 | Rite Aid Corp. Harrisburg. Pa. | (N5S)/(N5BP)/N290W/4X-CNZ |
| N29PC | Westwind-1124 | 263 | Pittway Corp. Northbrook, Il. | 4X-CNI |
| N29S | Sabre-65 | 465-65 | Sun Co. Philadelphia, Pa. | |
| N29SX | Sabre-60 | 306-49 | Aero Commander Acceptance Corp. Bethany, Ok. | N29S/N7522N |
| N29TC | Citation | 550-0127 | Teledyne Continental Motors, Muskegon, Mi. | N2631N |
| N29WS | Citation | 550-0226 | Wilson Industries Inc. Houston, Tx. | N6804F |
| N30AF | Sabre-40A | 282-113 | American Family Assurance Co. Columbus, Ga. | N40BT/N40SC/N8311N |
| N30AN | Westwind-1123 | 173 | Manville Forest Products Corp. W. Monroa, La. | N30JM/N680K/N1230 /4X-CJW |
| N30AP | Learjet | 25B-080 | Baltic Aviation Inc. Denver, Co. | (N90DH)/N1978L/N1976L |
| N30AV | HFB 320 | 1055 | American Velodur Metal Inc. Scituate, Ma. | N87950/N11NT/N897HJ /D-CORY |
| N30BK | Citation | 501-0251 | | |
| N30CC | Sabre-60A | 306-81 | Carrier Corp. Syracuse, NY. | N6ND/N6NR |
| N30CN | Falcon 10 | 161 | S W Jack Drilling Co. Indiana, Pa. | N230FJ/F-WZGM |
| N30DK | Learjet | 25B-154 | Fred Shaulis, Friedens, Pa. | N100K |
| N30EF | DH 125/1A | 25084 | Robert Brooks/Eastern Foods Inc. Charlotte, NC. | N154TR/N453CM /N1125G/G-ATNN |
| N30EM | Learjet | 24E-338 | Jay Roulier, Englewood, Co. | N30LM/N729GL |
| N30EV | Sabre-75 | 370-6 | Mid Continent Systems Inc. Memphis, Tn. | N29019/XA-SGR/N2TE/N7589N |
| N30FE | Falcon 20DC | 211 | 'Marianne' Federal Express Corp. Tn. | N4398F/F-WJMK |
| N30FL | Learjet | 24D-253 | Corporate Jet Aviation, Chamblee, Ga. | N711DB/N30FL/N999U/N123VW |
| N30JD | Citation | 550-0205 | Deere & Co. Moline, Il. | (N88727) |
| N30LM | Learjet | 25D-250 | Copperweld Corp. Pittsburgh, Pa. | |
| N30LS | Jet Commander-A | 125 | O L Scott Oil Properties. | N1121N |
| N30MR | Westwind-1124 | 225 | Mike Rutherford, Buda, Tx. | N1124U/4X-CLW |
| N30NS | Westwind-1124 | 329 | Accounting & Management Services Inc. Oklahoma City, Ok. | 4X-CRW |
| N30PN | Sabre 40 | 282-14 | Concentric Pipe Rentals Inc. Lafayette, La. | N30BE/N31BO/N31BC /N2009/N636RC |
| N30PR | HS 125/700A | NA0247 | P R Rutherford, Houston, Tx. | N130BC/G-5-11 |
| N30RL | Citation | 501-0109 | Roseburg Lumber Co. Or. | (N2647Y) |
| N30RP | Gulfstream 3 | 321 | RCA Corp. NY. | |
| N30TB | Falcon 10 | 171 | Tom Brown Inc. Midland, Tx. | N237FJ/F-WZGY |
| N30TH | Falcon 10 | 138 | Sony USA, New York. | N203FJ/F-WZGJ |
| N30UC | Citation | 550-0096 | Utah international Inc. SFO, Ca. | N550EW/N26632 |
| N30W | Learjet | 25D-214 | Worrell Newspapers Investment Co. Charlottesville. | |
| N31AA | Learjet | 25-041 | Alpha Aviation Inc. Dallas, Tx. | N205SA/N205SC/N960GA |
| N31AS | DH 125/3A | 25111 | American Standard, NY. | C-GKRL/N125GC/N1041B/G-ATYH |

| Regis-tration | Type | C/N | Owner/Operator | Previous Identities |
|---|---|---|---|---|
| N31B | DH 125/731 | 25108 | World Aircraft Exchange Inc. Mobile, Al. | N901TG/N901TC/N1025C/G-ATUY |
| N31BC | Sabre-65 | 465-16 | Heritage Oldsmobile Cadillac Inc. Somerset, Ky. | |
| N31CJ | Sabre-60 | 306-26 | Banner Energy Inc/Tiger Charter Inc. Midland, Tx. | N71CD/N323R /N644X/N4736N |
| N31CK | Learjet | 23-079 | Connie Kovitta Services Inc. Medford, Or. | N240AO/N240AG |
| N31DM | Falcon 50 | 59 | Pacific Holding Corp. Los Angeles, Ca. | N75FJ/F-WZHB |
| N31DP | Learjet | 23-059 | Innovation Data Processing, Clifton, NJ. | N364EJ |
| N31F | Citation | 550-0440 | | |
| N31FE | Falcon 20DC | 212 | 'Colleen' Federal Express Corp. Tn. | N4399F/F-WPXG |
| N31GS | Learjet | 25D-313 | MJI/First National Bank, Midland, Tx. | N31MJ |
| N31KW | Citation | 550-0078 | Kenneth Walker, Abilene, Tx. | (N2662B) |
| N31LB | Learjet | 24B-211 | Clint Priess Builder Inc. Houston, Tx. | N222AP/N30EH/N388P |
| N31LG | HS 125/700A | NA0249 | Landis Tool Co. Waynesboro, Pa. | N130BD/G-5-14 |
| N31LJ | JetStar-731 | 55/5087 | Double TV Inc. Abilene, Tx. | (N800J)/N800J/N41N |
| N31LT | Falcon 20C | 69 | Imperial Oil Co. of Delaware Inc. Tampa, Fl. | N176BN/N176NP/N893F /F-WMKF |
| N31MT | Citation | 501-0088 | Lewis T. Fowler, Hattiesburg, Ms. | N473CC/(N3181A) |
| N31RC | Citation | 501-0093 | Woodstock Aviation Inc. Santa Rosa, Ca. | N88CF/N3163M |
| N31RK | Citation | 550-0281 | R K Petroleum Corp. Midland, Tx. | N6864Z |
| N31S | | | Elmer Glause, Lyndhurst, Oh. | |
| N31SK | Learjet | 24-118 | Connie Kalitta Services Inc. Lakeview, Or. | N1919W/N1008S/N100GS N452LJ |
| N31TM | Falcon 10 | 160 | Morrisette/Taymor Inc. Mobile, Al. | N223HS/N225FJ/F-WZGK |
| N31V | Falcon 20C | 106 | El Paso L & G Services Co. Houston, Tx. | N9300M/F-GBPG/N987F/F-WJMM |
| N31WS | Learjet | 35-027 | Windstar Co. Stamford, Ct. | |
| N31WT | Falcon 20F | 446 | Mid-America Aviation Inc. Hillsboro, Or/Godfather's Pizza. | N454F /F-WJMN |
| N32BA | Learjet | 35A-190 | Centurion Investment Co. Denver, Co. | |
| N32BC | Sabre-60 | 306-62 | Heritage Oldsmobile Cadillac Inc. Somerset, Ky. | N905P/N905R/N7090 |
| N32BQ | Sabre-40 | 282-15 | A M Leasing Inc. Minneapolis, Mn. | (N19MS)/N32BC/N1062/N106G /N6369C |
| N32CA | Learjet | 24-132 | James Hall, Midland, Tx. | N238R/N233R/N658LJ |
| N32F | Citation | 550-0442 | | |
| N32FE | Falcon 20DC | 213 | 'Sarah' Federal Express Corp. Tn. | N4390F/F-WJMM |
| N32HE | DH 125/1A-522 | 25033 | Helpern Enterprises. | N63BL/(N700AB)/(N111AX)/N111AD/N111AG/N1125G /N125G/G-ATBD |
| N32HM | Learjet | 35A-187 | Southeastern Jet Corp. Fort Lauderdale, Fl. | N755GL |
| N32JC | Jet Commander | 32 | Pack River Management Co. Spokane, Wa. | N92BT/N92B |
| N32JJ | Citation | 550-0260 | ADM Leasco Inc/Cascade Oil. | N67986 |
| N32KR | JetStar-2 | 5220 | Knight-Ridder Newspapers, Miami, Fl. | N5546L |
| N32MJ | Citation | 501-0058 | S. Texas Aircraft Inc. Alice, Tx. | N36GC/N444AG/N44MC/N2627A |
| N32RP | HS 125/F600A | 6066 | RCA Corp. NY. | G-BDZH/G-5-15 |
| N32W | Citation | 500-0105 | EPPS Air Service Co. Atlanta, Ga. | N105JJ/N105CC |
| N32WE | Westwind 1123 | 164 | International Executive Aircraft Corp. NY. | N9114S/D-CAAS/4X-CJN |
| N32WT | Learjet | 24E-333 | Aviation Co. of America Inc. Hillsboro, Or. | N76TR |
| N33AH | Falcon 20F | 379 | American Hospital Supply Corp. Evanston, Il. | (N33AJ)/(N37AH) /N130F/F-WMKF |
| N33BC | Sabre-65 | 465-69 | Brunswick Corp. Skokie, Il. | |
| N33BK | HS 125/700A | NA0239 | Chaparrosa Aircraft Inc. San Antonio, Tx. | G-BGBL/G-5-17 |
| N33BQ | Sabre-60 | 306-13 | Brunswick Corp. Skokie, Il. | N33BC/N555SL/N6OY/N4723N |
| N33CJ | Learjet | 25-045 | Corporate Jet International, Opa Locka, Fl. | N815J/CF-DWW/N963GA |
| N33CP | HS 125/700A | NA0238 | Colonial Penn Group. | N700AR/G-5-20 |
| N33CX | Citation | 501-0079 | Conax Corp. Salem, NH. | N555EW/N3144M |
| N33D | Falcon 20C | 166 | Dow Chemical Corp. Midland, Mi. | N436RF/F-WLCS |
| N33FE | Falcon 20DC | 214 | 'Stacy' Federal Express Corp. Tn. | N4400F/F-WNGO |
| N33HM | Learjet | 25B-093 | Southeastern Jet Corp. Pompano Beach, Fl. | |
| N33L | Falcon 20D | 202 | Dow Chemical Corp. Midland, Mi. | N814PA/N4391F/F-WNGM |
| N33M | Gulfstream 2 | 106 | 3M Co. St. Paul, Mn. (r/c Mining Three). | N808GA |
| N33MQ | Citation | 500-0312 | McGraw-Edison Co. Elgin, Il. | (N233MF)/N33ME/N5312J |
| N33NH | Citation | 500-0206 | Harris Tire & Rubber Co. Troy, Al. | |
| N33NT | Sabre-75A | 380-41 | Northern Telecom Aviation Inc. Nashville. | N2113J |
| N33PT | Learjet | 35A-397 | Pel-Tex Oil Co. Houston Tx. | |
| N33RP | HS 125/600A | 6068 | Walter Probst, Palm Springs, Ca. | G-BDZR/(G-5-20) |
| N33SC | Falcon 20C | 71 | Harrison Interests Ltd. Houston, Tx. | N807PA/N807F/N967F/F-WNGM |
| N33TH | Citation | 500-0024 | Hirsch Corp. Columbus, Oh. | N524CA/N524CC |
| N33TP | Falcon 20C | 27 | F F Devine Jr. San Antonio, Tx. | N677SW/N847F/F-WMKJ |
| N33TR | Sabre-60 | 306-54 | Trinity Industries Inc. Dallas, Tx. | (N100EU)/N38JM/N1020P/N370VS |

40

| Regis-<br>tration | Type | C/N | Owner/Operator | Previous<br>Identities |
|---|---|---|---|---|
| | | | | /N7574N |
| N33WD | Westwind-1123 | 161 | Central States Energy Corp. Santa Fe, NM.N185G/(N653J)/D-CGLS/4X-CJK |
| N33WW | Citation | 501-0065 | W W Williams Co. Columbus, Oh. | N2888A |
| N34C | Falcon 20C | 31 | Consolidation Coal Co. Pittsburgh, Pa. | N806F/F-WNGM |
| N34DL | Citation | 501-0061 | LDH Leasing Inc. Midland, Tx. | N436CC/N2757A |
| N34FE | Falcon 20DC | 215 | 'Kellie' Federal Express Corp. Tn. | N4401F/F-WLCS |
| N34LP | Sabre-40 | 282-70 | Mid States Aviation Inc. Oklahoma City, Ok. | N17LT/N70SL/N22CH/N654E |
| | | | | /N111AB/N874AJ/N377P/N2236C |
| N34SS | Citation | 550-0200 | Sun Oil Co. Philadelphia, Pa. | (G-BHVA)/N67989 |
| N35AK | Learjet | 35A-314 | Fort Howard Paper Co. Green Bay, Wi. | |
| N35BK | Learjet | 35A-442 | Jet Airways Inc. Portland, Or. | N3799C/N40149 |
| N35CC | Sabre-40 | 282-79 | Crown Controls Corp. New Bremen, Oh. | N701NC/N797R/N2248C |
| N35CL | Learjet | 35A-113 | T C Services Inc. Wichita, Ks. | N763GL |
| N35D | HS 125/700A | NA0231 | Florida Gas Transmission Co. Winter Park, Fl. | G-BFYH |
| N35DL | Sabre-60 | 306-131 | R Lindner, Cincinnati, Oh. | N5DL/N2149J |
| N35FE | Falcon 20DC | 217 | 'Melanie' Federal Express Corp. Tn. | N4403F/F-WLCY |
| N35FM | Learjet | 35A-368 | First Mississippi Corp. Jackson, Ms. | |
| N35GC | Learjet | 35A-266 | G C Services Corp. Houston, Tx. | N922GL/SE-DDI/N39404 |
| N35HC | Citation | 550-0151 | Hoffman Contractors Inc. Portland, Or. | (N9852R) |
| N35KC | Learjet | 35A-144 | Marathon Air Inc. Miami, Fl. | N705US/D-CCAP/N39398 |
| N35LH | Westwind-1124 | 236 | Liberty Holmes, Goshen, In. | 4X-CMH |
| N35LJ | Learjet | 35A-181 | McTan Corp. Abilene, Tx. | |
| N35NB | Learjet | 35A-133 | Tulsa Aircraft Charter Corp. Sand Springs, Ok. | N728GL |
| N35RF | Learjet | 35A-201 | Geo A Rolfes Co. Boone, Ia. | |
| N35RT | Learjet | 35A-420 | Townsend Engineering Co. Des Moines, Ia. | N35RT/N79MJ/N39415 |
| N35SJ | Learjet | 24D-246 | US Petroleum Corp. Knoxville, Tn. | N5SJ/N21NA/N215Z |
| N35SL | Learjet | 35A-233 | Southland Life Insurance Co. Dallas, Tx. | |
| N35WB | Learjet | 35A-350 | Stoltz Wagner & Brown, Midland, Tx. | (N88NE) |
| N35WR | Learjet | 35A-234 | Rollins Inc. Atlanta, Ga. | |
| N36CC | Citation | 501-0036 | Cherne Contracting Corp. Ironwood, Mi. | N406CJ/N36918 |
| N36CW | Learjet | 36-012 | Skyflite Inc. Tulsa, Ok. | N666TB/C-GBWD/N2267Z/VR-BFR/N215RL/N139GL |
| N36FE | Falcon 20DC | 218 | 'Becky' Federal Express Corp. Tn. | N4372F/F-WMKJ |
| N36HH | Sabreliner | 306-18 | Helmsley Spear Inc. NY. | N18HH/N339GW/N908R/N4728N |
| N36JG | Citation | 501-0011 | JLG Industries, McConnellsburg, Pa. | (N1UB)/N36842 |
| N36MJ | Learjet | 36A-036 | ACM Aviation Inc. San Jose, Ca. | N610GE/N1426B |
| N36NP | HS 125/700A | NA0225 | Nationwide Mutual Insurance Co. Columbus, Oh. | G-5-16 |
| N36NW | Learjet | 25D-297 | Mid Ohio Aircraft Inc. Columbus, Oh. | N297EJ |
| N36SC | Learjet | 25D-209 | Lear Associates, Wilmington, De. | |
| N36SJ | Citation | 500-0306 | Royalty Smokeless Coal Co. Premier, WV. | N36CJ/N5306J |
| N36TA | Learjet | 36-003 | J & N Associates, New Orleans, La. | N363GL |
| N37BM | Citation | 551-0048 | Husky Aviation Co. Cody, Wy. | N6860R |
| N37DW | Citation | 500-0284 | Rinehart Wilke, Columbus, Oh. | N8508Z/YV-43CP/N284CC/(N5284J) |
| N37FE | Falcon 20DC | 270 | 'Theresa' Federal Express Corp. Tn. | N4435F/F-WMPIZ |
| N37GB | Learjet | 25-053 | Charter Leasing Corp. Las Vegas, Nv. | N37MB/N974M/N974GA |
| N37JF | Falcon 20D | 193 | Willis Moore, Dallas, Tx. | N930L/N4383F/F-WMKG |
| N37HW | Citation | 501-0186 | LI Charters Inc. Wilmington, De. | N95EW/(N6780A) |
| N37LB | Challenger | 1015 | TAG Flight Ltd. Wilmington, De. | C-GBLM |
| N37P | HS 125/700A | NA0210 | Nationwide Transport Inc. Columbus, Oh. | G-BFFL/G-5-18 |
| N37TA | Learjet | 35-034 | Keplinger & Associates, Tx. | |
| N38DJ | Learjet | 25B-191 | Sprite Flite Jets Inc. Kalispell, Mt. | N78BT/N1DD |
| N38DM | Learjet | 23-036 | Jet Air Inc. El Cajun, Ca. | N111WM/N210PC/N477K |
| N38JM | Sabre-75A | 380-39 | Cinco Investments/Gulf Central International Inc. Lafayette, La. | |
| | | | | N88JM/N102MJ/N7NR/N2110J |
| N38N | Gulfstream 2 | 41 | Union Carbide Corp. NY. | |
| N38WW | Westwind-1124 | 210 | Atlantic Aviation Corp. | N23AC/N662JB/N661CP/N69HM/N662JB/4X-CLH |
| N39BE | Citation | 501-0091 | Robert Elliott, Santa Ana, Ca. | N33BE/(N55BE)/(N887DM)/N3194M |
| N39DM | Learjet | 24D-302 | Flight International Inc. Atlanta, Ga. | N302EJ |
| N39E | Learjet | 55-018 | TRANSCO, Houston, Tx. | |
| N39GW | Westwind-1124 | 237 | Gulf & Western Industries Inc. Wilmington, De. | 4X-CMI |
| N39KM | Learjet | 24B-198 | Marvin Whiteman, McCall, Id. | N21XB/N21XL/N111GW/N66RP |
| N39LL | Citation | 501-0168 | Diamond Services Corp. Morgan City, La. | (N6777X) |
| N39MB | Learjet | 35A-216 | Richard Black, Chicago, Il. | N24MJ/D-CATE |
| N39N | Gulfstream 2 | 50 | Union Carbide Corp. NY. | |
| N39Q | JetStar-8 | 5126 | Transco, Houston, Tx. | N39E/N20S/N955HL/N955H/N7971S |
| N40 | B 727-25QC | 19854 | FAA, Oklahoma City, Ok. | N8171G |
| N40AB | Jet Commander | 106 | Diversified Metals inc. Oklahoma City, Ok. | N3711H |
| N40AS | NAL 1-11/401 | 17/061 | American Standard Inc. New York. | N5021 |

| Registration | Type | C/N | Owner/Operator | Previous Identities |
|---|---|---|---|---|
| N40BC | Learjet | 25D-288 | Ultra Aire/Wm. Chapman, Omaha, Ne. | N61WT/N31WT |
| N40BG | Westwind-1123 | 156 | Mel Powers, Houston, Tx. | (N666MP)/N40AS/N1123H |
| N40BP | Sabre-40 | 282-40 | Presant Industrial Supply Co. Leland, NC. | N715MR/N738R/N6395C |
| N40CE | Gulfstream 2 | 45 | Department of the Army, Baltimore, Md. | N115GA/VR-BHA/N215RL/N152RG /PK-PJG/N711R/N815GA |
| N40CH | Gulfstream 2 | 77 | Chase Manhattan Bank, NY. | N100WK/N824GA |
| N40CN | HS 125/700A | NA0285 | Champion International Corp. Stamford, Ct. | N125AT/G-5-13 |
| N40DC | JetStar-731 | 26/5120 | Daniel International Corp. Greenville, SC. | N7965S |
| N40ES | Learjet | 55-005 | Esmark Inc. Chicago, Il. | |
| N40GS | Citation | 550-0261 | Ambrion Aviation, Dallas, Tx. | N68616 |
| N40GT | HS 125/700A | NA0201 | General Transportation Corp. Dover, De. | N40WB/N700HS/G-5-20 |
| N40JE | Sabre-40A | 282-124 | Rockwell International Corp. | N2006/N200E/N193AT |
| N40JW | Sabre-40A | 282-122 | Walton Stations, Pebble Beach, Ca. | |
| N40MP | Westwind Two | 334 | Petrie Stores Corp. Secaucus, NJ. | (N45MP)/4X-CTB |
| N40N | Falcon 10 | 25 | Union Carbide Corp. NY. | N117FJ/F-WJMJ |
| N40NS | Sabre-40A | 282-126 | Jetco Joint Venture, Midland, Tx. | |
| N40PK | Learjet | 35A-260 | Porta Kamp Manufacturing Co. Inc. Houston, Tx. | |
| N40PL | Citation | 501-0242 | F P Lathrop-Shand Charter, Lafayette, La. | N2623B |
| N40SJ | Sabre-40 | 282-25 | American Air Transport Inc. Boyton Beach, Fl. | I-SNAK/HB-VAK /N6379C |
| N40SW | Learjet | 25D-238 | Stockham Valves & Fittings Inc. Birmingham, Al. | N39416 |
| N40TA | Learjet | 35A-208 | Bandag Inc. Muscatine, Ia. | N40149 |
| N40UA | Jet Commander | 40 | Rabie & Sindoni, Stanton, Ca. | N40AJ/N40JC/N913HB |
| N40WP | Sabre-40 | 282-32 | PSI Hydraulics Inc. Livonia, Mi. | N40SL/N711UC/N100HC/N100Y |
| N41BJ | Learjet | 24-178 | Island Helicopters Inc. Dover, De. | N24AJ/N56LS/N56LR/N55KX/N55KS /N674LJ |
| N41CP | Learjet | 55-037 | Chas Pfizer Inc. Trenton, NJ. | |
| N41ES | Learjet | 55-007 | Esmark Inc. Chicago, Il. | |
| N41GS | Sabre-40 | 282-16 | Pan Aviation Inc. Miami Beach, Fl. | N40GP/N227S/N227SW/N6370C |
| N41H | Learjet | 25D-217 | LJ Associates, Blairesville, Pa. | |
| N41MJ | Learjet | 35A-405 | Dharma Aircraft Ltd. Milwaukie, Or. | |
| N41ZP | Learjet | 25D-279 | Flight Transportation Corp. Eden Prairie, Mn. | |
| N42 | Convair 880 | 55 | FAA, Oklahoma City, Ok. | N112 |
| N42BL | MS 760 Paris | 50 | B L Jet Sales, Dover, De. | N111ER/N6068/CF-MAJ/CN-MAJ |
| N42C | JetStar 731 | 37/5150 | CONOCO Inc. Houston, Tx. | N200CG/N200CC/N516WC/N5514L |
| N42ES | Learjet | 55-009 | Esmark Inc. Chicago, Il. | |
| N42FE | Learjet | 35A-241 | Fritz Egger, Torrance, Ca. | |
| N42G | Falcon 10 | 20 | Bankers Life, Lincoln, Nb. | N113FJ/F-WLCV |
| N42GX | Learjet | 25B-140 | Oklahoma Aircraft Leasing Inc. Bethany, Ok. | N42G |
| N42QB | Jet Commander | 6 | White Industries Inc. Bates City, Mo. | N420P/CF-ULG/N5418 |
| N42ZP | Learjet | 28-003 | FTC Executive Air Charter Inc. Eden Prairie, Mn. | N157CB |
| N43AJ | Learjet | 24-141 | Beverly Hills Air Charter, Ca. | N348BJ/N348VL |
| N43D | Citation | 550-0171 | Dome Petroleum Corp. Denver, Co. | (C-GDPE)/(N88797) |
| N43DM | Learjet | 24D-305 | Flight International Inc. Atlanta, Ga. | N305EJ/N98DK/N305EJ |
| N43EL | Learjet | 35A-121 | Universal Underwriters Inc. Kansas City, Mo. | |
| N43ES | Falcon 50 | 49 | Esmark Inc. Chicago, Il. | N66FJ/F-WZHL |
| N43M | Gulfstream 2 | 126 | 3M Co. St Paul, Mn. (r/c Mining Four). | |
| N43R | Gulfstream 2 | 18 | Rockwell International Corp. Pittsburgh, Pa. | N205M/N838GA |
| N43TC | Citation | 550-0311 | Town & Country Food Markets, Wichita, Ks. | N6889L |
| N43W | Learjet | 24B-227 | H L Brown, Llano, Tx. | N10CB/N90797/XA-TIP |
| N43ZP | Learjet | 24-157 | Wm Rubin, St.Louis Park, Mn. | N124WL/N94HC/N191DA/N1919G/N1919W /N640GA |
| N44BB | Learjet | 25D-227 | AMI Aviation Inc. Shreveport, La. | |
| N44BW | Citation | 500-0048 | S & W Associates, Pittsburgh, Pa. | N5500S/N11DH/N727EE/N727LE/N54RCC |
| N44CP | Learjet | 24B-185 | International Jet Inc. Minneapolis, Mn. | N754M |
| N44EL | Learjet | 35A-255 | US Epperson Underwriting Co. Boca Raton, Fl. | |
| N44FC | Citation | 550-0197 | Fleming Companies Inc. Oklahoma City, Ok. | (N30F)/N6798Z |
| N44FE | Learjet | 25D-215 | Hop A Jet Inc. Fort Lauderdale, Fl. | |
| N44FH | Learjet | 25D-252 | F L Harcourt, Whittier, Ca. | N1468B |
| N44GL | Learjet | 36-009 | Combs-Gates Denver Inc. Co. | N704J/N2000M |
| N44GT | Citation | 550-0002 | General Telephone NW, Everett, Wa. | N552CC/N9R753 |
| N44HC | Citation | 500-0295 | CPT Corp. Eden Prairie, Mn. | N2274B/EP-KIA/EP-PAO/N5295J |
| N44JC | Falcon 10 | 22 | John Cox, Midland, Tx. | N114FJ/F-WLCX |
| N44LC | Citation | 501-0176 | Lowes Companies Inc. N. Wilkesboro, NC. | N6779L |
| N44LF | Citation | 550-0277 | Fritz Enterprises, Taylor, Mi. | N6864B |
| N44LJ | Learjet | 35A-276 | C W Culpepper, Oklahoma City, Ok. | |
| N44MC | Citation | 501-0058 | MJI, Lincoln, Nb. | N2627A |
| N44MD | Gulfstream 2 | 81 | Davis Oil Co. Denver, Co. | N777SW |

42

| Regis-tration | Type | C/N | Owner/Operator | Previous Identities |
|---|---|---|---|---|
| N44MW | Learjet | 35-044 | Helen Dow Whiting, Midland, Mi. | N38TA |
| N44NJ | Learjet | 24-120 | National Jets Inc. Ft. Lauderdale, Fl. | N44AJ/N633NJ/N633J/N457LJ |
| N44NT | Falcon 20F | 319 | Northern Telecom Aviation Inc. Nashville, Tn. | N730V/N4453F/F-WMKF |
| N44PA | Learjet | 25B-144 | Paul Anka, Las Vegas, Nv. | N10NT |
| N44PH | Sabre-40A | 282-136 | Spendthrift Aviation Inc. Lexington, Ky. | |
| N44PR | Westwind-1123 | 169 | Peninsular Resources Corp. Corpus Christi, Tx. | N1100D/N1500C/N1123U/4X-CJS |
| N44RD | Citation | 500-0334 | Royal Air Service Inc. Unionville, Mo. | N500DD/N5334J |
| N44SA | Citation | 500-0109 | John Anderson, Davis, Ca. | |
| N44WD | Sabre-60A | 306-116 | Guardian Industries, Northville, Mi. | N605RG/N2119J |
| N44WF | Citation | 550-0214 | Houston Hydrolance International Inc. Tx. | N13BJ/N6800S |
| N44ZP | Citation | 550-0192 | Wm. Rubin, St. Louis Park, Mn. | N88716 |
| N45AJ | Learjet | 24D-309 | American Jet Aviation Inc. Chesterfield, Mo. | N45FC/N310LJ |
| N45CP | Learjet | 25D-242 | Concrete Pipe & Products Co. Richmond, Va. | N1972G |
| N45EP | Citation | 550-0218 | A M Biedenhann, Boerne, Tx. | N98436 |
| N45ES | Falcon 50 | 75 | Esmark Inc. Chicago, Il. | N95FJ/F-WZHH |
| N45K | JetStar-8 | 5151 | Koppers Co. Inc. West Mifflin, Pa. | N46KJ/N711Z/N5515L |
| N45KK | Learjet | 25D-281 | K K Amini, Midland, Tx. | (N245KK) |
| N45MC | Citation | 550-0423 | Louisiana Gas Interstate Inc. Houston, Tx. | N12171 |
| N45SJ | Westwind-1124 | 289 | Richardson Carbon & Gas Co. Fort Worth, Tx. | N711CJ/4X-COI |
| N45Y | Gulfstream 2 | 69 | Manville Service Corp. Denver, Co. | N45JM/N33CR/N25JM/N69NG |
| N45ZP | Citation | 550-0159 | International Air Co. St. Louis Park, Mn. | (N88721) |
| N46B | BH 125/600A | 6044 | Beckwith Machinery Co. Pittsburgh, Pa. | N600MB/N42BH |
| N46F | JetStar-8 | 5124 | Hunt Oil Co. Dallas, Tx. | N7969S |
| N46MK | Citation | 550-0410 | Merillat Industries, Adrian, Mi. | (N258P)/N1216K |
| N46SC | Citation | 501-0137 | Salem Carpet Mills Inc. Winston Salem, NC. | N26503 |
| N46SD | Citation | 551-0060 | Bob Smith Dozer Service Inc. Clinton, Ok. | N6805T |
| N46WB | Learjet | 24-133 | World Jet Inc. Fort Lauderdale, Fl. | N555PV/N40JE/N40JF/N660LJ |
| N47AJ | Learjet | 25-023 | International Lease Finance Corp. Beverley Hills, Ca. | (N861L)/N13CR/N72CD/N577LJ |
| N47JE | Falcon 20D | 189 | Continental Telephone Service Corp. Atlanta, Ga. | N47JF/N950L/N4380F/F-WPUU |
| N47JR | Learjet | 35-007 | John Roberts, San Antonio, Tx. | N75DH/D-CONI |
| N47MJ | Learjet | 25-004 | MJI, Lincoln, Ne. | N7GJ/N1121C/N1121/N641GA |
| N47UC | JetStar-731 | 14/5123 | Union Camp Corp. Wayne, NJ. | N441A/N559GP/N1844S/N7968S |
| N48AJ | Learjet | 24-172 | American Jet Aviation, Chesterfield, Mo. | N234WR |
| N48BA | Learjet | 24-152 | Bass Aviation Inc. Hattiesburg, Pa. | N9LM/N98DK/N21U/N597GA/N3807G |
| N48CC | Falcon 20D | 200 | Centex Corp. Dallas, Tx. | N44CC/N44MC/N550MC/N4389F/F-WMKJ |
| N48CG | Sabre-40 | 282-75 | Corning Glass Works Inc. NY. | N2241C |
| N48L | Learjet | 24A-107 | Beach Club Booking Inc. Camden, SC. | |
| N48MJ | Learjet | 35A-448 | | |
| N48ND | Citation | 550-0074 | N48ND Corp. Midland, Tx. | N4754G |
| N48R | Falcon 10 | 80 | R J Reynolds/Amin Oil, Tx. | (N913CB)/N161FJ/F-WPXD |
| N48TC | Sabre-40 | 282-66 | Tiger Charter Inc. Midland, Tx. | N40HC/N40NR/N737R/N4943A/N355MJ/N2233B |
| N48TT | Falcon 10 | 16 | Cajun Equipment Co. Houston, Tx./Tatham Corp. | N110FJ/F-WLCT |
| N48UC | JetStar-731 | 31/5125 | Union Camp Corp. Wayne, NJ. | N47UC/N7970S |
| N48WS | Sabre-60A | 306-124 | Warner Swasey Co. Cleveland, Oh. | N60RS/N65NR/N2133J |
| N49BL | Citation | 501-0225 | R E & K B Leisy Incline Village, Nv. | N2614C |
| N49DM | Learjet | 24D-238 | Flight International, Atlanta, Ga. | N472EJ/N262GL |
| N49EA | Citation | 500-0017 | Ward Transformer Co. Raleigh, NC. | N49E/N508PB/N500PB/N317AB/N517CC |
| N49PE | Learjet | 35A-192 | Puma Engineering Co. Miami, Fl. | N2250C/N225CC/N4995A |
| N49R | Citation | 500-0281 | Miami Oil Producers Inc. Reno, Nv. | N5281J |
| N49UC | JetStar-731 | 47/5110 | Union Camp Corp. Morristown, NJ. | N788S/N2601/N2600/N7955S |
| N49WC | Citation | 501-0103 | Mid Continent Telephone Corp. Hudson, Oh. | (N2647U) |
| N50AL | Westwind-1124 | 190 | Allegheny Ludlum Industries Inc. Pittsburgh, Pa. | 4X-CKN |
| N50AM | Citation | 500-0041 | Charles Tolbert/American Aircraft Sales, Annapolis, Md. | N50AS/N541AG/N541CC |
| N50AS | DH 125/1A-522 | 25083 | American Standard Inc. NY. | N538/N533/N437T/N435T/N16777/G-ATOW |
| N50B | Learjet | 25D-224 | Ernst & Whinney, Cleveland, Oh. | |
| N50BA | Learjet | 24-043 | Air Capital Aircraft Sales Inc. Wichita, Ks. | N24MW/N39T/N368MJ |
| N50CR | Sabre-50 | 287-1 | Rockwell International, Cedar Rapids, Ia. | N287NA |
| N50DG | Sabre-60 | 306-19 | Mid Continent Systems Inc. Memphis, Tn. | N8000U/N918R/N4729N |
| N50DH | Learjet | 25XR-079 | Church's Fried Chicken Inc. San Antonio, Tx. | OE-GLA/D-CCAT |
| N50DM | Falcon 10 | 41 | NMCA of Texas Inc. Dallas, Tx. | N1HM/N129FJ/F-WLCS |
| N50DT | Learjet | 25-042 | Joseph Matherne, Lafayette, La. | (N429TJ)/N958DM/N958GA |
| N50DW | Westwind Two | 380 | Bancorp Leasing & Financial, Portland, Or. | 4X-CUM |

43

| Regis-<br>tration | Type | C/N | Owner/Operator | Previous<br>Identities |
|---|---|---|---|---|
| N50EC | JetStar-731 | 56/5033 | Enserch Corp. Dallas, Tx. | N25WA/XB-FIS/N200CG/N200CC/N100AC<br>/N100CC/N33EA/N16200/N1620 |
| N50FJ | Falcon 50 | 65 | Falcon Jet Corp. Teterboro, NJ. | F-WZHT |
| N50GG | Sabre-80A | 380-6 | Louisiana Interstate Gas Corp. Alexandria, La. | N5106 |
| N50HH | DH 125/1A-522 | 25022 | American Agronomics Corp. Tampa, Fl. | N100GB/N505PA/CF-SDA/G-ASZO |
| N50L | Learjet | 25B-152 | Jack Prewitt & Associates Inc. Dallas, Tx. | |
| N50M | Westwind 1124 | 327 | Multimedia Inc. Greenville, SC. | 4X-CRU |
| N50MM | Citation | 501-0215 | Majestic Energy Corp. Shreveport, La. | N1354G |
| N50PD | Learjet | 35A-409 | Cactus Enterprises Inc. Laredo, Tx. | |
| N50PG | Falcon 50 | 8 | Amax Inc. NYC. | N50FE/F-WZHC |
| N50PH | Learjet | 35A-246 | Regional Transportation Service, Portland, Or. | |
| N50PJ | Learjet | 23-076 | Southwestern Drilling Mud Service Inc/Petro Jet Aviation, Midland,<br>Tx. | N12GP/N801JA/N1966W |
| N50PM | Sabre-75A | 380-25 | Philip Morris Inc. St. Louis, Mo. | |
| N50PR | Citation | 500-0091 | Pester Corp. Des Moines, Ia. | (PT-LAW)/N76RE/N591CC |
| N50RL | Falcon 10 | 66 | Wright Enterprises, Lexington, Ky. | N150FJ/F-WJMN |
| N50SF | Learjet | 36-010 | Sequoia Ventures Inc. SFO, Ca. | |
| N50SK | Westwind Two | 309 | Drayton Associates Ltd. NYC. | N240S/4X-CRC |
| N50TB | Falcon 10 | 57 | Oncor Corp. Houston, Tx. | N142V/N142FJ/F-WJMJ |
| N50TN | HS 125/700A | NA0224 | Manville Services Corp. Denver, Co. | N50JM |
| N50TR | Citation | 500-0325 | Telles Ranch Inc. Firebaugh, Ca. | N25CJ/(N5325J) |
| N50TX | Sabre-40 | 282-23 | Victory Aviation Corp. Wilmington, De. | N301HA/N800M/N800M/N8400B<br>N282NA/N6377C |
| N50UD | JetStar-6 | 5019 | Omni, Washington DC. | N5UD/(N7OTP)/N105GN/N105GM/N9288R |
| N50US | Citation | 501-0132 | U S Companies Inc. Dallas, Tx. | N2651G |
| N50WM | Citation | 500-0246 | Jack Valenti, Oxnard, Ca. | N246CC |
| N51 | Sabre-75A | 380-5 | FAA, Oklahoma City, Ok. | |
| N51AJ | Learjet | 24D-273 | American Jet Aviation, Chesterfield, Mo. | 5Y-GEO/N118J/OH-GLA |
| N51B | Learjet | 24A-116 | Forest Beckett, Youngstown, Oh. | N40BP/N400EP/N8FM/N77GH/N52EN/N461F |
| N51BP | Falcon 10 | 51 | Iowa Beef Processors, Dakota City, Nb. | N137FJ/F-WJML |
| N51CA | Learjet | 25-030 | Chatham Corp. Denver, Co. | N45DM/N380LC/N48HM/N30PS/N745W/N999MK<br>/N999M/N951GA |
| N51CC | Citation | 501-0080 | Capsonic Group Inc. Elgin, Il. | N3145M |
| N51DB | Learjet | 25XR-246 | James Bath, League City, Tx. | N40162 |
| N51JT | Learjet | 24XR-283 | William Carr, Palm Beach, Fl. | D-IEGO/SE-DFA |
| N51MJ | Learjet | 25B-133 | MJI, Lincoln, Nb. | N1ORZ/N1ORE |
| N51SF | Falcon 20C | 12 | Sequoia Ventures Inc. SFO, Ca. | N221B/N803F/F-WMKI |
| N51V | DH 125/1A-522 | 25070 | SMB Joint Ventures, Midland, Tx. | N84W/N2148R/N214JR/N520M/G-ATKN |
| N51WP | Citation | 501-0133 | Weber Plywood & Lumber Co.Inc. Tustin, Ca. | (N955WP)/N2651J |
| N52 | Sabre-75A | 380-10 | FAA, Oklahoma City, Ok. | |
| N52AN | Citation | 500-0030 | ANA Ltd. Burlington, Vt. | N530CC |
| N52DC | Falcon 50 | 51 | Dow Chemical, Freeland, Mi. | N70FJ |
| N52FC | Westwind 1124 | 379 | Foremost Aviation Inc. Concord, NH. | 4X-CUJ |
| N52FJ | Falcon 50 | 26 | Masco Corp. Taylor, Mi. | F-WZHA |
| N52FP | Citation | 500-0052 | Flight Proficiency Service Inc. Dallas. | N52MA/N552CC |
| N52GW | Westwind Two | 330 | Gulf & Western/Cumberland Life Insurance Co. Dallas, Tx. | 4X-CRX |
| N52MJ | Learjet | 35A-363 | Matagorda Drilling, Corpus Christi, Tx. | |
| N52TC | Citation | 500-0324 | Erie Airways Inc.Pa. | N324C/(N5324J) |
| N53 | Sabre-75A | 380-14 | FAA, Oklahoma City, Ok. | |
| N53DM | Learjet | 35A-329 | Del Monte Bananas, Miami, Fl. | N39412 |
| N53SF | Falcon 20C | 102 | Sequoia Ventures Inc. SFO, Ca. | N223B/N985F/F-WMKI |
| N53WC | Sabre-40A | 282-137 | Watsonville Canning & Frozen Food, Ca. | N5512A/N5511A/N65763 |
| N54 | Sabre-75A | 380-16 | FAA, Oklahoma City, Ok. | |
| N54BW | JetStar-6 | 5014 | Great Plains Resources Inc. Miami, Fl. | N9MD/N58CG |
| N54CC | Citation | 550-0083 | Cherne Contracting Corp. Minneapolis, Mn. | N98718 |
| N54GL | Learjet | 55-054 | | |
| N54GP | Learjet | 25D-327 | Omega Industries Inc. Gary, NC. | |
| N54J | Falcon 20F | 289 | Doerr Electric, West Bend, Wi. | N20FJ/N4439F/F-WMKG |
| N54MC | Westwind 1124 | 202 | Tomlinson Petroleum Inc. Houston, Tx. | (N254MC)/N49968/D-CBAY/4X-CKZ |
| N54MH | Citation | 501-0146 | Monterey House, Houston, Tx. | N545CC/(N1782E) |
| N54MJ | Citation | 501-0208 | The Commercial Plastics Co. Mundelein, Il. | N6784P |
| N54RS | Falcon 10 | 94 | Rest Stop Ltd. Atlanta, Ga. | N171FJ/F-WNGO |
| N54SK | Citation | 500-0054 | Skyline Corp. Elkhart, In. | N554CC |
| N54TA | Learjet | 25D-258 | Pelham Corp. St. Louis, Mo. | N144FC |
| N54V | Falcon 10 | 35 | El Paso Natural Gas, Tx. | N125FJ/F-WLCV |
| N54YR | Learjet | 35A-356 | Phifer Wire Products Inc. Tuscaloosa, Al. | |
| N55 | Sabre-75A | 380-18 | FAA, Oklahoma City, Ok. | |

44

| Regis-tration | Type | C/N | Owner/Operator | Previous Identities |
|---|---|---|---|---|
| N55AS | Learjet | 35A-146 | Albertsons Inc. Boise, Id. | |
| N55BH | Citation | 550-0075 | Gilbert Imported Hardwood Inc. WV. | N3314M |
| N55CJ | JetStar-8 | 5090 | Alberto Duque/General Coffee Corp. Miami, Fl. | N1OMJ/N106G/N9246R |
| N55CR | Sabre-75 | 370-9 | Deutsche Aviation Corp. Tulsa, Ok. | N8NB/N8NR/N7592N |
| N55ES | Learjet | 25B-111 | Eugene Spitz, Morton, Pa. | N3OTP |
| N55F | Learjet | 35A-147 | Ford Motor Credit Co. Dallas, Tx. | N717W/N499G/HZ-KTC/N717W |
| N55FJ | Falcon 10 | 55 | Raymond Air Inc. Houston, Tx. | N141FJ/F-WPUV |
| N55G | DH 125/3A-RA | NA709 | General Tire & Rubber Co.Akron.Oh. | N208H/G-AWMV/G-5-16 |
| N55GG | Citation | 551-0047 | Business Real Estate Corp. NY. | N6805T |
| N55GH | Learjet | 55-012 | Sears Roebuck & Co. Chicago, Il. | |
| N55HD | Learjet | 55-026 | Howard Aviation Inc. NY. | N8565H |
| N55HF | Citation | 550-0114 | Hudson Foods Inc. Rogers, Ar. | (N89B)/N2745G |
| N55KC | Learjet | 55-014 | Kickerillo Co. Houston, Tx. | N90BS |
| N55KS | Sabre-75 | 370-5 | Kelly-Springfield Tire Co.Cumberland, Md. | N23G/N75NR/N7588N |
| N55LJ | Learjet | 25D-233 | Pre Cure Mud & Chemical Inc, Oklahoma City, Ok. | |
| N55ME | Falcon 20C | 83 | McGraw-Edison Co. | N1TC/N12WP/N22JW/N80506/N805CC/N974F/F-WJMQ |
| N55NC | JetStar-6 | 5060 | Omni International, Rockville, Md. | N31F/N9225R |
| N55NE | JetStar-731 | 32/5155 | Crowder Tank Inc. Drumright, Ok. | N4248Z/XA-FES/N711Z/N551GL |
| N55NJ | Learjet | 24-162 | National Jet Inc. Fort Lauderdale, Fl. | N835AG/N835AC/N919K/N91MK/N338DS/N841GA |
| N55PG | Challenger | 1045 | Geosurvey International Inc. Denver, Co. | |
| N55PP | Sabre-40A | 282-135 | Hal Clifford, Oklahoma City, Ok. | N7778L/N777SL/N4GV |
| N55PT | Learjet | 25B-171 | Tomlinson Interests Inc. Houston, Tx. | N55MF/N1DD/OY-ASP/N1DD/I-ELEN |
| N55RG | Gulfstream 2 | 1 | Motorola Inc. Wheeling, Il. | N801GA |
| N55SK | Citation | 500-0315 | Skyline Corp. Elkhart, In. | N5315J |
| N55SL | Learjet | 25D-219 | Sutherland Lumber & Material Co. Kansas City, Mo. | |
| N55SX | Citation | 550-0065 | Standex International Corp. Salem, NH. | N4191G |
| N55V | Learjet | 25B-185 | Morton Norwich Products Inc. Greenville, SC. | N666LP |
| N55VL | Learjet | 25C-176 | Virginia Log Co.Inc. Richmond, Va. | |
| N55WL | Citation | 550-0140 | Lane Air Inc. Northbrook, Il. | N2646Z |
| N56 | Sabre-75A | 380-20 | FAA, Oklahoma City, Ok. | |
| N56AG | Westwind-1124 | 201 | Atlanta Gas Light Co.Ga. | N1124N/N11240/4X-CKY |
| N56B | NAL 1-11/401 | 1/055 | Sharon Steel Corp. Hubbard, Oh. | N1JR/N111NA/N5015 |
| N56CC | Falcon 20F | 387 | Central Conference of Teamsters, Chicago, Il. | N162F/F-WJML |
| N56FJ | Falcon 50 | 33 | Emerson Electric Co. St. Louis, Mo. | F-WZHA |
| N56GT | Citation | 550-0137 | General Telephone Co. of NW.Everett, Wa. | N2638A |
| N56MC | Citation | 501-0023 | National Motor Club of America Inc. Dallas. | N36885 |
| N56MJ | Citation | 501-0209 | Nick Caporella/Carolina Executive Air, Inc. High Point, NC. | N6784X |
| N56NW | Sabre-65 | 465-62 | AMFAC Inc. San Francisco, Ca. | |
| N56RD | Learjet | 24D/A-286 | RDC Marine Inc. Houston, Tx. | N86GC/N59GL |
| N57 | Sabre-75A | 380-22 | FAA, Oklahoma City, Ok. | |
| N57FF | Learjet | 35-015 | Ore-Ida Foods Inc. Boise, Id. | N291BC |
| N57NB | Learjet | 24-145 | James Morse, Muskegon, Mi. | N57ND/N690J |
| N58 | Sabre-75A | 380-24 | FAA, Oklahoma City, Ok. | |
| N58AS | Learjet | 55-072 | | |
| N58CG | Sabre-60 | 306-42 | Corning Glass Works, N.Y. | N80L/N915R/N4755N |
| N58DM | Learjet | 24B-184 | Flight International, Atlanta, Ga. | N28DL/N78BH/N36RS/N84J/D-IMWZ/N950GA |
| N58GG | Citation | 551-0047 | Business Real Estate Corp. NY. | |
| N58H | Citation | 550-0312 | Harkins & Co. Alice, Tx. | N6889E |
| N58M | Learjet | 35-037 | Mutual of Omaha, Nb. | N100GL/N1462B |
| N58RD | B 707-441 | 18694 | Rowan Drilling Marine Inc. Houston, Tx. | PP-VJJ |
| N59 | Sabre-75A | 380-26 | FAA, Oklahoma City, Ok. | |
| N59BP | Learjet | 25B-124 | Combs-Gates Denver, Inc. | N39JE/N44MJ |
| N59CC | Citation | 501-0094 | Crain Automotive Group Inc. Detroit, Mi. | N103PC/N488CC/(N2646Z) |
| N59CL | Citation | 500-0173 | Colonial Life & Accident Insurance | N77CP |
| N59DM | Learjet | 35A-205 | Flight International, Atlanta, Ga. | N80SM/N3941R |
| N59JG | Learjet | 24B-221 | Oil Development Co. Aurora, Co. | (N57OJG)/N570P/N977GA |
| N59K | Sabre-60 | 306-82 | Genesco Inc. Nashville, In. | N60SL/N65759 |
| N59MJ | Citation | 550-0033 | MJI, Lincoln, Ne. | TR-LYE/(N3252M) |
| N59PC | Citation | 501-0053 | Transnational Motors Inc. Grand Rapids, Mi. | N98528 |
| N59RD | B707-441 | 17905 | Rowan Drilling Marine Inc. Houston, Tx. (Spares) | PP-VJA/N5090K |
| N60 | Sabre-75A | 380-28 | FAA, Oklahoma, Ok | |
| N60AH | Sabre-60 | 306-43 | Union Petroleum Corp. Houston, Tx. | N6NE/N6NP/N6NR/N5420/N4757N |
| N60AL | Westwind-1124 | 193 | Allegheny Ludlum Industries, Pittsburgh, Pa. | 4X-CKO |
| N60B | BH 125/400A | NA725 | Lease Air Inc/Forest Beckett, Youngstown, Oh. | N949CW/N111MB/G-AXDP |

| Registration | Type | C/N | Owner/Operator | Previous Identities |
|---|---|---|---|---|
| N60BB | Citation | 550-0207 | Fourway Aviation Co. Inc. Sidney, Oh. | N163CB/(N95CC)/N6800C |
| N60BC | JetStar-8 | 5116 | Baltimore Football Club Inc. Hunt Valley, Md | N3HB/N222QA/N7961S |
| N60BP | Sabre-60 | 306-91 | Advance Machine Co. Spring Park, Mn. | N204G/N204R/N65774 |
| N60CC | Citation | 550-0034 | Carrier Corp. Syracuse, NY. | N697A/N771A/N3258M |
| N60CH | JetStar-731 | 24/5037 | UFCW, Washington DC. | N60CN/N3060/N519L |
| N60CN | Falcon 50 | 79 | Champion International Corp. Stamford, Ct. | N86FJ/F-WZHE |
| N60CT | Gulfstream 2 | 113 | Continental Telephone, Atlanta, Ga. | N34RP/N30RP/N817GA |
| N60DD | Sabre-60 | 306-127 | FOA FINCO Inc/US Corp. Dover, De. | N5NE/N2142J |
| N60DG | Westwind Two | 364 | Geo A Hormell & Co. Austin, Mn. | 4X-CUR |
| N60DK | Learjet | 25D-231 | Koll Companies, Newport Beach, Ca. | N999ME/N999M/(OO-LFW) |
| N60HC | Sabre-60 | 306-21 | X-Cel Products Co. Houston, Tx. | N442A/N948R/N4731N |
| N60HJ | Gulfstream 2 | 119 | Sheraton Inns Inc. Wilmington, De. | N2991Q/C-FHBX/N825GA/TU-VAF /N824GA |
| N60JD | Citation | 550-0195 | John Deere & Co. Moline, Il. | N68032 |
| N60JF | Sabre-60 | 306-33 | Rockwell International Corp. | (N660BW)/N711TW/N30TC/N3FC/XA-APD /XB-APD/N600B |
| N60JP | Westwind 1124 | 320 | Michigan National Leasing Corp/Mountain Plains Oil Co. Billings, Mt. | 4X-CRN |
| N60MJ | Learjet | 55-060 | MJI, Lincoln, Ne. | |
| N60MM | Citation | 550-0179 | Minster Machine Co. Minster, Oh. | N88824 |
| N60MS | HS 125/700A | NA0209 | Melvin Simon & Associates Inc. Indianapolis. | N120GA/N46901/G-BFDW |
| N60PM | Sabre-75A | 370-7 | Philip Morris Inc. Teterboro, NJ. | N75NR/N7590N |
| N60PR | Citation | 501-0160 | Pester Corp. Des Moines, Ia. | (N58BD)/N1951E |
| N60RC | Sabre-40A | 282-134 | The Kenridge Co. Denver, De. | N40NR |
| N60RS | Sabre-60 | 306-44 | Rockwell International Corp. St. Louis, Mo. | N86Y/N45RS/N111VW /D-CEVW/N4760N |
| N60SL | Sabre-60 | | Rockwell International Corp. El Segundo, Ca. | |
| N60SM | JetStar-731 | 43/5161 | Smith International Inc. Newport Beach, Ca. | N22ES/N5525L |
| N60TG | Sabre-60 | 306-86 | Texas Gas Transmission Corp. Owensboro, Ky. | N60SL/N65765 |
| N60TN | HS 125/700A | NA0226 | Manville Services Corp. Denver, Co. | N60JM/G-5-17 |
| N61 | Sabre-75A | 380-29 | FAA, Frankfurt, W. Germany | |
| N61BL | DH 125/1A-522 | 25095 | BL Jet Sales, Dover, De. | N80CC/N5001G/N1923G/CF-SHZ/N125Y/G-ATSO |
| N61BP | Falcon 10 | 102 | Iowa Beef Processors Inc. Dakota City, Nb. | N178FJ/F-WPXK |
| N61DM | Learjet | 24B-224 | Flight International, Atlanta, Ga. | (N722DM)/N102PA/C-GPCL/N30DH N99606/D-IOGE |
| N61FC | Sabre-40 | 282-42 | International Fitness Center, Oklahoma City, Ok. | N904KB/N904K/N727R /N6397C |
| N61MS | | | Melvin Simon & Associates Inc. Indianapolis, In. | |
| N61MZ | BH 125/400A | NA752 | AiResearch Aviation Co. LAX, Ca. | N61MS/N914BD/N48BH |
| N61PR | Citation | 501-0234 | M O Rife, Fort Worth, Tx. | N2617B |
| N61SF | Learjet | 24E-346 | Spartan Food Systems Inc. Spartanburg, SC. | |
| N61SM | Gulfstream 2 | 122 | Smith International Inc. Newport Beach, Ca. | N4290X/N429JX/N832GA |
| N62 | Sabre-75A | 380-31 | FAA, Oklahoma City, Ok | |
| N62CB | Gulfstream 2 | 208 | St. Louis Southwestern Railway Co. San Francisco | N808GA |
| N62DM | Learjet | 24B-194 | Flight International, Atlanta, Ga. | N851BA/N77LS/N952GA |
| N62GG | Gulfstream 3 | 302 | Superior Oil Co. Midland, Tx. | N302GA |
| N62GL | Learjet | 55-062 | | |
| N62K | JetStar-731 | 5/5099 | Cook Industries Inc. Memphis, Tn. | N323P/N277NS/N594KR/N533EJ /N9255R |
| N62MS | HS 125/700A | NA0211 | M S Aircraft Inc. Wilmington, De. | G-BFFU/G-5-19 |
| N63 | Sabre-75A | 380-33 | FAA, Oklahoma City, Ok. | |
| N63CF | Citation | 500-0097 | Donald Slawson, Wichita, Ks. | N14CF/N597CC |
| N63ET | Learjet | 25B-110 | C W Alcorn, Victoria, Tx. | N50GL |
| N64 | Sabre-75A | 380-35 | FAA, Frankfurt, West Germany. | |
| N64C | JetStar-8 | 5131 | Norton Co. Tallmadge, Oh. | N31RP/N30RP/N7976S |
| N64CE | Learjet | 24B-205 | Combs-Gates Denver Inc. | N64CF/N974JD |
| N64CF | Learjet | 35A-461 | CF Industries Inc. Chicago, Il. | |
| N64GG | HS 125/700A | NA0310 | Superior Oil, Houston, Tx. | N700LL/G-5-20 |
| N64MC | Sabre-65 | 465-73 | Magic Chef Inc. Cleveland, Oh. | |
| N64MP | Learjet | 35A-490 | Mesa Petroleum Co. Amarillo, Tx. | |
| N64MR | Learjet | 35-060 | Mesa Petroleum Co. Amarillo, Tx. | N64MP |
| N64WM | Learjet | 55-022 | Waste Management Inc. Wilmington, De. | |
| N65 | Sabre 75A | 380-37 | FAA, Oklahoma City, Ok. | |
| N65A | Westwind-1124 | 235 | Assoc. Corp. Dallas, Tx. | (N24PP)/N1124E |
| N65AH | Sabre-65 | 465-68 | Allied Chemical Co. Morristown, NJ. | |
| N65AK | Sabre-65 | 465-35 | Allied Chemical Co. Morristown, NJ. | N2590E |
| N65AM | Sabre-65 | 465-58 | Allied Chemical Co. Morristown, NJ. | |

| Regis-tration | Type | C/N | Owner/Operator | Previous Identities |
|---|---|---|---|---|
| N65AN | Sabre-65 | 465-59 | Allied Chemical Co. Morristown, NJ. | |
| N65AR | Sabre-65 | 465-67 | Allied Chemical Co. Morristown, NJ. | |
| N65B | Falcon 50 | 10 | Bordens Inc. Morristown, NJ. | N50FG/F-WZHD |
| N65DD | Sabre-65 | 465-26 | Air Shamrock, Burbank, Ca. | N2548E/N465SL |
| N65DH | Learjet | 35A-381 | CMI Corp. Troy, Mi. | D-CORA |
| N65EC | DH 125/400A | NA737 | Pool Co. Houston, Tx. | N2500W/G-AXOE |
| N65FC | Sabre-65 | 465-31 | Fleming Companies, Bethany, Ok. | N2550E |
| N65L | Sabre-65 | 465-76 | Acopian Technical Co. Easton, Pa. | |
| N65LC | Citation | 550-0287 | Liebert Corp. Columbus, Oh. | N444MM/N68648 |
| N65LE | Falcon 20C | 40 | Business Aviation Inc. Sioux Falls, SD. | N65LC/N854WC/N354WC/N354H /N19BC/CF-BFM/N870F/F-WNGL |
| N65MK | DH 125/731 | 25032 | Morrison-Knudsen Co.Inc. Boise, Id. | G-ATBC |
| N65R | Sabre-65 | 306-114 | Rockwell International Corp. | (N60TF)/N2109J |
| N65RC | Sabre-65 | 465-19 | Robertshaw Controls, Richmond, Va. | |
| N65ST | Gulfstream 2 | 5 | GenStar, Montreal. | N100PJ/N100P |
| N65T | Citation | 501-0216 | Termicold Corp. Portland, Or. | N57MJ |
| N65WM | Learjet | 24-163 | Waste Management Inc. Fort Lauderdale, Fl. | N77AE/N65339/N1AP /N701AP |
| N66AG | Citation | 501-0136 | Phillips Travelstead, Greensboro, NC. | N66AT/(N26502) |
| N66AM | Learjet | 23-064 | Amjet Inc. Springfield, Il. | N73JT/N401RB/N400RB/N200G/N365EJ |
| N66AS | Learjet | 23-029 | McInerney Leasing Co. Oak Park, Mi. | N1BU/N715BC/N7000K |
| N66CC | Citation | 500-0066 | Hehr International Co. Van Nuys, Ca. | N566CC |
| N66ES | Sabre-80A | 380-32 | Starwood Air Service Inc. Englewood, Co. | N64MO/N64MP/N75RS/N2100J |
| N66FE | Learjet | 35A-383 | Ply Aircraft Co. Los Angeles Ca. | |
| N66JE | Westwind-1124 | 326 | NJE Aircraft Corp. Taneytown, Md. | (N88JE)/4X-CRT |
| N66KC | DH 125/731 | 25038 | Kimberly-Clarke Corp., Neenah, Wi. | N125G/N926G/G-ATCP |
| N66LE | Citation Eagle | 500-0170 | Liberty Exploration Co. Oklahoma City, Ok. | N818R/N90237/N60MS |
| N66LJ | Learjet | 35A-401 | C W Culpepper, Oklahoma City, Ok. | |
| N66LM | Learjet | 35A-306 | LLM Aircraft Co. Greensboro, NC. | N926GL |
| N66MJ | Learjet | 24E-334 | Corporate Air Inc. Hartford, Ct. | N6KM |
| N66MP | JetStar-6 | 5015 | Jet 66 Corp. Houston, Tx. | N9046F/N505T/N103KC/N172L/NASA4 |
| N66MR | Learjet | 24-159 | Lamont Bean, Seattle, Wa. | N661JB/N855W/N647GA |
| N66MS | Citation | 551-0053 | Modern Supply Co. Ponca City, Ok. | (N6890C) |
| N66MW | Learjet | 23-066 | Zircon Aviation Services Inc. Oklahoma City, Ok. | N72MK/N216RG |
| N66NJ | Learjet | 25-039 | WER Aviation Corp. Charlotte, NC. | N17JF/N959RE/N959GA |
| N66WM | Learjet | 35A-141 | Waste Management Inc. Ca. | N743GL |
| N67B | Challenger | 1066 | Federated Stores Inc. Cincinnati, Oh. | C-GLYH |
| N67EC | BH 125/731 | NA778 | Pool Co. Houston, Tx. | N2694C/C-GCEO/N733K/N555CB/N75BH |
| N67HW | Citation | 550-0421 | | |
| N67MA | Citation | 500-0277 | Somerset Acres Inc. Fort Wayne, In. | N67MP/N277CC/(N5277J) |
| N67MP | Citation | 550-0444 | Somerset Acres Inc. Fort Wayne, In. | |
| N67SG | Citation | 550-0235 | Gary Energy Corp. Englewood, Co. | (N6803T) |
| N67WW | Sabre-40 | 282-2 | Worldwide Energy Corp. Englewood, Co. | N57GS/N108U/N108W/N100WF /N577PM/N577R |
| N68BW | BH 125/400A | NA763 | AOPA, Washington DC. | N46R/N246N/(N91BH)/N58BH/(G-5-15) |
| N68DM | Learjet | 24-101 | Flight International Inc. Atlanta, Ga. | N473/N473EJ/N15PL/N316MF /N316M |
| N68DS | Citation | 550-0196 | TPA Inc./Drag Specialties, Minnetonka, Mn. | N6798Y |
| N68HC | Sabre-60 | 306-96 | HCA Properties Inc. Nashville, Tn. | N65784 |
| N68KM | Sabre-75A | 380-23 | Kerr McGee Corp. Oklahoma City, Ok. | N65776 |
| N68PJ | Learjet | 25-063 | Petro Jet Aviation Inc. Houston, Tx. | N680J/N184J/C-GPDZ/N919S |
| N68WM | Learjet | 23-074 | Waste Management Inc. Wilmington, De. | N23AN/N74MW/N23TC/D-IATD /5A-DAC |
| N69CG | Sabre-40 | 282-72 | Corporate General Ltd. Norman, Ok. | N744R/(N880HL) |
| N69CN | JetStar-731 | 2/5053 | Champion International Corp. Stamford, Ct. | N121CN/N12R/N9219R |
| N69GT | Jet Commander | 44 | Gregg Thompson, Broken Arrow, Ok. | N273LF/N273LP/N700CB/N700C/N200M |
| N69HM | JetStar-6 | 5004 | Aviation Equipment Corp. Washington DC. | N777EP/N524AC/N13304 /N9204R |
| N69KB | Learjet | 23-042 | White Industries Inc. Bates City, Mo. | N701RZ/N1ZA/N2932C/N293BC |
| N69WK | Sabre-75A | 380-30 | Kerr McGee Corp. Oklahoma City, Ok. | N65793 |
| N69MT | JetStar-8 | 5107 | Mortgage & Trust Inc. Houston, Tx. | N7788/YV-187CP/N7788/N337US/N11RK |
| N69X | MS 760 Paris | 90 | Flight Transportation Corp. Eden Prairie, Mn. | N454HC/D-INGE |
| N70CN | Learjet | 35A-277 | Cole National Corp. Cleveland, Oh. | N723LL/N925GL |
| N70FC | HS 125/700A | NA0339 | First National Chicago Association, Il/Emery Air Charter. | G-5-18 |
| N70GM | Citation | 550-0122 | Grove Manufacturing Co. Shady Grove, Pa. | N135CC/N2746E |
| N70HC | Citation | 551-0428 | | |
| N70JC | Learjet | 24-051 | Air Capital Sales, Wichita, Ks. | N990TM/(N69LL)/N100MJ /N1500G/N1500B |
| N70JF | Learjet | 25D-278 | Jet Fleet Corp. Dallas, Tx. | |

47

| Regis-tration | Type | C/N | Owner/Operator | Previous Identities |
|---|---|---|---|---|
| N70KM | Sabre-75A | 380-52 | Kerr-McGee, Oklahoma City, Ok. | N177NO/N177NC/N75A/N2136J |
| N70MD | Falcon 20D | 153 | J Ray McDermott & Co. New Orleans, La. | N4361F/F-WLCT |
| N70MP | Learjet | 25-051 | Montana Power Co. Butte, Mt. | N973GA |
| N70PM | HS 125/700A | NA0303 | Philip Morris Inc. Milwaukee, Wi. | (N80PM)/N125P/G-5-14 |
| N70PS | Gulfstream 3 | 327 | American International Group. | |
| N70TG | Citation | 500-0308 | Texas Gas Transmission Corp. Owensboro, Ky. | N38CJ/N308CC/(N5308J) |
| N70TP | JetStar-8 | 5156 | Phillippi Equipment Co. Golden Valley, Mn. | 9K-ACO/N5520L |
| N70U | Citation | 500-0304 | Brown & Root Inc. Houston, Tx. | N5253E/N5253A/N304CC/(N5304J) |
| N70WC | Falcon 10 | 140 | Wickes Leasing Corp. San Diego, Ca. | N205FJ/F-WZGL |
| N70WP | Citation | 501-0129 | W.H.Pease, Grand Junction, Ca. | (N50WP)/(N26499) |
| N71CC | Sabre-60A | 306-71 | Carlson Companies Inc. Minneapolis, Mn. | N1028Y/N370M/N31BM |
| N71CG | Citation | 550-0227 | Graham Leasing Corp. Royersgord, Pa. | N254CC/N68027 |
| N71DL | HFB 320 | 1026 | Caesars World Inc. Los Angeles, Ca. | N71CW/N890HJ/D-CARY |
| N71DM | Learjet | 25C-129 | Flight International, Atlanta, GA. (USN). | N551WC |
| N71LP | Falcon 20C | 89 | LCP Transportation Inc. Edison, NJ. | N345BM/N978F/F-WMKG |
| N71M | Westwind-1124 | 192 | International Multifoods, Minneapolis, Mn. | 4X-CKP |
| N71RB | Learjet | 25B-158 | Barnstormer Ltd/Richard Barnes, Chicago, Il. | N334LS/N85MJ/HZ-GP3 /N158GL |
| N71RC | Citation | 500-0184 | Lakeway Fuel Corp. Westlake, Oh. | N77RC |
| N71TP | Gulfstream 2 | 195 | Tesoro Petroleum Corp. San Antonio, Tx. | N212K |
| N72BC | Citation | 500-0270 | Bissel Inc. Grand Rapids, Mi. | N712N/N712J/N5270J |
| N72BB | Falcon 10 | 173 | KCM Company, Midland, Tx. | N239FJ/F-WZGA |
| N72CT | JetStar-731 | 45/5007 | Campbell Taggart Inc. Dallas, Tx. | N110G/N9205R |
| N72ET | Falcon 20C | 52 | International Jet Leasing Co. Fort Wayne, In. | N881F/F-WNGN |
| N72FJ | Falcon 50 | 58 | | |
| N72HC | BH 125/731 | NA780 | Harsco Corp. Camp Hill, Pa. | N78BH |
| N72HT | JetStar-731 | 50/5134 | Hughes Tool Co. Houston, Tx. | N50PS/N500S/N295AR/N7979S |
| N72JM | Learjet | 35A-183 | Levelor Lorentzen Inc. Lyndhurst, NJ. | N720M/N3802G |
| N72TB | Learjet | 35-014 | Tesoro Petroleum Corp. San Antonio, Tx. | N73TP/N71TP |
| N72TP | Learjet | 35A-140 | Tesoro Petroleum Corp. San Antonio, Tx. | N888BL/N742GL |
| N72TQ | Jet Commander | 4 | Oklahoma Aircraft Corp. Yukon, Ok. | N72TC/N77TC/N77F |
| N73B | Falcon 10 | 79 | The Kroger Co. Cincinnati, Oh. | N160FJ/F-BPXB/F-WPXB |
| N73FJ | Falcon 50 | 55 | | |
| N73FW | Citation | 501-0150 | Admiral Beverage Corp. Worland, Wy. | N95MJ/N2616G |
| N73G | Sabre-60 | 306-8 | Brown & Root Inc. Houston, Tx. | N4716N |
| N73HP | Sabre-40A | 282-120 | San Felipe Ranch, Palo Alto, Ca. | |
| N73LL | Citation | 500-0287 | Jet America International Inc. Cambridge, Md. | N287CC/(N5287J) |
| N73M | Gulfstream 2 | 128 | 3M Co. St. Paul, Mn. (r/c Mining Seven). | |
| N73PC | Sabre-40 | 282-11 | Jetex Inc. Abilene, Tx. | N167G/N167H/N6365C |
| N74G | Learjet | 25B-174 | MJI, Lincoln, Nb. | |
| N74JA | Citation | 550-0327 | Abercrombie Mineral Co. Houston, Tx. | N5474G |
| N74KV | Citation | 550-0298 | KVI Aviation Inc. Des Moines, Ia. | N68873 |
| N74MG | Citation | 550-0269 | MGF Oil Corp. Midland, Tx. | N6863G |
| N74MJ | Sabre-40A | 282-102 | Bill Burns, Midland, Tx. | N74MG/N800DC/N2WR/N7597N |
| N74RP | Gulfstream 2TT | 199 | General Transportation Corp. NY. | N75RP/N75WC/N829GA |
| N74TP | Learjet | 36A-030 | Tesoro Petroleum Corp. San Antonio, Tx. | N71TP |
| N74XL | Jet Commander-A | 128 | MBPXL Corp. Wichita, Ks. | N660RW |
| N75AG | Sabre-75A | 380-42 | Apache Corp. Minneapolis, Mn. | D-CHIC/N75RS/N2114J |
| N75CC | JetStar-8 | 5102 | Jed Air, Sidney, Oh. | N500ZB/N326K/N9235R |
| N75CS | DH 125/400A | NA722 | Chessie Services Inc. Baltimore, Md. | N1393/G-AXDO |
| N75FN | Citation | 500-0257 | First National Supermarkets Inc. Maple Heights, Oh. | N75MN/N5257J |
| N75HL | Sabre-75A | 380-36 | Husky Aviation Co. Cody, Wy. | JY-AFM/N75A/N2105J |
| N75HP | Sabre-60 | 306-48 | Hewlett Packard Co. San Jose, Ca. | N60AG/N284U/N234U/N93BR/N7519N |
| N75KR | Citation | 550-0060 | King Ranch Inc. Kingsville, Tx. | (N550KR)/N26610 |
| N75KV | Learjet | 24D-258 | Knape & Vogt Manufacturing Co. Grand Rapids, Mi. | |
| N75NL | Sabre-75A | 380-40 | Rockwell/Gulf Oil, Houston, Tx. | N4NB/N4NR/N2112J |
| N75PX | Citation | 500-0248 | Jasper Textiles Inc. Lumberton, NC. | (N5248J) |
| N75RD | BH 125/400A | NA751 | R R Donnelley & Sons, Chicago, Il. | N120GB/N120GA/G-BCLR/N640M /N47BH |
| N75RP | Gulfstream 3 | 328 | General Transportation Corp. NY. | N309GA |
| N75RS | Sabre-75A | 380-63 | Randall Stores, Mitchell, SD. | |
| N75TD | Learjet | 36A-028 | Teledyne Industries Inc. Los Angeles, Ca. | N731GA |
| N75TP | Learjet | 55-032 | Tesoro Petroleum Corp. San Antonio, Tx. | |
| N75U | Sabre-75 | 370-4 | Michigan Wisconsin Pipeline Co. Detroit, Mi. | N7587M |
| N75W | Sabre-40A | 282-129 | Michigan Wisconsin Pipeline Co. Detroit, Mi. | |

48

| Regis-tration | Type | C/N | Owner/Operator | Previous Identities |
|---|---|---|---|---|
| N75X | Sabre-75A | | | |
| N75Y | Sabre-75A | 380-64 | Michigan-Wisconsin Pipeline Co. Detroit, Mi. | N75NR |
| N76CS | Gulfstream 2 | 158 | Chessie Services Inc. Cleveland, Oh. | |
| N76FJ | Falcon 50 | 67 | Ayre Inc. Rockville, Md. | F-WZHG |
| N76GP | Learjet | 35-036 | Gerber Products Co. Fremont, Mi. | N76GL/N134GL |
| N76GT | Sabre-60 | 306-61 | Girod Trust Co. San Juan, PR. | (N1VC)/N961R/N965R |
| N76NX | Sabre-65 | 465-53 | NICOR, Napierville, Il. | |
| N77 | B727-30 | 18360 | FAA, Oklahoma City, Ok. | N68649/D-ABIB/N68649 |
| N77A | Sabre-65 | 465-1 | AMP Inc. Harrisburg, Pa. | N65RS/N465S/N2501E |
| N77AT | Sabre-60 | 306-23 | Alban Tractor Co.Inc. Baltimore, Md. | N15RF/CF-BLT/N908R/N4733N |
| N77C | BH 125/600A | 6038 | Parn Aviation Corp. Dover, De. | N40BH |
| N77CD | DH 125/3A | 25123 | Thiokol Corp. Brigham City, Ut. | N77C/N706M/N700M/G-AVAG |
| N77CP | Learjet | 35A-177 | Pfizer Inc. Trenton, NJ. | N1461R |
| N77D | JetStar-731 | 60/5097 | Mine Safety Appliances Inc. Pittsburgh, Pa. | N306L/N300L/N9253R |
| N77FD | Citation | 501-0250 | General Telephone Co. | |
| N77FK | Learjet | 35A-376 | K Services Inc. Wilmington, De. | N458JA |
| N77FV | Jet Commander | 26 | Seacrest Corp. Easton, Me. | N1OMC/N614JC |
| N77GJ | Citation | 501-0119 | Minnesota Automotive Inc. Mankato, Mn. | N53RC/N35TM/N35AA/(N26486) |
| N77HW | JetStar-6 | 5080 | Harrah Corp. Anaheim, Ca. | N914P/N914X |
| N77KT | Jet Commander | 7 | Kenneth Tureaud, Tulsa, Ok. | (N711VK)/N3ORJ/N22CH/N1173Z/N112JC |
| N77MR | Sabre-40R | 282-52 | AMP Inc. Harrisburg, Pa. | N40R/N2004/N2000/N200A/N7502V |
| N77ND | Citation | 550-0005 | University of N. Dakota, Grand Forks, ND. | OE-GKP/N98817 |
| N77NJ | Learjet | 25-033 | National Jets Inc. Fort Lauderdale, Fl. | YV-88CP/N786M/N143J/HB-VBP |
| N77RC | Citation | 550-0130 | Rudd Enterprises, Louisville, Ky. | (N88845) |
| N77RY | Learjet | 24-137 | John McClelland, Houston, Tx. | N73HG/N907CS |
| N77ST | Jet Commander | 108 | K E Tureund, Birmingham, Mi. | N12JX/N12JA/N1WP/N1121Z |
| N77SW | Gulfstream 2 | 15 | Joseph E Seagram & Sons Inc. N.Y. | N375PK |
| N77TC | Sabre-65 | 465-10 | Timken Co. Canton, Oh. | N65SL |
| N77TE | Learjet | 35-031 | American TV & Comms Corp. Englewood, Co. | N77U/N77FC |
| N77TG | Gulfstream 3 | 332 | Texasgulf Aviation Inc. Stamford, Ct. | N310GA |
| N77TW | Citation | 501-0135 | Transwestern Pipeline Co. Houston, Tx. | N2650Y |
| N78 | B727-30 | 18362 | FAA,. Oklahoma City, Ok. | N90558/D-ABID |
| N78AB | Citation | 501-0070 | Southern Union Co. Dallas, Tx. | (N444CW)/N3062A |
| N78BC | Sabre-40A | 282-104 | Beloit Corp. Beloit, Wi. | N40CH |
| N78CS | HS 125/700A | NA0297 | Chessie Service Inc. Baltimore, Md. | N125BD/G-5-16 |
| N78DT | Learjet | 25D-356 | Devin Aviation Inc. Lafayette, La. | |
| N78GL | Learjet | 25D-240 | Stanley Averch, Omaha, Nb. | |
| N78MC | Citation | 500-0150 | Cowan Aviation Inc. Odessa, Tx. | N501JG/OE-FAU/N5LG/VH-WRM/N5B/N150CC |
| N78MD | Falcon 10 | 18 | J Ray McDermott & Co. Inc. Singapore. | N111FJ/F-WJMJ |
| N78MN | Learjet | 35A-237 | Morris Newspaper Corp. Savannah, Ga. | N843GL |
| N78TC | Citation | 550-0246 | Timken Co. Canton, Oh. | N72TC/N6861E |
| N79HA | Falcon 10 | 128 | EAF/Houston Astros, Teterboro, NJ. | N1871R/N197FJ/F-WNGO |
| N79HC | HS 125/700A | NA0246 | Harsco Corp. Camp Hill, Pa. | N130BB/G-5-20 |
| N79RS | Learjet | 24XR-280 | Stern Investment Corp. Portland, Or. | D-ICHS |
| N79SF | Learjet | 36A-041 | Stahmann Farms Inc. Las Cruces, NM. | |
| N80 | Jet Commander-C | 144 | FAA, Oklahoma City, Ok. | N9044N/4X-CPK |
| N80A | Gulfstream 2 | 38 | U.S. Steel Corp. West Trenton, NJ. | |
| N80AB | Sabre-75A | 380-59 | Epps Air Service, Atlanta, Ga. | |
| N80AT | Challenger | 1036 | Taubman Air Inc. Troy, Mi. | C-GROO/C-GLYC |
| N80AW | Citation | 550-0186 | Sale, Houston. | N98418 |
| N80BS | Citation | 550-0119 | Briggs & Stratton Corp. Wauwatosa, Wi. | N27457 |
| N80BT | Learjet | 25D-248 | MJI, Lincoln, NB. | |
| N80CD | Learjet | 35A-215 | Baron Leasing, Charlotte, NC. | N2951P/VH-UPB |
| N80CR | Sabre-60 | 306-142 | Rockwell International Corp. Richardson, Tx. | N6ORS |
| N80DH | Learjet | 24B-191 | Marker Aviation Ltd. SLC. Ut. | (N44TL)/N44LJ/N855W |
| N80DR | Citation | 550-0184 | David Richardson, Incline Village, Nv. | N2619M |
| N80E | Gulfstream 2 | 184 | U.S. Steel Corp. West Trenton, NJ. | N861GA |
| N80ED | Learjet | 35A-337 | R E Job Cement Contractor Inc. Pomona, Ca. | (N337WC) |
| N80FH | Sabre-65 | 465-34 | Stephen Muss, Miami Beach, Fl. | N112KM/N500G |
| N80G | HS 125/700A | NA0293 | U S Steel Corp. Pittsburgh, Pa. | N700BA/G-5-11 |
| N80GM | Citation | 550-0147 | Grove Manufacturing Co. Pa. | (N155JK)/N98682 |
| N80J | Gulfstream 2 | 160 | U.S. Steel Corp. West Trenton, NJ. | |
| N80K | HS 125/700A | NA0298 | U.S. Steel Corp. Pittsburgh, Pa. | N125G/G-5-17 |
| N80MF | Citation | 501-0154 | McClean-Fogg/Caledonian Leasing Partnership, Dover, De. | N2613C |
| N80MP | Falcon 10 | 68 | Jenos Pizza, Duluth, Mn. | N91DH/N11DH/N7NL/N7NP/N152FJ/F-WLCV |
| N80PM | HS 125/700A | NA0300 | Philip Morris Inc. Teterboro, NJ. | N70PM/G-5-20 |
| N80WG | Learjet | 35A-281 | U.S. Fidelity & Guarantee Co. Baltimore, Md. | |
| N81 | Jet Commander-C | 143 | FAA, Oklahoma City Ok. | N9043N/4X-CPJ |

| Regis-tration | Type | C/N | Owner/Operator | Previous Identities |
|---|---|---|---|---|
| N81CC | Citation | 501-0104 | J F Wilbur Jr. Inc. Fayetteville, NC. | N312GK/(N2647Z) |
| N81DM | Diamond One | 002 | Mitsubishi Aircraft International Inc. Dallas, Tx. | J08002 |
| N81EB | Citation | 501-0003 | Elkhart Brass Manufacturing Co. Inc. In. | N781L/N55CJ/N5355J |
| N81HH | Diamond One | A013SA | | |
| N81HP | Sabre-60 | 306-100 | Hewlett Packard Co. Palo Alto, Ca. | N881MC/N65790 |
| N81JJ | JetStar-6 | 5002 | Georges International Equipment, Reno, Nv. | N69TP/N106GM/EP-VRP /N9202R |
| N81LB | Falcon 10 | 158 | Commercial Aviation Inc/LDB Corp. Kerrville, Tx. | N223FJ/F-WZGI |
| N81LJ | Learjet | 23-081 | Avia Jet Inc. Dallas, Tx. | N418LJ/XC-JOA/N437LJ/N369EJ |
| N81MC | Learjet | 24F-344 | Macton Corp. Danbury, Ct. | |
| N81TC | Citation | 550-0067 | The Trane Co. La Crosse, Wi. | N2663B |
| N81WT | Learjet | 24E-351 | MJI, Lincoln, Nb. | N31WT/N19MJ |
| N82 | Jet Commander-C | 142 | FAA, Oklahoma City, Ok. | N9042N/4X-CPI |
| N82A | Falcon 20D | 205 | EAF/Prudential Insurance Co. Newark, NJ. | N21W/N4393F/F-WPXF |
| N82AL | Gulfstream 3 | 363 | Allegheny International Corp. Pittsburgh, Pa. | |
| N82CF | Sabre-40A | 282-100 | Clark Financial Corp. Salt Lake City, Ut. | N19HF |
| N82CR | Falcon 100 | 183 | Rockwell Coillins Radio, Cedar Rapids, Ia. | N249FJ/F-WZGO |
| N82CS | Diamond One | A040SA | | |
| N82HH | Westwind | 383 | Hughes & Hughes Oil & Gas, Beeville, Tx. | |
| N82JL | Learjet | 35A-380 | Continental Aviation Services Inc/James Lennane, Londonderry, NH. | |
| N82MD | Falcon 10 | 77 | J Ray McDermott & Co. Inc. Dubai, UAE. | N158FJ/F-WNGN |
| N82MP | Falcon 50 | 42 | Mesa Petroleum, Amarillo, Tx. | N61FJ/F-WZHE |
| N82MW | Sabre-60 | 306-76 | Ohio Jet Services Inc. Cincinnati, Oh. | N333NC/N333PC/N67NR |
| N82R | Sabre-40A | 282-131 | Rebel Oil Co. Oklahoma City, Ok. | N30M/N3BM/N9251N |
| N82RP | Citation | 550-0126 | RER Equipment Co. Lake Worth, Fl. | N26863/OE-GHP/(N2747R) |
| N82UH | Learjet | 25-010 | United Home Builders, SFO, Ca. | N102PS/N671WM/N846HC/N846GA |
| N83 | Jet Commander-A | 131 | FAA, Oklahoma City, Ok. | N5039E/4X-CPE |
| N83AL | Gulfstream 3 | 363 | | |
| N83FJ | Falcon 50 | 74 | Anheuser-Busch Inc. St. Louis, Mo. | F-WZHA |
| N83M | Gulfstream 2 | 135 | 3M Co. St. Paul, Mn. (r/c Mining Eight). | |
| N83MD | Falcon 10 | 78 | J Ray McDermott & Co. Inc. New Orleans, La. | N159FJ/F-WLCT |
| N83ND | Citation | 501-0178 | Thomas Ryan & McCormick Business Jet, Grand Forks. Mn. | N4246A/LV-PML /N67799 |
| N83RG | Learjet | 24XR-243 | Rio Grande Aviation Services Inc. Pearsall, Tx.(N85DH)/N2909W/HB-VCI | |
| N83TC | Learjet | 25D-315 | Texas Commerce International Leasing Co. Houston, Tx. | N3798A/N10873 |
| N83TF | Citation | 500-0256 | Building Trades Dept. Washington DC. | SE-DDN/N256CC |
| N83V | Falcon 20F | 366 | El Paso Natural Gas, Tx. | N1020F/F-WMKG |
| N84 | Jet Commander-A | 130 | FAA, Oklahoma City, Ok. | N503RE/4X-CPD |
| N84AL | Gulfstream 2 | 166 | Allegheny International Corp. Pittsburgh, Pa. | N66AL/N515KA/N811GA |
| N84CF | Citation | 501-0082 | Carlton Forge Works, Paramount, Ca. | N460CC/N3150M |
| N84LA | Westwind 1124 | 378 | | 4X-CUI |
| N84TF | HS 125/3A-RA | 25169 | Omni International Corp. Rockville, Md. | G-AWWL/N3AL/VH-BBJ/G-AWWL /G-5-17 |
| N84V | Falcon 20E | 302 | El Paso Natural Gas, Tx. | OE-GDP/D-COMM/F-WROP |
| N84X | Gulfstream 2 | 43 | McGraw-Edison Co. Elgin, Il. | F-BRUY/N17583 |
| N85A | Falcon 50 | 92 | Burlington Industries Inc. Greensboro, NC. | N97FJ/F-WZHZ |
| N85AT | Citation | 500-0087 | On Wings of Song Inc. New York. | (N64792)/N587CC |
| N85CA | Learjet | 35A-421 | MHC Inc. Omaha, Ne. | N44MJ |
| N85CD | Learjet | 24D-250 | MJI, Omaha, Nb. | N85CA/N1U/N2U/N122CG/D-IMAR/N112C |
| N85FS | Citation | 501-0040 | Fuel Services Inc. Pascagoula, Ms. | N8725B |
| N85JM | Falcon 10 | 85 | John Murphy, Columbus, Oh. | N165FJ/F-WPXI |
| N85MA | Jet Commander | 48 | Reafund Advisors Inc. Cleveland, Oh. | N486G/N8LC/N444WL/N400LR/N541M /N541SG |
| N85MD | Falcon 50 | 76 | J Ray McDermott & Co. Inc. New Orleans, La. | N84FJ/F-WZHB |
| N85V | Falcon 20F | 412 | El Paso Natural Gas, Tx. | N409F/F-WMKI |
| N85W | Learjet | 24-135 | Fort Terrett Leasing Co. Odessa, Tx. | |
| N86 | Sabre-40 | 282-86 | FAA, Oklahoma City, Ok. | |
| N86CC | Learjet | 24-115 | M & N Co. Denver, Co. | N591DL/N591D/N665LJ/N458LJ |
| N86HM | JetStar-6 | 5039 | Howard McCormack, Oklahoma City, Ok. | N81MR/N600J/N600J |
| N86JJ | Citation | 501-0004 | Desert Eet Inc. Bend, Or. | N88JJ/N5356J |
| N86MJ | Learjet | 25-062 | MJI/Purolator Courier | HZ-GP4/N303JJ/N105BJ/N4981/OY-AKZ |
| N86PC | Learjet | 35A-108 | Pepsi Cola Bottling Co. Denver, Co. | F-GCLE/D-COCO |
| N86RM | Sabre-60 | 306-89 | Rocky Mountain Energy Co. Denver, Co. | N23DS/N65770 |
| N86SG | Citation | 550-0350 | Papercraft Inc. Santa Fe Springs, Ca. | |
| N86SS | Citation | 500-0285 | Stanley Shaw, Kemp, Tx. | N2U/(N285CC)/N5285J |
| N86TP | JetStar-8 | 5142 | Phillippi Equipment Co/Louisiana Land. | N9065B/HZ-SH3/N2OS/N1UP /N5113H/N5506L |

| Regis-tration | Type | C/N | Owner/Operator | Previous Identities |
|---|---|---|---|---|
| N86W | Falcon 20E | 298 | El Paso Products, Midland, Tx. | N4444F/F-WMKG |
| N87 | Sabre-40 | 282-87 | FAA, Far East | |
| N87AP | Learjet | 24D-290 | Roarr Enterprises, Cleveland, Oh. | N934H/N23JC/N462B |
| N87AT | Learjet | 35A-096 | Asplundh Tree Expert Co. Wilmington, De. | (N11JV)/N214LS |
| N87CF | Learjet | 24B-181 | Joe Featherstone, Roswell, NM. | N44PA/N651J/N10C/N2340 |
| N87CM | Sabre-40 | 282-21 | CMI Corp. Oklahoma City, Ok. | N168D/N168H/N6375C |
| N87DC | Jet Commander | 14 | Cable Holdings Aviation Corp. Glenville, Ct. | N121BN/N350M |
| N87GT | Falcon 10 | 181 | Gulf States Toyota, Houston, Tx. | N247FJ/F-WZGC |
| N87JL | Learjet | 24E-335 | Oregon Jet Aviation, Ashland, Or. | N721GL |
| N87W | Learjet | 35A-104 | El Paso Products, Odessa, Tx. | |
| N87Y | Sabre-75A | 380-1 | N L Petroleum Services, Houston, Tx. | N6K/N7593N |
| N88 | Sabre-40 | 282-88 | FAA, Oklahoma City, Ok. | |
| N88AE | Gulfstream 2 | 102 | National Express Co. Inc. N.Y. | N854GA |
| N88AT | Falcon 10 | 73 | Taubman Air Inc. Southfield, Mi. | N155FJ/F-WNGL |
| N88B | Learjet | 24-015 | Louise Timken, Canton, Oh. | |
| N88BY | Learjet | 25B-168 | Lone Elm Aviation Ltd. Dallas, Tx. | N88BT/N72TP |
| N88CH | Convair 880 | 58 | Sentinel Jets Ltd. Reno, Nv. | VR-HGF/JA8022 |
| N88CJ | Learjet | 25-006 | Air Charter Holidays Inc/First Interstate Bank of Ca. | (N88GJ)/N90MH /N256P |
| N88DD | Citation | 550-0217 | Transportation Corp. of America, Chicago Heights, Il. | N6804L |
| N88EA | Learjet | 23-077 | Sparkomatic Corp. Milford, Pa. | N90658/N500P/N868J/N812LJ |
| N88EP | Learjet | 35A-134 | El Paso National Bank, Tx. | N1473B |
| N88FE | Falcon 20F | 317 | Funk Exploration Inc. Oklahoma City, Ok. | N92K/N99E/N31CM/N4452F /F-WMKG |
| N88GA | Gulfstream 2 | 217 | Greyhound Armour Co. Phoenix, Az. | |
| N88JA | Learjet | 25D-305 | Kenny Rogers, Bel Air, Ca. | |
| N88JF | Learjet | 24A-110 | Hugh Preston/Jet Fleet Corp. Dallas, Tx. | N35FJ/N362AA/N1969H/N388R |
| N88JJ | Citation | 550-0172 | Agri Empire Corp. San Jacinto, Ca. | N72MM/(N28MM)/N88795 |
| N88JM | JetStar-731 | 1/5011 | Central Gulf International/Jay Menard, Lafayette, La. | N159B/N10461 /C-GKRS/N731A/PK-PJH/9V-BEE/PK-PJS/T17845/N9282R |
| N88ME | Falcon 10 | 8 | McGraw-Edison Co. Elgin, Il. | N21EK/N21ET/N21ES/N104FJ/F-WJMN |
| N88MJ | Citation | 550-0089 | MJI, Lincoln, Nb./Chrysler Corp. | (N26623) |
| N88MR | DH 125/1A | 25013 | Aircraft Component & Equipment Supplies Inc. Los Angeles, Ca. | N4646S/N7125J/N2426/N125J/G-ASSJ |
| N88NJ | Learjet | 25-008 | Vee Neal Inc. Latrobe, Pa. | N645L/N1976S/N744W/VP-BDM/N744W/N648GA |
| N88TC | Learjet | 23-022 | 88TC Inc. New Iberia, La. | N103TC/N400CS/N428EJ |
| N88WP | Westwind-1123 | 151 | Hill Top Developers Inc. Bakersfield, Ca. | N1123E/4X-CJD |
| N89 | Sabre-40 | 282-89 | FAA, Oklahoma City, Ok. | |
| N89AE | Gulfstream 3 | 349 | National Express Co. Inc. NY. | |
| N89B | Citation | 550-0092 | Midland Ross Corp. Cleveland, Oh. | (N26643) |
| N89FJ | Falcon 10 | 81 | Smith-Kline Beckman, Philadelphia, Pa. | F-WZHA |
| N89MR | Jet Commander | 9 | Albatross Products, Wa. | N66EW/N9BY/N45JD/N459JD/CF-WIIL/N450JD |
| N89PP | HS 125/700A | NA0269 | Pogo Producing Co. Houston, Tx. | N125Y/G-5-15 |
| N90B | HS 125/700A | NA0283 | Midland Ross Corp. Cleveland, Oh. | N125AS/G-5-20 |
| N90BA | Citation | 500-0117 | Executive Charter Services Ltd. Watsonville, Ca. | N617CC |
| N90C | Sabre-75A | 380-46 | Tom O'Connor, Victoria, Tx. | (N50K)/N2125J |
| N90CF | Citation | 501-0184 | Peter Karagines/Orange County Food Service Co. Anaheim. | N67786 |
| N90CP | JetStar 2 | 5232 | Chesebrough Ponds, Inc. Greenwich, Ct. | N4046M |
| N90DH | Learjet | 24-117 | Dee Howard, San Antonio, Tx. | HZ-SMB/N16MJ/F-BRAL/N288VW |
| N90E | Learjet | 55-004 | Transcontinental Gas Pipeline Co. Houston, Tx. | |
| N90EC | Sabre-60 | 306-73 | Elliott Co Flight Dept., Latrobe, Pa. | N601MG/N7NR |
| N90FJ | Falcon 50 | 85 | | F-WZHO |
| N90GM | Sabre-75A | 380-27 | Grove Manufacturing Co. Shady Grove, Pa. | N6NG/N6NR/N10CN/N8NB /N8NR/N65787 |
| N90GS | Falcon 20F | 388 | Song Bird Ltd. Miami Beach, Fl. | N169F/F-WJMM |
| N90HM | Westwind-1123 | 170 | Howard McCormack, Oklahoma City, Ok. | N150HR/N112RC/N1123W |
| N90J | Learjet | 24-060 | Bankers Union Life Insurance, Englewood, Co. | N899WF |
| N90JD | Citation | 550-0315 | Deere & Co. Moline, Il. | N6889Z |
| N90JF | Falcon 20C | 45 | Jet Fleet Corp. Dallas, Tx. | N159FC/N147X/N876F/F-WMKI |
| N90LP | Learjet | 35A-236 | Waukesha Pearce Industries Inc. Plains, Ks. | N8537B/G-ZOOM |
| N90MD | Gulfstream 2 | 241 | J Ray McDermott & Co. Inc. New Orleans, La. | (N801GA)/(N6OTA) /N830GA |
| N90ME | JetStar-6 | 5057 | McGraw Edison Co. Wilmington, De. | N90U/N1007 |
| N90N | Sabre-60 | 306-12 | Natural Gas Pipeline Co. Houston, Tx. | N4722N |
| N90R | Sabre-60 | 306-36 | Winn Dixie Stores Inc. Jacksonville, Fl. | N18N/N918R/N4749N |
| N90Z | Citation | 550-0336 | International Paper Co. Mobile, Al. | N6830Z |

| Regis-tration | Type | C/N | Owner/Operator | Previous Identities |
|---|---|---|---|---|
| N90ZP | JetStar-731 | 21/5055 | Executive Air Charter Inc. Minneapolis, Mn. | N303H/N296AR/N9222R |
| N91B | Citation | 550-0194 | Scott & Fetzer Co. Lakewood, Oh. | N88723 |
| N91CH | Learjet | 35A-021 | ICH Corp. Louisville, Ky. | N101GP |
| N91DH | Falcon 10 | 108 | ACME Air Corp. Van Buren, Ar. | N11DH/N246FJ/F-BIPC/F-WZGF/HZ-AKI /F-WPUZ |
| N91ED | Learjet | 25D-255 | Edward J DeBartolo Corp. Youngstown, Oh. | N1ED/N1433B |
| N91FJ | Falcon 50 | 87 | Kellogg Co. Battle Creek, Mi. | F-WZHS |
| N91MH | Falcon 10 | 23 | Texas Independent Oil Co. Houston, Tx. | N310FJ/N73B/N115FJ/F-WLCY |
| N91MJ | Citation | 550-0101 | Southwestern Bell Telephone, Dallas, Tx. | (N2664U) |
| N91W | Learjet | 35A-194 | Liberty Exploration, Ok. | |
| N91Y | HS 125/700A | NA0311 | Island Creek Coal Co. Lexington, Ky. | G-5-15 |
| N92CC | Citation | 501-0026 | Skylane Farms Inc. Woodburn, Or. | N93B |
| N92CS | Learjet | 25D-292 | Shuetz Enterprises Ltd, Oakbrook, Il. | N92MJ/N1088C |
| N92FA | Citation | 500-0068 | H C W Corp. Midland, Tx. | N53MJ/PT-LAY/N568CM/N568CC |
| N92FJ | Falcon 50 | 88 | | F-WZHU |
| N92MH | Falcon 20C | 3 | Texas Independent Oil Co. Houston, Tx. | HB-VAV/VR-BCG/F-WMKG |
| N93BE | Jet Commander | 27 | Business Aircraft Corp. Atlanta, Ga. | N93B |
| N93BR | Learjet | 24D-231 | Jet Components Inc. Houston, Tx. | N37DH/N693LJ/I-CART/HB-VBU |
| N93C | Learjet | 35A-159 | Greyhound Leasng & Financial Corp. Phoenix, Az. | |
| N93SC | Jet Commander | 90 | Standard Container Co. Homerville, Co. | N1121E/N188WP |
| N93WD | Citation | 500-0220 | Wilson Industries Inc. Houston, Tx. | N522QJ |
| N94B | HS 125/600A | 6055 | Beckett/Interlake Steel Inc. Chicago, Il. | G-BDOP/G-5-19 |
| N94BD | HS 125/700A | NA0217 | Dillard Department Stores, Little Rock. Ar. | G-BFLG |
| N94DE | Citation | 500-0094 | Corporate Air Inc. Hartford, Ct. | N594CC |
| N94MC | Falcon 10 | 166 | Riverside Aviation/James McManus, Wilmington, De. | N232FJ/F-WZGS |
| N94ME | Citation | 550-0368 | Montgomery Elevator Co. Moline, Il. | (N12155) |
| N94RS | Learjet | 25XR-141 | Jetflight Inc. Dallas, Tx. | N424JP/N424JR/N52L |
| N95B | Jet Commander | 19 | Wean United Inc. Pittsburgh, Pa. | |
| N95BS | Learjet | 25B-180 | B S Stillwell, Tucson, Az. | VH-BLJ |
| N95CC | Citation | 550-0367 | | |
| N95JK | Jet Commander | 95 | Consolidated Airways Inc. Fort Wayne, In. | N200MZ/N200MP/N100CA /N210FE/N709Q/N6412/N5412 |
| N95RE | Citation | 501-0124 | Reliance Electric Co. Cleveland, Oh. | N2650N |
| N96AC | Learjet | 35A-224 | Caravelle Corp. White Plains, NY. | |
| N96BB | JetStar-6 | 5049 | Solar Sportsystems Inc. Buffalo, NY. | N96B/N1230R |
| N96CE | Learjet | 55-033 | US Fidelity & Guarantee, Baltimore, Md. | |
| N96DM | Learjet | 35A-186 | J David Co. | N590/N753GL |
| N96FJ | Falcon 50 | 106 | Thoroughbred Management Services, Waterford, Va. | F-WZHT |
| N96RE | Citation | 500-0331 | Reliance Electric Co. Cleveland, Oh. | N86RE/N331CC/(N5331J) |
| N96RS | Learjet | 25XR-175 | Jet Flight Inc. Portland, Or. | N462BA/N462B |
| N96TC | Citation | 501-0125 | Tejas Warehousing Services, Laredo, Tx. | N45MC/(N501DP)/N2651Y |
| N96TD | Citation | 501-0140 | Teledyne Inc. Latrobe, Pa. | (N99TD)/(N2651R) |
| N97KR | BAC 1-11/201 | 005 | Kenny Rogers, Beverley Hills, Ca. | N3756F/VR-CAQ/XB-MUO/TP-0201 /XB-MUO/N734EB/G-ASJA |
| N97MC | Falcon 10 | 82 | Canton Co. Baltimore, Md. | N168FJ/F-WPXE |
| N97MJ | Learjet | 23-093 | Turbo-Porsche Inc. Ft. Lauderdale, Fl. | N101AD/N101AR/N486G/N38JD /N12TA/N416LJ/N3350/N416LJ |
| N97RE | Sabre-65 | 465-32 | Reliance Electric Co. Cleveland, Oh. | |
| N97RS | Learjet | 25XR-162 | Ray Stern/Jet Flight Inc. Dallas, Tx. | N663JB/N661MP/N62ZS |
| N97S | Citation | 550-0238 | Sun Oil Co. Philadelphia, Pa. | N67999 |
| N98DM | Citation | 500-0296 | Stephen Peskoff, Toledo, Oh. | (N5296J) |
| N98FJ | Falcon 50 | 93 | | F-WZHB |
| N98G | Gulfstream 2 | 24 | Weyerhauser Co. Gig Harbor, Wa. | N4S/N536CS |
| N98GC | Citation | 550-0244 | Grant Corp. Houston, Tx. | N6860C |
| N98KT | Caravelle 6R | 102 | E & H Associates Inc. Vero Beach, Ca. | N2296N/N555SL/PH-TRU/N1017U |
| N98MD | JetStar-6 | 5048 | Waynco, Las Vegas, Nv. | N98KR/N4ONC/N4ON/N4N |
| N98ME | Citation | 501-0191 | Moran Energy Inc. Houston, Tx. | N6780Y |
| N98R | Falcon 20F | 428 | R J Reynolds Co. Winston Salem, NC. | N426F/F-WMKI |
| N98RS | Learjet | 25XR-148 | Stern Investment Corp. Dallas, Tx. | N336WR/N58GL |
| N99AA | Sabre-60 | 306-53 | Consumers Power Inc. Jackson, Mi. | N957R/N7573N |
| N99BC | Citation | 500-0190 | Buckeye Cellulose Corp. Perry, Fl. | N190CC |
| N99DM | Learjet | 24-114 | Associates Leasing Inc. Chicago, Il. | N999M/N443LJ |
| N99E | JetStar-2 | 5216 | Transcontinental Gas Pipeline Co. Houston, Tx. | N95BA/N5542L |
| N99FJ | Falcon 50 | 94 | | F-WZHC |
| N99GA | Gulfstream 2 | 99 | Greyhound Armour & Co. Phoenix, Az. | N851GA |
| N99GC | Citation | 501-0012 | Grant Corp. Houston, Tx. | N99XY/N999RB/N190K/N36858 |
| N99GS | Jet Commander | 31 | Waggoner Aircraft Inc. Bethany, Ok. | N399D |

| Registration | Type | C/N | Owner/Operator | Previous Identities |
|---|---|---|---|---|
| N99HB | MS 760 Paris 2B | 102 | Bodmer Financing Co. Wilmington, De. | HB-VEU/N760E/PH-MSR/F-BJZO |
| N99KR | DH 125/3A-R | 25149 | Northrop University, Inglewood, Ca. | N99GC/N99SC/N1125E/G-AVRJ |
| N99KW | Citation | 550-0351 | Florida Wings Inc. Fort Lauderdale, Fl. | |
| N99ME | Learjet | 35A-204 | Moran Energy Inc, Wichita Falls, Tx. | N87MJ/D-COSY/N1466B |
| N99S | Sabre-65 | 465-64 | Sun Co. Inc. Philadelphia, Pa. | |
| N99TC | Learjet | 23-098 | National Leasing Corp. Pittsburgh, Pa. | N711AE/N711/N2DD/N11111/N112T |
| N99VA | Learjet | 35A-185 | Combs-Gates Denver Inc. | N99ME |
| N99WB | Citation | 500-0346 | B Battlestein, Houston, Tx. | N4234K/D-IJON/N5346J |
| N99WH | Westwind-1124 | 284 | Mar Flite Ltd, Portland, Or. | 4X-COD |
| N99XZ | Learjet | 25C-087 | R E Hibbert, Houston, Tx. | N777LF/N723LF |
| N100A | Gulfstream 2 | 89 | Exxon Corp. Newark, NJ. | N882GA |
| N100AD | Citation | 500-0226 | Joseph Spruit/Autodie Corp. Grand Rapids, Mi. | JA8418/N5226J |
| N100AG | Westwind Two | 346 | | 4X-CTN |
| N100AK | Westwind-Two | 295 | The Bergt Co. Anchorage, Ak. | N295WW/4X-COO |
| N100AQ | Citation | 500-0195 | Amvest Corp. Charlottesville, Va. | N100AC/N14JA |
| N100BG | Falcon 10 | 64 | Gelco Corp. Minneapolis, Mn. | N148FJ/F-WLCT |
| N100BX | Citation | 500-0366 | The Bendix Corp. Arlington, Va. | N2887A |
| N100CC | NAL 1-11/401 | 2/059 | Trinity Jet/Janmar Aviation Corp. Dover, De. | N5019/N112NA/N5019 |
| N100CE | Sabre-60 | 306-128 | Clark Equipment Co. South Bend, In. | N80CR/N2143J |
| N100CJ | Citation | 550-0167 | Cameron Iron Works, Houston, Tx. | N88737 |
| N100DE | Diamond One | A016SA | | N133RC |
| N100DL | Learjet | 24B-201 | Dan Lasater, Washington, D.C. | C-GTFA/D-CDDD/D-IDDD/N273GL/N3871J |
| N100EP | Learjet | 35A-150 | Avion Inc. Houston, Tx. | |
| N100FJ | Falcon 100 | 194 | Falcon Jet Corp. Teterboro, NJ. | N260FJ/F-WZGZ |
| N100FL | Sabre-60 | 306-46 | State of Florida, Tallahassee. | N3600X/N4764N |
| N100FS | Sabre-40 | 282-38 | Flight Systems Inc. Ca. | N299LR/N2997/N6393C |
| N100GL | JetStar-731 | 57/5132 | Great Lakes Carbon Corp. NY. | N1620N/N1620/N7977S |
| N100GN | Gulfstream 3 | 312 | Gannett Inc. NY. | N304GA |
| N100GP | Learjet | 24-106 | Geo Priester, Wheeling, Il. | N969J/N888NS |
| N100HB | Citation | 550-0058 | Heileman Brewing Co. Inc. La Crosse, Wi. | N71CJ/N5348J |
| N100HF | DH 125/731 | NA717 | Hardees Food Systems Inc. Rocky Mount, NC. | N162D/N162A/G-AWXB/G-5-18 |
| N100HP | Citation | 500-0280 | Don Love Aircraft Sales, Wichita, Ks. | N280CC/(N5280J) |
| N100K | Learjet | 35A-170 | Fred Shaulis, Friedens, Pa. | |
| N100KK | Learjet | 24B-219 | Herbert Kohler Jr. Kohler, Wi. | N711CE/N658AT |
| N100LR | DH 125/400A | NA732 | Leighton & Rosenthal, Cleveland, Oh. | N21ES/N44CN/N73JH/N500AG/G-AXOA |
| N100P | Gulfstream 3 | 301 | National Distillers & Chemical Corp. N.Y. | |
| N100PM | Gulfstream 2 | 114 | Philip Morris Inc. Richmond, Va. | N818GA |
| N100RA | Learjet | 24-180 | Rynes Aviation Inc. Melrose Park, Il. | N802JA/N556RB |
| N100SN | Citation | 501-0197 | A D Watson, Fort Lauderdale, Fl. | N6781Z |
| N100SQ | Learjet | 24-113 | Brandis Aircraft, Springfield, Il. (rebuild) | N204Y |
| N100SR | Jet Commander A | 127 | Steven Rayman, Big Rock, Il. | N20GB/N209RR/N34HD/N27X/N6B |
| N100SV | Citation | 501-0073 | Robert Lammerts, Oklahoma City, Ok. | N3117M |
| N100TR | Jet Commander | 76 | Environmental Equipment Corp. San Leandro, Ca. | N100DR/N100DG/CF-VVX /N1121C |
| N100VQ | Learjet | 24-140 | The Vollrath Co. Sheboygan, Wi. | N100VC/N252M/N593KR/N663LJ/N663L /N663LJ |
| N100VV | Citation | 550-0143 | E L Cox, Athens, Tx. | N2649D |
| N100WM | Jet Commander | 73 | Caruth C. Byrd Enterprises Inc. Dallas, Tx. | N100W/N98S/N98SA |
| N100X | Learjet | 23-035 | Conwood Corp. Memphis, Tn. | |
| N100Y | HS 125/700A | NA0259 | Purolator Inc. Rahway, NJ. | N125AH/G-5-12 |
| N101AR | Learjet | 36-008 | AMCA Resources, Ky. | N84MJ/VR-BJO/VR-BJD/N20JA |
| N101AW | JetStar-8 | 5103 | Advance World Services Corp. | N176BN/N672M/N23M |
| N101BG | Learjet | 35A-106 | National Tire Wholesalers, Woodbridge, Va. | |
| N101BX | Citation | 550-0157 | Bendix Corp. Arlington, Va. | N550K/N6799T |
| N101DB | Learjet | 23-070 | Massanutten Village Inc. McGaheysville, Va. | N111CT/N197GL/N1976L CF-ARE |
| N101FJ | Falcon 50 | 108 | | F-WZHU |
| N101HB | Learjet | 35A-152 | First Hawaiian Bank, Honolulu, Hi. | |
| N101HF | Citation | 500-0203 | Hardees Food Systems, Rocky Mountain, NC. | (N724CC)/N95DR |
| N101HK | Learjet | 35A-440 | H J Kalikow Development Co. NYC. | |
| N101KK | Citation | 500-0219 | Kohler Co. Kohler, Wi. | N25CS/N219CC |
| N101LB | Jet Commander | 8 | Liberty Baptist College Inc. Lynchburg, Va. | N749MP/N749MC/N31CF /N157JF |
| N101ME | Sabre-75A | 380-70 | American Continental Corp. Phoenix, Az. | (N15ME)/(N13ME) |
| N101NK | Jet Commander-B | 148 | John Morrell & Co. Chicago, Il. | N200DF/N200DE/N8536/N9048M/4X-CPL |
| N101PG | Learjet | 35A-228 | Geosurvey International Inc. Aurora, Co. | |

53

| Regis-tration | Type | C/N | Owner/Operator | Previous Identities |
|---|---|---|---|---|
| N101PP | Learjet | 23-085 | Air Continental, Elyria, Oh. | N385J/N825LJ |
| N101RL | Citation | 551-0058 | GECC/Robert P Lammerts. | N68027 |
| N101SV | Westwind-1124 | 246 | Super Valu Stores Inc. Hopkins, Mn. | 4X-CMR |
| N101US | Learjet | 24F-352 | U.S. Soil Conditioning, Salida, Co. | |
| N101VS | Learjet | 24B-218 | Advanced Technology Center, Buffalo, NY. | N682LJ |
| N102C | Learjet | 24E-343 | S A Camp Pump Co. Shafter, Ca. | N102B |
| N102FJ | Falcon 50 | 100 | | F-WZHN |
| N102GP | Learjet | 35A-105 | Allstate Insurance Co. Northbrook, Il. | N102GH/N720GH |
| N102HS | Gulfstream 2 | 112 | Hensley-Schmidt International Inc. Atlanta, Ga. | N102ML/N816GA |
| N102U | Westwind-1124 | 230 | B A Leasing Corp. SFO, Ca | XC-HCP/N4995N/4X-CMB |
| N103C | Learjet | 35A-273 | Adolph Coors Co. Vero Beach, Ca. | N35FH |
| N103F | HFB 320 | 1023 | McCollum Aviation Inc. Danville, Il. | N320AF/N1320U/N320J/D-CARI |
| N103FJ | Falcon 50 | 102 | | F-WZHO |
| N103GP | Learjet | 35A-148 | Allstate Insurance Co. Northbrook, Il. | N103GH |
| N103PJ | Falcon 10 | 148 | Professional Jet Leasing/General Dynamics. | N213FJ/F-WZGT |
| N103TC | Learjet | 24B-213 | PFC FAC of NY Inc. Chicago, Il. | N43KC/N999RA/N886WC/N986WC/N555MH |
| N103WV | Citation | 500-0028 | Willamette Valley Co. Eugene, Or. | N10DG/N528CC |
| N104CF | Citation | 501-0149 | Macomb Aviation Associates, Detroit, Mi. | (N1772E) |
| N104FJ | Falcon 50 | 103 | | F-WZHO |
| N104RS | Westwind-1124 | 273 | Tandy Corp. Fort Worth, Tx. | 4X-CNS |
| N105BJ | Learjet | 23-092 | Don Tidwell Aircraft Sales, Haleyville, Al. | N422JR/N415LJ |
| N105CF | Citation | 501-0153 | Macomb Aviation Associates, Detroit, Mi. | (N1930E) |
| N105FJ | Falcon 50 | 104 | Shearson, Loeb & Rhoades Inc. NYC. | F-WZHR |
| N105G | JetStar 2 | 5223 | Gulf Oil Corp. Pittsburgh, Pa. | N5549L |
| N105RK | B 727-51 | 19122 | Thunderbird Airways, Houston, Tx. | N476US |
| N105TW | Citation | 501-0198 | Truck World Inc/TWA Leasing, Denver, Co. | (N602CC)/N67822 |
| N105Y | Gulfstream 2 | 56 | Oxy Petroleum Inc. SFO, Ca. | N20XY/N10XY |
| N106CA | Learjet | 24-138 | Kay E Cohlmia, Dallas, Tx. | N45JF/N575G/N808D/N808DP/N37P |
| N106FJ | Falcon 50 | 105 | Champion International Corp. Stamford, Ct. | F-WZHS |
| N106G | JetStar 2 | 5217 | Gulf Oil Corp. Pittsburgh, Pa. | N5543L |
| N106WT | Westwind Two | 351 | Shearson American Express, NY. | 4X-CTS |
| N107A | Gulfstream 2 | 53 | ARAMCO, Jeddah, Saudi Arabia | |
| N107BB | Citation | 551-0021 | Beall Bros. Inc. Jacksonville, Tx. | N26639 |
| N107FJ | Falcon 50 | 112 | | F-WZHA |
| N107G | JetStar 2 | 5219 | Gulf Oil Corp. Pittsburgh, Pa. | N5545L |
| N107GL | Learjet | 24D-324 | Raymond Town/American Industries Inc. Portland, Or. | |
| N107GM | JetStar 2 | 5206 | General Mills Inc. Minneapolis, Mn. | N5532L |
| N107JM | Learjet | 35A-249 | HLM Enterprises, Irvine, Ca. | |
| N107SC | Citation | 500-0107 | Sundstrand Corp. Rockford, Il. | N107CC/(N607CC) |
| N107T | Citation | 550-0163 | Trunkline Gas Co. Houston, Tx. | N8881N |
| N108BN | B 707-138B | 18740 | TAG International, Europe-Middle East | VH-EBM |
| N108FJ | Falcon 50 | 113 | | F-WZHB |
| N108GM | Westwind-1124 | 221 | General Mills Inc. Minneapolis, Mn. | 4X-CLS |
| N108MC | Citation | 500-0322 | Gulf Coast Building & Supply, Mobile, Al. | N1AP/N5322J |
| N108NC | Falcon 20C | 168 | Nalco Chemical Co. Oak Brook, Il. | N100KW/N4369F/F-WLCX |
| N108PA | Learjet | 25B-195 | Northeast Jet Co. Allentown, Pa. | OB-M-1004 |
| N108TW | Learjet | 23-027 | | F-GAPY/HB-VES/JY-AEI/N430EJ |
| N109AL | Citation | 500-0037 | R Van Irvine, Casper, Wy. | N537CC |
| N109AP | Citation | 500-0046 | API Inc. St. Paul, Mn. | N50SL/N50SK/N546CC |
| N109FJ | Falcon 50 | 109 | | F-WZHV |
| N109G | HS 125/700A | NA0322 | Gulf Oil Corp. Pittsburgh, Pa. | |
| N109JC | Citation | 550-0099 | John Cassidy, Stroud, Ok. | N2664L |
| N109JM | HS 125/700A | NA0272 | JMAC Inc. Columbus, Oh. | N89PP/G-5-17 |
| N109JR | Learjet | 35A-101 | Ruan Cab Co. Des Moines, Ia. | N40149 |
| N109SJ | Learjet | 25D-269 | Grayback Leasing Corp. Grants Pass, Or. | |
| N110AN | JetStar-731 | 58/5092 | Daniel Industries Inc. Houston, Tx. | N901H/N372H/N9248R |
| N110CE | Falcon 20C | 7 | Clark Enterprises Inc. Bethesda, Md. | N12GH/N20GH/N777FA/CF-GWI/N740L N607S/N807F/F-WMKX |
| N110CG | Falcon 10 | 45 | Inland Container Corp. Minneapolis, Mn. | N120HC/N131FJ/F-WJML |
| N110FS | Sabre-40 | 282-58 | Flight Systems Inc. Newport Beach, Ca. | N11OG/N750RV |
| N110KS | Challenger | 1006 | Kalair USA Corp. NY. | C-GCSN |
| N110M | Falcon 10 | 34 | Olan Mills Inc. Chatanooga, Tn. | N124FJ/F-WLCS |
| N110MN | JetStar-731 | 11/5149 | Morton Norwich Products Inc. Chicago, Il. | N2222R/N524AC/N1570P /N157JF/N711Z/N5513L |
| N110TA | BAC 1-11/520 | 236 | TigerAir Inc. Los Angeles, Ca. | PP-SDS |
| N110TP | Citation | 501-0155 | Towner Petroleum/Gawain Associates, Hartford, Ct. | N110TV/(N108CT) /N2617B |
| N111AC | Gulfstream 2 | 74 | Worldwide Church of God, Pasadena, Ca. | N845GA |

| Regis-tration | Type | C/N | Owner/Operator | Previous Identities |
|---|---|---|---|---|
| N111AG | Westwind-1124 | 199 | Knickerbocker Corp. Houston, Tx. | N1124P/4X-CKW |
| N111AK | B 727-2L4 | 21010 | Adnan Khashoggi-Triad/American Capital Aviation. | |
| N111AM | Citation | 500-0135 | Allen Morrow, Harveys Lake, Pa. | N975EE/N902T/N900T/N135BC/N135CC |
| N111BP | Falcon 20C | 111 | Iowa Beef processors Inc. Sergeant Bluff, Ia. | N111AM/N111AC/N990F /F-WMKI |
| N111DC | HFB 320 | 1030 | Rancho del Cierva Estates Inc. Wilmington, De. | (N247GW)/D-CATE |
| N111EA | Sabre-40 | 282-27 | Wallace Companies Inc. Birmingham, Al. | N129GB/N129GP/N720R/N6381C |
| N111EK | B 727-77 | 19253 | Mark 111 Leasing Co Reno, Nv. | N110AC/VH-RMR |
| N111FJ | Falcon 50 | 115 | | F-WZHC |
| N111G | Challenger | 1025 | GTE Service Corp. Stamford, Ct. | N2636N/C-GLXF |
| N111GL | Learjet | 35A-084 | Gulf Life Insurance Co. Jacksonville, Fl. | |
| N111GS | BAC 1-11/422 | 126 | Geo Source, Houston, Tx. | N341TC/N18813/(N80GM)/N18813/PP-SRU |
| N111GU | JetStar-731 | 18/5114 | Gulf United Corp. Jacksonville, Fl. | N94K/N930M/N930MT/N7959S |
| N111JD | Learjet | 23-006 | Tampo Manufacturing Co. Inc. San Antonio, Tx. | N23CH/N578LJ/N505PF |
| N111KK | Learjet | 35A-425 | Kohler Co. Wi. | |
| N111M | Falcon 20C | 10 | Standard Fittings Co. Opelousas, La. | N81OF/F-WMKK |
| N111MF | B 707-321B | 18338 | Wistair Internationial Inc. Wilmington, De. | N763W/N763PA |
| N111MU | Citation | 500-0262 | Mustang Gas Products Co. Oklahoma City. Ok. | N44JF/N5262J |
| N111NF | Westwind-1123 | 168 | J E F Enterprises Inc. Houston, Tx. | N66SM/N973EJ/4X-CJR |
| N111QP | Citation Eagle | 500-0019 | Sale, High Point, NC. | N256WN/N11DQ/N11DH/N519CC/USCG519/N519CC |
| N111RB | DH 125/731 | NA734 | Reading & Bates Offshore Drilling, Tulsa, Ok. | N125J/G-AXOC |
| N111RF | Learjet | 35A-217 | R C Fisher, West Palm Beach, Fl. | |
| N111SF | Learjet | 25B-189 | Savannah Foods & Industries Inc. Ga. | |
| N111TD | Jet Commander | 11 | Tower Pipe & Steel Inc. Atlanta, Ga. | N1172L/N1172Z |
| N111TT | Learjet | 24D-301 | MJI, Lincoln, Ne. | N137GL |
| N111VW | Sabre-75A | 380-69 | Vorelco Inc. Englewood Cliffs, NJ. | N2542E |
| N111WW | Falcon 10 | 165 | R H Fulton, Lubbock, Tx. | N229FJ/F-WZGR |
| N111XB | Sabre-40A | 282-101 | Geneva International Ltd. Arlington, Va. | N1BX/N7596N |
| N111XL | Jet Commander | 34 | Jack Weiss, Boca Raton, Fl. | N13ORC/N777MH/N329HN/N102SY/N102SV /N1210G/N1210 |
| N111Y | Sabre-80A | 380-17 | Ingram Industries, Nashville, Tn. | N15RF/N7OTF/5N-AMM/N8ORS/N339K /N65768 |
| N111YL | Jet Commander | 42 | Jetwind Inc. Oklahoma City. Ok. | N111Y/N6361C/N3DL/N599KC/N6511V |
| N112AK | DC 9-15 | 47151 | Adnan Khashoggi-Triad/American Capital Aviation. | N228Z |
| N112CT | Learjet | 25B-090 | Certain-teed Products Corp. Valley Forge, Pa. | N265GL |
| N112EL | Learjet | 35A-078 | GECC, Stanford, Ct. | N440JB/N711SD/N711SW/N95BH/N95BA |
| N112FJ | Falcon 50 | 116 | | F-WZHD |
| N112KH | Sabre-75A | 380-34 | Hotelerama Association Inc. Teterboro, NJ. | N6LG/N114JK |
| N112M | DH 125/400A | NA736 | Montex Drilling Co. Ft. Worth, Tx. | N30PP/N30PR/G-AXOD |
| N112MC | Citation | 501-0035 | Wayne Newton, Bend, Or. | N500WN/(N800M)/N36915 |
| N112MR | Westwind-1124 | 174 | IMCO Services, Tomball, Tx. | N1123X |
| N113AK | Learjet | 25-020 | Mark 111 Leasing Co. Reno, Nv. | (N90TC)/N30TT/N215Z/N941GA |
| N113FJ | Falcon 50 | 118 | | F-WZHF |
| N113JS | Learjet | 24F-356 | S & G Helicopter Co. Inc. Castleton, NY. | N677SW |
| N113MR | Jet Commander-B | 126 | B M Rankin, Dallas, Tx. | N315SA/N4983E/4X-COM |
| N113RF | Learjet | 25B-143 | R C Fisher, West Palm Beach, Fl. | N111RF/(N33VF)/N96VF |
| N114B | DH 125/731 | NA727 | Blount Inc. Montgomery, Al. | N814M/G-AXDS |
| N114CC | Learjet | 25C-126 | W M Keck Jr. Reno, Nv. | N12WK |
| N114EL | Citation | 550-0292 | GECC/Pacific Telephone & Telegraph Co. | N6887X |
| N114FJ | Falcon 50 | 119 | | F-WZHN |
| N114HC | Gulfstream 2 | 92 | Southern Natural Service Co. Inc. Birmingham, Al. | N300U/N300L/N884GA |
| N114M | BAC 1-11/422 | 119 | Montex Drilling, Fort Worth, Tx. | N18814/PP-SRT |
| N115EL | Learjet | 55-035 | GECC/Aircraft Services Corp. Wilton, Ct. | |
| N115FJ | Falcon 50 | 121 | | F-WZHO |
| N115K | Citation | 500-0379 | First Chicago Leasing Inc. Il/Kaiserair Inc. | N2131A |
| N115MR | JetStar-8 | 5111 | McMoran Exploration Co. Metairie, La. | N11SX/N5111H/N7956S |
| N115RS | HS 125/700A | 7067 | FEDEX, Memphis, Tn. | N9113J/HZ-DA1 |
| N116EL | Learjet | 35A-173 | Flight International Inc. Atlanta, Ga. | N100GU/(HZ-NCI)/N750GL /HZ-MIB/N750GL |
| N116K | Citation | 550-0149 | Kaiser Aluminium, Oakland, Ca. | |
| N116KX | Jet Commander | 87 | Kirby Exploration Co. Houston, Tx. | N430DC/N430PC/N400PC/N920GP/N920G |
| N116MC | Jet Commander | 86 | Jetaway Management Inc. Bethany, Ok. | N13TV/N2JW/N1100M |
| N117CH | Learjet | 35-045 | 117CH Partners. Houston, Tx. | N45MJ/XA-HOS/N999M/N99786/N35HB/HB-VEN /N1461B |
| N117EL | Learjet | 55-061 | GECC, Wilton, Ct. | |
| N117EM | BH 125/F600A | 6046 | Intemedics, Houston, Tx. | N402HR/(N401HR)/N91HR/N43BH |
| N117FJ | Learjet | 35A-417 | First Jersey Securities, NYC. | N934GL |

| Regis-tration | Type | C/N | Owner/Operator | Previous Identities |
|---|---|---|---|---|
| N117JJ | Gulfstream 2 | 163 | Gavilan Corp. Dover, De. | PJ-ABA/(YV-60CP)/N17581 |
| N117K | Learjet | 24D-272 | Koch Industries Inc. Wichita, Ks. | N51GL |
| N117MR | NAL 111/401 | 5/065 | McMoran Properties Inc. Metairie, La. | N825AO/N825AC/N76GW/N5025 |
| | | | | /N111NA/N5025 |
| N118AF | Westwind-1123 | 177 | Prestige Aviation Inc. Indianapolis, In. | N777CJ/N11WC/N1123U/4X-CKA |
| N118B | JetStar-6 | 5091 | Four Star International Inc. Las Vegas, Nv. | N107GH/N107G/N9247R |
| N118K | Learjet | 35A-067 | Kaiser Industries Corp. Oakland, Ca. | |
| N118R | Falcon 20F | 385 | R J Reynolds Tobacco Co. Winston Salem, NC. | N139F/F-WJMJ |
| N118SE | Learjet | 25B-118 | Southland Executive Charter Inc. Florence, Ca. | N601J/OO-LFZ |
| N119BA | Learjet | 23-084 | Beckair Company Inc. Elkhart, In. | N101JR/N788DR |
| N119CC | BH 125/731 | NA749 | Wm. Keck, Reno, Nv. | N81T/N45BH/G-AXYH |
| N119EL | Citation | 650-0013 | | |
| N119R | Gulfstream 2 | 243 | R J Reynolds Industries, Winston Salem, NC. | |
| N120AR | JetStar-8 | 5089 | ASARCO/Western Leasing Co. Van Nuys, Ca. | N324K/N9245R |
| N120CG | Falcon 20F | 384 | Inland Container Corp. Indianapolis. | N384JK/OO-PSD/F-WROU |
| N120EL | Learjet | 55-067 | | |
| N120MB | Learjet | 35A-307 | Milton Bradley Co. Springfield, Mo. | N5016 |
| N120TA | NAL 1-11/401 | 14/056 | Congoleum Aviation Inc. Portsmouth, NH. | N5016 |
| N120YB | Sabre-75A | 380-12 | Bemis Co. Inc. Minneapolis, Mn. | D-CLAN/N75SL/D-CLAN/HB-VEC/N335K |
| | | | | /N65758 |
| N121AJ | Jet Commander | 57 | American Jet Industries Inc. Burbank, Ca. | N77OWL/N6544V |
| N121AM | Falcon 20E | 310 | IBM World Trade Asia Corp. Paris. | (N370ME)/N4450F/F-WMKH |
| N121C | Citation | 550-0209 | Charles Muench, Sylva, NC. | N67997 |
| N121CG | Citation | 550-0354 | Columbia Gas System Service Co. Columbus, Oh. | |
| N121EU | Falcon 20E | 297 | IBM World Trade Asia Corp. | (N370EU)/N4443F/F-WMKF |
| N121JW | Citation | 501-0006 | Jackson B Wolff, Sandusky, Oh. | N358CC/(N5358J) |
| N121PG | Jet Commander | 45 | Perry Gas Co. Inc. Odessa, Tx. | N340ER/N340DR/N920R |
| N122CG | Citation | 550-0355 | Columbia Gas System Service Co. Columbus, Oh. | |
| N122DJ | Gulfstream 2 | 6 | Dow Jones & Co. N.Y. | N430R/N834GA |
| N122EH | Sabre-60 | 306-57 | United Technologies Corp. E. Hartford, | N22EH/N53G/N7NR/N937R |
| | | | | /N7577N |
| N122JB | Jet Commander | 133 | Jet Wind Inc. Oklahoma City, Ok. | N161X/N666JM/N133JC/N56AZ/N56AG |
| | | | | /N1172Z/N5041E |
| N122M | Learjet | 23-065A | Fred Maxwell, Kilgore, Tx. | N1GZ/(N28BR)/(N28BP)/N3880 |
| N122RW | Learjet | 24D-321 | J B Hunt, Lowell, Ar. | N1OWF |
| N122TY | Challenger | 1035 | Tyco Laboratories, Exeter, NH. | C-GLYA |
| N123AC | DH 125/3A | 25122 | Perpetual Corp. Houston, Tx. | N255CB/N555CB/N12225/G-AVAF |
| N123CC | Learjet | 24D-268 | Circus Circus Hotels Inc. Las Vegas, Nv. | N111WW/N53GL |
| N123CG | Learjet | 25D-270 | TAG Services Inc. Savannah, Ga. | N842GL |
| N123DR | Westwind-1123 | 158 | Fick Foundary Co. Dallas, Tx. | N1123G |
| N123EB | Citation | 501-0020 | Darling Bolt Co. Warren, Mi. | N32JJ/N36873 |
| N123FG | Citation | 501-0156 | The Grupe Co. Stockton, Ca. | N26517 |
| N123H | BAC 1-11/414 | 163 | Hilton Hotels, Los Angeles, Ca. | D-AILY |
| N123HP | Citation | 501-0204 | Muncoco Co. El Dorado, Ar. | N6784L |
| N123RE | Falcon 20C | 150 | Retlaw Jet Charter, Glendale, Ca. | N679RE/N777XX/N8227V/(N95591) |
| | | | | /HB-VBO/F-WMKH |
| N123SF | Learjet | 25B-088 | Air Pegasus Inc. Los Angeles, Ca. | N88GO/N88GC |
| N124AR | HS 125/700A | NA0254 | ARCO, Dallas, Tx. | N125TR/N125AM/(G-BHKF)/G-5-13 |
| N124BN | Gulfstream 2 | 39 | Burlington Northern Inc. St. Paul, Mn. | N401HR/N8000/N800 |
| N124EZ | Learjet | 24E-347 | Aerocouncil Inc/Berkeley Controls Inc. Irvine, Ca. | N724GL |
| N124GS | BH 125/F600A | 6026 | Geosource Inc. Houston, Tx. | G-5-16/N37BH |
| N124KC | Citation | 501-0319 | | |
| N124MC | Learjet | 35A-453 | Air Charter Funding Inc. Long Beach, Ca. | |
| N124PA | Westwind-1124 | 244 | Presidential Airways, N. Philadelphia, Pa. | 4X-CMP |
| N124TY | Westwind-1124 | 223 | BT Equipment Leasing Inc. New York/Tyco Laboratories. | N1124P/4X-CLU |
| N124WK | Westwind-1124 | 291 | Kilroy Oil Corp. Houston, Tx. | 4X-COK |
| N124WW | Westwind-1124 | 203 | Omni/Alberta Energy | N1124G/4X-CLA |
| N125AR | BH 125/731 | NA745 | ARCO, Burbank, Ca. | N41BH/G-AXYE |
| N125AW | DH 125/1A | 25057 | American Way Service Corp. Southfield, Mi. | N188K/G-ATIL |
| N125AX | Learjet | 35A-415 | Amarex Inc/Fidelity Bank, Oklahoma City, Ok. | |
| N125BA | HS 125/700A | NA0316 | British Aerospace Inc. Washington DC. | N7OOPP/G-5-15 |
| N125CG | HS 125/700A | NA0289 | Columbia Gas Systems, Columbus, Oh. | N125AJ/G-5-17 |
| N125DH | DH 125/731 | NA739 | Burns Petroleum, Wichita Falls, Tx. | G-AXTR |
| N125E | DH 125/1A-522 | 25110 | Erasmus Inc. Houston, Tx. | N3125B/G-ATZE/G-5-11 |
| N125EH | BH 125/400A | NA747 | Joe Jet Inc. New York. | N43BH/G-AXYF |
| N125EM | Falcon 10 | 53 | U S Electrical Motors, Ct. | N810US/N8100E/N139FJ/F-WLCS |
| N125F | DH 125/3A-RA | 25151 | J M Foster Co. Gary, In. | G-AVTY |

56

| Registration | Type | C/N | Owner/Operator | Previous Identities |
|---|---|---|---|---|
| N125GP | HS 125/700A | NA0215 | The Garrett Corp. Los Angeles, Ca. | N54555/G-BFLF |
| N125GS | BH 125/F600A | 6040 | Geosource Inc. Houston, Tx. | N4224Y/C-GJCM/N41BH |
| N125HD | DH 125/731 | 25051 | Quantum Corp. Miami Beach, Fl. | N9300C/N9300/G-ATGU |
| N125JW | HS 125/400A | NA743 | Carl Johnson, Addison, Tx. | TP-108/TP-0206/XC-GOB/N9138/G-AXTV |
| N125KC | HS 125/731 | 25249 | K C Aviation, Dallas, Tx. | N107AW/N72HA/N72HT/N51993/G-AZAF/G-5-16 |
| N125MC | Sabre-60 | 306-10 | Musket Corp. Oklahoma City, Ok. | N19CM/N9001V/N9000V/N3OW/N4720N |
| N125N | Sabre-75 | 370-3 | Natural Gas Pipeline Co. Chicago, Il. | N7ONR/N7586N |
| N125PP | BH 125/400A | NA769 | Pay N Pak Stores Inc. Seattle, Wa. | N972D/N872D/N66BH |
| N125TA | HS 125/700A | NA0274 | TigerAir Inc. Los Angeles, Ca. | N125BA/(N125AB)/G-5-11 |
| N126AR | HS 125/700A | NA0291 | ARCO, Dallas, Tx. | N125BC/G-5-19 |
| N126HC | Falcon 20C | 148 | Standard Oil Co. of California, San Francisco. | N12OHC/N4358F /F-WMKG |
| N126JM | Falcon 20C | 28 | Mid Region Petroleum Inc. Eugene, Or. | (N28ORC)/N5OCA/YV-78CP /(JY-AEJ)/N573EJ/N1OWA/N367EJ/N848F/F-WMKG |
| N127DM | Learjet | 24-169 | Air Unlimited Inc/Robert Wood, Opa Locka, Fl. | (N127DN)/N9033X/D-ICAR |
| N127K | Learjet | 35A-447 | Kamyr Inc. Glen Falls, NY. | |
| N127LJ | Learjet | 24-127 | R J Kosi, Los Angeles, Ca. | (N127HG)/N111LJ/N654LD/N654JC/N654LJ |
| N127MW | HFB 320 | 1027 | Western Airmotive Co. Inc. Oakland, Ca. | N905MW/D-CITO/I-TALC/D-CASO |
| N127SC | Citation | 550-0115 | Sundstrand Corp. Rockford, Il. | N2745L |
| N127V | Gulfstream 2 | 130 | El Paso Natural Gas, Tx. | N872GA |
| N128DM | Learjet | 25-017 | Aries Aviation Inc. Dallas, Tx. | N55WJ/N666WL/N16JP/N101WR/N720AS |
| N128GA | BAC 1-11/401 | 058 | Gulfstream American Corp. Van Nuys, Ca. | N128TA/N711ST/N5018 |
| N129DM | Learjet | 24B-187 | Donald L McCoy, Dallas, Tx. | N5WJ/F-GAJD/ZS-SGH |
| N129GP | Sabre-65 | 465-50 | Singer Co. Flight Simulation Div. Binghampton, NY. | N2570E |
| N129K | Jet Commander | 70 | Oklahoma Gas & Electric Co. Bethany, Ok. | N1194Z |
| N130A | Gulfstream 3 | 322 | American Can Co. NY. | |
| N130B | Falcon 10 | 28 | American Can Co. N.Y. | N119FJ/F-WJML |
| N130MW | HFB 320 | 1033 | Air National Sales, Carmel, Ca. | N132MW/PH-HFB/D-CERI |
| N130TC | Citation | 550-0310 | Winters National Leasing Corp. Dayton, Oh. | N68887 |
| N131CA | Learjet | 24D-277 | Walter E Heller & Co. Chicago, Il. | |
| N131ET | Citation | 550-0118 | Blue Sky Aviation, Denver, Co. | LV-PHH/N2745X |
| N131G | Learjet | 25B-170 | Delford Smith, McMinnville, Or. | |
| N131WT | Falcon 50 | 28 | IBM World Trade Asia Corp. Paris. | N53FJ/F-WZHE |
| N132MW | HFB 320 | 1032 | Airborne Express Inc. Wilmington, Oh. | N130MW/PH-HFA/D-CERE |
| N133JA | Falcon 20E | 290 | IASCO, Burlingame, Ca. | N4440F/F-WMKH |
| N133JF | Learjet | 25D-264 | Southmark Properties, Norcross, Ga. | N716NC |
| N133ME | Jet Commander | 50 | Magna Energy Corp. Houston, Tx. | N612JC |
| N133W | Learjet | 23-021 | National Jets Inc. Tulsa, Ok. | N427NJ/N427EJ |
| N135AB | Learjet | 35A-414 | Robert Bass, Fort Worth, Tx. | N39MW |
| N135CP | Gulfstream 2 | 200 | Colgate Palmolive Co. NY. | N1806P/N826GA |
| N135J | Learjet | 35A-097 | Dana Corp. Toledo, Oh. | |
| N135MB | Learjet | 35A-343 | Oregon MB-35 Corp. Des Moines, Ia. | |
| N135RJ | Learjet | 35A-443 | Kanair Inc. Marco Island, Fl. | |
| N135ST | Learjet | 35A-169 | Southwest Toyota Distribution Inc. Pompano Beach, Ca. | |
| N135UT | Learjet | 35A-327 | Sharon Aviation Inc. Kansas City, Mo. | N3797N |
| N136LK | DH 125/3A | 25116 | E L Kay Industries Inc. | N93TC/G-ATZN |
| N136MW | HFB 320 | 1036 | Bay Aerostar Sales, San Jose, Ca. | N2MK/N380EX/N891HJ/D-CESA |
| N137BC | Learjet | 25-024 | O F D Inc. Lafayette, La. | N125ST/N425RD |
| N137K | Learjet | 25D-295 | Kamyr Inc. Glens Falls, N.Y. | N229AP |
| N138TA | B 707-138B | 17696 | TigerAir Inc. Los Angeles, Ca. | C-FPWV/VH-EBA/N31239 |
| N140AK | DH 125/1A-522 | 25104 | Kinnair Inc. Cincinnati, Oh. | N257H/G-ATUW |
| N140RC | Learjet | 23-048 | R J Clark Enterprises, Lake Havasu, Co. | N48MW/N147EJ/N805LJ |
| N140V | Citation | 550-0352 | Sterling Aircraft Sales Co. Little Rock, Ar. | (N140DV)/(N1214J) |
| N141CC | Citation | 500-0141 | Mary Williamson, Fort Worth, Tx. | |
| N141H | Sabre-40 | 282-60 | Navajo Refining Co. Dallas, Tx. | N555AB/N555AE/N256EA/N256EN /N256MA/N22TP/N66TP/N903G |
| N142B | DH 125/1A-522 | 25101 | Benjamin F Shaw Co. | G-ATXE |
| N142HC | Learjet | 25B-142 | Superiorgas Ltd. Des Moines, Ia. | N42HC/N515WH |
| N143CP | BH 125/400A | NA748 | Air Support Services, NY. | N199B/N189B/N144PA/N222RG/N222RR/N22DH N44BH/G-AXYG |
| N143EP | Citation | 501-0005 | Gary Norton, Atmol, Id. | N665JB/N661AA/N5357J |
| N144AR | Citation | 501-0098 | ARCO Pipe Line Co. Dallas, Tx. | N44RD/N3161M |
| N145G | Sabre-40 | 282-65 | La Paloma Leasing Inc. Boca Raton, Fl. | N2232B |
| N145ST | Gulfstream 2 | 22 | Car Crafts Inc. Fort Lauderdale, Fl. | N5152/N862GA |
| N145TA | Citation | 500-0145 | Thurston Aviation Inc. Charlotte, NC. | N145FC/N145CC |
| N146BF | Westwind-1124 | 287 | Jewel Companies Inc. Great Falls, Mt. | 4X-COG |
| N146J | Westwind-1124 | 313 | Jewel Companies Inc. Great Falls, Mt. | 4X-CRG |
| N146JC | Citation | 500-0160 | Jewel Companies Inc. Great Falls, Mt. | (N146BE)/N146BF |

| Regis-tration | Type | C/N | Owner/Operator | Previous Identities |
|---|---|---|---|---|
| N147CF | Sabre-40 | 282-94 | Aircraft Management Corp. Fort Lauderdale, FL. | N6TE/N216R/N16R/N4703N |
| N147DB | Citation | 500-0009 | Rockwell International Corp. St. Louis, Mo. | N147DA/N700JD/N500JD /N509CC |
| N147K | Learjet | 35A-462 | Richmor Aviation Inc. Hudson, NY. | N8562W |
| N147X | Falcon 20D | 185 | Quintana Petroleum Corp. Houston, Tx. | N3WN/I-IRIF/F-WMKF |
| N148J | Learjet | 24D-291 | Cotswolds Investments Corp. Fort Lauderdale, Fl. | N45862/ZS-GLD |
| N148JB | Citation | 501-0130 | Lease Northwest Inc. Minneapolis, Mn. | (N2650V) |
| N149BP | Jet Commander-B | 149 | Sunburst Leasing Inc. Oklahoma City, Ok. | (N9LP.)/N1121E/N700R/N78MN N489G/N45SL/N100PC/N100MC/N9049N/4X-CPM |
| N149J | Learjet | 25B-149 | EPPS Air Service Inc. Atlanta, Ga. | EC-CIM/HB-VDI |
| N150BG | Falcon 50 | 13 | Gelco Corp. Eden Prairie, Mn. | N5OFK/F-WZHF |
| N150HR | Citation | 550-0117 | Hussman Refrigerator Co. Bridgeton, Mo. | N575FM/N2745R |
| N150JP | Falcon 50 | 44 | American Aircraft Exchange Inc. Bethany, Ok. | N62FJ/F-WZHA |
| N150JT | Falcon 50 | 53 | Joseph E Seagram & Sons Inc. NY. | F-WZHS |
| N150WC | Falcon 50 | 47 | The Western Co. Fort Worth, Tx. | N65FJ/F-WZHP |
| N150WW | Learjet | 25B-147 | Builders Interests Inc. Houston, Tx. | N25KC/N55KC |
| N151AE | HS 125/700A | NA0263 | Aetna Life & Casualty Co. Hartford, Ct. | N130BL/G-5-18 |
| N151CR | Jet Commander | 33 | Richard Jagitsch, Atlanta, Ga. | N1180Z |
| N151WC | Falcon 10 | 163 | The Western Co. Fort Worth, Tx. | N227FJ/F-WZGP |
| N152AE | HS 125/700A | NA0314 | Aetna Life & Casualty Co. Hartford, Ct. | G-5-11 |
| N152GS | JetStar-731 | 48/5061 | R W Martin Inc. Carlsbad, Ca. | N67GT/N47BA/N506D/N506T/N9226R |
| N153SR | Challenger | 1034 | Southern Railway Co. Washington DC. | N2634Y/C-GLXY |
| N154G | Citation | 500-0110 | Channel Aviation Inc. NY. | N500AB/(N610CC) |
| N154X | Gulfstream 2 | 12 | Quintana Petroleum Corp. Houston, Tx. | N11UM/N500R |
| N155EC | Sabre-60 | 306-20 | Western Co. of N. America, Fort Worth, Tx. | N55BP/N78JP/N44SB /N22JW/N330US/N938R/N4730N |
| N155J | Learjet | 24B-182 | DEC International Inc. Madison, Wi. | N500ZH/N500ZA/N171L/N945GA |
| N155JC | Learjet | 55-071 | | (N155UT) |
| N155LP | Learjet | 55-055 | L B P Trading Co. Atlanta, Ga. | |
| N155NK | Falcon 20C | 107 | American Enka Co. Arden, NC. | N965BC/N988F/F-WMKJ |
| N155PT | Citation | 551-0049 | P J Taggares Co. Portland, Or. | N170CC/(N88848) |
| N155TA | Citation | 551-0023 | Torrey Jet Aviation, Portland, Or. | N98599 |
| N155TD | Learjet | 35A-335 | SAJ Inc. Lincoln, Nb. | N25MJ |
| N155VW | Jet Commander-A | 123 | Riviera Motors Inc. Hillsboro, Or. | N5410 |
| N158DP | JetStar-8 | 5013 | Air Capital Aircraft Sales, Wichita, Ks. | N8AD/N11JC/HZ-MAC/N11JC /N523AC/N322K/N9284R |
| N159B | Gulfstream 2 | 190 | Carter Hawley Hale Stores, Los Angeles, Ca. | N130K |
| N159DP | Jet Commander | 52 | OBI Enterprises, Ok. | N159MP/N159YC/N696GW/N1121G/N701AP |
| N160D | Citation | 551-0036 | Old Dominion Freight Line Inc. High Point, NC. | N162CC/N2661P |
| N160VE | Citation | 550-0303 | Valero Management Co. San Antonio, Tx. | (N281AM)/N6861D |
| N160WC | Jet Commander-B | 141 | Beker Industries, Greenwich, Ct. | N100CJ/N9041N/4X-CPH |
| N161MM | HS 125/700A | 7151 | Aircraft Associates/Berkshire Inn Inc. | G-5-12 |
| N161X | Westwind-1124 | 234 | Power Leasing Inc. Oklahoma City, Ok. | N1124Z/HC-BGL/(N1124Z)/4X-CMF |
| N162A | HS 125/700A | NA0208 | AMF Inc. N.Y. | N700HS/N125HS/G-BFBI/G-5-14 |
| N163A | Learjet | 35A-073 | AMF Inc. N.Y. | N108GL |
| N163DC | Jet Commander | 89 | Crain Industries/Aircraft International, Ft. Smith, Ar. | N10BK/N1195N /N6B |
| N164CB | Citation | 501-0239 | Tar River Communications, Rocky Mount, NC. | |
| N165BA | Citation | 500-0159 | SBA Corp. Gates Mills, Or. | N36MC |
| N166CB | Citation | 501-0141 | Ferris Hamilton, Denver, Co. | N26510 |
| N166RM | Learjet | 35A-336 | Intravia Inc. Englewood, Co. | N590J/HB-VGW |
| N167C | Westwind-1124 | 261 | Federated Department Stores Inc. Cincinnati, Oh. | 4X-CNG |
| N167H | Sabre-60A | 306-119 | Hanna Mining Co. Cleveland, Oh. | N2123J |
| N167J | Westwind-1124 | 265 | Federated Department Stores Inc. Cincinnati, Oh. | 4X-CNK |
| N168H | Sabre-60A | 306-122 | Hanna Mining Co. Cleveland, Oh. | N2131J |
| N170JL | Sabre-40 | 282-29 | Jet Time Inc. Oklahoma City, Ok. | N9IOE/N6383C |
| N170L | Learjet | 35A-156 | Dana Corp. Toledo, Oh. | |
| N171CB | Citation | 550-0021 | California Business Jets, SFO, Ca. | N296AB/N98871 |
| N171LE | Citation | 550-0324 | Lee Enright, SFO, Ca. | N5873C |
| N173A | Sabre-65 | 465-20 | Airco Inc. Montvale, NJ. | N2544E |
| N173LP | Learjet | 25B-163 | Louisiana Pacific Corp. Hillsboro, Or. | N70606/SE-DFC |
| N173SK | Citation | 501-0041 | BT Equipment Leasing, New York. | N5OMC/N36880 |
| N174B | Diamond One | A031SA | | |
| N174CB | Citation | 501-0241 | Homco International Inc. Houston, Tx. | (N2624L) |

58

| Regis-tration | Type | C/N | Owner/Operator | Previous Identities |
|---|---|---|---|---|
| N175BA | Learjet | 23-038 | SBA Corp. Fort Lauderdale, Fl. | (See N300TA) |
| N175BL | Falcon 10 | 168 | Liberty Mutual Insurance Co. Boston, Ma. | N234FJ/F-WZGU |
| N175FJ | Falcon 10 | 97 | Marmac Corp. Parkersburg, WV. | F-WPXF |
| N176BN | JetStar 2 | 5207 | Burlington Northern Inc. St. Paul, Mn. | N5533L |
| N176CP | Learjet | 24B-204 | Nordam, Tulsa, Ok. | N957E/N957GA |
| N176P | Gulfstream 2 | 176 | Pittston Corp. N.Y. | N806GA |
| N177CJ | Citation | 550-0131 | Max Pasley Inc. Sioux Falls, SD. | |
| N177CM | Citation | 550-0210 | QHL Aviation Leasing Associates Inc. Laconia, NH. | N762PF/N68018 |
| N177JC | Jet Commander | 77 | Houston Fabricating, Tx. | N121JC/N21JW/N11BK/N442WT/N523AC/N1121X |
| N177NC | JetStar-731 | 52/5070 | Natomas Energy Co. San Francisco, Ca. | N9921/C-GAZU/N9921/N992 |
| N178CP | Learjet | 35-005 | Coral Petroleum Co. Houston, Tx. | N175J/EC-CLS/TR-LXP/EC-CLS |
| N179AR | Gulfstream 2 | 37 | ARCO,Burbank, Ca. | |
| N179T | Gulfstream 2 | 86 | Texas Eastern Transmission Corp. Houston, Tx. | N880GA |
| N180AR | Sabre-60 | 306-77 | ARCO, Dallas, Tx. | N65751 |
| N180MC | Learjet | 35A-212 | International Jet Inc. Minneapolis, Mn. | N3803G |
| N180PF | Citation | 500-0047 | Earl Wilson, Johnson City, Tn. | N547CC |
| N180RN | B 737-2W8 | 22628 | NOGA/Chemco International Leasing Inc. NY. | |
| N181AR | Sabre-60 | 306-90 | ARCO. Dallas, Tx. | N65772 |
| N181CB | Falcon 20F | 436 | CBI Industries Inc. Oak Brook, Il. | N434F/F-WJMN |
| N181MA | MU-300 Diamond | 001SA | Mitsubishi Aircraft International, Dallas, Tx. | J08001 |
| N182AR | Sabre-60 | 306-93 | ARCO, Dallas, Tx. | N366N/N65777 |
| N182K | Learjet | 35A-293 | Koch Industries Inc. Wichita, Ks. | |
| N183AR | Sabre-40A | 282-127 | ARCO, Dallas, Tx. | N110PM |
| N184GP | JetStar-731 | 51/5064 | Georgia Pacific Corp. Portland, Or. | |
| N185FP | Learjet | 35A-360 | EAF/Federal Paper Board Co. Inc. Lexington, Ma. | |
| N185S | Falcon 20C | 56 | Wallace Leasing Corp/Sperry Corp. NY. | N100SR/N671SR/N882F/F-WNGM |
| N186G | Jet Commander | 43 | Prestige Aviation Inc/Indiana Electric Association, Indianapolis. N271E | |
| N186MW | Citation | 500-0186 | Hangar One Inc. Atlanta, Ga. | N186CC |
| N187G | Jet Commander | 41 | Carousel Enterprises Ltd. Reno, Nv. | N6510V |
| N187MW | Citation | 500-0187 | Tri-State Ready Mix Co. Inc. Kenova, WV. | (TI-ACB)/(HB-VDR)/N187CC |
| N187S | Falcon 50 | 18 | Sperry Flight Systems, Phoenix, Az. | N5OFN |
| N188DH | Falcon 10 | 188 | Dayton Hudson Corp. Minneapolis, Mn. | N253FJ/F-WZGS |
| N188TC | Learjet | 25D-276 | T C Aviation Inc. Portland, Or. | |
| N189AR | Sabre-40 | 282-77 | ARCO, Dallas, Tx. | N608AR/N608S/N2244B |
| N189B | BH 125/F600A | 6061 | Private Business Air Service, Los Angeles, Ca. | N169B/N707WB/N8253A /N5253A/N125HS/G-BDOB/G-5-14 |
| N190K | Citation | 501-0192 | R Klabzuba, Fort Worth, Tx. | (N6781G) |
| N190SC | Learjet | 24B-190 | Morris Shenker, Las Vegas, Nv. | F-GBLA/HZ-GP4/N50TC/N9HM/N4291G |
| N191C | Falcon 20D | 195 | Ingram, New Orleans, La. | N186S/N200SR/N4385F/F-WPXD |
| N192G | Citation | 500-0163 | Brown & Root Inc. Houston, Tx. | |
| N192MH | Learjet | 25D-239 | Michael T Halbouty, Houston, Tx. | |
| N194AT | Citation | 500-0146 | Figgie International Inc. Willoughby, Oh. | |
| N194MC | Falcon 20C | 135 | MASCO Corp. Taylor, Mi. | N9999E/N40XX/N40XY/N6820J/N4351F/F-WMKI |
| N196KC | JetStar 2 | 5231 | Kansas City Life Assurance Co. Mo. | N4043M |
| N197DA | Sabre-40 | 282-28 | AAHS Inc. Orlando, Fl. | N27DA/N524AG/N524AC/N6565K/N6565A/N6382C |
| N199AM | B 727-021 | 19262 | Abdul Madi/Jetex International Inc. Wilmington, De. | N727WE/N360PA |
| N199BT | Learjet | 25D-311 | Citizens Fidelity Bank, Louisville, Ky. | N39391 |
| N199GH | Westwind Two | 364 | Geo Hormer & Co. Austin, Md. | N60DG/4X-CUR |
| N199SP | Citation | 500-0199 | Sverdrup Corp. St. Louis, Mo. | |
| N200A | Gulfstream 2 | 94 | Exxon Corp. Newark, NJ. | N886GA |
| N200CC | BH 125/731 | NA766 | Luqa Inc. Jacksonville, Fl. | N300LD/N711YR/N711YP/N63BH |
| N200CE | Sabre-60 | 306-87 | Clark Equipment Co. Buchanan, Wy. | N400CE/N100MA/N60RS/N100CE /N65767 |
| N200CP | Falcon 20F | 410 | Coral Petroleum, Houston, Tx. | F-WROT |
| N200DE | Falcon 20D | 191 | Dunavant Enterprises Inc. Memphis, Tn. | N910L/N4381F/F-WPUX |
| N200DH | Learjet | 24-170 | Plaza Enterprise Ltd. Houston, Tx. | |
| N200FJ | Falcon 200 | 401 | Falcon Jet Corp. Teterboro, NJ. | F-GATF/F-WZAH |
| N200G | Learjet | 25-048 | Green Construction Co. of Indiana, Oaktown, In. | N965GA |
| N200GN | Falcon 20F | 339 | Gannett Inc. N.Y. | N100GN/N200GN/N4461F/F-WMKH |
| N200GP | Learjet | 24-134 | Geo Priester, Wheeling, Il. | N215J/N282R/N281R/N231R |
| N200HR | Westwind-1123 | 182 | Evan Construction Co. Houston, Tx. | N1123Q |
| N200JR | Citation | 550-0204 | Pearson American Drilling Inc. Burns Flat, Ok. | N820/(N6801H) |
| N200JW | Falcon 20C | 64 | Jim Walter Co. Tampa, Fl. | N806F/N889F/F-WMKG |
| N200KC | Citation | 500-0104 | Kimberly-Clark Corp. Neenah, Wi. | (N604CC) |
| N200LF | Jet Commander | 47 | L A Fritz, Corpus Christi, Tx. | N222HM/N222GL/N33GL/HB-VBX/N6513V |
| N200LH | Westwind-1124 | 312 | De Luxe Check Printers Inc. St. Paul, Mn. | 4X-CRF |

| Regis-tration | Type | C/N | Owner/Operator | Previous Identities |
|---|---|---|---|---|
| N200MH | Learjet | 25C-083 | Mark Hurd Aerial Surveys, Goleta, Ca. | N200Y/N31CS |
| N200MP | Sabre-40 | 282-36 | Petco Aircraft Corp. Dallas, Tx. | N88JM/N63A/N59KQ/N59K/N22BN /N1903W/N6391C |
| N200P | Gulfstream 2 | 121 | National Distillers & Chemical Corp. NY | |
| N200RG | Gulfstream 2TT | 216 | EAF/Reliance Group, Inc. NY. | |
| N200RT | Citation | 551-0419 | Torray, Clark & Co. Bethesda, Md. | N63SD/HB-IEZ |
| N200SX | Learjet | 35A-286 | Mitel Inc. Dover, De. | (N333XX)/N333X |
| N200WC | Westwind-1123 | 153 | Castleton Inc. Detroit, Mi. | N773EJ/4X-CJB |
| N200WK | Falcon 20F | 261 | L Rockefeller, NY. | N4368F/F-WLCU |
| N200Y | Learjet | 36-014 | Mark Hurd Aerial Surveys, Goleta, Ca. | N900Y |
| N200YM | Citation | 550-0411 | | N1216N |
| N202BA | Learjet | 24A-031 | National Air College Inc, San Diego, Ca. | N777TE/N777TF/N477BL /N175FS |
| N202BT | Learjet | 35-041 | Big Three Industries Inc, Houston, Tx. | |
| N202CH | HS 125/700A | NA0260 | Crouse Hinds Co. Mattydale, NY. | N130BK/G-5-14 |
| N202GA | Gulfstream 2 | 26 | Gulfstream American Corp. Savannah, Ga. | N328K |
| N202WM | Learjet | 25D-355 | Kero Sun Inc/Marcia Litwin, New Medford, Ct. | (N830WM) |
| N203BT | Falcon 50 | 22 | Big Three Industries, Houston, Tx. | N50FS/F-WZHF |
| N203CK | Learjet | 24B-203 | Croman Corp. Medford, Or. | N55MJ/N55LJ/(N43TL)/N3GW/N515WC |
| N203G | Challenger | 1069 | Grace Natural Resources Corp. Dallas, Tx. | C-GLXM |
| N203M | Jet Commander | 120 | Nevis Enterprises Inc. Carson City, Nv. | N200M |
| N204C | Gulfstream 2 | 143 | CONOCO Inc. Houston, Tx. | N334/N883GA |
| N204R | HS 125/700A | NA0279 | Raytheon Corp. Lexington, Ma. | N125AD/G-5-17 |
| N204TM | Sabre-40 | 282-56 | Globe Life & Insurance Co. OKC, Ok. | (N722ED)/N722FD/N722ST/N10CC /N322CS |
| N205FM | Citation | 500-0264 | Hesston Corp. Hesston, Ks. | N5264J |
| N205MM | HFB 320 | 1039 | Metromedia Inc. Secaucus, NJ. | N666LO/N666LC/CF-WDU/N893HJ/N118RA /D-CESO |
| N205SC | Citation | 550-0156 | South Central Bell Telephone, Birmingham, Al. | N205SG/(N31F)/N6567C /N98784 |
| N205X | Falcon 10 | 44 | AMAX Coal Co. Indianapolis, In. | N130FJ/F-WJMJ |
| N206EQ | Learjet | 25D-206 | Easco Corp. Baltimore, Md. | N206EC |
| N206FC | Learjet | 35A-467 | Arlington Integrated Holding, NY. | |
| N208N | Citation | 500-0021 | Norman Blankenship, Amarillo, Tx. | N550CC/N5B/JA8421/N521CC |
| N208TC | Citation | 550-0304 | Crown Aviation Leasing Co. Wilmington, De. | N6888D |
| N208W | Citation | 501-0062 | Norman Blankenship, Amarillo, Tx. | D-IBWB/N98599 |
| N209GA | Gulfstream 2 | 9 | GAC, Savannah, Ga. | (N115RS)/N320FE/C-FSBR |
| N209MW | Citation | 500-0209 | Hangar One Inc. Atlanta, Ga. | |
| N210F | Sabre-60 | 306-25 | Flint Steel Corp. Tulsa, Ok. | N4735N |
| N210GP | Learjet | 23-020 | McCollum Aviation Inc. Danville, Il. | N2GP/N338KK/N388R |
| N210MJ | Citation | 550-0093 | Mercantile National Bank, Dallas, Tx. | N95CC/(N108CT)/N2664F |
| N210MT | Citation | 500-0210 | GTC Inc. E Greenwich, RI. | N9011R/TR-LTI |
| N210ST | BH 125/600A | 6009 | Storage Technology, Louisville, Co. | N219ST/N3PW/N22BH |
| N211BY | Learjet | 55-059 | | |
| N211CD | Learjet | 25D-275 | Corwin Denney, Beverly Hills, Ca. | |
| N211DB | Citation Eagle | 500-0174 | Bogart Oil Aviation Inc. Bethany, Ok. | N21NA/N26HC |
| N211DH | Learjet | 35A-253 | Hagadone Newspapers Co. Coeur D'Alene, Id. | N40144 |
| N211FJ | Falcon 10 | 146 | National Medical Enterprises Inc. Los Angeles, Ca. | F-WZGR |
| N211JC | Learjet | 25D-310 | J C Enterprises, Ringgold, Pa. | N211PD/N1088C |
| N212AP | JetStar-8 | 5147 | Apex Aeronautics Inc. Wilmington, De. | N718R/N744UT/N5511L |
| N212C | Falcon 20C | 155 | 195 Broadway Corp. Morristown, NJ. | N205SC/N500Y/N4362F/F-WJMK |
| N212CW | Jet Commander | 75 | Crain Industries Inc. Fort Smith, Ar. | N1121R |
| N212H | Falcon 20F | 259 | 195 Broadway Corp. Morristown, NJ. | N4418F/F-WLCT |
| N212JP | Learjet | 55-006 | 195 Broadway Corp. Morristown, NJ. | N113EL |
| N212N | Falcon 10 | 150 | 195 Broadway Corp. Morristown, NJ. | N215FJ/F-WZGV |
| N | Falcon 50 | 89 | 195 Broadway Corp. Morristown, NJ. | N93FJ/F-WZHV |
| N212NE | Learjet | 25D-212 | RAS Aviation Aircraft Ltd. Allentown, Pa. | N911MG/N1450B |
| N212T | Falcon 20F | 273 | 195 Broadway Corp. Morristown, NJ. | N4432F/F-WPUU |
| N213H | DH 125/731 | 25119 | Hughes Aircraft Co. Culver City, Ca. | G-AVAD/G-5-11 |
| N214CC | Westwind-1124 | 197 | E C Aircraft Inc. Greenwich, Ct. | 4X-CKU |
| N214GP | Gulfstream 2 | 3 | The Gillette Co. Boston, Ma. | N831GA |
| N215G | HS 125/700A | NA0267 | Grace Natural Resources Corp. Dallas, Tx. | N125L/G-5-12 |
| N215JW | Learjet | 35A-223 | James Wilson, Montgomery, Al. | |
| N215M | Westwind-1124 | 206 | Burlington Northern Inc. Billings, Mt. | N215C/N215G/4X-CLD |
| N215RL | Challenger | 1068 | Citadel Air Inc. Dover, De. | C-GLXK |
| N216HB | Learjet | 24D-275 | H B E Corp, Midland, Tx. | N24TC/XB-NUR |
| N216SC | Westwind-1124 | 216 | Sundstrand Corp. Rockford, Il. | 4X-CLN |

60

| Regis-<br>tration | Type | C/N | Owner/Operator | Previous<br>Identities |
|---|---|---|---|---|
| N217A | Sabre-60 | 306-85 | Airco Alloys Inc, NY. | N65764 |
| N217E | Sabre-40A | 282-103 | BKN Corp. Cleveland, Oh. | N217TE/N217A/N9MS/N44P/N7598N |
| N217F | DH 125/400A | NA713 | The Federal Co. Memphis, Tn. | G-AWPC |
| N217FS | Citation | 550-0273 | Federal Signals Corp. Oakbrook, Il. | N68637 |
| N217RR | Citation | 501-0221 | Raymond Rutter, Rolling Hills, Ca. | N643MC/(N26228) |
| N218S | Falcon 20C | 32 | Oilfield Aviation Corp. NY. | N418S/N805F/F-WNGL |
| N218US | Sabre-75A | 380-45 | BT Equipment Leasing Inc. New York. | D-CCVW/N2117J |
| N219JA | HS 125/700A | 7013 | Storage Technology, Louisville, Co. | G-CBBI |
| N220CC | Citation | 550-0040 | The Coleman Co. Inc. Wichita, Ks. | (N3274M) |
| N220HS | Learjet | 25D-220 | Henry Siegel Co. Inc. NY | |
| N220RB | DC-8-21 | 45280 | Project ORBIS Inc. Houston, Tx. | N8003U/N8038D |
| N220S | Citation | 500-0192 | Stanmar Corp. Dover, De. | N508S/N4TK |
| N220ST | Jet Commander | 46 | Central Truck Sales Inc. Dallas, Tx. | N200GT/N200RM/N200BP<br>/N1500C |
| N220T | DH 125/731 | NA730 | Trunkline Gas Co. Houston, Tx. | G-AXJF |
| N220US | Learjet | | US Jet Corp. Englewood, Co. | |
| N220W | Citation | 500-0025 | T J McNerney, Lenexa, Ks. | N976EE/N745US/N70703/D-IMAN/N525CC |
| N221AC | Citation | 500-0364 | Aero Center Inc. Laredo, Tx. | HB-VFF/N36892 |
| N221MJ | Westwind-1124 | 204 | McJunkin Corp. Charleston, WV. | 4X-CLB |
| N221PH | Sabre-40 | 282-55 | Petroleum Helicopters Inc, Harahan, La. | N68HO/N68HC/N353WC/N353WB<br>/N2007/N7505V |
| N221UE | Learjet | 35-042 | United Engineers & Constructors Inc, Philadelphia. | |
| N221Z | Learjet | 35-059 | Zurn Inustries Inc. Erie, Pa. | |
| N222AG | Citation | 550-0148 | Groenvelt Enterprises Inc, Watertown, Wi. | |
| N222AP | Learjet | 25D-225 | Empire Lumber Co. Butte, Mt. | 9J-AED |
| N222B | Learjet | 25-047 | Clear Air Inc. Denver, Co. | |
| N222BE | Learjet | 35A-489 | Chesapeake Leasing Co. Norfolk, Va. | |
| N222BK | Learjet | 35A-180 | Combs-Gates Denver Inc. | N222BE/N3819G |
| N222BN | Learjet | 24D-296 | Richard Kekelsen, Omaha, Ne. | XA-FIW |
| N222FJ | Falcon 10 | 157 | Falcon Jet Corp. Teterboro, NJ. | F-WZGF |
| N222G | DH 125/1A-52 | 25064 | James Acridge, Phoenix, Az. | N33BK/N125JG/N230H/G-ATKK |
| N222LW | Learjet | 25D-299 | Leslie T Welsh Inc. Barrington, Il. | |
| N222MU | Falcon 10 | 164 | Mustang Gas Products Co. Oklahoma City, Ok. | N228FJ/F-WZGO |
| N222MW | Westwind-1124 | 255 | McWane Inc. Birmingham, Al. | 4X-CNA |
| N222Q | Diamond One | A021SA | | |
| N222RB | HS 125/700A | NA0218 | Reading & Bates Offshore Drilling Co. Tulsa, Ok. | N37975/G-BGDM<br>/G-5-15 |
| N222SG | Citation | 550-0110 | Sheller-Globe Corp. Toledo, Oh. | (N2665Y) |
| N222SL | Citation | 500-0096 | Great Planes Sales Inc. Tulsa, Ok. | N596CC |
| N222SR | Westwind-1124 | 194 | Stearns-Roger Corp. Denver, Co. | 4X-CKR |
| N222WA | Citation | 501-0007 | Ralph Kiewit, Sherman Oaks, Ca. | N5360J |
| N222WL | Citation | 550-0208 | Weatherford International, Houston, Tx. | N54RC/N6801P |
| N222Y | JetStar-731 | 40/5006 | The Permian Corp. Houston, Tx. | N731JS/N227K/N12R/N9280R |
| N223AS | Citation Eagle | 500-0212 | Alvin Siteman/Air Services Co. St. Louis, Mo. | N223LB/N222LB/N1LB |
| N223G | DH 125/3A-RA | NA710 | Grace Petroleum, Tulsa, Ok. | N228G/N226G/N1259K/G-AWMW |
| N223GC | Citation | 501-0164 | TRG Drilling Corp. Oklahoma City, Ok. | N57OCC/(N6778L) |
| N223RE | Citation | 501-0102 | John Bitterman, Hackessin, De. | N486CC/(N2646X) |
| N223S | Citation | 500-0233 | Sparks Enterprises Inc. Memphis, Tn. | N233VM/N233CC/N5233J |
| N224CC | Citation | 550-0178 | L C Metals, Dover, De. | N67988 |
| N224RP | Falcon 10 | 159 | Reidy International Inc. Houston, Tx. | N224FJ/F-WZGJ |
| N225AC | Learjet | 25XR-139 | Aero Center Inc. Laredo, Tx. | N618R |
| N225AD | Citation | 550-0107 | Alexander Dawson Inc. Las Vegas, Nv. | N550CB/N2665D |
| N225CC | Gulfstream 2 | 8 | Circo Resorts Inc. Las Vegas, Nv. | N5UD/N504TF/PJ-ARI/N777GG<br>/N400SA/HB-IMV/N400SA/N400SJ/N18N/N833GA |
| N225LS | Sabre-40 | 282-51 | Dan M Krausse, Dallas, Tx. | N227LS/N108X/N108G/N733R |
| N225MC | Learjet | 35A-225 | J N O McCall Coal Co. Inc, Baltimore, Md. | |
| N225SF | Gulfstream 2 | 55 | Standard Oil Co. of California, San Francisco, Ca. | N875GA |
| N226G | Falcon 20F | 244 | W R Grace Co. NY. | N11LB/N20FJ/N4420F/F-WMKI |
| N227G | Challenger | 1059 | W R Grace Co. NY. | C-GLXY |
| N227GC | Falcon 20DC | 59 | W R Grace Co. NY. | N710MT/N710MR/N710MW/N263MW/N971F/F-WNGO |
| N227GL | Gulfstream 2 | 76 | Mobil Saudi Arabia Inc. | N227G/N711LS |
| N227PC | Citation | 550-0113 | Petrolite Corp, St.Louis, Mo. | N2666A |
| N227RW | Learjet | 25B-201 | Erickson Jet Inc. Fairview, Mt. | |
| N228G | B 727-1H2 | 20533 | W R Grace & Co. NY. | N320HG |
| N228GC | BH 125/731 | NA777 | W R Grace Co. Memphis, Tn. | N571GH/N571CH/N74BH |
| N228LS | Sabre-65 | 465-43 | Lone Star Drilling, Houston, Tx. | N950CS |

61

| Registration | Type | C/N | Owner/Operator | Previous Identities |
|---|---|---|---|---|
| N228SW | Learjet | 25D-228 | Richards Motor & Equipment Co, Carrollton, Ga. | |
| N229GC | Challenger | 1043 | W R Grace & Co. Memphis, Tn. | |
| N229LS | Sabre-60 | 306-38 | Lone Star Steel Corp. Dallas, Tx. | N251MA/N253MZ/N4751N |
| N230R | Learjet | 35A-130 | Dart Industries Inc, West Bend, Wi. | |
| N230S | Falcon 50 | 70 | Norton Simon Properties Inc. NY. | N81FJ/F-WZHL |
| N230TL | Westwind-1124 | 279 | Time Aviation Inc. NY. | N885DR/N1126G/4X-CNY |
| N231R | Learjet | 35A-128 | Dart Industries Inc. Orlando, Fl. | |
| N232R | Learjet | 35A-102 | Dart Industries Inc. Los Angeles, Ca. | N1451B |
| N232T | Sabre-40 | 282-83 | Trinity Marine Marketing Inc. Metairie, La. | N642LR/N726R |
| N233R | Learjet | 35-048 | Dart Industries Inc. Teterboro, NJ. | |
| N233U | Falcon 50 | 14 | Combustion Engineering Co. Stamford, Ct. | N50FL/F-WZHG |
| N234EJ | Learjet | 25D-234 | E J Sales, Columbus, Oh. | N234KK/(N27GW)/N3815G |
| N234G | Jet Commander | 28 | Wyatt Cafeterias Inc. Dallas, Tx. | N77NR/N1190Z |
| N234U | Falcon 10 | 29 | Combustion Engineering Co. Stamford, Ct. | N120FJ/F-WJMM |
| N235HR | Learjet | 35A-082 | Hoffman La Roche Inc. Nutley, NJ. | |
| N235U | Gulfstream 3 | 305 | Combustion Engineering Inc, Stamford, Ct. | N305GA |
| N236FJ | Falcon 10 | 170 | | F-WZGX |
| N236R | Learjet | 55-025 | Dart Industries, Northbrook, Il. | |
| N237GA | Learjet | 35A-262 | George Argyros, Santa Ana, Ca. | |
| N237LM | Gulfstream 2 | 101 | WOTAN America Inc. Wilmington, De. | N1159K/N853GA |
| N237R | Learjet | 55-066 | Dart Industries, Northbrook, Il. | |
| N238U | Falcon 50 | 86 | Combustion Engineering Inc. Stamford, Ct. | N94FJ/F-WPXD |
| N239P | Gulfstream 2 | 63 | Air Combustion Inc. Stamford, Ct. | N238U/N835GA |
| N240AA | Citation | 500-0202 | Amarillo Aircraft Sales, Tx. | N202MW |
| N240AG | Learjet | 25B-197 | Aerojet-General Corp, Ontario, Ca. | N104GL |
| N240AR | Citation | 550-0216 | ARCO, Dallas, Tx. | N6801L |
| N240B | Learjet | 35A-240 | First Security Bank, Salt Lake City, Ut./Budd Co. | |
| N240CC | Citation | 500-0240 | T C Scales, Atlanta, Ga. | N5240J |
| N241AG | Learjet | 25B-075 | Aerojet-General Corp. Ontario, Ca. | |
| N241TC | DC-9-15 | 45775 | Tracinda Investment Co. Las Vegas, Nv. | N1061T |
| N242AG | Learjet | 25-025 | Cynthian Technology Inc. Lancaster, Ca. | N49BB/N92V/N920S/N928S/N920S |
| N242FJ | Falcon 10 | 176 | | F-WZGI |
| N242WT | Citation | 551-0066 | Wm T Burton Industries Inc. Sulphur, La. | N6825X |
| N244A | Falcon 10 | 145 | Archer Daniels Midland Co. Wilmington, De. | N209FJ/F-WZGO |
| N244CA | Falcon 20F | 321 | E J Aircraft Inc. OKC, Ok. | N702SC/N2525/N4454F/F-WMKJ |
| N244FC | Learjet | 35A-299 | Ammest Services Inc. San Antonio, Tx. | |
| N244WJ | Citation | 500-0252 | Bruce Gillis, Beverly Hills, Ca. | C-GZXA/N200WN/N10PS/N5252J |
| N245CC | Citation | 550-0212 | Hughes Aircraft Co. Culver City, Ca. | (N6801V) |
| N246N | BH 125/400A | NA763 | Zhobi Corp. Las Vegas, Nv. | N46B/N246N/(N91BH)/N58BH/(G-5-15) |
| N248FJ | Falcon 10 | 182 | | F-WZGN |
| N248HM | Learjet | 35A-164 | Herman Miller Inc. Zeeland, Mi. | N1473B |
| N248J | Learjet | 24B-220 | J M Aircraft Inc. Fort Lauderdale, Fl. | N292BC |
| N250AA | Citation | 500-0200 | Amarillo Aircraft Sales, Tx. | N200MW/N520CC |
| N250FJ | Falcon 10 | 184 | | F-WZGP |
| N250JP | Westwind-1124 | 196 | Therdale Corp. Van Nuys, Ca. | N1124E/4X-CKT |
| N250PM | Westwind-1124 | 227 | Pet Inc. St.Louis, Mo. | 4X-CLY |
| N250SP | Citation | 501-0181 | Sonoca Products Co. Hartsville, SC. | N6781C |
| N251FJ | Falcon 10 | 186 | | F-WZGB |
| N251JE | Sabre-65 | 465-2 | Jacobs Engineering Group Inc. Pasadena, Ca. | N465T |
| N252FJ | Falcon 10 | 187 | | F-WZGR |
| N252V | DH 125/3A | 25112 | MGM Grand Hotel Reno Inc, Las Vegas, Nv. | N2525/G-ATYI |
| N253J | Learjet | 25D-253 | Executive Jets Avia Inc. Columbus, Oh. | N97DK/N253EJ |
| N253L | Falcon 50 | 19 | N L Industries, Houston, Tx. | N63A/N50FM/F-WZHB |
| N253W | Citation | 550-0221 | Wolverine World Wide Inc. Rockford, Mi. | N68026 |
| N254AR | Gulfstream 2 | 254 | ARCO, Dallas, Tx. | |
| N254FJ | Falcon 10 | 189 | | F-WZGT |
| N254TW | Citation | 501-0147 | ATLO Inc. Los Angeles, Ca. | N1728E |
| N255CT | HS 125/700A | NA0207 | Caterpillar Tractor Co. Peoria, Il. | G-BFAJ/G-5-13 |
| N255FJ | Falcon 10 | 190 | | F-WZGU |
| N255ST | Learjet | 55-064 | | |
| N256EN | HS 125/700A | NA0292 | SOHIO, Cleveland, Oh. | (N256MA)/N125AK/G-5-20 |
| N256FJ | Falcon 10 | 191 | | F-WZGV |
| N256M | Falcon 20F | 274 | MAPCO Inc. Tulsa, Ok. | N121WT/N370WT/N4433F/F-WJMM |
| N256MA | Falcon 20C | 23 | MAPCO Inc. Tulsa, Ok.(N256M)/N256EN/N15CC/N424JX/N844F/F-BNKX/F-WNGL |
| N256TW | Learjet | 35A-218 | Tidewater Realty Inc, La Place, La. | |
| N256W | Citation | 550-0026 | Wendy's International Inc. Dublin, Oh. | N3240M |
| N257H | JetStar 2 | 5230 | H J Heinz & Co. Pittsburgh, Pa. | N4042M |
| N257W | Falcon 10 | 119 | Wendy's International Inc. Dublin, Oh. | N191FJ/F-WPXK |

| Regis-<br>tration | Type | C/N | Owner/Operator | Previous<br>Identities |
|---|---|---|---|---|
| N258CC | Citation | 550-0225 | Earl Slick, Greensboro, NC. | (N34SS)/(N6803Y) |
| N258FJ | Falcon 10 | 192 | | F-WZGX |
| N258G | Learjet | 25B-092 | GPI Aviation Inc, Dover, De. | N9671A/N1ED |
| N258P | Citation | 550-0454 | | N1216K |
| N259FJ | Falcon 100 | 193 | | F-WZGY |
| N260CC | Citation | 500-0260 | H E Butt Grocery Co. Corpus Christi, Tx. | (N5260J) |
| N260FJ | Falcon 10 | 194 | | F-WZGZ |
| N261FJ | Falcon 10 | 195 | | F-WZGA |
| N261WC | Learjet | 25D-261 | West Coast Air Charter, Pomona, Ca. | N24JK/N180MC/N3802G |
| N262FJ | Falcon 10 | 196 | | F-WZGB |
| N263C | Gulfstream 3 | 341 | CONOCO Inc. White Plains, NY. | |
| N263FJ | Falcon 10 | 198 | | F-WZGF |
| N263GL | Learjet | 35-009 | Gates Learjet Corp. Wichita, Ks. | N275J/N14EL/N44EL |
| N263K | Falcon 20F | 438 | Kellogg Co. Battle Creek, Mi. | N442F/F-WMKI |
| N264FJ | Falcon 10 | 199 | | F-WZGG |
| N265A | Sabre-65 | 465-47 | Armstrong World Industries, Lancaster, Pa. | |
| N265C | Sabre-60 | 306-120 | Rockwell International Corp. | N2124J |
| N265EJ | Learjet | 25D-265 | Executive Jet Aviation, Columbus, Oh. | N1462B |
| N265FJ | Falcon 10 | 200 | | |
| N265JS | Sabre-65A | 465-56 | J.S. Aviation, Enid, Ok. | N544PH |
| N265U | Sabre-60 | 306-132 | Cummins Engine Co. Inc. Columbus, Oh. | N60AG/N994W/N108W/N60RS/N2150J |
| N266BS | Learjet | 36A-035 | Stillwell Aviation Inc. Denver, Co. | VH-BIB/N3807G |
| N266FJ | Falcon 10 | 201 | | |
| N266GL | Learjet | 28-064 | Experimental 'Longhorn' prototype | |
| N267P | JetStar-731 | 22/5074 | Federated Stores Inc. Cincinnati, Oh. | N67B/N9234R |
| N268WC | Learjet | 25D-268 | West Coast Air Charter Inc. Pomona, Ca. | |
| N269MD | Citation | 501-0151 | Litton Industrial Products Inc. Hagerstown, Md. | (N1820E) |
| N270A | Westwind-1124 | 270 | Digital Equipment Corp. Maynard, Ma. | (N270WW)/4X-CNP |
| N270MC | HS 125/700A | NA0307 | Manufacturers Hannover Leasing, NY. | N700GG/G-5-18 |
| N270MH | HS 125/700A | NA0306 | Manufacturers Hannover Leasing, NY. | N700DD/G-5-17/(G-5-13) |
| N270MQ | HS 125/600A | 6067 | Manufacturers Hannover Leasing, NY. | N270MC/(N522C)/N522X/G-BEIN |
| N270SF | Citation | 501-0144 | Super Food Services Inc. Dayton, Oh. | N2652U |
| N271AC | Citation | 500-0218 | AMCA International Corp. Hanover, NH. | N4AC/(N218CC) |
| N272HS | Learjet | 35A-272 | Lanair, Philadelphia, Pa. | N39398 |
| N272JM | Learjet | 25D-272 | John McConnell, Worthington, Oh. | N272EJ |
| N272T | Learjet | 35A-349 | Sorenson Development, Salt Lake City, Ut. | |
| N273K | Falcon 20F | 349 | Kellogg Co. Battle Creek, Mi. | N4465F/F-WMKG |
| N273LP | Learjet | 25-058 | Louisiana-Pacific Corp. Hillsboro, Or. | N2366Y |
| N273MC | Learjet | 35A-149 | Meredith Corp. Des Moines, Ia. | N85351/HB-VGN/OO-KJG |
| N274JH | Learjet | 35A-274 | Bill Hodges Truck Co. Oklahoma City, Ok. | N274JS/N1087Y |
| N274K | Westwind-1124 | 274 | Oklahoma Gas & Electric Co. Oklahoma City, Ok. | N701W/N701Z/4X-CNT |
| N275AL | Citation | 500-0333 | Aeroquip Corp. Jackson, Mi. | (N5333J) |
| N275CC | Citation | 550-0220 | Coleman Co. Wichita, Ks. | N95CC/N6802S |
| N275CQ | Citation | 501-0122 | The Coleman Co. Wichita, Ks. | N275CC/(N26495) |
| N275E | Learjet | 24D-245 | Combs Gates Denver Inc. | JA8446/N275E/N275LE |
| N276AL | Citation | 550-0016 | Libby-Owens Ford Co. Toledo, Oh. | N3221M |
| N276JS | Learjet | 35A-458 | Mariner Equipment Inc. Portland, Or. | |
| N276LE | Learjet | 25B-078 | Rockford Motors Inc, Il. | N64MR/N64MP/N258GL |
| N277CT | HS 125/700A | NA0261 | Caterpillar Tractor Co. Peoria, Il. | N125AL/G-5-17 |
| N277HM | Citation | 551-0035 | Air Cruise/John W Myers, Long Beach, Ca. | N6860U |
| N277LE | Learjet | 25-028 | Rockford Motors Inc, Il. | N263GL/N592KR |
| N277NS | NAL 1-11/401 | 3/057 | EAF/Norton Simon Inc. NY. | N5017 |
| N277T | Gulfstream 2 | 209 | Trunkline Gas Co. Houston, Tx. | N806GA |
| N278A | Citation | 550-0153 | Burlington Industries Inc. Greensboro, NC. | N27BA/(N88842) |
| N278SP | Citation | 500-0278 | Southwestern Public Services Co. Amarillo, Tx. | N278CC/(N5278J) |
| N279DM | Learjet | 35A-214 | Domar Jet Charter Inc. Menlo Park, Ca. | |
| N279LE | Learjet | 25B-112 | Rockford Motors Inc. Rockford, Il. | N173J/OY-BFC |
| N279SP | Learjet | 35A-452 | Southwestern Public Service Co. Amarillo, Tx. | N25MJ |
| N280R | Learjet | 24B-188 | Dart Industries, West Bend, Wi. | N230R |
| N281AM | Citation | 550-0303 | | |
| N281FP | Learjet | 24D-281 | Flight Proficiency Service Inc. Dallas, Tx. | N23MJ/OY-BIZ/SE-DFB |
| N281R | Learjet | 25-026 | F & S Aviation Ltd. Pittsburgh, Pa. | N283R/C-GMAP/N7ZA/N4005S |
| N284JJ | Falcon 20E | 284 | Andorra Aviation, Santa Barbara, Ca. | N132JA/N4437F/F-WPXM |
| N285U | Falcon 20F | 364 | National Medical Enterprises Inc. Los Angeles, Ca. | N235U/N1013F<br>/F-WMKI |
| N286G | Citation | 550-0173 | Larry Mohr, Indianapolis, In. | (N36NW)/N88822 |
| N287W | Falcon 20D | 194 | S & W Aircraft Leasing Co. Seattle, Wa. | N297W/N555RA/N100M/N43R4F |

63

| Regis-tration | Type | C/N | Owner/Operator | Previous Identities |
|---|---|---|---|---|
| | | | | /F-WPUZ |
| N288DF | Learjet | 24D-288 | Exploring the Air Corp. Teterboro, NJ. | |
| N288J | Learjet | 24F-357 | Joy Manufacturing Co. Pittsburgh, Pa. | |
| N288WW | Westwind 1124 | 277 | Urban Development Investment Co. Chicago, Il. | (N2AJ)/4X-CNW |
| N289CA | Learjet | 29-003 | | |
| N289K | Gulfstream 2 | 225 | Crawford Fitting Co. Solon, Oh. | N55922/G-BGLT/N17585 |
| N290 | Learjet | 25D-251 | Braman Aviation Inc. Miami, Fl. | N78SD/N752GL |
| N290BC | Learjet | 35-064 | Boise Cascade Corp. Boise, Id. | |
| N290W | Falcon 50 | 90 | Kellogg Rust Inc. Hampton, NH. | F-WZHX |
| N292BC | Falcon 50 | 62 | Boise Cascade Corp. Boise, Id. | N77FJ/F-WZHE |
| N292JC | Westwind-1124 | 292 | Oil Field Rental Service Co. Houston, Tx. | 4X-COL |
| N293BC | Falcon 50 | 82 | Boise Cascade Corp. Boise, Id. | N88FJ/F-WZHU |
| N294NW | Learjet | 25-031 | Norfolk & Western Railway Co. Roanoke, Va. | |
| N294W | Westwind-1124 | 222 | The Rust Engineering Co. Hampton, NH. | 4X-CLT |
| N296BS | Learjet | 35A-296 | Gemini Aviation Inc. Denver, Co. | |
| N296PH | Citation | 550-0266 | Pizza Hut Inc. Wichita, Ks. | N296CC/N68622 |
| N297A | Westwind-1124 | 267 | Sinclair & Valentine Inc. Hampton, NH. | N297W/4X-CNM |
| N297W | Falcon 50 | 111 | Wheelabrator-Frye. | F-WZHZ |
| N298A | Westwind-1124 | 318 | Sigma Instrument Inc. Hampton, NH. | N298W/4X-CRL |
| N298CJ | Citation | 550-0268 | Don Bluth, Provo, Ut. | N68625 |
| N299CT | HS 125/700A | NA0264 | Caterpillar Tractor Co. Peoria, Il. | G-5-19 |
| N299FB | HS 125/700A | NA0287 | Fisher Bros. Financial & Development Corp. NYC. | N77LP/N125/G-5-15 |
| N299NW | Falcon 20C | 61 | Norfolk & Western Railway Co. Corp. Roanoke, Va. | N887F/F-WMKI |
| N299W | Falcon 50 | 21 | Wheelabrator-Frye Inc. Boston, Ma. | 9K-AEE/(9K-ACO)/F-WZHN |
| N300A | Falcon 10 | 59 | ICI Americas Inc. Wilmington, De. | N300GN/N144FJ/F-WJMN |
| N300AL | Falcon 20F | 330 | Abbott Laboratories, Wheelling, Il. | N4460F/F-WNGM |
| N300AG | JetStar-6 | 5056 | Saudi Royal Family. | N105GH/N105G/N9223R |
| N300CC | HS 125/731 | 25250 | Luqa Inc. Monterey, Ca. | N24S/N20S/G-AYOK/TR-LOU/G-AYOK |
| N300CF | BH 125/731 | NA770 | C F & I Steel Corp. Pueblo, Co. | N88GA/N67BH/G-5-11 |
| N300CH | Sabre-40 | 282-26 | Engineered Mechanical Service Inc. Baton Rouge, La. | N153G/N737E /N60R7/N60Y/N63ROC |
| N300CR | JetStar-6 | 5020 | Crane Co. NY. | N371H/N9207R |
| N300DH | Jet Commander | 74 | Harpair Corp. Oklahoma City, Ok. | N47DM/N535D |
| N300DM | Diamond One | A003SA | Mike Donahoe Aviation Co. Phoenix, Az. | |
| N300GA | Gulfstream 3 | 300 | Bristol Myers Co. NY. | |
| N300GB | DH 125/1A-522 | 25074 | General Battery Corp. Reading, Pa. | N400UW/N400NW/G-ATOV |
| N300HC | Westwind Two | 307 | Hardaway Construction Inc. Columbus, Ga. | N1124K/YV-388CP/4X-CRA |
| N300HH | Diamond One | A035SA | | |
| N300HR | Westwind Two | 335 | Hussman Refrigerator Co. Dover, De. | 4X-CTC |
| N300JA | Learjet | 24D-282 | ERA Helicopters Inc. Anchorage, Ak. | D-INKA |
| N300JJ | Falcon 20DC | 208 | Wallace Leasing Corp. Rochester, NY. | VH-BRR/HB-VCA/F-WPXD |
| N300L | Gulfstream 3 | 318 | Triangle Publications Inc. Radnor, Pa. | N308GA |
| N300LB | Learjet | 24-149 | Jet Air Inc. Jacksonville, Fl. | N300HH/N2945C/N294BC |
| N300LD | HS 125/700A | NA0232 | Lendee Co. Los Angeles, Ca. | N900CC/G-BFYV/(G-5-15) |
| N300LS | Westwind 1124 | 226 | Limited Stores Inc. Columbus, Oh. | N500LS/4X-CLX |
| N300M | Jet Commander B | 124 | Amcord Inc. Newport Beach, Ca. | N1300M |
| N300NL | Falcon 20DC | 221 | Sunstream Jet Express Inc. Port Chester, NY. | N25FE/N4406F/F-WPUV |
| N300PL | Learjet | 25D-247 | Continental Illinois Leasing Corp. Chicago, Il. | |
| N300PP | Learjet | 25-043 | Herndon Oil & Gas. Tulsa, Ok. | N808NP/N3OLJ |
| N300R | DH 125/1A-522 | 25043 | Howell Instruments, Fort Worth, Tx. | N3007/N1230V/N125J/G-ATGA |
| N300RC | Sabre-60 | 306-111 | Royal Crown Companies, Atlanta, Ga. | N2106J |
| N300TA | Learjet | 23-038 | SBA Corp. Ft. Lauderdale, Fl. | N100JZ/N100TA/N433JB/N433J/90-CHB /90-CGM/N1002B/LN-NPE/VR-BCF/N812LJ |
| N300TB | Sabre-60A | 306-24 | Asamera Oil U.S. Inc. Denver, Co. | N5419/N958R/N4734N |
| N300TK | Sabre-40 | 282-41 | Thomas Knox Associates, Willow Grove, Pa. | N57RM/N707JM/N300RG /N300RC/N661P/N6396C |
| N300WG | Learjet | 25D-346 | Greenleaf Corp. Saggerstown, Pa. | N379RV |
| N300WK | Citation | 500-0359 | N Rockefeller, NY. | N36863 |
| N301DM | Diamond One | A007SA | | |
| N301EC | Gulfstream 2 | 258 | Household Finance Corp. Prospect Heights, Il. | N823GA |
| N301HC | Citation | 500-0348 | ECSL 11, Wolfeboro, NH. | N300HC/(N534RJ) |
| N301L | Jet Commander | 98 | Wm Mason, Franklin, NC. | N482G/N101DE/N6DB/CF-WRN/N1121N |
| N301MC | Sabre-60 | 306-146 | Heron Associates, Lexington, Ma. | |
| N301PC | Westwind 1124 | 383 | Peabody Coal Co. Wilmington, De. | N82HH/4X-CUO |
| N301SC | Learjet | 35A-143 | M P Appleby, Oklahoma City, Ok. | |
| N302CE | Citation | 500-0302 | White Industries Inc. Bates City, Mo. | N5302J |

| Registration | Type | C/N | Owner/Operator | Previous Identities |
|---|---|---|---|---|
| N302DM | Diamond One | A004SA | | |
| N302H | Sabre-60A | 306-5 | Husky Aviation Co. Cody, Wy. | N365N |
| N303AF | Learjet | 24-144 | Air Partnership Ltd. Denver, Co. | N700C/N9KC/N397BC/N397L/N593GA |
| N303EC | Citation | 550-0306 | Household International, Wilmington, De. | N6888X |
| N303EJ | Learjet | 24D-303 | F H & H Aero Leasing, Dallas, Tx. | |
| N303GA | Gulfstream 3 | 357 | | |
| N303PC | Citation | 500-0124 | J C Pace & Co. Fort Worth, Tx. | N300HO/N300HC/N124CC |
| N303X | Citation | 550-0187 | Panhandle Eastern Pipeline, Kansas City, Mo. | N98432 |
| N304DM | Diamond One | A005SA | Hartford National Bank, Ct. | |
| N304E | Learjet | 36A-038 | Bamerilease Capital Corp. San Francisco, Ca. | |
| N304EJ | Learjet | 24D-304 | Executive Jet Aviation, Columbus, Oh. | |
| N304WW | Westwind-Two | 304 | The Whitewind Co. Greenwich, Ct. | 4X-COX |
| N305BB | Westwind-1124 | 228 | Badgett Brown, Central City, Ky. | 4X-CLZ |
| N305DM | Diamond One | A009SA | | |
| N305M | Citation | 501-0063 | Martin Marietta Corp. Bethesda, DC. | N2991A |
| N305SC | Learjet | 35A-322 | GECC, Orlando, Fl. | |
| N306CW | Sabre-40A | 282-108 | Williams Aviation Co. Midland, Tx. | N442WP/N442WT/N7596N |
| N306DM | Diamond One | A010SA | Valley International Properties Inc. Wolfboro, NH. | |
| N306EJ | Learjet | 24D-306 | Executive Jet Aviation, Columbus, Oh. | |
| N306M | Learjet | 35A-416 | Martin Marietta Corp. Bethesda, Md. | |
| N306PC | Sabre-40A | 282-112 | Peabody Coal Co. Wilmington, De. | N301PC/N6789D/N6789/N7667N |
| N306SC | Citation | 550-0286 | Sundstrand Corp. Rockford, Il. | N68631 |
| N307D | Sabre-60 | 306-31 | National Center for Atmospheric Research, Boulder. | |
| N307DM | Diamond One | A011SA | | |
| N307EJ | Learjet | 24D-307 | Executive Jet Aviation, Columbus, Oh. | |
| N308A | Gulfstream 2 | 155 | ARAMCO, Jeddah, Saudi Arabia. | |
| N308DM | Diamond One | A012SA | Campbell Taggart, Dallas, Tx. | |
| N308EJ | Learjet | 24D-308 | Executive Jet Aviation, Columbus, Oh. | |
| N308EL | Gulfstream 2 | 68 | Eli Lilly & Co. Indianapolis, In. | |
| N309EL | Gulfstream 2 | 250 | Eli Lilly & Co. Indianapolis, In. | N821GA |
| N310AD | JetStar-6 | 5051 | Modern World Export Finance Co. Boca Raton, Fl/Indimi Enterprises, Nigeria. | N31S/N44MF/N400KC/N9217R |
| N310BA | Learjet | 35-062 | Somerset Distributors Inc. Long Beach, Ca. | N701US/TL-ABD/ZS-LII /N217CS |
| N310EL | NAL 1-11/401 | 6/072 | Eli Lilly & Co. Indianapolis, In. | N5030 |
| N311DM | Diamond One | A019SA | | |
| N312CT | Learjet | 35A-403 | Centel Communications Co. Chicago, Il. | N37966 |
| N312DC | Citation | 550-0345 | GTE Directories Corp. Des Plaines, Il. | N6804Y |
| N312K | Sabre-40 | 282-105 | Wyco Inc. Omaha, Nb. | N22BJ/N20W/N2HW |
| N313BT | Citation | 551-0022 | Circle B Omni Inc. Medford, Or. | N26640 |
| N313DM | Diamond One | A022SA | | |
| N314DM | Diamond One | A023SA | | |
| N314TC | Citation | 500-0216 | Cherokee Services Aviation Inc. OKC, OK. | N216CC |
| N315DM | Diamond One | A015SA | | |
| N315MR | Citation | 501-0076 | Guy Mabee, Midland, Tx. | N451CJ/N3122M |
| N315S | Citation | 501-0038 | Stim Air Inc. Portland, Or. | N36923 |
| N316 | Learjet | 35-024 | Oman Construction Co. Ltd. Nashville, Tn. | |
| N316DM | Diamond One | A024SA | | |
| N316H | Citation | 550-0283 | Burlington Industries Inc. Greensboro, NC. | N316CC/N6861L |
| N317DM | Diamond One | A025SA | | |
| N317EM | DH 125/731 | 25115 | Intermedics Inc. Freeport, Tx. | N333MF/N333ME/N229P/G-ATYK |
| N317MR | Learjet | 24D-297 | Proform, Minneapolis, Mn. | N716US/XA-ACC/N297EJ |
| N318DM | Diamond One | A034SA | | |
| N318GA | Gulfstream 3 | 355 | | |
| N319DM | Diamond One | A027SA | | |
| N319EJ | Learjet | 25D-319 | Executive Jet Aviation, Columbus, Oh. | |
| N319GA | Gulfstream 3 | 370 | | |
| N319Z | Gulfstream 3 | 319 | Dana Corp. Toledo, Oh. | |
| N320DM | Diamond One | A028SA | | |
| N320EJ | Learjet | 25D-320 | Bruce G Sundlun, The Plains, Va. | |
| N320GA | Gulfstream 3 | 372 | | |
| N320S | JetStar-731 | 36/5082 | Texasgulf Inc. NY. | |
| N320V | Citation | 550-0180 | Orbit Valve Co/Jet Leasing Co. Little Rock, Ar. | N88825 |
| N320W | Jet Commander | 15 | White Industries, Bates City, Mo. | N125K/HB-VAX/N365G |
| N321AS | Learjet | 25D-273 | Alvin Siteman, St.Louis, Mo. | |
| N321DM | Diamond One | A029SA | | |
| N322CC | HS 125/F600 | 6070 | Crown Central Petroleum Corp. Baltimore, Md. | G-5-15/N322CC/G-BEDT |

65

| Regis-tration | Type | C/N | Owner/Operator | Previous Identities |
|---|---|---|---|---|
| | | | | /G-5-11 |
| N322CS | JetStar 2 | 5208 | Island Helicopters Corp. NY. | N5534L |
| N322DM | Diamond One | A030SA | | |
| N323CB | Citation | 501-0167 | C R B Oil & Gas, Dallas, Tx. | N563CC/(N2616L) |
| N323DM | Diamond One | A032SA | | |
| N323EC | Sabre-60 | 306-134 | Whiteland Inc. Malvern, Pa. | N2152J |
| N323EJ | Learjet | 25D-323 | Charles Carroll, Akron, Oh. | |
| N324K | HS 125/700A | NA0277 | Ford Motor Co. Dearborn, Mi. | N125AF/G-5-16 |
| N325DM | Diamond One | A006SA | | |
| N325K | Sabre-40 | 282-63 | Kiewit Co. Omaha, Nb. | |
| N326DM | Diamond One | A036SA | | |
| N326EJ | Learjet | 24D-326 | Charles Ogle, Middletown, Oh. | |
| N326K | HS 125/700A | NA0284 | Ford Motor Co. Dearborn, Mi. | N125AE/G-5-11 |
| N327DM | Diamond One | A037SA | | |
| N327EJ | Learjet | 24D-327 | Charles Ogle, Middletown, Oh. | |
| N327JB | Sabre-40 | 282-9 | Aero Services International, Teterboro, NJ. | N620K/N620M/N6363C |
| N327K | Gulfstream 2 | 25 | Ford Motor Co. Dearborn, Mi. | |
| N328CC | Citation | 500-0328 | Mid South Aviation, Little Rock, Ar. | (N571K) |
| N328DM | Diamond One | A039SA | | |
| N328TL | Learjet | 24B-212 | Husky Industries Inc. White City, Or. | N291BC |
| N329K | Gulfstream 2 | 180 | Ford Motor Co. Dearborn, Mi. | N859GA |
| N330CC | Citation | 500-0330 | SCM Corp. NY. | (N5330J) |
| N330DM | Diamond One | A041SA | | |
| N330J | Learjet | 24-130 | Rex Baker, Houston, Tx. | N33CJ/N130J/N1871P/N1871R/N420WR/N657LJ |
| N332DM | Diamond One | A041SA | | |
| N332GJ | Citation | 500-0015 | Ryan Aviation Corp. Wichita, Ks. | N979EE/N58CC/N5867/N515CC |
| N332H | Citation | 500-0144 | Halliburton Services, Dallas, Tx. | (N644CC) |
| N332LS | Learjet | 25B-122 | Lockheed Aircraft Corp. Ontario, Ca. | N23TA |
| N333AR | Gulfstream 2 | 189 | ARCO, Burbank, Ca. | |
| N333CG | Westwind Two | 339 | Aviation Trading Centre, W. Palm Beach, Fl. | 4X-CTG |
| N333GU | Gulfstream 3 | 875 | Gulf United Corp. Dallas, Tx. | N333GA |
| N333KN | JetStar-8 | 5118 | Kaneb Services Inc. York, Nb. | N3330A/N7963S |
| N333ME | HS 125/700A | NA0202 | Pacific Systems Inc. Portland, Or. | N64688/G-BERP/G-5-19 |
| N333MS | Citation | 501-0190 | Stovrolla Farms, Antony, Fl. | N584CC/(N6780M) |
| N333PC | Sabre-65 | 465-28 | Permian Corp. Houston, Tx. | N2549E |
| N333PP | Citation Eagle | 500-0050 | Ohio Scientific Inc. Aurora, Oh. | N471HH/N471MH/N471MM/N550CC |
| N333RB | Learjet | 35A-220 | Reading & Bates Corp. Tulsa, Ok. | N79BH |
| N333RW | JetStar-8 | 5138 | Marine Fabricators Inc. Houston, Tx. | N1301P/N5502L |
| N333SG | Learjet | 25D-226 | Comm-Scope Company, Catawba, NC. | |
| N333SV | Jet Commander | 114 | Commander Associates, Newport Beach, Ca. | N85MR/N10GR/N111ST /N448WT/N442WT/4X-CPC/N4743E |
| N333XX | Learjet | 35A-286 | Mitel Inc. Dover, De. | N333X |
| N334 | Westwind Two | 344 | John Galbeath, Columbus, Oh. | 4X-CTL |
| N334AM | Citation | 550-0201 | Amica Mutual Insurance, Providence, RI. | N6799E |
| N334DM | Diamond One | A044SA | | |
| N334JR | BH 125/600A | 6020 | Rollins Inc. Atlanta, Ga. | N125CU/N29BH |
| N334LP | Jet Commander | 20 | Louisiana Power & Light Co. New Orleans. | |
| N335H | Gulfstream 2TT | 238 | Halliburton Services, Dallas, Tx. | N831GA |
| N335WR | Falcon 20C | 122 | Orkin Extermination Co. Inc. Atlanta, Ga. | N779P/N4342F/F-WNGL |
| N338DB | Falcon 20D | 225 | N332FE/N37WT/N25MJ/OH-FFJ/F-BOFH/TR-LRU/TR-KHA/F-WPXD | |
| N338DM | Diamond One | A038SA | | |
| N338X | Learjet | 24D-251 | CECO Corp. Columbus, Ms. | N333X |
| N339GA | Gulfstream 3 | 374 | | |
| N340 | JetStar-731 | 38/5029 | National Steel Corp. West Mifflin, Pa. | N3EK/N3E |
| N340DR | Westwind-1124 | 242 | Donrey Inc. Las Vegas, Nv. | 4X-CMN |
| N341AG | Citation | 550-0041 | Anderson-Greenwood Co. Bellaire, Tx. | N8418B/N3279M |
| N341AP | Sabre-65 | 465-40 | Air Products & Chemicals Inc. Allentown, Pa. | |
| N341CC | Citation | 500-0320 | Westvaco Corp. NY. | N299WV/N341CC/N320CC/(N5320J) |
| N341FW | Learjet | 25D-341 | Fisher Webb Investments, Abilene, Tx. | |
| N341GA | Gulfstream 3 | 360 | | |
| N341NS | Gulfstream 2 | 64 | National Steel Corp. West Mifflin, Pa. | N950BS/N940BS/N836GA |
| N341TC | B 727-22 | 19148 | Tracinda Corp. Las Vegas, Nv. | N7084U |
| N342AP | Citation | 500-0077 | Butler Industrial Gas Co. Allentown, Pa. | N577CC |
| N342CC | Citation | 550-0414 | Westvaco Corp. NY. | |
| N342K | Falcon 20C | 101 | Midwest Aviation Inc. Omaha, Nb. | N984F/F-WMKJ |
| N343CC | Citation | 550-0320 | Glenn Martin, | (N6890D) |
| N343K | Gulfstream 2 | 10 | Eastman Kodak Co. NY. | |

| Regis-tration | Type | C/N | Owner/Operator | Previous Identities |
|---|---|---|---|---|
| N344A | Falcon 10 | 153 | Archer Daniels Midland Co. Wilmington, De. | N218FJ/F-WZGZ |
| N344K | Sabre-60 | 306-97 | Peter Kiewit/Midwest Aviation Inc. Omaha, Nb. | N3WO/I-FBCA/N65785 |
| N344UP | Sabre-40 | 282-45 | Union Pacific Railroad Co. Columbus, Nb. | N747UP |
| N345CP | Gulfstream 2 | 123 | 711 Aviation/Columbia Pictures, NY. | N805CC |
| N345EJ | Learjet | 25D-345 | E J A, Columbus, Oh. | |
| N345MC | Learjet | 25-046 | MCOCO, Houston, Tx. | N33PT/N55KO/N55KC/N964GA |
| N345PA | Falcon 50 | 36 | Bristol-Myers Co. NY. | N54FJ/F-WZHJ |
| N345UP | Gulfstream 2 | 159 | Union Pacific Railroad Co. NY. | |
| N347EJ | Learjet | 25D-347 | E J A, Columbus, Oh. | |
| N347WW | Westwind Two | 347 | Reed Rock Bit Co. Houston, Tx. | 4X-CTO |
| N348SJ | Westwind-1124 | 348 | Jet East, Dallas, Tx. | N348WW/4X-CTP |
| N349EJ | Learjet | 25D-349 | E J A, Columbus, Oh. | N40146 |
| N349M | Jet Commander | 23 | Midland Mortgage Co. Oklahoma City, Ok. | N2100X |
| N350AG | Learjet | 25D-350 | Aaron Giebel, Midland, Tx. | |
| N350E | Sabre-40 | 282-76 | Erie Manufacturing Co. Milwaukee, Wi. | N415GS/N415CS/N124H/N787R D-CAVW/N474VW/N2242B |
| N350JF | Learjet | 35A-219 | Barton & Barton Co. Atlanta, Ga. | N502G/VH-BJO/N39416 |
| N350M | Citation | 501-0112 | Murphy Oil Corp. El Dorado, Ar. | (N900LL)/N2649E |
| N350PM | Westwind Two | 338 | Pet Inc. St. Louis, Mo. | N338W/4X-CTF |
| N351C | Westwind-1124 | 264 | Ingram Corp. Nashville, Tn. | 4X-CNJ |
| N351GL | Learjet | 35-001 | Gates Learjet Corp. Wichita, Ks. (Winglets). | N731GA |
| N351N | Learjet | 23-054 | Epps Air Service Inc. Atlanta, Ga. | N351NR/N351WC/N351WB/CF-TEL |
| N352WC | Citation | 500-0275 | The Williams Companies, Tulsa, Ok. | (N38MM)/N40MM/N600SR/(N5275J) |
| N353EJ | Learjet | 25D-353 | E J A, Columbus, Oh. | |
| N353WC | HS 125/700A | NA0223 | The Williams Companies, Tulsa, Ok. | N700BA/G-BFUE |
| N354WC | HS 125/700A | NA0245 | The Williams Companies, Tulsa, Ok. | N700BA/N125HS/G-5-15 |
| N355WC | Falcon 20C | 44 | The Williams Companies, Tulsa, Ok. | N355WB/N873F/F-WNGN |
| N355WW | Westwind Two | 355 | P C Aviation Co. Rockville, Md. | 4X-CUI |
| N356P | Learjet | 35-006 | Potlatch Corp. Lewiston, Id. | |
| N356WC | Falcon 20C | 80 | The Williams Companies, Tulsa, Ok. | N356WB/N115K/N972F/F-WMKI |
| N357H | JetStar 2 | 5234 | H J Heinz & Co. Pittsburgh, Pa. | N4049M |
| N358CT | Westwind Two | 358 | Continental Tool Corp. Rockville, Md. | 4X-CUL |
| N359V | Falcon 10 | 120 | Valmont Industries, Nb. | N20ES/N192FJ/F-WPXM |
| N360CH | Sabre-60 | 306-15 | Chart House Inc. Lafayette, La. | N60BK/N101L/N4725N |
| N360DJ | Citation | 501-0182 | Denver Jet Inc. Englewood, Co. | N6780J |
| N360N | Citation | 550-0072 | Ottaway Newspapers Inc. Cambell Hall, NY. | (N2661H) |
| N360X | HS 125/700A | NA0230 | Panhandle Eastern Pipeline Co. Kansas City, Mo. | G-5-13 |
| N361DJ | Citation | 550-0037 | Denver Jets Inc. Co. | N37HG/(N3268M) |
| N362DJ | Citation | 550-0050 | Denver Jets Inc. Co. | N102FC/(N3298M) |
| N363BC | Learjet | 24D-241 | Sierra Lima Jet Service, Georgetown, Tx. | N120J/HB-VCT |
| N363HA | Learjet | 25D-242 | Holiday Inns Inc. Memphis, Tn. | N749GL |
| N365G | Gulfstream 2TT | 198 | General Electric Co. NY. | N825GA |
| N365N | Learjet | 35A-300 | Nielson Enterprises, Cody, Wy. | |
| N366F | Falcon 50 | 77 | Figgie International, Willoughby, Oh. | N85FJ/F-WZHC |
| N366G | Falcon 20C | 9 | General Electric Co. NY. | N809F/F-WMKI |
| N366MP | DH 125/3A-RA | NA700 | Powers Air, Houston, Tx. | N338/N514VA/N514V/G-AVHA/G-5-11 |
| N367G | Gulfstream 2 | 125 | General Electric Co. NY. | N870GA |
| N368G | Falcon 20C | 29 | General Electric Co. NY. | N849F/F-WMKI |
| N368S | Westwind-1124 | 271 | Victor Alhadeff, Bellevue, Wa. | 4X-CNO |
| N369G | Falcon 20C | 34 | General Electric Co. NY. | N808F/F-WMKJ |
| N369N | Sabre-40 | 282-8 | Chinook Pipeline Inc. Douglas, Wy. | N366N/N520S/N6362C |
| N369XL | Learjet | 35A-423 | L J Ltd. St. Petersburg, Fl. | |
| N370EC | Learjet | 35-003 | R T Thompson, Cashier, NC. | N263GL/N931BA/N731GA |
| N370M | HS 125/700A | NA0213 | Murphy Oil Corp. El Dorado, Ar. | (G-BFGV) |
| N371H | Westwind-1124 | 315 | Hercules Inc. Wilmington, De. | 4X-CRI |
| N371HH | Citation | 500-0214 | Heussler Helicopter Corp. Buffalo, NY. | N214CC |
| N372BC | HS 125/700A | NA0219 | Berwind Corp. Philadelphia, Pa. | N1230A/G-BFMO |
| N372CC | Citation | 550-0332 | | (N6803L) |
| N372CM | Gulfstream 3 | 338 | Cordelia Scaife May, Ligonier, Pa. | N862GA |
| N372H | JetStar 2 | 5228 | Hercules Inc. Wilmington, De. | N4034M |
| N372WW | Westwind-1124 | 372 | Aircraft Equipment Resources Inc. Bethesda, Md. | 4X-CUB |
| N373CM | Westwind Two | 373 | Charter Medical Corp. Wilmington, De. | 4X-CUK |
| N373KC | Falcon 20F | 264 | Kraftco Corp. Glenview, Il. | N4428F/F-WJMN |
| N373LP | Gulfstream 2 | 13 | Louisiana-Pacific Corp. Hillsboro, Or. | N2GP/5N-AMN/N98AM/N678RZ /N678RW |
| N374FC | Citation | 550-0340 | Falk Corp. Milwaukee, Wi. | N6804F |
| N374GS | Citation | 501-0227 | G S Equipment Inc. Midland, Tx. | N2614H |

| Regis-tration | Type | C/N | Owner/Operator | Previous Identities |
|---|---|---|---|---|
| N376D | Sabre-60A | 306-101 | Salyer Land Co. Corcoran, Ca. | N68NR/N65791 |
| N376RP | Sabre-40A | 282-115 | Whitney Investors Co. Menlo Park, Ca. | N376DD/N376D/N8333N |
| N376SC | Falcon 20F | 391 | Steelcase Inc. Grand Rapids, Mi. | N175F/F-WLCS |
| N377C | Learjet | 35A-389 | Commonwealth Aviation Partnership, Lincoln, Nb. | N59MJ |
| N377Q | Learjet | 25D-257 | Nubo Ltd, Kansas City, Mo. | N377C/N700BJ |
| N377KC | Citation Eagle | 501-0032 | Century Aircraft Corp. Amarillo, Tx. | N33AA/N388CJ/N36887 |
| N379JR | Westwind Two | 353 | Nexxus Products Co. Santa Barbara, Ca. | 4X-CTU |
| N379TH | Jet Commander | 109 | Bluestreak Inc. Oklahoma City, Ok. | N9DC/N350X |
| N380T | Sabre-75A | 380-58 | Litton Industries Inc. Van Nuys, Ca. | N75RS/N2148J |
| N380X | DH 125/731 | NA733 | Panhandle Eastern Pipeline Co. Kansas City. | G-AXOB |
| N382BL | Learjet | 35A-382 | BLC Corp. San Mateo, Ca. | |
| N390F | Gulfstream 2 | 178 | Faberge Inc. NY. | N819GA |
| N392T | Learjet | 25B-104 | Thompson & Green Machinery Co. Inc. Nashville, Tn. | N101JR/N1JR |
| N393RC | Citation | 550-0313 | Ransburg Corp. Indianapolis, In. | N6889K |
| N395CC | Citation | 550-0314 | | |
| N395SC | Citation | 501-0031 | Steiner Corp. Salt lake City, Ut. | N36896 |
| N398CC | Citation | 551-0062 | Davis Mud Co. & Chemical Inc. Sidney, Mt. | |
| N398RP | Citation | 500-0316 | Ring Power Corp. Jacksonville, Fl. | N5316J |
| N399CB | Gulfstream 2 | 118 | Film Properties Inc. Chicago, Il. | N823GA |
| N399DM | Diamond One | A008SA | Information Industries Inc/Capitol Aero, Helena, Mt. | (N56SK)/N303DM |
| N399RP | Diamond One | A020SA | | |
| N399SW | Falcon 20D | 197 | EAF/First National City Bank of NY. | N4387F/F-WPXF |
| N399W | Learjet | 35A-209 | Williams Research Corp. Walled Lake, Mi. | |
| N400 | Learjet | 25B-137 | Island Helicopters Inc. Long Island, NY. | |
| N400AG | DH 125/400A | NA735 | A G Spanos Construction Inc. Las Vegas, Nv. | N125AJ/VP-BDH/G-AXPX |
| N400BH | Citation | 500-0244 | Lesea, South Bend, In. | N244WJ/SE-DDM/(N5244J) |
| N400CS | Sabre-40 | 282-34 | Coastal Corp. Houston, Tx. | N5PO/N5PC/N575R/N6389C |
| N400CX | Gulfstream 2 | 100 | Skybird Aviation Inc. Van Nuys, Ca. | N4000X/N852GA |
| N400DT | Citation | 550-0095 | Bedford Aviation Inc. NY. | N26631 |
| N400EP | Learjet | 24XR-215 | Enterprise Products Co. Houston, Tx. | (N57JR)/N29CA/N10EC/N201WL /N971GA |
| N400GN | Falcon 20F | 325 | Gannett Inc. NY. | N100GN/N4457F/F-WMKG |
| N400GP | BH 125/731 | NA762 | Citation Builders, San Leandro, Ca. | N523M/N57BH |
| N400HC | Jet Commander | 117 | Hallmark & Son Coal Co. Warrior, Al. | N200BP/N237JF |
| N400J | Gulfstream 2 | 196 | Johnson & Johnson, New Brunswick, NJ. | |
| N400JD | Gulfstream 2 | 67 | John Deere & Co. Moline, Il. | N10HR/EL-WRT/N711S/N839GA |
| N400JE | Learjet | 35A-120 | Public Service Co. Albuquerque, NM. | |
| N400JS | Learjet | 25D-235 | Jet South Inc. Fort Myers, Fl. | N400PC |
| N400K | Citation | 500-0102 | King Radio Corp. Olathe, Ks. | N800PL/(N602CC) |
| N400KC | DH 125/731 | NA728 | Kimberly Clark Corp. Neenah, Wi. | N24CH/G-AXJD |
| N400M | Gulfstream 2 | 132 | Fluor Corp, Los Angeles, Ca. | N873GA |
| N400NW | HS 125/700A | NA0229 | Northwest Industries Inc. Chicago, Il. | N700BR/G-5-12 |
| N400PG | Learjet | 23-068 | Freedom International Inc. Detroit. | N9RA/N575HW/N902AB/N902AR /N460F |
| N400RB | Learjet | 35-011 | Badgett Rogers Sr. Madisonville, Ky. | N3816G |
| N400SJ | Westwind-1124 | 240 | Raritan Aviation Co. New Brunswick, NC. | (N4000)/N240WW/4X-CML |
| N400SP | Falcon 10 | 125 | Boomer Oil Co. Inc. Tulsa, Ok. | N195FJ/F-WNGD |
| N400WT | BH 125/731 | NA779 | Northwestern Leasing Co. Chicago, Il. | N84CP/N33CP/N488SJ/N76BH |
| N401AB | Falcon 20C | 66 | Nabisco, Morristown, NJ. | N891F/F-WNGL |
| N401BP | Westwind-1124 | 260 | Best Ashland Inc. Va. | 4X-CNF |
| N401DE | Jet Commander | 92 | Gold Coast Jet Leasing Inc. Fort Lauderdale, Fl. | N33PS/N524X /N5420 |
| N401JE | Learjet | 55-041 | Connell Finance Co. Inc. Westfield, NJ. | |
| N401M | Gulfstream 2 | 174 | Fluor Corp. Los Angelse, Ca. | N805GA |
| N404CB | Westwind-1124 | 245 | Greymac Aircraft Corp. Wilmington, De. | N1124P/4X-CMO |
| N404DB | Learjet | 23-026 | Heath Construction Corp. Santa Ana, Ca. | N222GH/N404AJ/N26008 /F-BSTP/HB-VBA/N706L |
| N404G | Citation | 550-0097 | P H Glatfelter Co. York, Pa. | N26634 |
| N404M | Gulfstream 2 | 220 | Martin Marietta Corp. NY. | N805GA |
| N407PC | Falcon 20C | 30 | Bassett & Tesini Inc. Fort Lauderdale, Fl. | N368EJ/YV-126CP/(JY-AEK) /N368EJ/N804F/F-WMKF |
| N408CS | Sabre-40 | 282-13 | Coastal States Gas (Europe Based). | N40RS/N899TG/N6367C |
| N408M | Gulfstream 3 | 362 | Fluor Corp. Los Angeles, Ca. | |
| N408PC | Falcon 20C | 98 | Bassett & Tesini Inc. Ft. Lauderdale, Fl. | OY-AZT/TU-VAD/F-WNGN |
| N408TR | Sabre-40 | 282-4 | The Lubrizol Corp. Ypsilanti, Mi. | N111MS/N75JD/N14J |
| N409M | Gulfstream 2 | 83 | Martin Marietta Corp. Bethesda, DC. | N404M |
| N409WT | Jet Commander | 3 | Jet Wind Inc. Oklahoma City, Ok. | N400WT/N316E/N316/N612JC |

| Registration | Type | C/N | Owner/Operator | Previous Identities |
|---|---|---|---|---|
| N410CC | Citation | 550-0412 | | N12160 |
| N410NA | Citation | 500-0345 | Noble Drilling Corp. Tulsa, Ok. | N23ND/(N5345J) |
| N410ND | Citation | 500-0259 | Florida Wings, Fort Lauderdale, Fl. | N5259J |
| N410US | Falcon 20C | 120 | U.S. Gypsum Co. Chicago, Il. | N4340F/F-WMKI |
| N410WW | Falcon 10 | 86 | Wm Wrigley Jr. Co. Chicago. Il. | N166FJ/F-WPXJ |
| N411CC | Falcon 20C | 159 | EAF/Asterion Inc. Dover, De. | N5RC/N4364F/F-WMKJ |
| N411DR | Citation | 500-0249 | Ransome Air Inc. Philadelphia, Pa. | N27PA/N5249J |
| N411LC | Learjet | 35A-366 | Calabras Inc. Winston Salem, NC. | |
| N411MM | Learjet | 24F-353 | Peregrino, Abilene, Tx. | N711PD/N740GL |
| N411SP | Learjet | 24B-216 | Radcliff Co. Cincinnati, Oh. | N711DB/N723LL/N212LF |
| N411WC | Citation | 501-0029 | Westcor Ltd. Phoenix, Az. | (N411CJ)/N87253 |
| N413GH | DH 125/1A | 25030 | Osmond Family, Provo, Mt. | G-ATBA |
| N414CB | Citation | 501-0179 | Richard Bertea, Corona del Mar, Ca. | N589CJ/(N6781D) |
| N414GC | Citation | 550-0086 | John Duncan, Houston, Tx. | N2663G |
| N415CS | Sabre-65 | 465-42 | Central Soya Co. Inc. Fort Wayne, In. | N2561E |
| N416F | Falcon 20F | 416 | Crown Zellerbach/BT Equipment Leasing Inc. NY. | N415F/F-WLCT |
| N416G | Learjet | 24D-325 | Security Pacific Equipment Leasing, SFO. | N76RV |
| N416RM | Learjet | 25D-301 | Black Jack Aviation Inc. Houston, Tx. | |
| N418S | Falcon 50 | 64 | Oilfield Aviation/Schlumberger, NY. | N79FJ/F-WZHH |
| N419GL | Learjet | 25D-294 | Gates Learjet Corp. Wichita, Ks/Air Fleet International. | N27K |
| N420A | JetStar-6 | 5063 | AVCO Corp. NY. | N420L/N9228R |
| N420L | Challenger | 1027 | AVCO Corp. NY. | C-GLXK |
| N420P | Citation | 550-0213 | AVCO Corp. Nashville, Tn. | N6802X |
| N421CJ | Citation | 550-0422 | | |
| N421ZC | Falcon 20C | 117 | Zollner Corp. Fort Lauderdale, Fl. | N171PF/N995F/F-WMKH |
| N422B | Learjet | 25D-331 | Bovairds Supply Co. Tulsa, Ok. | N462B |
| N422CC | Citation | 501-0051 | Valhi Inc. New Orleans, La. | N98601 |
| N422X | HS 125/700A | NA0253 | Field Crest Mills, Eden, NC. | G-5-19 |
| N423D | Citation | 550-0158 | Pittsburgh & Shawmut Coal Co. Manchester, NH. | (N662AA)/N88738 |
| N425DC | DH 125/731 | 25079 | Daniel Construction Co. Greenville, SC. | N40DC/N448DC/N440DC /G-ATLL |
| N426NA | Learjet | 24D-292 | PCI Transportation Inc. Chicago, Il. | (N600PC) |
| N426PS | Learjet | 24-148 | Aifam Enterprises Inc. Wichita, Ks. N8482B/HB-VDH/N133TW/N80CB/N406L | |
| N428JX | Learjet | 25B-103 | S.Central Aviation Inc. Springfield, Il. | |
| N429RC | Citation | 500-0078 | Ralph Cooke, Los Angeles, Ca. N21TV/N54531/TL-AAW/ZS-IYY/N2HD/N578CC | |
| N431CB | Citation | 550-0369 | C R Bard Inc. Murrayhill, NJ. | N324CC |
| N431CC | Citation | 501-0059 | Kenrue & Melroe Aircraft Ltd. Irvine, Ca. | N2079A |
| N431M | Learjet | 35A-132 | Motorola Inc. Wheeling, Il. | |
| N434CC | Citation | 550-0435 | | |
| N435M | Learjet | 35A-086 | Motorola Inc. Schaumburg, Il. | |
| N435N | Learjet | 35A-435 | Norfolk & Western Railway Co. Roanoke, Va. | |
| N435T | Falcon 20F | 357 | Chicago Tribune, Chicago, Il. | N4469F/F-WMKI |
| N438 | Jet Commander | 118 | Fish Engineering & Construction Inc. Ft. Stockton. | N312S |
| N439ME | Learjet | 35A-439 | | |
| N440DM | Learjet | 25D-348 | Don Mullins/Thunderbird Airways, Houston, Tx. | N37949 |
| N440MC | Learjet | 35A-495 | | |
| N441A | Gulfstream 3 | 342 | ARMCO Steel Corp. Middletown, Oh. | |
| N441T | Citation | 550-0302 | Continental Protection Systems, Houston, Tx. | N329CC/N6888T |
| N442A | Gulfstream 2TT | 255 | ARMCO Steel Corp. Middletown, Oh. | |
| N442WT | Sabre-65 | 465-45 | Wilson Trailer Co. Sioux City, Ia. | |
| N443A | Westwind-1124 | 354 | ARMCO Inc. Middletown, Oh. | 4X-CTV |
| N444AG | Learjet | 24B-208 | LAGCO, Beeville, Tx. | N32MJ/N444AG/N42HC/N72335/D-ILDE |
| N444BF | Learjet | 35A-391 | Ben Forston, Oakland, Va. | N3793D |
| N444J | Citation | 500-0179 | Centennial Credit Co. Fresno, Ca. | |
| N444JH | JetStar-731 | 42/5036 | Bill Hodges Truck Co. Bethany, Ok. | N776JM/N41TC/N1622D/N1622 |
| N444LP | Citation | 500-0223 | Lucerne Products Inc. Hudson, Oh. | N223CC |
| N444MW | Citation | 501-0034 | McWane Inc. Birmingham, Al. | N36911 |
| N444RP | Citation | 500-0250 | Rich Products, Lake Worth, Fl. | XA-JEL/N25CK/N25PA/N250CC/N5250J |
| N444SC | Falcon 20F | 324 | Southern Conference of Teamsters, Hallandale, Fl. | N4456F/F-WMKF |
| N444WB | Learjet | 35A-318 | Bauer Development Co. Newport Beach, Ca. | |
| N444WC | Learjet | 23-047 | Bard Air Freight Inc. Detroit, Mi. N9260A/YV-15CP/YV-E-GPA/N347J /N2503L | |
| N444WS | Learjet | 25-038 | ITTCO Enterprises Inc. Odessa, Tx. N36MW/N738GL/HB-VRR/EC-CKD/HB-VBR | |
| N445 | Jet Commander | 37 | N445 Associates, Long Beach, Ca. | N723JB/N123JB/N967L |
| N445A | Westwind-1124 | 362 | ARMCO Inc. Middletown, Oh. | 4X-CUP |
| N446A | Westwind-1124 | 367 | ARMCO Inc. Middletown, Oh. | 4X-CUD |
| N448DC | DH 125/3A | 25078 | Daniel Construction Co. Greenville, SC. | N40DC/G-ATLK |
| N448EC | Citation | 500-0191 | Westmoreland Coal Co. Philadelphia, Pa. | N5600M |

| Regis-tration | Type | C/N | Owner/Operator | Previous Identities |
|---|---|---|---|---|
| N448GC | Learjet | 35A-472 | Litirsa Corp. Matoon, Il. | |
| N448GG | Learjet | 23-057 | Westmoreland Coal Co. Philadelphia, Pa. | N448GC |
| N449A | Falcon 10 | 49 | Armco Steel Corp. Middletown, Oh. | N49AS/(N490A)/N136FJ/F-WLCV |
| N450 | Learjet | 25B-127 | Island Helicopter Corp. NY. | (N42BJ)/N83JM/N93CE/N93C |
| N450JD | DH 125/3A-R | 25148 | B F Shaw Inc/Budget Jet Inc. Oneida, Tn. | N8125J/G-AVRI/G-5-13 |
| N450KK | Learjet | 35A-450 | K K Associates, Columbus, Oh. | |
| N450X | Falcon 50 | 54 | Jet Leasing/Rose Associates Inc. Miami, Fl. | N71FJ/F-WZHT |
| N454LJ | Learjet | 24B-226 | Texas Instruments Inc. Dallas, Tx. | |
| N454SR | Jet Commander | 79 | Defender Chemical Industries, Columbia, SC. | |
| N455DM | Citation | 551-0018 | Acme Air Corp. Sparta, NC. | (N666AJ)/N2663F |
| N455H | Citation | 501-0162 | Fram Corp. Lake Providence, RI. | N1959E |
| N455JA | Learjet | 24XR-300 | ERA Helicopters Inc. Anchorage, Ak. | N300EJ |
| N455SF | Sabre-65 | 465-49 | Standard Oil, SFO. | |
| N455SR | Challenger | 1032 | Drum Financial Corp/St. Regis Paper Co. NY. | C-GLXU |
| N456AS | Gulfstream 2 | 17 | Firemans Fund Insurance Co. | N819GA/N119K |
| N456JA | Learjet | 24D-265 | ERA Helicopters, Anchorage, Ak. | N32WL/N2WL |
| N456N | Citation | 550-0061 | Nordstrom Inc. Seattle, Wa. | (N26614) |
| N456SR | Falcon 20F | 299 | St.Regis Paper Co. NY. | N21FJ/N734S/F-WMKI |
| N456SW | Gulfstream 3 | 337 | Sentry Insurance Co/Pittway Corp. North Brook, Il. | |
| N457F | Falcon 20 | 449 | | F-WLCT |
| N457JA | Learjet | 24XR-207 | ERA Helicopters, Anchorage, Ak. | N878W/N851JH |
| N457SW | Gulfstream 2 | 115 | SENCO Inc. Steven's Point, Wi. | N677S/N819GA |
| N458A | Falcon 10 | 58 | Armco Steel Corp. Middletown, Oh. | N58AS/N76FJ/N143FJ/F-WJMM |
| N458SW | Falcon 20C | 68 | SENCO Inc. Steven's Point, Wi. | N577S/N892F/F-WMKJ |
| N460F | Falcon 20F | 453 | | F-WJMK |
| N460MC | Falcon 20C | 105 | DALCO Petroleum, Ok. | N97FJ/N77GR/N243K/N986F/F-WNGL |
| N464CL | Learjet | 24A-096 | Clay Lacy, Van Nuys, Ca. | N1972L/N33BK/N527ER/N1967W/N421LJ |
| N464EC | Westwind-Two | 305 | Erickson Aircrane Co. Central Point, Or. | 4X-COY |
| N464HA | Learjet | 35A-304 | Holiday Inns Inc. Memphis, Tn. | |
| N465NW | Learjet | 35A-465 | Norfolk & Western Railway Co. Roanoke, Va. | |
| N465R | HS 125/700A | NA0221 | Gulf Resources & Chemical Corp. | |
| N466F | Falcon 20F | 459 | | F-WMKJ |
| N466MP | DH 125/3A-RA | 25155 | Powers Air, Houston, Tx. | N32F/G-AVXN/(G-5-12) |
| N467H | Sabre-40 | 282-3 | Hughes Aircraft Co. Culver City, Ca. | (N570R)/N570R |
| N469F | Falcon 20 | 461 | | |
| N469JR | HS 125/700A | NA0321 | Aircraft Leasing Corp. | N710BL/G-5-18 |
| N471F | Falcon 20 | 463 | Falcon Jet/Japan Air Lines. | |
| N471H | Citation | 501-0089 | The Catamore Co. Inc. Providence, RI. | (N3175M) |
| N472SP | JetStar 731 | 3/5078 | Omni International, Washington DC. | N7105/N711Z |
| N473 | Learjet | 24-101 | Flight International Inc. Atlanta, Ga. | N473EJ/N15PL/N316MF/N316M |
| N473LP | Citation | 500-0276 | Louisiana Pacific Corp. Portland, Or. | N100CM/N276CC/(N5276J) |
| N474F | Falcon 20 | 467 | | |
| N474L | Citation | 500-0323 | Ladish Malting Co. Milwaukee, Wi. | N300PB/N5323J |
| N476VC | Learjet | 35A-476 | Corporate Funding Inc. Grand Rapids, Mi. | |
| N476X | Citation | 501-0166 | Executive Airways Inc. Oklahoma City, Ok. | N2614C |
| N477JB | Learjet | 24D-230 | J R Brown Enterprises, Sierra Blanca, Tx. | N18SD/N433JA/N433J N93CB/N93C/N329HN/N252GL |
| N477X | Sabre-40A | 282-110 | Dillon Real Estate Co. Inc. Hutchinson, Ks. | N7597N |
| N479CC | Citation | 501-0097 | Maurer Development Co. Tustin, Ca. | N3198M |
| N480CC | Citation | 501-0096 | Central States Investment Co. Bartlesville, Ok. | N660AA/N3202A |
| N480LR | HFB 320 | 1054 | Latham Resources Corp. Shreveport, La. | N896HJ/D-CORU |
| N481DH | Jet Commander-B | 139 | IDSO Investments, Metaire, La. | N188G/I-ARNT/N8535/4X-CPF/N5047E |
| N481EZ | Learjet | 24A-139 | Robert Lazier, Vale, Co. | N42AJ/N52JH/N590GA |
| N482U | Learjet | 35A-482 | UPALI (USA) Inc/ARMCO Pacific Ltd. Singapore. | |
| N483G | Citation | 550-0295 | GECC/Avtex Fibers Inc. | N68876 |
| N484KA | Citation Eagle | 500-0387 | Kawneer Co. Inc. Niles, Oh. | N3206M |
| N485S | Learjet | 35A-485 | | |
| N487HR | Citation | 501-0120 | Hotel Research Laboratories Inc. Longwood, Fl. | N2646Y |
| N490MP | HS 125/700A | NA0296 | HBO & Co. Atlanta, Ga. | G-5-15 |
| N490WC | Citation | 501-0131 | Citation Industries Inc. Roseburg, Or. | N2650X |
| N491N | Citation | 550-0329 | Indium Corp. NY. (1000th Citation). | N6800C |
| N492CB | HS 125/700A | NA0241 | Crocker National Bank, San Francisco, Ca. | N700NT |
| N494G | Citation | 500-0147 | E R Ginn & Assoc. Inc. Charlotte, NC. | N404G |
| N495G | DH 125/1A-522 | 25017 | American International Airways, | N123JB/N306MP/N3060F/N3060/G-ASSH |
| N499AS | JetStar-8 | 5146 | A A S Corp. New York. | N4990D/C-GWSA/N80GM/N5510L |
| N499G | Learjet | 35A-202 | Caruth C Byrd Enterprises Inc. Dallas, Tx. | VH-MIO |

| Registration | Type | C/N | Owner/Operator | Previous Identities |
|---|---|---|---|---|
| N500AD | Citation | 500-0006 | AMS/Air Corp. Inc. Portland, Or. | N506SR/N506MX/N500MX/N506TF/N506CC /OE-FGP/N506CC |
| N500BE | Learjet | 55-058 | Bucyrus-Erie Corp. | (N55BE) |
| N500BF | Learjet | 23-010 | Broyhill Furniture Industries Inc. Lenoir, NC. | N400BF/N29BF /N333BF/N2920C/N292BC/N805LJ |
| N500CD | Learjet | 35A-083 | H D R Inc. Omaha, Nb. | (N45SL)/(N400MJ)/N400CC/(N600CC) |
| N500CS | NAL 1-11/401 | 8/086 | Coastal States Gas Co. Houston, Tx. | N111NA/N5040 |
| N500E | Sabre-65 | 465-52 | Exxon Corp. Newark, NJ. Jet Way Inc. Jackson, Mi. | |
| N500FM | Learjet | 23-088 | (N500LH)/N48AS/N804JA/N11JK/N616PS/N816LJ | |
| N500GA | Citation | 500-0217 | Griffin Industries Inc. Butler, Ky. | N217CC |
| N500GE | Citation | 500-0004 | James Berry, Titusville, Pa. | N500GS/N504CC |
| N500GJ | Jet Commander | 64 | Jet Wind Inc. Oklahoma City, Ok. | N6512V |
| N500GK | Westwind-Two | 301 | GK Technologies Inc. Greenwich, Ct. | 4X-COU |
| N500GS | Falcon 10 | 132 | General Signal Corp. NY. | N198FJ/F-WZGD |
| N500J | Westwind-Two | 303 | Johnson & Johnson, West Trenton, NJ. | 4X-COW |
| N500JC | Citation | 501-0057 | Cornell Equipment Co. Inc. Salem, Or. | N98751 |
| N500JD | JetStar-8 | 5152 | John Deere & Co. Moline, Il. | N5516L |
| N500JJ | B 707-138 | 17699 | Sunnyside Holdings Inc. New York. | G-AVZZ/VH-EBD |
| N500JS | Learjet | 35A-404 | Jet South Inc. Fort Myers, Fl. | |
| N500JW | Learjet | 23-005 | Jet Way Inc. Jackson, Mi. | N15BE/N721GB/N721HW/N994SA/N570FT/N232R |
| N500K | Citation | 501-0127 | H & L Tooth Co. Montebello, Ca. | N2649H |
| N500LS | HS 125/700A | NA0320 | Limited Stores Inc. Columbus, Oh. | N710BN/G-5-17 |
| N500M | Westwind-Two | 300 | Schoenfield Industries Inc. Seattle, Wa. | 4X-COT |
| N500MH | Learjet | 24-158 | Cardinal Aviation Inc. Tulsa, Ok. | N855GA/N392T/N642GA |
| N500ML | Westwind-1123 | 175 | P & M Rentals Inc. Houston, Tx. | N500M/N1123R/4X-CJY |
| N500P | Learjet | 24-119 | Jet Way Inc. Jackson, Mi. (N500PJ)/N500PP/N110W/N994SA/N605GA/N453SA | /N453LJ |
| N500PB | Citation | 500-0232 | Pabst Brewing Corp. Milwaukee, Wi. | N5232J |
| N500PC | Falcon 20C | 19 | Pepsico Inc. NY. | N841F/F-WNGN |
| N500PP | Learjet | 35A-390 | Patrick Petroleum Co. Jackson, Mi. | |
| N500OC | JetStar-2 | 5205 | Cargill Inc. Minneapolis, Mn. | N5000C/N5531L |
| N500RE | Learjet | 24B-193 | Regal Air, Fresno, Ca. | N500RP/N31TC/D-IOGI |
| N500RP | Learjet | 35A-341 | Penske Jet Inc. Reading, Pa. | |
| N500RR | Learjet | 24E-345 | Penske Jet Inc. Reading, Pa. | N500RP |
| N500S | JetStar 2 | 5209 | Freeport Minerals, NY. | N5535L |
| N500SB | Learjet | 24-166 | International Air Leases Inc. Miami, Fl. | N993KL |
| N500SS | Citation | 501-0189 | Simpson Sports, Torrance, Ca. | N80SF/N6780C |
| N500T | JetStar 2 | 5211 | Tenneco Inc. Houston, Tx. | N5537L |
| N500TD | Citation | 500-0070 | Twin Disc Inc. Racine, Wi. | N570CC |
| N500TF | Sabre-75A | 380-19 | Mutual Savings Life Insurance Co. New Orleans, La. | D-CLUB/N65771 |
| N500VB | Citation | 550-0132 | Westwind II Inc. Las Vegas, Nv. | N13627/G-CJHH/N2633Y |
| N500WH | Westwind 1124 | 215 | Wm. Hagerman/Overland Express, Minneapolis, Mn. | N215DH/4X-CLM |
| N500WP | Citation | 550-0215 | Woods Petroleum Corp. Oklahoma City, Ok. | N68003 |
| N500WR | Citation | 500-0166 | Wire Rope Corp. of America, St.Joseph, Mo. | |
| N500XY | Citation | 500-0347 | Hudson Oxygen Therapy Sales Co. Temecula, Ca. | |
| N500Z | JetStar-731 | 22/5072 | Intratex Gas Co. Houston, Tx. | N9233R |
| N500ZA | Learjet | 24F-350 | Wm. Roden/HNG Oil Co. Midland, Tx. | N741GL |
| N500ZC | Citation | 501-0060 | Zeto Industries Inc. Chicago, Il. | N435CC/N2741A |
| N501BL | Citation | 550-0028 | Midwest Corp. Aviation Inc. Wichita, Ks. | OE-GAU/(G-BFLY)/(N3246M) |
| N501CC | Citation | 670 | Cessna Aircraft Co. Wichita, Ks. | |
| N501CM | Citation | 501-0228 | Ceres Marine Terminals Inc. Chicago, Il. | (N999CB)/N2612N |
| N501CX | Citation | 501-0066 | Champlin Exploration Inc. Enid, Ok. | N501BG/D-IHEY/(N209RA) |
| N501EF | Citation | 501-0069 | Mark Eden Inc. Pebble Beach, Ca. | N2906A |
| N501FM | Citation | 501-0152 | First Mississippi Corp. Jackson, Ms. | N547CC/(N1874E) |
| N501HM | Citation | 501-0206 | McAllister Trucking Co. Elkin, NC. | N6784Y |
| N501KR | Citation | 501-0071 | King Ranch Oil and Gas Inc. Kingsville, Tx. | N501SR/N3105M |
| N501MM | Citation | 501-0199 | Citizens Fidelity Bank & Trust Co. Louisville, Ky. | N6782X |
| N501NC | Falcon 50 | 11 | Internorth Inc. Omaha, Nb. | N50FH/F-WZHE |
| N501SC | Citation | 500-0314 | Inland Steel Corp. Chicago, Il. | (N314CC)/N5314J |
| N501SP | Citation | 501-0019 | Don Love, Wichita, Ks. | (N301MC)/N368R2 |
| N501T | JetStar-2 | 5213 | Tenneco Inc. Houston, Tx. | N5539L |
| N502CC | Citation | 501-0113 | Davis Mud & Chemical Inc. Sidney, Mt. | (N515CC)/(N2649S) |
| N502GP | Citation | 500-0027 | Georgia Pacific Co. Portland, Or. | N527CC |
| N502MH | Learjet | 25C-098 | MJI, Lincoln, Nb. | N96MJ/YV-26CP/VR-BGF/N139J/VR-BEM/N7JN |
| N502T | BAC 1-11/212 | 083 | Tenneco Inc. Houston, Tx. | |

| Regis-tration | Type | C/N | Owner/Operator | Previous Identities |
|---|---|---|---|---|
| N503CC | Citation | 500-0003 | H R Sharpe Jr. Wilmington, De. | |
| N503GP | Citation | 500-0086 | Georgia Pacific Co. Portland, Or. | N586CC |
| N503T | BAC 1-11/212 | 183 | Tenneco Inc. Houston, Tx. | |
| N504GP | Citation | 500-0265 | Georgia Pacific Co. Augusta, Ga. | N5265J |
| N504T | BAC 1-11/211 | 084 | Tenneco Inc. Houston, Tx. | D-ABHH |
| N504Y | Learjet | 35A-282 | Southwest Forest Industries Inc. Phoenix, Az. | |
| N505C | JetStar-731 | 25/5113 | Celtran Inc. Corpus Christi, Tx. | N795RS |
| N505GP | Citation | 500-0272 | Georgia Pacific Co. Portland, Or. | N5272J |
| N505JH | Citation | 501-0126 | Richard Sugden, Wilson, Wy. | N505SP/N26492 |
| N505T | B 727-31 | 20115 | Tenneco Inc. Houston, Tx. | N7893 |
| N505W | BH 125/600A | 6013 | S J Groves & Sons, Minneapolis, Mn. | N25BE/N25BH |
| N506C | Learjet | 35A-094 | Celanese Corp. New York. | |
| N506GP | Learjet | 35A-109 | Georgia Pacific Co. Portland, Or. | |
| N506TF | Citation | 501-0001 | McGough & Associates, Las Vegas, Nv. | N51CJ/N5351J |
| N507CC | Challenger | 1026 | Celanese Corp. NYC. | C-GLXH |
| N507GP | Citation | 550-0252 | Georgia Pacific Corp. Portland, Or. | N6862R |
| N508M | Learjet | 23-025 | NMCA of Texas Inc. Dallas, Tx.   N50DM/N37DM/N3JL/N5DM/N600G/N600G | |
| N508T | JetStar-731 | 29/5119 | Tenneco Inc. Houston, Tx. | N11HM/N7964S |
| N509G | Learjet | 25-054 | Paso Grande Aviation Co. Houston, Tx. | N500JW/N12373/0Y-AKL |
| N509T | JetStar 2 | 5222 | Tenneco Inc. Houston, Tx. | (N509TF)/N5548L |
| N510AA | Sabre-80A | 380-4 | General Motors Corp. Detroit, Mi. | N5105 |
| N510CP | Falcon 10 | 43 | Cluett Peabody Co. Inc. NY. | N1515P/N135FJ/F-WJMN |
| N510LJ | Learjet | 35-025 | Texas International Co. Oklahoma City, Ok. | N135TX/N40TF/9K-ACT |
| N510PC | Challenger | 1011 | Pepsico Inc. NY. | N42137/C-GBHS |
| N510US | Gulfstream 2 | 223 | U.S.Gypsum Co. Wilmington, De. | |
| N510X | DH 125/3A | 25126 | Madden Aircraft Sales, | G-AVDL/G-5-11 |
| N511AT | Learjet | 24E-330 | Ferris Aviation Corp. East Palestine, Oh. | |
| N511BX | HS 125/3A | 25150 | Borax/Pacific Coast Molybdenum Co, Los Angeles, Ca. | G-AWMS/G-5-13 |
| N511CC | Westwind-1124 | 253 | Cabot Corp. Manchester, NH. | 4X-CMY |
| N511NC | Sabre-65 | 465-6 | Northern Natural Gas, Omaha, Nb. | N65NC |
| N511S | Falcon 10 | 115 | Jada Corp. Cincinnati, Oh. | N188FJ/F-WPXH |
| N511T | Falcon 20C | 142 | Tenneco Inc. Houston, Tx.   N777WJ/N298W/N1BF/N100S/N4355F/F-WJMM | |
| N511WC | Citation | 550-0234 | Westcor Aviation Inc. Phoenix, Az. | N8879R |
| N511WP | Falcon 20F | 341 | EAF/West Point Pepperell Inc. West Point, Ga. | N66GA/N20FJ/N4462F /F-WMKF |
| N512T | Falcon 20C | 118 | Tenneco Inc. Racine, Wi. | N996F/F-WMKG |
| N513T | Falcon 20C | 123 | Tenneco Inc. Racine, Wi. | N4343F/F-WNGM |
| N514B | HS 125/700A | NA0251 | Burroughs Corp. Detroit, Mi. | N130RF/G-5-17 |
| N514T | Falcon 20C | 130 | Tenneco Inc. Houston, Tx. | N4347F/F-WMKJ |
| N514V | BH 125/600A | 6023 | Burroughs Corp. Detroit, Mi. | N35BH |
| N515AA | Citation | 500-0085 | Aronov Realty Leasing Co. Inc. Montgomery, Al. | N51MW/N585CC |
| N516WP | Sabre-40A | 282-98 | Washington Water Power Co. Spokane, Wa. | N40SC/N4707N |
| N518S | Falcon 10 | 74 | Oilfield Aviation Corp. Houston, Tx.   N34TH/N30TH/N156FJ/F-WJMJ | |
| N519ME | Westwind-1124 | 207 | Mellon National Leasing Corp. Pittsburgh, Pa. | N330PC/N6053C /N1124P/4X-CLE |
| N520M | JetStar-8 | 5159 | Phillippi Equipment Co. Golden Valley, Mn. | N5523L |
| N520RP | Citation | 501-0202 | P B & S Chemical Co. Henderson, Ky. | N6783V |
| N520TT | Diamond One | A033SA | | N3120M |
| N521JP | Learjet | 25D-330 | Paris Enterprises Partnership, Raleigh, NC. | (N523JP) |
| N521NC | Sabre-60A | 306-109 | Northern Natural Gas Co. Omaha, Nb. | N64NC/N522N/N2101J |
| N522M | HS 125/700A | NA0326 | Marathon Oil Co. Findlay, Oh. | G-5-11 |
| N522SB | Gulfstream 3 | 339 | Bank of America, Oakland, Ca. | N302GA |
| N522TA | Learjet | 25D-318 | Caldwell Enterprises, Boca Raton, Fl. | N522JP |
| N523AC | BAC 1-11/203 | 015 | Amway Corp. Ada, Mi.   N8LG/N5LC/N541BN/N1110A/N1541/G-ASUF | |
| N523M | HS 125/700A | NA0333 | Marathon Oil Co. Findlay, Oh. | |
| N523SA | Learjet | 25D-325 | A & M Properties Inc. Baton Rouge, La. | N123MC |
| N524AC | BAC 1-11/419 | 120 | Amway Corp. Ada, Mi. | N44R/N270E |
| N524HC | Learjet | 35A-358 | Harbert Construction Corp. Birmingham, Al. | |
| N525AC | Citation | 500-0343 | Amway Corp. Ada, Mi. | (N5343J) |
| N525AW | Jet Commander-A | 129 | International Multifoods Inc. Minneapolis, Mn. | N5032F |
| N526AC | Citation | 550-0038 | Amway Corp. Ada, Mi. | (N3271M) |
| N526D | Falcon 10 | 84 | Digicon Inc. Houston, Tx.   N8447A/JA8447/N8447A/N164FJ/F-WPXH | |
| N527AC | Citation | 550-0091 | Amway Corp. Ada, Mi. | (N2665S) |
| N530G | JetStar-731 | 10/5096 | CONOCO, Houston, Tx. | N9252R |
| N530M | JetStar 2 | 5214 | Marathon Oil Co. Cleveland, Oh. | N5540L |
| N530TL | Citation | 500-0342 | Temple Eastex Inc. Diboll, Tx. | (N5342J) |

72

| Regis-tration | Type | C/N | Owner/Operator | Previous Identities |
|---|---|---|---|---|
| N531M | JetStar 2 | 5236 | Marathon Oil Co. Cleveland, Oh. | N4056M |
| N531NC | Sabre-60 | 306-7 | T C Leasing Corp. Wilmington, De. | N63NC/N523N/N4715N |
| N532M | Citation | 550-0344 | Marathon Oil Co. Findlay, Oh. | N6808X |
| N533 | HS 125/700A | NA0281 | Marion Corp. Mobile, Al. | N125AN/G-5-18 |
| N533CS | Falcon 10 | 177 | Campbell Soup Co. Camden, NJ. | N243FJ/F-WZGJ |
| N533M | Citation | 550-0024 | Marathon Oil Co. Findlay, Oh. | N3276M |
| N534M | Citation | 550-0048 | Marathon Oil Co. Findlay, Oh. | N3288M |
| N534MW | Citation | 550-0052 | Myrna Lopez, Las Cruces, NM. | N90MJ/OY-ASV/(OO-LFX)/N4620G |
| N535MC | Learjet | 35A-385 | Mississippi Chemical Corp. Yazoo City, Ms. | |
| N536M | Citation | 550-0128 | Marathon Oil Co. Findlay, Oh. | N2631V |
| N537M | Citation | 550-0129 | Marathon Oil Co. Findlay, Oh. | N2632Y |
| N538M | Citation | 550-0299 | Marathon Oil Co. Findlay, Oh. | N6888L |
| N540B | HS 125/700A | NA0255 | Jucamcyn Theaters Corp. Minneapolis, Mn. | N125AJ/G-5-14 |
| N540G | JetStar-731 | 19/5075 | CONOCO, Houston, Tx. | N397B |
| N540HP | Learjet | 35A-399 | PIP Capital Inc. Los Angeles, Ca. | N37965 |
| N541MM | Challenger | 1044 | Bowater North America Corp. Greenwich, Ct. | |
| N544X | Falcon 20F | 258 | Pillsbury Co. Minneapolis, Mn. | N20JM/N4426F/F-WNGM |
| N545GA | Citation | 500-0357 | State of Georgia, Atlanta, Ga. | N120RD/YV-120CP/N36854/N5368J |
| N545S | DH 125/731 | NA719 | Scovill Manufacturing Co. Waterbury, Ct. | G-AWXD |
| N546EX | Falcon 50 | 41 | Bristol-Myers Co. NY. | N60FJ/F-WZHI |
| N550CC | Citation | 550-686 | Cessna's Citation 2 Prototype. | |
| N550CF | Citation | 550-0346 | Cosden Oil & Chemical Co. Dallas, Tx. | |
| N550DD | Citation | 550-0258 | Nevada National Leasing Inc. Las Vegas, Nv. | N172CB/N6861S |
| N550J | Citation | 550-0418 | Justiss Oil Co. Inc. Jena, La. | |
| N550JR | Citation | 550-0275 | J. Redman/Addison Piper Inc. | N6799L |
| N550KC | Citation | 550-0264 | Carland Inc. Kansas City, Mo. | N6862L |
| N550KP | Citation | 550-0162 | GFI Air Inc. Wilmington, De. | VH-UOH/N2745T |
| N550LP | Citation | 550-0177 | Mar-Flite Ltd. Portland, Or. | (N200MR)/N98468 |
| N550RL | Citation | 550-0240 | TODCO Inc. Portland, Or. | N6804S |
| N550TP | Citation | 550-0170 | Tecumseh Products Co. Tecumseh, Mi. | N88791 |
| N550WR | Citation | 550-0359 | Wire Rope Corp. of America, St. Joseph, Mo. | N67983 |
| N551AB | Citation | 551-0030 | Algernon Blair Inc. Montgomery, Al. | (N98718) |
| N551AS | Learjet | 24B-229 | Albertsons Inc. Boise, Id. | N298H/N293BC |
| N551BC | Citation | 551-0012 | Boyne USA Inc. Boyne Falls, Mi. | N1955E |
| N551CC | Learjet | 35-017 | Intercontinental Consolidated, Houston, Tx. | N119GS |
| N551DP | Learjet | 25D-213 | Sandair Inc. Houston, Tx. | |
| N551GL | Learjet | 55-001 | Gates Learjet Corp. Wichita, Ks. | |
| N551HB | Learjet | 55-038 | First Hawaii Bank, Honolulu, Hi. | |
| N551MC | Citation | 551-0019 | Marie Callender Pie Shops Inc. Long Beach, Ca. | (N26621) |
| N551MD | Gulfstream 2TT | 212 | Tiger Oil Co. Denver, Co. | N807GA |
| N551PL | Learjet | 551-0029 | Silsbee Cattle Co. El Centro, Ca. | N168CB/N26369 |
| N551R | Citation | 550-0377 | Ralph Rogers Co.Inc. Bloomington, In. | (N26648) |
| N551SC | Learjet | 55-008 | Sabine Corp. Billings, Mt. | |
| N551SE | Citation | 551-0359 | Scribner Equipment Co. Amory, Ms. | N67983 |
| N551UT | Learjet | 55-069 | | |
| N551WC | Learjet | 35A-441 | Westchase Corp & Patheco Inc. Wilmington, De. | |
| N552GL | Learjet | 55-002 | Gates Learjet Corp. Wichita, Ks. | |
| N552MD | Citation | 501-0055 | Majestic Mining Inc. Widen, WV. | N98682 |
| N552N | DH 125/3A | 25124 | Bender Building. | N125J/G-AVAH |
| N552TF | Citation | 550-0176 | Tyson Foods Inc. Springdale, Ar. | N98563 |
| N553GP | Learjet | 55-003 | Garrett AiResearch, Los Angeles, Ca. | |
| N555AE | Sabre-60 | 306-102 | Albert Equipment Co. Inc. Tulsa, Ok. | N108G/N65792 |
| N555CB | HS 125/700A | NA0228 | Cleveland Bros. Equipment Co. Wilmington, De. | G-5-11 |
| N555CC | Citation | 500-0039 | Nevada National Leasing Co. Inc. Reno, Nv. | N539CC |
| N555CS | Gulfstream 2 | 73 | Bank of America, Oakland, Ca. | N116K |
| N555DM | Jet Commander | 25 | Ford, Bacon and Davis Construction Corp. Monroe, La. | |
| N555EW | Citation | 550-0271 | Employers Insurance, Wausau, Wi. | (N303EC)/N6863J |
| N555GL | Learjet | 55-036 | | N3803G |
| N555J | Westwind-1124 | 213 | Furrs Cafeterias Inc. Lubbock, Tx. | N213WW/4X-CLK |
| N555JM | HFB 320 | 1037 | United Engines Inc. Oklahoma City, Ok. | N6ML/N6MK/N5ZA/N892HJ /D-CESE |
| N555LA | Learjet | 24-177 | Jet Air Inc. Jacksonville, Fl. | N555LB/N104MB/N3210 |
| N555PB | JetStar-6 | 5047 | Paul Broadhead & Associates, Meridian, Ms. | N409MA/N409M/N9214R |
| N555PT | Falcon 20F | 426 | Petro Royal, Houston, Tx. | N123WH/N427F/F-WJMK |
| N555RR | Sabre-60 | 306-60 | Royal Aviation, Mesquite, Tx. | N31BC/N115L/N947R |
| N555SD | Learjet | 25D-333 | A R Sanchez, Laredo, Tx. | N34MJ |

| Regis-tration | Type | C/N | Owner/Operator | Previous Identities |
|---|---|---|---|---|
| N555TD | Citation | 550-0438 | | |
| N556N | Westwind-1124 | 331 | GECC, Seattle, Wa. | |
| N557CC | Citation | 501-0165 | North American Plastics Inc. Aberdeen, Ms. | (N2OKW)/N2612N |
| N558CB | Citation | 551-0014 | C B Industries Inc. Oakbrook, Il. | N558CC/N3319M |
| N558E | Learjet | 35A-100 | Consolidated Airways Inc. Fort Wayne, In. | N550E |
| N559BC | Citation | 500-0059 | Cooper Industries Inc. Houston, Tx. | N559CC |
| N560MC | Jet Commander | 24 | Philip Rivera, Houston, Tx. | N360MC/N7GW/N360MC/N360M/N94B |
| N560R | Falcon 20F | 313 | Thomas O'Malley, Chicago, Il. | N56CC/N744CC/N220FJ/N4449F/F-WMKJ |
| N564CC | Citation | 550-0070 | Pacific Gas/Aviation Equipment Leasing Inc. Rockville, Md. | N2072A |
| N564CL | Learjet | 25-060 | Clay Lacy, Boise, Id. | N695LJ |
| N565CC | Citation | 500-0065 | R A Underwood & Co. Terre Haute, In. | |
| N566CC | Citation | 550-0279 | Oscar Wyatt, Houston, Tx. | (N88838) |
| N566MP | Westwind 1123 | 156 | Powers Air, Houston, Tx. | (N666MP)/N4OBG/N4OAS/N1123H/4X-CJF |
| N567DW | Sabre-40 | 282-35 | Production Service Inc. Oklahoma City, Ok. | N341AR/N341AP/N6390C |
| N570R | Sabre-65A | 465-75 | Jetco Joint Venture, Midland, Tx. | N2581E |
| N571CH | HS 125/700A | NA0256 | W R Grace & Co. Chemed Division, Cincinnati, Oh. | N125AK/G-5-15 |
| N571E | HS 125/600A | 6071 | Dupont de Nemours Inc. Wilmington, De. | N571DU/(N91884)/G-BEES/G-5-14 |
| N571NC | Sabre-60 | 306-1 | James Keenan, McClean, Va. | N521N/N978R/N306NA |
| N573LP | Learjet | 24B-196 | Louisiana Pacific Corp. Hillsboro, Or. | N173LP/N99E/N99ES/N1125E /N99SC |
| N573P | Westwind-1124 | 257 | Dupont de Nemours Inc. Wilmington, De. | 4X-CNC |
| N575 | DH 125/400A | NA744 | Dupont de Nemours Inc. Wilmington, De. | N575DU/G-AXTW |
| N575CC | Citation | 500-0075 | Sundstrand Corp. Rockford, Il. | |
| N575SF | Gulfstream 2 | 221 | Standard Oil Co. San Francisco, Ca. | |
| N575W | Citation | 550-0008 | Worthington Industries Inc. Columbus, Oh. | N98840 |
| N577JB | B 727-29 | 19401 | Joe R Brown, Sierra Blanca, Ca. | D-AHLO/OO-STC |
| N577SW | Sabre-80A | 380-21 | Joseph Seagram, New York. | N25AT/N22NT/N75A/N711A/N65773 |
| N577VM | Sabre-40 | 282-31 | Cleveland Newspapers Inc. Austin, Tx. | N70OR/N80OY/N23G |
| N578W | Citation | 550-0077 | Worthington Industries Inc. Columbus, Oh. | N582CC/(N2662A) |
| N580AV | Citation | 550-0146 | Atwood Vacuum Machine Co. Rockford, Il. | N26610 |
| N586 | JetStar-6 | 5085 | Bendix Corp. Detroit, Mi. | N9241R |
| N586RE | Citation | 550-0199 | Royce Beal, Jacksonville, Tx. | N67983 |
| N589CC | Citation | 500-0089 | FPSI Leasing Inc. Dallas, Tx. | |
| N590RB | Citation | 550-0202 | Reeves Bros. Inc. Spartanburg, SC. | N6799Y |
| N591D | Learjet | 35A-069 | Walston Airbusiness Inc. Elgin, Il. | N103GL |
| N591GA | Learjet | 24-142 | Green Bay Packaging Inc. Green Bay, Wi. | |
| N592DC | Falcon 10 | 26 | Dow Corning Corp. Midland, Mi. | N118FJ/F-WJMK |
| N593DC | Falcon 10 | 180 | Dow Corning, Midland, Mi. | N245FJ/F-WZGM |
| N600AG | HS 125/600A | 6069 | A G Spanos, Stockton, Ca. | N350MH/G-BEIO |
| N600AN | Corvette | 10 | Airborne Freight Corp. Cleveland, Oh. | F-BVPO |
| N600B | Gulfstream 2 | 82 | International Brotherhood of Teamsters, Washington DC. | N9040/N10LB N711DP |
| N600BE | Learjet | 35A-348 | Blocker Energies Corp. Houston, Tx. | N3798B/(N17ND) |
| N600BP | Sabre-40 | 282-53 | Lowell Anderson, Incline Village, Nv. | N67201/ZS-PTJ/(ZS-GSB)/N620 N62K/N101T/N123MS/N999BS/N7503V |
| N600C | Learjet | 55-047 | | |
| N600CL | Challenger | 1005 | ICOS Construction, NY. | C-GBDH-X |
| N600CN | Learjet | 35A-235 | Coca Cola Bottling Co. Coral Gables, Fl. | N841GL |
| N600CR | Citation | 550-0407 | Crutcher Resources. | (N1215S) |
| N600CS | B 707-312B | 19739 | Coastal States Gas, Houston, Tx. | 9V-BBR |
| N600EZ | Citation | 550-0185 | E-Z Serve Inc. Abilene, Tx. | N815GK/N6799L |
| N600FL | BH 125/600A | 6034 | Family Lines System, Jacksonville, Fl. | N9OBL/N9OB/N39BH |
| N600HT | Learjet | 25B-101 | Hughes Tool Co. Houston, Tx. | N156CB/N30AP/N269AS/N575GD/N26RGL |
| N600J | Westwind-Two | 302 | Johnson & Johnson, West Trenton, NJ. | 4X-COV |
| N600JJ | B 707-138B | 17702 | Trafalgar Leasing, NY. | G-AWDG/VH-EBG |
| N600JW | Challenger | 1061 | S C Johnson & Son Inc. Racine, Wi. | C-GLYO |
| N600KC | Challenger | 1012 | K C Aviation Inc. Appleton, Wi. | C-GBKE |
| N600LC | Learjet | 35A-211 | Lincoln National Corp. Fort Wayne, In. | N15MJ/D-CATY/N1461B |
| N600LN | Learjet | 35A-332 | Lincoln National Corp. Fort Wayne, In. | |
| N600MB | Gulfstream 2 | 108 | Mary O'Connor Braman, Victoria, Tx. | N60GG/N11UC/N810GK |
| N600MK | Challenger | 1050 | Morrison Knudsen Co. Boise, Id. | C-GLXO |
| N600PC | Learjet | 25B-116 | P C I Transportation Inc. Chicago, Il. | C-FCXY |
| N600PM | Gulfstream 3 | 333 | Philip Morris Inc. Teterboro, NJ. | |
| N600R | Sabre-40 | 282-6 | World Enterprises of Florida Inc./Apex Aviation Co. St. Louis, Mo. | |
| N600SR | Citation | 500-0236 | ARSA Investments Inc/Sankar Ramani, Dallas, Tx. | N8O1K/NRO1L/N2801L /N24PA/N236CC/N5236J |

74

HS-125 C6-BPC                                                                    J. Birch

Gulfstream 3 F-249                                               Gulfstream American Corp.

Westwind 1 N84LA                                                        Atlantic Aviation

*Falcon 10 PT-KTO*                                    *Nelson de Barros Pereira*

*Learjet 55 N3794C*                                        *Gates Learjet Corp.*

*Sabreliner 40R XA-LEL*                                            *B. Gates*

Citation PT-FXB                                          Nelson de Barros Pereira

Citation 2 G-BJIR                                                    I. McFarlane

Learjet 35A VH-BQR                                                      D. Daw

JetStar 8 XB-CXO

J. Birch

Falcon 50 N65B

I. McFarlane

Westwind Two N464EC

Atlantic Aviation

| Regis-tration | Type | C/N | Owner/Operator | Previous Identities |
|---|---|---|---|---|
| N600TP | JetStar-731 | 4/5058 | Apex Oil Co. | N600TT/N50AS/N1500M/N100AL/N100A |
| N600TT | Challenger | 1048 | Gulf States Oil & Refining, Houston, Tx. | N29687/C-GLXK |
| N601AN | Corvette | 13 | Airborne Express Inc. Wilmington, Oh. | F-BVPD |
| N601CL | Challenger 601 | 3001 | Canadair Inc. Westport, Ct. | C-GBUU |
| N601UU | DH 125/1A-522 | 25103 | Union Underwear Co. Inc. Bowling Green, Ky. | N210M/N533/G-ATUV |
| N601WW | Challenger | 1047 | Whitewind Co. Ltd. White Plains, NY. | N2741Q/C-GLXH |
| N602AN | Corvette | 31 | Midwest Air Charter Inc. Elyria, Oh. | F-BTTK/F-WNGZ |
| N602CL | Challenger | 1020 | Canadair USA Inc. Westport, Ct. | N36LB/C-GLWV |
| N604AN | Corvette | 18 | Air National, Elyria, Oh. | F-BTTO/N615AC/F-WNGR |
| N604NA | B 727-51 | 19124 | International Executive Aircraft Corp. NY. | N478US |
| N605CL | Challenger | 1057 | Canadair Inc. Westport, Ct. | C-GBTK/C-GLXU |
| N605RP | Falcon 20C | 100 | Ralston-Purina Co. St.Louis, Mo. | N983F/F-WJMN |
| N606AB | Westwind-1124 | 268 | Abex Corp. NY. | N821H/(N13HH)/4X-CNN |
| N606RP | Falcon 20F | 265 | Ralston-Purina Co. St.Louis, Mo. | N4429F/F-WLCX |
| N610GE | Learjet | 35A-338 | Odin Corp. Las Vegas, Nv. | RP-C7272/N1473B |
| N610JA | Westwind-1124 | 298 | Jaco Enterprises, Houston, Tx. | 4X-CQR |
| N611DB | Learjet | 24D-318 | Skybird Aviation Inc. Van Nuys, Ca. | N114JT |
| N611ER | Citation | 550-0236 | Cyclops Corp. Mansfield, Oh. | N68033 |
| N611MC | HS 125/700A | NA0257 | May Department Stores, St. Louis, Mo. | N125HS/G-5-18 |
| N612DS | Citation | 501-0095 | Drag Specialties Inc. Minnetonka, Mn. | N3172M |
| N616NA | Learjet | 25-035 | National Aeronautics, Cleveland, Oh. | N33TR/N33GF/N683LJ |
| N617CC | Citation | 501-0211 | Jack Prewitt & Assoc. Dallas, Tx. | N6785C |
| N618S | Falcon 10 | 156 | Oilfield Aviation/Schlumberger, NY. | N221FJ/F-WZGE |
| N620M | HS 125/700A | NA0203 | Olin Corp. Stamford, Ct. | G-BERV |
| N620S | Challenger | 1031 | Texasgulf Inc. Stamford, Ct. | C-GLXS |
| N623RM | Citation | 501-0217 | R M Marketing Assoc. Knoxville, Tx. | N1710E |
| N626P | Citation | 500-0267 | Philips Industries Inc. Dayton, Oh. | N1UT/N28PA/N5267J |
| N627L | Citation | 501-0123 | Lord Corp. Erie, Pa. | N513CC/N2650C |
| N628CH | Citation | 501-0220 | Coachmen Industries Inc. Middlebury, In. | N2052A |
| N630CC | Citation | 501-0224 | Kittiwake Corp/Three Seven Corp. Midland, Tx. | N2611Y |
| N630M | Challenger | 1023 | Olin Corp. Stamford, Ct. | C-GLXB |
| N630N | Sabre-40 | 282-73 | Olin Corp. Stamford, Ct. | N630M |
| N631SC | Gulfstream 2TT | 224 | Stauffer Chemical Co. Westport, Ct. | N810GA/N17584 |
| N631SQ | BH 125/600A | 6002 | Page Gulfstream Inc. Rochester, NY. | N631SC/N79BH/(N92BH) |
| N632PB | DH 125/1A | 25058 | Modern Welding Co. Inc. Owenboro, Ky. | N470R/N215G/N9308Y/D-COMI |
| N632SC | Citation | 550-0357 | Stauffer Chemical Co. Westport, Ct. | N6808C |
| N634H | Learjet | 35A-292 | Hillenbrand Industries Inc. Batesville, In. | |
| N636 | JetStar 8 | 5127 | E F MacDonald Co. Dayton, Oh. (N636MC)/N636C/N3GR/N42GB/N42G/N7972S | |
| N636CC | Citation | 501-0229 | MJI, Lincoln, Ne. | (N2615L) |
| N636MC | Sabre-60 | 306-140 | E F MacDonald Co. Dayton, Oh. | N636 |
| N636SC | Citation | 500-0222 | Stauffer Chemical Co. Westport, Ct. | N222CC |
| N637ML | Challenger | 1024 | Dacion Corp. NY. | C-GLXD |
| N640BS | Citation | 501-0237 | Alpine Aviation Inc. Zanesville, Oh. | (N2617K) |
| N641FG | Westwind 1124 | 370 | Britt Aviation Inc. Burlington, NC. | 4X-CUG |
| N642BB | Citation | 550-0318 | Britt Aviation Inc. Burlington, NC. | N6889Y |
| N644X | Falcon 20C | 36 | Pillsbury Co. Minneapolis, Mn. | N711BC/N900P/N810F/F-WMKI |
| N645G | Learjet | 35-056 | Gates Rubber Co. Denver, Co. | N106GL/(JY-AEX) |
| N646G | Learjet | 55-016 | Gates Rubber Co. Denver, Co. | |
| N647JP | Falcon 20C | 70 | Sunstream Jet Express, Port Chester, NY. | N966F/F-WMKH |
| N650 | Citation | 650-697 | Citation 3 Second prototype. | |
| N650C | Sabre-60 | 306-194 | Crystal Oil Co. Shreveport, La. | N60SL/N2506E |
| N650CC | Citation | 650-696 | Cessna Aircraft Co. Citation 3 prototype. | |
| N650NL | Learjet | 35A-154 | National Life & Accident Insurance Co. Nashville, Tn. | |
| N650TF | Citation | 500-0142 | The Krystal Co. Chattanooga, Tn. | VH-UCC/N142CC |
| N650WC | Citation | 550-0007 | Towne Management Co. Youngstown, Oh. | (N447FM)/N300PB/N98830 |
| N650X | Falcon 50 | 69 | AMAX Inc. NY. | N80FJ/F-WZHJ |
| N651CC | Citation | 650-0001 | | |
| N651GL | Sabre-65 | 465-36 | IMC Corp. Waukegan, Il. | |
| N651LJ | Learjet | 24A-125 | Steven Lysdale, Bellevue, Wa. | |
| N651S | Sabre-65 | 465-14 | I T & T Corp. NY. | |
| N651TF | B 707-351C | 18586 | Air Separation Inc. Las Vegas, Nv. | VR-CAO/VR-HGO/N353US |
| N652CC | Citation | 650-0002 | | |
| N653DR | Citation | 501-0185 | D F Tully & Assoc. Melrose, Ma. | N2614K |
| N653F | Citation | 501-0230 | This End Up Furniture Co. Raleigh, NC. | N2616G |
| N654DN | Learjet | 24-019 | Carrows Restaurants Inc. Santa Barbara, Ca. | N889JF/HB-VAI/N464LJ |
| N654E | Falcon 20C | 164 | Elgin National Industries, Chicago, Il. | N4367F/F-WJMN |
| N654PC | Falcon 10 | 131 | Wingspan Leasing Inc Holland, Mi. | N196FJ/F-WZGC |
| N655PC | Citation | 550-0121 | Prince Corp. Holland, Mi. | N2746C |

79

| Regis-<br>tration | Type | C/N | Owner/Operator | Previous<br>Identities |
|---|---|---|---|---|
| N656CC | Citation | 650-0006 | | |
| N659HX | Learjet | 25D-300 | Hecks Inc. Charleston, WV. | (N46BA) |
| N660A | Learjet | 24-155 | M G C Corp. Satellite Beach, Fl. | N210FP/N833GA/N462BA/N462B/N422U |
| | | | | /N598GA |
| N660CJ | Learjet | 35A-079 | WTCR Assoc. Bethesda, Md. | N6000J |
| N660P | Falcon 20F | 430 | Phillips Petroleum Co. Bartlesville, Ok. | N428F/F-WMKG |
| N660SA | Learjet | 35A-469 | Sale, Oakland, Ca. | |
| N660W | Jet Commander | 58 | Bank of Commerce of Tulsa, Ok. | N120GH/N721AS/N90B |
| N661AA | Learjet | 36A-049 | Central States Investment. | |
| N661JB | HS 125/700A | NA0275 | Fuqua Industries Inc. Atlanta, Ga. | N125V/G-5-13 |
| N661MP | Westwind-1123 | 176 | PowersAir Inc. Houston, Tx. | C-GJCD/N1123T/4X-CJY |
| N661TV | Citation | 501-0255 | World Publishing Co. | |
| N662AA | Learjet | 35A-315 | Adams Energy, Tulsa, Ok. | N927GL |
| N662D | Falcon 10 | 87 | Dow Chemical Co. Midland, Mi. | (N200AF)/N167FJ/F-WPXK |
| N662F | Sabre-60A | 306-6 | Mosbacher Aviation Co. Houston, Tx. | N662P/N4712N |
| N662G | Gulfstream 2 | 188 | General Dynamics, St. Louis, Mo. | N862G/N823GA |
| N662JB | Westwind-1124 | 209 | Fuqua Industries Inc. Atlanta, Ga. | N663JB/N661JB/4X-CLG |
| N662P | Falcon 20F | 378 | Phillips Petroleum Co. Bartlesville, Ok. | (N662PP)/N107F/F-WROT |
| N663B | Gulfstream 2 | 14 | Phillips Petroleum Co. Bartlesville, Ok. | N663P |
| N664B | Falcon 20C | 95 | Falcon Jet Corp. Teterboro, NJ. | N664P/N802F/N980F/F-WNGO |
| N664CC | Citation | 501-0258 | | |
| N664CL | Learjet | 24-167 | Clay Lacy, Boise, Id. | N888B/N841LC/N847GA |
| N664J | Citation | 550-0025 | Bricmont & Bricmont, McMurray, Pa. | N664JB/N9014S/EP-KIC/N3239M |
| N664JB | Falcon 10 | 162 | Lano Corp. Bandera, Tx. | N226FJ/F-WZGN |
| N664P | Gulfstream 3 | 343 | Phillips Petroleum Corp. Bartlesville, Ok. | N305GA |
| N665B | Falcon 20C | 88 | I C Deal, Dallas, Tx. | N665P/N130B/N977F/F-WNGN |
| N665P | Falcon 20F | 444 | Phillips Petroleum Corp. Bartlesville, Ok. | N453F/F-WJMJ |
| N666BP | Jet Commander-B | 122 | T Smith & Son, Metairie, La. | N122JC/N801NM/N4940E |
| N666CC | Learjet | 35A-254 | Corrao Construction Co. Reno, Nv. | |
| N666JM | Westwind-1124 | 283 | Joe Morten, Sioux City, Nb. | N483A/4X-COC |
| N666JR | Learjet | 35A-074 | Mercury Oil Co. Dallas, Tx. | N530J/N5000B |
| N666KK | Learjet | 25D-285 | Getty Western Crude Oil Co. Denver, Co. | N6666K/(N28RW)/N6666R |
| N666LC | HS 125/600A | 6064 | Clinton Court Corp. NYC. | N105AS/HZ-AMM/G-5-17 |
| N666RB | Learjet | 35A-393 | GECC, Dallas, Tx. | N932GL |
| N666RC | Citation | 550-0042 | Roper Corp. Kankakee, Il. | (N3283M) |
| N666WW | Citation | 550-0174 | T G I Fridays Inc. Dallas, Tx. | N201CC/(N98510) |
| N667P | Falcon 20F | 432 | Phillips Petroleum Co. Bartlesville, Ok. | N430F/F-WJMK |
| N668MC | Learjet | 24B-214 | Marnell Corrao Associates Inc. Las Vegas, Nv. | N666CC/N192MB |
| | | | | /N192MH |
| N668P | Falcon 20F | 308 | Phillips Petroleum Co. Bartlesville, Ok. | N4447F/F-WMKF |
| N671B | Citation | 550-0231 | I B W Transportation Inc. Laredo, Tx. | (N221BW)/N28RF/N6860A |
| N673LP | Citation | 501-0114 | Louisiana Pacific Corp. Hillsboro, Or. | N2649Y |
| N673M | Learjet | 35-008 | Omaha Indemnity Co. Omaha, Nb. | |
| N678BM | Falcon 20F | 345 | Bristol-Myers Inc. NY. | N4463F/F-WMKI |
| N678DG | Citation | 501-0219 | Abbott Building Co. Midland, Tx. | N25CJ/N1772E |
| N678RW | Gulfstream 2 | 192 | Coca Cola Co. Atlanta, Ga. | N811GA |
| N678SP | Learjet | 24F-354 | Deutsche Luftwege GmbH, Glen, NH. | |
| N679RW | Gulfstream 2 | 109 | Coca Cola Co. Atlanta, Ga. | N811GA |
| N680RW | Gulfstream 2 | 191 | Coca Cola Co. Atlanta, Ga. | N810GA |
| N684HA | Citation | 500-0113 | Harlan Anderson, New Canaan, Ct. | N113CC/(N613CC) |
| N690 | Learjet | 24E-339 | Prestige Jet, Orlando, Fl. | N851CC/N15MJ |
| N695CC | Citation | 501-0180 | Silicon Valley Express Inc. Palo Alto, Ca. | (N593CC)/(N6781T) |
| N696A | Citation | 550-0331 | GECC/Albany International Corp. | |
| N700AA | HS 125/700A | NA0302 | SARSA, Mexico City. | G-5-19 |
| N700AC | HS 125/700A | NA0290 | Perpetual Corp. Houston, Tx. | G-5-18 |
| N700BA | HS 125/700A | NA0331 | | |
| N700BD | Falcon 10 | 81 | Becton Dickinson & Co. East Rutherford, NJ. | N162FJ/F-WPXF |
| N700BF | Jet Commander-B | 137 | Great Planes Sales Inc. Tulsa, Ok. | N5BP/N300LS/N500LS |
| | | | | /N873/N3VF/N5OVF/SE-DCZ/N5045E |
| N700BW | HS 125/700A | NA0288 | Borg Warner Acceptance Corp. Chicago, Il. | N125AH/G-5-16 |
| N700C | Learjet | 24-123 | On Mark Aviation Inc. Knoxville, Tn. | N262HA |
| N700CC | DH 125/400A | NA731 | Lendee Co. Monterrey, Ca. | N65LT/G-AXJG |
| N700CF | Sabre-40A | 282-109 | H & K Construction, Sinton, Tx. | N4NP |
| N700CW | Citation | 500-0205 | Winn Exploration Co. Inc. Eagle Pass, Tx. | (N541NC)/N520N |
| N700ER | Citation | 501-0148 | Refco Transport Equipment Inc. Chicago, Il. | N167CB/(OO-ECT)/N1758E |

| Regis-tration | Type | C/N | Owner/Operator | Previous Identities |
|---|---|---|---|---|
| N700HH | HS 125/700A | NA0240 | Hilton Hotels Corp. Santa Monica, Ca. | N130BA/G-BFZJ |
| N700HS | HS 125/700A | NA0305 | British Aerospace Inc/Storer Broadcasting. | G-5-11 |
| N700JC | Sabre-65 | 465-74 | Oxley Petroleum Co. Tulsa, Ok. | |
| N700JD | Citation | 500-0009 | John Deere & Co. Moline, Il. | N500JD/N509CC |
| N700LB | Citation | 551-0057 | Baker Machine Corp. Ingleside, Tx. | N6830X |
| N700MD | Westwind-1124 | 212 | Bill McDavid Oldsmobile Inc. Houston, Tx. | N900CS/N212WW/4X-CLJ |
| N700MM | Westwind-1124 | 311 | Arthur Goldberg/Integrated Resources Inc. NYC. | 4X-CRE |
| N700NN | HS 125/700A | NA0312 | New York Times Co/AMF Corp. Westfield, Ma. | G-5-18 |
| N700NP | Learjet | 23-082 | Heitman Realty Corp. Wilmington, De. | N7GP/N805JA/N280C |
| N700PM | Gulfstream 2TT | 207 | Philip Morris Inc. Teterboro, NJ. | |
| N700RD | DH 125/3A-RA | NA701 | Rust Aviation/Austin Avia Inc. Tx. | N700RG/N605W/N505W/N506N/N501W /G-AVHB |
| N700SS | HS 125/700A | NA0317 | | G-5-20 |
| N700WM | Westwind Two | 319 | Miller & Miller Auctioneers, Fort Worth, Tx. | N560SH/XA-LOR/4X-CRM |
| N701AS | Learjet | 35A-047 | AID Corp. Des Moines, Ia. | N13MJ/XA-ALE |
| N701MG | Falcon 20D | 196 | Midland Glass Co. Cliffwood, NJ. | N811PA/N4386F/F-WPXE |
| N701SC | Learjet | 24XR-235 | Sigmor Inc. San Antonio, Tx. | N51VL |
| N701VF | Citation | 501-0244 | | (N711VF)/N650CJ/N2626J |
| N701Z | HS 125/F600A | 6058 | Zapata Corp. Houston, Tx. | N9043U/G-5-16/G-BGKN |
| N702D | DH 125/400A | NA738 | Sears Roebuck & Co. Dallas, Tx. | G-AXOF |
| N702H | Gulfstream 2 | 229 | Sears Roebuck & Co. Chicago, Il. | N821GA |
| N702M | BH 125/400A | NA759 | Sears Roebuck & Co. Chicago, Il. | N6702/N54BH/G-5-20 |
| N702P | DH 125/400A | NA740 | Sears Roebuck & Co. Los Angeles, Ca. | G-AXTS |
| N702R | Citation | 550-0014 | Rea Magnet Wire Co. Inc. Fort Wayne, In. | N3212M |
| N703SC | Falcon 20C | 24 | Viking Petroleum/McKenzie Enterprises Inc. Tulsa, Ok. | N60SN/N60SM /N738RH/N22550/N30JM/N297AR/N845F/F-WNGM |
| N705NA | Learjet | 24A-102 | NASA, Moffett Field, Ca. | N365EJ |
| N707AR | B 707-123B | 17634 | ARCO, Burbank, Ca. | N7507A |
| N707HD | B 707-321 | 18084 | Quantum Inc. Miami, Fl. | N433MA/C6-BDG/VP-BDG/G-AYRZ/N758PA |
| N707RZ | B 707-328 | 18375 | Intercontinental Airways Inc. Wilmington, De. | F-BHSU/CN-RMA /F-BHSU |
| N707TG | Sabre-40 | 282-74 | Texas Gas Transmission Corp. Owensboro, Ky. | N572R/N2241B |
| N707TR | Learjet | 25-005 | West Texas Marketing Corp. Houston, Tx.(N707TP)/N777RA/N1969W/N646GA |  |
| N707US | Citation | 500-0339 | Jack Silberberg, Maplewood, NJ. | G-JEAN/(N5339J) |
| N707WB | JetStar 2 | 5210 | First Interstate Bancorp. Los Angeles, Ca. | N400KC/N5536L |
| N708A | B707-331B | 20060 | ARAMCO, Houston, Tx. | N8731 |
| N708BW | BH 125/731 | NA765 | Melvin Simon & Associates Inc. Indianapolis, In. N700RW/N125PA/N62BH |  |
| N708TR | Learjet | 25-015 | West Texas Marketing Corp. Abilene, Tx. | N713US/CF-HMV/N858GM |
| N709AB | Sabre-60 | 306-75 | Allen Bradley Co. Milwaukee, Wi. | N666WL/N110G |
| N709Q | Sabre-40 | 282-30 | Westland Oil Development Corp. Tx. | N7090/N526N/N6384C |
| N710BA | HS 125/700A | NA0336 | | |
| N710BC | HS 125/700A | NA0332 | Halliburton Co. Dallas, Tx. | G-5-11 |
| N710BD | HS 125/700A | NA0330 | S. Jernigan, OKC, Ok. | |
| N710BF | HS 125/700A | NA0329 | Chemgraphics Systems Inc. Secaucus, NJ. | G-5-17 |
| N710BG | HS 125/700A | NA0328 | Helmerich & Payne, Tulsa, Ik. | G-5-16 |
| N710BJ | HS 125/700A | NA0324 | J B & A Aircraft Inc. League City, Tx. | G-5-11 |
| N710BP | HS 125/700A | NA0319 | Mid Atlantic Leasing, Houston, Tx. | G-5-15 |
| N710JW | Jet Commander | 35 | Martinez Garrido, Miami, Fl. | N7HL/N189G/N101GS/N100TH/N22AC/N6504V |
| N710K | MS 760 Paris | 112 | E G Martin, Orefield, Pa. | N7277X/N65218/F-BOJY/HB-PAC/F-EXAA |
| N711 | Learjet | 35A-207 | William Carpenter, Palm Beach, Fl. | N40146 |
| N711AE | Citation | 501-0086 | Alpha Energy Corp. OKC, Ok. | N88CF/N8LG/N3195M |
| N711BF | Learjet | 25D-324 | Wm. Fiore, Pittsburgh, Pa. | |
| N711BY | Sabre-75A | 380-51 | Geo Priester/Bally Manufacturing Co. Chicago, Il. N4343/N43R/N2135J |  |
| N711CD | Learjet | 35A-456 | Condor (Dorsey & Coca Cola), Chattanooga, Tn. | |
| N711CH | Learjet | 35-032 | The Carborundum Co. Niagara Falls, N.Y. | |
| N711CU | HS 125/700A | NA0258 | The Carborundum Co. Niagara Falls, N.Y. | (N125AM)/G-5-19 |
| N711CW | Learjet | 24-055 | Warren Francis, Portland, Or. | N511WH/N2366Y/N809LJ |
| N711DS | Learjet | 24B-189 | Evergreen Helicopters Inc. McMinnville, Or. | N14MJ/D-CONA/D-IKAF /D-CJET |
| N711DZ | JetStar 2 | 5201 | Solar Sportsystems Inc. Buffalo, NY. | N711Z/N5527L |
| N711EV | Learjet | 25-016 | Evergreen Helicopters Inc. McMinnville, Or. | N424RD/CF-KAX/N145JN |
| N711FJ | Falcon 10 | 149 | Louisiana Land & Exploration Co. New Orleans, La. | N214FJ/F-WZGU |
| N711GW | Jet Commander | 12 | Jack Franks, Reno, Nv. | N37BB/N777V/N613J/N8300 |
| N711JS | JetStar-731 | 61/5153 | Louisiana Land & Exploration Co. New Orleans, La. | N5517L |
| N711JT | Learjet | 25D-243 | JPAC Enterprises Inc. El Dorado, Ar. | |
| N711KG | Falcon 20C | 57 | Argent Corp. Las Vegas, Nv. | N76RY/N3JJ/N677BM/N678BM/N499MJ/N883F |

| Regis-tration | Type | C/N | Owner/Operator | Previous Identities |
|---|---|---|---|---|
| | | | | /F-WNGO |
| N711L | Learjet | 35A-151 | The Carborundum Co. Niagara Falls, NY. | N39399 |
| N711MB | Westwind-1124 | 282 | Larry Mohr/Merchants National Bank, Indianapolis, In. | 4X-COB |
| N711MM | Gulfstream 2 | 61 | McLean Co. Inc. NY. | N18N |
| N711MR | Westwind-1124 | 191 | Matthews McCracken Rutland Corp. Baton Rouge, La. | N13VF/N3VF/4X-CKO |
| N711MT | Gulfstream 2B | 16 | Southland Corp. Dallas, Tx. | N697A/N890A |
| N711NR | Citation Eagle | 501-0024 | Falconaire Corp. Oklahoma City, Ok. | N1CA/(N1OCA)/N36886 |
| N711PD | Learjet | 25B-138 | Dunigan Enterprises Inc. Abilene, Tx. | N777PD/N36204/N100EP/N11BU |
| N711R | Learjet | 35-035 | Cockrell Corp. Houston, Tx. | |
| N711RL | HS 125/700A | NA0301 | Polo Fashions Inc. NYC. | N700HB/G-5-13 |
| N711S | Sabre-60 | 306-92 | Southland Corp. Dallas, Tx. | N65775 |
| N711SC | Gulfstream 2B | 70 | Southland Corp. Dallas, Tx. | |
| N711SE | Citation | 500-0261 | Robert Merson, Meridian, Ms. | N55LF/N55HF/N261CC/N5261J |
| N711ST | Sabre-60 | 306-129 | Southland Corp. Dallas, Tx. | N2144J |
| N711SW | DC-9-15 | 45740 | Golden Nugget Inc. Las Vegas, Nv. | N310MJ/N1059T |
| N711T | Sabre-40 | 282-67 | Southland Corp. Dallas, Tx. | N2234B |
| N711TG | Learjet | 25D-298 | JJJ Associates Inc. Dallas, Tx. | N923GL |
| N711TJ | Learjet | 24A-011 | Orco Aviation Inc. Riverside, Ca. | N711PJ/N5OJF/N150WL/N1966K |
| | | | | /N233VW/N806LJ |
| N711VF | Citation | 501-0236 | | N26227 |
| N711WD | Learjet | 25D-282 | Jet East Inc. Midland, Tx. | |
| N711WJ | DH 125/1A | 25021 | Rynes Aviation Inc. Chicago, Il. | N125KC/N125BT/N228GL/N228G/N2504 |
| | | | | /N575DU/G-ASZN |
| N711WM | Citation | 551-0388 | Barbary Coast Hotel and Casino, Las Vegas, Nv. | |
| N711YP | HS 125/700A | NA0234 | L M Berry & Co. Dayton, Oh. | G-5-16 |
| N712DC | Learjet | 25-032 | Combs-Gates Denver Inc. | N711DB/N373M |
| N712GW | JetStar-6 | 5016 | Jack Franks, Palm Springs, Ca. | N425BP/HZ-SH2/HZ-AFS/N20TF/(N222R) |
| | | | | /N2222R/N9210R |
| N712J | Citation | 550-0365 | Eagle-Picher Industries Inc. Cincinatti, Oh. | (N12159) |
| N712JA | Learjet | 25B-134 | Johnson Armstrong Leasing Co. Austin, Tx. | N15BH/N52GL |
| N712L | Learjet | 35A-256 | Eagle-Picher Industries Inc. Cincinnati, Oh. | |
| N712R | Learjet | 24-156 | Royal Cake Co. Inc. Winston Salem, NC. | N111RP/N111RF/N468DM |
| | | | | /N599GA |
| N712SJ | Learjet | 25D-296 | Sunjet Associates, Dallas, Tx. | N712RW |
| N712US | Citation | 500-0044 | Associated Utilities, West Chester, Pa. | N942B/N544CC |
| N713Q | Learjet | 25B-105 | Pacific Executive Jet Charter Ltd. Long Beach, Ca. | N711WE/N1RA/N1BR |
| N713RR | Learjet | 25D-241 | R R Investments Inc. Dallas, Tx. | N712BW/N711WD/N25TB/N25TA/N432SL |
| N714K | Learjet | 35A-230 | BLC Corp. San Mateo, Ca. | |
| N714S | Learjet | 35A-367 | General Telephone Co. of SW San Angelo, TX. | |
| N715A | B 737-2S2C | 21928 | ARAMCO, Houston, Tx. | N204FE |
| N715DG | Citation | 501-0033 | Gebron Oil & Gas Corp. Wichita Falls, Tx. | N300PB/N400GR/N36908 |
| N715JF | Learjet | 25B-132 | Aircharter Inc. Dallas, Tx. | N54MQ/N54MC/N132GL/N202BT |
| N715JM | Citation | 501-0009 | McFarlane Aviation, Houston, Tx. | N715EK/N67CC/N36850 |
| N716A | B 737-2S2C | 21929 | ARAMCO, Houston, Tx. | N205FE |
| N716RD | JetStar 2 | 5218 | Readers Digest Sales & Service, NY. | N5544L |
| N717 | JetStar 2 | 5202 | Allied Stores Corp. NY. | N5528L |
| N717A | Gulfstream 3 | 308 | ARAMCO, Houston, Tx. | |
| N717DB | Learjet | 24-179 | United Aviation Exchange Inc. El Toro, Ca. | N410PB/N410PD/N111RE |
| | | | | /N111RA/N300CC/N920FF |
| N717DS | Learjet | 35A-302 | ALCOA, Pittsburgh, Pa. | |
| N717HB | Learjet | 24XR-295 | HBE Corp. St. Louis Mo. | |
| N717JM | JetStar-6 | 5009 | K C Aviation Inc. Dallas, Tx. | (HB-VET)/N717/N717X/N767Z/N540G |
| | | | | /N9206R |
| N717RB | Citation | 501-0074 | Vetter Corp. Rantoul, Il. | N888DS/YV-232CP/N3118M |
| N718SW | Learjet | 35A-179 | Scotland Oil Co. Inc. Laurel Hill, NC. | D-CAPD/D-CCAR/N39412 |
| N718VA | Citation | 550-0029 | Vac Air Alloys, NY. | N502AL/G-JEEN/(N3247M) |
| N719A | Gulfstream 3 | 310 | ARAMCO, Houston, Tx. | |
| N719GA | Gulfstream 2 | 79 | Exxon Corp. Newark, NJ. | N826GA |
| N720A | B 737-2S2C | 21926 | ARAMCO, Houston, Tx. | N201FE |
| N720C | Citation | 500-0073 | International Paper Co. Dallas, Tx. | (N881M)/N573CC |
| N720CC | B 720-022 | 17915 | Agro Air International Inc. West Palm Beach, Fl. | N7209U |
| N720E | Gulfstream 2 | 65 | IBM Corp. NY. | N837GA |
| N720F | Gulfstream 2 | 66 | IBM Corp. NY. | N838GA |
| N720M | Learjet | 55-020 | Levelor Lorentzen Inc. Lyndhurst, NJ. | |
| N720ML | Falcon 10 | 48 | Northwestern Mutual Life Insurance Co. Milwaukee. | N133FJ/F-WJMM |
| N720UA | Learjet | 23-067 | First Missouri Bank/United Air Leasing Corp. Tulsa, Ok. | N703DC/N2ZA |
| | | | | /N815LJ |
| N721CP | Gulfstream 2TT | 46 | Caesers World, Los Angeles, Ca. | N9272K/C-GSLK/N111RF/N40CC/N806CC |

| Registration | Type | C/N | Owner/Operator | Previous Identities |
|---|---|---|---|---|
| N721J | Learjet | 24B-200 | Continental Jet Aviation Inc. Il. | (N24NP) |
| N721MF | B 727-2X8 | 22687 | Wedge Aviation Inc. Houston, Tx. | N4523N |
| N722Q | MS 760 Paris | 9 | Kendall Aviation Inc. Sylmar, Ca. | N300ND |
| N722W | Westwind-1123 | 159 | Wheaton industries Inc. Milville, NJ. | N1123E |
| N723GL | Learjet | 35A-107 | General Telephone Co. San Angelo, Tx. | |
| N723ST | JetStar-6 | 5023 | Jack Lombardi, Syracuse, NY. | N879RA/N979RA/N767Z/N1107Z/I-SNAL /N9221R |
| N724B | HS 125/700A | NA0204 | Blount Inc. Montgomery, Al. | G-BERX/G-5-18 |
| N725P | Learjet | 35A-167 | Butler Manufacturing Co. Inc. Kansas City, Mo. | |
| N726RW | B 727-2M7 | 21655 | Government of Congo. | |
| N727C | Citation | 550-0337 | Consumers Power Co/KJL Ltd. Sparks, Nv. | N6802S |
| N727DG | B 727-021 | 19261 | International Executive Aircraft Corp. NY. | N359PA |
| N727GL | Learjet | 35A-127 | Anheuser Busch Inc. St.Louis, Mo. | |
| N727HC | B 727-35 | 19835 | Hardesty Corp. Tulsa, Ok. | N1959 |
| N727MB | B 727-44 | 19318 | International Executive Aircraft Corp. NY. | N2689E/ZS-SBF/ZS-EKW |
| N727SG | B 727-021 | 19260 | International Executive Aircraft Corp. NY. | N358PA |
| N727TA | B 727-51 | 19122 | Thunderbird Airways, Houston, Tx. | N105RK/N476US |
| N727UD | B 727-30 | 18367 | U Dantata, Nigeria. | N2703J/D-ABIL |
| N728C | Sabre-65 | 465-71 | KJL Ltd Inc. Sparks, Nv. | |
| N729S | Falcon 20F | 173 | Shell Aviation Corp. Houston, Tx. | N70PA/F-BLCU/F-WLCU |
| N730CA | Sabre-40A | 282-103 | BKN Corp. Cleveland, Oh. | N217E/N217TE/N217A/N9MS/N44P/N759RN |
| N730PV | Jet Commander | 36 | Peavey Co. Minneapolis, Mn. | N1121M |
| N730S | Falcon 20F | 247 | Shell Aviation Corp. Houston, Tx. | N4419F/F-WPXE |
| N731F | Falcon 50 | 45 | AiResearch Aviation, Los Angeles, Ca. | N63FJ/F-WZHE |
| N731FJ | Falcon 10 | 3 | IMC/UOP Inc. Des Plaines, Il. | N100FJ/F-WJMJ |
| N731G | DH 125/731 | 25153 | AiResearch Aviation, Los Angeles, Ca. | N30FD/N30F/G-AVXM |
| N731KC | DH 125/3A | 25118 | K C Aviation Inc. Appleton, Wi. | N45PM/N743UT/G-ATYL |
| N731X | BH 125/400A | NA760 | Sears Roebuck & Co. Chicago, Il. | N55BH/G-5-12 |
| N732S | Falcon 20F | 272 | Shell Aviation Corp. Houston, Tx. | N2OFJ/N4431F/F-WMKF |
| N733H | HS 125/700A | NA0212 | Humana Inc. Wilmington, De. | G-BFGU |
| N733K | Challenger | 1041 | HAC-Humana Inc. Wilmington, De. | |
| N733M | HS 125/700A | NA0265 | HAC-Humana Inc. Wilmington, De. | |
| N733S | Falcon 20F | 292 | Shell Aviation Corp. Houston, Tx. | N4441F/F-WMKI |
| N734 | Learjet | 55-051 | | |
| N734S | Falcon 20F | 316 | Shell Aviation Corp. Houston, Tx. | N4451F/F-WMKF |
| N735A | Learjet | 35A-323 | ALCOA, Pittsburgh, Pa. | |
| N737FN | Learjet | 24-171 | Amerada Hess Corp. NY. | |
| N737X | HS 125/700A | NA0237 | John T Dorrance, Gladwyne, Pa. | G-BGBJ/G-5-19 |
| N740E | Learjet | 24B-222 | Eaton Corp. Cleveland, Oh. | N692LJ |
| N740R | Sabre-60 | 306-112 | TRW Inc. Cleveland, Oh. | N2107J |
| N741E | Learjet | 25B-100 | Eaton Corp. Cleveland, Oh. | N262E/N262JE |
| N741JB | Citation | 500-0213 | Justice Builders Inc. Myrtle Beach, SC. | N355H/N62HB |
| N741R | Sabre-60 | 306-143 | TRW Inc. Cleveland, Oh. | N800M/N800M |
| N741RL | Sabre-60 | 306-28 | Rockwell International Corp. | N741P |
| N742E | Learjet | 25B-096 | Eaton Corp. Cleveland, Oh. | |
| N742R | Sabre-60 | 306-45 | TRW Inc. Cleveland, Oh. | N4763N |
| N743E | Learjet | 25B-169 | Eaton Corp. Cleveland, Oh. | N471MM |
| N744CC | Falcon 20F | 347 | International Brotherhood of Teamsters, Washington DC. | N4464F /F-WMKF |
| N744CF | Learjet | 23-082A | Teterboro Aircraft Service Inc. NJ. | N255ES/N823LJ |
| N744E | Learjet | 35A-203 | Eaton Corp. Cleveland, Oh. | |
| N744JC | Learjet | 24D-323 | James & Linda Chavers, Mobile, Al. | N61AW |
| N744JR | Westwind-1124 | 198 | Robbie Airways Inc. Ennis, Mt/Miami Dolphins. | N800Y/4X-CKV |
| N744LC | Learjet | 25D-232 | Teterboro Aircraft Service Inc. NJ. | |
| N744SW | Citation | 550-0009 | Statewide Sales Co. Los Angeles, Ca. | N98853 |
| N745DM | Citation | 500-0131 | Citation Associates, SLC, Mt. | (N725DM)/N1045T/D-IDAU |
| N745E | Learjet | 35A-294 | Eaton Corp. Salt Lake City, Ut. | (1000th Learjet) |
| N746E | Learjet | 35A-297 | Eaton Corp. Milwaukee, Wi. | |
| N746UP | Sabre-60 | 306-22 | Union Pacific Railroad Co. Omaha, Nb. | N4732N |
| N746UT | JetStar-2 | 5225 | United Telecom Systems Inc. Shawnee Mission, Ks. | N4021M |
| N747 | Falcon 50 | 50 | FMC Corp. Wheeling, Il. | N67FJ/F-WZHO |
| N747E | Sabre-40 | 282-22 | Pilliod Cabinet Co. Swanton, Oh. | N747/N6376C |
| N747G | Gulfstream 2 | 49 | National Gypsum Co. NY. | |
| N747T | Falcon 20C | 81 | FMC Corp. Chicago, Il. | N661J/N661JB/N799G/N973F/F-WNGN |
| N747UP | Sabre-60 | 306-39 | Union Pacific Railroad Co. White Plains, NY. | N507TF/N888MC/N10PF /N4752N |
| N747W | Falcon 20C | 5 | FMC Corp. Philadelphia, Pa. | N804F/F-WMKI |

| Regis-tration | Type | C/N | Owner/Operator | Previous Identities |
|---|---|---|---|---|
| N747WA | Citation | 500-0301 | Concord Aviation Ltd. Burlington, Ia. | N81MJ/EP-PAP/N5301J |
| N748MN | Gulfstream 2 | 215 | Merle Norman Cosmetics Inc. Los Angeles, Ca. | N816GA |
| N748VA | Citation | 500-0148 | Top Line Sales Corp. Nevada, Ia. | N718VA/(N100JC) |
| N750CS | Sabre-65 | 465-37 | Coastal Petroleum (Far East) Pte. Ltd. Singapore. | |
| N750R | Falcon 20D | 187 | Oral Roberts, Tulsa, Ok. | N40AC/N4379F/F-WLCV |
| N750SB | HFB 320 | 1031 | Araz Leasing Corp. Hicksville, NY. | N300SB/D-CERA |
| N750SS | Falcon 20C | 6 | Sunshine Mining Co. Dallas, Tx. | N497/N65311/C-G00G/N21DT/N21JM /N20JM/N805F/F-BMKH/F-WMKH |
| N750WJ | Learjet | 24-065 | W & R Leasing Co. Naples, Fl. | (N7500K)/N7500K/N200DM/N2000M |
| N751CC | Citation | | | |
| N751CR | Jet Commander | 88 | Gary Eyler, Indianapolis, In. | N70CS/N963WM |
| N752CC | Citation | 550-0018 | US Customs Service, Washington DC. | (N3225M) |
| N752RT | Citation | 550-0056 | Republic of Texas, Houston, Tx. | N5342J |
| N753CC | Citation | 550-0109 | US Customs Service, Washington DC. | N2665N |
| N754GL | Learjet | 35A-197 | Armored Transport Inc. Los Angeles, Ca. | |
| N754S | Falcon 50 | 39 | Shell Aviation Corp. Houston, Tx. | N59FJ/F-WZHL |
| N755S | Gulfstream 2 | 20 | Shell Aviation Corp. Houston, Tx. | N2PG |
| N756 | JetStar-8 | 5154 | Cleveland Cliffs Iron Co. Oh. | N3031/N5518L |
| N756N | DH 125/3A-RA | NA708 | Nekoosa-Edwards Paper Co. Wi. | N9149/G-AWKI |
| N756S | Gulfstream 3 | 348 | Shell Aviation Corp. Houston, Tx. | |
| N759A | Gulfstream 2 | 131 | ARAMCO Overseas Co. Houston, Tx. | 9M-ATT/N17582 |
| N760AC | Learjet | 55-017 | Auxiliary Carrier Inc. NJ. | |
| N760AR | MS 760 Paris 2B | 108 | Investment One Ltd. Kailua Kona, Hi. | PH-MSX/F-BJZX |
| N760J | MS 760 Paris | 6 | Don Hansen, Fort Worth, Tx. | N84J |
| N760LP | Learjet | 35A-155 | Penley Associates, Philadelphia, Pa. | |
| N760R | MS 760 Paris 2B | 104 | N Pacific Aircraft Development, Helena, Mt. | N760P/PH-MST/F-BJZS |
| N760S | MS 760 Paris | 43 | Arnold Barr, Longmeadow, Ma. | N760C/N776K |
| N760T | MS 760 Paris 2B | 103 | Visalia Airmotive, Ca. | N760N/YV-163CP/N760N/PH-MSS/F-BJZR |
| N760U | Gulfstream 2 | 75 | Union Oil Co. Los Angeles, Ca. | N600CS/N100CC/N100AC/N1000/N823GA |
| N760X | MS 760 Paris | 28 | LGW Inc. Albuquerque, NM. | I-SNAI |
| N761A | Learjet | 36A-022 | IBM Corp. NY. | |
| N762L | Learjet | 36A-033 | IBM Corp. NY. | |
| N763R | Learjet | 36A-034 | IBM Corp. NY. | |
| N764G | Learjet | 35A-406 | IBM Corp. NY. | |
| N765A | Gulfstream 2 | 111 | ARAMCO Overseas Co. The Hague. | N13LB/N10LB/N815GA |
| N766R | Sabre-40R | 282-1 | Aircraft Parts & Development Corp. Laredo, Tx. | N177A/N7820C |
| N767PC | Citation | 500-0080 | Mercer Beverage Co. Fort Wayne, Inc. | N222KW/N59019/C-GJAP/N419K /N50CC/N580CC |
| N767RV | B 727-17 | 20512 | EAF/Asterion Inc. Dover, De. | N99548/CP-1339/N99548/CF-CUR |
| N769K | Citation | 500-0228 | Airco Speer Carbon Graphite, St.Marys, Pa. | N6365C/(N228CC) |
| N770AC | Gulfstream 2 | 57 | Auxiliary Carrier Inc. Hasbrouck Heights, NJ. | N876GA |
| N770CA | Challenger | 1042 | Valley Line Supply & Equipment Co. Pittsburgh, Pa. | |
| N770DA | DH 125/731 | NA705 | Interfirst Corp. Dallas, Tx. | N822CC/N7440C/N744CC/N9040/N688CC /N9040/N7055/G-AVOL |
| N770JM | Learjet | 55-039 | M Air Inc. Houston, Tx. | N39418 |
| N771A | Learjet | 35A-303 | ALCOA, Pittsburgh, Pa. | |
| N771CB | Learjet | 25D-326 | Champagne Limousine Service Inc. Dallas, Tx. | |
| N772C | Citation | 500-0180 | Gloria Delzer, Rapid City, SD. | N61MJ/PT-LAZ/N31079/HB-VFH/SE-DDO /N31079/I-AMBR/N180CC |
| N773FR | Citation | 501 0042 | Fresh International Corp. Salinas, Ca. | N87185 |
| N773LP | Citation | 501-0075 | Louisiana Pacific Corp. Hillsboro, Or. | N3120M |
| N773WB | Jet Commander | 112 | Wm Brian Egolf Co. Oklahoma City, Ok. | N44WG/N4WG/N91WG/N91B |
| N776DS | Falcon 20C | 76 | D-S Corp. Palm Springs, Ca. | N937GC/N970F/F-WMKF |
| N777AJ | Citation | 501-0108 | Al Johnson Construction Co. Minneapolis, Mn. | (N56CJ)/(N264RZ) |
| N777CF | Westwind-1124 | 231 | UGI Corp. Pa. | N8514Y/HB-VFP/4X-CMC |
| N777FC | Citation | 500-0038 | Chino Jet Services Inc. Pomona, Ca. | N81BA/N2EL/HR-VCU/N53RCC |
| N777FE | Citation | 501-0111 | Furnas Electric Co. Batavia, Il. | (N333RB)/N140WC/N26490 |
| N777JF | Falcon 20F | 249 | Valley Line Supply & Equipment Co. St.Louis, Mo. | N11AK/N4421F /F-WJMM |
| N777LF | Learjet | 35A-449 | Levitz Furniture Co. Miami, Fl. | N37947 |
| N777MC | Learjet | 35A-125 | Meredith Corp. Des Moines, Ia. | N3803G |
| N777PV | Falcon 20C | 137 | Garrett Corp. Phoenix, Az. (ATF3-6 Test aircraft). | N8999A/N4352F /F-BLLK/F-WLLK |
| N777RA | Learjet | 35A-285 | Ramada Airways Inc. Wilmington, De. | |
| N777SA | Learjet | 24B-228 | Mid South Bottling, Tx. | D-IIPD/(D-1IDD)/N7DL/N4292G/N245GL |
| N777SL | Citation | 500-0307 | Sanders Lead Co. Troy, Mi. | N2613/N2607/N5307J |
| N777SW | Gulfstream 3 | 306 | Seagrams Whiskey, New York. | N306GA |

| Regis-<br>tration | Type | C/N | Owner/Operator | Previous<br>Identities |
|---|---|---|---|---|
| N777TX | Falcon 20F | 365 | Textron Inc. Providence, RI. | N1018F/F-WMKJ |
| N777VZ | Sabre-40 | 282-69 | Challenge 2 Inc. Owensboro, Ky. N777V/N43NR/N1MN/N125NL/N256MA/N125N<br>/N2236B |  |
| N777XX | Challenger | 1017 | TAG/Aviation Methods, SFO. | N4247C/C-GBPX |
| N780AC | Learjet | 25XR-173 | Auxiliary Carrier Inc. Hasbrouck Heights, NJ. |  |
| N780RH | JetStar-731 | 30/5095 | Roy Huffington Inc. Houston, Tx. | N78MP/N9251R |
| N788C | Gulfstream 2 | 165 | Jet Aviation of America Inc. Washington DC. | N7000C/N810GA |
| N789TE | Westwind-1124 | 241 | Temple-Eastex, Diboll, Tx. | 4X-CMM |
| N790FA | B 707-138B | 17697 | Private Jet Services/Lowa Ltd. Washington, DC. | TC-JBN/N790SA/D-ADAP<br>N790SA/VH-EBB |
| N793JR | Westwind Two | 365 | Blinder Robinson Co. Englewood, Co. | 4X-CUS |
| N793NA | B 707-138B | 17700 | T A G International. | VP-BDE/N793SA/CF-PWW/N793SA/VH-EBE |
| N797AS | B 727-90C | 19169 | BP/Alaska Airlines, Seattle, Wa. |  |
| N800BD | Falcon 50 | 35 | Beckton Dickinson Co. Teterboro, NJ. | N57FJ/F-WZHF |
| N800BH | Citation | 501-0039 | Home Interiors & Gifts Inc. Dallas, Tx. | N800DC/N403CC/N36914 |
| N800CB | HS 125/700A | NA0216 | Western Leasing Co. Van Nuys, Ca. | N72505/G-BFFH |
| N800CF | Falcon 20F | 368 | U S Fire Insurance Co. Morristown, NJ. | N1036F/F-WMKI |
| N800CS | Sabre-40 | 282-64 | Coastal States Gas Co. Houston, Tx. | N9000S/N9000V |
| N800DA | DH 125/1A-522 | 25047 | First National Bank, Dallas, Tx. | N75CT/N580WS/N778SM/G-ATGT |
| N800DC | Falcon 20C | 75 | Home Interiors & Gifts Inc. Dallas, Tx. | N2568/N256MA/N100V/N969F<br>/F-WNGL |
| N800J | Gulfstream 3 | 359 | Johnson & Johnson, W.Trenton, NJ. |  |
| N800JJ | Westwind-1124 | 290 | Johnson & Johnson, W.Trenton, NJ. | 4X-COJ |
| N800KC | Citation | 500-0083 | Kimberly-Clark Corp. Neenah, Wi. | N10U0/N10UC/N583CC |
| N800LS | Falcon 20C | 144 | National Medical Enterprises, Riyadh, Saudi Arabia. | N888JR/N888L |
| N800M | Sabre-65 | 465-41 | Montgomery Drilling Inc. Bakersfield, Ca. | N2556E |
| N800MC | Falcon 20C | 74 | Personal Way Aviation Inc. Dallas, Tx. | N57HH/N1MB/N1851T/N968F<br>/F-WMKG |
| N800W | Citation | 500-0014 | Wilse Kleckey, Cameron, La. | N900W/N766FT/N514CC/N6565C |
| N801G | Citation | 550-0100 | Burt Sugarman, Los Angeles, Ca. | (N801L)/N2664T |
| N801L | Citation | 501-0201 | Five K Corp. Columbia, Ms. | N6783U |
| N802GA | Gulfstream 2 | 2 | Grumman Aerospace Corp. Bethpage, NY. |  |
| N802W | Learjet | 24-128 | Robert Graf Inc. Fort Lauderdale, Fl. | N37594/HB-VBK/N4CR/N383X<br>/N333X/N914BA/HB-VBK/N655LJ |
| N805C | Challenger | 1037 | A E Staley MFG Co. Decatur, Il. | C-GLYE |
| N805RG | Sabre-80A | 380-48 | Procter & Gamble, Cincinnati, Oh. | N8NG/N8NR/N2127J |
| N806C | Citation | 550-0010 | A E Staley Manufacturingf Co. Decatur, Il. | N550PL/OE-GEP/N98R58 |
| N806LJ | Learjet | 23-073 | EPPS Air Service Inc. Atlanta, Ga. |  |
| N807F | Falcon 10 | 114 | A E Staley Manufacturing, Decatur, Il. | N100YM/N200YM/N187FJ/F-WPXF |
| N807G | DH 125/731 | 25121 | Southern Bell Telephone Co. | N307G/N795J/G-AVAE |
| N807GA | Gulfstream 2 | 233 | Security Pacific National Bank, Los Angeles, Ca. |  |
| N808DM | Citation | 550-0084 | Diamond M Co. Houston, Tx. | N222LB/N26629 |
| N808JA | Learjet | 23-050A | Jet America International, Cambridge, Md. | NR08LJ |
| N809F | Falcon 20F | 393 | A E Staley Manufacturing Co. Decatur, Il. | N76TA/N21NL/N176F/F-WLCT |
| N809LS | Gulfstream 2 | 47 | Lear Siegler, Ca. | N809GA/N553MD/N35JM/N803GA |
| N809P | Falcon 20C | 35 | A E Staley "anufacturing, Decatur, Il. | N809F/F-WMKG |
| N810E | Falcon 10 | 60 | Emerson Electric Co. St. Louis, Mo. | N77GT/N145FJ/F-WJML |
| N810SC | HS 125/700A | NA0327 | Southern California Gas Inc. Los Angeles, Ca. | G-5-15 |
| N810SG | Citation | 550-0032 | Southern California Gas Inc. Los Angeles, Ca. | N810SC/N3251M |
| N812JA | Learjet | 35A-394 | Joseph Imparato/Houston Oil, Tx. | N1466K |
| N812N | DH 125/1A | 25052 | NASCAR, Daytona Beach, Fl. | N812M/N816MC/N816M/G-ATIK |
| N812TT | DH 125/1A-522 | 25046 | Thousand Trails Inc. Seattle, Wa. | N666AE/N125P/N4886/N48UC/G-ATGS |
| N813H | HS 125/700A | NA0206 | Hughes Aircraft Co. Culver City, Ca. | G-REYC/G-5-12 |
| N813PR | DH 125/3A-RA | NA702 | Duncan Aviation Canada Ltd. Lincoln, Nb. | N13MJ/CF-KCI/CF-AAG/G-AVJD |
| N814M | Learjet | 35A-077 | Standard Oil Co. of Ohio, Cleveland, Oh. |  |
| N814NA | JetStar-6 | 5003 | NASA, Edwards AFB, Ca. | NASA14/N9203R |
| N815A | Learjet | 35A-142 | Amerock Corp. Rockford. Il. |  |
| N815AC | Falcon 20D | 206 | Allis Chalmers Corp. West Allis, Wi. | N4394F/F-WLCS |
| N816JA | Learjet | 35A-394 | Joseph Imparato, Houston, Tx. | N1466K |
| N816M | Learjet | 35-030 | Standard Oil Co. Cleveland, Oh. |  |
| N816S | Westwind 1124 | 360 | Sale, Houston, Tx. | 4X-CUN |
| N817M | Falcon 50 | 24 | Standard Oil Co. Cleveland, Oh. | N51FJ/F-WZHL |
| N818CD | Citation | 500-0311 | British Motor Car Distributors Ltd. SFO, Ca. | N5311J |
| N819GA | Gulfstream 2TT | 228 | United Brands/Air Services Transportation Co. NY. | (N30B)/(N700CO) |
| N819H | Citation | 500-0263 | Bruce-Anderson Co. Inc. Bozeman, Mt. | (N126KP)/N126KR/N5263J |
| N819JA | Westwind-Two | 328 | John Jumonville, Ventress, La. | N816JA/4X-CRV |

| Registration | Type | C/N | Owner/Operator | Previous Identities |
|---|---|---|---|---|
| N819M | HS 125/700A | NA0318 | Standard Oil Co. Cleveland, Oh. | G-5-14 |
| N820FJ | Citation | 500-0310 | Fred Jones Manufacturing Co. Oklahoma City, Ok. | N1851N/N1851T /N510CC/(N5310J) |
| N821LM | Learjet | 25D-317 | Black Jack Aviation Inc. Houston, Tx. | |
| N821PC | Learjet | 35A-486 | | |
| N823J | Learjet | 35A-171 | Associated Inns & Restaurants Co. of America. Denver, Co. | C-GNSA /N747GL |
| N823M | Learjet | 24-050 | Ken Davis Industries Inc. Tulsa, Ok. | N828M/N828MW |
| N824GA | Learjet | 24F-342 | Parker Drilling Co. Tulsa, Ok. | YV-178CP/N40144 |
| N824LJ | Learjet | 23-083 | Clement Brothers Inc. Hickory, NC. | |
| N827GA | Gulfstream 2 | 80 | PPG Industries Inc. Pittsburgh, Pa. | |
| N828B | Citation | 550-0316 | Boettcher & Co. Denver, Co. | N5428G |
| N828M | Learjet | 35-063 | Ken Davis Industries International Inc. Portland, Or. | |
| N828QA | Learjet | 25-052 | Gates Learjet Corp. Tucson, Az. | N8280/N232MD |
| N829GA | Gulfstream 2 | 245 | Texas Commerce Bank, Houston, Tx./Emirates Air Service. | |
| N829JM | Citation | 550-0249 | James Moore, Livonia, La. | N88718 |
| N830G | Gulfstream 2 | 44 | CONOCO, NY. | N814GA |
| N830TL | Gulfstream 2 | 35 | Time Inc. NY. | N1004T |
| N831CJ | Learjet | 35A-166 | Great Lakes Corp. Chicago, Il. | |
| N831WM | Learjet | 25B-076 | Combs Gates Denver Inc. | N711CA/N160J/D-CCWK/HB-VCL |
| N833JL | Citation | 501-0045 | J Lewis Investments, Birmingham, Al. | N833/N98468 |
| N835AC | Learjet | 35A-158 | Allis Chalmers Corp. Milwaukee, W. | |
| N835F | Falcon 10 | 135 | P L Lloyd, Little Rock, Ar. | N199FJ/F-WZGG |
| N835GA | Learjet | 35A-087 | Parker Drilling Co. Tulsa, Ok. | N720GL |
| N835WB | Learjet | 25-027 | SWAB, Midland, Tx. | N35WB/N423RD/N7000G |
| N836GA | Learjet | 36A-027 | Parker Drilling Co. Tulsa, Ok. | |
| N837F | Falcon 10 | 137 | Commercial Union Corp. Boston, Ma. | N200FJ/F-WZGI |
| N839F | Falcon 50 | 55 | Clark Rental System/Commercial Union Corp. Boston, Ma. | N73FJ/F-WZHU |
| N840GL | Learjet | 35A-210 | Southeastern Jet Corp. Fort lauderdale, Fl. | (N35HM) |
| N840H | BH 125/400A | NA753 | Halliburton Services Inc. Oh. | N400BH/N49BH |
| N841F | Falcon 50 | 63 | Commercial Union Corp. Boston, Ma. | N78FJ/F-WZHF |
| N846YT | Learjet | 25-012 | Belle Fourche Pipeline Co. Casper, Wy. | N191DA/N853DS/N853GA |
| N848C | Jet Commander | 54 | Pennsylvania Glass Sand Corp, Wilmington, De. | |
| N848GL | Learjet | 35A-488 | | N8563G |
| N850CS | Sabre-65 | 465-38 | Coastal Corp. Houston, Tx. | |
| N851BA | Learjet | 24B-194 | Bass Aviation Inc. | N77LS/N952GA |
| N853KB | Citation | 501-0232 | Cape Smythe Air Service, Barrow, Ak. | N2616C |
| N855W | Learjet | 24B-199 | L W Rozzo Inc. Fort Lauderdale, Fl. | N333CR |
| N856JB | Learjet | 23-052 | Bird Leasing Inc. Bradford, Ma. | N360EJ/HB-VBD/N360EJ |
| N856W | Gulfstream 2 | 104 | Travelers Insurance Co. Hartford, Ct. | N856GA |
| N857W | Sabre-65 | 465-72 | Travelers Insurance Co. Hartford, Ct. | |
| N861L | Learjet | 25-023 | International Lease Finance Corp. Beverley Hills, Ca. | N47AJ/N13CR /N72CD/N577LJ |
| N862G | Gulfstream 3 | 329 | General Dynamics Co. St. Paul, Mn. | N301GA |
| N866DH | Jet Commander | 78 | Precision Instrument Co. Inc. Spring, Tx. | N1121E |
| N866JM | Westwind-1123 | 184 | New Park Aviation, Lafayette, La. | N666JM/N1123T/4X-CKH |
| N869KM | HS 125/700A | NA0315 | Colleen Corp. Philadelphia, Pa. | G-5-14 |
| N871D | HS 125/700A | NA0295 | Diamond International Corp. NY. | G-5-13 |
| N871E | Gulfstream 2 | 145 | I T & T Corp. Wilmington, De. | N871D/N894GA |
| N872D | | | Diamond International Corp. NY. | |
| N872E | Gulfstream 2 | 257 | I T & T Corp. Wilmington, De. | N822GA |
| N873D | Citation | 500-0337 | Diamond International Corp. N.Y. | N5337J |
| N873E | Gulfstream 3 | 320 | I T & T Corp. Wilmington, De. | |
| N873G | DH 125/3A-RA | NA707 | Brown & Root Inc. Houston, Tx. | N873D/N350MC/G-AWKH/G-5-15 |
| N874RA | Gulfstream 3 | 361 | | (N875E) |
| N877BP | Citation | 500-0255 | Blandin Paper Co. Grand Rapids, Mi. | N37643/D-INCI/N5255J |
| N877C | Citation | 501-0017 | Norman Fink Engineering Co. Los Angeles, Ca. | |
| N878DE | Learjet | 24-153 | James Brock, Odessa, Tx. | (N53DE)/N159J/N1TK/N524SC |
| N878ME | Learjet | 25D-351 | Wickes Leasing Co. Minneapolis, Mn. | |
| N880CM | Citation | 501-0050 | Ben Mason, Victoria, Tx. | N20SP/N36901 |
| N880EP | Convair 880 | 38 | LM Corp. Nashville, Tn. | N8809E |
| N880F | Falcon 50 | 3 | Anheuser-Busch, St.Louis, Mo. | N50EJ/N50FJ/F-GBIZ/F-WFJC |
| N880KC | Sabre-60 | 306-121 | Charles Redwine/Business Jet Service, Dallas, Tx. | N2130J |
| N880P | Falcon 20C | 51 | Crawford Enterprises, Tx. | N880F/F-WMKJ |
| N880SC | BH 125/600A | 6018 | General Air Transportation Corp. Wilmington, De. | N500GD/N28BH |
| N881G | Falcon 20F | 399 | International Paper Co. NY. | N184F/F-WMKI |

| Regis-tration | Type | C/N | Owner/Operator | Previous Identities |
|---|---|---|---|---|
| N881J | Falcon 20F | 396 | International Paper Co. NY. | N179F/F-WMKG |
| N881M | Falcon 50 | 83 | International Paper Co. NY. | N88U/F-WZHJ |
| N881P | Falcon 10 | 33 | International Paper Co. NY. | N123FJ/F-WJMJ |
| N881W | Learjet | 35A-269 | L R French, Midland, Tx. | |
| N886WC | Learjet | 35-023 | Teamsters, Los Angeles, Ca. | N986WC |
| N887PL | Westwind-1124 | 195 | Provident Life & Accident Insurance, Chattanooga, Tn. | 4X-CKS |
| N888AC | Citation Eagle | 500-0349 | Arthur Corp. Phoenix, Az. | (N5349J) |
| N888CR | DH 125/400A | 25180 | Crutcher Resources Corp. Houston, Tx. | N196KQ/N196KC/G-AWPF |
| N888DH | Learjet | 35-010 | R D Hubbard, Wichita, Ks. | |
| N888DL | HFB 320 | 1051 | Richard Sparks, Midland, Tx. | N6ZA/N895HJ/D-CORE |
| N888EB | Citation | 551-0055 | Johnson Bates Drilling, Konawa, Ok. | N350CC/N5492G |
| N888GA | Citation | 500-0132 | Don Love, Wichita, Ks. | N888JD/(N10GR)/N80CC/N35LT/(N632CC) |
| N888MC | Gulfstream 3 | 351 | View Top Corp. NY. | |
| N888MV | Learjet | 35A-362 | R E C Aircraft Inc. NYC. | N3794M |
| N888PM | Sabre-40 | 282-12 | PPJ Leasing Co. Houston, Tx. | N905M/N6366C |
| N888R | Westwind-1124 | 254 | Murco Drilling Corp. Shreveport, La. | N600TD/4X-CMZ |
| N888RB | Learjet | 25R-150 | Lear 25 Partners, San Jose, Ca. | N714KP/N714K |
| N888RW | JetStar-6 | 5040 | Consolidated Airways Inc. Fort Wayne, In. | N7SZ/N518L/N505CC |
| N888SW | Gulfstream 2 | 117 | View Top Corp. NY. | N580RA/N822GA |
| N888WL | Sabre-60 | 306-27 | Bradford Aviation Co. Fort Worth, Tx. | N11AL/I-SNAD/N978R/N4737N |
| N889WF | Learjet | 24D-237 | Wm Farah, El Paso, Tx. | N353J/N32AA/N112J/N25TA/N111TT/N902AR |
| N890A | Gulfstream 3 | 325 | ALCOA, Pittsburgh, Pa. | |
| N894F | Falcon 20C | 133 | J P Stevens & Co. Greer, SC. | N4349F/F-WNGO |
| N897D | Falcon 20C | 134 | Deering Milliken Inc. Greer, SC. | N897DM/N895F/N4350F/F-WMKH |
| N899N | Citation | 500-0114 | General Service Operations Inc. Cleveland, Oh. | N999JB/(N614CC) |
| N900AR | Falcon 10 | 157 | Jet Leasing Corp. Middleton, Oh. | N222FJ/F-WGAF |
| N900BA | Citation | 550-0223 | Rubbermaid Inc. Wooster, Oh. | N6R010 |
| N900BD | Learjet | 24-143 | Burton Davis, Charlotte, NC. | N49AJ/N778GA/N145JN/N592GA |
| N900BE | Westwind 1124 | 382 | Mahan & Rowsey Aviation Co. OKC, Ok. | 4X-CUP |
| N900D | Falcon 10 | 141 | TCB Leasing Co. Houston, Tx. | (N10AH)/N206FJ/F-WZGM |
| N900EL | BH 125/731 | NA747 | Country Club Aventura, Miami, Fl. | N125EH/N43BH/G-AXYF |
| N900GC | Citation | 500-0298 | Granite Construction Co. Watsonville, Ca. | N5298J |
| N900H | JetStar-8 | 5135 | Summa Corp. Las Vegas, Nv. | N636/N7980S |
| N900JD | Citation | 500-0023 | John Deere & Co. Moline, Il. | N523JD/N523CC |
| N900JE | Learjet | 35A-123 | Jack Eckerd Corp. Clearwater, Fl. | N3802G |
| N900JL | Falcon 20D | 171 | Jones & Laughlin Steel Co. Pittsburgh, Pa. | N570L/N4371F/F-WMKG |
| N900KC | DH 125/731 | NA723 | K C Aviation, Appleton, Wi. | N511YP/G-AXDP |
| N900LH | Diamond One | A018SA | | |
| N900MC | Citation | 501-0052 | Continental Telephone Service Corp. Merrifield, Va. | N98715 |
| N900MD | Learjet | 36A-045 | Interrad International Inc. Stamford, Ct. | |
| N900MM | Citation | 501-0128 | Browning-Ferris Industries, Houston, Tx. | N522CC/(N26504) |
| N900MP | Citation | 500-0055 | Pennco Inc. Ashland, Ky. | N900KC |
| N900MR | HS 125/700A | NA0252 | Moore McCormack Resources Inc. Stamford, Ct. | N700HS/G-5-18 |
| N900NA | Learjet | 24A-111 | Northern Air Service Inc. Grand Rapids, Mi. | N44WD/N500FM/N900Y |
| N900P | Learjet | 35A-457 | Pickands Mather & Co. Cleveland, Oh. | |
| N900Q | Learjet | 25-049 | Combs Gates Denver Inc. | N900P/N966GA |
| N900SF | Gulfstream 2 | 167 | Santa Fe Air Transport Inc. Long Beach, Ca. | N204GA/VR-CBC/5V-TAC/N17583 |
| N900T | Falcon 10 | 134 | Browning Ferris Industries, Memphis, Tn. | N202FJ/F-WZGF |
| N900WW | Westwind-1124 | 321 | Connecticut General Insurance Corp. Hartford, Ct. | 4X-CRO |
| N901B | DC-9-15 | 45731 | Westinghouse Electric Corp. Pittsburgh, Pa. | N60FM/N8500/HB-IFA |
| N901BM | Gulfstream 2 | 120 | Bristol-Myers Co. NY. | NR25GA |
| N901GA | Gulfstream 3 | 249 | Gulfstream American Corp. Savannah, Ga. | N300GA |
| N901MH | Falcon 10 | 110 | Texas Independent Oil Co. Houston, Tx. | N90MH/N184FJ/F-WNGO |
| N901TC | Falcon 20F | 335 | Southwestern Bell Telephone Co. St.Louis, Mo. | N4459F/F-WMKF |
| N901YP | Falcon 20F | 360 | Bell Telephone Co. St.Louis, Mo. | N1010F/F-WMKJ |
| N902 | Gulfstream 2 | 11 | Owens Illinois Inc. Toledo, Oh. | N835GA |
| N902K | JetStar-731 | 6/5104 | Westinghouse Electric Corp. Pittsburgh, Pa. | |
| N903G | Gulfstream 2 | 172 | Owens Illinois Inc. Toledo, Oh. | N804GA |
| N903K | Sabre-65 | 465-57 | Westinghouse Electric Corp. Pittsburgh, Pa. | |
| N903KB | Sabre-40 | 282-33 | Westinghouse Electric Corp. Pittsburgh, Pa. | N903K/N737R |
| N904K | Sabre-65 | 465-23 | Westinghouse Electric Corp. Pittsburgh, Pa. | |
| N905K | Sabre-65 | 465-17 | Westinghouse Electric Corp. Pittsburgh, Pa. | N2537E |
| N905LC | Learjet | 35A-320 | Air Treks Inc. Greenville, SC. | |
| N907KH | Citation | 501-0172 | Pacific States Aviation Inc/K Hoffman, Concord, Ca. | (N6782P) |
| N907SW | Gulfstream 2 | 71 | Golden Nugget Inc. Las Vegas, Nv. | N711SW/N4CO/N4CP |
| N908EF | Falcon 50 | 46 | REFCO/Ray Friedman & Co./R & T Partnership. | N64FJ/F-WZHK |

| Regis-tration | Type | C/N | Owner/Operator | Previous Identities |
|---|---|---|---|---|
| N909CH | NAL 1-11/401 | 16/067 | Hemmeter Investment Co. Honolulu, Hi. | HZ-GRP/N5027 |
| N910A | Gulfstream 3 | 367 | | |
| N910G | JetStar-731 | 7/5112 | Standard Oil Realty Corp. Chicago, Il. | N7957S |
| N910M | JetStar-731 | 20/5069 | Standard Oil Realty Corp. Chicago. Il. | |
| N910S | Gulfstream 2TT | 234 | Standard Oil Realty Corp. Chicago, Il. | N808GA |
| N910W | Falcon 20D | 192 | Willis Moore, Dallas, Tx. | N57JF/N920L/N4382F/F-WPUY |
| N910Y | Falcon 20C | 48 | Standard Oil Realty Corp. Chicago, Il. | N878F/F-WMKG |
| N911DB | Learjet | 35A-231 | Skybird Aviation Inc. Van Nuys, Ca. | (N712DM)/(N10AB) |
| N911RF | Falcon 10 | 46 | R & T Partnership, Wilmington, De. | N134FJ/F-WLCT |
| N912DA | Jet Commander-B | 147 | Westside Airways, Houston, Tx. | N147JK/N728MC/N720ML/N9047N |
| N914X | Challenger | 1021 | Xerox Corp. NY. | C-GLWX |
| N918A | Citation | 500-0168 | Burlington Industries Inc. Greenboro, NC. | N91BA |
| N919AT | Citation | 500-0209 | Albert Thomasson, Birmingham, Al. | N209MW |
| N919G | Gulfstream 2 | 29 | Western Electric International Inc. Greensboro, NC. | N930BS/N869GA |
| N920C | Learjet | 35A-283 | Sky City Stores Inc. Asheville, NC. | |
| N920CC | Learjet | 25B-136 | Thomas Daly, Ossinig, NY. | |
| N920G | Falcon 20F | 352 | Anchor Hocking Corp. Lancaster, Oh. | N4466F/F-WMKF |
| N921ML | Falcon 20C | 99 | Marion Laboratories Inc. Kansas City, Mo. | N982F/F-WJMK |
| N922CR | Westwind-1124 | 299 | C R Anthony & Co. Oklahoma City, Ok. | 4X-COS |
| N922DS | Falcon 20F | 373 | Diamond Shamrock Corp. Dallas, Tx. | N53DS/N1041F/F-WMKI |
| N923DS | Falcon 10 | 117 | Diamond Shamrock Corp. Dallas, Tx. | N23DS/N190FJ/F-WPXG |
| N923JA | Jet Commander-B | 146 | Texas Energy Petroleum Corp. Houston, Tx. | N99CK/N99CV/N9046N |
| N924BW | Learjet | 24-164 | Robert Wood/Air Unlimited Inc. Opa Locka, Fl. | N464J/N711L |
| N924DS | Gulfstream 2 | 181 | Diamond Shamrock Corp. Cleveland, Oh. | N24DS/N860GA |
| N924ED | Learjet | 24-104 | E H Derby Co. Sheffield, Al. | N433LJ |
| N925CT | DH 125/1A | 25066 | Cooper Tire & Rubber Co. Findlay, Oh. | G-ATKM |
| N925DS | B 727-23 | 20046 | Harbor Land Co. Dallas, Tx. | N2914 |
| N925R | Jet Commander | 80 | A P St.Philip Inc. Tampa, Fl. | N173AR/N900JL/N87B |
| N925Z | Sabre-60 | 306-3 | Rockwell International. | N1001G/N177A |
| N926DS | Westwind-1124 | 189 | BT Leasing Services Inc. NY. | N26DS/4X-CKM |
| N926LR | DH 125/731 | 25098 | UMC Industries, Stamford, Ct. | N45SL/N11AR/N57G/N666SC/N10121 /G-ATNS |
| N927DS | Falcon 10 | 116 | Diamond Shamrock Corp. Dallas, Tx. | N4DS/N189FJ/F-WNGL |
| N928DS | Citation | 550-0247 | Diamond Shamrock Corp. Dallas, Tx. | (N18DD)/N6860T |
| N929A | Citation | 500-0207 | Burlington Industries Inc. Greenboro, NC. | N92BA |
| N929DS | Citation | 550-0232 | Land Sea Air Leasing Corp. Oregon City, Or. | N6861P |
| N930BS | Citation | 550-0079 | Bethlehem Steel Corp. Pa. | (N26622) |
| N930GL | Learjet | 35A-330 | Airplane Services Inc. New York. | |
| N933 | DH 125/731 | NA721 | Morrison Inc. Mobile, Al. | N93BH/N125G/G-AWXF |
| N933NA | Learjet | 23-049 | NSTL/Earth Resources Laboratory, NSTL Station, Ms. | N701NA/NASA701 |
| N934F | DC-9-32CF | 47148 | American International/Bally's Park Place Casino Hotel, Atlantic City, NJ. | |
| N937GL | Learjet | 25G-337 | | |
| N937J | Falcon 10 | 19 | Shelby Drilling Ltd. Englewood, Co. | N36JM/(N36KA)/(N30JH)/N30JM |
| N940BS | Gulfstream 2 | 157 | Bethlehem Steel Corp. Pa. | N914BS/N805GA |
| N942B | Falcon 10 | 105 | Northwestern Bell Telephone Co. Omaha, Nb. | N180FJ/F-WPUV |
| N944B | Citation | 500-0318 | Northwestern Bell Telephone Co. Omaha, Nb. | N518CC/N5318J |
| N944H | Gulfstream 2 | 251 | Honeywell Inc. Minneapolis, Mn. | |
| N946NA | Gulfstream 2 | 146 | NASA Johnson Space Center, Houston, Tx. | N897GA |
| N947NA | Gulfstream 2 | 147 | NASA Johnson Space Center, Houston, Tx. | N898GA |
| N948N | Citation | 500-0352 | Nibco Inc. Elkhart, In. | N5354J |
| N952 | Learjet | 25D-291 | G E MacDonald, St. Louis, Mo. | N666RB/N1088D |
| N954S | Learjet | 24-136 | Central Flying Service Inc. Little Rock, Ar. | N222RB/N664LJ |
| N955H | Gulfstream 2 | 98 | Honeywell Inc. Minneapolis, Mn. | N93M/N850GA |
| N956 | Sabre-40 | 282-50 | Colorado Interstate Corp. Colorado Springs. | N757E/N6557C |
| N957 | Sabre-40 | 282-71 | Colorado Interstate Corp. Colorado Springs. | N2239B |
| N959AT | Learjet | 35-019 | Golden Jet, Ca. | |
| N959SA | Learjet | 35A-076 | Aviation Equipment Leasing Inc. Washington DC. | |
| N961JC | Westwind-1124 | 208 | Cooper Industries Inc. Houston, Tx. | 4X-CLF |
| N962 | Learjet | 25B-102 | American Jet Aviation, Chesterfield, Mo. | N52AJ/N311CC/N999ML/N999M /N267GL |
| N964C | Sabre-65 | 465-66 | National Can Corp. Chicago, Il. | |
| N966H | Gulfstream 2 | 150 | Honeywell Inc. Minneapolis, Mn. | N803GA |
| N966L | Falcon 20D | 181 | Frito-Lay Inc. Dallas, Tx. | N836UC/N4376F/F-WNGL |
| N967A | Westwind-1124 | 205 | Burlington Industries Inc. Greensboro, NC. | N96BA/4X-CLC |
| N968BN | JetStar-731 | 13/5109 | Burlington Northern Inc. St.Paul, Mn. | N968GN/N7954S |
| N968DM | Citation | 501-0207 | Dairymen Inc. Louisville, Ky. | N67839 |

| Regis-tration | Type | C/N | Owner/Operator | Previous Identities |
|---|---|---|---|---|
| N971H | Learjet | 35A-095 | Harris Corp. Melbourne, Fl. | |
| N972 | Learjet | 24D-252 | G MacDonald, St.Louis, Mo. | N711LD/N711L |
| N972H | Learjet | 24D-322 | Harris Corp. Melbourne, Fl. | N105GL/XA-DAT |
| N972JD | Citation | 500-0118 | ABKO Properties Inc. Wichita, Ks. | N221CC/N220CC/(N618CC) |
| N972TF | Jet Commander-B | 138 | Hamlin Inc. Lake Mills, Wi. | N5BA/4X-COB/N5046E |
| N973 | Learjet | 25D-254 | Richmor Aviation Inc. Hudson, NY. | |
| N973JD | Learjet | 25B-123 | Ryan Aviation Corp. Wichita, Ks. | N360AA |
| N974JD | Learjet | 25B-106 | Jet Dividers Associates, Wichita, Ks. | N10FL/N10NP |
| N978E | Learjet | 36A-024 | Black & Decker Mfg. Co. Fayetteville, NC. | N38D |
| N978EE | Citation | 500-0018 | Emery Express. | (N58AN)/N5QZ/(N5QC)/N5Q/N518CC |
| N979F | Falcon 20C | 91 | S C Johnson & Sons Inc. Racine, Wi. | F-WMKJ |
| N979RA | Gulfstream 2 | 151 | Ogden Corp. NY. | N804GA |
| N980A | Learjet | 25D-340 | Omni Air Inc. Louisville, Ky. | |
| N980EE | Citation | 500-0034 | Emery Express. | N25HC/N534CC |
| N981EE | Citation | 500-0005 | Emery Express. | N501PC/N505CC |
| N984JD | Learjet | 25D-342 | Residence Inn Corp. Wichita, Ks. | N820M/N39391 |
| N986WC | Learjet | 55-030 | Western Conference of Teamsters, Los Angeles, Ca. | |
| N991 | JetStar-731 | 54/5139 | Reynolds Metals Co. Richmond, Va. | N5503L |
| N992 | Sabre-60 | 306-88 | Reynolds Metals Co. Richmond, Va. | N65769 |
| N993 | Falcon 50 | 38 | Reynolds Metals Co. Richmond, Va. | N58FJ/F-WZHK |
| N994 | Sabre-65 | 465-33 | Reynolds Metals Co. Richmond, Va. | |
| N994F | Falcon 20C | 116 | Russell Stover Candies Inc. Kansas City, Mo. | F-WMKJ |
| N996W | Sabre-65 | 465-22 | Wettarau Inc. Keene, NH. | |
| N999CB | Citation | 500-0211 | Charles Brewer Ltd. Phoenix, Az. | N990CB |
| N999CM | Citation | 500-0158 | Cyprus Mines Inc. Los Angeles, Ca. | |
| N999DC | Sabre-60 | 306-95 | Riviera Corp. Birmingham, Al. | N65783 |
| N999JR | Learjet | 24-174 | Riverside Inc. Richmond, Va. | N661JG/N661CP/N854GA |
| N999M | Learjet | 24D-249 | C M I Corp. Troy, Mi. | N27MJ/9J-ADF |
| N999MF | Learjet | 24B-202 | Samuel Grossman, Portland, Or. | N26MJ/F-BUFN/N77JN/N3816G |
| N999RA | Jet Commander | 93 | Rig Air Inc. Oklahoma City, Ok. | N50LB/N221CF/N619JC |
| N999RB | Learjet | 35A-301 | Reading & Bates Corp. Tulsa, Ok. | N301TP |
| N999RW | BH 125/731 | NA757 | Robert Waltrip, Anderson, Tx. | (N44BH)/N154/N10C/N125BH/N52BH |
| N999TH | Learjet | 25D-293 | Journal Publishing Co. Albuquerque NM. | |
| N999U | Westwind-1123 | 178 | Aerojet Charter/John Mason, Washington DC. | N1123Z/4X-CKB |
| N1000E | Sabre-40R | 282-19 | Rockwell International Corp. | N100CE/N881MD/N881MC/N6373C |
| N1001A | Learjet | 23-071 | Daniel Hanna, Portland, Or. | |
| N1001L | Learjet | 35A-357 | Triton Oil & Gas Corp. Dallas, Tx. | N3797S |
| N1001U | Caravelle 6R | 86 | Litton Industries-Aero Service Corp-Goodyear, Houston, Tx. | |
| | | | (Photo Survey). | PT-DUW/N1001U |
| N1010A | Learjet | 36-017 | Texas Instruments Inc. Dallas, Tx. | |
| N1010G | Learjet | 36A-043 | Texas Instruments Inc. Dallas, Tx. | |
| N1010H | Learjet | 36A-044 | Texas Instruments Inc. Dallas, Tx. | |
| N1019K | Westwind-1123 | 180 | Miami Aviation Service Inc. Fl. | HP-1A/4X-CKD |
| N1021T | Citation Eagle | 501-0047 | Century Aircraft Inc. Amarillo, Tx. | HB-VFI/N87496 |
| N1024G | Sabre-60 | 306-64 | Sabre Associates Ltd, Chicago, Il. | N370L/N21BM/N8357N |
| N1036N | Learjet | 25B-121 | Victory Transfer Co. Inc. Laredo, Tx. | N500PP/N39JJ/HZ-MRP/N7GA |
| N1039 | Gulfstream 2 | 40 | Dantata, Kano, Nigeria. | (N5040)/N1040 |
| N1040 | Gulfstream 3 | 314 | Cox Enterprises Inc. Vandalia, Oh. | |
| N1047T | Falcon 20C | 126 | Ambassador Airways Inc. Wilmington, De. | PH-BAG/HB-VBL/F-WMKH |
| N1064 | T-39A | 265-52 | Reason for civil reg?. | 61-0649 |
| N1103 | HS 125/700A | NA0244 | Gould Inc. Chicago, Il. | N130BG/G-5-18 |
| N1107M | Falcon 20C | 38 | EAF/Heublein Inc. Hartford, Ct. | N842F/F-WMKF |
| N1107Z | JetStar-8 | 5122 | Pennzoil Co. Houston, Tx. | N7967S |
| N1109 | Citation | 550-0434 | Gould inc. Chicago, Il. | |
| N1116A | Sabre-60 | 306-30 | General Dynamics Corp. Fort Worth, Tx. | N2440C/N2440G/N905BG/N905R /N4742N |
| N1121G | Jet Commander | 67 | Clover Aviation Inc. Houston, Tx. | N650M |
| N1123H | Westwind-1123 | 167 | Joseph Imparato, Montgomery, Tx. | N873EJ |
| N1123Y | Westwind-1123 | 179 | Windsor Gas Co. Houston, Tx. | 4X-CKC |
| N1124G | Westwind-1124 | 243 | GTE Service Corp. Stamford. Ct. | 4X-CMO |
| N1124L | Westwind 1124 | 340 | CPN Leasing Co. Concord, Ca. | 4X-CUA |
| N1124P | Westwind 1124 | 341 | Alberto Culver Co. | 4X-CUB |
| N1124X | Westwind-1124 | 233 | Gaylord Broadcasting Co. Oklahoma City, Ok. | 4X-CME |
| N1125 | DH 125/731 | 25023 | National Steel Corp. Pittsburgh, Pa. | G-ASZP |
| N1125G | Westwind-1124 | 247 | GTE Services Corp. Stamford, Ct. | 4X-CMS |
| N1127M | Learjet | 35A-226 | Miles Laboratories Inc. Elkhart, In. | |

| Regis-tration | Type | C/N | Owner/Operator | Previous Identities |
|---|---|---|---|---|
| N1141G | Westwind-1124 | 275 | Getty Refining & Marketing Co. Tulsa, Ok. | 4X-CNU |
| N1181G | Falcon 50 | 72 | Getty Refining & Marketing Co. Tulsa, Ok. | N82FJ/F-WZHM |
| N1210 | Sabre-60 | 306-4 | A Parravano, Los Angeles, Ca. | N178W |
| N1212G | Westwind-1124 | 229 | Getty Refining & Marketing Co. Tulsa, Ok. | 4X-CMA |
| N1214H | Citation | 551-0393 | Sklar & Phillips. | (N18CC) |
| N1214S | Citation | 550-0363 | N J Leasing Co. NYC. | |
| N1215G | Citation | 550-0366 | W R Osborn Jr. Santa Elena, Tx. | |
| N1216H | Citation | 550-0408 | | |
| N1217D | Citation | 550-0417 | Aircraft Facilities Ltd. Wichita, Ks. | |
| N1217H | Citation | 550-0418 | | |
| N1217N | Citation | 550-0419 | | |
| N1217P | Citation | 551-0419 | | |
| N1217V | Citation | 550-0422 | | |
| N1218A | Citation | 550-0425 | | |
| N1230B | DH 125/1A | 25088 | Norman Spivock, Beaverton, Or. | G-ATNO |
| N1234X | Citation | 501-0028 | Taylor Industries Inc. Des Moines, Ia. | N36895 |
| N1270F | Falcon 20C | 72 | Kearney & Trecker Corp. Milwaukee, Wi. | HB-VAW/F-WNGO |
| N1288 | B 737-2A6 | 20195 | United Technologies Corp. East Hartford, Ct. | |
| N1306T | DC-9-15F | 47061 | Nelson Steel & Wire Co. Inc. Franklin Park, Il. | |
| N1333Z | Citation | 550-0243 | James Haldane, Glenbrook, Nv. | VR-BHG/TI-APZ/N6860L |
| N1382C | Citation | 500-0309 | Clover Club Foods Co. Kaysville, Ut. | N1UG/N1JN/(N1GB)/N5309J |
| N1424 | Westwind-Two | 345 | J W Galbreath, Columbus, Oh. | 4X-CTM |
| N1424Z | Jet Commander | 94 | J W Galbreath, Columbus, Oh. | N1424 |
| N1454H | Gulfstream 3 | 350 | Amerada Hess Corp. NY. | N317GA |
| N1500 | Falcon 20C | 8 | Continental Group, Morristown, NJ. | N150CG/N1500/N806F/F-WMKJ |
| N1500B | Learjet | 25-055 | Bucyrus-Erie Co. South Milwaukee, Wi. | |
| N1500E | Learjet | 35A-124 | Bucyrus-Erie Co. South Milwaukee, Wi. | |
| N1501 | Falcon 20C | 15 | Continental Can Co. Morristown, NJ. | N151CG/N1502/N622R/N806F/F-WMKK |
| N1502 | Learjet | 35A-328 | Greenwich Aviation, Ct. | N3807G |
| N1503 | Learjet | 35A-316 | Continental Group, Morristown, NJ. | N39398 |
| N1515E | DH 125/1A | 25035 | F J Boutell Driveway Co. Inc. Flint, Mi. | N1515P/G-ATCO |
| N1515P | BH 125/600A | 6022 | Hoover Universal, Ann Arbor, Mi. | N701A/N701Z/N34BH |
| N1543 | BAC 1-11/203 | 017 | Cerro Industries, Rockville, Md. | VR-BAC/N1543 |
| N1620 | HS 125/700A | NA0308 | Texaco Inc. NY. | N700KK/G-5-19 |
| N1621 | Gulfstream 2 | 31 | Texaco Inc. NY. | |
| N1622 | Challenger | 1030 | Texaco Inc. NY. | C-GLXQ |
| N1624 | Gulfstream 2 | 33 | Texaco Inc. NY. | |
| N1625 | Gulfstream 2 | 154 | Texaco Inc. NY. | |
| N1707Z | Gulfstream 2 | 213 | Pennzoil Co. Houston, Tx. | |
| N1776F | Jet Commander | 38 | MEI Aviation Inc. Newbury Park, Ca. | (N200WN)/N217AL/N217PM/N901JL |
| N1807Z | Gulfstream 2 | 27 | Pennzoil Co. Houston, Tx. | |
| N1812C | Challenger | 1018 | EAF/Cityflight Inc. Wilmington, De. | C-GLWR |
| N1818S | Falcon 20C | 149 | Stephens Inc. Little Rock, Ar. | N4359F/F-WNGO |
| N1823B | Citation | 551-0050 | Duane Stranahan, Toledo, Oh. | N98403 |
| N1823D | Gulfstream 2 | 59 | Champion Spark Plug Co. Toledo, Oh. | N879GA |
| N1823F | Falcon 20C | 129 | Champion Spark Plug Co. Toledo, Oh. | N4346F/F-WJMM |
| N1841D | Gulfstream 2 | 227 | Dun & Bradstreet Companies Inc. NY. | N818GA |
| N1847B | Citation | 550-0325 | Boatmans National Bank, St. Louis, Mo. | N6829Y |
| N1851T | Citation | 550-0019 | New York Times Co. NY. | N3232M |
| N1863T | Sabre-40 | 282-62 | Westinghouse Electric Corp. Baltimore, Md. | |
| N1868M | HS 125/700A | NA0214 | Metropolitan Insurance Co. NYC. | N900KC/N34CH |
| N1868N | Falcon 20C | 139 | Superior Training, Indianapolis, In. | N1868M/N926LR/N334JR/N4353F/F-WNGM |
| N1871P | Learjet | 36A-023 | Aragua Services Inc. NY. | N1871R |
| N1871R | Falcon 50 | 6 | Ingersoll Rand Service Co. Woodcliff Lakes, NJ. | N5OFB/F-WZHB |
| N1875P | Gulfstream 2 | 137 | EAF/Prudential Assurance Co. Newark, NJ. | N875GA |
| N1880S | Citation | 500-0183 | Shelby Mutual Insurance Co. Oh. | N1VC/(N721CC)/(VH-FRM) |
| N1881Q | Falcon 20F | 414 | Oneida Ltd/Oriole Assoc. Ltd. Lexington, Ma. | N412F/F-WJML |
| N1884Z | Jet Commander-B | 150 | Gulf States Paper Corp. Tuscaloosa, Al. | N9050N/4X-CPN |
| N1896T | HS 125/700A | NA0312 | AFM Corp./New York Times Co. NY. | N700NN/G-5-18 |
| N1902P | Gulfstream 2 | 226 | J C Penney Co. Inc. NY. | |
| N1902W | Falcon 20F | 269 | Whirlpool Corp. Benton Harbor, Mi. | N4430F/F-WPUX |
| N1909D | Sabre-40 | 282-57 | P & S Partners, Denver, Co. | N1909R/N545C/N27C/N7507V |
| N1909R | Sabre-60 | 306-41 | Business Mens Assurance Co. Kansas City, Mo. | N173A/N925R/N4754M |
| N1923M | DH 125/1A | 25031 | American Management Association Inc. NY. | G-ATBB |
| N1924G | JetStar 2 | 5224 | Ideal Basic Industries Inc. Denver, Co. | N4016M |
| N1924L | BH 125/400A | NA761 | Texas Commerce Barcshares Inc. Houston, Tx. | N125BH/N56BH |

| Registration | Type | C/N | Owner/Operator | Previous Identities |
|---|---|---|---|---|
| N1929S | Learjet | 35A-388 | Standard Brands Inc. NY. | |
| N1929Y | Gulfstream 2 | 19 | Paul Mellon, Upperville, Va. | N839GA |
| N1955E | Citation | 501-0161 | Gamely Corp. Middleburg, Va. | |
| N1963A | Learjet | 23-097 | Combs Gates Denver Inc. Denver, Co. | N1968A/N79LS/N425SC |
| N1966G | JetStar-6 | 5065 | Ethyl Corp. Richmond, Va. | |
| N1966J | Jet Commander | 66 | Bruton Smith, Rockford, Il. | |
| N1968W | Learjet | 23-089 | GAR Inc. Cochranville, Pa. | N969B/N869B |
| N1969L | Learjet | 24-012 | Sale, Oregon City, Or. | N1967L/N1965L |
| N1971R | Falcon 20F | 322 | Ingersoll Rand Services Co. Woodcliff Lakes, NJ. | N4455F/F-WMKH |
| N1976L | Learjet | 35-053 | Coad Inc. Philadelphia, Pa. | |
| N1978L | Learjet | 35A-162 | Coad Inc. Philadelphia, Pa. | N711HH/(HB-VFO)/N751GL |
| N1982G | HS 125/700A | NA0282 | Ethyl Corp. Sandston, Va. | N125AP/G-5-19 |
| N2000 | Sabre-65 | 465-7 | Swiflite Aircraft Corp. Tulsa, Ok. | N10580 |
| N2000M | Learjet | 35A-396 | Brunner & Lay Inc. Asheville, NC. | |
| N2013M | Gulfstream 2 | 51 | Monsanto Co. St.Louis, Mo. | |
| N2015M | Learjet | 35A-072 | Monsanto Co. Decatur, Al. | |
| N2022L | Learjet | 35A-290 | Rexnord Inc. Milwaukee, Wi. | |
| N2022R | Learjet | 25B-200 | Rexnord Inc. Milwaukee, Wi. | |
| N2259V | T-39 | | | |
| N2265Z | Sabre-75A | 380-43 | Norman Lively, Chicago, Il. | N6NR/N2115J |
| N2296C | T-39 | | | |
| N2297B | Learjet | 35-033 | Gates L Corp. Wichita, Ks. | HZ-KA1/N7KA |
| N2426 | Learjet | 25D-216 | Owens Corning Fiberglass Corp. Toledo, Oh. | N3556F |
| N2427F | Learjet | 25B-157 | Owens Corning Fiberglass Corp. Toledo, Oh. | |
| N2428 | Challenger | 1013 | Owens Corning Fiberglass Corp. Toledo, Oh. | C-GBHZ |
| N2440G | Sabre-80A | 380-44 | General Dynamics Corp. St.Louis, Mo. | N2116J |
| N2586E | Sabre-65 | 465-21 | Howard McCormack, OKC, Ok. | |
| N2600 | Gulfstream 3 | 315 | Mobil Oil Corp. NY. | N315GA |
| N2601 | Gulfstream 3 | 316 | Mobil Oil Corp. NY. | N316GA |
| N2605 | Falcon 20F | 312 | Mobil Oil Corp. NY. | N4448F/F-WMKH |
| N2607 | Gulfstream 2 | 30 | Mobil Oil Corp. NY. | N2601/N788S/N870GA |
| N2613C | Citation | 501-0260 | Hope-Air, Houma, La. | |
| N2614 | Falcon 20F | 376 | Mobil Oil Corp. NY. | N2624M/N103F/F-WROS |
| N2615 | Gulfstream 2 | 148 | Mobil Saudi Arabia Inc. Jeddah. | N710MP/N710MR |
| N2617U | Citation | 501-0235 | Folsum Metal Products Inc. McCalla, Al. | |
| N2622M | Falcon 20F | 242 | Mobil Administration Services Co. NY. | (N320FJ)/N800CF/N4418F /F-WPUZ |
| N2624Z | Citation | 501-0243 | San Diego Iron & Steel, Ca. | |
| N2626A | Citation | 501-0238 | Hydro Line Co. | |
| N2626M | Sabre-60 | 306-113 | MASCO, Wilmington, De. | N712MR/N2108J |
| N2627M | Sabre-60 | 306-123 | MASCO, Wilmington, De. | N710MR/N2132J |
| N2627N | Citation | 501-0246 | | |
| N2628Z | Citation | 501-0252 | Libby Welding Co. Kansas City, Mo. | |
| N2630 | Citation | 500-0340 | Mobil Oil Corp. NY. | (N5340J) |
| N2631V | Citation | 501-0257 | Northwestern Supply Co. McCook, Ne. | |
| N2634B | HS 125/700A | 7020 | | VR-BHE/G-EFPT/(G-BFVN)/(G-BFTP) |
| N2635M | Sabre-60 | 306-118 | MASCO, Wilmington, De. | N711MR/N65NR/N2122J |
| N2637Z | Learjet | 35A-413 | Citicorp Leasing International Inc. Wilmington, De. | HB-VHE |
| N2642F | Challenger | 1033 | TAG International. | C-GLXW |
| N2648X | Citation | 501-0105 | Cleo Slater, Fort Lauderdale, Fl. | |
| N2649E | Citation | 550-0144 | Asian Aviation Services Inc. Wichita, Ks. | |
| N2650 | Citation | 500-0341 | Mobil Pipeline Co. Dallas, Tx. | (N5341J) |
| N2650S | Citation | 501-0134 | Robert Masket, Los Angeles, Ca. | |
| N2651 | Citation | 500-0401 | Mobil Oil Corp. NY. | N2617K |
| N2652Z | Citation | 501-0145 | Michael Miller, Bel Air, Ca. | (ZS-KGF) |
| N2653R | Citation | 550-0145 | Silicon Valley Express Inc. Palo Alto, Ca. | |
| N2697V | B 720-027 | 18066 | NASA Dryden Flight Research. | N23/N36860 |
| N2710T | Sabre-60 | 306-2 | Sale, Lincoln, Ne. | N277CT/N22MA/N968R/N307NA |
| N2711B | Falcon 50 | 84 | Zhobi Corp. Las Vegas, Nv. | F-WZHK |
| N2741A | B 727-14 | 18990 | International Executive Aircraft Corp. NY. | D-AHLP/N975PS |
| N2743T | Learjet | 35A-193 | UCO Aviation Inc, Whittier, Ca.VH-SBJ/N620J/VH-SBJ/(YV-131CP)/N1465B | |
| N2815 | Learjet | 35A-334 | Texas Eastern Transmission Corp. Houston, Tx. | |
| N2844 | Learjet | 35A-424 | Texas Eastern Transmission Corp. Houston, Tx. | |
| N2855 | Learjet | 55-079 | | |
| N2913 | B 727-23 | 20045 | Parker Drilling Co. Tulsa, Ok. | (N2550) |
| N2915 | B 727-1A7C | 20143 | Walter E. Heller & Co. Chicago, Il. | |
| N2954T | Falcon 20C | 58 | Urich Oil/UCO Aviation, Big Timber, Mt. | HB-VDG/F-BTOZ/N600KC/N884F |

| Regis-tration | Type | C/N | Owner/Operator | Previous Identities |
|---|---|---|---|---|
| N2979 | Falcon 20D | 183 | General Foods Corp. NY. | /F-WNGL N4377F/F-WLCY |
| N2989 | Falcon 20C | 112 | General Foods Corp. NY. | N991F/F-WJMJ |
| N2998 | Gulfstream 2TT | 236 | General Foods Corp. NY. | N812GA |
| N3000 | Sabre-65 | 465-11 | Swiflite Aircraft Corp. Tulsa, Ok. | |
| N3007 | BH 125/600A | 6007 | Empire Gas Corp. Lebanon, Mo. | N125KR/N125BH/N21BH |
| N3008 | Sabre-60 | 306-29 | Sun Co. Inc. Pa. | N3000/N4741N |
| N3030 | JetStar 2 | 5212 | Republic Steel Corp. Cleveland, Oh. | N5538L |
| N3031 | Westwind-1124 | 269 | Republic Steel Corp. Cleveland, Oh. | 4X-CNO |
| N3032 | Citation | 550-0066 | Republic Steel Corp. Cleveland, Oh. | (N3031)/N26619 |
| N3056R | Citation | 500-0138 | Richard Irwin, Homewood, Il. | |
| N3080 | JetStar-6 | 5094 | World Carpet Enterprises Inc. Dalton, Ca. | N3030/N9250R |
| N3082B | Jet Commander | 97 | Mid Region Petroleum Inc. Tulsa, Ok. | N3032/N96B/N4644E |
| N3100X | Falcon 10 | 12 | Xerox Corp. NY. | N107FJ/F-WJML |
| N3118M | HS 125/400B | 25199 | | HB-VBW/HB-VGU/G-AXLX/HB-VBW/G-AXLX |
| N3131G | Learjet | 25D-274 | Unilease No. 6 Inc. NY. | D-CEPD/N600CD |
| N3155B | Learjet | 35A-117 | Budd Leasing Corp. Troy, Mi. | |
| N3160M | Citation | 501-0084 | Aviation Equipment Leasing Inc. Rockville, Md. | (N11JC)/(N463CJ) |
| N3197M | Citation | 501-0092 | Cin Air Inc, Cincinnati, Oh. | (HB-VGD) |
| N3234S | HS 125/700A | NA0262 | ComAir Inc. Portland, Or. | C-GKRS/(N130BL)/G-5-16 |
| N3237S | Challenger | 1070 | TAG Flight Ltd. Wilmington, De. | C-GLXS |
| N3250 | Learjet | 35A-250 | Vulcan Materials Co. Birmingham, Al. | |
| N3278 | Sabre-60 | 306-32 | Armstrong Cork Co. Lancaster, Pa. | N4743N |
| N3280E | Learjet | 36-013 | Eidal International Inc. Albuquerque, NM. | SE-DDH/(N852WC)/N352WC |
| N3280G | Sabre-40 | 282-70 | Aero UVA International Corp. Miami, Fl. (See N34LP) | |
| N3298D | Sabre-40 | 282-20 | Donham Oil Tool Co. Inc. Dallas, Tx. | N265R/N6374C |
| N3300L | Citation | 500-0256 | Linclay Corp. St. Louis, Mo. | N6861X |
| N3300M | Citation | 500-0338 | Meredith Air Inc. Weyers Cave, Va. | N8499B/HB-VEX/(N868D)/N5338J |
| N3320G | Westwind-1124 | 363 | Getty Refining & Marketing Co. Tulsa, Ok. | 4X-CUO |
| N3330M | Challenger | 1052 | Olan Mills Inc. Chattanooga, Tn. | C-GLXS |
| N3333M | B 737-2A6 | 20194 | John Mecom, Houston, Tx. | N8527S/VR-BEH/N520L |
| N3402 | Learjet | 35A-402 | Vulcan Materials Co. Birmingham, Al. | |
| N3444G | Falcon 20C | 21 | Gates Rubber Co. Denver, Co. | N843F/F-WMKI |
| N3456L | Learjet | 36A-050 | Kaiserair Inc. Ca. | |
| N3526 | Citation | 550-0044 | K B I Corp. Findley, Oh. | N3286M |
| N3533 | Sabre-60 | 306-34 | Thomas D Coffman Inc. Austin, Tx. | N4746N |
| N3600X | Falcon 10 | 88 | Xerox Corp. NY. | N169FJ/F-WPXL |
| N3711H | Jet Commander | 106 | R S G Development Inc. Aspen, Co. | N4690E |
| N3711L | BH 125/400A | NA711 | J T Trotter, Fort Stockton, Tx. | N125J/G-AWMX |
| N3793P | Learjet | 35A-407 | Public Service Co. Albuquerque, NM. | |
| N3794B | Learjet | 55-021 | James Bath, League City, Tx./Bin Laden Aviation. | |
| N3794C | Learjet | 55-028 | | |
| N3794P | Learjet | 25G-352 | | |
| N3794U | Learjet | 35A-455 | | |
| N3794W | Learjet | 35A-454 | | |
| N3794Z | Learjet | 35A-364 | Howard Hughes, Pasadena, Ca. | (N981TH)/(N65TA) |
| N3795U | Learjet | 25D-354 | | |
| N3795Y | Learjet | 55-034 | | |
| N3796B | Learjet | 55-023 | Dan Urschel, Caradian, Tx. | |
| N3796P | Learjet | 35A-473 | | |
| N3796U | Learjet | 55-042 | Omni International Corp. Rockville, Md. | |
| N3796X | Learjet | 55-027 | | |
| N3797A | Learjet | 35A-398 | | |
| N3797B | Learjet | 35A-477 | | |
| N3797C | Learjet | 55-044 | | |
| N3797L | Learjet | 25D-343 | Aero Leasing Group, NY. | |
| N3797U | Learjet | 25D-357 | | |
| N3798L | Learjet | 25D-344 | | |
| N3798P | Learjet | 35A-408 | | (N33VG) |
| N3871J | Learjet | 24XR-274 | James Lyon, Houston, Tx. | |
| N3946A | B 727-191 | 19394 | Burlington Northern Inc. Seattle, Wa. | N300BN |
| N4000X | Challenger | 1058 | Xerox Corp. NY. | C-GLXW |
| N4002M | B 727-17 | 20327 | Fluor Corp. Irving, Ca. | N115TA/CF-CPN |
| N4110S | Citation | 550-0090 | Samedan Oil Corp. Ardmore, Ok. | N2662Z |
| N4209K | Citation | 500-0164 | Truman Trading Co. Inc. Miami, Fl. | D-IHSV/N164CC |
| N4227Y | Falcon 20D | 237 | TAG Aviation Inc. Wilmington, De. | D-CITY/(D-CALM)/(D-CHCH)/F-WPXF |

| Registration | Type | C/N | Owner/Operator | Previous Identities |
|---|---|---|---|---|
| N4245S | B 727-46 | 19282 | Resebury Corp. | D-AHLO/JA8325 |
| N4246N | Learjet | 35-061 | Dana Corp. Toledo, Oh. | N424DN |
| N4246R | Falcon 20D | 175 | Consolidated Airways Inc. Fort Wayne, In. | I-CAIB/F-GBMS/F-ODHA |
| | | | | /D-COFG/F-BUFG/N866MM/N4373F/F-WMKF |
| | | | | D-ICFA/N290CC/(N5290J) |
| N4246Y | Citation | 500-0290 | Executive Air Charter, Tx. | |
| N4247C | Challenger | 1017 | TAG International, Paris. | C-GBPX |
| N4260K | Sabre-75A | 380-60 | ASCO Aircraft Corp. Wilmington, De. | D-CBVW/N2521E |
| N4263X | Citation | 501-0249 | Clark Pipe & Supply Inc. Odessa, Tx. | RP-C237/N2650M |
| N4339D | Convair 880 | 61 | General Dynamics Corp. Fort Worth, Tx. | N5866/HR-TNP/JA8025 |
| N4345F | Falcon 20C | 127 | Alav Inc. NY. | F-WNGN |
| N4350M | Falcon 20C | 140 | Distribution Export Merchandising, Dayton, Oh. | N4354F/F-WNGN |
| N4351M | Falcon 20F | 457 | Mead Corp. Dayton, Oh. | N463F/F-WJMM |
| N4351N | Falcon 20C | 11 | T Helicopter Corp. NY. | N4351M/N30CO/N30CC/N220CM/N2200M/CF-SRZ |
| | | | | /N808F/F-WMKH |
| | | | | N425DN |
| N4358N | Learjet | 35-065 | Dana Corp. Toledo, Oh. | |
| N4366F | Falcon 20D | 163 | EAF/Gillman Paper Co. Concord, NH. | F-WNGM |
| N4400E | DH 125/1A | 25026 | Jed Air Inc. Owasso, Ok. | N225LL/N225K/N225KJ/G-ATAY |
| N4401 | Learjet | 35A-434 | Red Lobster Inns of America, Orlando, Fl. | |
| N4402 | Learjet | 25B-117 | Red Lobster Inns of America, Orlando, Fl. | N170RL/N170GT/N40AS |
| N4403 | Citation | 500-0271 | Red Lobster Inns of America, Orlando, Fl. | N168RL/N5271J |
| N4411 | Gulfstream 2 | 48 | Texas Eastern Trans Corp. Houston, Tx. | N109G |
| N4444U | Westwind-1123 | 163 | Phelps Dodge Magnet Wire Corp. Fort Wayne, In. | N1123T |
| N4503W | B 737-247 | 19600 | Lockheed Aircraft Services, Ca. | |
| N4646S | Citation | 500-0051 | Steuart Investment Co. Washington DC. | N61BR/N51BR/N51BP/N551CC |
| N4875 | Falcon 10 | 54 | Jefferson Industries Inc. Birmingham, Al. | N464AC/(XA-SAR)/N140FJ |
| | | | | /F-WPUU |
| N4993H | T-39A | | B K Robinson, Oklahoma City, Ok. | |
| N5022 | BAC 1-11/401 | 062 | Dresser Industries, Dallas, Tx. | C6-BDN/VP-BDN/N5022 |
| N5033 | BAC 1-11/401 | 075 | Dresser Industries, Dallas, Tx. | N55JT/N5033 |
| N5034 | NAL 1-11/401 | 15/076 | TAG International, Europe Based. | |
| N5037 | BAC 1-11/401 | 079 | Dresser Industries, Dallas, Tx. | |
| N5038 | B 707-123B | 17652 | Dresser Industries Inc. Dallas Tx. | N7525A |
| N5050J | Citation | 550-0001 | Cessna Aircraft Co. Wichita, Ks. | (N551CC)/(N98751) |
| N5071L | Sabre-60 | 306-9 | United Technologies Corp. East Hartford, Ct. | N32UT/N129R/N958R |
| | | | | /N998R/N4717N |
| | | | | N36872 |
| N5072L | Citation | 501-0272 | United Technologies Corp. East Hartford, Ct. | N33UT/N16764/D-ABIV |
| N5073L | B 727-30 | 18936 | United Technologies Corp. East Hartford, Ct. | N38UT/N33UT/N105UA |
| N5075L | Sabre-60A | 306-16 | United Technologies Corp. West Palm Beach, Fl. | /N160RW/N100PW/N5415/N787R/N4726N |
| | | | | N1967G/N9254R |
| N5098G | JetStar-731 | 28/5098 | G T & E Service Corp. Stamford, Ct. | |
| N5101 | Gulfstream 2 | 84 | General Motors Corp. Detroit, Mi. | |
| N5102 | Gulfstream 2 | 85 | General Motors Corp. Detroit, Mi. | |
| N5108 | Sabre-80A | 380-9 | General Motors Corp. Detroit, Mi. | |
| N5109 | Sabre-80A | 380-11 | General Motors Corp. Detroit, Mi. | |
| N5113H | Gulfstream 2 | 107 | Amerada Hess Corp. Woodbridge, NJ. | N809GA |
| N5117H | Gulfstream 2 | 197 | Amerada Hess Corp. Woodbridge, NJ. | N800GA |
| N5152 | Falcon 20F | 440 | C B S Inc. NY. | N452F/F-WROO |
| N5253A | Gulfstream 2 | 222 | C B S Inc. NY. | NR17GA |
| N5400G | Gulfstream 2B | 36 | G A C, Savannah, Ga. | N26LA/N26L |
| N5430G | Citation | 550-0321 | Intertec Data System Corp. Columbia, SC. | |
| N5451G | Citation | 550-0317 | Western Equipment Co. Inc. Midland, Tx. | |
| N5500F | Citation | 550-0125 | S Flickinger Co. Inc. NYC. | N2746Z |
| N5511A | Sabre-65 | 465-39 | Amana Refrigeration Inc. Amana, Ia. | N2551E |
| N5541L | JetStar 2 | 5215 | Bowater N.American Corp., Greenwich, Ct. | |
| N5543G | Learjet | 55-043 | Universal Equipment Gathering Co. Rockville, Md. | |
| N5574 | Learjet | 55-074 | | |
| N5594U | HS 125/F400A | 25219 | TigerAir Inc. Los Angeles, Ca. | G-5-12/9K-AEA/4W-ACA/G-AYEP/G-5-14 |
| N5627 | HFB 320 | 1038 | John Franks, Shreveport, La. | N110WS/D-CESI |
| N5863 | Convair 880 | 48 | RDC Marine Inc. Houston, Tx. | N58RD/N5863/TF-AVB/N5863/JA8027 |
| | | | | /NR490H |
| N5878 | MS 760 Paris 2B | 106 | M K Enterprises Inc. Punta Gorda, Fl. | PH-MSV/F-BJZU |
| N5879 | MS 760 Paris 2B | 107 | Hyde Aircraft Inc., Kansas City, Mo. | PH-MSW/F-BJZV |
| N6000J | Sabre-65 | 465-54 | Ashland Oil Co. Ky. | N2579F |
| N6001L | Citation | 550-0169 | Producers Gas Co. Dallas, Tx. | N185CC/(N8R743) |
| N6034F | Citation | 500-0239 | D T I Rental, Houston, Tx. | N239CC/(N5239J) |
| N6053C | Westwind-Two | 361 | Culbro Corp. NY. | 4X-CUO |
| N6550V | Jet Commander | 56 | Career Aviation Academy Inc., Hayward, Ca. | |

| Regis-tration | Type | C/N | Owner/Operator | Previous Identities |
|---|---|---|---|---|
| N6666K | Learjet | 35A-481 | Burnett Aviation Co. Fort Worth, Tx. | |
| N6666R | Learjet | 35A-412 | Burnett Aviation Co. Fort Worth, Tx. | N37980 |
| N6701 | Falcon 20D | 177 | Sears Roebuck & Co. Chicago, Il. | N4374F/F-WMKI |
| N6709 | BH 125/731 | NA758 | Sears Roebuck & Co. Chicago, Il. | N53BH/G-5-19 |
| N6782B | Citation | 501-0196 | Norton Drilling Co. Lubbock, Tx. | (N575SR)/(N597JV) |
| N6783C | Citation | 501-0231 | K & W Charters Inc. Coos Bay, Or. | |
| N6784T | Citation | 501-0205 | Southern Environmental Industries, Wilmington, De. | |
| N6785L | Citation | 501-0212 | Gem Airplane Leasing Inc. Florissant, Mo. | |
| N6800S | Citation | 550-0334 | Summitville Tiles Inc. Oh. | |
| N6801Z | Citation | 550-0356 | Larken Inc., Cedar Rapids, Ia. | |
| N6802Z | Citation | 550-0258 | Excalibur Oil Co. Tulsa, Ok. | |
| N6803E | Citation | 550-0229 | Lanair Inc. Philadelphia, Pa. | |
| N6804C | Citation | 550-0248 | Geo Reintjes Co. Inc. Kansas City, Mo. | |
| N6862Q | Citation | 550-0265 | McCrae Oil Corp. Houston, Tx. | |
| N6863L | Citation | 550-0290 | Traders Intercontinental Corp. El Paso, Tx. | |
| N6864L | Citation | 550-0278 | Fleetwing Aviation Inc. Wilmington, De. | (N819Y)/(N990Y) |
| N6864X | Citation | 551-0056 | Kilauea Aviation Inc. Bend, Or. | (N312CC) |
| N6864Y | Citation | 550-0280 | Emerald Holding Co. Wilmington, De. | |
| N6887R | Citation | 501-0214 | James Wood, Refugio, Tx. | |
| N6887Y | Citation | 550-0293 | Overnight Transportation Co. Richmond, Va. | |
| N6888Z | Citation | 551-0065 | Antlers Natural Gas Inc. Colorado Springs, Co. | |
| N6889T | Citation | 551-0064 | Floair Inc. Wichita, Ks. | |
| N7000C | Gulfstream 3 | 344 | Cargill Inc. Minneapolis, Mn. | N306GA |
| N7004 | Citation | 550-0428 | B.F. Goodrich Co., Akron, Oh. | |
| N7008 | JetStar-731 | 15/5101 | B F Goodrich Co. Akron, Oh. | N9208R |
| N7085U | B 727-22 | 19149 | Reliance Group, NY. | |
| N7110K | Citation Eagle | 500-0016 | ROC Aviation Inc. Oklahoma City, Ok. | N711CR/N15FS/N3JJ/N516CC |
| N7111H | Citation | 501-0195 | Victor Leasing Co. Bakersfield, Ca. | N161CB/N67814 |
| N7200K | Learjet | 23-099 | Kaman Corp. Windsor Locks, Ct. | |
| N7224U | B 720-022 | 18077 | Sinclare Air Service Inc. Las Vegas, Nv. | |
| N7300K | Learjet | 24B-186 | Air Kaman Inc. Windsor Locks, Ct. | N18G/N1SS/N100AJ/N266P |
| N7600 | JetStar-731 | 59/5054 | Union Oil Co. of California, Los Angeles, Ca. | N760OJ/N9220R |
| N7600K | Learjet | 25B-135 | Sigmet Inc. Morristown, Tn. | G-BBEE |
| N7602 | Gulfstream 2B | 32 | Union Oil Co. of California, Los Angeles, Ca. | |
| N7638S | Jet Commander | 134 | Frontier Ford Inc. Rockford, Il. | 4X-COP/5X-AAB/UAF 1/4X-FVN/N111E |
| N7682V | Sabre-60 | 306-79 | Dravo Corp. Pittsburgh, Pa. | N768DV/N4NE/N4NR |
| N7777B | DH 125/400A | NA712 | Butler International, Mountvale, NJ. | N496G/N60JC/N511WP/N1199G /N1199M/G-AWMY |
| N7789 | Gulfstream 2 | 90 | Dresser Industries, Dallas, Tx. | N883GA |
| N7962S | JetStar-731 | 35/5117 | Exxon Corp. Houston, Tx. | |
| N8000J | Gulfstream 2 | 42 | Northrop Corp. Los Angeles, Ca. | |
| N8000U | Sabre-65 | 465-24 | Ashland Oil, Ky. | N2545E/N65NR |
| N8010X | Challenger | 1038 | Xerox Corp. NY. | C-GLYH |
| N8025X | Sabre-60 | 306-84 | Royal Aviation, Mesquite, Tx. | PT-KOU/N65762 |
| N8100E | Falcon 10 | 52 | Emerson Electric Co. St.Louis, Mo. | N52TJ/N342G/N138FJ/F-WLCX |
| N8102N | B 727-25 | 18253 | | |
| N8200E | Falcon 10 | 111 | Emerson Electric Co. St.Louis, Mo. | N185FJ/F-WNGO |
| N8280 | Learjet | 35A-310 | McDonnell-Douglas Corp. St.Louis, Mo. | (N13HQ)/N13HB/N97JL |
| N8281 | Learjet | 35A-232 | McDonnell-Douglas Corp. St.Louis, Mo. | (900th Learjet) |
| N8300E | JetStar-731 | 39/5115 | Emerson Electric Co. St.Louis, Mo. | N40XY/N26TR/N933CY/N933LC |
| N8414 | B 707-323C | 19577 | MME Farms Maintenance Corp., Warrenton, Va. | |
| N8417B | Citation | 550-0035 | | /N7960S |
| N8520J | Citation | 550-0136 | The Western Co. Fort Worth, Tx. | |
| N8534 | Jet Commander | 113 | United Aviation Inc. Teterboro, NJ. | N3278M |
| N8562Y | Learjet | 35A-483 | OFT Collection & Container Corp. Odessa, Tx. | 4X-CPB/N4732E |
| N8563A | Learjet | 35A-480 | Richmor Aviation Inc. Hudson, NY. | |
| N8563B | Learjet | 25D-360 | | |
| N8563E | Learjet | 55-056 | | (VH-ALH)/N3819G |
| N8563N | Learjet | 35A-491 | | |
| N8563P | Learjet | 55-063 | | (N854GA) |
| N8565J | Learjet | 35A-479 | | |
| N8565K | Learjet | 55-065 | | |
| N8733 | B 707-331B | 20062 | TWA/ARAMCO, Houston. | |
| N8860 | DC-9-15 | 45797 | Richard Mellon Scaife, Pittsburgh. | N8953U/(EC-BAX) |
| N9000F | Sabre-65 | 465-25 | Ash Property Inc. Dublin, Oh. | |

| Regis-<br>tration | Type | C/N | Owner/Operator | Previous<br>Identities |
|---|---|---|---|---|
| N9023W | Jet Commander | 10 | Ammest Service Inc. San Antonio, Tx. | N5BP/N600CD/N31SB/N31S |
| N9060Y | Citation | 500-0241 | Southport Construction Inc. S Padre Island, Tx. | XA-KAJ/N241CC |
| N9071M | Challenger | 1019 | H C Airlease Inc/Hyatt Corp. Rosemont, Il. | C-GLWT |
| N9231R | JetStar-731 | 27/5068 | Exxon Corp. Houston, Tx. | |
| N9300 | Gulfstream 2 | 7 | Crown Cork & Seal, Philadelphia, Pa. | CF-HOG |
| N9871R | Citation | 500-0121 | Air Co Inc. Wichita, Ks. | |
| N10108 | Citation | 500-0035 | Joe Jet Inc. NYC. | N535CC |
| N10122 | DH 125/1A-522 | 25029 | H K Porter Co. Pittsburgh, Pa. | G-ATAZ |
| N10123 | JetStar-6 | 5012 | H K Porter Co. Pittsburgh, Pa. | D-BABE/N9283R |
| N10726 | Falcon 20C | 54 | Southern Natural Services Co. Inc. Birmingham, Al. | N2005/N200P/N886F<br>/F-WMKI |
| N11827 | Falcon 20C | 26 | Southern Natural Services Co. Inc. Birmingham, Al. | N802F/N846F/F-WNGO |
| N12109 | Learjet | 35A-410 | M H Whittier Corp. Los Angeles, Ca. | |
| N12142 | Citation | 550-0362 | United Technologies Corp., Hartford, Ct. | |
| N12157 | Citation | 550-0364 | AmVest Corp. | |
| N12160 | Citation | 550-0413 | | |
| N12162 | Citation | 550-0414 | | |
| N12164 | Citation | 550-0415 | | |
| N12167 | Citation | 550-0416 | Hughes Aircraft Co. | |
| N26178 | Citation | 550-0160 | A W Alloys Inc. Stansted, UK. | (9V-PUW) |
| N26232 | Citation | 501-0240 | Leo A Stater, Fort Lauderdale, Fl. | |
| N26263 | Citation | 501-0245 | | |
| N26440 | Challenger | 1039 | Metropolitan Life Insurance Co. NY. | C-GLYK |
| N26498 | Citation | 500-0398 | Ster Disposables Group, Netherlands. | (PH-JOB) |
| N26540 | Citation | 500-0115 | Mutschler Farms, Jamestown, ND. | N501GF/N26494 |
| N28686 | DH 125/3A-RA | 25152 | Aircraft Conversions Inc. San Antonio, Tx. | XA-IIT/N123RZ/N45793<br>/CF-QNS/G-AVTZ |
| N28968 | Citation | 551-0016 | Lisle Aircraft Inc. Dallas, Tx. | HB-VGE/N22RJ/(N71RL)/(D-ICWB)<br>/(N2661P) |
| N29858 | Citation Eagle | 500-0112 | Eagle North Inc. Durham, NC. | C-GRJC/N3LG/VH-DRM/N512CC |
| N29977 | DH 125/1A | 25028 | White Industries Inc. Bates City, Mo. | XA-ESQ/N50SS/N48172/C-GLFI<br>/G-5-11 |
| N29984 | Challenger | 1060 | TAG International. | C-GLYK |
| N29991 | Citation | 500-0254 | Hubert Hoffman, Alexandria, Va. | C-GJTX/N26PA/N5254J |
| N29995 | Westwind-1124 | 250 | Winnebago Inc. Wilmington, De. | C-GFAO/N250WW/4X-CMV |
| N31240 | Challenger | 1063 | Mid Atlantic Aviation Corp. Wilmington, De. | C-GLWX |
| N32654 | Sabre-40A | 282-111 | Milburn Investments Inc. Austin, Tx | XA-SAG/N9NR/N7662N |
| N36861 | Citation | 501-0013 | Refiners & Producers Marketing Inc. Midland, Tx. | |
| N37489 | Citation | 500-0317 | Atlantic Aviation Corp. Wilmington, De. | D-ICCA/N5317J |
| N37516 | HS 125/400A | 25271 | White Industries/Royal Aviation, Dallas, Tx. | EC-CMU/G-BABL/XX506<br>/G-BABL/G-5-14 |
| N37951 | Learjet | 55-011 | J & N Associates, New Orleans, La. | |
| N37962 | Learjet | 35A-446 | | |
| N37971 | Learjet | 25D-358 | | |
| N37973 | Learjet | 25D-359 | | |
| N37975 | Learjet | 35A-474 | Air Support Corp. Miami, Fl. | N39413 |
| N37984 | Learjet | 35A-384 | Four Winds Air Inc. San Diego, Ca. | |
| N37988 | Learjet | 35A-436 | | |
| N42622 | BH 125/600A | 6011 | ChemGraphics Inc. Secaucus, NJ. | VR-BGS/N555GB/N555CB/N6001H/N24BH |
| N58937 | B 707-138B | 18334 | TAG Aviation Ltd. Wilmington, De. | 9Y-TDB/VH-EBK |
| N67848 | Citation | 501-0210 | Jonathan L Greene, Van Nuys, Ca. | |
| N67986 | Citation | 550-0260 | ADM Leasing Inc./Cascade Oil Co. | |
| N68607 | Citation | 550-0245 | Andrew Mathieson, Ligonier, Pa. | |
| N68609 | Citation | 550-0257 | | |
| N68615 | Citation | 550-0251 | Asian Aviation Services Inc. Wichita, Ks. | |
| N68624 | Citation | 550-0267 | Quantum Leasing/Lanair Inc. Philadelphia, Pa. | |
| N68888 | Citation | 550-0397 | Cotton & Carden, Covington, La. | |
| N72700 | B 727-30 | 18368 | Boeing Equipment Holding Co. Seattle, Wa. | N9234Z/D-ABIM |
| N77111 | Citation | 501-0259 | | |
| N80639 | Citation | 500-0258 | Jon Stiteler, Phoenix, Az. | (N76AM)/TI-AFB/(N5258J) |
| N85653 | Learjet | 55-053 | | |
| N88822 | Citation | | Monticello Flying Service Inc. | |
| N91669 | Jet Commander | 17 | McCollum Aviation, Danville, Il. | C-FSUA/(HB-VAL) |
| N93146 | B 720-047B | 18452 | Volpar Inc. Van Nuys, Ca. | |
| N98688 | Citation | 501-0056 | Negley Air Inc. E.Palestine, Oh. | (N501SF)/(N426CC) |

95

## DH - BH 125 NA SERIES C/N TIE UP

| | | | | |
|---|---|---|---|---|
| NA700/25134 | NA716/25180 | NA732/25203 | NA748/25224 | NA764/25262 |
| NA701/25136 | NA717/25183 | NA733/25204 | NA749/25225 | NA765/25263 |
| NA702/25137 | NA718/25187 | NA734/25205 | NA750/25226 | NA766/25265 |
| NA703/25139 | NA719/25188 | NA735/25206 | NA751/25228 | NA767/25267 |
| NA704/25141 | NA720/25185 | NA736/25207 | NA752/25229 | NA768/25273 |
| NA705/25142 | NA721/25186 | NA737/25208 | NA753/25230 | NA769/25275 |
| NA706/25146 | NA722/25190 | NA738/25210 | NA754/25232 | NA770/25276 |
| NA707/25160 | NA723/25191 | NA739/25211 | NA755/25233 | NA771/25278 |
| NA708/25161 | NA724/25192 | NA740/25212 | NA756/25234 | NA772/25279 |
| NA709/25163 | NA725/25193 | NA741/25213 | NA757/25236 | NA773/25280 |
| NA710/25170 | NA726/25195 | NA742/25214 | NA758/25239 | NA774/25281 |
| NA711/25173 | NA727/25196 | NA743/25216 | NA759/25241 | NA775/25282 |
| NA712/25174 | NA728/25198 | NA744/25218 | NA760/25244 | NA776/25283 |
| NA713/25175 | NA729/25200 | NA745/25220 | NA761/25237 | NA777/25284 |
| NA714/25176 | NA730/25201 | NA746/25221 | NA762/25245 | NA778/25285 |
| NA715/25179 | NA731/25202 | NA747/25222 | NA763/25261 | NA779/25286 |
| | | | | NA780/25287 |

## CITATION 500/501 UNIT NUMBERS WITH C/N TIE UP

| | | | | | | | | | |
|---|---|---|---|---|---|---|---|---|---|
| 350 | 501-0027 | 391 | 501-0026 | 432 | 501-0066 | 473 | 501-0088 | 514 | 501-0249 |
| 351 | 501-0001 | 392 | 500-0364 | 433 | 500-0379 | 474 | 501-0087 | 515 | 501-0124 |
| 352 | 500-0351 | 393 | 500-0362 | 434 | 501-0058 | 475 | 501-0085 | 516 | 501-0134 |
| 353 | 501-0002 | 394 | 501-0028 | 435 | 501-0060 | 476 | 501-0091 | 517 | 501-0130 |
| 354 | 500-0352 | 395 | 501-0031 | 436 | 501-0061 | 477 | 501-0086 | 518 | 501-0131 |
| 355 | 501-0003 | 396 | 500-0370 | 437 | 501-0064 | 478 | 501-0092 | 519 | 501-0135 |
| 356 | 501-0004 | 397 | 501-0262 | 438 | 501-0068 | 479 | 501-0097 | 520 | 501-0136 |
| 357 | 501-0005 | 398 | 501-0050 | 439 | 500-0366 | 480 | 501-0096 | 521 | 501-0137 |
| 358 | 501-0006 | 399 | 500-0367 | 440 | 501-0065 | 481 | 500-0389 | 522 | 501-0128 |
| 359 | 500-0353 | 400 | 501-0033 | 441 | 501-0069 | 482 | 501-0107 | 523 | 501-0121 |
| 360 | 501-0007 | 401 | 501-0034 | 442 | 501-0067 | 483 | 500-0391 | 524 | 501-0142 |
| 361 | 500-0361 | 402 | 500-0368 | 443 | 501-0063 | 484 | 500-0387 | 525 | 501-0138 |
| 362 | 501-0008 | 403 | 501-0039 | 444 | 501-0070 | 485 | 501-0100 | 526 | 501-0139 |
| 363 | 500-0354 | 404 | 501-0035 | 445 | 500-0381 | 486 | 501-0102 | 527 | 501-0132 |
| 364 | 501-0011 | 405 | 501-0046 | 446 | 501-0071 | 487 | 501-0120 | 528 | 501-0133 |
| 365 | 500-0355 | 406 | 501-0036 | 447 | 501-0072 | 488 | 501-0094 | 529 | 501-0140 |
| 366 | 500-0356 | 407 | 500-0371 | 448 | 501-0073 | 489 | 500-0392 | 530 | 500-0395 |
| 367 | 501-0009 | 408 | 501-0037 | 449 | 501-0074 | 490 | 501-0103 | 531 | 501-0125 |
| 368 | 500-0357 | 409 | 501-0038 | 450 | 501-0075 | 491 | 501-0109 | 532 | 501-0141 |
| 369 | 501-0012 | 410 | 501-0042 | 451 | 501-0076 | 492 | 501-0104 | 533 | 500-0396 |
| 370 | 501-0010 | 411 | 501-0029 | 452 | 501-0077 | 493 | 501-0105 | 534 | 501-0156 |
| 371 | 501-0014 | 412 | 501-0040 | 453 | 501-0078 | 494 | 500-0394 | 535 | 501-0143 |
| 372 | 501-0013 | 413 | 501-0047 | 454 | 500-0369 | 495 | 501-0108 | 536 | 501-0144 |
| 373 | 501-0015 | 414 | 501-0048 | 455 | 500-0374 | 496 | 501-0110 | 537 | 501-0159 |
| 374 | 500-0359 | 415 | 500-0373 | 456 | 501-0079 | 497 | 501-0119 | 538 | 501-0145 |
| 375 | 501-0016 | 416 | 501-0045 | 457 | 501-0080 | 498 | 501-0111 | 539 | 501-0163 |
| 376 | 501-0017 | 417 | 501-0043 | 458 | 501-0081 | 499 | 501-0112 | 540 | 500-0403 |
| 377 | 500-0358 | 418 | 501-0053 | 459 | 500-0375 | 500 | 501-0127 | 541 | 501-0147 |
| 378 | 501-0018 | 419 | 501-0054 | 460 | 501-0082 | 501 | 501-0106 | 542 | 501-0148 |
| 379 | 501-0272 | 420 | 501-0049 | 461 | 500-0378 | 502 | 501-0113 | 543 | 501-0149 |
| 380 | 501-0020 | 421 | 501-0062 | 462 | 501-0083 | 503 | 501-0114 | 544 | 501-0150 |
| 381 | 501-0041 | 422 | 501-0051 | 463 | 501-0084 | 504 | 501-0118 | 545 | 501-0146 |
| 382 | 500-0363 | 423 | 500-0372 | 464 | 501-0098 | 505 | 501-0126 | 546 | 501-0151 |
| 383 | 501-0019 | 424 | 501-0044 | 465 | 501-0093 | 506 | 501-0117 | 547 | 501-0152 |
| 384 | 501-0021 | 425 | 501-0055 | 466 | 501-0090 | 507 | 501-0115 | 548 | 501-0153 |
| 385 | 501-0022 | 426 | 501-0056 | 467 | 501-0099 | 508 | 501-0122 | 549 | 501-0160 |
| 386 | 501-0023 | 427 | 501-0052 | 468 | 501-0101 | 509 | 501-0116 | 550 | 501-0161 |
| 387 | 501-0024 | 428 | 500-0376 | 469 | 501-0095 | 510 | 501-0239 | 551 | 500-0397 |
| 388 | 501-0032 | 429 | 500-0377 | 470 | 500-0386 | 511 | 500-0398 | 552 | 501-0162 |
| 389 | 501-0025 | 430 | 501-0057 | 471 | 501-0089 | 512 | 501-0129 | 553 | 501-0157 |
| 390 | 501-0030 | 431 | 501-0059 | 472 | 500-0383 | 513 | 501-0123 | 554 | 500-0399 |
| | | | | | | | | | |
| 555 | 501-0175 | 563 | 501-0167 | 571 | 501-0193 | 579 | 501-0174 | 587 | 500-0408 |
| 556 | 501-0158 | 564 | 501-0155 | 572 | 501-0173 | 580 | 501-0178 | 588 | 501-0181 |
| 557 | 501-0165 | 565 | 500-0401 | 573 | 501-0170 | 581 | 501-0186 | 589 | 501-0179 |
| 558 | 501-0154 | 566 | 501-0169 | 574 | 501-0171 | 582 | 501-0189 | 590 | 501-0192 |

| | | | | | | | | | |
|---|---|---|---|---|---|---|---|---|---|
| 559 | 501-0166 | 567 | 501-0183 | 575 | 501-0184 | 583 | 501-0182 | | |
| 560 | 500-0404 | 568 | 501-0168 | 576 | 501-0187 | 584 | 501-0190 | | |
| 561 | 501-0185 | 569 | 501-0188 | 577 | 501-0176 | 585 | 501-0191 | | |
| 562 | 501-0150 | 570 | 501-0164 | 578 | 501-0177 | 586 | 501-0187 | | |
| | | | | | | | | | |
| 591 | 501-0194 | 597 | 501-0196 | 603 | 500-0406 | 609 | 501-0203 | 615 | 501-0206 |
| 592 | 501-0222 | 598 | 500-0412 | 604 | 501-0231 | 610 | 501-0207 | 616 | 501-0210 |
| 593 | 501-0180 | 599 | 501-0172 | 605 | 501-0200 | 611 | 501-0204 | 617 | 501-0211 |
| 594 | 501-0197 | 600 | 500-0405 | 606 | 501-0201 | 612 | 501-0208 | 618 | 501-0213 |
| 595 | 501-0195 | 601 | 501-0199 | 607 | 501-0202 | 613 | 501-0205 | 619 | 501-0212 |
| 596 | 500-0409 | 602 | 501-0198 | 608 | 500-0413 | 614 | 501-0209 | 620 | 500-0414 |
| | | | | | | | | | |
| 621 | 501-0214 | 628 | 501-0220 | 635 | 501-0226 | 642 | 501-0236 | | |
| 622 | 501-0215 | 629 | 500-0415 | 636 | 501-0229 | 643 | 501-0221 | | |
| 623 | 501-0217 | 630 | 501-0224 | 637 | 501-0232 | 644 | 501-0240 | | |
| 624 | 501-0216 | 631 | 501-0228 | 638 | 501-0230 | 645 | 500-0411 | | |
| 625 | 501-0219 | 632 | 501-0260 | 639 | 501-0234 | 646 | 501-0242 | | |
| 626 | 501-0218 | 633 | 501-0225 | 640 | 501-0237 | 647 | 501-0241 | | |
| 627 | 501-0223 | 634 | 501-0227 | 641 | 501-0235 | 648 | 501-0243 | | |

## CITATION 550/551

| | | | | | | | |
|---|---|---|---|---|---|---|---|
| 401 | 550-0407 | 406 | 550-0408 | 411 | 550-0355 | 416 | 550-0417 |
| 402 | 550-0368 | 407 | 550-0409 | 412 | 550-0413 | 417 | 550-0418 |
| 403 | 550-0364 | 408 | 550-0410 | 413 | 550-0414 | 418 | 550-0419 |
| 404 | 550-0365 | 409 | 550-0411 | 414 | 550-0415 | 419 | 551-0419 |
| 405 | 550-0367 | 410 | 550-0412 | 415 | 550-0416 | 420 | |

## AIRCRAFT WRITTEN-OFF

| | | | | |
|---|---|---|---|---|
| 01 | HS 125/400B | 25177 | 26/MAY/71, Devil's Peak, South Africa. | G-AWXN |
| 02 | HS 125/400B | 25181 | 26/MAY/71, Devil's Peak, South Africa. | G-AXLU/(G-5-13) |
| 03 | HS 125/400B | 25182 | 26/MAY/71, Devil's Peak, South Africa. | G-AXLV |
| 39 | Falcon 10MER | 39 | 30/JAN/80, Toul-Rosieres, France. | F-WPUX |
| 154 | Mystere 20C | 154 | 22/JAN/76, Rambouillet, France. | F-WLCV |
| IAC236 | HS 125/F600B | 25256 | 27/NOV/79, Casement-Dublin, Ireland. | G-AYBH/G-5-13/RP-C111/G-AYBH |
| 16+22 | HFB 320 | 1059 | 27/NOV/76, Schwabmunchen, West Germany. | D-COSO |
| 157352 | Sabre-40 | 282-46 | 21/DEC/75, Alameda AFB, Ca. USA. | N339NA/N6553C |
| 4X-COJ | Jet Commodore | 29 | 21/JAN/70, Tel Aviv, Israel. | N615J |
| 5A-DAD | Learjet | 23-075 | 05/JUN/67, Damascus, Syria. | |
| 5N-AMF | HFB 320 | 1028 | 25/JUL/77, Abidjan, Ivory Coast. | D-CASU |
| 5V-TAA | Gulfstream 2 | 149 | 26/DEC/74, Lome, Togo, W.Africa. | N17586/N896GA |
| 59-5961 | JetStar-6 | 5030 | 07/NOV/62, Robins AFB, Ga. USA. | |
| 60-3506 | Sabreliner | 265-34 | 09/FEB/74, Colorado Springs, Co. USA. | |
| 61-0672 | Sabreliner | 265-75 | 13/MAR/79, Kunsong, Korea. | |
| 62-4448 | Sabreliner | 276-1 | 28/JAN/64, Erfurt, East Germany. | |
| 62-4458 | Sabreliner | 276-11 | 25/MAR/65, Clark AFB, Philippines. | |
| 7T-VHB | Gulfstream 2 | 230 | 03/MAY/82, Nr. Ootur, NW Iranian Border. | N17586 |
| 7T-VRE | Mystere 20C | 156 | 30/MAY/81, Bamako, Mali. | F-WMKI |
| T-24 | Learjet | 35A-333 | /82, Falklands, S. Atlantic. | |
| VC-93-2122 | HS 125/3B-RA | 25166 | 18/JUN/79, Brasilia, Brazil. | |
| CA+102 | JetStar-6 | 5035 | 16/JAN/68, Bremen, West Germany. | (62-12167) |
| CF-BRL | Sabre-40A | 282-107 | 27/FEB/74, Frobisher Bay, NWT, Canada. | N40NR/N7584N |
| CF-CFL | DH 125/400A | NA725 | 11/NOV/69, Labrador, Newfoundland. | |
| C-FCFL | DH 125/400A | NA741 | 09/DEC/77, Labrador, Newfoundland. | G-AXTT |
| C-FEYG | Jet Commander | 81 | 26/MAY/78, Winnipeg, Manitoba. | CF-KBI/N6617V |
| C-GCGR-X | Challenger | 1001 | 03/APR/80, Mojave, Ca. USA. | |
| D-CASY | HFB 320 | 1029 | 29/JUN/72, Blackpool, England. | |
| D-CDFA | Learjet | 36-006 | 25/MAR/80, Libya, North Africa. | D-CAFO/HB-VEA/(I-CRYS) |
| D-CHFB | HFB 320 | V1 | 12/MAY/65, Torrejon, Spain. | |
| D-CIRO | HFB 320 | 1044 | 18/DEC/70, Texel Island, Netherlands. | |
| D-IHAQ | Learjet | 23-007 | 12/DEC/65, Zurich, Switzerland. | N826L |
| D-IHLZ | Learjet | 24B-225 | 18/JUN/73, Mariensiel, West Germany. | N6188 |
| D-IJHM | Citation | 551-0033 | 19/MAY/82, Kassel, West Germany. | N88692 |
| EC-CGG | Citation | 500-0108 | 22/NOV/74, Barcelona, Spain. | N108CC |
| EC-DFA | Learjet | 35A-196 | 13/AUG/80, Palma, Spain. | HB-VFU |

| Regis-tration | Type | C/N | | Previous Identities |
|---|---|---|---|---|
| EP-AGX | Mystere 20E | 283 | 21/NOV/74, Kermanshah, Iran. | F-WROS |
| F-BKMF | DH 125/1 | 25007 | 05/JUN/66, Nice, France. | HB-VAH/G-ASTY/(G-ASSH) |
| F-WFAL | Falcon 10 | 01 | 31/OCT/72, Romorantin, France. | |
| F-WRSN | Corvette | 01 | 23/MAR/71, Marseilles, France. | |
| G-AVGW | HS 125/3B | 25120 | 23/DEC/67, Luton, England. | |
| G-AXPS | HS 125/3B | 25135 | 20/JUL/70, Edinburgh, Scotland. | HB-VAY/G-5-14 |
| G-BCUX | HS 125/600B | 6043 | 20/NOV/75, Dunsfold, England. | |
| G-BPCP | Citation | 500-0403 | 01/OCT/80, Jersey, Channel Islands. | N1710E |
| HB-VAM | Learjet | 23-044 | 28/AUG/72, Innsbruck, Austria. | N22B |
| HB-VAP | Mystere 20C | 37 | 01/OCT/67, Goose Bay, Newfoundland. | F-WMKF |
| | | | (Sub. N7922/N11WA, never flew again). | |
| HB-VCG | Mystere 20D | 231 | 20/FEB/72, St.Moritz, Switzerland. | F-WPXE |
| HZ-GP5 | Learjet | 25XR-199 | 11/JAN/82, Narssarssuaq, Greenland. | HZ-RI1/HB-VEI |
| I-AIFA | Learjet | 36A-021 | 10/DEC/79, Forli, Italy. | N3524F |
| I-AMME | Learjet | 24D-310 | 06/FEB/76, Bari, Italy. | HB-VDU |
| I-MCSA | Learjet | 35A-099 | 22/FEB/78, Palermo, Sicily. | HB-VFC/N40146 |
| I-PIAI | PD 808 | 503 | 18/JUN/68, San Sebastian, Spain. | |
| I-SNAP | MS 760 Paris | 99 | 27/OCT/62, Milan, Italy. | |
| JY-AEW | Learjet | 35-052 | 28/APR/77, Riyadh, Saudi Arabia. | |
| JY-AFC | Learjet | 36A-020 | 21/SEP/77, Amman, Jordan. | |
| LN-FOE | Mystere 20C | 62 | 12/DEC/73, Norwich, England. | (N17401)/F-BOLX/F-WMKJ |
| OH-FFW | Mystere 20F | 243 | 01/MAR/72, Montreal, Canada. | F-WMKH |
| OY-SBS | Corvette | 21 | 03/SEP/79, Nice, France. | F-BVPE |
| PP-FMX | Learjet | 23-090 | 30/AUG/69, Rio de Janeiro, Brazil. | |
| PT-CXK | Learjet | 24-122 | 04/MAY/73, Rio-Galeon, Brazil. | N461LJ |
| PT-DVL | Learjet | 25B-077 | 12/NOV/76, Sao Paulo, Brazil. | |
| PT-DZU | Learjet | 24D-244 | 23/AUG/79, Sao Paulo, Brazil. | |
| PT-IBR | Learjet | 25C-072 | 26/SEP/76, Sao Paulo, Brazil. | N256GL |
| PT-JBQ | Learjet | 25B-119 | 04/SEP/82, Rio Branco, Brazil. | N3810G |
| PT-JDX | Learjet | 25C-131 | 26/DEC/78, Congonhas, Brazil. | N3803G |
| PT-JXS | Citation | 500-0162 | 16/MAR/75, Belem, Brazil. | |
| PT-KIU | Citation | 500-0172 | 12/NOV/76, Aracatuba, Brazil. | N172CC |
| PT-KZY | Learjet | 25B-204 | 16/MAY/82, Uberaba, Brazil. | N472J/N373SC/N376SC |
| SA-R-7 | DH Comet 4C | 6461 | 20/MAR/63, Cuneo, Italy. | |
| SE-DCY | Jet Commander | 136 | 04/DEC/69, Stockholm, Sweden. | N5044E |
| SX-ASO | Learjet | 25B-074 | 18/FEB/72, Antibes, France. | N251GL |
| TN-ADB | Corvette | 22 | 30/MAR/79, Nkayi, Congo Republic. | F-ODFE/F-BTTU/N617AC/F-WNGT |
| TR-KHB | Gulfstream 2 | 127 | 06/FEB/80, Ngaoundere, Cameroun. | N17581 |
| TY-BBK | Corvette | 29 | 16/NOV/81, Lagos, Nigeria. | F-OBZP/F-BVPJ/F-OBZP/F-BVPJ/F-WNGY |
| XA-COL | DH 125/1A | 25086 | 12/OCT/73, Acapulco, Mexico. | N3699T/CF-DSC |
| XA-EEU | Sabre-40 | 282-54 | ground accident Mexico 1980 (details ?) | N256CT/N255CT/N7504V |
| XA-ESQ | DH 125/1A | 25028 | 10/DEC/81, Laredo, Tx. USA. | N50SS/N48172/C-GLFI/G-511 |
| XA-CUZ | BH 125/400A | NA772 | 26/DEC/80, Cancun, Mexico. | N69BH/G-5-12 |
| XA-KEW | HS 125/700A | NA0276 | 02/MAY/81, Norte, Monterrey, Mexico. | G-5-14 |
| XB-JOY | Learjet | 24D-263 | 29/JUN/76, Mexico City, Mexico. | N3812G |
| YU-BJH | Learjet | 25B-186 | 18/JAN/77, Sarajevo, Yugoslavia. | |
| YV-O-MAC-1 | Citation | 500-0336 | 1979 , Caracas, Venezuela (details ?) | N336CC |
| N1EM | JetStar-6 | 5077 | 25/MAR/76, Chicago. Il. USA. | N1924V/N9236R |
| N12MK | Learjet | 24B-192 | 06/JAN/77, Palm Springs, Ca. USA. | N1919W |
| N15NY | Citation | 501-0110 | 02/AUG/79, Akron, Oh. USA. | (N26481) |
| N20M | Learjet | 23-094 | 15/DEC/72, Detroit, Mi. USA. | N417LJ |
| N25TA | Learjet | 25B-196 | 11/APR/80, ? NM. USA. | N711WD |
| N27R | Falcon 20E | 303 | 12/NOV/76, Naples, Fl. USA. | N4445F/F-WMKH |
| N29LB | Jet Commander | 61 | 19/DEC/80, Many Airport, La. USA. | N29LP/N999FB/N100NR/N51CH/N666DC/N1196Z |
| N30W | Sabre-40 | 282-5 | 21/DEC/67, Perryville, Mo. USA. | |
| N34W | Sabre-40 | 282-47 | 04/JAN/74, Midland, Tx. USA. | N740R |
| N36MK | DH 125/1A | 25073 | 28/DEC/70, Boise, Id. USA. | N372GM/N372CM/G-ATLI |
| N40BC | Learjet | 25B-128 | 06/JUL/79, Pueblo, Co. USA. | N1MX/N67PC |
| N40LB | Learjet | 25-009 | 25/SEP/73, Omaha, Nb. USA. | 9Q-CHC/N670LJ/N843GA |
| N40PC | BH 125/600A | 6010 | 28/APR/77, McLean, Va. USA. | N23BH |
| N40SN | Learjet | 25-021 | 20/DEC/78, Minneapolis, Mn. USA. | N40SW/N1LL/N1JR/N111LL/N942GA |
| N44CJ | Learjet | 24-146 | 01/OCT/81, Felt, OK. USA. | N235Z/N672LJ |
| N57TA | Learjet | 55-010 | 13/NOV/81, Johannesburg, S. Africa. | |
| N60MB | Falcon 10 | 15 | 03/APR/77, Denver, Co. USA. | N109FJ/F-WJMM |
| N67KM | Sabre-75A | 380-7 | 14/JUN/75, Watertown, SD. USA. | |
| N77AP | Sabre-40 | 282-37 | 07/NOV/77, New Orleans, La. USA. | N265W/N6392C |

| Regis-tration | Type | C/N | | Previous Identities |
|---|---|---|---|---|
| N77RS | Learjet | 25C-094 | 04/DEC/78, Anchorage, Ak. USA. | N97J/VR-BFV/SX-CBM |
| N85 | Sabre-40 | 282-97 | 14/JAN/76, Nr. Recife, Brazil. | N4706N |
| N100MK | Learjet | 25-019 | 21/OCT/78, Sandusky, Oh. USA. | N88FP/N88EP/N591KR |
| N100RC | Jet Commander | 60 | 14/NOV/70, Lexington, Ky. USA. | N6545V |
| N100TA | Learjet | 23-045 | 06/MAY/82, Savannah, Ga. USA. | N711MR/N242F |
| N121GW | Falcon 20C | 4 | 18/MAY/78, Memphis, Tn. USA. | N116JD/N801F/F-WMKF |
| N123CB | Learjet | 24D-232 | 17/APR/71, Butte, Mt. USA. | |
| N123RE | Learjet | 24-154 | 17/OCT/78, Lancaster, Ca. USA. | N11AK/N7HA/N424RD/N12315/N123VW |
| N125NE | Learjet | 25D-271 | 21/MAY/80, Gulf of Mexico. | N183AP |
| N137GL | Learjet | 25D-237 | 19/JAN/79, Detroit, Mi. USA. | (N28BP) |
| N148E | Jet Commander | 22 | 13/SEP/68, Burbank, Ca. USA. | |
| N196KC | Jet Commander | 68 | 01/JUL/68, Fayetteville, Ar. USA. | |
| N200RC | Jet Commander | 140 | 25/SEP/73, Tampa, Fl. USA. | N9040N |
| N211MB | Learjet | 25-059 | 03/MAR/80, Port au Prince. Haiti. | N425JX |
| N234F | Learjet | 23-063 | 14/NOV/65, Palm Springs, Ca. USA. | |
| N235KC | DH 125/1A | 25096 | 21/NOV/66, Grand Bahama. | G-ATNR |
| N235R | Learjet | 23-032 | 23/APR/66, Clarendon, Tx. USA. | |
| N236JP | Jet Commander | 116 | 31/OCT/69, Marion, Va. USA. | N4743E |
| N250UA | Jet Commander-A | 121 | 27/APR/78, Flatwood, La. USA. | N1121R/N250JP/N840AR/N1121X |
| N253K | Falcon 10 | 10 | 30/JAN/80, Meigs-Chicago, Il. USA. | N105FJ/F-WJMJ |
| N267L | JetStar-6 | 5067 | 29/MAR/81, Luton, England. | N207L/N711Z/N871D |
| N316M | Learjet | 23-061 | 19/MAR/66, Lake Michigan, USA. | |
| N320MC | HFB 320 | 1034 | cancelled USCAR 9/FEB/81 as Broken-up. | N320J/D-CERO |
| N332PC | Learjet | 23-056 | 06/JAN/77, Flint, Mi. USA. | N362EJ |
| N366AA | Learjet | 25B-151 | 31/AUG/74, Briggsdale, Co. USA. | |
| N397F | Gulfstream 2 | 72 | 22/FEB/76, Burlington, Vt. USA. | |
| N400CP | Jet Commander | 30 | 21/JAN/71, Burlington, Vt. USA. | N401V |
| N400M | JetStar-6 | 5008 | 27/DEC/72, Saranac Lake, NY. USA. | N500Z |
| N403M | Jet Commander | 132 | 16/DEC/69, Salt Lake City, Ut. USA. | N200M |
| N432EJ | Learjet | 23-028A | 25/OCT/67, Muskegon, Mi. USA. | N803LJ |
| N434EJ | Learjet | 23-046 | 09/MAY/70, Pellston, Mi. USA. | |
| N454RN | Learjet | 24-121 | 26/FEB/73, Atlanta, Ga. USA. | N454GL/N454LJ |
| N500J | Gulfstream 2 | 60 | 26/SEP/76, Hot Springs, Va. USA. | N892GA |
| N500JR | Jet Commander | 65 | 26/SEP/66, N.Platte, SD. USA. | |
| N501GP | Citation | 500-0026 | 21/JAN/81, Bluefield, WV, USA. | N526CC |
| N501PS | Learjet | 25B-153 | 26/MAY/77, Detroit, Mi. USA. | |
| N515VW | Learjet | 25-013 | 17/APR/69, Delemont, Switzerland. | N856GA |
| N520S | JetStar-731 | 8/5084 | 11/FEB/81, Westchester, NY, USA. | N901E/N732M/N83M/N9240R |
| N521M | DH 125/3A | 25129 | 12/DEC/72, Findlay, Oh. USA. | G-AVDM/G-5-12 |
| N555AJ | Citation | 500-0007 | 19/NOV/79, Denver, Co. USA. | N500LF/N507CC |
| N658TC | Learjet | 25-044 | 18/JAN/72, Victoria, Tx. USA. | N962GA |
| N690LJ | Learjet | 23-078 | 30/NOV/67, Orlando, Fl. USA. | |
| N711AF | Learjet | 35-029 | 11/AUG/79, en-route Athens-Jeddah. | |
| N711JT | Jet Commander | 91 | 13/MAR/75, Tullahoma, Tn. USA. | N73535/N1972W/N365RJ |
| N711ST | BAC 1-11/401 | 058 | 09/FEB/75, Lake Tahoe, NV. USA. (See N128TA). | N5018 |
| N720Q | Gulfstream 2 | 58 | 24/JUN/74, Kline, SC. USA. | N87RGA |
| N739R | Sabre-60 | 282-78 | 16/MAY/67, Ventura, Ca. USA. | |
| N743R | Sabre-60 | 306-11 | 13/APR/73, Montrose, Co. USA. | N723R/N4721N |
| N760M | MS 760 Paris | 49 | 03/MAY/69, Evadale, Tx. USA. | |
| N801L | Learjet | 23-001 | 04/JUN/64, Wichita, Ks. USA. | |
| N805F | Falcon 20C | 60 | 05/JUL/71, Boca Raton, Fl. USA. | N885F/F-WMKJ |
| N822LJ | Learjet | 23-080 | 09/DEC/67, Detroit, Mi. USA. | |
| N804LJ | Learjet | 23-015A | 21/OCT/65, Jackson, Mi. USA. | |
| N866JS | Learjet | 23-018 | 06/MAY/80, Richmond, Va. USA. | N866DB/N652J/D-IKAA/N661FS/N807LJ |
| N888AR | Falcon 20C | 33 | 07/AUG/76, Acapulco, Mexico. | N369FJ/N807F/F-WNGO |
| N920G | Sabre-60 | 306-74 | 27/DEC/74, Lancaster, Pa. USA. | |
| N990L | Falcon 20C | 43 | 08/MAR/75, Dallas NAS, Tx. USA. | N872F/F-WMKJ |
| N999HG | Learjet | 25B-178 | 08/SEP/77, Sanford, NC. USA. | N999MV/N999M/N75B |
| N1021B | Learjet | 23-086 | 06/NOV/69, Racine, Wi. USA. | |
| N1135K | DH 125/1A | 25019 | 24/FEB/66, Des Moines, Ia. USA. | N1125G/G-ASYX |
| N1846 | Falcon 20C | 47 | 13/MAR/68, Parkersburg, WV. USA. | N875F/F-WNGM |
| N5107 | Sabre-75A | 380-8 | 23/FEB/75, Oakland Pontiac Airport, Ca. USA. | |
| N5565 | Sabre-40A | 282-119 | 15/JAN/74, Oklahoma City, Ok. USA. | N8341N |
| N7824M | Falcon 20C | 42 | 16/JAN/74, Fort Worth, Tx. USA. | N1503/N871F/F-WNGO |
| N9503Z | Sabre-40 | 282-10 | 07/MAR/73, Blaine, Mn. USA. | N525N/N6364C |

| Regis-<br>tration | Type | C/N | | Previous<br>Identities |
|---|---|---|---|---|

AIRCRAFT WITHDRAWN FROM USE

| Registration | Type | C/N | Notes | Previous Identities |
|---|---|---|---|---|
| 5N-AER | DH 125/1B-522 | 25099 | Located Sao Tome Island, W. Africa since 1968 Biafran War. | (N121AC)/(N2246)/HB-VAU |
| D-CARE | HFB 320 | 1022 | C of A expiry 28/APR/72. German Air Force Museum, Uetersen, Hamburg wef APR/78 | |
| D-CLOU | HFB 320 | V2 | Stored at Erding Air Base. | |
| F-BLKB | Mystere 20 | 01 | Last flight 06/FEB/76, engineering mock-up for Gardian project. | F-WLKB |
| F-WAMD | Mystere 30 | 01 | Project shelved 1975, wfu Bordeaux. | |
| G-ARYA | HS 125/1 | 25001 | C of A expiry 01/OCT/65. Kelsterton College N.E. Wales Institute of Technology ground instructional airframe. Noted FEB/82 as no longer a complete aircraft. | |
| G-ARYB | HS 125/1 | 25002 | C of A expiry 22/JAN/68. Module training section, Hatfield. | |
| G-ARYC | HS 125/1 | 25003 | C of A expiry 01/AUG/75. Mosquito Museum, Hatfield. | |
| (G-BBRT) | HS 125/600B | 6036 | Fuselage used in paint spraying trials, Chester. | |
| N3MF | DH 125/1A-522 | 25093 | Accident New Mexico 26/JAN/79. Front end used in repair of EC-CMU following accident Ivory Coast 10/DEC/79. Flew W.Africa-USA via Shannon 12/MAY/80 as N37516. | |
| N10EA | Jet Commander | 39 | As for N121HM, arrived Copenhagen 15/MAY/82. | N16FP/N1BC/N80TF/N66TS /N666JD/N550NM/N6505V |
| N38B | Beech 200 | BB-1 | Beech fan-jet prototype. Project shelved 1978. | |
| N121HM | Jet Commander | 18 | Cancelled USCAR 26/MAR/80 Last Flight Prestwick-Copenhagen 17/DEC/78. Located at the Skolen For Luftfartsuddannelserne, Kastrup, south of the airport gate outside the airport boundary. Owned and used by Dansk Metal Arbedjer for Bund primarily for mechanic training. | |
| N172AC | Jet Commander | 1 | Dismantled. Details required. | N112AC/N610JC |
| N220N | McDonnell 220 | 1 | Wfu Albuquerque, NM. See Aviation Convention News 29/APR/77. | N119M |
| N329J | JetStar | 1001 | Last flight 16/AUG/82. Donated to Pacific Vocational Institute, Vancouver | |
| N463LJ | Learjet | 25-001 | Used in construction of Learjet C/n 25-002 | |
| N500CC | Citation | 500-669 | Last flight SEP/76. Fuselage at the Wallace Division 'bone yard', Wichita. Ks. Still there as of FEB/82. | |
| N611JC | Jet Commander | 2 | Test Aircraft for static fatigue. | |
| N661LJ | Learjet | 25-002 | AiResearch engine tests, wfu JUL/72. | |
| N711Z | JetStar | 1002 | Atlanta Area Technical School, Ga. | N329K |
| N802L | Learjet | 23-002 | Last flight 17/JUN/66. At Smithsonian Institute, Washington DC. | |
| N804LJ | Learjet | 23-004 | Re-certificated C/n 23-015A. W/O 21/OCT/65. | |
| N2600 | JetStar-6 | 5037 | Overpressurized and redesignated C/n 5128S | N9211R |
| N4060K | Sabre-UTX | 246-1 | Last flight 62 or early 63. Shipped ex-Los Angeles to St.Louis 63. Retained as mock-up until 67 when it was broken-up at St.Louis. | |
| N7201U | B 720-022 | 17907 | Broken-up for scrap at Luton, UK. 13/JUL/82. | |
| N7572N | Sabre-75 | 370-1 | Used as parts in other test aircraft. | |
| N7775 | JetStar-6 | 5073 | Fuselage used as interior mock-up by K C Aviation at Dallas, Tx. | |
| VH-ECE | HS 125/3B | 25-062 | Located The Oaks, Camden Airport Museum, NSW. Completed 53,882 Landings, 13936 hours as of mid-1982. | |
| NO.141 | Caravelle 3 | 141 | Musee de l'Air, Le Bourget-Paris 1980. | F-BJTK |

AIRFORCE OPERATED

ARGENTINA

| Registration | Type | C/N | Notes | Previous Identities |
|---|---|---|---|---|
| 5-T-10-0740 | F-28-3000M | 11147) | | PH-EXW |
| 5-T-20-0741 | F-28-3000C | 11145) | Armada, Argentina, Buenos Aires. | PH-EXV |
| 5-T-21-0742 | F-28-3000M | 11150) | | PH-EXX |
| 5-T-30-0653 | HS 125/400B | 25251 | Comando do Aviacion Naval, Ezeiza. | |
| AE-129 | Citation | 550-0106 | Fabricaciones Militares, Buenos Aires. | N2665A |
| AE-175 | Sabre-75A | 380-13 | Comando de Aviacion Ejercito, Comision Especial do Adquisiciones, Buenos Aires. | N65761 |
| AE-185 | Citation | 500-0356 | Comando de Aviacion Ejercito, Instituto Geografico Militar. | N36848/N5366J |
| T-02 | F-28-1000 | 11028 | FAA=Fuerza Aerea Argentina, Presidential. | T-01/PH-EXA |
| T-03 | F-28-1000 | 11048 | Fuerza Aerea Argentina. | LV-LZN/PH-ZBM/TG-CAO/N280FH/PH-EXF |
| T-10 | Sabre-75A | 380-3 | Fuerza Aerea Argentina. | N8467N |
| T-21 | Learjet | 35A-115 | FAA, Photo reconnaissance. ) | |
| T-22 | Learjet | 35A-136 | FAA, Photo reconnaissance. ) Dept. de Aviones Precidenciales | |
| T-23 | Learjet | 35A-319 | FAA, Photo reconnaissance. ) 1 Brigada Aerea, El Palomar. | |
| VR-17 | Learjet | 35A-369 | FAA, Navigational Aid Calibration. | |

| Regis-tration | Type | C/N | Owner/Operator | Previous Identities |
|---|---|---|---|---|
| **AUSTRALIA** | | | | |
| A11-078 | Mystere 20C | 78 | VM-NLD). (r/c Envoy) | VM-NSD/F-WNGM |
| A11-085 | Mystere 20C | 85 | VM-NLE) Royal Australian Air Force. | VM-NSE/F-WMKH |
| A11-090 | Mystere 20C | 90 | VM-NLF) 34 Squadron. | VM-NSF/F-WNGL |
| A12-124 | BAC 1-11/217 | 124 | VM-NLG) Fairbairn, Canberra. | VM-NSG |
| A12-125 | BAC 1-11/217 | 125 | VM-NLH) (r/c Nightbird) | VM-NSH |
| A20-624 | B 707-338C | 19624 | VM-NUQ( Govt. of Australia, Canberra. | VH-EAD |
| A20-627 | B 707-338C | 19627 | VM-NUR( (r/c Aussie overseas) (r/c Windsor internal flight)VH-EAG | |
| | | | Wef 01/JAN/81 all VM- radio callsigns were replaced by Squadron r/cs | |
| **BELGIUM** | | | | |
| CB-01 | B 727-29C | 19402 | BAF 21) Belgische Luchtmacht, | OO-STB |
| CB-02 | B 727-29C | 19403 | BAF 22) Force Aerienne Belge, | OO-STD |
| CM-01 | Mystere 20E | 276 | BAF 31) No.15 Wing, 21 Squadron, | F-WNGL |
| CM-02 | Mystere 20E | 278 | BAF 32) Melsbroek, Brussels. | F-WNGM |
| **BOLIVIA** | | | | |
| FAB 001 | Sabre-60 | 306-115 | Presidencia de la Republica Bolivia, Departmento Aereo Palacio de Govierno, La Paz. | N2118J |
| FAB 008 | Learjet | 25B-192 | Direccion de Fotogrametria, Aero Andes Bolivia Ltd. La Paz. | |
| FAB 010 | Learjet | 25D-211 | FAB=Fuerza Aerea Boliviana, La Paz. | N3514F |
| FAB | Sabre 65A | 465-60 | Presidencia de la Republica Bolivia, La Paz. | N2580E |
| **BRAZIL** | | | | |
| EU93-2119 | HS 125/403B | 25274 | FAB=Forca Aerea Brasileira, calibration. | G-5-20 |
| VC93-2120 | HS 125/3B-RC | 25162 | ) | |
| VC93-2121 | HS 125/3B-RC | 25165 | ) | |
| VC93-2123 | HS 125/3B-RC | 25167 | ) FAB, GTE=Grupo do Transporte Especiale, Brasilia. | |
| VC93-2124 | HS 125/3B-RC | 25168 | ) | |
| EC93-2125 | HS 125/3B-RC | 25164 | FAB, flight inspection. | |
| VU93-2126 | HS 125/403B | 25277 | ) | |
| VU93-2127 | HS 125/403B | 25288 | ) | |
| VU93-2128 | HS 125/403B | 25289 | ) FAB, GTE=Grupo do Transporte Especiale, Brasilia. | G-5-16 |
| VU93-2129 | HS 125/403B | 25290 | ) | |
| VC96-2115 | B 737-2N3 | 21165 | ) | |
| VC96-2116 | B 737-2N3 | 21166 | ) | |
| **BURMA** | | | | |
| | Citation | 550-0358 | Burmese Air Force | N68010 |
| **CANADA** | | | | |
| 117501 | Falcon 20C | 82 | ) | 20501/F-WJMM |
| 117502 | Falcon 20C | 87 | ) Type CC117, Canadian Armed Forces, | 20502/F-WJMJ |
| 117503 | Falcon 20C | 92 | ) No 412 (Transport) Squadron, | 20503/F-WJMM |
| 117504 | Falcon 20C | 97 | ) CFB Ottawa, Ontario. | 20504/F-WJMJ |
| 117505 | Falcon 20ECM | 103 | ( | 20505/F-WMKH |
| 117506 | Falcon 20ECM | 109 | ( No. 414 Squadron. | 20506/F-WNGM |
| 117507 | Falcon 20ECM | 114 | ( CFB North Bay, Canada. | 20507/F-WNGM |
| 13701 | B 707-347C | 20315 | ) Type CC137, CAF. | (N1506W) |
| 13702 | B 707-347C | 20316 | ) No. 437 Squadron. | N1785B/(N1507W) |
| 13703 | B 707-347C | 20317 | ) Boeing VIP Kit fits these aircraft. | (N1508W) |
| 13704 | B 707-347C | 20318 | ) Two of these converted to | (N1509W) |
| 13705 | B 707-347C | 20319 | ) drogue tankers for CF-5 support. | (N1510W) |
| | Challenger | 1040 | ( Type CC144, Canadian Armed Forces | C-GLYM |
| | Challenger | 1065 | ( No 412 (Transport) Squadron, CFB Ottawa, Ontario | C-GBVE |
| **CHILE** | | | | |
| 901 | B 727-22C | 19196 | Fuerza Aerea de Chile | N7421U |

| Regis-<br>tration | Type | C/N | Owner/Operator | Previous<br>Identities |
|---|---|---|---|---|
| **CHINA** | | | | |
| 090 | Citation | 550-0305 | ) | N67999 |
| 092 | Citation | 550-0297 | ) Government of Chinese People's Republic. | N68003 |
| 091 | Citation | 550-0301 | ) | N6799T |
| **COLOMBIA** | | | | |
| FAC 001 | F-28-1000 | 11992 | FAC=Fuerza Aerea Colombiana, Presidential. | |
| | | | Operated by SATENA, Bogota. | PH-EXA/PH-ZAU |
| **DENMARK** | | | | |
| F-249 | Gulfstream 3 | 249 | ) | N901GA/N300GA |
| F-313 | Gulfstream 3 | 313 | ) RDAF Maritime Surveillance. | |
| F-330 | Gulfstream 3 | 330 | ) No. 721 Sqn. Vaerlose, Copenhagen. | |
| **ECUADOR** | | | | |
| ANE 201 | Citation | 500-0389 | Armada del Ecuador, Guayaquil. | N3202M |
| | | | ANE=Aviacion Naval Ecuatoriana. | |
| IGM 401 | Learjet | 24D-312 | Ejercito, Ecuadorian Army for photo survey. | |
| | | | IGM=Instituto Geographico Militar. | |
| **EGYPT** | | | | |
| SU-AYD | Mystere 20F | 361 | Egyptian Air Force, Cairo. | |
| | | | (was in USCG colours at Paris Salon 1977). | F-WMKF |
| **FINLAND** | | | | |
| LJ-1 | Learjet | 35A-430 | ) | N10870 |
| LJ-2 | Learjet | 35A-451 | ) Finnish Air Force | |
| LJ-3 | Learjet | 35A-470 | ) | N3810G |
| **FRANCE** | | | | |
| 02 | Falcon 10 | 02 | F-ZACB, CEV Bretigny. Larzac test bed. | F-ZJTA/F-WTAL |
| 1 | Mystere 20 | 1 | F-ZACV, CEV. Variable Characteristics. | F-WMSH/F-BMSH/F-WMSH |
| 5 | Falcon 50 | 5 | F-RAFI, Presidential aircraft. | F-WZHB |
| 22 | Mystere 20 | 22 | F-ZACS, CEV. | F-BMSS/F-WMSS |
| 32 | Falcon 10MER | 32 | ) MER=Marine Entrainment Radar, Aeronavale, | |
| | | | ) SRL=Section Reacteur de Landivisiau, | |
| | | | ) uses callsign block F-YETA to F-YETZ. | |
| 48 | Gardian | 448 | F-ZWVF, Paris 1981 Gardian demonstrator for Marine Nationale. | |
| 49 | Mystere 20C | 49 | F-RAFJ, A de l'Air, GLAM 1/60, Villacoublay. | F-WNGN |
| 79 | Mystere 20 | 79 | F-ZACT, CEV. | F-BNRH/F-WMKH |
| 86 | Mystere 20C | 86 | F-ZACG, CEV=Centre d'Essais en Vol, Cazaux. | F-WRGO/HB-VDW |
| | | | /G-BBEK/F-BUYI/(G-BBEK)/N622R/N808F/N976F/F-WMKI | |
| 93 | Mystere 20C | 93 | F-RAFN, A de l'Air, GLAM 1/60, Villacoublay. | F-RBQA/F-RAFN |
| | | | | /F-WMKF |
| 101 | Falcon 10 | 101 | Marine Nationale, 3S Hyeres. | F-WPXJ |
| 115 | Mystere 20SNA | 115 | F-UGWL, A de l'Air, CPIR339, Luxeuil. Mirage IIIE simulator. | |
| | | | SNA=Systeme Navigation et d'Attaque. | F-WJML |
| 124 | Mystere 20C | 124 | F-ZACC, CEV, Cazaux, Istres & Bretigny. | F-WJMJ |
| 129 | Falcon 10 | 129 | Marine Nationale. | F-WZGA |
| 131 | Mystere 20C | 131 | F-ZACD, CEV, Cazaux, Istres & Bretigny. | F-WJMJ |
| 133 | Falcon 10 | 133 | F-ZGTI, Marine Nationale. | F-WZGE |
| 138 | Mystere 20C | 138 | F-ZACR, CEV, Cazaux. F-BUIC/(G-BAOA)/D-CGJH/D-CALL/F-WLCS | |
| 143 | Falcon 10MER | 143 | Marine Nationale, Landivisiau. | F-WZGO |
| 145 | Mystere 20C | 145 | F-ZACU, CEV F-GCGY/OO-PJB/F-BPJB/F-WNGN | |
| 167 | Mystere 20C | 167 | F-RAFL, A de l'Air, GLAM 1/60. | F-WMKG |
| 182 | Mystere 20C | 182 | F- , A de l'Air. F-BVFV/I-ROBM/F-WTDJ/HB-VCB/F-WNGN | |
| 185 | Falcon 10 | 185 | Marine Nationale. | F-WZGO |
| 201 | Caravelle 10B | 201 | F-RAFH, A de l'Air, GLAM. | F-BNRA/TU-TXQ/F-BNRA |

| Regis-<br>tration | Type | C/N | Owner/Operator | Previous<br>Identities |
|---|---|---|---|---|
| 238 | Mystere 20C | 238 | F-RAFM, A de l'Air, GLAM 1/60. | F-WROP |
| 260 | Mystere 20E | 260 | F-RAEA, A de l'Air, GAEL 1/65, Villacoublay. | F-WMKJ |
| 268 | Mystere 20E | 268 | F-RAFK, A de l'Air, GLAM 1/60. | F-RAEB/F-WNGN |
| 291 | Mystere 20E | 291 | F-RCAP, A de l'Air EdC57, Villacoublay. | F-RAEC/F-WROT |
| 422 | Mystere 20F | 422 | F-RCAL, GAEL, Villacoublay. | F-ZJTJ/F-WROU |
| 463 | Mystere 20SNA | 186 | F-UGWM, A de l'Air, CPIR339, Luxeuil. | F-WPXL |

Mirage IIIE simulator. CPIR=Centre Prediction et Instruction
Radar GAEL=Groupe Aerien d'Entrainment et de Liaison.
FM=Commandement des Transports Aeriens Militaires GLAM=Groupe des
Liaisons Aeriennes Ministerielles. (FM plus four numbers is used
as a radio callsign for GLAM/GAEL aircraft).

| | | | | |
|---|---|---|---|---|
| 45570 | DC-8-53 | 45570 | F-RAFE, A de l'Air, ET 3/60, Roissy. | F-ZARK/F-BIUZ |
| 45692 | DC-8F-55 | 45692 | F-RAFB, A de l'Air, ET 3/60, Roissy. | N801SW |
| 45819 | DC-8F-55 | 45819 | F-RAFC, A de l'Air, ET 3/60, Roissy. | F-BNLD/TU-TXK/F-RCFA<br>/TU-TXG/F-BNLD |
| 45820 | DC-8F-55 | 45820 | F-RAFA, A de l'Air, ET 3/60, Roissy. | F-BLKX |
| 46013 | DC-8-62CF | 46013 | F-RAFG, A de l'Air, ET 3/60, Roissy. | OH-LFT |
| 46043 | DC-8-62CF | 46043 | F-RAFD, A de l'Air, ET 3/60, Roissy. | OH-LFV/OH-LFS |
| 46130 | DC-8-62CF | 46130 | F-RAFF, A de l'Air, ET 3/60, Roissy. | OH-LFY |

WEST GERMANY

| | | | | |
|---|---|---|---|---|
| 10+01 | B 707-307C | 19997 | ) (were allocated procurement serials 68-11071 to 074) | |
| 10+02 | B 707-307C | 19998 | ) Luftwaffe, Fl Ber BMVg Koln-Wahn, VIP Unit. | |
| 10+03 | B 707-307C | 19999 | ) Boeing VIP kit fits these aircraft. | |
| 10+04 | B 707-307C | 20000 | ) | |
| 11+01 | JetStar-6 | 5025 | Luftwaffe, Koln-Wahn ) | CA+101/(62-12166) |
| 11+02 | JetStar-8 | 5121 | Luftwaffe, Koln-Wahn ) VIP Unit. | N7966S |
| 11+03 | JetStar-6 | 5071 | Luftwaffe, Koln-Wahn ) | CA+103 |
| 16+01 | HFB 320 | 1041 | ) | D-CIRA |
| 16+02 | HFB 320 | 1042 | ) Luftwaffe, | D-CIRE |
| 16+03 | HFB 320 | 1043 | ) Flugbereitschaft BMVg, | D-CIRI |
| 16+04 | HFB 320 | 1046 | ) Fl Ber BMVg, | D-CISA |
| 16+05 | HFB 320 | 1047 | ) Koln-Wahn. | D-CISE |
| 16+06 | HFB 320 | 1048 | ) | D-CISI |
| 16+07 | HFB 320 | 1024 | Luftwaffe, Erprobungsstelle 61, Manching. | D-9536/D-CARO |
| 16+08 | HFB 320 | 1025 | Luftwaffe, Erprobungsstelle 61, Manching. | D-9537/D-CARU |
| 16+21 | HFB 320 | 1058 | Luftwaffe ) | D-COSI |
| 16+23 | HFB 320 | 1060 | Luftwaffe ) GFVS, Lechfeld. | D-COSU |
| 16+24 | HFB 320 | 1061 | Luftwaffe ) | D-CANI |
| 16+25 | HFB 320 | 1062 | ( JaboG 32 | D-CANO |
| 16+26 | HFB 320 | 1063 | ( | D-CANU |
| 16+27 | HFB 320ECM | 1064 | ( | D-CAMA |
| 16+28 | HFB 320ECM | 1065 | ( | D-CAME |
| 17+01 | VFW 614 | G14 | ) | |
| 17+02 | VFW 614 | G18 | ) Luftwaffe, Fl Ber BMVg, Koln-Wahn, VIP Unit. | |
| 17+03 | VFW 614 | G19 | ) | |

GHANA

| | | | | |
|---|---|---|---|---|
| G-530 | F-28-3000IP | 11125 | Government of Ghana, Accra. | PH-ZBP/PH-EXP |

GREAT BRITAIN

| | | | | |
|---|---|---|---|---|
| XS709/M | Dominie T1 | 25011 | ) | |
| XS710/O | Dominie T1 | 25012 | ) | |
| XS711/L | Dominie T1 | 25024 | ) | |
| XS712/A | Dominie T1 | 25040 | ) | |
| XS713/C | Dominie T1 | 25041 | ) | |
| XS714/P | Dominie T1 | 25054 | ) | |
| XS726/T | Dominie T1 | 25044 | ) | |
| XS727/D | Dominie T1 | 25045 | ) | |
| XS728/E | Dominie T1 | 25048 | ) | |
| XS729/G | Dominie T1 | 25049 | ) Royal Air Force, 6FTS, Finningley. | |
| XS730/H | Dominie T1 | 25050 | ) | |
| XS731/J | Dominie T1 | 25055 | ) | |
| XS732/B | Dominie T1 | 25056 | ) | |

| Regis-<br>tration | Type | C/N | Owner/Operator | Previous<br>Identities |
|---|---|---|---|---|
| XS733/Q | Dominie T1 | 25059 | ) | |
| XS734/N | Dominie T1 | 25061 | ) | |
| XS735/R | Dominie T1 | 25071 | ) | |
| XS736/S | Dominie T1 | 25072 | ) | |
| XS737/K | Dominie T1 | 25076 | ) | |
| XS738/U | Dominie T1 | 25077 | ) | |
| XS739/F | Dominie T1 | 25081 | ) | |
| XW788 | HS 125/CC1 | 25255 | ( | |
| XW789 | HS 125/CC1 | 25264 | ( Royal Air Force, | |
| XW790 | HS 125/CC1 | 25266 | ( No 32 Squadron, Northolt. | |
| XW791 | HS 125/CC1 | 25268 | ( | |
| XW930 | HS 125/1 | 25009 | Royal Aeronautical Establishment, Bedford. | G-ATPC |
| XX507 | HS 125/CC2 | 6006 | ) Royal Air Force, | |
| XX508 | HS 125/CC2 | 6008 | ) No 32 Squadron, Northolt. | |

HONDURAS

| | | | | |
|---|---|---|---|---|
| HR-001 | Westwind-1123 | 183 | FAH=Fuerza Aerea Honduras, Tegucigalpa. | FAH 318/4X-CKG |
| HR-002 | Westwind-1124 | 333 | FAH=Fuerza Aerea Honduras, Tegucigalpa. | 4X-CTA |

INDIA

| | | | | |
|---|---|---|---|---|
| K2370 | B 737-2A8 | 21498 | Indian Air Force | VT-EFM |
| K2371 | B 737-2A8 | 21497 | Indian Air Force | VT-EFL |

INDONESIA

| | | | | |
|---|---|---|---|---|
| T1645 | JetStar-6 | 5059 | ) TNI-AU=Tentara Nasional Indonesia | |
| T9446 | JetStar-6 | 5046 | )         Angkatan Udura. | N9282R |
| AI-7301 | B 737-2X9 | 22777 | ( | |
| AI-7302 | B 737-2X9 | 22778 | ( For maritime patrol. | |
| AI-7303 | B 737-2X9 | 22779 | ( | |

IRELAND

| | | | | |
|---|---|---|---|---|
| IAC 238 | HS 125/700B | 7082 | Irish Air Corps. Dublin. | |

ITALY

| | | | | |
|---|---|---|---|---|
| MM577 | PD 808-TA | 501 | RS-40 ) AMI=Aeronautica Militare Italiana, | |
| MM578 | PD 808-TA | 502 | RS-5  ) RSV=Reparto Sperimentale Volo, Practica di Mare. | |
| | | | (Code changes, details required ?) | |
| MM61958 | PD 808-ECM | 505 | AMI, 14 Stormo-71 Gruppo, Practica di Mare. | |
| MM61948 | PD 808-VIP | 506 | 31-48 ) | |
| MM61949 | PD 808-VIP | 507 | 31-49 ) | |
| MM61950 | PD 808-VIP | 508 | 31-50 ) | |
| MM61951 | PD 808-VIP | 509 | 31-51 ) | |
| MM61952 | PD 808-TA | 510 | 31-52 ) VIP=Seats 7. TA=10 seats, | |
| MM61953 | PD 808-TA | 511 | 31-53 ) AMI, 31 Stormo, Roma-Ciampino. | |
| MM61954 | PD 808-TA | 512 | 31-54 ) | |
| MM61955 | PD 808-TA | 513 | 31-55 ) | |
| MM61956 | PD 808-TA | 514 | 31-56 ) | |
| MM61957 | PD 808-TA | 515 | 31-57 ) | |
| MM61959 | PD 808-ECM | 516 | ) | |
| MM61960 | PD 808-ECM | 517 | ) | |
| MM61961 | PD 808-ECM | 518 | ) AMI, 14 Stormo-71 Gruppo. | |
| MM61962 | PD 808-ECM | 519 | ) | |
| MM61963 | PD 808-ECM | 520 | ) | |
| MM62012 | DC-9-32 | 47595 | 31-12 ( AMI, Transporti Speciali, | N54635 |
| MM62013 | DC-9-32 | 47600 | 31-13 ( 31 Stormo, Roma-Ciampino. | |
| MM62014 | PD 808-RM | 521 | CR-14 ) AMI, RM=Radio Misure,        ) | |
| MM62015 | PD 808-RM | 522 | CR-15 ) AMI, CR=Centro Radiomisure, ) Practica | I-PIAY |
| MM62016 | PD 808-RM | 523 | CR-16 ) AMI, 14 Stormo-8 Gruppo.     ) di Mare | |
| MM62017 | PD 808-RM | 524 | CR-17 ) AMI, Calibration aircraft.  ) | |

IRAN

| Regis-tration | Type | C/N | Owner/Operator | Previous Identities |
|---|---|---|---|---|
| 1001 | B 707-386C | 21396 | Govt. of Iran, Teheran. | EP-HIM |
| 1003 | JetStar-8 | 5137 | Govt. of Iran, Teheran. | EP-VRP/N5501L |
| 1004 | JetStar-2 | 5203 | Govt. of Iran, Teheran. | EP-VLP/N5529L |
| 5-2801 | Mystere 20E | 333 | ) | F-WNGL |
| 5-2802 | Mystere 20E | 336 | ) IN=Iranian Navy, | F-WROP |
| 5-2803 | Mystere 20E | 340 | ) Mehrabad. | F-WROX |
| 5-2804 | Mystere 20E | 346 | ) | F-WROP |
| 5-3020 | Mystere 20E | 348 | ( IAA=Iranian Air Army, | 5-4039/F-WROR |
| 5-3021 | Mystere 20E | 350 | ( Mehrabad. | 5-4040/F-WROS |
| 5-9001 | Mystere 20F | 351 | ) IAF=Iranian Air Force, | F-WMKJ |
| 5-9002 | Mystere 20F | 353 | ) 1st Transport Base, | F-WROP |
| 5-9003 | Mystere 20F | 354 | ) Mehrabad. | F-WROR |

### ISRAEL

| | | | | |
|---|---|---|---|---|
| 4X-JYF | Westwind Sea Scan | 152 | Israeli Defence Force/AF, '029', Tel Aviv. | 4X-CJC |
| 4X-JYG | Westwind-1123 | 107 | Israeli Defence Force/AF, '064', Tel Aviv. | (4X-COK)/4X-COL |
| | | | | /N4691E |
| 4X-JYJ | Westwind-1124 | 185 | Israeli Defence Force/AF, Tel Aviv. | N1123U/4X-CKI |
| 4X-JYO | Westwind-1123* | 186 | Israeli Defence Force/AF, Tel Aviv. | N1123R/4X-CKJ |

* (retrofit 1123 for Coast Guard duties)

### IVORY COAST

| | | | | |
|---|---|---|---|---|
| TU-VAB | F-28-1000C | 11099 | Force Aerienne de Cote d'Ivoire, GATL, Abidjan. | PH-EXL |
| TU-VAC | Gulfstream 2 | 218 | Government of Ivory Coast, Abidjan. | |
| TU-VAF | Gulfstream 3 | 303 | Government of Ivory Coast, Abidjan. | N303GA/N300GA |
| TU-VAJ | F-28-4000VIP | 11124 | Government of Ivory Coast, Abidjan. | TU-VAZ/PH-EXY |

### JORDAN

| | | | | |
|---|---|---|---|---|
| JY-HAH | Falcon 50 | 52 | Govt/Jordanian Air Force, Amman. | F-BMER/F-WZHV |
| JY-HZH | Falcon 50 | 61 | Govt/Jordanian Air Force, Amman. | F-WZHI |

### KUWAIT

| | | | | |
|---|---|---|---|---|
| KAF 320 | DC-9-32 | 47691 | Government of Kuwait/Air Force. | 160749 |
| KAF 321 | DC-9-32 | 47690 | Government of Kuwait/Air Force. | 160750 |

### MALAWI

| | | | | |
|---|---|---|---|---|
| MAAW-J1 | HS 125/700B | 7076 | Govt/Malawi Air Force, Blantyre. | 70-YJI/G-5-17 |

### MALAYSIA

| | | | | |
|---|---|---|---|---|
| FM1801 | HS 125/400B | 25189 | 9M-EDA, ) Royal Malaysian AF, | FM1200/(G-AXFY)/G-5-20 |
| FM1802 | HS 125/400B | 25209 | 9M-EDC, ) No 2 Squadron, Kuala Lumpur. | FM1201 |
| FM2101 | F-28-1000 | 11088 | 9M-EBS, RMAF, ) VIP transport for Govt use. | PH-EXI |
| FM2102 | F-28-1000 | 11089 | 9M-EBT, RMAF, ) No 2 Squadron, Kuala Lumpur. | PH-EXL |
| FM | Challenger | 1062 | 9M-    , RMAF, ) | C-GBTT/C-GLWV |
| FM | Challenger | 1064 | 9M-    , RMAF, ) | C-GBUB |

### MEXICO

| | | | | |
|---|---|---|---|---|
| FAM DN-01 | JetStar-8 | 5144 | Ministry of Defence, Mexico City. | JS 10201/N5508L |
| MTX-01 | Learjet | 24D-313 | Mexican Navy, Mexico City. (500th Learjet delivered) | |
| TP-01 | B 727-51 | 19123 | Government of Mexico, Mexico City. XC-UJA. | N477US |
| TP-02 | B 727-51 | 19121 | Government of Mexico, Mexico City. XC-UJB. | N475US |
| TP-03 | B 737-247 | 20127 | Government of Mexico, Mexico City. | N4523W |
| TP-04 | B 737-112 | 19772 | Government of Mexico, Mexico City. | N48AF/9V-BFF/9M-AOW |
| TP-103 | Sabre-75A | 380-67 | XC-UJC ) | N2528E |
| TP-104 | Sabre-75A | 380-68 | XC-UJD ) UTAPEF, | N2538E |
| TP-105 | Sabre-60 | 306-139 | XC-UJE ) Mexico City. | |
| TP-106 | Sabre-60 | 306-144 | XC-UJF ) | N2519E |
| TP-107 | Sabre-40A | 282-130 | XC-UJG ) | XC-SRA/N44NR/N33LB |
| TP-10501 | B 727-64 | 19427 | Mexican Air Force.) | XA-SEM |
| TP-10502 | B 727-14 | 18908 | Mexican Air Force.) | XA-SER |
| TP-10503 | B 727-14 | 18909 | Mexican Air Force.) Confirmation required ? | XA-SEU |

| Registration | Type | C/N | Owner/Operator | Previous Identities |
|---|---|---|---|---|
| TP-10504 | B 727-14 | 18911 | Mexican Air Force.) | XA-SEA |
| TP-10505 | B 727-14 | 18912 | Mexican Air Force.) | XA-SEP |

MOROCCO

| Registration | Type | C/N | Owner/Operator | Previous Identities |
|---|---|---|---|---|
| CN-ANL | Gulfstream 2TT | 182 | Government of Morocco, Rabat. | N17589 |
| CN-ANN | Mystere 20ECM | 152 | Ministry of Defence, Rabat. | CN-MBG/F-WJMJ |
| CN-ANO | Falcon 50 | 12 | Government of Morocco, Rabat. | F-WZHC |
| CN- | Mystere 20ECM | 165 | Ministry of Defence, Rabat. | CN-MBH/F-WJMJ |
| CN-ANR | B 707-3W6C | 21956 | Government of Morocco, Rabat. | N7070T |

NEW ZEALAND

| Registration | Type | C/N | Owner/Operator | Previous Identities |
|---|---|---|---|---|
| NZ7271 | B 727-22C | 19892 | ) | N7435U |
| NZ7272 | B 727-22C | 19895 | ) RNZAF. | N7438U |
| NZ7273 | B 727-22C | 19893 | ) | N7436U |

NIGER

| Registration | Type | C/N | Owner/Operator | Previous Identities |
|---|---|---|---|---|
| 5U-BAG | B 737-2N9C | 21499 | Government of Niger Republic, Niamey. | (5U-MAF) |

NORWAY

| Registration | Type | C/N | Owner/Operator | Previous Identities |
|---|---|---|---|---|
| 041 | Mystere 20ECM | 41 | ) Royal Norwegian AF, | LN-FOI/F-BOED/SAAF431/F-WNGL |
| 053 | Mystere 20ECM | 53 | ) No 335 Squadron, Gardemoen, Oslo. | LN-FOD/F-BNRE/F-WNGO |
| 0125 | Mystere 20 | 125 | ) | LN-FOE/N812PA/N6810J/N4344F/F-WJMN |

PAKISTAN

| Registration | Type | C/N | Owner/Operator | Previous Identities |
|---|---|---|---|---|
| J 753 | Mystere 20E | 277 | Government of Pakistan No 12 Squadron, Karachi. | F-WPXD |

PANAMA

| Registration | Type | C/N | Owner/Operator | Previous Identities |
|---|---|---|---|---|
| HP-1A | Falcon 20F | 382 | FAP=Fuerza Aerea Panamena, Tocumen. | N138F/F-WMKG |

PERU

| Registration | Type | C/N | Owner/Operator | Previous Identities |
|---|---|---|---|---|
| FAP 390 | F-28-1000 | 11100 | FAP=Fuerza Aerea del Peru, Lima. | PH-EXY |
| FAP 522 | Learjet | 25B-159 | ) FAP, Las Palmas AFB, Lima. | |
| FAP 523 | Learjet | 25B-164 | ) National Aerophotography Service. | |

SAUDI ARABIA

| Registration | Type | C/N | Owner/Operator | Previous Identities |
|---|---|---|---|---|
| 101 | JetStar-8 | 5129 | ) Royal Saudi Air Force, | N7974S |
| 102 | JetStar-8 | 5130 | ) Royal Flight No 1 Squadron. Riyadh. | 103/N7975S |
| HZ-106 | Learjet | 35A-374 | McDonnell-Douglas/Royal Saudi Air Force, Riyadh. | |
| HZ-107 | Learjet | 35A-375 | McDonnell-Douglas/Royal Saudi Air Force, Riyadh. | |

SOUTH AFRICA

| Registration | Type | C/N | Owner/Operator | Previous Identities |
|---|---|---|---|---|
| 04 | HS 125/400B | 25184 | ) South African Air Force, VIP Unit, | G-AXLW |
| 07 | HS 125/400B | 25269 | ) No 21 Squadron, Zwartkop, Pretoria. | G-AZEM |
| ZS-JBA | HS 125/400B | 25259 | Government of Republic of South Africa. | 05/G-AZEK |
| ZS-JIH | HS 125/400B | 25260 | Government of Republic of South Africa. | 06/G-AZEL |

SPAIN

| Registration | Type | C/N | Owner/Operator | Previous Identities |
|---|---|---|---|---|
| T 15-1 | DC-8-52 | 45814 | 401-01 ) | EC-BAV/N45814/EC-BAV |
| T 15-2 | DC-8-52 | 45658 | 401- ) | EC-ATP |
| T 11-1 | Mystere 20E | 253 | 401-02 ) Ejercito del Aire, | EC-BZV/F-WROS |
| TM 11-2 | Mystere 20D | 222 | 401-03 ) Esc 401, Getafe. | EC-BXV/F-WNGL |
| TM 11-3 | Mystere 20D | 219 | 401-04 ) | EC-BVV/F-WPXH |
| TM 11-4 | Mystere 20E | 332 | 401-05 ) | EC-CTV/F-WROP |

(Radio callsigns EC-ZCI/J/K/L/M)

SWEDEN

| Registration | Type | C/N | Owner/Operator | Previous Identities |
|---|---|---|---|---|
| 86001 | Sabre 40 | 282-49 | Defense Material Administration, Swedish AF, Linkoping. | N905KB /N905K/N757R/N6556C |
| 86002 | Sabre 40 | 282-91 | Defence Material Administration, Swedish AF, Linkoping. | N40NR /N66ES/N5511Z/N5511A/N9500B |

## SYRIA

| | | | | |
|---|---|---|---|---|
| YK-ASA | Mystere 20F | 328 | Syrianair/Government of Syria, Damascus. | F-WMKJ |
| YK-ASB | Mystere 20F | 331 | Syrianair/Government of Syria, Damascus. | F-WROS |

## TAIWAN FORMOSA

| | | | | |
|---|---|---|---|---|
| 18351 | B 720-051B | 18351 | Government of Republic of China (Taiwan). | N721US |
| 2721 | B 727-109 | 19399 | Taiwan Air Force | B-1818 |
| 2722 | B 727-109 | 19520 | Taiwan Air Force | B-1820 |
| 2723 | B 727-109C | 20111 | Taiwan Air Force | B-1822 |
| 2724 | B 727-121C | 19818 | Taiwan Air Force | B-188/XV-NJB/N388PA |

## TOGO

| | | | | |
|---|---|---|---|---|
| 5V-MAB | F-28-1000 | 11079 | Force Aerienne Togolaise/Government, Lome. | 5V-TAB/PH-ZBK /PH-EXB |

## UNITED STATES OF AMERICA

| | | | | |
|---|---|---|---|---|
| 01 | Gulfstream 2 | 23 | VC11A, USCG, Washington DC. | N863GA |
| 150542 | Sabreliner | 277-1 | T39D, U.S.Navy. | |
| 150543 | Sabreliner | 277-2 | T39D, U.S.Navy. | |
| 150544 | Sabreliner | 277-3 | T39D, U.S.Navy. | |
| 150545 | Sabreliner | 277-4 | T39D, U.S.Navy. | |
| 150546 | Sabreliner | 277-5 | T39D, U.S.Navy. | |
| 150547 | Sabreliner | 277-6 | T39D, U.S.Navy. | |
| 150548 | Sabreliner | 277-7 | T39D, U.S.Navy. | |
| 150549 | Sabreliner | 277-8 | T39D, U.S.Navy. | |
| 150550 | Sabreliner | 277-9 | T39D, U.S.Navy. | |
| 150551 | Sabreliner | 277-10 | T39D, U.S.M.C. | |
| 150969 | Sabreliner | 285-1 | T39D, U.S.Navy. | |
| 150970 | Sabreliner | 285-2 | T39D, U.S.Navy. | |
| 150971 | Sabreliner | 285-3 | T39D, U.S.Navy. | |
| 150972 | Sabreliner | 285-4 | T39D, U.S.Navy. | |
| 150973 | Sabreliner | 285-5 | T39D, U.S.Navy. | |
| 150974 | Sabreliner | 285-6 | T39D, U.S.Navy. | |
| 150975 | Sabreliner | 285-7 | T39D, U.S.Navy. | |
| 150976 | Sabreliner | 285-8 | T39D, U.S.Navy. | |
| 150977 | Sabreliner | 285-9 | T39D, U.S.Navy. | |
| 150978 | Sabreliner | 285-10 | T39D, U.S.Navy. | |
| 150979 | Sabreliner | 285-11 | T39D, U.S.Navy. | |
| 150980 | Sabreliner | 285-12 | T39D, U.S.Navy. | |
| 150981 | Sabreliner | 285-13 | T39D, U.S.Navy. | |
| 150982 | Sabreliner | 285-14 | T39D, U.S.Navy. | |
| 150983 | Sabreliner | 285-15 | T39D, U.S.Navy. | |
| 150984 | Sabreliner | 285-16 | T39D, U.S.Navy. | |
| 150985 | Sabreliner | 285-17 | T39D, U.S.Navy. | |
| 150986 | Sabreliner | 285-18 | T39D, U.S.Navy. | |
| 150987 | Sabreliner | 285-19 | T39D, U.S.Navy. | |
| 150988 | Sabreliner | 285-20 | T39D, U.S.Navy. | |
| 150989 | Sabreliner | 285-21 | T39D, U.S.Navy. | |
| 150990 | Sabreliner | 285-22 | T39D, U.S.Navy. | |
| 150991 | Sabreliner | 285-23 | T39D, U.S.Navy. | |
| 150992 | Sabreliner | 285-24 | T39D, U.S.Navy. | |
| 151336 | Sabreliner | 285-25 | T39D, U.S.Navy. | |
| 151337 | Sabreliner | 285-26 | T39D, U.S.Navy. | |
| 151338 | Sabreliner | 285-27 | T39D, U.S.Navy. | |
| 151339 | Sabreliner | 285-28 | T39D, U.S.Navy. | |
| 151340 | Sabreliner | 285-29 | T39D, U.S.Navy. | |
| 151341 | Sabreliner | 285-30 | T39D, U.S.Navy. | |
| 151342 | Sabreliner | 285-31 | T39D, U.S.Navy. | |
| 151343 | Sabreliner | 285-32 | T39D, U.S.Navy. | |

| Regis-tration | Type | C/N | Owner/Operator | Previous Identities |
|---|---|---|---|---|
| 157353 | Sabre-40 | 282-84 | CT39E, U.S.Navy. | N2254B |
| 157354 | Sabre-40 | 282-85 | CT39E, U.S.Navy. | N2255B |
| 158380 | Sabre-40 | 282-95 | CT39E, U.S.Navy. | N4704N |
| 158381 | Sabre-40 | 282-93 | CT39E, U.S.Navy. | N4701N |
| 158382 | Sabre-40 | 282-92 | CT39E, U.S.Navy. | N2676B |
| 158383 | Sabre-40 | 282-96 | CT39E, U.S.Navy. | N4705N |
| 158843 | Sabre-40 | 306-52 | CT39G, U.S.Navy. | N955R/N7571N |
| 158844 | Sabre-60 | 306-55 | CT39G, U.S.Navy. | N5419/N908R/N7575N |
| 159361 | Sabre-60 | 306-65 | CT39G, U.S.Navy. | N8364N |
| 159362 | Sabre-60 | 306-66 | CT39G, U.S.Navy. | N8365N |
| 159363 | Sabre-60 | 306-67 | CT39G, U.S.Navy. | |
| 159364 | Sabre-60 | 306-69 | CT39G, U.S.M.C. Cherry Point, NC. | |
| 159365 | Sabre-60 | 306-70 | CT39G, U.S.M.C. Cherry Point, NC. | |
| 160053 | Sabre-60 | 306-104 | CT39G, U.S.Navy, New Orleans, La. | N65795 |
| 160054 | Sabre-60 | 306-105 | CT39G, U.S.M.C. Cherry Point, NC. | N65796 |
| 160055 | Sabre-60 | 306-106 | CT39G, U.S.M.C. Cherry Point, NC. | N65797 |
| 160056 | Sabre-60 | 306-107 | CT39G, U.S.M.C. Cherry Point, NC. | N65798 |
| 160057 | Sabre-60 | 306-108 | CT39G, U.S.Navy, New Orleans, La. | N65799 |
| 59-2868 | Sabreliner | 265-1 | T39A, USAF. Serv-Air Inc. Bronxville, Tx. | |
| 59-2869 | Sabreliner | 265-2 | T39A, USAF. | |
| 59-2870 | Sabreliner | 265-3 | T39A, USAF. | |
| 59-2871 | Sabreliner | 265-4 | T39A, USAF. | |
| 59-2872 | Sabreliner | 265-5 | T39A, USAF. Serv-Air Inc. Bronxville, Tx. | |
| 59-5958 | JetStar-6 | 5010 | C140A, USAF) | |
| 59-5959 | JetStar-6 | 5026 | C140A, USAF) HQ AFCS, Scott AFB, Il. | |
| 59-5960 | JetStar-6 | 5028 | C140A, USAF) 1866th Facility Checking Squadron, | |
| 59-5962 | JetStar-6 | 5032 | C140A, USAF) | |
| 59-2873 | Sabreliner | 270-1 | T39B, USAF. | |
| 59-2874 | Sabreliner | 270-2 | T39B, USAF. | |
| 60-3474 | Sabreliner | 270-3 | T39B, USAF. | |
| 60-3475 | Sabreliner | 270-5 | T39B, USAF. | |
| 60-3476 | Sabreliner | 270-5 | T39B, USAF. | |
| 60-3477 | Sabreliner | 270-6 | T39B, USAF. | |
| 60-3478 | Sabreliner | 265-6 | T39A, USAF. | |
| 60-3479 | Sabreliner | 265-7 | T39A, USAF. | |
| 60-3480 | Sabreliner | 265-8 | T39A, USAF. | |
| 60-3481 | Sabreliner | 265-9 | T39A, USAF. | |
| 60-3482 | Sabreliner | 265-10 | T39A, USAF. | |
| 60-3483 | Sabreliner | 265-11 | T39A, USAF | |
| 60-3484 | Sabreliner | 265-12 | T39A, USAF | |
| 60-3485 | Sabreliner | 265-13 | T39A, USAF | |
| 60-3486 | Sabreliner | 265-14 | T39A, USAF | |
| 60-3487 | Sabreliner | 265-15 | T39A, USAF | |
| 60-3488 | Sabreliner | 265-16 | T39A, USAF | |
| 60-3489 | Sabreliner | 265-17 | T39A, USAF | |
| 60-3490 | Sabreliner | 265-18 | T39A, USAF | |
| 60-3491 | Sabreliner | 265-19 | T39A, USAF | |
| 60-3492 | Sabreliner | 265-20 | T39A, USAF | |
| 60-3493 | Sabreliner | 265-21 | T39A, USAF | |
| 60-3494 | Sabreliner | 265-22 | T39A, USAF | |
| 60-3495 | Sabreliner | 265-23 | T39A, USAF | |
| 60-3496 | Sabreliner | 265-24 | T39A, USAF | |
| 60-3497 | Sabreliner | 265-25 | T39A, USAF | |
| 60-3498 | Sabreliner | 265-26 | T39A, USAF | |
| 60-3499 | Sabreliner | 265-27 | T39A, USAF | |
| 60-3500 | Sabreliner | 265-28 | T39A, USAF | |
| 60-3501 | Sabreliner | 265-29 | T39A, USAF | |
| 60-3502 | Sabreliner | 265-30 | T39A, USAF | |
| 60-3503 | Sabreliner | 265-31 | T39A, USAF | |
| 60-3504 | Sabreliner | 265-32 | T39A, USAF | |
| 60-3505 | Sabreliner | 265-33 | T39A, USAF | |
| 60-3506 | Sabreliner | 265-34 | T39A, USAF | |
| 60-3507 | Sabreliner | 265-35 | T39A, USAF | |
| 60-3508 | Sabreliner | 265-36 | T39A, USAF | |
| 61-0634 | Sabreliner | 265-37 | T39A, USAF | |
| 61-0635 | Sabreliner | 265-38 | T39A, USAF | |
| 61-0636 | Sabreliner | 265-39 | T39A, USAF | |
| 61-0637 | Sabreliner | 265-40 | T39A, USAF | |

| Regis-tration | Type | C/N | Owner/Operator | Previous Identities |
|---|---|---|---|---|
| 61-0638 | Sabreliner | 265-41 | T39A, USAF | |
| 61-0639 | Sabreliner | 265-42 | T39A, USAF | |
| 61-0640 | Sabreliner | 265-43 | T39A, USAF | |
| 61-0641 | Sabreliner | 265-44 | T39A, USAF | |
| 61-0642 | Sabreliner | 265-45 | T39A, USAF | |
| 61-0643 | Sabreliner | 265-46 | T39A, USAF | |
| 61-0644 | Sabreliner | 265-47 | T39A, USAF | |
| 61-0645 | Sabreliner | 255-48 | T39A, USAF | |
| 61-0646 | Sabreliner | 265-49 | T39A, USAF (W.O. ?) | |
| 61-0647 | Sabreliner | 265-50 | T39A, USAF | |
| 61-0648 | Sabreliner | 265-51 | T39A, USAF | |
| 61-0649 | Sabreliner | 265-52 | T39A, USAF | |
| 61-0650 | Sabreliner | 265-53 | has civil reg. N1064. T39A, USAF | |
| 61-0651 | Sabreliner | 265-54 | T39A, USAF | |
| 61-0652 | Sabreliner | 265-55 | T39A, USAF Serv-Air Inc. Bronxville, Tx. | |
| 61-0653 | Sabreliner | 265-56 | CT39A, USAF Ramstein, West Germany. | |
| 61-0654 | Sabreliner | 265-57 | CT39A, USAF. Ramstein, West Germany. | |
| 61-0655 | Sabreliner | 265-58 | T39A, USAF. | |
| 61-0656 | Sabreliner | 265-59 | T39A, USAF. | |
| 61-0657 | Sabreliner | 265-60 | T39A, USAF. | |
| 61-0658 | Sabreliner | 265-61 | T39A, USAF. | |
| 61-0659 | Sabreliner | 265-62 | T39A, USAF. | |
| 61-0660 | Sabreliner | 265-63 | T39A, USAF. | |
| 61-0661 | Sabreliner | 265-64 | T39A, USAF. (W.O. ?) | |
| 61-0662 | Sabreliner | 265-65 | T39A, USAF. | |
| 61-0663 | Sabreliner | 265-66 | T39A, USAF. | |
| 61-0664 | Sabreliner | 265-67 | T39A, USAF. | |
| 61-0665 | Sabreliner | 265-68 | T39A, USAF. | |
| 61-0666 | Sabreliner | 265-69 | T39A, USAF. | |
| 61-0667 | Sabreliner | 265-70 | T39A, USAF. | |
| 61-0668 | Sabreliner | 265-71 | T39A, USAF. | |
| 61-0669 | Sabreliner | 265-72 | T39A, USAF. | |
| 61-0670 | Sabreliner | 265-73 | T39A, USAF. | |
| 61-0671 | Sabreliner | 265-74 | T39A, USAF. | |
| 61-0673 | Sabreliner | 265-76 | T39A, USAF. | |
| 61-0674 | Sabreliner | 265-77 | T39A, USAF. | |
| 61-0675 | Sabreliner | 265-78 | T39A, USAF. | |
| 61-0676 | Sabreliner | 265-79 | T39A, USAF. | |
| 61-0677 | Sabreliner | 265-80 | CT39A, USAF. Stuttgart, West Germany. | |
| 61-0678 | Sabreliner | 265-81 | T39A, USAF. | |
| 61-0679 | Sabreliner | 265-82 | CT39A, USAF. Ramstein, West Germany. | |
| 61-0680 | Sabreliner | 265-83 | T39A, USAF. | |
| 61-0681 | Sabreliner | 265-84 | T39A, USAF. | |
| 61-0682 | Sabreliner | 265-85 | T39A, USAF. | |
| 61-0683 | Sabreliner | 265-86 | T39A, USAF. | |
| 61-0684 | Sabreliner | 265-87 | T39A, USAF. Ramstein, West Germany. | |
| 61-0685 | Sabreliner | 265-88 | CT39A, USAF. Stuttgart, West Germany. | |
| 61-2488 | JetStar-6 | 5017 | VC140B, U.S. Air Force, SAM, Andrews AFB. | N9286R |
| 61-2489 | JetStar-6 | 5022 | VC140B, U.S. Air Force, West Germany. | |
| 61-2490 | JetStar-6 | 5024 | VC140B, U.S. Air Force, SAM, Andrews AFB. | |
| 61-2491 | JetStar-6 | 5027 | VC140B, U.S. Air Force, West Germany. | |
| 61-2492 | JetStar-6 | 5031 | VC140B, U.S. Air Force, SAM, Andrews AFB. | |
| 61-2493 | JetStar-6 | 5034 | VC140B, U.S. Air Force, SAM, Andrews AFB. | |
| 62-4197 | JetStar-6 | 5041 | C140B, U.S. Air Force, SAM, Andrews AFB. | |
| 62-4198 | JetStar-6 | 5042 | C140B, U.S. Air Force, West Germany. | |
| 62-4199 | JetStar-6 | 5043 | C140B, U.S. Air Force, SAM, Andrews AFB. | |
| 62-4200 | JetStar-6 | 5044 | C140B, U.S. Air Force, West Germany. | |
| 62-4201 | JetStar-6 | 5045 | C140B, U.S. Air Force, West Germany. | |
| 62-4449 | Sabreliner | 276-2 | T39A, USAF. | |
| 62-4450 | Sabreliner | 276-3 | T39A, USAF. | |
| 62-4451 | Sabreliner | 276-4 | T39A, USAF. | |
| 62-4452 | Sabreliner | 276-5 | T39A, USAF. | |
| 62-4453 | Sabreliner | 276-6 | T39A, USAF. Frankfurt, West Germany. | |
| 62-4454 | Sabreliner | 276-7 | T39A, USAF. | |
| 62-4455 | Sabreliner | 276-8 | T39A, USAF. | |
| 62-4456 | Sabreliner | 276-9 | T39A, USAF. | |
| 62-4457 | Sabreliner | 276-10 | T39A, USAF. | |
| 62-4458 | Sabreliner | 276-11 | T39A, USAF. | |

| Regis-tration | Type | C/N | Owner/Operator | Previous Identities |
|---|---|---|---|---|
| 62-4459 | Sabreliner | 276-12 | T39A, USAF. | |
| 62-4460 | Sabreliner | 276-13 | T39A, USAF. (W.O. ?) | |
| 62-4461 | Sabreliner | 276-14 | CT39A, USAF. Ramstein, West Germany. | |
| 62-4462 | Sabreliner | 276-15 | CT39A, USAF. Ramstein, West Germany. | |
| 62-4463 | Sabreliner | 276-16 | T39A, USAF. | |
| 62-4464 | Sabreliner | 276-17 | T39A, USAF. | |
| 62-4465 | Sabreliner | 276-18 | T39A, USAF. | |
| 62-4466 | Sabreliner | 276-19 | T39A, USAF. | |
| 62-4467 | Sabreliner | 276-20 | T39A, USAF. | |
| 62-4468 | Sabreliner | 276-21 | T39A, USAF. | |
| 62-4469 | Sabreliner | 276-22 | T39A, USAF. | |
| 62-4470 | Sabreliner | 276-23 | T39A, USAF. | |
| 62-4471 | Sabreliner | 276-24 | CT39A, USAF. Ramstein, West Germany. | |
| 62-4472 | Sabreliner | 276-25 | T39A, USAF. | |
| 62-4473 | Sabreliner | 276-26 | T39A, USAF. | |
| 62-4474 | Sabreliner | 276-27 | T39A, USAF. Ramstein, West Germany. | |
| 62-4475 | Sabreliner | 276-28 | T39A, USAF. | |
| 62-4476 | Sabreliner | 276-29 | T39A, USAF. | |
| 62-4477 | Sabreliner | 276-30 | T39A, USAF. | |
| 62-4478 | Sabreliner | 276-31 | T39A, USAF. | |
| 62-4479 | Sabreliner | 276-32 | T39A, USAF. | |
| 62-4480 | Sabreliner | 276-33 | T39A, USAF. | |
| 62-4481 | Sabreliner | 276-34 | T39A, USAF. | |
| 62-4482 | Sabreliner | 276-35 | T39A, USAF. | |
| 62-4483 | Sabreliner | 276-36 | T39A, USAF. | |
| 62-4484 | Sabreliner | 276-37 | T39A, USAF. | |
| 62-4485 | Sabreliner | 276-38 | T39A, USAF. | |
| 62-4486 | Sabreliner | 276-39 | T39A, USAF. | |
| 62-4487 | Sabreliner | 276-40 | T39A, USAF. | |
| 62-4488 | Sabreliner | 276-41 | T39A, USAF. | |
| 62-4489 | Sabreliner | 276-42 | T39A, USAF. | |
| 62-4490 | Sabreliner | 276-43 | T39A, USAF. | |
| 62-4491 | Sabreliner | 276-44 | T39A, USAF. | |
| 62-4492 | Sabreliner | 276-45 | T39A, USAF. | |
| 62-4493 | Sabreliner | 276-46 | T39A, USAF. | |
| 62-4494 | Sabreliner | 276-47 | T39A, USAF. | |
| 62-4495 | Sabreliner | 276-48 | T39A, USAF. | |
| 62-4496 | Sabreliner | 276-49 | T39A, USAF. | |
| 62-4497 | Sabreliner | 276-50 | T39A, USAF. | |
| 62-4498 | Sabreliner | 276-51 | T39A, USAF. | |
| 62-4499 | Sabreliner | 276-52 | T39A, USAF. | |
| 62-4500 | Sabreliner | 276-53 | T39A, USAF. | |
| 62-4501 | Sabreliner | 276-54 | T39A, USAF. | |
| 62-4502 | Sabreliner | 276-55 | T39A, USAF. | |
| 58-6970 | VC137B | 17925 | Andrews AFB. Md. | |
| 58-6971 | VC137B | 17926 | Andrews AFB. Md. | |
| 58-6972 | VC137B | 17927 | Andrews AFB. Md. | |
| 60-0376 | C135B | 18151 | HQAFLC, Wright-Patterson AFB. Oh. | |
| 60-0378 | C135B | 18153 | HQAFCS, Scott AFB. Il. | |
| 62-4125 | VC135B | 18465 | HQUSAFE, Ramstein, West Germany. | |
| 62-4126 | VC135B | 18466 | Andrews AFB. Md. | |
| 62-4127 | VC135B | 18467 | Andrews AFB. Md. | |
| 62-4129 | VC135B | 18469 | Andrews AFB. Md. | |
| 62-4130 | VC135B | 18470 | Andrews AFB. Md. | |
| 71-0874 | C9A | 47467 | USAF, Rhein-Main, West Germany. | |
| 71-0876 | C9A | 47475. | USAF, Rhein-Main, West Germany. | |
| 71-0879 | C9A | 47537 | USAF, Frankfurt. | |
| 71-0880 | C9A | 47538 | USAF, Frankfurt. | |
| 71-0881 | C9A | 47540 | USAF, Frankfurt. | |
| 71-0882 | C9A | 47541 | USAF, Frankfurt. | |
| 73-1681 | VC9C | 47668 | Andrews AFB. Md. | |
| 73-1682 | VC9C | 47670 | Andrews AFB. Md. | |
| 73-1683 | VC9C | 47671 | Andrews AFB. Md. | |
| 62-6000 | B 707-353B | 18461 | Presidential aircraft, 89th MAW, Andrews AFB. Md. | |
| 72-7000 | B 707-353B | 20630 | Presidential aircraft, 'Air Force One'. | N8459 |
| 2101 | HU-25A Guardian | 374 | US Coast Guard | N1045F/F-WROP |
| 2102 | HU-25A Guardian | 386 | US Coast Guard | N149F/F-WJMK |

| Regis-tration | Type | C/N | Owner/Operator | Previous Identities |
|---|---|---|---|---|
| 2103 | HU-25A Guardian | 394 | US Coast Guard | N178F/F-WMKF |
| 2104 | HU-25A Guardian | 390 | US Coast Guard | N173F/F-WJMN |
| 2105 | HU-25A Guardian | 398 | US Coast Guard | N183F/F-WMKF |
| 2106 | HU-25A Guardian | 402 | US Coast Guard | N187F/F-WJMJ |
| 2107 | HU-25A Guardian | 409 | US Coast Guard | N407F/F-WMKJ |
| 2108 | HU-25A Guardian | 405 | US Coast Guard | N405F/F-WMKI |
| 2109 | HU-25A Guardian | 407 | US Coast Guard | N406F/F-WJMJ |
| 2110 | HU-25A Guardian | 411 | US Coast Guard | N408F/F-WMKG |
| 2111 | HU-25A Guardian | 413 | US Coast Guard | N410F/F-WJMK |
| 2112 | HU-25A Guardian | 415 | US Coast Guard | N413F/F-WLCV |
| 2113 | HU-25A Guardian | 417 | US Coast Guard | N416FJ/N416F/F-WJMM |
| 2114 | HU-25A Guardian | 418 | US Coast Guard | N417F/F-WJMN |
| 2115 | HU-25A Guardian | 419 | US Coast Guard | N419F/F-WMKJ |
| 2116 | HU-25A Guardian | 420 | US Coast Guard | N420F/F-WMKG |
| 2117 | HU-25A Guardian | 421 | US Coast Guard | N422F/F-WMKI |
| 2118 | HU-25A Guardian | 423 | US Coast Guard | N423F/F-WJMJ |
| 2119 | HU-25A Guardian | 424 | US Coast Guard | N424F/F-WMKF |
| 2120 | HU-25A Guardian | 425 | US Coast Guard | N425F/F-WMKG |
| 2121 | HU-25A Guardian | 431 | US Coast Guard | N429F/F-WMKJ |
| 2122 | HU-25A Guardian | 433 | US Coast Guard | N432F/F-WJML |
| 2123 | HU-25A Guardian | 435 | US Coast Guard | N433F/F-WJMM |
| 2124 | HU-25A Guardian | 437 | US Coast Guard | N435F/F-WMKG |
| 2125 | HU-25A Guardian | 439 | US Coast Guard | N443F/F-WMKJ |
| 2126 | HU-25A Guardian | 441 | US Coast Guard | N445F/F-WJMK |
| 2127 | HU-25A Guardian | 443 | US Coast Guard | N447F/F-WMKG |
| 2128 | HU-25A Guardian | 445 | US Coast Guard | N449F/F-WJMM |
| 2129 | HU-25A Guardian | 447 | US Coast Guard | N455F/F-WLCS |
| 2130 | HU-25A Guardian | 450 | US Coast Guard | N458F/F-WMKG |
| 2131 | HU-25A Guardian | 452 | US Coast Guard | N459F/F-WMKI |
| 2132 | HU-25A Guardian | 454 | US Coast Guard | N461F/F-WJML |
| 2133 | HU-25A Guardian | 456 | US Coast Guard | N462F/F-WJMJ |
| 2134 | HU-25A Guardian | 458 | US Coast Guard | N465F/F-WJMN |
| 2135 | HU-25A Guardian | 460 | US Coast Guard | N467F/F-WJML |
| 2136 | HU-25A Guardian | 462 | US Coast Guard | N470F/F-WMKI |
| 2137 | HU-25A Guardian | 464 | US Coast Guard | N472F/F-WJMK |
| 2138 | HU-25A Guardian | 466 | US Coast Guard | N473F/F-WJML |
| 2139 | HU-25A Guardian | 468 | US Coast Guard | |
| 2140 | HU-25A Guardian | 469 | US Coast Guard | |
| 2141 | HU-25A Guardian | 371 | US Coast Guard | N1039F/F-WMKJ |

URUGUAY

| FAU 500 | Learjet | 35A-378 | FAU | |
|---|---|---|---|---|

VENEZUELA

| 0001 | B 737-2N1 | 21167 | Presidential aircraft, Caracas. | ) |
| 0002 | Citation | 550-0011 | FAV, MoD, Comando Aereo Logístico. | ) Esc/2, GTE. (N98876) |
| 0004 | Gulfstream 2 | 124 | FAV, MoD, Comando Aereo Logístico. | ) N203GA |
| | | | | /VR-BGO/(VR-BGL)/HB-IEW/N834GA |
| 0222 | Citation | 500-0092 | FAV, MoD, Comando Aereo Logístico. | ) N592CC |

YUGOSLAVIA

| 70401 | Learjet | 25B-202 | JRV/Government of Yugoslavia, Belgrade. | 10401/N3807G |
| 70402 | Learjet | 25B-203 | JRV/Government of Yugoslavia, Belgrade. | 10402/N3811G |
| 72101 | Falcon 50 | 25 | Government of Yugoslavia, Belgrade. | F-WZHI |
| 74301 | B 727-2L8 | 21080 | YU-AKH, JRV/Government of Yugoslavia, Belgrade. | 14301 |
| 74302 | B 727-2L8 | 21040 | YU-AKD, JRV/Government of Yugoslavia, Belgrade. | 14302 |

PRODUCTION LISTS

Appended below are Falcon, Gulfstream, HS 125/700, Challenger, Learjet 35 and Cessna 550/551 production lists in brief format. Dates quoted are generally from official sources. However, these sources are not uniform in their choice of date, and may select the registration, bill of sale, customer acceptance, delivery to completion centre or delivery on completion date as their reference point. To specifiy each date is outside the scope of this publication, but the variance should be no more than a few months from the dates given.

The abbreviations FJC, GAC, BAe and GLC have been used for Falcon Jet Corp., Gulfstream American Corp, British Aerospace and Gates Learjet Corp. respectively. Others are standard and should be familiar to most readers.


FALCON 10


01    F-WFAL Prototype. Ff 1/DEC/70. W/O Romorantin-France 31/OCT/72.
02    F-WTAL Ff 15/OCT/71. F-ZJTA CEV Larzac Test-bed 1973
03    F-WSQN OCT/72. F-BSQN AMD-BA JUL/73
1     F-WSQU 1973. F-BSQU AMD-BA demo JUN/73. PH-ILT Philips SEP/78. F-WJLH AMD-BA NOV/80.
      F-BJLH EFS/Leadair DEC/80
2     F-WJMM 1973. N10FJ FJC NOV/73. N103JM Jas H Matthews & Co. SEP/75. C-GRIS Skycharter JAN/79.
3     F-WJMJ 1973. N100FJ FJC DEC/73. N731FJ AiResearch DEC/73. BA Leasing Corp. MAR/79.
      UOP-Signal Co/International Minerals & Chemical JUL/79.
4     F-WJMK 1973. N101FJ FJC DEC/73. XB-SII Cementos Mexicanos S.A. APR/74.
5     F-WLCT 1973. F-BVPR EFS JAN/75.
6     F-WJML 1973. N102FJ FJC DEC/73. N600BT International Brotherhood of Teamsters AUG/74. (N110FJ) FJC
      JAN/77. N10AG A.G. Spanos/Aviation Methods JUL/79. Aviation Methods/AMAX Inc. AUG/79.
7     F-WJMN 1974. VR-BFF Euralair/Korreda OCT/74. F-BXAG EFS/Korreda MAY/75. Euralair International/Ste.
      Eurofer 1980.
8     F-WJMN 1974. N104FJ FJC FEB/74. N21ES Esmark Inc. AUG/74. N21ET FJC SEP/78. N21EK FJC MAR/79. N88ME
      McGraw-Edison Co. JUN/79.
9     F-WJMM 1974. N103FJ FJC FEB/74. N10TX Texas Industries Inc. MAY/74.
10    F-WJMJ 1974. N105FJ FJC MAR/74. N253K Kellogg Co. MAY/74. W/O Meigs-Chicago, USA 20/JAN/80. Tt 3196
      Hours.
11    F-WJMK 1974. N106FJ FJC APR/74. N23ES Esmark Inc. AUG/74. N23ET FJC DEC/78.
12    F-WJML 1974. N107FJ FJC APR/74. N3100X Xerox Corp. JUN/74.
13·   F-WLCS 1974    N108FJ FJC APR/74. N734S Shell Oil Co. JUL/74. N210FJ FJC Various leases JAN/75. N72EU
      Euclid Air Inc. MAY/78. N10JZ J Zenko/Telemedia Inc. AUG/79.
14    F-WJMK 1974. SE-DEL SAAB-Scania AB. JUL/74.
15    F-WJMM 1974. N109FJ FJC MAY/74. N60MB Mountain Bell SEP/74. W/O Stapleton-Denver, USA 3/APR/77. Tt
      1425 Hours.
16    F-WLCT 1974. N110FJ FJC JUN/74. N48TT Centex Corp. SEP/74. Mid-American Oil MAR/75. Cajun Equipment
      Co. Tatham Corp. FEB/79.
17    F-WLCS 1974. OH-FFB Nielsen OY. SEP/74. VH-FFB Hancock Prosepecting NOV/78. N29966 General Aviation
      Services Inc. MAR/82. SAAHS APR/82. N27DA SEP/82.
18    F-WJMJ 1974. N111FJ FJC JUN/74. N78MD J. Ray McDermott SEP/74.
19    F-WLCU 1974. N112FJ FJC JUN/74. N30JM Johns-Manville OCT/74. (N30JH) OCT/78. (N36KA) OCT/78. N36JM
      Cole National Corp. OCT/78. N937J Combs-Gates JUL/81. Shelby Drilling Ltd. AUG/81.
20    F-WLCV 1974. N113FJ FJC JUL/74. N42G Bankers Life OCT/74.
21    F-WJMK 1974. (HB-VDT) 1974. 3D-ACB Rembrandt Tobacco NOV/76.
22    F-WLCX 1974. N114FJ FJC JUL/74. N44JC John L. Cox AUG/75.
23    F-WLCY 1974. N115FJ FJC JUL/74. N73B Kroger Co. NOV/74. N310FJ FJC JUN/77. N91MH Uni Oil NOV/79.
      Texas Independent Oil Co. JUN/81.
24    F-WJML 1974. N116FJ FJC JUL/74. N1924V Genesco Inc. AUG/74. F-GBTI Technal International JUL/78.
25    F-WJMJ 1974. N117FJ FJC SEP/74. N40N Union Carbide Corp. OCT/74.
26    F-WJMK 1974. N118FJ FJC SEP/74. N592DC Dow Corning JAN/75.
27    F-WLCX 1974. SE-DDF Volvo AB. FEB/75.
28    F-WJMJ 1974. N119FJ FJC OCT/74. N130B American Can Co. APR/75.
29    F-WJMM 1974. N120FJ FJC NOV/74. N234U Combustion Engineering Co. MAR/75.
30    F-WLCT 1974. N121FJ FJC OCT/74. N294W Wheelabrator-Frye FEB/75. N3OFJ Atlantic Aviation OCT/77. N156X
      Quintana Petroleum Corp. JUN/78. N73WZ Washington Jet Inc. DEC/79. Masco Corp. JAN/80.
31    F-WLCU 1974. N122FJ FJC NOVC/74. N2MP Missouri Pacific MAR/75.
32    F-W... 1974. No. 32 French Marine Entrainement Radar APR/75.
33    F-WJMJ 1974. N123FJ FJC DEC/74. N881P International Paper Co. DEC/74.
34    F-WLCS 1974. N124FJ FJC DEC/74. N110M Olan Mills JUL/75.
35    F-WLCV 1975. N125FJ FEB/75. N54V El Paso Natural Gas MAY/75.


112

36  F-WJMJ 1975. HB-VDD Air Charter/Kraus & Naimer AUG/75.
37  F-WJML 1975. C-GFCS Canadian Superior Oil FEB/75.
38  F-WJMM 1975. N127FJ FJC JAN/75. N20ES Esmark Inc. JUL/75. N20ET FJC SEP/78. F-GBRF Ste Roquette
    Freres JUN/79.
39  F-WPUX 1975. No. 39 French Marine Entrainement Radar JUL/75. W/O Toul-Rosieres, France 30/JAN/80. Tt
    2659 Hours.
40  F-WJMN 1975. N128FJ FJC MAY/75. N10XX Furrs Realty JUN/75. N15SJ Steve Jernigan OCT/79. XA-LIO
    Protexa S.A. de C.V. MAR/81.
41  F-WLCS 1975. N129FJ FJC MAR/75. N1HM Houston Oil & Minerals/Permian Mud SEP/75. N5ODM NMCA of Texas Inc.
    SEP/82
42  F-WLCU 1975. N126FJ FJC MAR/75. N18X Joy Manufacturing Co. DEC/75.
43  F-WJMN 1975. N135FJ FJC MAY/75. N1515P Hoover Ball & Bearing Co. NOV/75. N510CP Cluett Peabody Co.
    SEP/79.
44  F-WJMJ 1975. N130FJ FJC APR/75. AMAX Inc. AUG/75. N205X AMAX Coal Co. SEP/82
45  F-WJML 1975. N131FJ FJC MAR/75. N120HC Inland Container Corp. NOV/75. N110CG
46  F-WLCT 1975. N134FJ FJC APR/75. N911RF Ray Friedman & Co. AUG/75.
47  F-WLCY 1975. N132FJ FJC APR/75. YV-O7CP CEDICA NOV/75. PJ-AYA CEDICA MAR/76. YV-221CP Constructora
    Maya SEP/78. Hopreca C.A. OCT/80. Gustavos Zingg JUN/81.
48  F-WJMM 1975. N133FJ FJC JUN/75. N720ML Northwestern Mutual Life Insurance Co. DEC/75.
49  F-WLCV 1975. N136FJ FJC MAY/75. (N490A) AUG/77. N49AS Armco Steel AUG/77. N449A SEP/80.
50  F-WLCS 1975. VH-MEI Mount Enid Iron JUL/77.
51  F-WJML 1975. N137FJ FJC JUN/75. N51BP Iowa Beef Processors NOV/75.
52  F-WLCX 1975. N138FJ FJC JUN/75. N342G Granite Steel Co. FEB/76. National Steel Corp. JUL/78. N52TJ
    Lester Industries MAR/79. N8100E Emerson Electric NOV/80.
53  F-WLCS 1975. N139FJ FJC JUL/75. N8100E Emerson Electric Co. OCT/75. N810US U.S. Electrical Motors
    NOV/80. N125EM JAN/81.
54  F-WPUU 1975. N140FJ FJC JUL/75. (XA-SAR) S.A. Regio Montanos 1975. N464AC Erikson Aircrane Co.
    MAR/77. N4875 Southern Natural Gas/Jefferson Industries Inc. MAY/80.
55  F-WPUV 1975. N141FJ FJC JUL/75. N55FJ Raymond International Builders Inc. JUL/76.
56  F-WPUY 1975. HB-VDX JUL/75. Dr. Legler/Air Material/Holegro Consulting JUL/76. ALAG
57  F-WJMJ 1975. N142FJ FJC AUG/75. N142V Valmont Industries APR/76. N5OTB Tom Brown JUL/80. Oncor Corp.
    JUL/81.
58  F-WJMM 1975. N143FJ FJC SEP/75. N76FJ FJC 1976. N58AS Armco Steel MAR/77. N458A SEP/80.
59  F-WJMN 1975. N144FJ FJC SEP/75. N300GN Gannett Co. OCT/75. N300A Management Air Services/ICI Americas
    Inc. DEC/77.
60  F-WJML 1975. N145FJ FJC OCT/75. N77GT Gulf States Toyota JAN/77. N810E Emerson Electric Co. OCT/81.
61  F-WPUV 1975. D-CBMB  Mercedes-Benz JAN/76. F-WZGD AMD-BA JUN/79. (F-BIPF) DEC/79. F-BFDG Euralair/Ste
    Korreda JUN/80. 3D-ART Rembrandt Tobacco OCT/81.
62  F-WJMM 1975. N146FJ FJC NOV/75. N12LB Lindner Bros. 1976. N6VG Deverian/General Dynamics APR/77.
    Deverian Airways MAR/81.
63  F-WLCX 1975. N147FJ FJC NOV/75. PT-KTO Camargo Correia S.A. NOV/76.
64  F-WLCT 1975. N148FJ FJC DEC/75. N100BG Gelco Corp. SEP/76.
65  F-WJMJ 1975. N149FJ FJC DEC/75. XB-BAK Protexa S.A. de C.V. NOV/76.
66  F-WJMN 1975. N150FJ FJC DEC/75. N50RL Riviere de Loup Industries JUL/76. Wright Enterprises SEP/82
67  F-WLCU 1975. N151FJ FJC JAN/76. Robert Carr Aircraft Sales APR/76. D-COME H. Bauer/Air Service-Hamburg
    MAY/76.
68  F-WLCV 1976. N152FJ FJC JAN/76. N7NP Northwest Pipeline Co. JUL/76. N7NL 1978. N11DH Acme Air Corp.
    MAY/79. N91DH FEB/81. N80MP Jenos Pizza APR/81.
69  F-WJML 1976. N153FJ FJC FEB/76. N43CC COREMCO-Continental Resources & Mineral Co. NOV/76. N3RC Roy
    Carver Aero Inc. MAY/79.
70  F-WJMM 1976. HB-VEG Starjet-Vaduz MAY/76.
71  F-WJMM 1976. D-CMAN Moebel Mann APR/77.
72  F-WLCX 1976. N154FJ FJC FEB/76. N10TB Tom Brown MAR/77.
73  F-WNGL 1976. N155FJ FJC FEB/76. N88AT Taubman Air DEC/76.
74  F-WJMJ 1976. N156FJ FJC MAR/76. N30TH Sony-USA DEC/76. N34TH DEC/79. N518S Oilfield
    Aviation/Schlumberger Technology Corp. JAN/80.
75  F-WNGM 1976. N157FJ FJC MAR/76. N12U Mountain Bell DEC/76.
76  F-WPUU 1976. F-BYCC EFS JUL/76.
77  F-WNGN 1976. N158FJ FJC APR/76. N82MD J Ray McDermott OCT/76.
78  F-WLCT 1976. N159FJ FJC APR/76. N83MD J Ray McDermott OCT/76.
79  F-WPXB 1976. F-BPXB AMD-BA demo JUN/76. N160FJ FJC JUN/76. N73B Kroger Co. JUL/77.
80  F-WPXD 1976. N161FJ FJC JUL/76. N48R RJR Foods Inc. APR/77. RJR/Del Monte DEC/77. Amin Oil JUN/81.
81  F-WPXF 1976. N162FJ FJC JUL/76. N700BD Beckton-Dickinson SEP/76.
82  F-WPXE 1976. N168FJ FJC MAR/77. N97MC Canton Co. AUG/77.
83  F-WPXG 1976. N163FJ FJC JUL/76. N5GD Gould Inc. DEC/76. XA-FIU Aeropersonal S.A. APR/79.
84  F-WPXH 1976. N164FJ FJC OCT/76. N8447A Sony-Japan SEP/77. JA8447 FEB/78. N8447A Sony-USA MAR/81. N526D
    Digicon Inc. OCT/81.

```
85   F-WPXI 1976. N165FJ FJC JUL/76. N85JM Murphy Oil/U S Jet Aviation Inc. AUG/77.
86   F-WPXJ 1976. N166FJ FJC SEP/76. N410WW Wm Wriggley Co. MAR/77.
87   F-WPXF 1976. N167FJ FJC SEP/76. (N200AF) 1977. N662D Dow Chemical DEC/77.
88   F-WPXL 1976. N169FJ FJC OCT/76. N3600X Xerox Corp. SEP/77.
89   F-WPXM 1976. D-CADB Daimler-Benz APR/77. F-WZGF AMD-BA JUN/79. I-CAIC Soc. CAI JUL/79.
90   F-WNGD 1976. N170FJ FJC DEC/76. N14U Mountain Bell JAN/78.
91   F-WJMJ 1976. D-CBAG Bertelsmann AG. JUL/77.
92   F-WNGM 1976. N172FJ FJC JAN/77. (N61BP) 1977. N1PB Palm Beach Co. MAY/78.
93   F-WNGN 1977. F-BYCV BSN/Merieux DEC/77. Natio Equipment 1980.
94   F-WNGO 1977. N171FJ FJC JAN/77. N54RS Rest Stop Ltd. DEC/77.
95   F-WPXD 1977. N173FJ FJC MAR/77. PT-ASJ Serv-Jet JUL/78.
96   F-WNGD 1977. N174FJ FJC APR/77. XA-SAR SARSA DEC/77. OE-GLG Montana Flug OCT/81.
97   F-WPXF 1977. N175FJ FJC MAR/77. McDonough Co. OCT/78. Marmac Corp. AUG/81.
98   F-WPXG 1977. D-CBUR Burda GmbH JUN/77.
99   F-WPXH 1977. N176FJ FJC MAR/77. N1OTJ National Fire Insurance APR/78. Thoroughbred Jet Aviation Inc.
     MAY/78.
100  F-WPXI 1977. N177FJ FJC MAR/77. N1OFJ SEP/77. YV-17CP Banco de la Construccion y de Oriente C.A.
     OCT/78.
101  F-WPXJ 1977. No. 101 French Marine FEB/78.
102  F-WPXK 1977. N178FJ FJC APR/77. N61BP Iowa Beef Processors Inc. FEB/78.
103  F-WPXL 1977. F-GBMH Moet et Chandon FEB/78. Natio Equipment/Lyons Air 1980.
104  F-WPUU 1977. N179FJ FJC JUN/77. N90DM Donaghmore Inc. AUG/78. VR-BHJ Guildford Ltd. DEC 1981.
105  F-WPUV 1977. N180FJ FJC JUN/77. N942B Northwestern Bell Telephone Co. MAY/78.
106  F-WPUX 1977. N181FJ FJC AUG/77. N1JN Jack Nicklaus/Air Bear Inc. JUN/78. N1OFJ FJC JAN/81.
107  F-WPUY 1977. N182FJ FJC NOV/77. XB-ZRB Zefero Romero Bringas OCT/78.
108  F-WPUZ 1977. HZ-AKI TAG MAR/78. F-WZGF AMD-BA JUN/79. F-BIPC EFS JAN/80. N246LJ FJC SEP/80. N11DH Acme
     Air Corp/Doyle Hopkins OCT/80. N91DH APR/82.
109  F-WNGD 1977. N183FJ FJC FEB/78. N77NR Petroclor Services Inc. JUN/78. C6-BEN JAN/81.
110  F-WNGO 1977. N184FJ FJC APR/78. N90MH Uni Oil AUG/78. Texas Independent Oil Co. JUN/81. N901MH SEP/82.
111  F-WNGO 1977. N185FJ FJC DEC/77. N8200E Emerson Electric AUG/78.
112  F-WPXD 1978. N186FJ FJC APR/78. N12XX Wm O. Morrow NOV/78. N12MB Wing Corp. MAR/79.
113  F-WPXE 1978. (I-SHOP) SEP/78. I-CHOC VIP-Air OCT/78.
114  F-WPXF 1978. N187FJ FJC MAY/78. N200YM American Industry & Resources Corp. OCT/78. N100YM AUG/79.
     N807F A E Stanley Manufacturing Co. JAN/81.
115  F-WPXH 1978. N188FJ FJC MAY/78. N511S Stone Oil Corp. OCT/78. Jada Corp. FEB/79.
116  F-WNGL 1978. N189FJ FJC MAY/78. N4DS Diamond Shamrock NOV/78. N927DS DEC/81.
117  F-WPXG 1978. N190FJ FJC JUN/78. N23DS Diamond Shamrock NOV/78. N923DS DEC/81.
118  F-WPXI 1978. HZ-AMA TAG SEP/78. HZ-NOT OCT/78. HZ-AO2 Akaram Ojjeh/TAG MAR/80.
119  F-WPXK 1978. N191FJ FJC SEP/78. N257W Wendys International Inc. MAR/79.
120  F-WPXM 1978. N192FJ FJC JUN/78. N2OES Esmark Inc. DEC/78. N359V Valmont Industries AUG/81.
121  F-WPUU 1978. (HB-VFS) OCT/78. HB-VFT TIL Management OCT/78. F-GDLR EFS/Leadair JUN/81.
122  F-WPUV 1978. N193FJ FJC JUL/78. N22ES Esmark Inc. DEC/78.
123  F-WPUX 1978. N194FJ FJC JUL/78. N23ES Esmark Inc. DEC/78.
124  F-WPUY 1978. F-GBTC Thomson-CSF NOV/78.
125  F-WNGD 1978. N195FJ FJC SEP/78. N4OOSP BPM Ltd. APR/79. Boomer Oil Co. Inc. AUG/82.
126  F-WNGM 1978. I-CHIC VIP-Air SEP/79.
127  F-WNGN 1978. F-GCTT EFS-Unijet OCT/80.
128  F-WNGO 1978. N197FJ FJC JUL/78. N1871R Ingersoll Rand MAR/79. N79HA EAF/Houston Astros JUL/80.
129  F-WZGA 1978. No. 129 French Marine APR/79.
130  F-WZGB 1978. I-SFRA Soc. Ferruzzi MAR/81.
131  F-WZGC 1978. N196FJ FJC OCT/78. N654PC Wing Span Leasing/Prince Corp. APR/79.
132  F-WZGD 1978. N198FJ FJC NOV/78. N5OOGS General Signal Corp. AUG/79.
133  F-WZGE 1978. F-ZGTI/No. 133 French Marine JUN/79.
134  F-WZGF 1978. N202FJ FJC NOV/78. N900T Browning Ferris Industries JUL/79.
135  F-WZGG 1978. N199FJ FJC DEC/78. N835F Commercial Union/AFM Corp. JUL/79. P L Lloyd JAN/82.
136  F-WZGH 1978. I-MUDE CAI-Rome JUN/81.
137  F-WZGI 1978. N200FJ FJC JAN/79. N837F Commercial Union/AFM Corp. JUL/79.
138  F-WZGJ 1979. N203FJ FJC JAN/79. N3OTH Sony-USA OCT/79.
139  F-WZGK 1979. N204FJ FJC JAN/79. N1OAH American Hospital Supply Corp. NOV/79.
140  F-WZGL 1979. N205FJ FJC MAR/79. N7OWC Wickes Leasing Corp. NOV/79.
141  F-WZGM 1979. N206FJ FJC MAR/79. (N1OAH) NOV/79. N9OOD Browning Ferris Industries FEB/80.
142  F-WZGN 1979. N207FJ FJC APR/79. N1OHK Hobart Corp. NOV/79. ACME Air Corp. DEC/81. N11DH AUG/82.
143  F-WZGO 1979. No. 143 French Marine APR/80.
144  F-WZGP 1979. N208FJ FJC APR/79. N1TC Toro Co. DEC/79.
145  F-WZGQ 1979. N209FJ FJC MAY/79. N244A Archer Daniels Midland Co. DEC/79.
146  F-WZGR 1979. N211FJ FJC MAY/79. National Medical Enterprises Inc. JUN/80.
147  F-WZGS 1979. N212FJ FJC JUN/79. N12TX Texas Industries Inc. DEC/79.
```

148 F-WZGT 1979. N213FJ FJC JUN/79. N103PJ Professional Jet Leasing DEC/79. Field Properties/General
Dynamics MAY/80.
149 F-WZGU 1979. N214FJ FJC AUG/79. N711FJ Louisiana Land & Exploration Co. APR/80.
150 F-WZGV 1979. N215FJ FJC JUL/79. N212N 195 Broadway Corp. MAR/80.
151 F-WZGX 1979. N217FJ FJC SEP/79. N26CP Consolidated Petroluem Industries Inc. SEP/80. OE-GAG Nikki Lauda
JUL/82.
152 F-WZGY 1979. N216FJ FJC SEP/79. N8463 Sony Corp-Japan OCT/80. JA8463 OCT/80.
153 F-WZGZ 1979. N218FJ FJC OCT/79. N344A Archer Daniels Midland Co. JUL/80.
154 F-WZGA 1979. N219FJ FJC NOV/79. Nepacamti Air Services Corp. DEC/80. Omnium Agency (Brazil) MAR/81.
PT-LCO NOV/81.
155 F-WZGC 1979. (N220FJ) 1980. D-CIEL Hertie Waren u Kaufhaus GmbH. DEC/80.
156 F-WZGE 1979. N221FJ FJC JAN/80. N618S Oilfield Aviation/Schlumberger Technology DEC/80.
157 F-WZGF 1979. N222FJ FJC JAN/80. N900AR Songbird/Jet Leasing-Armco DEC/80.
158 F-WZGI 1980. N223FJ FJC FEB/80. N81LB LDB Corp. OCT/80.
159 F-WZGJ 1980. N224FJ FJC MAR/80. N224RP Reidy International Inc. DEC/80.
160 F-WZGK 1980. N225FJ FJC MAR/80. N223HS Hiram T. Morrissette DEC/80. N31TM JUN/81.
161 F-WZGM 1980. N230FJ FJC APR/80. N30CN SW Jack Drilling Co. FEC/80.
162 F-WZGN 1980. N226FJ FJC MAY/80. N664JB Fuqua Industries Inc. DFC/80.
163 F-WZGP 1980. N227FJ FJC APR/80. N151WC The Western Co. DEC/80.
164 F-WZGQ 1980. N228FJ FJC JUN/80. N222MU Mustang Gas Products Co. DEC/80.
165 F-WZGR 1980. N229FJ FJC JUN/80. N111WW R H Fulton DEC/80.
166 F-WZGS 1980. N232FJ FJC JUN/80. N94MC James McManus DEC/80.
167 F-WZGT 1980. N233FJ FJC JUL/80. N39K Knoell Bros. Construction MAR/81. VR-    Continental Dynamics
JAN/82. 5V-TAE Govt. of Togo JAN/82.
168 F-WZGU 1980. N234FJ FJC AUG/80. N175BL AFM Corp. FEB/81.
169 F-WZGV 1980. N235FJ FJC SEP/80. VH-DJT Drayton Investments JUN/81.
170 F-WZGX 1980. N236FJ FJC SEP/80. (For South America).
171 F-WZGY 1980. N237FJ FJC NOV/80. N30TB Tom Brown Inc. MAR/81.
172 F-WZGZ 1980. N238FJ FJC NOV/80. YV-99CP Fab. Nac. de Ascensores (National Elevator) JUN/81.
173 F-WZGA 1980. N239FJ FJC DEC/80. N72BB KCM Co. OCT/81.
174 F-WZGE 1980. N240FJ FJC DEC/80.
175 F-WZGF 1980. N241FJ FJC JAN/81. XA-LOK Aero Personal AUG/81.
176 F-WZGI 1981. N242FJ FJC FEB/81.
177 F-WZGJ 1981. N243FJ FJC FEB/81. N533CS Campbell Soup Co. OCT/81.
178 F-WZGK 1981. N244FJ FJC MAR/81. Quarles Drilling/Indrex Aviation Inc. DEC/81. N100D JUN/82.
179 F-WZGL 1981. I-DJMA Soc. CAI-Rome (For 1982 delivery).
180 F-WZGM 1981. N245FJ FJC APR/81. N593DC Dow Corning Corp. OCT/81.
181 F-WZGC 1981. N247FJ FJC APR/81. N87GT Gulf States Toyota JUN/82.
182 F-WZGN 1981. N248FJ FJC JUN/81.
183 F-WZGO 1981. N249FJ FJC SEP/81. N82CR Collins Radio AUG/82.
184 F-WZGP 1981. N250FJ FJC JUL/81.
185 F-WZGQ 1981. No. 185 French Marine FEB/82.
186 F-WZGB 1981. N251FJ FJC SEP/81.
187 F-WZGR 1981. N252FJ FJC NOV/81.
188 F-WZGS 1981. N253FJ FJC NOV/81. N188DH Dayton Hudson Corp. JUN/82.


FALCON 20


01 F-WLKB Prototype. Ff 4/MAY/63. F-BLKB AMD-BA DEC/67. Gardian Mock-up 1977.
1  F-WMSH 1965. F-BMSH AMD-BA SEP/65. EFS 1968. CEV JUN/73. F-ZACV 1980 Variable Stability research.
2  F-WMSS 1965. F-BMSS AMD-BA MAY/65. EFS 1970. IGN APR/72.
3  F-WMKG 1965. VR-BCG Niarchos JAN/66. HB-VAV Rothel AG. MAY/67. Travelair AG. JUL/67. Transcommerce
   Leasing & Charter Estab. DEC/67. Wienerwald Betriebs AG. JUN/70. Travelair AG. JUN/70. Balair/UNO
   JUN/71. Aeroleasing SA. AUG/76. N92MH Uni Oil MAY/80. Texas Independent Oil Co. JUN/81.
4  F-WMKF 1965. N801F Pan Am JUN/65. N116JD Associated Leasing Inc. JUN/69. N121GW Gulf & Western Food
   Products Co. JAN/71. Flight Safety International AUG/76. W/O Memphis, Tn. 18/MAY/78.
5  F-WMKI 1965. N804F Pan Am AUG/65. N747W FMC Corp. AUG/65.
6  F-WMKH 1965. F-BMKH AMD-BA AUG/65. N805F Pan Am AUG/65. N20JM Johns-Manville Corp. AUG/65. N21JM MAR/73.
   Jet Traders Inc. JUN/73. N21DT Darrell Tomblin JUN/73 ntu. Robert Moffat JUL/73. Estate of R. Moffat
   JUN/74. Cancelled USA JUN/74. C-GOOG Commander Aviation JUN/74. Glenway Home Builders Ltd JUN/74. N65311
   MAY/76. N497 IASCO MAY/76. Western Skyways/AAR Corp. NOV/76. N750SS Sunshine Mining Co. OCT/80.
7  F-WMKK 1965. N807F Pan Am AUG/65. N607S Sinclair Oil Corp. SEP/65. N740L JAN/70. CF-GWI Hashman/Great
   Western International APR/70. N777FA Greyhound Leasing/York International/Dankho Associates JUN/71. Omni
   JAN/74. N20GH Hyman Construction Co. MAY/74. N12GH JAN/75. N110CE Clark Enterprises Inc. FEB/80.
8  F-WMKJ 1965. N806F Pan Am AUG/65. N1500 Continental Can Co. SEP/65. N150CG Continental Group Inc.
   MAY/80. N1500 APR/81


115

9  F-WMKI 1965. N809F Pan Am OCT/65. N366G GEC Corp. OCT/65.
10 F-WMKK 1965. N810F Pan Am OCT/65. N111M Gambles Skogmo Inc. FEB/66. Arthur Roland Equip. Co. JAN/78. Standard Fittings MAY/78
11 F-WMKH 1965. N808F Pan Am OCT/65. CF-SRZ Home Oil Co. FEB/66. Mannix Co. APR/68. Loram Corp JUL/69. N2200M Continental Telephone Corp JUN/70. N220CM MAR/72. Bryant Air Conditioning APR/72. N30CC Carrier Corp. AUG/72. N30CQ AUG/76. Mead Corp. OCT/76. N4351M APR/77. N4351N NOV/81. C T Helicopter Corp. JAN/82.
12 F-WMKI 1965. N803F Pan Am DEC/65. N221B Bechtel Corp. N51SF FEB/77. Sequoia Ventures Inc. APR/80.
13 F-WMKH 1965. F-BOEF AMD-BA SEP/66. TR-LOL Air Service Libreville MAY/69. F-BOEF EFS JUL/69. D-CILL Travelair DEC/69. F-BTCY EFS APR/72
14 F-WMKJ 1965. N804F Pan Am NOV/65. CF-DML Denison Mines Ltd. FEB/66. Royal Bank of Canada AUG/68. Canadian Inspection & Testing JUL/69. Royal Bank of Canada APR/70. Atlantic Aviation to USA SEP/73. N22DL RELCO SEP/73. N22HC Hardesty Construction NOV/77
15 F-WMKK 1965. N806F Pan Am DEC/65. N622R Winrock Farms MAY/66. N1502 Continental Can Co. SEP/68. N151CG Continental Group Inc. JUN/80. N1501 APR/81.
16 F-WNGL 1965. N807F Pan Am JAN/66. N354H Armour Co. JAN/66. Page Airways/Arkansas Aviation FEB/72. N1OFE FEC APR/72
17 F-WMKF 1965. N802F Pan Am JAN/66. N545C Celanese Corp. JAN/66. Celtran Inc. FEB/69. N5450 Champlin Petroleum Co. DEC/69. N5C 1970.
18 F-WNGM 1965. N840F Pan Am DEC/65. N803LC Life & Casualty Insurance JAN/66. D-COLO Travelair AUG/70. Civil Air Charter FEB/72. N777JF Jet Charter of California JAN/73. Valley Line & Supply Equipment Co. FEB/73. N9DM Dynamark Corp. AUG/74
19 F-WNGN 1965. N841F Pan Am JAN/66. N500PC Pepsico Inc. JAN/66
20 F-WMKJ 1966. N842F Pan Am JAN/66. N367G GEC Corp JAN/66. N367GA Arkansas Aviation JAN/72. N5FE FEC APR/72
21 F-WMKI 1966. N843F Pan Am FEB/66. N3444G Gates Rubber Co. FEB/66
22 F-WMKK 1966. F-BMKK EFS JUN/66. SFA/DGAC JUL/66. St. Yan Training School 1972. Cocooned JUL/77. F-ZACS CEV 1980.
23 F-WNGL 1966. F-BNKX AMD-BA FEB/66. N844F Pan Am MAR/66. N424JX Dana Corp. MAR/66. N15CC Collier Cobb & Assoc. JUL/73. N256EN MAPCO APR/77. N256MA MAY/81. (N256M) NOV/81
24 F-WNGM 1966. N845F Pan Am FEB/66. N297AR ARCO JUL/66. N3OJM Johns-Manville Corp. MAY/69. Tidwell Aircraft Sales JUL/72. Arkansas Aviation SEP/72. N2255Q lease FEC 72-73 as N13FE, lease Fluor Corp. 73-74. N738RH Ray Henderson & Assoc 1975. IASCO SEP/75. N60SM Smith International DEC/75. N60SN JAN/78. N703SC Sigmore Corp. JUL/78. Viking Petroleum/McKenzie Enterprises MAY/81.
25 F-WNGN 1966. F-BOON Prince Aga Khan APR/66. HB-VCO Air Jet SA MAY/72. SATA SA. MAY/74. Uni Jet SEP/74. F-BSYF IGN DEC/75.
26 F-WNGO 1966. N846F Pan Am MAR/66. N802F demo APR/66. N11827 Southern Natural Gas DEC/66. Jefferson Industries Inc. 1978. Southern Natural Services Co. Inc. 1981.
27 F-WMKJ 1966. N847F Pan Am MAR/66. N677SW Seagram's Whiskey AUG/66. N33TP Texas Pacific Oil Co. 1972. F.F. Devine/Tampo Manufacturing Co. MAY/81.
28 F-WMKF 1966. N848F Pan Am MAR/66. N367EJ EJA MAR/66. Accident 28/JUL/68. American Contract Co. 1969. Omni 1969. N1OWA Wheelair OCT/69. CJS Air Cargo AUG/70. Brandis Aircraft 1970. Rebuild from s/n 28, 37 & 60. N573EJ EJA JUN/73. (JY-AEJ) APR/75. Arab Wings few months lease from MAY/75. Starbright Management Corp. APR/76. N50CA Carolina Aircraft Corp. JUL/77. Morgan Rourke Aircraft Sales OCT/77. United Aviation Exchange JAN/78. Security Pacific National Bank FEB/79. Ron Clarke Enterprises FEB/80. (N280RC) 1980. Mid Region Petroleum Inc. OCT/81. N126JM DEC/81.
29 F-WMKI 1966. N849F Pan Am MAR/66. N368G GEC Corp. APR/66.
30 F-WMKF 1966. N804F Pan Am APR/66. N368EJ EJA JUN/66. (JY-AEK) APR/75. Arab Wings few months lease from MAY/75. Elvis Presley DEC/75. Omni DEC/76. YV-126CP Industries Yukery S.A. MAY/77. N368EJ T. Reese Inc. JUL/79. Bassett & Tesini Inc./Professional Jet Charter MAY/80. N407PO OCT/81.
31 F-WNGM 1966. N806F Pan Am APR/66. N34C Consolidation Coal Co. MAY/66.
32 F-WNGL 1966. N805F Pan Am MAY/66. N418S Schlumberger Technology/Oilfield Aviation MAY/66. N218S AUG/81.
33 F-WNGO 1966. N807F Pan Am MAY/66. N369EJ EJA JUL/66. N888AR Colonial Alliance JAN/72. Arlen Realty & Development Corp. JAN/74. W/O Acapulco, Mexico 07/AUG/76.
34 F-WMKJ 1966. N808F Pan Am MAY/66. N369G GEC Corp. MAY/66.
35 F-WMKG 1966. N809F Pan Am MAY/66. A.E. Staley Manufacturing Co. AUG/66. (N1777R). N809P MAR/81.
36 F-WMKI 1966. N810F Pan Am MAY/66. N900P Pickands Mather Co./Diamond Shamrock AUG/66. N711BC Omni MAR/71. N644X Pillsbury Co. MAY/71.
37 F-WMKF 1966. HB-VWW requested FEB/66. HB-VAP Wienerwald Betriebs AG. OCT/66. Accident 01/OCT/67. N7922 Omni OCT/69, not in FAA file. N11WA Wheelair DEC/69. W.D. Shepherd FEB/70. CJS Air Cargo Inc. AUG/70. Brandis Aircraft OCT/71. Used in rebuild of s/n 28. CofA cancelled NOV/73.
38 F-WMKF 1966. N842F Pan Am MAY/66. N1107M Theodore Hamm Brewing MAY/66. Heublein Inc. OCT/74.
39 F-WNGM 1966. N843F Pan Am MAY/66. N5555U Universal American Corp. MAY/66. Robre Manufacturing Corp. JAN/68. Gulf & Western Industries/Associates Leasing Inc. N6565A AUG/72. N5OMM McMartin Industries MAY/79. N91OU Tenneco Inc. 1980. XA-LOB Construcciones Protexa APR/81.
40 F-WNGL 1966. N870F Pan Am JUN/66. CF-BFM West Coast Transmission Ltd. SEP/66. N19BC Omni AUG/71. N354H The Williams Companies SEP/71. N354WC JAN/72. N854WC APR/80. N65LC Bancohio National Bank/Liebert Corp. JUN/80. AAR/Two Jacks/Business Aviation Inc. AUG/81. N65LE OCT/81.

116

41  F-WNGL 1966. F-BOED AMD-BA AUG/66. (SAAF 431). LN-FOI Fred Olsen Executive Service OCT/69. 041 RNoAF
    DEC/72
42  F-WNGO 1966. N871F Pan Am JUN/66. N1503 Continental Can Co. SEP/66. N7824M Cauble Enterprises SEP/73.
    W/O Meacham Fort Worth, Tx. 16/JAN/74.
43  F-WMKJ 1966. N872F Pan Am JUN/66. N990L LTV Inc. NOV/66. W/O Dallas Naval Station, Tx. 03/MAR/75. FEC
    spares APR/75.
44  F-WNGN 1966. N873F Pan Am JUN/66. Skelly Oil Co. SEP/66. N355WB Williams Brothers Co. APR/70. N355WC
    Williams Companies MAY/71
45  F-WMKI 1966. N876F Pan Am JUL/66. N147X Quintana Petroleum Corp. JUL/66. N159FC Fleming Companies Inc.
    AUG/74. N9OJF Travis Ward/Jet Fleet NOV/80
46  F-WMKG 1966. CF-ESO Imperial Oil Ltd. OCT/66. N23555 Omni AUG/72. N7FE FEC AUG/72.
47  F-WNGM 1966. N875F Pan Am JUL/66. N1846 Mead Corp. W/O Parkersburg, WV. 13/MAR/68.
48  F-WMKG 1966. N878F Pan Am AUG/68. N910Y Standard Oil Realty Corp. AUG/66.
49  F-WNGN 1966. No.49 French Air Force.
50  F-WNGO 1966. N879F AUG/66. N804F demo 1966. N6565A Associates Leasing Inc. AUG/69. N6FE FEC MAR/73.
51  F-WMKJ 1966. N880F Pan Am SEP/66. Anheuser Busch Inc. SEP/68. N880P Crawford Enterprises OCT/79.
52  F-WNGN 1966. N881F Pan Am SEP/66. International Paper Co. OCT/66. Consolidated Airways AUG/80. Speedbird
    Aircraft Corp. OCT/80. Southwind Aviation MAR/81. N72ET JAN/82. International Jet Leasing Co. JUL/82.
53  F-WNGO 1966. F-BNRE AMD-BA NOV/66. LN-FOD Fred Olsen Executive Service APR/69. 053 RNoAF DEC/72.
54  F-WMKI 1966. N886F Pan Am OCT/66. N200P National Distillers Chemical Corp. OCT/66. N2005 APR/68. N10726
    Southern Natural Gas JUL/68. Jefferson Industries 1978. Southern Natural Services Co. Inc. 1981.
55  F-WNGO 1966. VR-BCJ Niarchos DEC/66. HB-VBS Travelair AG OCT/69. Fred Air AG/Aeroleasing SA JAN/72.
56  F-WNGM 1966. N882F Pan Am OCT/66. N671SR Sperry Rand Corp. FEB/67. N100SR FEB/67. N185S Sperry Corp
    1981.
57  F-WNGO 1966. N883F Pan Am SEP/66. N499MJ Mead-Johnson Corp. SEP/66. N678BM Bristol-Myers Corp. MAR/69.
    N677BM FEB/77. N3JJ IASCO FEB/77. N76RY Las Vegas Jet Charter Service JAN/78. N711KG NOV/78.
58  F-WNGL 1966. N884F Pan Am NOV/66. N600KC Kimberley-Clark Co. APR/67. F-BTQZ EFS/Euralair International
    FEB/73. HB-VDG Aeroleasing SA SEP/74. N2954T UCO Aviation MAY/82.
59  F-WNGO 1967. N971F Pan Am MAR/67. N263MW Upward Co. JUL/67. N710MW Montgomery Ward AUG/67. N710MR Marcor
    Inc. DEC/70. N710MT JUN/74. N227GC W.R. Grace Corp. AUG/74.
60  F-WMKJ 1966. N885F Pan Am NOV/66. N805F demo NOV/66. Associates Leasing Inc. JUN/69. General
    Transportation Corp JUN/70. W/O Boca Raton, Fl. 05/JUL/71. Used as FEC spares and rebuild of s/n 28
61  F-WMKI 1966. N887F Pan Am NOV/66. N299NW Norfolk & Western Railway MAY/67.
62  F-WMKJ 1967. F-BOLX EFS APR/67. LN-FOE Fred Olsen Executive Service DEC/72. W/O Norwich, UK. 12/DEC/73.
    N17401 AJI JAN/74 ntu. Used as FEC spares.
63  F-WMKI 1967. PH-LPS N V Philips JAN/67.
64  F-WMKG 1966. N889F Pan Am DEC/66. N806F demo MAR/67. N200JW Jim Walter Corp. JUN/67.
65  F-WNGN 1966. N890F Pan Am NOV/66. N383RF Rayette-Faberge Inc. JAN/67. (N393RF). N393F Faberge Inc.
    SEP/69. York International/Dankho Industries JUL/73. N777WJ W.J. Runyon APR/75. Wylain Corp. MAY/77.
    N777WL JAN/78. N1U Urich Oil/UCO Aviation Inc. MAY/80.
66  F-WNGL 1966. N891F Pan Am DEC/66. N401AB NABISCO JAN/67.
67  F-WJMN 1967. F-BOOA EFS JUN/67. F-BTML Ste Martell MAR/72.
68  F-WMKJ 1966. N892F Pan Am JAN/67. N577S Sentry Insurance Co. JAN/67. N458SW SEP/82.
69  F-WMKF 1966. N893F Pan Am DEC/66. N176NP Northern Pacific Railroad JAN/67. N176BN Burlington Northern
    Railroad JUL/70. Arkansas Aviation JUL/71. N31LT Leisure Technology OCT/71. Imperial Oil Co. OCT/73.
70  F-WMKH 1966. N966F Pan Am JUL/67. N647JP Northland Foods Inc. MAY/67. Jenos Inc. APR/68.
71  F-WNGM 1967. N967F Pan Am FEB/67. N807F demo FEB/67. N807PA DEC/69. N33SC Southern Conference of
    Teamsters DEC/72. FJC DEC/75. Dan J Harrison Interests Ltd. SEP/76.
72  F-WNGO 1967. HB-VAW Sardi AG. MAY/67. N1270F American Metal Climax Inc. OCT/68. AMAX Inc. 1975.
    Universal Jet Exchange/Kearney & Trecker NOV/81.
73  F-WJML 1967. VH-BIZ Business Jets Pty Ltd. JUL/67. Air Nauru FEB/70-DEC/71. F-BRHB AMD-BA DEC/72-FEB/73.
    VH-BIZ to France JUL/73. 9Q-CKZ Republic of Zaire AUG/74.
74  F-WMKG 1967. N968F Pan Am MAY/67. N1851T New York Times Inc. DEC/67. N1MB Murchison Bros. FEB/70. N57HH
    Home Interiors & Gifts Inc. JUL/75. N800MC JAN/77. Personal Way Aviation Inc. FEB/80.
75  F-WNGL 1967. N969F Pan Am MAY/67. N100V C.V. Starr & Co. AUG/67. Shell Oil Co. OCT/73. FJC JUL/74.
    N256MA MAPCO NOV/74. N2568 Personal Way Aviation Inc. MAY/81. N800DC JAN/82.
76  F-WMKF 1967. N970F Pan Am JUN/67. N937GC National General Amusement Corp. NOV/67. NGC AUG/73. K & S
    Corp. MAY/74. N776DS D S Corp/Daniel Schwartz APR/76
77  F-WNGO 1967. I-RIED Soc Rizzoli Editore MAY/67.
78  F-WNGM 1967. A11-078 RAAF MAY/67.
79  F-WMKH 1967. F-BNRH DGAC APR/67. St. Yan Training School 1972. Cocooned JUL/77. F-ZACT CEV 1980.
80  F-WMKI 1967. N972F Pan Am APR/67. N115K Kaiser Steel Corp APR/67. N356WB Williams Brothers Co. MAR/71.
    N356WC The Williams Companies JUN/72.
81  F-WNGN 1967. N973F Pan Am APR/67. N799G Cars Unlimited MAY/67. GAC Rental Corp. FEB/70. N661JB Fuqua
    Industries JUN/72. N661J DEC/72. N747T FMC Corp. DEC/72.
82  F-WJMM 1967. 20501 RCAF MAY/67. CAF FEB/68. 117501 JAN/70.

117

83 F-WJMJ 1967. N974F Pan Am MAY/67. N805CC Chrysler Corp. MAY/67. N80506 U.S.Pipe & Foundry Co. DEC/70.
   N22JW Jim Walter Corp. NOV/71. N12WP Wm Perry Racing Stables NOV/73. Omni FEB/76. N1TC Turbodyne Corp.
   APR/76. N55ME McGraw Edison Co. OCT/80.
84 F-WJMK 1967. N975F Pan Am JUN/67. N530L LTV JUN/67. Arkansas Aviation Sales MAR/72. N1FE FEC MAR/72.
85 F-WMKH 1967. A11-085 RAAF JUN/67.
86 F-WMKI 1967. N976F Pan Am JUL/67. N808F demo NOV/67. N622R Winn Rock Farms OCT/68. Estate of W.
   Rockefeller APR/73. Two Jacks Aircraft Sales/J T Barta Associates MAY/73. (G-BBEK) Trader Airways Ltd
   AUG/73. F-BUYI EFS/Trader Airways NOV/73. G-BBEK Trader Airways (Horley) Ltd JUL/74. Regent Airways Ltd.
   NOV/74. HB-VDW Jet Aviation AG DEC/74. F-WRGO AMD-BA MAY/76. F-ZACG CEV MAY/76.
87 F-WJMJ 1967. 20502 RCAF JUL/67. CAF FEB/68. 117502 JAN/70.
88 F-WNGN 1967. N977F Pan Am JUL/67. N130B American Can Co. DEC/67. N665P Phillips Petroleum NOV/70. N665B
   AUG/81. I C Deal NOV/81.
89 F-WMKG 1967. N978F Pan Am JUL/67. N345BM Bristol-Myers Corp. JUL/67. Linden Chemical JAN/82. N71CP
   MAR/82.
90 F-WNGL 1967. A11-090 RAAF AUG/67.
91 F-WMKJ 1967. N979F Pan Am JUN/67. S C Johnson & Son Inc. SEP/67.
92 F-WJMM 1967. 20503 RCAF JUL/67. CAF FEB/68. 117503 JAN/70
93 F-WMKF 1967. No. 93 French Air Force.
94 F-WNGO 1967. I-ATMO Soc VIP-AIR OCT/67. Soc Nicomede S.R.L. 1978.
95 F-WNGO 1967. N980F Pan Am JUL/67. N802F demo JAN/68. N664P Phillips Petroleum MAR/68.
96 F-WNGN 1967. N981F Pan Am AUG/67. Cluett Peabody Corp. AUG/67. AMEX DEC/68. The Westgate Co. MAY/72.
   N511S Stone Oil Co. JUL/75. N5RT Richmond Tank Car Co. SEP/78.
97 F-WJMJ 1967. 20504 RCAF JUL/67. CAF FEB/68. 117504 JAN/70.
98 F-WNGN 1967. TU-VAD Ivory Coast Air Force OCT/67. OY-AZT Air Marine JUN/78. N407PC Professional Jet
   Charter JUL/81.
99 F-WJMK 1967. N982F Pan Am AUG/67. N921ML Marion Laboratories Inc. AUG/67.
100 F-WJMN 1967. N983F Pan Am AUG/67. N605RP Ralston Purina Co. AUG/67.
101 F-WMKJ 1967. N984F Pan Am AUG/67. N342K WYCO Inc./Peter Kiewit Inc. FEB/68.
102 F-WMKI 1967. N985F Pan Am SEP/67. N223B Bechtel Corp. SEP/67. N53SF FEB/77. Sequoia Ventures Inc.
   APR/80.
103 F-WMKH 1967. 20505 RCAF SEP/67. CAF FEB/68. 117505 JAN/70.
104 F-WJMK 1967. (OT-JFA). F-BOXV Euralair/EFS NOV/67. EFS 1975.
105 F-WNGL 1967. N986F Pan Am SEP/67. N243K Kellogg Co. SEP/67. N77GR Oral Roberts Evangelistic Association
   JAN/77. N97FJ Araphoe Datsun Inc. JUL/79. N460MC Viking Petroleum OCT/80. Dalco Petroleum MAY/81.
106 F-WMKJ 1967. N988F Pan Am SEP/67. El Paso Natural Gas Co. OCT/67. F-GBPG EFS/El Paso Natural Gas MAR/79.
   N9300M Energy Service Co. SEP/81. N31V El Paso L & G Services Co. JAN/82.
107 F-WMKJ 1967. N988F Pan Am OCT/67. N965BC Barber Colman Co. OCT/67. Omni MAR/74. N155NK American Enka Co.
108 F-WNGO 1967. D-CBAT Battenfeld Maschinen Fabriken GmbH. DEC/67. N5CA Omni DEC/71. Arkansas Aviation
   Sales JAN/72. N4FE FEC APR/72
109 F-WNGM 1967. 20506 RCAF NOV/67. CAF FEB/68. 117506 JAN/70.
110 F-WMKG 1967. N989F Pan Am OCT/67. CF-WRA Massey Ferguson Industries Inc. OCT/67. Sugra Ltd. DEC/70.
   Argus Corp. DEC/71.
111 F-WMKI 1967. N990F Pan Am OCT/67. N111AC Ambassador College MAR/68. N111AM JUL/70. N111BP Iowa Beef
   Processors APR/72.
112 F-WJMJ 1967. N991F Pan Am OCT/67. N2989 General Foods Corp. MAR/68.
113 F-WNGL 1967. N993F Pan Am NOV/67. leased IBC NOV/67. PP-FOH Brazilian Coffee Institute APR/69. PT-FOH
   1974.
114 F-WJMM 1967. 20507 RCAF NOV/67. CAF FEB/68. 117507 JAN/70.
115 F-WJML 1967. No. 115 French Air Force NOV/67.
116 F-WMKJ 1967. N994F Pan Am NOV/67. Ward Paper Box Co. AUG/68. Russell Stover Candies 1970.
117 F-WMKH 1967. N995F Pan Am DEC/67. N171PF Perfe ct Film & Chemical Corp. OCT/68. N421ZC Zollner Corp.
   JUL/69.
118 F-WMKG 1967. N996F Pan Am DEC/67. N512T Tenneco Inc. APR/68.
119 F-WJMK 1967. I-SNAV SNAM/ENI JAN/68.
120 F-WMKI 1967. N4340F Pan Am DEC/67. N410US U.S.Gypsum Corp. JAN/69.
121 F-WJMJ 1967. N4341F Pan Am JAN/68. N242LB ACLC SEP/68. N813PA Pan Am/EAF JUL/70. N813P Provident Bank of
   Cincinnati APR/72. N1199M EAF/Neil McConnell JAN/73. N25CP Cotton Petroleum Corp. NOV/78.
122 F-WNGL 1967. N4342F Pan Am JAN/68. N779P PAC JAN/68. Charter Jet Inc. DEC/68. Four Seasons Nursing
   Centres FEB/70. N335WR Orkin Extermination/Rollins Inc. DEC/70.
123 F-WNGM 1967. N4343F Pan Am JAN/68. N513T Tenneco Inc. MAY/68.
124 F-WJMJ 1968. No. 124 French AF JAN/68.
125 F-WJMN 1967. N4344F Pan Am JAN/68. N681OJ AFLC DEC/68. Olympic Jet Inc. DEC/68. N812PA Pan Am AUG/72.
   LN-FOE Fred Olsen Executive Service MAY/74. O125 RNAF DEC/78.
126 F-WMKH 1968. HB-VBL Bernhard Cornfeld MAY/68. Aeroleasing SA. DEC/70. PH-BAG Business Air Services
   NOV/77. N1041T Midwest Aircraft Sales JUN/79. FJC/Kellogg APR/80.
127 F-WNGN 1967. N4345F Pan Am JAN/68. EAF/Goldfield Corp. REMCO Aviation Inc. JAN/72. New England Petroleum
   SEP/79. ALAV Inc. OCT/80.
128 F-WMKJ 1968. 5A-DAF KLA FEB/68. Libyan Arab Airlines 1969.

129  F-WJMM 1967. N4346F Pan Am FEB/68. N1823F Champion Spark Plug Co. MAR/68.
130  F-WMKJ 1968. N4347F Pan Am FEB/68. N514T Tennecco Inc. MAY/68.
131  F-WJMK 1968. No. 131 French AF. MAR/68.
132  F-WMKG 1968. N4348F Pan Am FEB/68. N560L LTV Aerospace Corp. FEB/68. N2FE FEC MAY/72.
133  F-WNGO 1968. N4349F Pan Am APR/68. N894F J P Stevens & Co. Inc. AUG/68.
134  F-WMKH 1968. N4350F Pan Am MAY/68. N895F MAY/68. N897DM Deering Milliken Inc. AUG/68. N897D JUL/81.
135  F-WMKI 1968. N4351F Pan Am JUN/68. N6820J AFLC DEC/68. Olympic Jet Inc. DEC/68. Pan Am JUN/70. Precision
     Valve Co. MAR/73. FJC FEB/74. N4OXY Hooker Chemical Corp. 1974. N9999E Engelhard Minerals & Chemical
     Corp. JUL/75. Circus Circus Aviation MAY/76. Masco Corp. FEB/77. N194MC SEP/82
136  F-WMKJ 1968. HB-VBM Lonrho Ltd. MAY/68. 9K-ACQ Gulf International AUG/74. Muburak Al Hassawi & Co.
     AUG/76. F-GCGU Gulf Management Services JUN/79. HB-VBM Ilaair AG/ALAG MAY/81.
137. F-WLLK 1968. F-BLLK AMD-BA MAR/68. F-WLLK DEC/68. N4352F Pan Am APR/69. N8999A Edward Balf Co. MAR/71.
     N777PV EAF/Precision Valve Co. JUN/72. Hansa Jet Corp. 1976. Garrett Corp. MAY/77. ATF-3-6 test
     aircraft.
138  F-WLCS 1968. D-CALL Travelair APR/68. Teer Strassenbau GmbH JUL/68. D-CGJH Gruner u Jahr JUL/70. G-BAOA
     Trader Airways FEB/73. F-BUIC EFS JUL/73. F-ZACR CEV MAY/76.
139  F-WNGM 1968. N4353F Pan Am APR/68. N334JR Rollins International DEC/68. N926LR EAF/UMC Industries
     MAY/74. N1868M EAF/Metropolitan Life Insurance Co. APR/76. N1868N SEP/81. Continental Training Services
     NOV/81.
140  F-WNGN 1968. N4354F Pan Am APR/68. N4350M Mead Corp. AUG/68.
141  F-WMKF 1968. F-BPIO EFS APR/68. F-BIHY Soc. Hennessy MAR/72.
142  F-WJMM 1968. N4355F Pan Am APR/68. N100S Sangamo Electric Co. MAY/68. N1BF B R Firestone AUG/72. N298W
     Wheelabrator-Frye Inc. MAR/75. N777WJ Runyon Construction FEB/78. N511T Tennecco Inc. JUL/79.
143  F-WMKH 1968. 5A-DAG KLA MAY/68. Libyan Arab Airlines 1969.
144  F-WJMJ 1968. N4356F Pan Am JUN/68. N888L Royal Industries Inc. DEC/68. N888JR MAY/74. Jack Schafer
     Aircraft Sales APR/80. N800LS Lear Siegler ntu. National Medical Enterprises, Saudi Arabia 1980.
145  F-WNGN 1968. F-BPJB EFS JUN/68. OO-PJB Uni-Jet SA. MAY/79. F-GCGY EFS MAR/80. F-ZACU CEV 1982.
146  F-WJMN 1968. N4357F Pan Am DEC/68. N964M Chase Manhattan/Deltona Corp. MAY/70. N777EG C.E. Gengras
     MAR/72. EAF/Textron Inc. OCT/73. FJC NOV/77. N11TC Teledyne Industries Inc. NOV/78.
147  F-WLCU 1968. PH-ILF N V Philips JUN/68.
148  F-WMKG 1968. N4358F Pan Am DEC/68. Bank of America/Republic Corp. APR/69. N120HC Inland Container Corp.
     MAR/71. N126HC Standard Oil Co. of Ca. AUG/75.
149  F-WNGO 1968. N4359F Pan Am JUL/68. N1818S Stephens Inc. NOV/68.
150  F-WMKH 1968. HB-VBO C-Plane SA. FEB/69. Travelair AG. SEP/70. Jet Aviation AG. AUG/71. Fred Air AG.
     MAR/72. (N95591) SEP/74. N8227V Helena Chemical Co. SEP/74. N777XX TAG-Europe APR/77. N679RE Retlaw
     Enterprises Inc. JUL/79. N123RE FEB/80.
151  F-WMKI 1968. N4360F Pan Am AUG/68. N810F SEP/68. N810PA MAR/71. N3FE FEC JUL/72.
152  F-WJMJ 1968. CN-MBG MoD Morocco JUL/68. CN-ANN 1981.
153  F-WLCT 1968. N4361F Pan Am MAR/69. N70MD J. Ray McDermott Co. NOV/69.
154  F-WLCV 1968. No. 154 French Air Force JUL/68.
155  F-WJMK 1968. N4362F Pan Am DEC/68. N500Y South West Forest Industries OCT/69. N205SC South Central Bell
     Telephone Co. FEB/78. N212C 195 Broadway Corp. FEB/81.
156  F-WMKI 1968. 7T-VRE Govt. of Algeria JAN/69. W/O Bamako, Mali 30/MAY/81.
157  F-WJMM 1968. N4363F Pan Am MAR/69. N166RS Remote Sensing Inc. DEC/69. Robert Warren JAN/70. Aurora
     Associates FEB/70. 117508 CAF JUN/71. C-GRSD-X Dept. of Energy Mines & Resources NOV/75. C-GRSD AUG/76.
158  F-WMKJ 1968. D-CMAX Grundig Werke GmbH. JAN/69.
159  F-WMKJ 1968. N4364F Pan Am JAN/69. N5RC Carlton Industries Inc. JUL/72. Robintech Inc. 1975. N411CC
     EAF/Coca Cola Bottling Co. JUN/76. EAF/Asterion Inc. SEP/80.
160  F-WMKG 1968. I-DKET Soc. Fiat. DEC/68.
161  F-WMKF 1968. N4365F Pan Am JAN/69. N93CD Farm & Home Savings Association MAR/73. N19BD Black & Decker
     Manufacturing Co. JUN/76.
162  F-WNGO 1969. OO-WTB Brussels Airways MAR/69. D-CBBT Battenfeld GmbH. DEC/70. Gerling Versicherungsgruppe
     AUG/74. HB-VED Aeroleasing SA. MAY/75. Salvador Sanz MAY/81. F-ODOK MAY/82.
163  F-WNGM 1968. N4366F Pan Am JAN/69. Celanese Corp. MAY/69. EAF/Gilman Paper Co. SEP/70.
164  F-WJMN 1968. N4367F Pan Am APR/69. The Pittston Co. DEC/69. N654E Elgin National Industries Inc. AUG/76.
165  F-WJMJ 1969. CN-MBH MOD Morocco JUN/69. CN-A 1981.
166  F-WLCS 1968. N4368F Pan Am APR/69. N33D Dow Chemical Co. OCT/71.
167  F-WMKG 1968. No. 167 French AF OCT/68.
168  F-WLCX 1968. N4369F Pan Am MAY/69. GAC Rental Corp. NOV/69. FJC MAR/73. N100KW Kewanee Oil OCT/73.
     N108NC Nalco Chemical Co. MAR/76.
169  F-WNGN 1968. N4370F Pan Am JUN/69. XC-SEY Ministry of Education JUL/71.
170  F-WPUV 1969. I-EKET Soc. Fiat MAR/69.
171  F-WMKG 1968. N4371F Pan Am JUL/68. N570L LTV Inc. JUL/68. N900JL Jones & Laughlin Steel Corp. NOV/71.
172  F-WNGM 1968. F-BRHB EFS OCT/68. I-LIAB ALI 1978.
173  F-WLCU 1968. F-BLCU AMD-BA SEP/69. N70PA Pan Am JUN/70. N729S Shell Oil Co. MAY/71.
174  F-WNGL 1969. TL-AAY Govt. of Central African Republic APR/69. TL-KAZ APR/69. HB-VER De Chambrier
     Aviation SA. FEB/76. F-WSHT AMD-BA 1976. HZ-KA3 Kamal Adham JUN/76.

175 F-WMKF 1968. N4373F Pan Am OCT/68. N866M Marsh & McLennon Inc. JAN/69. Tidwell Aircraft Sales MAR/73.
    F-BUFG TAT, Lyons 1973. D-COFG VFW-Fokker GmbH. JUL/76. F-ODHA Itavia/Uni-Jet JUN/77. F-GBMS AMD-BA
    1978.I-CAIB Soc. CAI Rome MAR/79.
176 F-WMKG 1969. I-SNAM SNAM/ENI NOV/69.
177 F-WMKI 1968. N4374F Pan Am NOV/68. N6701 Sears Roebuck & Co. JAN/69.
178 F-WPXF 1970. OH-FFA Nordair OY. JUN/70. Finnaviation OY. 1979.
179 F-WNGO 1968. N4375F Pan Am DEC/68. N1OLB AFLC JUN/69. N12LB Lind-Air/Marathn Manufacturing Co. DEC/71.
    N12MF OCT/74.
180 F-WMKF 1970. OY-BDS Danfoss Aviation SEP/70.
181 F-WNGL 1968. N4376F Pan Am DEC/68. N836UC Sigma Airways DEC/68. N966L Frito Lay Co. MAY/71.
182 F-WNGN 1970. HB-VCB Optiplast Holding AG. MAY/70. F-WTDJ AMD-BA MAY/75. I-ROBM Soc. Melpi OCT/76. F-BVFV
    EFS DEC/81. French AF 1982.
183 F-WLCY 1968. N4377F Pan Am FEB/69. N2979 General Foods Corp. JUN/69.
184 F-WRQQ 1972. F-BTMF EFS MAY/72. TAT, Lyons JAN/74. D-COMF VFW-Fokker GmbH. JUL/76. F-GAPC Air Gefco
    MAR/77.
185 F-WMKF 1968. I-IRIF Soc. VIP-Air MAY/69. N3WN Washington Jet Inc. DEC/79. N147X Quintana Petroleum Corp.
    JAN/80.
186 F-WPXL 1970. NO. 463 French AF NOV/71.
187 F-WLCV 1968. N4379F Pan Am OCT/69. N40AC Allied Chemical Corp. OCT/69. N750R Oral Roberts FEB/81.
188 F-WJMK 1969. F-BRPK EFS MAY/69.
189 F-WPUU 1968. N4380F Pan Am MAR/69. N950CL AFLC/LTV Jet Fleet Corp. JUN/69. Jet Fleet Corp. JUN/73. N47JF
    SEP/73. Estate of A F Chisholm AUG/7w4. Continental Telephone Service Corp. JUL/76.
190 F-WNGN 1970. LAAFOO2/5A-DAH Libyan AF OCT/71. 5A-DCO Libyan Arab Airlines 1978.
191 F-WPUX 1968. N4381F Pan Am FEB/69. N91OL LTV Aerospace Inc. MAY/69. Wilson Industries MAR/71. N200DE
    Dunavant Enterprises MAR/74.
192 F-WPUY 1969. N4382F Pan Am MAR/69. N920L LTV Aerospace Inc. JUN/69. Jet Fleet Corp. JUN/73. N57JF
    SEP/73. N91OW Wilson & Co. SEP/74. Willis Moore 1977.
193 F-WMKG 1969. N4383F Pan Am JUN/69. N930L AFLC/LTV Aerospace Inc. SEP/69. N37JF MAR/73. Jet Fleet Corp.
    JUN/73. Willis Moore 1977. Jet Fleet Corp. JAN/81.
194 F-WPUZ 1969. N4384F Pan Am APR/70. N100M AiResearch Aviation Co. JUL/70. N555RA Rapid American/Viewtop
    Corp. NOV/73. N297W Wheelabrator-Frye/Sinclair & Valentine JAN/77. N287W Atlantic Aviation NOV/79. S & W
    Aircraft Leasing Co. DEC/79.
195 F-WPXD 1969. N4385F Pan Am MAY/69. N200SR ASperry Rand Corp. MAY/69. N186S Sperry Corp. JUN/81. N191C
    Ingram Corp. JAN/82.
196 F-WPXE 1969. N4386F Pan Am JUL/69. N811PA demo/Charter AUG/69. N701MG Midland Glass Co. JUL/72.
197 F-WPXF 1969. N4387F Pan Am APR/69. N399SW EAF/Citti Bank JUN/70.
198 F-WNGO 1969. VR-BDK Niarchos JUN/69. FEC-14 OCT/72. N74196 Arkansas Aviation/Tidwell Aircraft Sales
    OCT/72. XC-BIN PEMEX JAN/73.
199 F-WMKH 1969. N4388F Pan Am APR/70. N8FE FEC MAY/72.
200 F-WMKJ 1969. N4389F Pan Am SEP/69. N550MC McCulloch Properties JAN/70. N44MC ? N44CC Centex Service Co.
    APR/73. N48CC 1975.
201 F-WLCY 1969. D-CELL Travelair JUL/69. Fa. Globus JUL/69. Transalpina Flugzeughalter GmbH. JAN/70.
202 F-WNGM 1969. N4391F Pan Am APR/70. N814PA demo/charter APR/71. N33L Dow Chemical Co. FEB/73.
203 F-WPXH 1969. N4378F Pan Am JUL/69. N1857B Borden Inc. NOV/69. Consolidated Airways MAR/81. N20BE
    Beatrice Foods MAY/81.
204 F-WMKI 1969. N4392F Pan Am APR/70. N26FE FEC MAY/73.
205 F-WPXF 1969. N4393F Pan Am SEP/69. N21W Transco AUG/70. N82A Anaconda Co. SEP/74. EAF/Prudential
    Assurance Co. AUG/76.
206 F-WLCS 1969. N4394F Pan Am AUG/69. N815AC Allis Chalmers Corp. JAN/70.
207 F-WMKF 1969. N4395F Pan Am MAY/71. N27FE FEC MAY/73.
208 F-WPXD 1970. HB-VCA Air Charter/JKraus & Naimer MAY/70. VH-BRR Wards Express JUL/79. N300JJ IASCO
    SEP/80. Wallace Leasing Corp. JUN/82.
209 F-WLCX 1969. N4396F Pan Am MAY/70. N28FE FEC MAY/73.
210 F-WNGL 1969. N4397F Pan Am JUN/70. N29FE FEC MAY/73.
211 F-WJMK 1969. N4398F Pan Am JUN/70. N3OFE FEC MAY/73.
212 F-WPXG 1969. N4399F Pan Am JUN/70. N31FE FEC MAY/73.
213 F-WJMM 1969. N4390F Pan Am SEP/70. N32FE FEC MAY/73.
214 F-WNGO 1969. N4400F Pan Am SEP/70. N33FE FEC MAY/73.
215 F-WLCS 1969. N4401F Pan Am JAN/71. N34FE FEC MAY/73.
216 F-WLCT 1969. N4402F Pan Am MAR/71. N9FE FEC JUN/72.
217 F-WLCY 1969. N4403F Pan Am MAY/71. N35FE FEC MAY/73.
218 F-WMKJ 1969. N4372F Pan Am MAY/71. N36FE FEC MAY/73.
219 F-WPXH 1970. EC-BVV Secretariat of Civil Aviation JUN/70. TM 11-3/401-04 Spanish AF JUN/78.
220 F-WPUU 1969. N4404F Pan Am JUL/71. N24FE FEC MAY/73.
221 F-WPUV 1969. N4406F Pan Am JUL/71. N25FE FEC MAY/73. Accident Green Apt. Warwick, RI 3/OCT/75. N300NL
    Sunstream Jet Express/Emery Express MAY/79.
222 F-WNGL 1971. EC-BXV Secretariat of Civil Aviation MAR/71. TM 11-2/401-03 Spanish AF JUN/78.
223 F-WPUX 1969. N4407F Pan Am OCT/71. N22FE FEC MAY/73.

224 F-WPUY 1970. N4408F Pan Am MAR/72. N23FE FEC MAY/73
225 F-WPXD 1970. TR-KHA Govt. of Gabon OCT/70. TR-LRU DEC/73. F-BOFH AMD-BA JUL/75. OH-FFJ Salora TV JAN/76.
    N25MJ MJI MAY/78. N37WT Godfathers Investments JUN/78. Mid American Aviation Inc. DEC/79. N332FE FEC
    JAN/80. N338DB Atlantic Aviation SEP/82
226 F-WPXI 1970. N4409F Pan Am JUN/72. N21FE FEC SEP/72.
227 F-WMKG 1970. N4410F Pan Am APR/72. N14FE FEC OCT/72.
228 F-WNGL 1970. ZS-LAL SKK JUN/70. ZS-LLG LLG Jet Charters SEP/70. 3D-LLG Louis Luyt Group FEB/72. FJC
    MAY/75. C-GWSA Sam Hashman DEC/75. HB-VEZ Private Jet Services JAN/77.
229 F-WJMJ 1970. N4411F Pan Am SEP/72. N15FE OCT/72.
230 F-WJML 1970. N4412F Pan Am OCT/72. N16FE FEC OCT/72.
231 F-WPXE 1970. HB-VCG Travelair AG. AUG/70. Fred Air Ag. JAN/72. W/O St. Morritz, Switzerland 20/FEB/72.
232 F-WJMN 1970. N4413F Pan Am OCT/72. N17FE FEC NOV/72.
233 F-WLCV 1970. N4414F Pan Am OCT/72. N18FE FEC MAY/73.
234 F-WLCU 1970. (D-CIBM) APR/70. D-COLL Friedrich Flick GmbH. NOV/70. I-LIAC Soc. ALI 1979.
235 F-WPXJ 1970. N4415F Pan Am NOV/72. N2OFE FEC MAY/73.
236 F-WPXK 1970. (N4416F). CF-JES Distillers Corp. JUL/70.
237 F-WPXF 1970. (D-CALM) & (D-CHCH) DEC/70. D-CITY Hertie Waren u Kaufhaus APR/71. N4227Y TAG Aviation Ltd.
    Europe MAR/81.
238 F-WRQP 1971. NO. 238 French AF JUN/71.
239 F-WPXM 1970. N4417F Pan Am JUL/70. AiResearch Aviation JUL/70. N1OMT Mack Trucks Inc. SEP/72. C-GBFL
    B.C. Forest Products JUL/76.
240 F-WLCX 1970. I-SNAG SNAM NOV/70.
241 F-WRQP 1971. SE-DCO Handelsbolaget Skato, Ehrenstrom Flyg MAR/71. Crownair Swedish Ltd. FEB/74. N48AD
    Triple D Corp. MAY/77. Hirschmann Corp. JUN/78. HZ-HE4 Sheikh Hassan Enany. HZ-PL7 Mobil Oil JAN/82.
242 F-WPUZ 1970. N4418F Pan Am SEP/70. N800CF Crum & Forster Insurance Co. SEP/70. (N320FJ) 1978. N2622M
    MASCO Inc. JUL/78.
243 F-WMKH 1970. OH-FFW Finnwings JAN/71. W/O St. Francois de Laval, Montreal, Canada 1/MAR/72. Spares as
    simulator for FEC.
244 F-WMKI 1970. N4420F Pan Am JUN/72. N2OFJ FJC OCT/72. N11LB Lindair DEC/72. N226G W R Grace Co. DEC/74.
245 F-WLCS 1971. SX-ABA Falcon Enterprises Ltd. MAR/72. F-BUIX EFS MAY/73. HB-VDP ATES MAR/74. HB-VDY
    VDP/Private Jet Services DEC/79. Schweizerische Kreditanstalt FEB/82.
246 F-WJMK 1971. F-BSTR EFS JUN/71. Air Inter APR/74-OCT/74. AMD-BA Flight Test Development 1975. EFS FEB/82
247 F-WPXE 1970. N4419F Pan Am MAR/71. N730S Shell Oil Co. MAY/71.
248 F-WRQV 1972. OH-FFV Finnwings APR/72. N37JJ IASCO AUG/78. XB-AQU Mario Vasquez Rana 1978. XB-OEM
    Organization Editorial Mexicana 1980.
249 F-WJMM 1971. N4421F Pan Am FEB/72. N11AK Alaska Interstate Co. MAY/72. N777JF Valley Line Supply &
    Equipment Co. APR/74.
250 F-WMKF 1971. N4422F Pan Am JAN/72. N111AM Ambassador College MAY/72. XA-HEW Commercial Aerea S.A.
    AUG/77.
251 F-WRQR 1971. EP-VAP Govt. of Iran NOV/71. EP-FIE Civil Aviation Organization JAN/81.
252 F-WRQP 1971. I-GIAZ Soc. Zanussi OCT/71.
253 F-WRQS 1971. EC-BZV Secretariat of Civil Aviation DEC/71. T 11-1/401-02 Spanish AF JUN/78.
254 F-WNGO 1971. N4423F Pan Am DEC/72. CF-YPB Tele Direct Ltd. JAN/73.
255 F-WRQP 1972. 122 RJAF JUN/72. HB-VDZ Omar Yehia/Mission Permanente d'Oman JUN/75.
256 F-WNGL 1971. N4416F Pan Am FEB/72. N3RC Carver Pump Co. MAY/72. C-GNTZ Northern Telecom JUL/78.
257 F-WMKH 1971. N4425F Pan Am FEB/72. N781W Winnebago Industries FEB/72. FJC SEP/73. N300CC Luqa Inc.
    DEC/73. C-GNTL Northern Telecom JUN/76.
258 F-WNGM 1971. N4426F Pan Am JUL/72. N2OJM Johns Manville Corp. APR/73. N544X Pillsbury Co. NOV/78.
259 F-WLCT 1972. N4418F Pan Am FJC MAR/72. N212H 195 Broadway Corp. AUG/72.
260 F-WMKJ 1972. No. 260 French AF JUL/72.
261 F-WLCU 1972. N4368F Pan Am JUL/72. N200WK Wayfarer Ketch Corp. JAN/73.
262 F-WMKK 1972. N4427F FJC FEB/73. N720ML Northwestern Mutual Life Insurance Co. JUL/73. N750ME Brundred &
    Snyder DEC/75. VH-WLH Lang Hancock Prospecting Pty Ltd. OCT/76. N501AS Omni SEP/78. C-GTLU Bell Canada
    FEB/79. Al Hickman Aviation, Saudi Arabia OCT/80.
263 F-WJMH 1972. HB-VCR Falcon International SA. APR/72. F-BSBU EFS MAY/72. Air Inter APR/74-OCT/74.
    Aerogulf Services Co. JAN/77-APR/77. EFS MAY/77.
264 F-WJMN 1972. N4428F FJC JUL/72. N373KC Kraft Inc. DEC/72.
265 F-WLCX 1972. N4429F MAR/73. N606RP Ralston Purina Co. MAR/73.
266 F-WRQR 1972. PH-ILX N V Philips SEP/72.
267 F-WRQZ 1972. I-REAL Soc. SARAS Raffinazione DEC/72.
268 F-WNGN 1972. No. 268 French AF DEC/72.
269 F-WPUX 1972. N4430F FJC MAR/73. N1902W Whirlpool Corp. AUG/73.
270 F-WPUZ 1972. N4435F FJC JAN/73. N37FE FEC MAY/73.
271 F-WNGN 1973. 7T-VRP Govt. of Algeria JUL/73.
272 F-WMKF 1972. N4431F FJC FEB/73. N2OFJ FEB/73. N732S Shell Oil Co. DEC/73.
273 F-WPUU 1972. N4432F FJC MAR/73. N212T 195 Broadway Corp. MAR/73.
274 F-WJMM 1973. N4433F FJC MAR/73. N37OWT IBM, Europe JUL/73. N121WT 1973. MAPCO APR/82. N256M SEP/82
275 F-WMKH 1972. N4434F FJC OCT/72. N661JB Fuqua Industries DEC/72. N9FB Frank Basil Aviation, Athens
    DEC/76.

276  F-WNGL 1973. CM-01 Belgian AF FEB/73.
277  F-WPXD 1972. J-753 Pakistan AF DEC/72.
278  F-WNGM 1973. CM-02 Belgian AF APR/73.
279  F-WMKJ 1973. I-FKET Soc. Fiat APR/73.
280  F-WPXK 1973. I-EDIS Soc. VIP-Air OCT/73.
281  F-WRQR 1973. D-CORF Korf Transport GmbH. JUL/73. N2OCG Washington Jet Inc/GATX Leasing Corp. FEB/81.
282  F-WMKG 1973. N4436F FJC APR/73. N131JA IASCO/Japan Air Lines DEC/73. N282JJ IASCO AUG/78. Colgate
     Palmolive DEC/78. XC-DIP Banco Nacional Credito Rural OCT/80.
283  F-WRQX 1973. EP-AGX Govt. of Iran JUN/73. W/O Kermanshah, Iran 21/NOV/74.
284  F-WPXM 1973. N4437F FJC MAY/73. N132JA IASCO/Japan Air Lines JAN/74. N284JJ IASCO SEP/78. Andorra
     Aviation JUL/80.
285  F-WRQT 1973. A40-AA Govt. of Oman JUL/73. A40-GA DEC/76. C-in-C SOAF 1981.
286  F-WRQU 1973. EP-AGY Govt. of Iran OCT/73.
287  F-WMKF 1973. N4438F FJC JUL/73. YV-TAVA CEDICA DEC/73. YV-38CP OCT/75.
288  F-WRQZ 1973. F-BUYE EFS NOV/73.
289  F-WMKG 1973. N4439F FJC JUL/73. N2OFJ SEP/74. N54J Doerr Electric SEP/74.
290  F-WMKH 1973. N4440F FJC NOV/73. N133JA International Jet Leasing Corp. FEB/74.
291  F-WRQT 1974. No. 291 French AF JUL/74.
292  F-WMKI 1973. N4441F FJC OCT/73. N733S Shell Oil Co. DEC/73.
293  F-WMKJ 1973. N4442F FJC DEC/73. N2615 Mobil Saudi Arabia Inc. AUG/74. N2613 JAN/78. HZ-PL1 1981.
294  F-WRQT 1973. F-BVPM EFS JUN/74. SU-AXN Govt. of Egypt SEP/74.
295  F-WRQQ 1974. I-EDIM Soc. VIP-Air FEB/74.
296  F-WRQP 1973. HB-VDB Air Charter AG/Kraus & Naimer DEC/73. Aerorent SA. FEB/76. D2-EBB Govt. of Angola
     AUG/76. J5-GAS Govt. of Guinea Bissau MAR/79.
297  F-WMKF 1974. N4443F FJC FEB/74. (N37OEU). N121EU IBM, Europe JAN/75.
298  F-WMKG 1974. N4444F FJC FEB/74. N86W El Paso Products Co. NOV/74.
299  F-WMKI 1973. FJC JAN/74. (N734S). N21FJ JAN/74. N456SR St. Regis Paper Co. AUG/74.
300  F-WRQP 1974. I-EDIF Soc. VIP-Air MAY/74. Soc. Pirelli FEB/78. Soc. Locatrice Italiana 1979.
301  F-WNGL 1974. EP-AKC National Iranian Oil Co. JUN/74.
302  F-WRQP 1974. D-COMM Super Magazin OCT/74. Quick Air GmbH. JUN/76. OE-GDP Dr. Polsterer AUG/76. N84V El
     Paso Natural Gas Co. AUG/79.
303  F-WMKH 1974. N4445F FJC MAR/74. N27R R J Reynolds Tobacco JUL/74. W/O Naples, Fl. 12/NOV/76.
304  F-WRQP 1975. G-BCYF Falcon Jet Centre Ltd. MAR/75. Nidiva Services (UK) Ltd. SEP/81.
305  F-WMKJ 1974. N4446F FJC APR/74. N16R R J Reynolds Tobacco. AUG/74. RJR Aircraft Inc. NOV/81.
306  F-WRQS 1974. D-CGSO Giesecke u Devrient GmbH. OCT/74.
307  F-WRQT 1974. HB-VDV Avegim SA. NOV/74. I-GCAL Soc. Gaetano Caltagirone JAN/77. Soc. Patrimoniale
     Finanziara 1979. OE-GLL Luftfahrzeug Service AUG/81.
308  F-WMKF 1974. N4447F FJC MAY/74. N668P Phillips Petroleum OCT/74.
309  F-WRQT 1975. TR-LUW Govt. of Gabon JUL/75.
310  F-WMKH 1974. N4450F FJC OCT/74. (N37OME). N121AM IBM, Europe MAR/75.
311  F-WRQS 1975. F-BVPNB Soc. Michelin FEB/75.
312  F-WMKH 1974. N4448F FJC JUL/74. N2605 Mobil Oil Corp. JUL/74.
313  F-WMKJ 1974. N4449F FJC SEP/74. N22OFJ SEP/74. N744CC Central Conference of Teamsters JUN/75. N56CC
     MAR/75. N560R allocated JUL/79.
314  F-WNGL 1974. D-COTT Super Magazin NOV/74. Air Flight GmbH. JUN/76. Dornier Reparaturwerft GmbH. 1980.
315  F-WRQP 1975. F-BVPQ EFS JAN/75. OO-VPQ Uni-Jet Benelux MAR/80. Benelux Falcon Service JUN/82.
316  F-WMKF 1974. N4451F FJC OCT/74. N734S Shell Oil Co. JAN/75.
317  F-WMKG 1974. N4452F FJC NOV/74. N31CM TRANSCO DEC/75. N99E MAY/77. N92K AUG/81. Funk Exploration MAY/82.
     N88FE AUG/82.
318  F-WRQT 1975. (EP-VAS). EP-VSP Red Lion & Son Organization FEB/75. Govt. of Iran 1980. EP-FIG Civil
     Aviation Organisation noted APR/82.
319  F-WMKF 1974. N4453F FJC DEC/74. N730V LTV Corp/Vought Corp. AUG/75. Gustavos Zingg, Caracas APR/77.
     N44NT Northern Telecom Aviation Inc. AUG/78.
320  F-WRQS 1975. EP-AHV Govt. of Iran MAY/75. EP-FIF Civil Aviation Organization JAN/81.
321  F-WMKJ 1974. N4454F FJC JAN/75. N2525 C F Braun Co. APR/75. N702SC Sigmor Corp. APR/80. N244CA E J
     Aircraft Inc. JUN/82.
322  F-WMKH 1975. N4455F FJC FEB/75. N1971R Ingersoll Rand Services Co. SEP/75.
323  F-WRQS 1975. HB-VEB Mig SA JUL/75. I-FCIM Soc. Francesco Caltagirone OCT/76. OE-GLF Lauda Air JAN/81.
324  F-WMKF 1975. N4456F FJC MAY/75. N444SC Southern Conference of Teamsters.
325  F-WMKG 1975. N4457F FJC APR/75. N1OOGN Gannett Newspapers Inc. DEC/75. N4OOGN NOV/76.
326  F-WRQQ 1975. PH-ILY N V Philips SEP/75.
327  F-WMKI 1975. N4458F FJC JUN/75. (N9H). N3H Harrah's JUN/75. N2H MAY/76.
328  F-WMKJ 1975. (N4459F). YK-ASA Govt. of Syria OCT/75.
329  F-WRQV 1975. D-CMET DFVLR Met Research SEP/75.
330  F-WNGM 1975. N4460F FJC JUL/75. N3OOAL Abbott Laboratories DEC/75.
331  F-WRQS 1975. YK-ASB Govt. of Syria NOV/75.
332  F-WRQP 1975. EC-CTV Secretariat 'of Civil Aviation OCT/75. TM 11-4/401-05 Spanish AF JUN/78.

```
333  F-WNGL 1975. 5-2801 Iranian Navy NOV/75.
334  F-WRQU 1975. EP-FIC Dept. of Civil Aviation OCT/75.
335  F-WMKF 1975. N4459F FJC OCT/75. N901TC Southwestern Bell Telephone Co. APR/76.
336  F-WRQP 1975. 5-2802 Iranian Navy DEC/75.
337  F-WRQR 1976. YI-AHH Iraqi Airways FEB/76.
338  F-WMKG 1975. EP-FID Dept. of Civil Aviation DEC/75.
339  F-WMKH 1975. N4461F FJC NOV/75. N200GN Gannett Newspapers Inc. DEC/75. N100GN DEC/76. N200GN OCT/80.
340  F-WRQX 1976. 5-2803 Iranian Navy FEB/76.
341  F-WMKF 1975. N4462F FJC FEB/76. N2OFJ JUN/76. N66GA Greyhound Armour AUG/76. N511WP West Point Peperell
     Inc.
342  F-WRQP 1976. YI-AHI Iraqi Airways MAR/76. J2-KAC Govt. of Djibouti JUL/80.
343  F-WRQR 1976. YI-AHJ Iraqi Airways MAY/76.
344  F-WRQP 1976. A6-HEM Dubai Air Wing FEB/77.
345  F-WMKI 1976. N4463F FJC JUN/76. N678BM Bristol Myers Co. MAY/77.
346  F-WRQP 1976. 5-2804 Iranian Navy JUL/76.
347  F-WMKF 1976. N4464F FJC MAY/76. N744CC International Brotherhood of Teamsters.
348  F-WRQR 1976. N4461F FJC JUL/76. 5-3020 NOV/78.
     F-WRQR 1976. 5-4039 Iranian Army JUL/76. 5-3020 NOV/78.
349  F-WMKG 1976. N4465F FJC JUL/76. N273K Kellogg Co. JAN/77.
350  F-WRQS 1976. 5-4040 Iranian Army JUL/76. 5-3021 NOV/78.
351  F-WMKJ 1976. 5-9001 Iranian AF NOV/76.
352  F-WMKF 1976. N4466F FJC OCT/76. N920G Anchor/Hocking Corp. FEB/77.
353  F-WRQP 1976. 5-9002 Iranian AF DEC/76.
354  F-WRQR 1976. 5-9003 Iranian AF JAN/77.
355  F-WMKF 1976. N4467F FJC JUN/77. N2OFJ SEP/77. N27AC AMCA International Corp. FEB/78.
356  F-WMKG 1976. N4468F FJC FEB/77. N27R R J Reynolds Tobacco JUL/77.
357  F-WMKI 1976. N4469F FJC DEC/76. N435T Chicago Tribune MAY/77.
358  F-WRQS 1977. SU-AZJ Arab Organization for Industrialisation JUL/77. F-WROY AMD-BA JAN/78. SU-AZJ AOI
     1978.
359  F-WRQR 1977. (N64769) JUL/77. HZ-TAG TAG International AUG/77. HZ-AO1 MAR/80.
360  F-WMKJ 1977. N1010F FJC MAR/77. N901YP Bell Telephone Co. SW Region SEP/77.
361  F-WMKF 1977. SU-AYD Govt. of Egypt OCT/77.
362  F-WZAS 1977. F-WATF AMD-BA NOV/77. 20G/Gardian using ATF3-6 turbofans.
363  F-WRQV 1977. HZ-DC2 Sheikh El Khereiji OCT/77.
364  F-WMKI 1977. N1013F FJC MAY/77. N235U Combustion Engineering Inc. APR/78. N285U National Medical
     Enterprises JAN/81.
365  F-WMKJ 1977. N1018F FJC JUN/77. N777TX Textron Inc. NOV/77.
366  F-WMKG 1977. N1020F FJC JUL/77. N83V El Paso Natural Gas Co. NOV/77.
367  F-WRQR 1977. EP-SEA Atomic Energy Organization of Iran OCT/77.
368  F-WMKI 1977. N1036F FJC SEP/77. N800CF U S Fire Insurance Co. MAY/78.
369  F-WRQP 1977. N1037F FJC SEP/77. N2OSR Shelton Ranch Corp. MAR/78.
370  F-WMKF 1977. N1038F FJC JAN/78. HL7234 Korean Air Lines SEP/78.
371  F-WMKJ 1977. N1039F FJC OCT/77. 2141 USCG Prototype.
372  F-WRQV 1977. ST-PRS Govt. of Sudan JAN/78.
373  F-WMKI 1977. N1041F FJC DEC/77. N53DS Diamond Shamrock DEC/78. N922DS DEC/81.
374  F-WRQP 1977. N1045F FJC NOV/77. 2101 USCG MAR/82
375  F-WRQR 1978. F-GBMD EFS MAR/78.
376  F-WRQS 1978. N103F FJC FEB/78. N2624M MASCO Inc. OCT/78. N2614 AUG/81.
377  F-WRQP 1978. D-CCMB Daimler Benz AG. MAY/79.
378  F-WRQT 1978. N107F FJC MAR/78. (N662PP). N662P Phillips Petroleum OCT/78.
379  F-WMKF 1978. N130F FJC FEB/78. (N37AH). (N33AJ). N33AH American Hospital Supply Corp. DEC/78.
380  F-WMKI 1978. N136F FJC JUN/78. N8BX Travenol Laboratories Inc. MAR/79. N1BX JUN/80.
381  F-WRQS 1978. (I-LAFA). D-CCDB Daimler Benz AG. MAY/79.
382  F-WMKG 1978. N138F FJC JUL/78. HP-1A Govt. of Panama JUN/79.
383  F-WRQR 1978. D-CONU Contact Air SEP/78. Dornier Reparaturweft GmbH. 1980.
384  F-WRQU 1978. OO-PSD Cie. Europ Recherches FEB/79. N384JK Jim Kelly OCT/80. N120HC Inland Container Corp.
     JAN/81.
385  F-WJMJ 1978. N139F FJC JUN/78. N119R R J Reynolds Industries Inc. DEC/78.
386  F-WJMK 1978. N149F FJC APR/78. 2102 USCG FEB/82.
387  F-WJML 1978. N162F FJC JUN/78. Lease Govt. of Panama JAN/79. N56CC Central Conference of Teamsters
     JUN/79.
388  F-WJMM 1978. N169F FJC JUL/78. N9OGS Song Bird Ltd NOV/78.
389  F-WRQV 1978. I-CMUT Soc. Comau MAY/79.
390  F-WJMN 1978. N173F FJC MAY/79. 2104 USCG MAR/82.
391  F-WLCS 1978. N175F FJC SEP/78. N376SC Steelcase Inc. SEP/79.
392  F-WRQT 1978. D-CALL Friedrich Flick GmbH. APR/79.
393  F-WLCT 1978. N176F FJC JAN/79. N21NL National Lease Co. JUL/79. N76TA Thunderbird Airways NOV/79. N809F
     A E Staley Manufacturing Co. DEC/80.
```

```
394  F-WMKF 1978. N178F FJC SEP/78. 2103 USCG MAR/82.
395  F-WRQX 1979. (HZ-AKI). OD-PAL Govt of Lebanon NOV/79.
396  F-WMKG 1979. N179F FJC MAR/79. N881J International Paper Co. NOV/79.
397  F-WRQP 1979. F-GBTM EFS FEB/80.
398  F-WMKF 1978. N183F FJC NOV/78. 2105 USCG MAR/82.
399  F-WMKI 1978. N184F FJC JAN/79. N881G International Paper Co. SEP/79.
400  F-WRQR 1979. RP-C1980 Central Bank of Philippines DEC/79.
401  F-WZAH AMD-BA 20H prototype, redesignated 200 1981. F-GATF SEP/82. N200FJ FJC OCT/82
402  F-WJMJ 1978. N187F FJC JAN/79. 2106 USCG MAR/82.
403  F-WMKJ 1979. N189F FJC APR/79. N15AT ATO Inc. NOV/79. Figgie International AUG/81.
404  F-WJMK 1979. N404F FJC MAY/79. N28C Edwin L Cox FEB/80.
405  F-WMKI 1979. N405F FJC MAR/79. 2108 USCG JUN/82.
406  F-WMKF 1979. G-BGOP Datsun UK Ltd. SEP/79.
407  F-WJMJ 1979. N406F FJC APR/79. 2109 USCG JUL/82.
408  F-WRQS 1979. PK-CAG Directorate of Civil Aviation MAY/80.
409  F-WMKJ 1979. N407F FJC MAY/79. 2107 USCG APR/82.
410  F-WRQT 1979. N200CP Coral Petroleum JUL/81.
411  F-WMKG 1979. N408F FJC JUN/79. 2110 USCG APR/82.
412  F-WMKI 1979. N409F FJC JUL/79. N85V El Paso Natural Gas Co. APR/80.
413  F-WJMK 1979. N410F FJC JUL/79. 2111 USCG.
414  F-WJML 1979. N412F FJC DEC/79. N1881Q Oriole Assoc/Oneida Ltd. MAY/80.
415  F-WLCV 1979. N415F FJC OCT/79. 2112 USCG.
416  F-WLCT 1979. N415F FJC DEC/79. B T Equipment Leasing Inc/Crown Zellerbach Corp. JUN/80. N416F JUL/80.
417  F-WJMM 1979. N416F FJC NOV/79. N416FJ MAR/80. 2113 USCG.
418  F-WJMN 1979. N417F FJC NOV/79. 2114 USCG.
419  F-WMKJ 1979. N419F FJC DEC/79. 2115 USCG.
420  F-WMKG 1980. N420F FJC JAN/80. 2116 USCG.
421  F-WMKI 1980. N422F FJC JAN/80. 2117 USCG.
422  F-WRQU 1980. No. 422 F-ZJTJ/F-RCAL French AF MAY/81.
423  F-WJMJ 1980. N423F FJC MAR/80. 2118 USCG.
424  F-WMKF 1980. N424F FJC APR/80. 2119 USCG.
425  F-WMKG 1980. N425F FJC MAY/80. 2120 USCG.
426  F-WJMK 1980. N427F FJC MAY/80. N123WH Songbird/Rose Associates AUG/80. N555PT Petro Royal/Tomlinson
     Interests MAY/81.
427  F-WRQV 1980. 5N-AYM Imani & Sons OCT/82
428  F-WMKI 1980. N426F FJC JUL/80. N98R Reynolds Industries JAN/81.
429  F-WMKF 1980. VR-BHL Sioux Co. Ltd. FEB/82.
430  F-WMKG 1980. N428F FJC SEP/80. N660P Phillips Petroleum APR/81.
431  F-WMKJ 1980. N429F FJC OCT/80. 2121 USCG.
432  F-WJMK 1980. N430F FJC OCT/80. N667P Phillips Petroleum MAY/81.
433  F-WJML 1980. N432F FJC NOV/80. 2122 USCG.
434  F-WRQP 1980.
435  F-WJMM 1980. N433F FJC DEC/80. 2123 USCG.
436  F-WJMN 1980. N434F FJC OCT/80. N181CB CBI Industries Inc. 1981.
437  F-WMKG 1981. N435F FJC DEC/80. 2124 USCG.
438  F-WMKI 1981. N442F FJC JAN/81. N263K Kellogg Co. MAY/81.
439  F-WMKJ 1981. N443F FJC JAN/81. 2125 USCG.
440  F-WRQQ 1981. N452F FJC FEB/81. N5152 CBS Inc. 1981.
441  F-WJMK 1981. N445F FJC FEB/81. 2126 USCG.
442  F-WJML 1981. N446F FJC MAR/81. Hawker Pacific NOV/81. VH-FJZ Bond Corp. JAN/82.
443  F-WMKG 1981. N447F FJC MAR/81. 2127 USCG.
444  F-WJMJ 1981. N453F FJC APR/81. N665P Phillips Petroleum AUG/81.
445  F-WJMM 1981. N449F FJC APR/81. 2128 USCG.
446  F-WJML 1981. N454F FJC MAY/81. N31WT OCT/81.
447  F-WLCS 1981. N455F FJC MAY/81. 2129 USCG.
448  F-        1981. No. 48 French Navy Gardian 1981. F-WZVF Noted JUL/82.
449  F-WLCT 1981. N457F FJC MAY/81.
450  F-WMKG 1981. N458F FJC MAY/81. 2130 USCG.
451  F-WRQR 1981.
452  F-WMKI 1981. N459F FJC JUL/81. 2131 USCG.
453  F-WJMK 1981. N460F FJC JUL/81.
454  F-WJML 1981. N461F FJC SEP/81. 2132 USCG.
455  F-WRQS 1981.
456  F-WJMJ 1981. N462F FJC SEP/81. 2133 USCG.
457  F-WJMM 1981. N463F FJC OCT/81. N4351M Mead Corp. AUG/82.
458  F-WJMN 1981. N465F FJC OCT/81. 2134 USCG.
459  F-WMKJ 1981. N466F FJC NOV/81.
460  F-WJML 1981. N467F FJC NOV/81. 2135 USCG.
```

```
461  F-      1981. N469F FJC DEC/81.
462  F-WMKI  1982. N470F FJC JAN/82. 2136 USCG.
463  F-      1982. N471F FJC FEB/82. Japan Air Lines JUL/82.


                              FALCON 50


1   F-WAMD Prototype. Ff 7/NOV/76. F-BNDB AMD-BA APR/80.
2   F-WINR 1978. F-BINR EFS FEB/81.
3   F-WFJC 1978. F-GBIZ AMD-BA SEP/78. N5OFJ JUL/79. N5OEJ NOV/79. N880F Anheuser Busch Companies Inc.
    MAR/80.
4   F-WZHA 1979. N11OFJ FJC MAR/79. N5OFJ SEP/80. YV-452CP Petrovan AUG/81.
5   F-WZHB 1979. No. 5 French Presidential 1979.
6   F-WZHB 1979. N5OFB FJC JUL/79. N1871R Ingersoll Rand Service Co. SEP/80.
7   F-WZHA 1979. HZ-AKI TAG FEB/80. HZ-AO3 MAR/80. N8516Z Great American Life Insurance Co. DEC/80. N26LB
    MAY/81.
8   F-WZHC 1979. N5OFE FJC SEP/79. N5OPG AMAX Inc. SEP/80.
9   F-WZHD 1979. I-SAFP Soc. Fiat OCT/80. XA-LOH Aero Personal SA. APR/81.
10  F-WZHE 1979. N5OFG FJC DEC/79. N65B Bordens Inc. DEC/80.
11  F-WZHE 1980. N5OFH FJC APR/80. N5O1NC Internorth nc. DEC/80.
12  F-WZHC 1980. CN-ANO Govt. of Morocco MAY/80.
13  F-WZHF 1980. N5OFK FJC FEB/80. N150BG Gelco Corp. FEB/80.
14  F-WZHG 1980. N5OFL FJC MAR/80. N233U Combustion Engineering Inc. MAR/80.
15  F-WZHM 1980. PH-ILR N V Philips JUL/80.
16  F-WZHH 1980. (N5OFM). D-BIRD Deutsche BVV JUL/80.
17  F-WZHI 1980. 5A-DGI Govt. of Libya AUG/80. TY-BBM Govt. of Benin OCT/82
18  F-WZHJ 1980. N5OFN FJC APR/80. N187S Sperry Corp. MAY/81.
19  F-WZHB 1980. N5OFM FJC MAY/80. N63A Superior Oil MAY/81. N253L NL Industries JUL/82.
20  F-WZHK 1980. N5OFR FJC MAY/80. C6-BER Petroclor Services JUN/81.
21  F-WZHN 1980. (9K-ACQ). 9K-AEE Muburak Al Hassawi, Kuwait OCT/80. N299W Wheelabrator-Frye DEC/80.
22  F-WZHF 1980. N5OFS FJC JUN/80. N203BT Big Three Industries DEC/80.
23  F-WZHG 1980. (D-BBAD). D-BBWK W Korf GmbH. AUG/80.
24  F-WZHL 1980. N51FJ FJC JUL/80. N817M Standard Oil Co. DEC/80.
25  F-WZHI 1980. 72101 Govt. of Yugoslavia NOV/80.
26  F-WZHA 1980. N52FJ Masco Corp. JUL/80.
27  F-WZHN 1980. HB-IEU Gatair FEB/81.
28  F-WZHE 1980. N53FJ FJC SEP/80. N131WT IBM, Europe MAY/81.
29  F-WZHB 1980. I-SAFR Soc. Fiat FEB/81.
30  F-WZHD 1980. I-SNAC SNAM/ENI MAR/81.
31  F-WZHC 1980. (N54FJ). I-KIDO Soc. Gitanair/VIP-Air FEB/81.
32  F-WZHJ 1980. VR-BTT Inter Insurance APR/81.
33  F-WZHA 1980. N56FJ FJC DEC/80. Caribbean Falcon Inc. MAR/81. Emerson Electric Co. JUL/82.
34  F-WZHH 1980. HB-IEV Aerogulf SA. MAR/81. Ilair/EJA SA JAN/82.
35  F-WZHF 1980. N57FJ FJC DEC/80. N800BD Beckton Dickinson Co. JUL/81.
36  F-WZHJ 1980. N54FJ FJC DEC/80. N345PA Bristol-Myers Co. JUL/81.
37  F-WZHM 1980. (I-CAIK). I-SAME Soc. CAI, Rome MAR/81.
38  F-WZHK 1980. N58FJ FJC DEC/80.
39  F-WZHL 1981. N59FJ FJC JAN/81. N754S Shell Oil Co. JUN/81.
40  F-WZHG 1981. 9K-AEF Gulf International MAY/81.
41  F-WZHI 1981. N6OFJ FJC JAN/81. N546EX JUL/81. Bristol-Myers Co. JAN/82.
42  F-WZHE 1981. N61FJ FJC FEB/81. N82MP Mesa Petroleum 1981.
43  F-WZHO 1981. 72102 Yugoslav Govt. MAY/81.
44  F-WZHA 1981. N62FJ FJC FEB/81. Wrather Corp. JAN/82. N150JP American Aircraft Exchange Inc. JUL/82.
45  F-WZHF 1981. N63FJ FJC FEB/81. N731F AiResearch Aviation MAY/81.
46  F-WZHK 1981. N64FJ FJC MAR/81. N908EF REFCO SEP/81.
47  F-WZHP 1981. N65FJ FJC APR/81. N150WC The Western Co. DEC/81.
48  F-WZHK 1981. HB-IET Sarl Azemco JUL/81.
49  F-WZHL 1981. N66FJ FJC APR/81. N43ES Esmark Inc. SEP/81.
50  F-WZHQ 1981. N67FJ FJC APR/81. N747 FMC Corp. SEP/81.
51  F-WZHR 1981. N7OFJ FJC APR/81. N52DC Dow Chemical NOV/81.
52  F-WZHV 1981. F-BMER AMD-BA JUN/81. JY-HAH Govt. of Jordan SEP/81.
53  F-WZHS 1981. N150JT MAY/81. Joseph E Seagrams & Sons Inc. JAN/82.
54  F-WZHT 1981. N71FJ FJC MAY/81. N450X Rose Associates Inc. MAR/82.
55  F-WZHU 1981. N73FJ FJC MAY/81. N839F Commercial Union Corp. SEP/81.
56  F-WZHR 1981. F-GDFE AMD-BA NOV/81.
57  F-WZHC 1981. HB-IER Giesecke & Devrient JUN/81.
58  F-WZHA 1981. N72FJ FJC JUN/81.
```

```
59  F-WZHB 1981. N75FJ FJC JUN/81. N31DM Pacific Holding Corp. SEP/81.
60  F-WZHD 1981. JY-HZH Govt. of Jordan 1981.
61  F-WZHI 1981. HB-IES Logarcheo Anstult Vaduz 1981.
62  F-WZHE 1981. N77FJ FJC JUN/81. N92BC Boise Cascade Corp. OCT/81.
63  F-WZHF 1981. N78FJ FJC JUL/81. N841F Commercial Union Corp. SEP/81.
64  F-WZHH 1981. N79FJ FJC JUL/81. N418S Oilfield Aviation MAR/82.
65  F-WZHT 1981. Falcon International SA 1981. N5OFJ FJC FEB/82.
66  F-WZHP 1981. PH-SDL Film Air. MAY/82.
67  F-WZHG 1981. N76FJ FJC SEP/81. AYRE Inc. SEP/82.
68  F-WZHQ 1981. 5A-DCM Govt. of Libya SEP/81.
69  F-WZHJ 1981. N8OFJ FJC SEP/81. N650X AMAX Inc. MAR/82.
70  F-WZHL 1981. N81FJ FJC SEP/81. N230S Norton Simon Properties Inc. FEB/82.
71  F-WZHF 1981. YI-ALB Iraqi Govt. MAR/82.
72  F-WZHM 1981. N82FJ FJC OCT/81. N1181G Getty Refining & Marketing Co. FEB/82.
73  F-WPXE 1981.
74  F-WZHA 1981. N83FJ FJC DEC/81. Anheuser Busch Inc. MAR/82.
75  F-WZHH 1981. N95FJ FJC JAN/82. N45ES Esmark Inc. JUL/82.
76  F-WZHB 1981. N84FJ FJC DEC/81. N85MD J Ray McDermott MAR/82.
77  F-WZHC 1981. N85FJ FJC NOV/81. N366F Figgie International Inc. JAN/82.
78  F-WPXF 1981. F-ODEO Ministry of Cooperation, Gabon, MAR/82. TR-LAK OCT/82
79  F-WZHE 1981. N86FJ FJC DEC/81. N6OCN Champion International FEB/82.
80  F-WZHN 1981. N87FJ FJC DEC/81. XB-OEM OEM JUN/82.
81  F-WZHA 1981. N89FJ FJC JAN/82. Smith-Kline Beckman. JUN/82.
82  F-WZHG 1981. N88FJ FJC JAN/82. N293BC Boise Cascade MAR/82.
83  F-WZHJ 1981. (N881M). N88U International Paper Co. JUN/82. N881M International Paper Co. SEP/82.
84  F-WZHK 1981. N2711B Zhobi Corp. MAY/82.
85  F-WZHO 1981. N9OFJ FJC JAN/82.
86  F-WPXD 1981. N94FJ FJC JAN/82. N238U Combustion Engineering JUN/82.
87  F-WZHS 1982. N91FJ FJC FEB/82. N    Kellogg Co. SEP/82.
88  F-WZHU 1982. N92FJ FJC FEB/82.
89  F-WZHV 1982. N93FJ FJC FEB/82. N    195 Broadway Corp. OCT/82
90  F-WZHX 1982. N290W Kellogg Rust Inc. JUL/82.
91  F-WZHY 1982. ZS-BMB Govt. of RSA
92  F-WZHZ 1982. N97FJ FJC FEB/82. N85A NBAA demo SEP/82
93  F-WZHB 1982. N98FJ FJC MAR/82.
94  F-WZHC 1982. N99FJ FJC APR/82.
95  F-WPXD 1982. VR-CBL ARAVCO AUG/82.
```

## GULFSTREAM 2

```
1   N801GA Ff 2/OCT/66. Demo. N55RG R W Galvin/Motorola Inc. SEP/70.
2   N802GA Ff 6/JAN/67. Grumman Aerospace Corp/Gulfstream American.
3   N831GA 1967. N214GP Gillette Products JUN/68.
4   N832GA 1967. N68ORW Coca Cola Co. JUN/68. N68ORZ DEC/76. 9K-ACY Gulf International Group JAN/77. VR-CAS
    Petromin/Mobil Oil, Saudi Arabia DEC/79. HZ-MPM JUL/80.
5   N100P National Distillers & Chemical Co. JAN/68. N100PJ GenStar Corp. MAY/79. N65ST JUN/80.
6   N834GA 1967. N430R Dow Jones & Co. Inc. FEB/68. N122DJ MAR/68.
7   CF-HOG Home Oil Co. FEB/68. Omni AUG/72. N9300 Crown Cork & Seal SEP/72.
8   N833GA 1967. Pulitzer Publishing Corp. DEC/67. N18N G-2 International/Winn Dixie Stores AUG/72. N400SJ
    Seward Johnson DEC/73. N400SA MAY/75. HB-IMV ATES/Agusta, Milan JUL/75. N400SA Seward Johnson MAY/77.
    N777GG CEDICA, Venezuela/Gavilan Corp. DEC/77. PJ-ARI Growth Aircraft, Aruba SEP/79. N504TF Omni FEB/80.
    N5UD U Dantata AUG/80. N225CC Circo Resorts Inc. SEP/80.
9   N890A Mines Ltd. JUN/68. N320FE Federal Express DEC/81. (N115RS) FEB/82. N209GA GAC OCT/82.
10  N343K Eastman Kodak Co. FEB/68.
11  N835GA 1968. N902 Owens Illinois Inc. APR/68.
12  N5OOR Superior Oil Co. APR/68. N11UM 1970. N154X Quintana Petroleum Corp. AUG/74.
13  N678RW Coca Cola Co. MAY/68. N678RZ Omni FEB/77. N98AM NAMCO, Nigeria MAY/77. 5N-AMN DEC/77. N2GP
    Washington Jet/Paul Heim MAY/79. UNO Charter 1980. N373LP Louisiana Pacific Corp. JUL/80.
14  N663P Phillips Petroleum MAY/68. N663B NOV/81.
15  N375PK Seagram's Whisky JUL/68. N77SW JUN/75.
16  N890A ALCOA MAY/68. N697A SEP/81. Southland Corp. DEC/81. 2B Conversion 1982. N711MT SEP/82.
17  N119K Kaiser Industries Inc. MAY/68. N819GA Grumman JAN/77. N456AS ITEL Corp. MAY/77. Firemans Fund
    Insurance Co. AUG/79.
18  N838GA MAY/68. N205M Richard Mellon FEB/69. Constance Burrell 1971. N43R Rockwell International APR/81.
19  N839GA 1968. N1929Y Paul Mellon DEC/68.
20  N2PG Procter & Gamble Co. NOV/68. N755S Shell Oil Co. MAR/80.
```

21  N4PG Procter & Gamble Co. NOV/68. N3PG 1969. N7ZX APR/81. N8PG DEC/81.
22  N826GA 1968. N5152 CBS Inc. JUL/68. SW Toyota/Car Crafts Inc. OCT/80.
23  01 USCG JUL/68.
24  N536CS Campbell Soup Co. AUG/68. N4S Weyerhauser Co. MAY/74. N98G FEB/82.
25  N327K Ford Motor Co. SEP/68.
26  N328K Ford Motor Co. OCT/68. N202GA GAC JUL/81.
27  N1807Z Union Producing Co. SEP/68. Pennzoil Co. 1969.
28  N695ST Minneapolis Star & Tribune SEP/68. N700ST 1969. N7004T Coastal States Gas DEC/75. C-GCFB Canadian
    MoT NOV/76.
29  N869GA 1968. N930BS Bethlehem Steel Corp. NOV/68. N919G Western Electric International Inc. JAN/78.
30  N870GA 1968. N788S Signal Companies 1969. N2601 Mobil Oil Corp. JAN/71. N2607 AUG/81.
31  N1621 Texaco Inc. NOV/68.
32  N7602 Union Oil Co. of Ca. DEC/68. 2B conversion 1982.
33  N1624 Texaco Inc. DEC/68.
34  N230E American Can Co. OCT/68. N130A 1969. N11SX Saxon Oil/G-34 Corp. DEC/80. VR-CBM ARAVCO SEP/82.
35  N1004T Time Inc. DEC/68. N830TL Time-Life JAN/69.
36  N26L Square D Co. N26LA Omni JAN/77. N5400G Oster Corp. MAY/77. Sunbeam Corp. JUN/79. 2B Conversion
    1982. GAC SEP/82.
37  N179AR ARCO MAR/69.
38  N80A U S Steel Corp. JAN/69.
39  N80Q U S Steel Corp. JAN/69. N8000 Northrop Corp. AUG/78. N401HR International Harvester/Harco Leasing
    DEC/79. N124BN Burlington Northern Inc. SEP/82.
40  N1040 Cox Enterprises/Dayton Newspapers Inc. JAN/69. N1039 Omni SEP/80. Dantata Nigeria JUL/81.
41  N38N Union Carbide Corp. JAN/69.
42  N8000J Northrop Corp. JAN/69.
43  N17583 1969. F-BRUY Prince Aga Khan, Paris JAN/69. N84X Page AvJet Corp. JUL/82. McGraw-Edison Co.
    AUG/82.
44  N841GA 1969. N830G CONOCO Inc. FEB/69.
45  N815GA 1969. N711R E Cockrell Jr. FEB/69. Cockrell Estate AUG/72. PK-PJG Pertamina Petroleum/Robin Air,
    Singapore JAN/73. N152RG Robin Loh, Singapore 1975. N215RL R Loh/Ednasa Air Inc. JAN/77. VR-BHA FEB/80.
    N115GA GAC OCT/80. N40CE Dept. of the Army FEB/81.
46  N806CC Chrysler Corp. FEB/69. N40CC Carrier Corp/Bryant Air Conditioning AUG/73. Union Pacific Railroad
    JUN/74. N111RF Robert Fisher MAY/75. C-GSLK Kaiser Resources Ltd. NOV/75. N9272K Ceasars World OCT/81.
    N721CP JAN/82.
47  N803GA 1969. Grumman Demo. N35JM Johns-Manville Corp. 1971. N553MD Mike Davis/Tiger Oil MAY/77. N809GA
    GAC APR/78. N809LS Lear Siegler Inc. DEC/79.
48  N109G Gulf Oil Corp. APR/69. N4411 Texas Eastern  Transmission Corp. AUG/68.
49  N871GA 1969. N747G National Gypsum Co. NOV/69.
50  N39N Union Carbide Corp. MAY/69.
51  N2013M Monsanto Chemical Co. APR/69.
52  C-FFNM Falconbridge Nickel Mines Ltd. OCT/69.
53  N107A ARAMCO Saudi Arabia APR/69.
54  N123H Hilton Hotels MAY/69. C-FNOR Noranda Mines Ltd. SEP/73.
55  N875GA 1969. N225SF Standard Oil Co. of Ca. JUN/69.
56  N1OXY Occidental Petroleum/OXY MAY/69. N2OXY JUL/80. N105Y NOV/80.
57  N876GA 1969. N770AC American Cyanamid Co. JUL/69. Auxiliary Carrier Inc. FEB/79.
58  N878GA 1969. N720Q IBM Corp. OCT/69. W/O Kline, SC. 24/JUN/74.
59  N879GA 1969. N1823D Champion Spark Plug Co. AUG/69.
60  N892GA 1969. N500J Johnson & Johnson AUG/69. W/O Ingalls Field, Hot Springs, Va. 26/SEP/76.
61  N18N A D Davis/Winn Dixie Stores JUL/69. N711MM McLean Securities Inc. JUL/69.
62  N834GA 1969. N372CM Cordelia Scaife May DEC/69. N372GM 1976. N1PG Procter & Gamble Co. FEB/77. N3ZO
    APR/81. N7PG DEC/81.
63  N835GA 1969. N238U Combustion Engineering Inc. AUG/69. N239P APR/82.
64  N836GA 1969. N940BS Bethlehem Steel Corp. 1969. N950BS JAN/76. N341NS National Steel Corp. JUN/76.
65  N837GA 1969. N720E IBM Corp. SEP/69.
66  N838GA 1969. N720F IBM Corp. SEP/69.
67  N839GA 1969. N711S Cal-Jet/Frank Sinatra SEP/69. Connex Press JAN/73. Omni DEC/73. EL-WRT Govt. of
    Liberia JAN/74. N1OHR Omni NOV/75. N4OOJD John Deere & Co. DEC/75.
68  N308EL Eli Lilly International Corp. SEP/69.
69  N69G NGC Amusement Corp. SEP/69. N25JM Johns Manville Corp. JAN/71. N33CR Deutsch Co/C Rittenberry 1974.
    N45JM Johns-Manville Corp. JUL/76. N45Y FEB/81.
70  N711SC Southland Corp. OCT/69.
71  N4CP Chas Pfizer & Co. OCT/69. N4CQ Golden Nuggett Inc. JUL/78. N711SW 1980. N907SW APR/82.
72  N397F Faberge Inc. OCT/69. W/O Burlington, Vt. 22/FEB/76.
73  N116K Bank of America/Kaiser Industries NOV/69. N555CS Bank of America JAN/76.
74  N845GA 1969. N111AC Ambassador College/Worldwide Church of God NOV/69.
75  N823GA 1969. N1000 Swiflite/Cities Service Oil JUL/70. N100AC Luqa Inc/Charter Oil Co. AUG/72. N100CC
    SEP/72. N600CS Coastal States Gas DEC/76. N760U Union Oil Co. of Ca. APR/77.


127

775 N804GA 1969. demo. N13GW Gulf & Western Industries Inc. FEB/72.
76  N711LS Lear Siegler Inc. DEC/69. N227G PHH Leasing Inc/W R Grace & Co. OCT/71. N227GL Mobil Saudi Arabia Inc. JUN/82.
77  N824GA 1969. N100WK Wayfarer Ketch/Rockefeller JAN/70. N40CH Chase Manhattan Bank JUN/79.
78  N17585 1969. PH-FJP N V Philips JUL/70. C-FIOT Imperial Oil FEB/72.
79  N826GA 1970. N719GA Humble Oil & Refining Co. JAN/70. Exxon Corp. OCT/72.
80  N827GA 1970. Pittsburgh Plate Glass Industries Inc. MAY/70
81  N777SW Seagram's Whisky FEB/70. N44MD Mike Davis Oil Co. JAN/76.
82  N711DP AFLC/Mid Western Airlines FEB/70. N10LB Lindner Bros. JAN/71. N9040 International Brotherhood of Teamsters MAR/72. N600B OCT/72.
83  N404M Martin-Marietta Corp. FEB/70. N409M AUG/79.
84  N5101 General Motors Corp. MAR/70.
85  N5102 General Motors Corp. MAR/70. Lease RDAF FEB/81-AUG/81.
86  N880GA 1970 N179T Texas Eastern Transmission Corp. SEP/70.
87  Built as C/n 775.
88  N881GA 1970. N2600 Mobil Oil Corp. SEP/70. N2637M JUL/81. Natascha Estab. Vaduz OCT/81.
89  N882GA 1970. N100A Esso Air Inc. JUL/70. Exxon Corp. OCT/72.
90  N883GA 1970. N7789 Dresser Industries Inc. JUL/70.
91  N17586 1970. G-AYMI Rio Tinto Zinc Ltd. JUL/70. VH-ASM Associated Airlines APR/72.
92  N884GA 1970. N300L Triangle Publications Inc. JUL/70. N300U Southern Natural Service Co. Inc. APR/81. N114HC JUL/81.
93  N885GA 1970. N8785R JUL/70. TJ-AAK Govt. of Cameroun OCT/70. W/O Yaounde, Cameroun 22/APR/71.
94  N886GA 1970. N200A Esso Air Inc. JUL/70. Exxon Corp. OCT/72.
95  N887GA 1970. VH-ASG Associated Airlines APR/71.
96  N888GA 1970. N100KS Kinney Services/General Transportation Co. JUN/71. N100WC Warner Communications OCT/71. N75WC JUN/72. N75SR AUG/77. XC-MEX Bank of Mexico SEP/77.
97  N889GA 1970. I-SMEG Soc. VIP-Air SEP/71. N66TF Omni MAR/78. N11AL Allegheny Ludlum Industries APR/78. Emra Corp. JAN/82.
98  N850GA 1970. N93M W L McKnight/3M Co. MAR/71. N955H Honeywell Inc. JUN/75.
99  N851GA 1971. N99GA Greyhound Armour & Co. AUG/71.
100 N852GA 1970. N4000X Xerox Corp. NOV/71. N400CX Skybird Aviation Inc. JAN/82.
101 N853GA 1970. N1159K R Kroc/McDonald's Hamburgers AUG/71. WOTAN America Inc. NOV/80. N237LM JAN/82.
102 N854GA 1971. N88AE National Express Co. Inc. JUN/71.
103 N885GA 1971. N801GA Grumman demo MAR/72. G-BDMF Rolls Royce (1971) Ltd. DEC/75. N833GA GAC MAY/80. P2-PNF Govt. of Papua New Guinea JAN/81. P2-PNG MAR/81.
104 N856GA 1971. N856W Travelers Corp. JAN/72.
105 N807GA 1971. N23M 3M Co. JAN/72.
106 N808GA 1971. N33M 3M Co. JAN/72.
107 N809GA 1971. N5113H Amerada Hess Corp. FEB/72.
108 N810GA 1972. N11UC Superior Oil Co. FEB/72. N60GG SEP/76. Alexander Dawson MAR/81. D H Braman AUG/81. Beckwith Machinery AUG/81. N600MB Mary Braman APR/82.
109 N811GA 1972. N679RW Coca Cola Co. MAR/72.
110 N814GA 1972. N500G Gannett Newspapers Inc. MAR/72. N200GN MAR/77. N200PB Page Inc. NOV/80. N21AM Airmark Corp. JAN/81.
111 N815GA 1972. N10LB Lindner Bros. APR/72. N13LB 1976. N765A ARAMCO JUN/76.
112 N816GA 1972. N102ML C V Starr & Co/American International Aviation Corp. AUG/72. Hensley-Schmidt Insurance Co/SENCO Inc. AUG/72. N457SW SEP/82.
116 N821GA 1972. 9M-ARR Govt. of Saba, East Malaysia OCT/72. N2OXY Occidental Petroleum/OXY MAY/77. N23W First Security Bank of Utah/Hooker Chemicals APR/78.
117 N822GA 1972. N580RA Rapid American/View Top Corp. SEP/72. N888SW 1975.
118 N823GA 1972. N399CB First National City Bank OCT/72. Film Properties Inc. AUG/81.
119 N824GA 1972. TU-VAF Govt. of Ivory Coast NOV/72. N825GA GAC MAR/80. C-FHBX Hudson's Bay Oil & Gas JAN/81. N29910 Sheraton Inns Inc. APR/82. N60HJ AUG/82.
120 N825GA 1972. N901BM Bristol Myers Co. JAN/73.
121 N200P National Distillers & Chemical Corp. DEC/72.
122 N832GA 1972. N429JX Dana Corp. APR/73. N4290X OCT/76. GAC AUG/81. N61SM Smith International Inc. FEB/82.
123 N805CC 1973. Chrysler Corp. MAR/73. N345CP G-11 Corp/Allen & Co. AUG/81. 711 Aviation/Columbia Pictures DEC/81.
124 N834GA 1973. HB-IEW Aztec SA. AUG/73. VR-BGO Sioux Corp/Livanos MAY/77. N203GA GAC MAY/81. 0004 Venezuelan AF. AUG/81.
125 N870GA 1973. N367G GEC Corp. APR/73.
126 N43M 3M Co. APR/73.
127 N17581 1973. TR-KHB Govt. of Gabon APR/73. W/O Ngaoundere, Nr. Yaounde, Cameroun 6/FEB/80.
128 N73M 3M Co. JUN/73.
129 N871GA 1973. N1H Harrahs' Club NOV/73.
130 N872GA 1973. N127V El Paso Natural Gas Co. JUL/73.
131 N17582 1973. 9M-ATT Govt. of Sabah, East Malaysia FEB/74. N759A ARAMCO JUN/76.

132 N873GA 1973. N400M Fluor Corp. AUG/73.
133 N17583 1973. N88906 Page Gulfstream AUG/73. 5X-UPF Govt. of Uganda MAR/74.
134 N806CC Chrysler Corp. AUG/73. C-FROC Ranger Oil (Canada) Ltd. JAN/81.
135 N83M 3M Co. OCT/73.
136 N874GA 1973. N65M Motorola Corp. OCT/73. ZS-JIS Anglo American Corp. FEB/75. 3D-AAC Swaziland Iron Ore
    Development Corp. JUN/75. Peak Timber Sales (Pty) Ltd. 1981.
137 N875GA 1973. N1875P Prudential Insurance Co. NOV/73.
138 N6JW Jim Walter Corp. DEC/73.
139 N880GA 1973. N18N A D Davis/Winn Dixie Stores/G-11 International DEC/73. HZ-PET Petromin/Mobil Oil,
    Saudi Arabia MAY/80.
140 N881GA 1974. C-GTWO International Nickel/INCO Ltd & ALCAN Ltd. JUN/74.
141 N17584 1974. JA8431 JCAB, Tokyo. JUN/74.
142 N882GA 1974. N6OCC Carrier Corp. AUG/74. N5RD RDC Marine Inc. FEB/81.
143 N883GA 1974. N334 J W Galbreath AUG/74. N204C CONOCO Inc. OCT/80.
144 N17585 1974. HB-ITR Tiny Rowland/Lonair SA/Lonrho Ltd. AUG/74.
145 N894GA 1974. N871D Diamond International Corp. MAY/74. I T & T Corp. 1978. N871E FEB/80.
146 N897GA 1974. N946NA NASA Shuttle Trainer MAY/74.
147 N898GA 1974. N947NA NASA Shuttle Trainer JUN/74.
148 N710MR MARCOR JUN/74. N710MP FEB/77. N2615 Mobil Saudi Arabia Inc. MAR/78.
149 N896GA 1974. N17586 JUL/74. 5V-TAA Govt. of Lome NOV/74. W/O Lome, Togo 27/DEC/74.
150 N803GA 1974. N966H Prulease Inc/Honeywell Inc. OCT/74.
151 N804GA 1974. N979RA Ogden American Corp. OCT/74.
152 N17587 1974. XA-FOU Jet Ejecutivos/Televisa SA. OCT/74.
153 N881GA 1974. N23A Superior Oil Co. FEB/75.
154 N1625 Texaco Inc. DEC/74.
155 N308A ARAMCO DEC/74.
156 N806GA 1974. N400SJ Seward Johnson JAN/75. N7000G Ashland Oil Inc. JUL/79. N16NK Castor Trading Co.
    FEB/82.
157 N805GA 1975. N914BS Bethlehem Steel Corp. FEB/75. N940BS FEB/75.
158 N76CS Chessie Services Inc. MAR/75.
159 N345UP Union Pacific Corp. MAR/75.
160 N8OJ U S Steel Corp. APR/75.
161 N17589 1975. XA-ABC Aviones Banco Comercio AUG/75. XC-FEZ Comision Federal de Electricidad DEC/80.
    XC-CFE AUG/81.
162 (C-GANE) 1975. N530SW Studebaker Worthington JAN/76. N74RV Tripco Inc. JUN/78. C-GTCB Trans Canada
    Pipeline MAY/80.
163 N17581 1975. (YV-60CP) CEDICA DEC/75. PJ-ABA Cia Aerea del Caribe/CEDICA FEB/76. N117JJ Gavilan
    Corp/CEDICA DEC/77.
164 N17582 1975. 9K-ACX Sheikh Zayed, UAE DEC/75. A6-HHZ 1976.
165 N810GA 1975. N7000C Cargill Inc. JUL/75. N788C Jet Aviation of America Inc. MAR/82.
166 N811GA 1975. N515KA Kirby Leasing/Alghanim/Star Jet Corp. NOV/75. N66AL Allegheny International Credit
    Corp. AUG/81. N84AL SEP/82.
167 N17583 1975. 5V-TAC Govt. of Togo JAN/76. VR-CBC Continental Dynamics NOV/81. N204GA GAC/Santa Fe Air
    Transport Inc. DEC/81. N900SF MAR/82.
168 N812GA 1975. N1OLB Lindner Bros. AUG/75.
169 N17584 1975. HB-IEX Interjet AG/Helmut Horten, Seestern Spedition AG/Private Jet Services MAR/76.
170 N991GA 1975. N14PC Pepsico Inc. NOV/75.
171 N17585 1975. HZ-AFH Saudia MAY/76.
172 N804GA 1975. N903G Owens Illinois Inc. NOV/75.
173 N801GA 1975. Tip tank development aircraft. XC-PET PEMEX 1979.
174 N805GA 1975. N401M Fluor Corp. DEC/75.
175 N17586 1975. HZ-AFG Saudia AUG/76.
176 N806GA 1976. N176P Pittston Corp. JAN/76.
177 N17587 1976. 5N-AGV Govt. of Nigeria NOV/76.
178 N819GA 1976. N390F Faberge Inc. APR/76.
179 N17588 1976. HZ-CAD Saudi Civil Aviation Directorate DEC/76. HZ-PCA 1978.
180 N859GA 1976. N329K Ford Motor Co. APR/76.
181 N860GA 1976. N24DS Diamond Shamrock Corp. OCT/76. N924DS DEC/81.
182 N17589 1976. CN-ANL Govt. of Morocco APR/77.
183 N17581 1976. A40-AA Govt. of Oman NOV/76.
184 N861GA 1976. N80E U S Steel Corp. NOV/76.
185 N862GA 1976. N372CM Cordelia Scaife May JUL/76. N372GM NOV/81. Cameron Iron Works FEB/82. N3E SEP/82.
186 N17582 1976. (D-ACVG) D-AFKG Friedrich Flick Gmbh AUG/76. 5N-AML Al Hadji Deribe JAN/82.
187 N17583 1976. N804GA AUG/76. HZ-ADC Raytheon Middle East Systems/Air Defence Command SEP/77.
188 N833GA 1976. N862G General Dynamics Corp. SEP/76. N662G allocated JAN/81.
189 N333AR ARCO SEP/76.
190 N130K American Can Co. SEP/76. N159B Carter Hawley Hale Stores FEB/82.
191 N810GA 1976. N680RW Coca Cola Co. OCT/76.

```
192   N811GA 1976. N678RW Coca Cola Co. OCT/76.
193   N808GA 1976. N26L Square D Co. NOV/76.
194   N17584 1976. HB-IMW ATES/Count Agusta DEC/76. C6-BEJ Chartair DEC/81.
195   N212K 195 Broadway Corp. DEC/76. N71TP Tesoro Petroleum NOV/80.
196   N400J Johnson & Johnson JAN/77.
197   N800GA 1977. N5117H Amerada Hess Corp. JAN/77.
198   N825GA 1977. N365G GEC Corp. FEB/77.
199   N829GA 1977. N75WC Warner Communications/General Transportation Corp. MAR/77. N75RP AUG/78. N74RP
      JUL/81.
200   N826GA 1977. N1806P Colgate Palmolive Co. NOV/77. N135CP FEB/81.
201   N17585 1977. HZ-AFI Saudia DEC/77.
202   N17586 1977. A9C-BG Govt. of Bahrain FEB/78.
203   N17587 1977. HZ-AFJ Saudia DEC/77.
204   N17588 1977. G-CXMF Gulfstream Investments Ltd. CI. AUG/78.
205   N25UG United Gas Pipeline Co. MAY/77.
206   N2PK Halcon Scientific Design Group Inc. JUN/77. Listowel Corp. SEP/82
207   N700PM Philip Morris Inc. SEP/77.
208   N808GA 1977. N62CB St. Louis Southwestern Railway Co. SEP/77.
209   N806GA 1977. N277T Trunkline Gas Co. AUG/77.
210   HB-IEY Petrolair, Athens MAY/78.
211   N17581 1978. VR-BGT Ditco Air Ltd/Sheikh El Khereiji MAY/78.
212   N807GA 1978. N551MD Mike Davis/Tiger Oil MAY/78.
213   N1707Z Pennzoil NOV/77.
214   N17588 1978. G-BSAL Shell Aircraft Ltd. JUL/78.
215   N816GA 1978. N748MN Merle Norman Cosmetics Inc. JAN/78.
216   HB-IEZ Sit Set AG/Aeroleasing/Intermaritime Service 1978. N63SD Luna Films JUN/78. Pan Eastern Corp.
      NOV/78. N200RG Reliance Group MAR/79.
217   N88GA Armour & Co. 1978.
218   TU-VAC Govt. of Ivory Coast AUG/78.
219   N84V El Paso Natural Gas MAR/78. VR-BJD Joc Oil/Transworld Oil AUG/79.
220   N805GA 1978. N404M Martin Marietta Corp. JUN/79.
221   N575SF Standard Oil Co. of Ca. APR/78.
222   N817GA 1978. N5253A CBS Inc. AUG/78.
223   N510US U S Gypsum Co. AUG/78.
224   N17584 1978. N810GA 1978. N631SC Stauffer Chemical Co. NOV/78.
225   N17585 1978. G-BGLT The Marconi Co. Ltd. MAY/79. N55922 FEB/80. N289K Crawford Fitting Co. MAR/80.
226   N1902P J C Penney JUL/78.
227   N818GA 1978. N1841D Dun & Bradstreet Corp. NOV/78.
228   N819GA United Brands/Air Services Transportation Co. NOV/78. (N700CQ). (N30B).
229   N821GA 1978. Sears Roebuck & Co. FEB/79.
230   N17586 1978. 7T-VHB Govt. of Algeria JUL/79. W/O Iran 03/MAY/82.
231   N808GA 1978. N1102 Gould Inc. 1979. VR-CAG 231 Gulfstream Ltd/NOGA OCT/80. VR-BHD Nimex Co. Ltd JUL/81.
      N18RN NOGA/Chemco International Leasing Inc. AUG/81.
232   N806GA 1978. C-GDPB Dome Petroleum 1979.
233   N807GA 1978. Security Pacific National Bank FEB/79.
234   N808GA 1979. N910S Standard Oil Realty Corp. MAR/79.
235   N17581 1979. G-HADI Al Tajit Bank/Arab Express Ltd. JUL/79.
236   N812GA 1978. N2998 General Foods Corp. JUN/79.
237   N816GA 1979. N25BH Riley Stoker Co. JUL/79. US Filter Corp. DEC/81. XA-MIX Moctezuma Brewery FEB/82.
238   N831GA 1979. N335H Halliburton Co. JUL/79.
239   N17582 1979. HZ-AFK Saudia JAN/80.
240   5A-DDR Govt. of Libya DEC/79.
241   N830GA 1979. (N60TA) Tigerair Inc 1979. (N801GA). N90MD J Ray McDermott Inc. FEB/80.
242   5A-DDS Govt. of Libya JAN/80.
243   N119R R J Reynolds Inc. JAN/80.
244   N17584 1979. 9K-AEB Govt. of Kuwait JAN/80.
245   N829GA James Bath AUG/79. Emirates Air Service, UAE FEB/80.
246   N17587 1979. HB-IEZ Sit Set AG. NOV/79.
247   N828GA 1979. N888MC View Top Corp. SEP/79. C-GTEP Tele Direct Ltd. OCT/81.
248   N17589 1979. 9K-AEC Govt. of Kuwait MAR/80.
249   Gulfstream 3 Airframe.
250   N821GA 1979. N309EL Eli Lilly International Corp. DEC/79.
251   N944H Honeywell Inc. NOV/79.
252   Gulfstream 3 Airframe.
253   N15TG Texas Gas Transmission Corp. DEC/79.
254   N254AR ARCO FEB/80.
255   N442A ARAMCO Inc. FEB/80.
256   N17581 1980. HZ-MSD Armed Forces Medical Services SEP/80.
```

```
257    N822GA 1979. N872E I T & T Corp. JAN/80.
258    N823GA 1979. N301EC Household Finance Corp. JAN/80.
```

GULFSTREAM 3

```
249    N300GA roll-out 21/SEP/79. N901GA Ff 2/DEC/79. F-249 R Danish AF. JAN/82.
252    (N777SL) NOV/80. N17582 NOV/80. XA-MEY Aviones B.C. 1981.
300    N300GA 1980. Alexander Dawson Inc. MAR/81. Bristol Myers Co. APR/82.
301    N100P National Distillers & Chemical Co. 1980.
302    N302GA 1980. N62GG Superior Oil Co. JUL/80.
303    N300GA 1980. N303GA GAC JUN/80. TU-VAF Govt. of Ivory Coast 1981.
304    N17583 1980. HZ-NR2 Rashid Engineering JUN/81.
305    N305GA 1980. N235U Combustion Engineering DEC/80.
306    N306GA 1980. N777SW Seagram's Whiskey DEC/80.
307    N17584 1980. C-GSBR Denison Mines Ltd. SEP/81.
308    N717A ARAMCO OCT/80.
309    N18LB ACSC Inc/Lind Air Inc. DEC/80. ACSC/United Dairy Farmers Inc. NOV/81.
310    N719A ARAMCO OCT/80.
311    N17585 1980. HZ-AFL Saudia MAY/81.
312    N304GA 1980. N100GN Gannett Inc. APR/81.
313    F-313 R Danish AF. APR/82.
314    N1040 Cox Enterprises Inc. OCT/80.
315    N315GA 1980. N2600 Mobil Oil Corp. SEP/81.
316    N316GA 1980. N2601 Mobil Oil Corp. SEP/81.
317    C-GKRL Kaiser Resources Ltd. SEP/81. N344GA GAC JUL/82. A6-CKZ Govt. of UAE OCT/82
318    N308GA 1980. N300L Triangle Publications MAY/81.
319    N319Z Dana Corp. AUG/81.
320    N873E I T & T Corp. 1981.
321    N3ORP CIT Corp. JUL/81. RCA Corp. DEC/81.
322    N130A American Can Co. FEB/81.
875    N333GA MAR/81. Gulf United Corp. MAR/82. N333GU OCT/82.
323    XA-MIC Aviones Televisa 1981.
324    HZ-AFM Saudia OCT/81.
325    N890 ALCOA 1981.
326    N17582 1981. TR-KHC Govt. of Gabon FEB/82
327    N7OPS American International Aviation Co. AUG/81.
328    N309GA 1981. N75RP General Transportation Corp. SEP/81.
329    N301GA 1981. N862G General Dynamics Corp. NOV/81.
330    F-330 R Danish AF.
331    N307GA 1981. N17LB Great American Insurance Co. NOV/81. HZ-RC3 Royal Commission AUG/82.
332    N310GA 1981. N77TG Texasgulf Aviation Inc. DEC/81.
333    N600PM Philip Morris Inc. NOV/81.
334    N1PG Procter & Gamble Co. NOV/81.
335    HB-IMX Sit Set AG. MAY/82.
336    N3PG Procter & Gamble Co. NOV/81.
337    N456SW Sentry Insurance Co. NOV/81. Pittway Corp. SEP/82
338    N862GA 1981. N372CM Cordelia Scaife May NOV/81.
339    N302GA 1981. Bank of America DEC/81. N522SB JUL/82.
340    F-GDHK Prince Aga Khan, Paris. JUL/82.
341    N263C Conoco Inc. DEC/81.
342    N441A ARMCO Steel Corp. DEC/81.
343    N305GA 1981. N664P Phillips Petroleum Co. MAR/82.
344    N306GA 1981. Cargill Inc. MAR/82. N7000C AUG/82.
345    G-BSAN Shell Aviation Ltd.
346    HZ-RH2 Saudi Oger Ltd. SEP/82.
```

HS 125 SRS 700

```
7001        G-BEFZ HSA demo NOV/76. McAlpine Aviation JAN/79. VR-HIM McAlpine Aviation (Asia) Ltd. 1979.
            G-BEFZ McAlpine Aviation JAN/81.
7002/NA0201 G-5-20 1977. N700HS Business Jet Aviation Co. JUN/77. HSA Inc. FEB/78. N4OWB Warner
            Brothers/General Transportation Corp. APR/78. N4OGT DEC/78.
7003/NA0202 G-5-19 1977. G-BERP BAe APR/77. N64688 Pacific Systems Inc. JUN/77. N333ME Morgan Equipment
            JAN/78.
```

7004/NAO218 G-BGDM Wavertree Ltd. AUG/77. G-5-15 HSA for 'A' conversion SEP/77. N37975 SEP/77. N222RB Reading
& Bates OCT/77.
7005/NAO203 G-BERV 1977. N620M Olin Corp. JUN/77.
7006/NAO204 G-5-18 1977. G-BERX HSA APR/77. N724B Blount Inc. JUL/77.
7007 HB-VFA Chartag, Zurich NOV/77.
7008/NAO205 G-5-11 1977. (G-BEWV) HSA JUL/77. C-GYYZ Gulf Oil JUL/77. Alberta Gas Trunkline Ltd. SEP/78.
7009/NAO206 G-5-12 1977. G-BEYC HSA JUL/77. N813H Hughes Aircraft Co. AUG/77.
7010 (G-5-16) 1977. HZ-MMM Sheikh Al Midani NOV/77.
7011/NAO207 G-5-13 1977. G-BFAJ HSA AUG/77. N255CT Caterpillar Tractor SEP/77.
7012/NAO208 G-5-14 1977. G-BFBI HSA SEP/77. N125HS HSA Inc/Business Jet Aviation Co. OCT/77. N700HS BAe Inc.
FEB/78. N162A AMF Inc. DEC/78.
7013 G-CBBI Barclays Bank International NOV/77. 'A' Conversion AUG/81. N219JA Storage Technology SEP/81.
7014/NAO209 G-5-17 1977. G-BFDW HSA OCT/77. N46901 GATX Third Aircraft Corp. NOV/77. N120GA AUG/78. N6OMS
Melvin Simon & Associates MAR/79.
7015/NAO210 G-5-18 1977. G-BFFL HSA NOV/77. N37P Nationwide Transport Inc. NOV/77.
7016/NAO216 G-BFFH 1977. N72505 Western Leasing Co. DEC/77. N8OOCB NOV/78.
7017/NAO211 G-5-19 1977. G-BFFU HSA DEC/77. N62MS Melvin Simon & Associates DEC/77.
7018/NAO212 G-BFGU 1977. N733H HAC Inc. DEC/77. Humana Inc. OCT/78.
7019/NAO213 (G-BFGV) 1977. N37OM Murphy Oil Corp. DEC/77.
7020 (G-BFTP) 1978. (G-BFVN) Finnamet Ltd. 1978. G-EFPT MAM/Castolin Eutectic Institute/Save Energy
Services Ltd. JUL/78. VR-BHE Air St. George Ltd. Bermuda MAR/81. N2634B JAN/82.
7021/NAO214 N34CH Cutler Hammer Inc. JAN/78. Eaton Corp. JUN/79. Kimberly-Clark Corp. 1980. N1868M
Metropolitan Life Insurance Co. OCT/81.
7022 (G-5-11) 1978. F-GASL Ste. Schlumberger MAR/78.
7023/NAO215 G-BELF 1978. N54555 Garrett AiResearch MAR/78. N125GP 1978.
7024/NAO217 G-BFLG 1978. N94BD Dillard Department Stores MAR/78.
7025 (G-5-12) 1978. G-BFPI McAlpine Aviation APR/78. VR-HIN McAlpine Aviation (Asia) Ltd/Neptunia 1979.
G-BFPI McAlpine Aviation JAN/81.
7026/NAO219 G-BFMO 1978. N1230A Uni Royal Inc. MAR/78. N572BC Berwind Corp. SEP/80.
7027/NAO220 G-BFMP 1978. C-GPPS Pacific Petroleum APR/78.
7028 G-BFSO De Beers International/Dravidian Air Services Ltd. MAY/78.
7029/NAO221 N465R Gulf Resources & Chemical Corp. MAY/78.
7030/NAO222 G-BFSI 1978. C-GSCL Shell Canada Ltd. MAY/78.
7031 G-BFSP De Beers International/Dravidian Air Services Ltd. JUN/78.
7032/NAO223 G-BFUE 1978. N700BA BAe Inc. JUN/78. N354WC Williams Companies DEC/78.
7033/NAO224 N5OJM Johns-Manville Corp. JUN/78. N5OTN DEC/80.
7034 G-5-14 1978. G-BFXT Coca Cola Exporting Co. OCT/78.
7035/NAO225 G-5-16 1978. N36NP Nationwide Mutual Insurance Co. JUL/78.
7036/NAO226 G-5-17 1978. N6OJM Johns Manville Corp. JUL/78. N6OTN DEC/80.
7037 G-5-18 1978. G-BFVI Bristows Helicopters Ltd. AUG/78.
7038/NAO227 G-5-19 1978. N1OCZ Congoleum Inc. JUL/78.
7039/NAO228 G-5-11 1978. N555CB Cleveland Bros. Equipment Co. AUG/78.
7040 HZ-RC1 Saudi Parsons/Royal Commission NOV/78.
7041/NAO229 G-5-12 1978. N700BB BAe Inc. SEP/78. N4OONW Northwest Industries Inc.
7042/NAO230 G-5-13 1978. N36OX Pan Handle Eastern Pipeline Co. SEP/78.
7043/NAO232 (G-5-15) 1978. G-BFYV BAe SEP/78. N9OOCC Luqa Inc. NOV/78. N3OOLD Lendee Co. SEP/82
7044/NAO231 G-BFYH 1978. N35D Florida Gas Transmission Co. OCT/78.
7045 G-BFZJ 1978. N130BA BAe Inc. FEB/79. N700HH Hilton Hotels Corp. JUN/79.
7046 4W-ACE Shaher Traders, Cairo DEC/78.
7047/NAO233 G-BFZI 1978. C-GABX Alberta Gas Trunkline/NOVA NOV/78.
7048/NAO234 G-5-16 1978. N711YP L M Berry & Co/Yellow Pages NOV/78.
7049/NAO239 G-5-17 1978. G-BGBL BAe NOV/78. N33BK B K Johnson/Chaparrosa Aircraft Inc. DEC/78.
7050/NAO235 G-5-18 1978. N7OOGB BAe Inc. DEC/78. N1OC Dennis O'Connor MAY/79.
7051/NAO236 G-5-11 1978. N7OOUK BAe Inc. JAN/79. N14JA J A Jones Construction Co. MAY/79.
7052/NAO237 G-5-19 1978. G-BGBJ BAe Inc. OCT/78. N737X John T Dorrance DEC/78.
7053/NAO238 G-5-20 1978. N7OOAR BAe Inc. JAN/79. N33CP Colonial Penn Group MAR/79.
7054 C6-BET Norwest SA Ltd. Bahamas JUN/79.
7055 G-5-16 1979. HZ-RC2 Saudi Parsons/Royal Commission MAY/79.
7056/NAO241 N7OONT BAe Inc. JAN/79. N492CB Crocker National Bank MAR/79.
7057/NAO242 G-5-14 1979. N7OOUR BAe Inc. FEB/79. N6OHJ Sheraton Inns Inc. AUG/79. C-GPCC Pancanadian
Petroleum Ltd. AUG/82
7058/NAO245 G-5-15 1979. N125HS BAe Inc. FEB/79. N700BA AUG/79. N354WC The Williams Companies OCT/79.
7059/NAO243 G-5-17 1979. N130BH BAe Inc. MAR/79. N20S Storer Broadcasting Co. MAY/79.
7060/NAO244 G-5-18 1979. N130BG BAe Inc. MAR/79. N1103 Gould Inc. JUN/79.
7061 G-5-19 1979. G-BGGS BAe MAY/79. G-OJOY H Goodman OCT/81.
7062 G-5-16 1979. HB-VGF Bosch GmbH. Stuttgart SEP/79.
7063/NAO246 G-5-20 1979. N130BB BAe Inc. APR/79. N79HC Harsco Corp. JUN/79.
7064 HZ-NAD NADCO, Saudi Arabia JUN/79.

7065/NAO247 G-5-11 1979. N130BC BAe Inc. MAY/79. N30PR P R Rutherford Oil JUL/79.
7066/NAO248 G-5-13 1979. G-BGSR BAe 1979. C-GKCI Irving Oil DEC/79.
7067        HZ-DA1 Dallah-AVCO DEC/79. N9113J Atlantic Aviation OCT/81. N115RS FEDEX SEP/82.
7068/NAO249 G-5-14 1979. N130BD BAe Inc. JUL/79. N31LG Landis Tool Co. SEP/79.
7069/NAO250 G-5-15 1979. N130BE BAe Inc. 1979. N29GP Genuine Parts Co. 1979.
7070        HS-VGG Bosch GmbH. Stuttgart 1979.
7071/NAO251 G-5-17 1979. N130BF BAe Inc. JUL/79. N514B Burroughs Corp. JUL/79.
7072/NAO252 G-5-18 1979. N700HS BAe Inc. AUG/79. N900MR Moore McCormack Resources Inc. OCT/80.
7073        G-5-12 1979. G-BGTD Rank Xerox (UK) Ltd. NOV/79.
7074/NAO253 G-5-19 1979. N422X Field Crest Mills.
7075/NAO254 G-5-13 1980. (G-BHKF) 1980. N125AM BAe Inc. APR/80. N125TR ARCO MAR/81.
7076        G-5-17 1979. 7Q-YJI Govt. of Malawi DEC/79. MAAW-J1 Malawi Army Air Wing JAN/80.
7077/NAO255 G-5-14 1979. N125AJ BAe Inc. NOV/79. N540B Jucamcyn Theaters Corp. JAN/80.
7078/NAO256 G-5-15 1979. N125AK BAe Inc. DEC/79. N571CH Chemed Corp. JAN/80.
7079/NAO256 G-5-16 1979. XA-JIX SARSA DEC/79.
7080/NAO257 G-5-18 1979. N125HS BAe Inc. DEC/79. N611MC May Department Stores Co. MAR/80.
7081/NAO258 G-5-19 1979. (N125AM) 1979. N711CU The Carborundum Co. DEC/79.
7082        IAC238 Irish Govt. FEB/80.
7083/NAO259 G-5-12 1980. N125AH BAe Inc. JAN/80. N100Y Purolator Inc. MAR/80.
7084/NAO260 G-5-14 1980. N130BK BAe Inc. JAN/80. N202CH Crouse Hinds Co. MAR/80.
7085        G-5-15 1980. G-BHIO McAlpine Aviation (Asia) Ltd/San Miguel Corp. Philippines MAR/80. RP-C1714 1980.
7086/NAO261 G-5-17 1980. N125AL BAe Inc. MAR/80. N277CT Caterpillar Tractor Co. MAY/80.
7087/NAO262 G-5-14 1980. (N130BL) 1980. C-GKRS Kaiser Resources Ltd. FEB/80. British Columbia Coal JAN/81. N3234S ComAir Inc. SEP/82
7088        HZ-DA2 Dallah-AVCO MAR/80.
7089/NAO263 G-5-18 1980. N130BL BAe Inc. FEB/80. N151AE Aetna Life Corp. APR/80.
7090/NAO264 G-5-19 1980. N299CT Caterpillar Tractor Co. MAR/80.
7091        G-BHLF GEC-Marconi/McAlpine Aviation APR/80.
7092/NAO265 G-5-20 1980. N733M HAC-Humana Inc. MAR/80.
7093/NAO266 G-5-11 1980. G-BHMP BAe FEB/80. C-GBRM Gulf Oil Canada NOV/80.
7094        G-OBAE BAe demo MAY/80.
7095/NAO267 G-5-12 1980. N125L BAe Inc. APR/80. N215G Grace Natural Resources Corp. MAR/81.
7096/NAO276 G-5-14 1980. XA-KEW SARSA Mexico MAY/80. W/O 2/MAY/81 Norte, Monterrey, Mexico.
7097        (G-BHTJ) 1980. G-HHOI Trust House Forte Ltd. JUL/80.
7098/NAO269 G-5-15 1980. N125Y BAe Inc. MAY/80. N89PP Pogo Producing Co. AUG/80.
7099/NAO270 G-5-16 1980. G-BHSK BAe JUN/80. C-GDAO Daon Development Corp. NOV/80.
7100        (G-5-19) 1980. D-CLVW Volkswagenwerke AG. AUG/80.
7101/NAO272 G-5-17 1980. N89PP BAe Inc. JUN/80. N109JM JMAC Inc. AUG/80.
7102/NAO280 G-5-18 1980. XA-KIS SARSA Mexico JUN/80.
7103        G-5-12 1980. G-BHSU Shell Aviation Ltd. SEP/80.
7104/NAO273 G-5-20 1980. N10PW Pennwalt Corp. JUL/80.
7105/NAO274 G-5-11 1980. (N125AB) 1980. N125BA BAe Inc. JUL/80. TigerAir Inc. MAR/81. N125TA FEB/82.
7106/NAO275 G-5-13 1980. N125V BAe Inc. AUG/80. N661JB Fuqua Industries Inc. OCT/80.
7107        G-BHSV Shell Aviation Ltd. OCT/80.
7108/NAO278 G-5-14 1980. XA-KON SARSA Mexico AUG/80.
7109        G-BHSW Shell Aviation Ltd OCT/80.
7110        G-5-15 1980. XA-KAC SARSA Mexico OCT/80.
7111/NAO277 G-5-16 1980. N125AF BAe Inc. SEP/80. N304K Ford Motor Co. NOV/80.
7112        D-CMVW Volkswagenwerke AG. OCT/80.
7113/NAO279 G-5-17 1980. N125AD BAe Inc. OCT/80. N204R Raytheon Co. FEB/81.
7114/NAO281 G-5-18 1980. N125AN BAe Inc. OCT/80. N533 Marion Corp. FEB/81.
7115        HZ-DA3 Dallah-AVCO DEC/80.
7116/NAO282 G-5-19 1980. N125AP BAe Inc. NOV/80. N1982G Ethyl Corp. FEB/81.
7117/NAO283 G-5-20 1980. N125AS BAe Inc. NOV/80. N90B Midland Ross Corp. FEB/81.
7118        (G-BIHZ) 1980. 5N-AVJ Nigerian National Oil Co. MAR/81.
7119/NAO284 G-5-11 1980. N125AE BAe Inc. DEC/80. N326K Ford Motor Co. MAR/81.
7120/NAO285 G-5-13 1980. N125AT BAe Inc. DEC/80. N40CN Champion International Corp. MAR/81.
7121/NAO286 G-5-14 1980. N125AU BAe Inc. DEC/80. N2OFX Twentieth Century Fox Films Corp. AR/81.
7122/NAO287 G-5-15 1980. N125U BAe Inc. JAN/81. N77LP Langham Petroleum MAR/81. N299FB Fisher Bros. Financial development Corp. JUN/82.
7123/NAO288 G-5-16 1981. N125AH BAe Inc. JAN/81. N700BW Borg Warner Leasing MAR/81.
7124        HZ-DA4 Dallah-AVCO MAR/81.
7125/NAO289 G-5-17 1981. N125AJ BAe Inc. FEB/81. N125CG Columbia Gas Systems APR/81.
7126/NAO290 G-5-18 1981. N700AC Perpetual Corp. MAR/81.
7127        G-TJCB JCB Excavators Ltd. MAR/81.
7128/NAO291 G-5-19 1981. N125BC BAe Inc. MAR/81. N126AR ARCO JUN/81.
7129/NAO292 G-5-20 1981. N125AK BAe Inc. MAR/81. N256EN MAPCO JUN/81. (N256MA) NOV/81. SOHIO JUL/82.

133

7130          G-DBBI Barclays Bank International APR/81.
7131/NA0293 G-5-11 1981. N700BA BAe Inc. demo MAR/81. N80G U S Steel FEB/82.
7132/NA0294 G-BIMY 1981. C-FIPG Interprovincial Pipeline Co. AUG/81.
7133          G-5-14 1981. LV-PMM YPF Argentina JUN/81. LV-ALW JUL/81.
7134/NA0295 G-5-13 1981. N871D Diamond International Corp. APR/81.
7135/NA0296 G-5-15 1981. N490MP WBD Associates MAY/81.
7136          G-BIRU Barclay Mercantile/MAM Aviation JUN/81.
7137/NA0297 G-5-16 1981. N125BD BAe Inc. JUN/81. N78CS Chessie Services Inc. AUG/81.
7138/NA0298 G-5-17 1981. N125G U S Steel JUL/81. N80K JAN/82.
7139          G-5-18 1981. (G-GAIL) 1981. G-BKAA Saudi Catering & Contracting SEP/81.
7140/NA0299 G-5-19 1981. N125BE BAe Inc. JUN/81. VR-BHH Caroana, Bermuda 1981.
7141/NA0300 G-5-20 1981. N70PM Philip Morris Inc. JUN/81. N80PM OCT/81.
7142          G-5-12 1981. G-BJDJ Consolidated Contractors Co. (based Athens) JUL/81.
7143/NA0325 G-5-20 1981. N700HA BAe Inc. JUL/81. N26H Halliburton Co. SEP/81.
7144/NA0326 G-5-11 1981. N522M Marathon Oil Co. AUG/81.
7145/NA0339 G-5-18 1981. N70FC First National Chicago Association/Emery Air Charter NOV/81. N711RL SEP/82.
7146/NA0301 G-5-13 1981. N700HB BAe Inc. SEP/81. (XA-    SARSA Mexico NOV/81). Polo Fashions Inc. FEB/82.
7147/NA0303 G-5-14 1981. N125P Philip Morris Inc. SEP/81. (N80PM) N70PM JAN/82.
7148/NA0304 G-5-17 1981. N700BB BAe Inc. SEP/81. VR-    Caroana, Bermuda 1981 .
7149/NA0302 G-5-19 1981. N700AA BAe Inc. OCT/81. XA-    SARSA Mexico 1981.
7150/NA0305 G-5-11 1981. N700HS BAe Inc. 1981.
7151          G-5-12 1981. N161MM Aircraft Associates/Berkshire Inn Inc. DEC/81.
7152/NA0306 (G-5-13) G-5-17 1981. N700DD BAe Inc. OCT/81. N270MH Manufacturers Hanover Leasing NOV/81.
7153/NA0313 G-5-14 1981. G-BJOW BAe OCT/81. XB-XKC Novedades Editores NOV/81.
7154/NA0307 G-5-18 1981. N700GG BAe Inc. NOV/81. N270MC Manufacturers Hanover Leasing NOV/81.
7155/NA0308 G-5-19 1981. N700KK BAe Inc. NOV/81. Texaco Inc. DEC/81. N162O FEB/82.
7156/NA0309 G-5-17 1981. N15AG Liggett Group/Amstar Corp. DEC/81.
7157/NA0310 G-5-20 1981. N700LL BAe Inc. DEC/81. Superior Oil JAN/82. N64GG FEB/82.
7158          G-5-14 1981. G-BJWB Opencity Ltd/McAlpine/Artoc FEB/82.
7159/NA0311 G-5-15 1982. N91Y Island Creek Coal JAN/82.
7160          G-5-19 1982. 5N-AVK Nigerian CAFU.
7161/NA0323 G-5-17 1982. N700RR BAe Inc. FEB/82. C-GZZX Canadian Superior Oil MAR/82.
7162/NA0312 G-5-18 1982. N700NN BAe Inc. FEB/82. N1896T New York Times Co. MAR/82.
7163          G-5-12 1982. 7T-VCW Algerian Met Research MAY/82.
7164/NA0314 G-5-11 1982. N152AE Aetna Life Corp. MAR/82.
7165/NA0315 G-5-14 1982. N869KM Colleen Corp. MAR/82.
7166          G-5-18 1982. F-BYFB Groupement International de Commerce JUN/82.
7167/NA0316 G-5-15 1982. N700PP BAe Inc. MAY/82. N125BA JUN/82.
7168/NA0317 G-5-20 1982. N700SS BAe Inc. APR/82.
7169          G-5-12 1982. (V4-SOA) VH-HSS Shell Aviation.
7170/NA0318 G-5-14 1982. N819M Standard Oil Co. MAY/82.
7171/NA0319 G-5-15 1982. N710BP BAe Inc. MAY/82. Mid Atlantic Leasing SEP/82
7172          5H-SMZ Zanzibar Govt. JUN/82. G-BKFS for delivery JUL/82. 5H-SMZ AUG/82.
7173/NA0320 G-5-17 1982. N710BN BAe Inc. JUN/82. N500LS Retail Leasing Corp. SEP/82


                              CANADAIR CHALLENGER


1001      C-GCGR-X Prototype. Ff 08/NOV/78. W/O Mojave, Ca. USA. 03/APR/80.
1002      C-GCGS-X MAR/79. Experimental.
1003      C-GCGT-X JUL/79. Experimental. Ff 10/APR/82 as CL601 with GEC CF-34 engines, redesignated C/N 3991.
1004      C-GXKQ-X SEP/79. Experimental.
1005      C-GBDH-X APR/80. N600CL ICOS Construction Corp. MAY/81.
1006      C-GCSN JUN/80. N110KS Kalair USA Corp. JUN/81.
1007      C-GBKC MAR/80. HZ-TAG TAG JUN/81. C-GBKC Canadair OCT/81. Canadian MOT FEB/82.
1008      C-GBEY JUL/80. MOT, Ottawa JUN/81.
1009      C-GBFY JUL/80. Winglet Prototype Ff 13/NOV/81.
1010      C-GCIB SEP/80. Canadian Imperial Bank JUL/81.
1011      C-GBHS JAN/81. N42137 Film Properties Inc. MAY/81. N510PC Pepsico Inc. MAR/82.
1012      C-GBKE MAR/81. N600KC K C Aviation Inc. MAY/81.
1013      C-GBHZ DEC/80. N2428 Owens Corning Fiberglass JUL/81.
1014      C-GBLL-X NOV/80. N97941 TAG SEP/81. HZ-TAG DEC/81.
1015      C-GBLN DEC/80. N37LB ASCS Inc. OCT/81. TAG Flight Ltd. MAR/82.
1016      C-GWRT APR/81. Sugra Ltd. FEB/82.
1017      C-GBPX MAY/81. N4247C TAG Aviation Inc. JUN/81. N777XX TAG/Aviation Methods JAN/82.
1018      C-GLWR JUN/81. N1812C Citiflight Inc. JUL/81.
1019      C-GLWT JUN/81. N9071M Hyatt Corp. SEP/81.

```
1020    C-GLWV 1981. N36LB ASCS Inc. SEP/81. N602CL Canadair USA Inc. NBAA SEP/82.
1021    C-GLWX 1981. N914X Xerox Corp. SEP/81.
1022    C-GLWY 1981. C-GOGO AUG/81. Ontario Ministry of Natural Resources JAN/82.
1023    C-GLXB 1981. N630M Olin Corp. OCT/81.
1024    C-GLXD 1981. N637ML Merrill Lynch Leasing JUN/81. Dacion Corp. DEC/81.
1025    C-GLXF 1981. N2636N GTE Service Corp. JAN/82. N111G FEB/82.
1026    C-GLXH 1981. N507CC Celanese Corp. NOV/81.
1027    C-GLXK 1981. N420L AVCO Financial Services Leasing Inc. NOV/81.
1028    C-GLXM 1981. HB-VHC Kontinair AG 1982.
1029    HB-VGA Air Charter AG. DEC/81.
1030    N1622 Texaco Inc. DEC/81.
1031    N620S Texasgulf Inc. DEC/81.
1032    N455SR St. Regis Paper Co. DEC/81. Drum Financial Corp. SEP/82
1033    N2642F Canadair Inc. JAN/82. TAG International AUG/82.
1034    N2634Y Southern Railway Co. DEC/81. N153SR FEB/82.
1035    N122TY Tyco Laboratories JAN/82.
1036    C-GBOQ FEB/82. N80AT Taubman Air Inc. MAR/82.
1037    N805C A E Staley Mfg. Co. FEB/82.
1038    N8010X Xerox Corp. FEB/82.
1039    N26440 FEB/82. Metropolitan Life Insurance Co. MAR/82.
1040    C-GLYM MAR/82.
1041    N733K HAC Inc. MAR/82.
1042    N770CA Valley Line Supply & Equipment Co. MAR/82.
1043    N229GC W R Grace & Co. MAR/82.
1044    N541MM Bowater North America Corp. MAR/82.
1045    N55PG Geosurvey International Inc. APR/82.
1046    C-GTXV Petro-Canada Explorations. APR/82.
1047    C-GLXH 1982. N2741Q JUN/82. N601WW Whitewind Co. Ltd. JUL/82.
1048    N29687 Clinton Aviation Group Inc. APR/82. N600TT Gulf States Oil & Refining JUN/82.
1049    N2720B Sandor Kvassay. APR/82.
1050    N600MK Morrison Knudsen Co. APR/82.
1051    C-GLXQ 1982. N27341 Clorox Co. JUL/82. N2OCX OCT/82
1052    C-GLXS 1982. N3330M Olan Mills Inc. SEP/82
```

LEARJET 35/35A

(Serial numbers 1-410)

```
001    N731GA GLC/The Garrett Corp. Ff 22/AUG/73. N351GL GLC Experimental JAN/75.
002    1974 N352GL GLC. N35SC Superior Continental Corp. 1975. C-GVVA Von Van Aviation MAR/76. Sulaero Ltd.
       1979.
003    1974 N731GA GLC/The Garrett Corp. N931BA GLC May/77. N263GL MAY/79. N370EC CMI Corp. MAY/80. R T
       Thompson SEP/81.
004    N74MP Mesa Petroleum NOV/74. N74MB 1978. N74MJ MJI NOV/78. C-GIRE Northgate Exploration Ltd. MAR/79.
       Central Trust Co. NOV/81.
005    EC-CLS Actividades Aereas Aragonensas 1974. TR-LXP Air Affaires, Gabon APR/77. return EC-CLS AUG/77.
       N175J Combs-Gates JUL/78. N178CP Coral Petroleum Co. DEC/78.
006    N356P Potlatch Corp. DEC/74.
007    D-CONI Contact Air/G Eheim MAR/75. N75DH Dee Howard FEB/81. N47JR Roberts Iterests SEP/82.
008    N673M Omaha Indemnity Co. FEB/75.
009    N44EL Management Services Inc. DEC/74. N14EL U.S. Epperson Underwriting Co. SEP/78. N275J
       Combs-Gates JAN/80. N263GL GLC OCT/80.
010    N888DH R Hubbard/Alpha Investments MAR/75.
011    N3816G GLC JUN/75. N400RB Rogers Badgett Mine Stripping Corp. AUG/75.
012    N711 W K Carpenter APR/75. N71LA Combs-Gates DEC/78. C-GVCB Business Flights Ltd. MAR/79.
013    N1DA Don Anderson Oil Corp. APR/75.
014    N71TP Tesoro Petroleum Corp. APR/75. N73TP APR/77. N72TB FEB/82.
015    N291BC Boise Cascade Corp. MAY/75. Ore-Ida Foods Inc. DEC/81. N57FF MAR/82.
016    1975 N136GL GLC. N5867 Bendix Corp. MAY/75. N9CN South Carolina State Development Board FEB/80.
017    N119GS Slab Fork Coal Co. MAY/75. Ramada Inns MAY/79. N551CC Combs-Gates MAY/80. Intercontinental
       Consolidated Petroleum JUL/80.
018    D-CORA Holstenflug MAY/75. F-GBMB Uni-Air DEC/78.
019    N959AT Peoples National Bank MAY/75.
020    XA-BUX Assessoria Empresas/Aerotaxis de Mexico 1975.
021    N101GP Interdec-Oceanic Air Inc. AUG/75. MJI MAY/77. Cvtd. 35A SEP/77. N91CH ICH Corp. SEP/78.
022    OY-BLG Grundfos A/S JUN/75.
```

023    N986WC Western Conference of Teamsters AUG/75. N886WC FEB/82.
024    N316 Oman Construction Co. Inc. JUL/75.
025    9K-ACT Alghanim & Sons JUL/75. Muburak Hassawi APR/76. Sid Nasser JUL/76. N40TF Omni's Trading Floor
       DEC/76. N135TX Texas International Co. JUN/77. N510LJ MAR/82.
026    D-CDHS Bomin & Bochumer Mineraloeges Mbh. AUG/75. D-CBRK German Red Cross AUG/77.
027    N31WS John Denver/Windstar Co. JUL/75.
028    1975 N135GL GLC. N20BG Bandag Inc. 1975. TigerAir Inc. AUG/79. XC-IPP Productores Pesquenos 1981.
029    N711AF Hydroplanes Inc/Transcontinental Log & Export Cop. JUL/75. Bahri Aviation Inc. Athens
       JAN/77. W/O Egypt JUL/79 aircraft never found.
030    N816M The Standard Oil Co. 1975.
031    N77FC Omni 1975. GLC SEP/75. N77U not confirmed. N77TE Temple Industries APR/76. American TV &
       Comms. Corp. FEB/80.
032    N711CH Carborundum Co. SEP/75.
033    N7KA Interedec/Sheikh Kamal Adham OCT/75. HZ-KA1 JAN/76. N2297B SABR Aeronautics SEP/78. Combs-Gates
       NOV/79. GLC FEB/80.
034    N37TA LPC Leasing Inc./Thunderbird Airways 1975. Norman Johnson NOV/80. J & N Associates JAN/82.
035    N711R E H Cockerell/ECEE Inc. OCT/75.
036    1975 N134GL GLC. N76GL Bi-Centennial colour-Scheme 1976. N76GP Gerber Products Co. APR/76.
037    1975 N1462B GLC. N100GL CSE Aviation Ltd. UK OCT/75. MJI APR/76. N58M Mutual of Omaha JUL/76.
038    1975 (VH-UDC). VH-ELJ Utah Development Corp. NOV/75. C-GBFP Business Flights Ltd. FEB/82.
039    N1HP Helmerich & Payne Inc. NOV/75.
040    C-GGYV Canada Learjet Ltd. DEC/75. Business Flights Ltd. AUG/77.
041    N202BT Big Three Industries Inc. DEC/75.
042    N221UE United Engineers & Constructors Inc. DEC/75.
043    C-GVCA Business Flights Ltd. MAR/76.
044    N38TA Helen Dow Whiting APR/76. N44MW 1977.
045    1976 N1461B GLC. HB-VEN Transair JAN/76. N35HB MJI FEB/76. N99786 1976. N999M Capitol Pipe & Steel
       APR/76. XA-HOS Aerotaxis de Mexico 1978. N45MJ MJI MAY/81. Texas Oilfield Supply NOV/81. N117CH
       117CH Partners JUN/82
046    VH-SLJ B S Stillwell & Co. FEB/76. Wards Express 1979.
047    XA-ALE Mexican customer ntu. N13MJ MJI 1976. N701AS AID Corp. AUG/76.
048    N233R Dart Industries Inc. MAY/76. (600th Learjet).
049    JY-AEV Arab Wings MAY/76. N3759C MAR/80. C-GBWL Brooker-Wheaton Avioation MAY/80.
050    CC-ECO Corporacion de Fomento, Chile. 1976.
051    SE-DEA Allamanna Svenska Electriska AB. MAR/76. Basair AB. SEP/80.
052    JY-AEW Arab Wings MAY/76. W/O Riyadh, Saudi Arabia 28/APR/77.
053    N1976L ARA Services/COAD Inc. FEB/76.
054    VR-BFX Olympic Maritime/Somers Navigation/Springfield Shipping, Athens APR/76.
055    D-CONO Contact Air/G Eheim AUG/76.
056    (JY-AEX) 1976. N106GL GLC MAY/76. N645G Gates Rubber Co. JUN/76.
057    N551MD Mike Davis Oil 1976. N57GL Combs-Gates AUG/77. Hobaugh Aviation Inc. NOV/77. C-GHOO Home Oil
       Co. Ltd. NOV/77. 058
058    C-GPUN Canada Learjet Ltd. APR/76.
059    N221Z Zurn Industries Inc. APR/76.
060    N64MP Mesa Petroleum Co. APR/76. N64MR APR/82.
061    N424DN Dana Corp. APR/76. N4246N JUL/76.
062    N217CS Charles Suhr 1976. U S Aircraft Sales 1978. ZS-LII/TL-ABD Engineering Design & Construction
       Co. APR/78. N701US U S Aircraft Sales APR/81. N310BA Somerset Distributors Inc. MAY/81.
063    N828M Ken Davis Industries International Inc. APR/76.
064    N290BC Boise Cascade Corp. MAY/76.
065    N425DN Dana Corp. MAY/76. N4358N JUL/76.
066    CC-ECP Corporacion de Fomento, Chile, 1976.
067    N118K Ford Motor Credit CO/Kaiser Industries SEP/76.
068    HB-VEM Swiss Air Rescue SEP/76.
069    1976 N103GL GLC. N591D Dixico Inc. OCT/76. Walston Airbusiness Inc. JUN/81. Sky Flite Inc. AUG/81.
070    D-CITA Holstenflug JUL/76. ACV-Allgemeine Computer Vermietungs GmbH. JUN/78.
071    JY-AFD Arab Wings JUL/76. F-WDCP Uni-Air AUG/80. F-GDCP AUG/80.
072    N2015M Monsanto Co. AUG/76.
073    1976 N108GL GLC. N163A AMF Inc. DEC/76.
074    N5000B Ashland Oil Co. DEC/76. N530J Omni/Combs-Gates AUG/80. N666JR Mercury Oil Co. OCT/80.
075    1976 N3503F GLC. HB-VEV 1976. JY-AFE Arab Wings DEC/76.
076    N959SA Aviation Equipment Leasing/International Teamsters 1976.
077    N814M Standard Oil Co. SEP/76.
078    N95BA Burlington Industries 1976. N95BH Omni MAR/77. N711SW Golden Nuggett Inc. MAY/77. N711SD
       SEP/78. N44OJB Blocker Energy Corp. FEB/79. N112EL GECC/Standard Brands JAN/80.
079    N6000J Ashland Oil Co. DEC/76. N660CJ WTCR Associates SEP/81.
080    1976 N109GL GLC. N23HB Hamilton Brothers Petroleum/Delaware Airjet Inc. 1976. N10AZ The Anschutz
       Corp. APR/79.

136

```
081    1976 N3523F GLC. JY-AFF Arab Wings DEC/76.
082    N235HR Hoffman La Roche Inc. NOV/76.
083    (N600CC) 1976. N400CC Luqa Inc/Charter Oil 1976. (N400MJ) MJI 1979. N45SL Sutherland Lumber Co.
       SEP/79. N500CD Lear Leasing Inc. APR/80. HDR Inc. OCT/80.
084    N111GL Gulf Life Insurance Co. NOV/76.
085    N15WH F & D Enterprises Inc. JAN/77.
086    N435M Motorola Inc. DEC/76.
087    N720GL Goodyear ntu 1976. Presidential Airways APR/77. Combs-Gates FEB/79. N835GA Parker Drilling
       SEP/79. Parker Aviation Inc. NOV/81.
088    1977 N3545F GLC. HB-VEW Jet Air Services AG. JAN/77.
089    1976 N3547F GLC. D-CCHB Bauhaus GmbH. DEC/76.
090    HB-VEY Ste. de Leasing Aerea SA/Sub Alpina, Milan. MAR/77. I-FIMI Soc. Finanziara Milanese/Air Fimi
       MAY/77.
091    VH-TLJ B S Stillwell & Co. MAR/77. Cold Storage Transport Co. SEP/77. C-GBLF Loram International
       Ltd. JAN/80.
092    N722GL Jet Sales & Management Corp. 1977. N424JR Randall Investments OCT/77. MJI 1978. Glovers Mills
       Co. 1978. C-GPFC Pocklington Financial Corp. JUL/81.
093    N804CC Chrysler Corp. JUN/77. (700th Learjet). C-GFRK Execaire Aviation Ltd. SEP/81.
094    N506C Celanese Corp. MAY/77.
095    N971H Harris Corp. APR/77.
096    N214LS Dynamic Development Corp. 1977. Hart & Associates FEB/79. Universal Health Care Inc. AUG/80.
       MJI APR/81. (N11JV) OCT/81. N87AT Asplundh Tree Expert Co. FEB/82.
097    N135J Dana Coprp. MAR/77.
098    N2OCR NCR Corp. MAY/77.
099    1977 N40146 GLC. HB-VFC Transair MAY/77. I-MCSA Maniglia Construzioni MAY/77. W/O Palermo, Sicily
       22/FEB/78.
100    N550E Taft Broadcasting Co. APR/77. N558E Consolidated Airways Inc. SEP/81.
101    1977 N40149 GLC. N109JR Ruan Cab Co. JUL/77.
102    1977 N1451B GLC. N232R Dart Industries Inc. MAY/77.
103    N96RE Reliance Electric Co. APR/77. N50MJ MJI MAY/80. Air Support Services MAR/81. PT-LCD Taxi Aereo
       Marilia JUN/81.
104    N87W El Paso Products Co. MAY/77.
105    (N720GH) Allstate Insurance Co. MAY/77. N102GH MAY/77. N102GP MAR/82.
106    N101BG Barnes Group Inc. JUN/77. NTW Inc. AUG/82.
107    N723GL Presidential Jet Corp. SEP/77. General Telephone Co. Southwest JUL/79.
108    D-COCO Holstenflug JUL/77. F-GCLE Ste. Regourd JUL/79. N86PC Combs-Gates to Pepsi Cola Bottling
       MAR/82.
109    N506GP Georgia Pacific Corp. SEP/77.
110    (N12EP) 1977. N4J Interstate Constructors Inc. JUN/77.
111    1977 N3815G GLC. (HB-VFE) Fraissinet 1977. (I-SIDU) Siderurgica Duina 1977. OE-GMA Alp-Air AUG/77.
       Air Charter Austria 1980. I-LIAD ALI-Aeroleasing Italiana 1981.
112    1977 N38i0G GLC. D-CCAY Gustav Schickendanz KG. JUL/77.
113    N763GL MJI SEP/77. Collier Cobb & Associates Inc. SEP/77. T-C Services Inc. NOV/77. N35CL SEP/82
114    1977 N3807G GLC. D-CONA Contact Air/G Eheim AUG/77.
115    T-21 Argentine AF photographic OCT/77.
116    I-MMAE Soc. Locatelli Estramed AUG/77.
117    N3155B Budd Leasing Corp. AUG/77.
118    1977 N39391 GLC. HB-VFK Transair OCT/77. John von Neumann 1977. Koci S.A. AUG/82.
119    HB-VFG Transair AUG/77. D-CHER Holstenflug NOV/77. N93MJ MJI MAR/80. OY-ASO Kali A/S SEP/82
120    N400JE Public Service Co. of NM. AUG/77.
121    N43EL Universal Underwriters Inc. AUG/77.
122    D-CCHS Bochumer Mineral GmbH. AUG/77. OE-GMP Air Charter Austria 1980.
123    1977 N3802G GLC. N900JE Jack Eckerd Corp. SEP/77.
124    N1500E Bucyrus Erie Co. SEP/77.
125    1977 N3803G GLC. N777MC Meredith Corp. SEP/77.
126    1977 N744GL GLC. N15EH Sinclair Marketing Inc. JAN/78.
127    N727GL Anheuser Busch Cos. Inc. 1977.
128    N231R Dart Industries Inc. OCT/77.
129    N22BX Bendix Corp. OCT/77. N229X SEP/78. XA-ZAP Aerotaxis de Mexico MAR/79.
130    N230R Dart Industries Inc. JAN/78.
131    1977 N3812G GLC. N26GB George Brown/Hibos Co. OCT/77.
132    N431M Motorola Inc. NOV/77.
133    1977 N728GL GLC. N35NB Braman Cadillac. AUG/78. Tulsa Aircraft Charter Corp. AUG/80.
134    1977 N1473B GLC. N88EP Great Western Management & Realtry Corp. OCT/77. El Paso National Bank
       MAR/79.
135    (OO-LFX) Abelag OCT/77. N22MJ MJI 1977. D-CDAX Blendax Werke JAN/78.
136    T-22 Argentine AF JAN/78.
137    1977 N3819G GLC. HB-VFL Transair JAN/78. EC-DEB Gestair SEP/78.
```

| | |
|---|---|
| 107 | N7∠3GL Presidential Jet Corp. SEP/77. General Telephone Co. Southwest JUL/79. |
| 108 | D-COCO Holstenflug JUL/77. F-GCLE Ste. Regourd JUL/79. N86PC Combs-Gates to Pepsi Cola Bottling MAR/82. |
| 109 | N506GP Georgia Pacific Corp. SEP/77. |
| 110 | (N12EP) 1977. N4J Interstate Constructors Inc. JUN/77. |
| 111 | 1977 N3815G GLC. (HB-VFE) Fraissinet 1977. (I-SIDU) Siderurgica Duina 1977. OE-GMA Alp-Air AUG/77. Air Charter Austria 1980. I-LIAD ALI-Aeroleasing Italiana 1981. |
| 112 | 1977 N3810G GLC. D-CCAY Gustav Schickendanz KG. JUL/77. |
| 113 | N763GL MJI SEP/77. Collier Cobb & Associates Inc. SEP/77. T-C Services Inc. NOV/77. N35CL SEP/82 |
| 114 | 1977 N3807G GLC. D-CONA Contact Air/G Eheim AUG/77. |
| 115 | T-21 Argentine AF photographic OCT/77. |
| 116 | I-MMAE Soc. Locatelli Estramed AUG/77. |
| 117 | N3155B Budd Leasing Corp. AUG/77. |
| 118 | 1977 N39391 GLC. HB-VFK Transair OCT/77. John von Neumann 1977. Koci S.A. AUG/82. |
| 119 | HB-VFG Transair AUG/77. D-CHER Holstenflug NOV/77. N93MJ MJI MAR/80. OY-ASO Kali A/S SEP/82 |
| 120 | N400JE Public Service Co. of NM. AUG/77. |
| 121 | N43EL Universal Underwriters Inc. AUG/77. |
| 122 | D-CCHS Bochumer Mineral GmbH. AUG/77. OE-GMP Air Charter Austria 1980. |
| 123 | 1977 N3802G GLC. N900JE Jack Eckerd Corp. SEP/77. |
| 124 | N1500E Bucyrus Erie Co. SEP/77. |
| 125 | 1977 N3803G GLC. N777MC Meredith Corp. SEP/77. |
| 126 | 1977 N744G GLC. N15EH Sinclair Marketing Inc. JAN/78. |
| 127 | N727GL Anheuser Busch Cos. Inc. 1977. |
| 128 | N231R Dart Industries Inc. OCT/77. |
| 129 | N22BX Bendix Corp. OCT/77. N229X SEP/78. XA-ZAP Aerotaxis de Mexico MAR/79. |
| 130 | N230R Dart Industries Inc. JAN/78. |
| 131 | 1977 N3812G GLC. N26GB George Brown/Hibos Co. OCT/77. |
| 132 | N431M Motorola Inc. NOV/77. |
| 133 | 1977 N728GL GLC. N35NB Braman Cadillac. AUG/78. Tulsa Aircraft Charter Corp. AUG/80. |
| 134 | 1977 N1473B GLC. N88EP Great Western Management & Realtry Corp. OCT/77. El Paso National Bank MAR/79. |
| 135 | (OO-LFX) Abelag OCT/77. N22MJ MJI 1977. D-CDAX Blendax Werke JAN/78. |
| 136 | T-22 Argentine AF JAN/78. |
| 137 | 1977 N3819G GLC. HB-VFL Transair JAN/78. EC-DEB Gestair SEP/78. |
| 138 | N7735A GTE Services Corp. OCT/77. N31FB Rumike Corp. SEP/79. NCRA Sales and Services Inc. NOV/81. N3RA SEP/82. |
| 139 | N15SC Sea Containers Associates DEC/77. |
| 140 | 1978 N742GL GLC. N888BL Bayliner Marine Corp. APR/78. N72TP Tesoro Petroleum NOV/79. |
| 141 | 1978. N743GL GLC. N66WM Waste Management Inc. MAR/78. |
| 142 | N81SA Amerock Corp. JAN/78. |
| 143 | N301SC Sabine Corp. FEB/78. Combs-Gates SEP/81. M P Appleby OCT/81. |
| 144 | 1978 N39398 GLC. D-CCAP Aerodienst/West Deutsche Landesbank FEB/78. N705US U S Aircraft Sales SEP/81. Marathon Air Inc. NOV/81. N35KC St. Lucie Skyways Inc. MAR/82. Marathon Air Inc. JUL/82. |
| 145 | 1978 N39394 GLC. HB-VFB Swiss Air Rescue FEB/78. |
| 146 | N55AS Albertsons Inc. FEB/78. |
| 147 | N717W John Hanson JAN/78. MJI FEB/78. HZ-KTC Al Khodair Trading & Contracting MAR/78. N499G Walston Airbusiness OCT/81. Fox Drilling & Rykoff NOV/81. N717W FEB/82. N55F Ford Motor Credit Co. SEP/82 |
| 148 | N103GH Allstate Insurance Co. AUG/78. N103GP MAR/82. |
| 149 | OO-KJG Abelag FEB/78. HB-VGN Total (Suisse) SA. JAN/80. N85351 Combs-Gates JAN/81. N273MC Meredith Corp. MAY/81. |
| 150 | N100EP Avion Inc. MAR/78. |
| 151 | 1978 N39399 GLC. N711L The Carborundum Co. MAR/78. |
| 152 | N101HB First Hawaiian Bank APR/78. |
| 153 | C-GZVV Perimeter Aviation Ltd. FEB/78. |
| 154 | N650NL National Life & Accident Insurance Co. MAR/78. |
| 155 | N760LP Penley Associates MAY/78. |
| 156 | N170L Dana Corp. APR/78. |
| 157 | 1978 N746GL GLC. YV-O1CP Dr. Albert Finol/Transporte Transilac SA. APR/78. |
| 158 | N835AC Allis Chalmers Corp. APR/78. |
| 159 | N93C Greyhound Leasing & Financial Corp. APR/78. |
| 160 | D-CCCA Maschinen Fabrik E Moellers GmbH. MAY/78. (800th Learjet). |
| 161 | 1978 N39415 GLC. YV-65CP C.A. de Edificaciones - Resid D Paulo 1978. |
| 162 | 1978 N751GL GLC. (HB-VFO) 1978. N711HH Hilton Hotels Corp. JUN/78. N1978L ARA Services/COAD Inc. JUL/79. |
| 163 | YV-173CP Terrenaca C.A. MAY/78. N27BL B L Jet Sales Inc. FEB/79. |
| 164 | 1978 N1473B GLC. N248HM Herman Miller Inc. JUN/78. |
| 165 | 1978 N40144 GLC. A40-CA Inspector General of Police, Oman. APR/78. |
| 166 | N831CJ GL Corp. JUN/78. Great Lakes Corp. SEP/82 |

| | |
|---|---|
| 167 | N725P Butler Manufacturing Co. JUN/78. |
| 168 | N22SF State Farm Mutual Auto Insurance Co. MAY/78. |
| 169 | N135ST Southeats Toyota Distributors JUN/78. |
| 170 | N100K Fred Shaulis MAY/78. |
| 171 | 1978 N747GL GLC. C-GNSA Nabors Drilling Ltd. NOV/78. N823J Combs-Gates JUN/81. Associated Inns & Restaurants Co. of America. MAR/82. |
| 172 | 1978 N748GL GLC. SE-DDG Swedair MAR/79. |
| 173 | 1978 N750GL GLC. MJI 1978. HZ-MIB Mohammed Imran Bamieh DEC/78. N750GL NCI Aviation Inc. FEB/79. (HZ-NCI) 1979. N100GU GECC/Grand Union FEB/80. N116EL GECC AUG/82. Flight International Inc. SEP/82 |
| 174 | TR-LYC Air Affaires/Business Flyers JUL/78. N65DH Dee Howard NOV/80. D-CAVI Avia Luftreederei GmbH. DEC/80. |
| 175 | D-CDWN Diehl Werke JUL/78. |
| 176 | N317MR MJI SEP/78. Blue River Alloys Inc/Corprojet MAR/79. Proform APR/80. XA-ACC Intervuelo S.A. SEP/82 |
| 177 | 1978 N1461B GLC. N77CP Pfizer Inc. JUL/78. |
| 178 | 1978 N40146 GLC. N22CP Pfizer Inc. JUN/78. |
| 179 | 1978 N39412 GLC. D-CCAR Aero Dienst 1978. D-CAPD P Dreidoppel JUL/78. N718SW Memphis Aero International Aircraft Sales MAY/81. Scotland Oil Co. Inc. AUG/82. |
| 180 | 1978 N3819G GLC. N222BE Chesapeake Leasing Co. SEP/78. N222BK JUL/82. |
| 181 | N35LJ McTan Corp. SEP/78. |
| 182 | 1978 N1450B GLC. N35HB Delaware Airjet Inc. AUG/78. N3HB NOV/78. |
| 183 | 1978 N3802G GLC. N720M Levelor Lorentzen Inc. AUG/78. N72JM DEC/81. |
| 184 | 1978 N1462B GLC. HB-VFO Transair S.A. AUG/78. Citticorp International Finance SA. FEB/82. |
| 185 | N99ME H C Price Co. 1978. Ryan Aviation/Magnum Land Corp. APR/79. N99VA Geo Jablah JUN/79. Abko Properties Inc. NOV/79. |
| 186 | N753GL GLC JUN/78. N590 Braman Aviation Inc/Prestige Jet JAN/79. N96DM J David Co. AUG/82. |
| 187 | N755GL GLC AUG/78. N32HM Southeastern Jet Corp. JAN/79. |
| 188 | VH-AJS B S Stillwell JUN/78. Australian Jet Charter 1979. |
| 189 | 1978 N3811G GLC. VH-AJV B S Stillwell 1978. Australian Jet Charter 1979. |
| 190 | N32BA Centurion Investment Co. SEP/78. |
| 191 | 1978 N3810G GLC. (YV-15CP) 1978. HB-VFX Latisair/Petrolair Systems S.A. OCT/78. |
| 192 | N4995A Circo Resorts Inc. 1978. N225CC SEP/78. N225QC SEP/80. N49PE Puma Engineering Co. JUN/81. |
| 193 | 1978 N1465B GLC. (YV-131CP) 1978. VH-SBJ Swan Brewery OCT/78. N620J Combs-Gates MAR/81. VH-SBJ Westkim Holdings Ltd. 1981. N2743T UCO Aviation Inc. JUN/82. |
| 194 | N91W Bamerilease Inc. NOV/78 |
| 195 | 1978 N1471B GLC. D-CONY G Eheim/Contact Air 1978 |
| 196 | HB-VFU Transair SA. OCT/78. EC-DFA Spantax SA. FEB/79. W/O Palma, Spain 13/AUG/80. |
| 197 | N754GL GLC 1978. Braman Aviation Inc. NOV/78. Armored Transport Inc. JUL/81. |
| 198 | N25FS Great Western Management & Realty Corp. OCT/78. |
| 199 | 1978 N40144 GLC. N9HM Holt Machinery Co. OCT/78. |
| 200 | 1978 N3818G GLC. D-CCAR Aero Dienst NOV/78. OO-LFY Abelag DEC/79. |
| 201 | 1978 N39415 GLC. N79MJ MJI SEP/78. N35RT Townsend Engineering Co. FEB/79. N35RF APR/81. Geo A Rolfes Co. DEC/81. |
| 202 | VH-MIQ Mount Isa Mines Ltd. DEC/78. N499G Walston Air Business MAR/82. |
| 203 | N744E Eaton Corp DEC/78. |
| 204 | 1978 N1466B GLC. D-COSY Holstenflug JAN/79. N87MJ MJI JAN/80. N99ME Moran Bros. Inc. MAR/80. Moran Energy AUG/82. |
| 205 | 1978 N39418 GLC. N80SM GLC Special Mission 1979. N59DM Flight International Inc. NOV/81. |
| 206 | N760GL GLC demo 1978. (N66HM) Southeastern Jet Corp FEB/79. HB-VGH EJA JUL/79. Air Leman Ecole les Ailes Heli-Ski SA. SEP/81. |
| 207 | 1978 N40146 GLC. N711 Wm. K Carpenter JAN/79. |
| 208 | 1978 N40149 GLC. N40TA Bandag Inc. JAN/79. |
| 209 | N399W Williams Research Corp. JAN/79. |
| 210 | N840GL Southeastern Jet Corp. JAN/79. (N35HM). |
| 211 | 1978 N1461B GLC. D-CATY Holstenflug 1978. N15MJ MJI 1980. N600LC Lincoln National Corp. JAN/80. |
| 212 | 1978 N3803G GLC. N180MC Hughes International Financial Corp. MAY/79. International Jet Inc. JAN/82. |
| 213 | N800RD Procurement & Contracts Office JUN/79. N935NA ? XC-CUZ Procurad General 1981. |
| 214 | N279DM Domar Jet Charter Inc. FEB/79. |
| 215 | VH-UPB Narich Pty Ltd. 1979. Stillwell Aviation/Publishing & Broadcasting Pty Ltd. 1981. N2951P Omni International Corp. APR/82. N80CD Baron Leasing AUG/82. |
| 216 | D-CATE Holstenflug MAY/79. N24MJ MJI 1980. N39MB Richard Black JAN/80. |
| 217 | N111RF R C Fisher MAR/79. |
| 218 | N256TW Tidewater Realty Inc. JUL/79. |
| 219 | 1979 N39416 GLC. VH-BJQ Barclay Jet Charter MAR/79. N502G Walston Airbusiness JAN/82. Barton & Barton Co. FEB/82. N350JF APR/82. |
| 220 | N79BH AWECO Inc. MAR/79. N333RB Reading & Bates Corp. NOV/80. |
| 221 | 1979 N845GL GLC. VH-WFE Wards Express NOV/79. |
| 222 | HB-VFZ EJA MAR/79. |

223     N215JW James Wilson Jr. APR/79.
224     N96AC Wabash Enterprises Inc. APR/79. Oxmill Inc. JAN/82.
225     N225MC JNO McCall Coal Co. MAY/79.
226     N1127M Miles Laboratories Inc. JUN/79.
227     N211BY Institute of Basic Youth Conflicts Inc. JUN/79. N25RF Combs-Gates SEP/80.
228     N101PG Geosurvey International Inc. MAY/79.
229     N8MA The ARO Corp. MAY/79.
230     N714K Gulf States Utilities/Beaumont Car Leasing Corp. JUN/79. BLC Corp. JAN/81.
231     (N10AB) DEC/78. (N712DM) MAR/79. N911DB Skybird Aviation Inc. JAN/80.
232     N8281 McDonnell-Douglas Corp. MAY/79. (900th Learjet).
233     N35SL Southland Life Insurance Co. JUN/79. Southland Corporate Services FEB/81.
234     N35WR Rollins Inc. MAY/79.
235     1979 N841GL GLC. N600CN The Coca Cola Bottling Co. of Miami. MAY/79.
236     G-ZOOM Falmer International Ltd. AUG/9. N8537B Lisle Aircraft Inc. JAN/81. N90LP Waukesha Pearce Industries Inc. APR/81.
237     1979 N843GL GLC. N78MN Morris Newspaper Corp. OCT/79.
238     1979 N844GL GLC. N80HK Food Development Corp. AUG/79. ZS-INS Aaron Searl JUN/80.
239     1979 N847GL GLC. (HB-VGC) 1979. VH-KTI Katies Pty Ltd. JUN/79.
240     N240B Budd Co/First Security Bank, SLC. JUL/79.
241     N42FE Fritz Egger JAN/80.
242     1979 N846GL GLC. VH-WFJ Wards Express 1979.
243     1979 N3812G GLC. HZ-ABM Sheikh Ali Bin Hussein Al Mussallam JUL/79.
244     1979 N1451B GLC. RP-57 Philippines National Oil Co. 1979.
245     N2WL Cardinal Associates AUG/79.
246     N50PH Regional Transportation Service SEP/79.
247     YV-265CP Paicosa Co. 1979.
248     1979 N3811G GLC. C-GBFA Business Flights Ltd. AUG/79.
249     N107JM HLM Enterprises AUG/79.
250     N3250 Vulcan Materials Co. AUG/79.
251     N27NB        Nolan Bushnell AUG/79.
252     N28CR GLC JUL/79. PT-KZR Lider Air Taxi 1979. Banco Bamerindus SA 1981.
253     1979 N40144 GLC. N211DH Hagadone Newspapers Service Co. AUG/79.
254     N666CC Corrao Construction Co. OCT/79.
255     N44EL US Epperson Underwriting Co. SEP/79.
256     N712L Eagle-Picher Industries Inc. NOV/79.
257     F-GCMS Air Pamys/Air Affaires International OCT/79.
258     (N1700) GLC MAY/79. N28BG Konfara Co. JUL/79.
259     1979 '139413 GLC. HB-VGC Fidinam SA OCT/79.
260     N40PK Porta Kamp Manufacturing Co. Inc. OCT/79.
261     N900RD GLC SEP/79. XA-ELU AVEMEX NOV/79.
262     N237GA Geo Argyros JAN/80.
263     D-CCAD Minitrans GmbH. OCT/79.
264     XA-ATA Minera Autlan SA de CV. NOV/79.
265     1979 N1462B GLC. G-ZEST CSE MAY/79. G-LEAR Northern Executive Aviation DEC/79.
266     1979 N39404 GLC. SE-DDI Joint Trawlers OCT/79. N922GL 35A-266 Ltd Partnership DEC/79. N35GC G C Services Corp. JUL/80.
267     1979 N39418 GLC. XA-LAN AVEMEX NOV/79.
268     1979 N10870 GLC. YV-286CP J V Persand & Co. NOV/79.
269     N881W L R French Jr. JAN/80.
270     1979 N10871 GLC. YV-O-MRI-1 Ministry of Interior Relations NOV/79.
271     1979 N1088A GLC. LV-OAS Ledesma NOV/79.
272     1979 N39398 GLC. N272HS Lanair inc. JUL/80.
273     N35FH GLC JAN/80. N103C Adolph Coors Co. MAY/80.
274     1979 N1087Y GLC. N274JS Bill Hodges Truck Co. Inc. JAN/80. N274JH APR/80.
275     1979 N10872 GLC. G-ZEAL Fairflight Charter/Jointair FEB/80.
276     N44LJ C W Culpepper JAN/80.
277     N925GL GLC FEB/80. N723LL Gary Levitz MAR/80. N7OCN Cole National Corp. JUN/81.
278     1979 N1476B GLC. HB-VGL Transair SA. JAN/80. ECT-028 Gestair JAN/80. EC-DJC APR/80.
279     N19LH Hillair Inc. MAR/80.
280     N80MJ MJI SEP/79. HP-912 Leybda CA. FEB/80. YN-BVO Aerotaxi Ejecutivo SA. APR/80.

## CITATION 550/551 UNIT NO/CONSTRUCTION NO.

550-686     N550CC Prototype. Ff 31/JAN/77.
001/550-0001     (N98751) 1977. (N551CC) 1978. N5050J Cessna Aircraft Co. JUL/80.
002/550-0002     N98753 1977. N552CC Cessna Hanover demo APR/78. N44GT General Telephone NW APR/78.
003/551-0004     (Was originally assigned 550-0003). N98784 1977. N553CJ APR/78. YV-19CP Dr. Alfonso Riverol 1978.

| | | |
|---|---|---|
| 004/550-0004 | N98786 1977. C-GPAW Pratt & Whitney Aircraft of Canada Ltd. DEC/77. | |
| 005/550-0005 | N98817 1977. OE-GKP Mercedes-Benz AG. APR/78. N77ND University of N. Dakota JUN/80. | |
| 006/550-0006 | N98820 1977. N2 FAA MAY/78. | |
| 007/550-0007 | N98830 1977. N300PB Permatex Co/Air Cab Inc. MAY/78. (N447FM) Fred McGilvray NOV/78. N650WC Towne Management Co. JUL/79. | |
| 008/550-0008 | N98840 1978. N575W Worthington Industries Inc. JUN/78. | |
| 009/550-0009 | N98853 1978. N744SW State Wide Sales Co. Inc. JUN/78. | |
| 010/550-0010 | N98858 1978. OE-GEP Dr. Polsterer JUN/78. N550PL Don Love DEC/79. N806C A E Staley Mfg. Co. FEB/80. | |
| 011/550-0021 | (Was originally assigned 551-0001 APR/78 then 550-0021 APR/78 then 551-0001 MAY/78 to 550-0021 AUG/80). N98871 1978. N296AB Algernon Blair Inc. JUN/78. SFO Commuter Group Inc. AUG/80. N171CB California Business Jets JUL/82. | |
| 012/550-0011 | (N98876) 1978. FAV 0002 Venezuelan Air Force 1978. | |
| 013/550-0012 | N3208M 1978. N513CC Cessna MAR/78. C-GHOL Husky Oil 1978. | |
| 014/551-0002 | (Was originally assigned 550-0013). N3210M 1978. YV-140CP SAECA 1978. | |
| 015/550-0014 | N3212M 1978. N702R Rea Wire Magnet Co. Inc. JUL/78. | |
| 016/551-0005 | (Was originally assigned 551-0002 then 550-0022). N3216M 1978. YV-151CP Dayco C.A. 1978. | |
| 017/550-0016 | N3221M 1978. N276AL Libbey Owens Ford Co. JUL/78. | |
| 018/551-0007 | (Was originally assigned 551-0003 then 550-0023). N3223M 1978. YV-169CP Pavimentadora Life C.A. 1978. | |
| 019/550-0018 | (N3225M) 1978. N752CC U.S. Customs Service 1978. | |
| 020/551-0006 | (Was originally assigned 550-0015). N3227A 1978. YV-O6CP Siderurgica del Orinoco 1978. | |
| 021/550-0017 | (Was originally assigned 550-0015). N3230M 1978. VH-MAY Southbank Aviation AUG/78. Australian Jet Charter 1980. | |
| 022/550-0019 | N3232M 1978. N1851X N.Y. Times Co. OCT/78. | |
| 023/550-0020 | N3236M 1978. PH-HES Heerema Engineering Service AUG/78. | |
| 024/551-0003 | (Was originally assigned 551-0004 then 550-0024). N3237M 1978. YV-205CP Fernando Zubillaga SEP/78. | |
| 025/550-0025 | N3239M 1978. (EP-KID). EP-KIC Kish Island Development SEP/78. N9014S Robey Smith 1978. Fuqua Industries Inc. NOV/78. N664JB MAY/79. N664J OCT/80. Bricmont & Bricmont NOV/81. | |
| 026/550-0026 | N3240M 1978. N256W Wendys International Inc. NOV/78. | |
| 027/550-0027 | N3245M 1978. N527CC Cessna SEP/78. G-BFRM Marshalls of Cambridge JAN/79. | |
| 028/550-0028 | (N3246M) 1978. (G-BFLY) Northair 1978. OE-GAU Aircraft Innsbruck 1978. Tyrollean Airways 1979. N501BL Don Love Aircraft Sales SEP/81. Professional Marketing APR/82. | |
| 029/550-0029 | (N3247M) 1978. G-JEEN Falmer Aircraft Ltd. JAN/79. N502AL Aviation Equipment Leasing Inc. AUG/79. N718VA Vac Air Alloys Corp. SEP/79. | |
| 030/550-0030 | (N3249M) 1978. G-DJBI DJB Engineering Ltd. AUG/78. G-FERY European Ferries JUL/80. | |
| 031/550-0031 | N3250M Flo Air/Heli Orient 1978. RP-C-580 Ayala Corp. 1978. | |
| 032/550-0032 | N3251M 1978. N810SC S. California Gas OCT/78. N810SG FEB/82. | |
| 033/550-0033 | (N3252M) 1978. TR-LYE Air Services Gabon OCT/78. N59MJ MJI JUN/82. | |
| 034/550-0034 | N3258M 1978. N771A ALCOA OCT/78. N697A DEC/78. National Aircraft Sales SEP/80. Unitech NOV/80. N60CC Carrier Corp. JAN/81. | |
| 035/551-0008 | (N3261M) 1978. N108WG International Association of the Age of Enlightenment JAN/79. HB-VGK OCT/80. | |
| 036/550-0036 | (N3262M) 1978. N58AN Air North JAN/79. N5Q Pioneer Corp. APR/79. | |
| 037/550-0037 | (Was originally assigned 550-0037 then 551-0013 DEC/78 to 550-0037 NOV/81) (N3268M) 1978. N37HG The Glimcher Co. DEC/78. John Koegel MAR/81. Two Jacks AUG/81. N361DJ Denver Jet Inc. NOV/81. | |
| 038/550-0038 | (N3271M) 1978. N526AC Amway Corp. DEC/78. | |
| 039/550-0039 | (N3273M) 1978. G-BJHH Armstrong Aviation Ltd. JAN/79. EI-BJL Helicopter Maintenance/Carrow More Ltd. JUL/80. | |
| 040/550-0040 | (N3274M) 1978. N220CC Coleman Co. DEC/78. | |
| 041/550-0024 | N3276M 1978. N533M Marathon Oil Co. FEB/79. | |
| 042/550-0035 | N3278M 1978. N8417B ARAMCO Saudi Arabia FEB/79. American Aircraft Exchange Inc. MAR/82. United Aviation Inc. SEP/82. | |
| 043/550-0041 | N3279M 1978. N8418B ARAMCO Saudi Arabia FEB/79. American Aircraft Exchange Inc. MAR/82. N341AG Anderson Greenwood & Co. AUG/82. | |
| 044/550-0042 | (N3283M) 1978. N666RC Roper Corp. FEB/79. | |
| 045/550-0045 | N3284M 1978. N4CH Pendleton Truck & Trailer Leasing FEB/79. N4CR MAY/80. 5N-AMR I Rabiu & Sons AUG/80. | |
| 046/550-0043 | N3285M 1978. N6Q Pioneer Corp. JAN/79. | |
| 047/550-0044 | N3286M 1978. N3526 O H Materials MAR/79. K B I Corp. JUN/81. | |
| 048/550-0048 | (Was originally assigned 551-0009) N3288M 1978. N534M Marathon Oil Co. FEB/79. | |
| 049/551-0010 | N3291M 1978. YV-137CP Ireol C.A. 1979. Charter Ejecutivo S.R.L. 1981. | |
| 050/550-0046 | (N3292M) 1978. C-GRHC Standard Developments MAR/79. | |
| 051/550-0049 | N3296M 1979. N1AP Arnold Palmer FEB/79. | |
| 052/550-0050 | (Was originally assigned 551-0011 to 550-0050 MAR/79). (N3298M) 1979. N102FC Comfortair Charter Co. Inc. MAR/79. Denver Jet Inc. JUL/78. N362DJ SEP/82 | |

```
053/550-0053   (N3300M) 1979. N4VF H D Lee Co. Inc. MAR/79.
054/550-C054   (N3301M) 1979. N501AA MAR/79. VH-WGJ Williams General Aviation Pty. Ltd. APR/79. Flightways
               Air Service AUG/82
055/550-0055   (N3308M) 1979. N55CC Cessna 1979. N2JZ International Transport & Earthmoving Equipment 1979.
               Atlantic Aviation AUG/79. (N1466K) Knoell Brothers Construction Inc. JAN/80. U.S. Dept of
               Energy JAN/81.
056/550-0047   N3313M 1979. (N66VM) 1979. Martin Aviation Inc. MAR/79. OB-M-1171 Southern Peru Copper Corp.
               MAY/79.
057/550-0075   (Was originally assigned 551-0009 to 550-0075 MAR/79). N3314M 1979. N55BH Gilbert Imported
               Hardwoods Inc. SEP/79.
058/551-0014   (Was originally 551-0012 then 550-0066 to 551-0014). N3319M 1979. N558CC Airflite South
               MAR/79. N558CB C B I Industries Inc. NOV/79.
059/551-0012   (Was originally assigned 550-0050 then 551-0012, to 550-0050 JAN/79 & back to 551-0012
               MAR/79). N1955E 1979. N551BC Boyne USA Inc. APR/79.
060/550-0051   N1958E 1979. C-GJAP Taggart Services Ltd. APR/79. C-GBCB Province of British Columbia JUN/80.
061/551-0009   (Was originally assigned 550-0067 to 551-0009 MAR/79). N1959E 1979. D-IMTM Mini Transport
               GmbH. MAY/79 Heinrich Then FEB/81.
062/551-0017   (Was originally assigned 550-0068 to 551-0017 APR/79). N2052A 1979. N1UH Martin Aviation Sales
               APR/79. Aviation Equipment Leasing Inc. JUN/79.
063/550-0069   N2069A 1979. F-GBPL Euralair APR/79. 3A-MWA Air Mediteranee MAY/79. HZ-AAA Sheikh Zaid Sudairi
               JUN/79. HZ-ALJ Abdul Latis Jameer Establishment 1980.
064/550-0070   N2072A 1979. N564CC Aviation Equipment Leasing Inc. 1980.
065/550-0065   N4191G 1979. N55SX Standex International Corp. MAY/79.
066/550-0071   N4308G 1979. G-GDPD Dome Petroleum Ltd. MAY/79.
067/550-0052   (Was originally 550-0052 to 550-0072 JAN/79 back to 550-0052 MAR/79). N4620G 1979. (00-LFX)
               Abelag Aviation MAY/79. OY-ASV Alkair MAY/79. N9OMJ MJI AUG/79. Lear Leasing Inc. SEP/79.
               N534MW Myrna Zaragoza JUN/80.
068/550-0073   N4621G 1979. F-GBTL Euralair MAY/79.
069/550-0074   N4754G 1979. N48ND N48ND Corp. MAY/79.
070/550-0056   N5342J 1979. N752RT Repulic of Texas JUN/79.
071/550-0058   N5348J 1979. N71CJ (P T Brahim Bros. Jakarta) MAY/79. N100HB Heileman Brewing Co. Inc. JUL/79.
072/550-0072   (Was originally assigned 550-0052). (N2661H) 1979. N360N Ottaway Newspapers Inc. JUN/79.
073/550-0057   (N2661N) 1979. VH-WNZ Rex Aviation MAY/79. United Jet Charter Western Australia JUN/79.
               Skywest Airlines 1981.
074/551-0016   (Was originally assigned 550-0059 to 551-0016 MAR/79). (N2661P) 1979. (D-ICWB) 1979. (N71RL)
               1979. N22RJ JUN/79. HB-VGE Crossair AG. JUL/79. N28968 Lisle Aircraft Inc. MAR/82.
075/550-0060   N26610 1979. (N55OKR) MAY/79. N75KR King Ranch Inc. JUN/79.
076/551-0015   (Was originally assigned 550-0059 to 551-0016 MAR/79). (N26613) 1979. YV-213CP Fundo
               Agropecuario el Retiro 1979.
077/550-0061   (N26614) 1979. N456N Nordstrom Inc. JUL/79.
078/550-0062   (N26615) 1979. (N77SF) Seneca Foods 1979. C-GDLR Woodward Stores (BC) Ltd. JUN/79.
079/550-0063   (N26616) 1979. C-GHYD B.C. Hydro & Power JUN/79.
080/550-0064   N26617 1979. YV-36CP Servicios Tecnicos Maracaibo C.A. 1979.
081/550-0066   N26619 1979. (N3031) 1979. N3032 Republic Steel Corp. AUG/79.
082/550-0077   (N2662A) 1979. N582CC Cessna JUN/79. N578W Worthington Industries DEC/79.
083/550-0078   (N2662B) 1979. N31KW Kenneth Walker AUG/79.
084/550-0059   (N2662F) 1979. N10LR Rinco Aviation Inc. JUL/79.
085/550-0090   (Was originally allocated 551-0018 to 550-0090 JUN/79). N2662Z 1979. N4110S Samedan Oil Co.
               AUG/79.
086/551-0019   (N26621) 1979. N551MC Marie Callender Pie Shops Inc. AUG/79.
087/550-0079   (N26622) 1979. N930BS Bethlehem Steel Corp. OCT/79.
088/550-0089   (Was originally assigned 551-0020 to 550-0089 JUN/79). (N26623) 1979. N88MJ MJI AUG/79.
089/550-0080   (N26624) 1979. G-BFLY Northair Ltd. JUL/79. HB-VGR Private Jet Services JAN/80.
090/550-0081   N26626 1979. I-FBCT Soc. Fabocart S.P.A. AUG/79.
091/550-0082   N26627 1979. G-BMCL Micro Consultants Ltd. AUG/79. Yewlands Executive Transport SEP/82.
092/551-0024   (Was originally assigned 550-0083 to 551-0024 JUL/79). N26628 1979. N2CA Coin Acceptors Inc.
               SEP/79.
093/550-0084   N26629 1979. N222LB L B Smith Inc. SEP/79. N808DM Diamond M Co. DEC/80.
094/550-0067   N2663B 1979. N81TC Trane Co. SEP/79.
095/551-0018   (Was originally assigned 550-0085 to 551-0018 JUN/79). N2663F 1979. N455DM Acme Air Corp.
               SEP/79. (N666AJ) SEP/79.
096/550-0086   N2663G 1979. N414GC John Duncan SEP/79.
097/550-0087   N2663J 1979. (C-FCFP) 1979. C-GTBR Canadian Forest Products Ltd. SEP/79.
098/550-0088   N2663N 1979. G-JRCi IDS Aircraft Ltd. SEP/79.
099/550-0076   (N2663X) 1979. LN-HOT Helikopter Service A/S OCT/79.
100/550-0085   (N2663Y) 1979. OY-GKC Lego Systems OCT/79.
101/550-0094   (N26630) 1979. G-JETA IDS Aircraft Ltd. OCT/79.
102/550-0095   N26631 1979. N400DT Bedford Aviation Inc. OCT/79.
```

103/550-0096    N26632 1979. N550EW N American Investments OCT/79. Thomas Richards MAY/80. N30UC Utah
International Inc. JUL/82.
104/550-0097    N26634 1979. N404G P H Glatfelter Co. DEC/79.
105/550-0098    (N26635) 1979. N17S Sperry Corp. NOV/79.
106/551-0020    N26638 1979. YV-147CP Inversiones Menil S.A. 1979.
107/551-0021    N26639 1979. N107BB Beall Brothers Inc. DEC/79.
108/550-0093    N2664F 1979. (N108CT) AUG/79. N95CC Cessna SEP/79. N210MJ Southwest Petrolease Inc. JAN/80.
Mercantile National Bank Dallas. FEB/82.
109/550-0099    N2664L 1979. N109JC John Cassidy Jr. DEC/79.
110/550-0100    N2664T 1979. (N801L) Martin Aviation Inc. NOV/79. N801G Burt Sugarman FEB/80.
111/550-0101    (N2664U) 1979. N91MJ MJI/SW Bell Telephone NOV/79.
112/550-0102    N2664Y 1979. VH-WNP Skywest Jet Charter NOV/79. Skywest Airlines 1981.
113/551-0022    N26640 1979. N313BT Circle B Omni Inc. DEC/79.
114/550-0092    (N26643) 1979. N89B Midland Ross Corp. JAN/80.
115/551-0026    (Was originally allocated 550-0103 to 551-0026 AUG/79). (N26648) 1979. N551R Ralph Rogers &
Co. Inc. DEC/79.
116/550-0105    N26649 1979. N116CC Cessna 1979. D-CNCP Nixdorf Computer AG. MAR/80.
117/550-0106    N2665A 1979. AE-129 Argentine Army DEC/79.
118/550-0107    N2665D 1979. N550CB 1979. N225AD Alexander Dawson Inc. JAN/80.
119/550-0108    (N2665F) 1979. N4TL Amory Garment Co. JAN/80.
120/550-0109    N2665N 1979. N753CC US Customs Service JAN/80.
121/550-0091    (N2665S) 1979. N527AC Amway Corp. FEB/80.
122/550-0110    (N2665Y) 1979. N222SG Sheller-Globe Corp. FEB/80.
123/550-0111    N26652 1979. N3R Weyerhauser FEB/80.
124/550-0112    (N26656) 1979. (C-GDPE) 1980. C-GDPF Dome Petroleum Ltd. JAN/80.
125/550-0113    N2666A 1979. N227PC Petrolite Corp. FEB/80.
126/550-0114    N2745G 1979. (N89B) 1979. N55HF James Hudson DEC/79.
127/550-0115    N2745L 1979. N127SC Sundstrand Corp. MAR/80.
128/550-0116    N2745M 1979. HZ-AAA Arabian International Services Co. FEB/80.
129/550-0117    N2745R 1979. N575FM Fed Mart Corp. FEB/80. N150HR Hussman Refrigerator Co. AUG/81.
130/550-0162    (Was originally assigned 550-0162 DEC/79 to 551-0023 APR/80 but delivered as 550-0162). N2745T
1980. VH-UOH Rex Aviation MAY/80. Hazelton Air Service Pty Ltd. MAY/80. N550KP GFI Air Inc.
DEC/80.
131/550-0118    N2745X 1980. LV-PHH Cygnus S.A. AUG/80. N131ET California Business Jets Inc. MAR/81. Blue Sky
Aviation DEC/81.
132/550-0119    N27457 1980. N80BS Briggs & Stratton Corp. APR/80.
133/551-0025    (Was originally assigned 550-0120) N2746B 1980. YV-299CP Fabrica Nacional de Ascensores
APR/80.
134/550-0121    N2746C 1980. N655PC Martin Aircraft Sales 1980. Prince Corp. MAY/80.
135/550-0122    N2746E 1980. N135CC Cessna 1980. Marin Aviation Inc. SEP/80. National Community Bank of NJ.
JUN/81. N70GM Kidde Inc. FEB/82.
136/550-0123    N2746F 1980. (CC-CGX) Linea Aerea Linahua JUN/80. N36CJ Cessna 1980. N81TF Belmont
International Inc. SEP/81. SE-DEV Kungsair/Blidberg & Metcalfe Shipping AB. NOV/81.
137/550-0124    N2746U 1980. LN-VIP Helikopter Service A/S MAR/80.
138/550-0125    N2746Z 1980. N5500F S M Flickinger Co. Inc. MAY/80.
139/550-0126    (N2747R) 1980. OE-GHP Automobilvertriebs mbH. MAR/80. N26863 California Business Jets JAN/82.
RER Equipment Co. FEB/82. N82RP JUL/82.
140/550-0103    N2747U 1980. XA-JEZ Aerotaxi Villa Rica SA. MAR/80.
141/550-0160    (Was originally assigned 551-0027) N26178 Upali USA Inc. APR/80. (9V-PUW). A W Alloys Inc.
AUG/82.
142/550-0184    (Was originally assigned 550-0083 then 551-0029 to 550-0184). N2619M 1980. N80DR David
Richardson MAY/80.
143/550-0127    N2631N 1980. N29TC Teledyne Continental Motors JUL/80.
144/550-0128    N2631V 1980. N536M Marathon Oil Co. MAY/80.
145/550-0129    N2632Y 1980. N537M Marathon Oil Co. MAY/80.
146/550-0104    N2633N 1980. CC-ECN Aeroservicios Ltda. 1980.
147/550-0132    N2633Y 1980. G-CJHH Armstrong Aviation Ltd. APR/80. N13627 Westwind II Inc. OCT/81. N500VB
MAY/82.
148/550-0133    N2634Y 1980. G-BHBH Rio Tinto Zinc Services Ltd. APR/80. C-GRIO Air Niagara (1978) Ltd.
MAR/82.
149/550-0134    N2635D 1980. HZ-AAI Arabian International Services 1980. HZ-ZTC JUL/82.
150/551-0029    (Was originally assigned 550-0135). N26369 1980. N168CB California Business Jets MAY/80.
N551PL William Duflock JUL/80.
151/550-0136    (D-CACS) Interdean International not imported 1980. N8520J Interjet Inc. DEC/80. Ray
Industries JUN/82.
152/550-0137    N2638A 1980. N56GT General Telephone Co. of NW. JUL/80.
153/550-0138    N2646X 1980. XC-SCT Secretariat of Communications & Transport 1980.

| | |
|---|---|
| 154/550-0139 | N2646Y 1980. ZS-KOO Natal Ammonium JUN/80. |
| 155/550-0140 | N2646Z 1980. N55WL Lane Air Inc. JUN/80. |
| 156/550-0141 | N26461 1980. VH-ING Inghams Enterprises Pty Ltd. JUN/80. |
| 157/550-0142 | N2648Z Cessna 1980. PT-LCR Taxi Aereo Marilia MAY/82. |
| 158/550-0143 | N2649D 1980. N1OOVV Edwin Cox Jr. AUG/80. |
| 159/550-0144 | N2649E 1980. Asian Aviation Services Inc. JUL/80. |
| 160/550-0145 | N2653R 1980. Asian Aviation Services Inc. AUG/80. Silicon Valley Express Inc. AUG/82. |
| 161/550-0146 | N26610 1980. N580AV Atwood Vacuum Machine Co. AUG/80. |
| 162/551-0036 | (Was originally assigned 550-0147 then 551-0032 then 550-0185 to 551-0036). N2661P 1980. N162CC Cessna JUN/80. Expeditor Systems Inc. AUG/80. N160D Old Dominion Freight Line Inc. DEC/80. |
| 163/550-0148 | N 1980. N222AG Groenevelt Enterprises Inc. AUG/80. |
| 164/550-0149 | N 1980. N116K Kaiser Aluminium & Chemical Co. AUG/80. |
| 165/550-0150 | N2668A 1980. N1SV Cochran Vierson Drilling Co. AUG/80. |
| 166/550-0279 | (Was originally assigned 551-0028 to 550-0279 APR/81). (N88838) 1980. N566CC Airflite Inc. South JUL/80. Oscar Wyatt Jr. APR/81. |
| 167/550-0152 | N88840 1980. (N1O7). RP-C-581 Manila Electric JUL/80. |
| 168/550-0153 | (N88842) 1980. N27BA Burlington Industries Inc. AUG/80. N278A JAN/82. |
| 169/550-0130 | (N88845) 1980. N77RC Rudd Enterprises AUG/80. |
| 170/551-0049 | (Was originally assigned 550-0157 to 550-0219 to 551-0049). (N88848) 1980. N170CC Cessna 1980. N155PT P J Taggares Co. FEB/81. |
| 171/550-0154 | (N8777N) 1980. G-DJBE DJB Engineering Co. AUG/80. |
| 172/551-0032 | (Was originally allocated 550-0159). (N98715) 1980. YV-300CP Aero Charter Aviation C.A. 1980. |
| 173/551-0030 | (N98718) 1980. N551AB Algernon Blair Inc. AUG/80. |
| 174/551-0031 | (Was originally assigned 550-0160). (N98749) 1980. N6565C 1980. YV-301CP Inversiones Finalven C.A. 1980. |
| 175/550-0155 | N6566C 1980. (YV-209CP). YV-298CP Servicios Tecnicos Maracaibo C.A. 1980. |
| 176/550-0156 | N98784 1980. N6567C 1980. (N31F) AUG/80. N205SG South Central Bell Telephone Co. NOV/80. N205SC AUG/81. |
| 177/550-0131 | N 1980. N177CJ Max Pasley Inc. SEP/80. |
| 178/550-0175 | N 1980. N1OJK Lee Bangerter DEC/80. |
| 179/550-0165 | (Was originally assigned 551-0040). N98871 1980. 3D-ACQ Diamcor Ltd. 1980. |
| 180/550-0166 | N88731 1980. PH-MBX Martinair AUG/80. |
| 181/550-0161 | N88732 1980. N999AU Intl. Trade & Investments 1980. XA-KIQ Aerogisa SA. 1981. |
| 182/550-0167 | N88737 1980. N1OOCJ Cameron Iron Works Inc. NOV/80. |
| 183/550-0158 | N88738 1980. (N662AA). N423D Pittsburgh & Shawmut Coal Co. OCT/80. |
| 184/550-0168 | N88740 1980. (VH-ICT) Intercity Airlines SEP/80. VH-TNP Transwest Air Charter JUL/81. Skywest Airlines 1982. |
| 186/550-0169 | (N88743) 1980. N185CC Cessna demo 1980. N6001L Producers Gas Co. NOV/81. |
| 187/550-0172 | N88795 1980. (N28MM). N72MM Downey Savings Loan Association OCT/80. N88JJ Agri Empire Corp. JUN/81. |
| 188/550-0171 | (N88797) 1980. (C-GDPE). N43D Dome Petroleum Corp. OCT/80. |
| 189/550-0234 | (Was originally assigned 551-0027). N88798 1980. N511WC Westcor Aviation Inc. NOV/80. |
| 190/550-0163 | N8881' 1980. N1O7T Trunkline Gas Co. NOV/O. |
| 191/550-0173 | N88822 1980. (N36NW). MFS Associates NOV/80. N286G Larry Mohr MAR/81. |
| 192/550-0179 | N88824 1980. N6OMM Minster Machine Co. FEB/81. |
| 193/550-0180 | N88825 1980. N320V Orbit Valve Co. NOV/80. |
| 194/550-0181 | N88826 1980. RP-C- Tagum Agricultural Development NOV/80. |
| 195/550-0182 | N88830 1980. (F-BKFB). F-GCSZ Groupement International de Commerce NOV/80. |
| 196/550-0233 | (Was originally assigned 550-0185 to 550-0195 to 551-0043 to 550-0233 to 551-0050 MAY/81). N98403 1980. N1823B Duane Stranahan NOV/81. |
| 197/550-0186 | N98418 1980. N80AW Supron Energy Corp. DEC/80. |
| 198/550-0187 | N98432 1980. N303X Panhandle Eastern Pipeline Co. DEC/80. |
| 199/550-0218 | (Was originally assigned 551-0023 to 550-0194 to 550-0218) N98436 1980. N45EP Eugene Perri JAN/81. |
| 200/550-0177 | N98468 1980. (N2OOMR). N55OLP Lanier Business Products Inc. NOV/81. |
| 201/550-0174 | (N98510) 1980. N201CC Cessna 1980. N666WW T G I Fridays Inc. MAR/81. |
| 202/550-0151 | (N98528) 1980. N35HC Hoffman Contractors Inc. DEC/80. |
| 203/550-0176 | N98563 1980. N552TF Tyson Foods JAN/81. |
| 204/551-0023 | N98599 1980. N155TA Torrey Jet Aviation Inc. DEC/80. |
| 205/550-0189 | N98601 1980. MJI DEC/80. D-CAAT P Dreidoppel/Consilia GmbH. SEP/81. HB-VGP Private Jet Services AG. MAY/82. |
| 206/550-0183 | N98630 1980. (XC-DUF). HB-VGS Private Jet Services DEC/80. |
| 207/550-0188 | N98675 1980. VH-SWL Sea World/Surfer's Paradise DEC/80. |
| 208/550-0147 | N98682 1980. (N155JK). N80GM Kidde Inc. JAN/81. |
| 209/550-0190 | N98715 1980. F-PTEL Euralair International DEC/80. |
| 210/550-0083 | N98718 1980. N54CC Cherne Contracting Corp. DEC/80. |
| 211/550-0164 | N 1980. N164CC Cessna 1980. N7YP State of Alabama Transportation Dept. MAY/81. |

| | |
|---|---|
| 212/551-0033 | N88692 1980. D-IJHM J Hurler Flugdienst KG. DEC/80. W/O Kassel 19/MAY/82. |
| 213/550-0191 | N88707 1980. C-GWCR Weldwood Canada Ltd. JAN/81. |
| 214/550-0192 | N88716 1980. N44ZP Wm Rubin JAN/81. |
| 215/550-0249 | (Was originally assigned 550-0195 to 551-0034 to 550-0249). N88718 1980. N829JM James Moore JAN/81. |
| 216/550-0159 | (N88721) 1980. N45ZP International Air Co. JAN/81. |
| 217/550-0194 | N88723 1980. N91B Scott & Fetzer Co. JAN/81. |
| 218/550-0205 | (N88727) 1980. N3OJD Deere & Co. JAN/81. |
| 219/550-0196 | N6798Y 1980. N68DS TPA Inc. MAY/81. |
| 220/550-0197 | N6798Z 1980. (N3OF). N44FC Fleming Companies Inc. MAR/81. |
| 221/550-0198 | (N67980) 1980. XC-DOK Pemex 1981. |
| 222/550-0199 | N67983 1980. N586RE Royce Beall MAR/81. |
| 223/550-0260 | (Was originally assigned 551-0034). N67986 1980. N32JJ ADM Leasco Inc. MAR/81. |
| 224/550-0178 | N67988 1980. N224CC SEP/80. L C Metals JUL/81. |
| 225/550-0200 | N67989 1980. (G-BHVA) 1980. N34SS Sun Refining & Marketing Co. JAN/81. |
| 226/550-0206 | N6799C 1980. XC-DUF PEMEX 1981. |
| 227/550-0201 | N6799E 1980. N334AM Amica Mutual Insurance Co. FEB/81. |
| 228/550-0185 | N6799L 1980. N815GK Mitchell Aero Inc. MAR/81. N600EZ E-Z Service Inc. JUL/82. |
| 229/550-0157 | N6799T 1980. N550K Bendix Corp. MAY/81. N101BX JUL/81. |
| 230/550-0202 | N6799Y 1980. Reeves Bros. MAY/81. N590RB SEP/81. |
| 231/550-0203 | N67990 1981. N12JA J A Jones Construction APR/81. |
| 232/550-0209 | N67997 1981. Citation Holding Group. MAR/81. N121C Charles Muench NOV/81. |
| 233/550-0238 | (Was originally assigned 551-0035) N67999 1981. N97S Sun Oil Co. MAR/81. |
| 234/550-0207 | N6800C 1981. (N95CC) 1981. N163CB California Business Jets JAN/81. N60BB Fourway Aviation Co. Inc. MAR/81. |
| 235/550-0135 | N6800J 1981. VH-KDI Southern Pacific Petroleum AUG/81. |
| 236/550-0214 | N6800S 1981. N13BJ Houston Hydrolance International Inc. MAR/81. N44WF JUN/81. |
| 237/550-0222 | N6800Z 1981. N17RG Ryan Group Insurance Co. MAR/81. |
| 238/550-0215 | N68003 1981. N500WP Woods Petroleum Corp. APR/81. |
| 239/550-0204 | (N6801H) 1981. N820 Jones Mfg/Jack Prewitt MAR/81. N200JR Pearson American Drilling Inc. APR/81. |
| 240/550-0216 | N6801L 1981. N240AR ARCO MAR/81. |
| 241/550-0208 | N6801P 1981. N54RC Weatherford Services Inc. APR/81. N222WL JUN/81. |
| 242/550-0223 | N6801Q 1981. N900BA Omni International MAY/81. Rubbermaid Inc. JUN/81. |
| 243/550-0284 | (Was originally assigned 550-0217 then 551-0041) N6801R 1981. I-ARIB Soc. Aer-Marche MAR/81. |
| 244/550-0211 | N6801T 1981. XA-LOT Aeropyc S.A. APR/81. |
| 245/550-0212 | (N6801V) 1981. N245CC Hughes Aircraft Co. SEP/81. |
| 246/551-0038 | N6801Z 1981. D-IBPF Pfleuger Flug. APR/81. |
| 247/550-0210 | N68018 1981. N762PF QHL Aviation Leasing Assoc. APR/81. (N177CM) APR/81. Walston Airbusiness * Inc. JAN/82. N3PC Paccar Inc. AUG/82. |
| 248/550-0220 | N6802S 1981. N95CC 1981. Coleman Co. Inc. AUG/81. N275CC MAR/82. |
| 249/550-0193 | N6802T 1981. (N47RP) 1981. XC-FOO Governor of State of Quintana Roo 1981. |
| 250/550-0213 | N6802X 1981. N420P AVCO Corp. MAY/81. |
| 251/550-0224 | N6802Y 1981. YV-O-MTC Ministry of Communications APR/81. YV-O-MTC-20 AUG/81. |
| 252/550-0258 | (Was originally assigned 550-0228 then 551-0052 back to 550-0228 SEP/82) N6802Z 1981. Great Planes Sales/Excalibur Oil Co. JAN/81. |
| 253/550-0221 | N68026 1981. N253W Wolverine World Wide Inc. JUN/81. |
| 254/550-0227 | N68027 1981. N254CC Graham Leasing Corp. OCT/81. N71CG reserved NOV/81. |
| 255/550-0229 | N6803E 1981. Omni International MAY/81. Lanair Inc. AUG/81. |
| 256/550-0239 | N6803L 1981. 8P-BAR Barclays Bank International 1981. |
| 257/550-0235 | (N6803T) 1981. N67SG Gary Energy Corp. JUN/81. |
| 258/550-0225 | (N6803Y) 1981. (N34SS) 1981. N258CC Earl Slick NOV/81. |
| 259/550-0195 | N68032 1981. N6OJD Deere & Co. JUN/81. |
| 260/550-0236 | N68033 1981. N611ER Greyhound Leasing MAY/81. Cyclops Corp. JUN/81. |
| 261/550-0248 | (Was originally assigned 551-0045) N6804C 1981. Geo P Reintjes Co. Inc. AUG/81. |
| 262/550-0226 | N6804F 1981. N29WS Wilson Industries Inc. MAY/81. |
| 263/550-0217 | N6804L 1981. N88DD Transportation Corp. of America JUN/81. |
| 264/550-0237 | N6804M 1981. 3D-ACT Peak Timber Sales (Pty) Ltd. 1981. |
| 265/550-0230 | (N6804N) 1981. G-OTKI |
| 266/550-0240 | N6804S 1981. Todco Inc. Portland Or. AUG/81. N550RL reserved AUG/81. |
| 267/551-0046 | N6804Y 1981. C-GDDC Pal Air Ltd. MAY/81. |
| 268/550-0241 | N6804Z 1981. N1OFN First National Bank of St. Louis JUL/81. |
| 269/551-0047 | N6805T 1981. N58GG Business Real Estate Corp. JUN/81. |
| 270/550-0250 | N68599 1981. N9LR Jetstream Corp. JUL/81. |
| 271/550-0231 | N6860A 1981. N28RF MAR/81. (N221BW) N671B International Bonded Warehouses Inc. SEP/81. IBW Transportation inc. AUG/82. |
| 272/550-0244 | N6860C 1981. N98GC Grant Corps. MAY/81. |
| 273/550-0243 | N6860L 1981. TI-APZ Air Finance Ltd. 1981. VR-BHG 1981. N1333Z James Haldan MAR/82. |

```
274/551-0048    N6860R 1981. N37BM Husky Aviation Co. SEP/81.
275/550-0254    N6860S 1981. N171CB California Business Jets MAY/81. XA-TEL Alquiladora de Casas. JUN/81.
276/550-0247    N6860T 1981. (N18DD). N928DS Diamond Shamrock Corp. OCT/81.
277/551-0035    N6860U 1981. Airflite Inc. South 1981. N277HM John Myers APR/82.
278/551-0039    N6860Y 1981. ECT-023 Spanish del. reg. OCT/81. EC-DOH Terrain Iberica S.A. NOV/81.
279/550-0245    N68607 1981. Andrew mathieson JUL/81.
280/550-0257    N68609 1981.
281/550-0303    (Was originally allocated 551-0044) N6861D 1981. (N281AM). N160VE Valero Management Co. *
                AUG/81.
282/550-0246    N6861E 1981. N72TC Timken Co. JUN/81. N78TC FEB/82.
283/550-0255    N6861L 1981. I-DEAF Soc. Ital-Avio SPRL JUN/81.
284/550-0232    N6861P 1981. N929DS The Harbor Land Co. AUG/81.
285/550-0258    N6861S 1981. N172CB California Business Jets JUL/81. Nevada National Leasing Co. JUL/82.
286/550-0256    N6861X 1981. N3300L Linclay Corp. JUL/81.
287/550-0251    N68615 1981. Asian Aviation Services Inc. OCT/81.
288/550-0261    N68616 1981. Great Planes Sales Inc. SEP/81. N40GS Geo Search Corp. APR/82.
289/550-0259    N68617 1981. VH-KDP Aviation Centre Charter AUG/81.
290/550-0262    N6862C 1981. G-DJHH Armstrong Aviation Ltd. JUN/81. Humber Kitchens Ltd. MAY/82.
291/551-0054    (Was originally assigned 550-0263) N6862D 1981. N12GK Omni Inc. SEP/81.
292/550-0264    N6862L 1981. N550KC Carland Inc. SEP/81.
293/550-0265    N6862Q 1981. McCrae Oil Corp. OCT/81.
294/550-0252    N6862R 1981. N507GP Georgia Pacific Co. SEP/81.
295/550-0253    N68621 1981. N23ND Noble Drilling Corp. AUG/81.
296/550-0266    N68622 1981. N296CC Cessna 1981. N296PH Pizza Hut Inc. JUL/82.
297/550-0267    N68624 1981. Lanair Inc. NOV/81.
298/550-0268    N68625 1981. N298CJ Cessna 1981. Don Bluth FEB/82.
299/550-0289    (Was originally assigned 551-0052). N68629 1981. D-CBAT Peter Dreidoppel AUG/81.
300/550-0270    N6863B 1981. OE-GLS Tyrolean Airways JUL/81.
301/551-0051    N6863C 1981. D-ICTA Wiking Helikopters Service GmbH. AUG/81.
302/550-0269    N6863G 1981. MGF Oil Corp. FEB/82. N74MG AUG/82.
303/550-0271    N6863J 1981. (N303EC). N555EW Employers Insurance of Wausau SEP/81.
304/550-0290    (Was originally assigned 551-0053). N6863L 1981. Traders International Corp. AUG/81.
305/550-0285    N6863T 1981. N20CN Consolidated Gas Supply Corp. SEP/81.
306/550-0286    N68631 1981. N306SC Sundstrand Corp. OCT/81.
307/550-0272    N68633 1981. 9M-WAN Hornbill Skyways SEP/81.
308/550-0273    N68637 1981. N217FS Federal Signal Corp. JUL/82.
309/550-0277    No864B 1981. N44LF Fritz Enterprises Inc. SEP/81.
310/550-0274    N6864C 1981. ZS-LDK AECI Ltd. JUN/82.
311/550-0278    N6864L 1981. (N990Y). (N819Y). Fleetwing Aviation Inc. OCT/81.
312/551-0056    (Was originally assigned 550-0275). N6864X 1981. (N312CC) Kilauea Aviation Inc. OCT/81.
313/550-0280    N6864Y 1981. Emerald Holding Co. AUG/82.
314/550-0281    N6864Z 1981. N31RK First National Bank of Midland OCT/81.
315/550-0282    N6864 1981. G-JETC IDS Aircraft Ltd. SEP/81.
316/550-0283    N       1981. N316CC Cessna 1981. N316H Burlington Industries Inc. DEC/81.
317/550-0287    N68648 1981. N444MM AAR Co. 1981. N65LC Liebert Corp. JAN/82.
318/550-0276    N68649 1981. C-GGFW B. C. Hydro & Power SEP/81.
319/550-0288    N6865C 1981. G-JETB IDS Aircraft Ltd. SEP/81.
320/550-0291    N6887T 1981. ZP-PNB Nicolas Santiago Bo. SEP/81.
321/550-0292    N6887X 1981. N114EL GECC DEC/81.
322/550-0293    N6887Y 1981. Overnight Transportation Co. MAR/82.
323/550-0294    N68872 1981. PH-HET Heerema Engineering OCT/81.
324/550-0298    N68873 1981. N74KV KVI Aviation Inc. NOV/81.
325/550-0295    N68876 1981. N483G GECC/Avtex Fibers DEC/81.
326/550-0296    N6888C 1981. G-BJIR Royco Homes OCT/81.
327/550-0304    N6888D 1981. N208TC Crown Aviation Leasing Co. FEB/82.
328/550-0299    N6888L 1981. N538M Marathon Oil Co. DEC/81.
329/550-0302    N6888T 1981. N329CC Cessna 1981. N441T Continental Protection Systems JUN/82.
330/550-0306    N6888X 1981. N303EC Household International FEB/82.
331/551-0065    (Was originally assigned 550-0309) N6888Z 1981. Antlers Natural Gas Enterprises Inc. JAN/82.
332/550-0300    N68881 1981. YV-162CP Aeroservicios Alas Ca. 1982.
333/550-0310    N68887 1981. N130TC Winters National Leasing Corp/CTC Corp. DEC/81.
334/550-0397    (Was originally assigned 550-0307 then 551-0059, to 550-0397 APR/82). N68888 R E Cotten
                APR/82.
335/550-0312    N6889E 1981. N58H Harkins & Co. JAN/82.
336/550-0313    N6889K 1981. N393RC Ransburg Corp. DEC/81.
337/550-0311    N6889L 1981. N43TC Town & Country Food Markets DEC/81.
338/551-0064    (Was originally 550-0314). N6889T 1981. VH-BRX (Australia) Pty Ltd. JAN/82.
339/550-0318    N6889Y 1981. Britt Aviation JAN/82. N642BB reserved MAY/82.
```

```
340/550-0315    N6889Z 1981. N9OJD John Deere & Co. JAN/82.
341/550-0308    N68891 1981. 3D-AVH ATAIR, RSA. DEC/81.
342/551-0053    (N6890C) 1981. N66MS Modern Supply Co. JAN/82.
343/550-0320    (N6890D) 1981. N343CC Cessna 1982. Glenn Martin AUG/82.
344/550-0322    (N6890E) 1981. N7FD Federal Data Corp. FEB/82. Amdahl Corp. JUL/82.
345/550-0319    N6890G 1981. N8BX Travenol Aircraft Inc. JAN/82.
346/550-0316    N5428G 1981. Boettcher & Co. JAN/82.
347/550-0321    N5430G 1981. Intertec Data System Inc. MAY/82.
348/550-0317    N5451G 1981. Western Equipment Co. Inc. JUN/82.
349/550-0327    N5474G 1981. N74JA J S Abercrombie Mineral Co. Inc. FEB/82.
350/551/0055    (Was originally assigned 550-0275) N5492G 1981. N350CC Cessna 1981. N888EB Johnson Bates *
                Drilling JAN/82.
351/550-0323    (N5703C) 1981. OE-GCP Automobilvertriebs AG. FEB/82.
352/550-0324    N5873C 1981. N171LE L Enright MD. FEB/82.
353/551-0359    (Was originally assigned 550-0325). N67983 1981. Scribner Equipment Co. Inc. FEB/82. N551SE
                reserved MAR/82.
354/550-0328    N67988 1981. G-BJIL RTZ Services Ltd. JAN/82.
355/551-0361    (Was originally assigned 550-0330). N6799C 1981. LV-PNB Cittibank NA. 1982.
356/550-0275    N6799L 1981. N55OJR James Redman FEB/82.
357/550-0301    N6799T 1982. 091 Govt. of Chinese Peoples Republic MAY/82.
358/550-0333    N67990 1982. Yellow Express Service 1982. PT-LCW Itamarati SA/Taxi Aereo Marilia APR/82.
359/550-0305    N67999 1982. 090 Govt. of Chinese Peoples Republic MAY/82.
360/550-0329    N6800C 1982. N491N Indium Aviation Inc. MAR/82. (1000th Citation delivery).
361/550-0334    N6800S 1982. Summitville Tiles Inc. MAR/82.
362/550-0297    N68003 1982. 092 Govt. of Chinese Peoples Republic MAY/82.
363/550-0331    N      1982. N696A GECC Albany International FEB/82.
364/551-0066    (Was originally assigned 550-0338). N6825X 1982. N242WT W T Burton Industries Inc. MAR/82.
365/550-0335    N6829Y 1982. Boatman's National Bank of STL. APR/82. N1847B SEP/82.
366/551-0057    N6830X 1982. Baker's Aviation Inc. MAY/82. N7OOLB SEP/82.
367/550-0336    N6830Z 1982. N9OZ International Paper Co. MAR/82.
368/550-0337    N6802S 1982. N727C KJL Ltd Inc/Consumers Power MAR/82.
369/550-0326    N6802T 1982. N12FC Federal Intermediate Credit bank MAY/82.
370/550-0339    N6802Y 1982. Ryan International Airways Co. MAR/82. VH-
371/551-0058    (Was criginally assigned 550-0297). N68027 1982. N101RL Robert Lammerts MAY/82.
372/550-0332    (N6803L) 1982. N372CC Cessna 1982.
373/550/0341    N68032 1982. C-GJAP Air Niagara (1978) Ltd. JUN/82.
374/550-0340    N6804F 1982. N374FC The Falk Corp. MAY/82.
375/550-0342    N6804L 1982. G-BJVP Jet Save FEB/82. Caixos Ltd. MAR/82. Fairflight Ltd. MAY/82.
376/550-0345    N6804Y 1982. N312DC GTE Directories Corp. JUL/82.
377/551-0060    N6805T 1982. N46SD Bob Smith Dozer Services Inc. MAR/82.
378/550-0344    N6806X 1982. N532M Marathon Oil Co. APR/82.
379/550-0357    (Was originally 550-0343). N6808C 1982. N632SC Stauffer chemical Co. MAY/82.
380/550-0347    N6826U 1982. ZS-LEE APR/82.
381/550-0348    N      1982. N381CC Cessna 1982. I-VIKI Soc. Italiana Const. Elettriche MAY/82.
382/550-0346    N      1982. N55OCF Corden Oil & Chemical Co. MAY/82.
383/550-0349    N      1982. N8FD Federal Data Corp. JUN/82.
384/550-0350    N      1982. N86SG Papercraft Inc. AUG/82.
385/550-0405    (Was originally assigned 550-0356 then 551-0063 and to 550-0405) N    1982. YV-276CP *
                Consolid-Air SA. 1982.
386/550-0351    N      1982. N99KW Florida Wings Inc. /82.
387/551-0388    (Was originally assigned 551-0061 then 550-0361). N    1982. N711WM Barbary Coast Hotel and
                Casino MAY/82.
388/550-0354    N      1982. N121CG Columbia Gas System Service Co. JUL/82.
389/550-0358    N6801Q 1982. Burmese Air Force AUG/82.
390/550-0356    N6801Z 1982. KBI Corp. JUL/82.
391/550-0343    (N1214D) 1982. G-MINE Mining Supplies Ltd. MAR/82.
392/551-0393    (Was originally assigned 550-0360) N1214H 1982. (N18CC) Sklar & Phillips /82.
393/550-0352    (N1214J) 1982. (N14ODV). N14OV Sterling Aircraft Sales co. JUL/82.
394/550-0363
395/550-0314    N      1982. N395CC Cessna 1982.
396/550-0362    N12142 1982.
397/550-0353    N      1982. G-GAIL Heron Aviation Ltd. MAY/82.
398/551-0062    N      1982. N398CC Cessna 1982. Davis Mud & Chemical Inc. AUG/82.
399/550-0366    N1215G 1982.
400/550-0359    (N67983) 1982. N55OWR Wire Rope Corp. AUG/82.
```

*a tradition in flying . . .*

*"for people who are going places"*

AVIATION CONSULTANTS
AIRCRAFT MANAGEMENT
JET CHARTER
EXECUTIVE TRANSPORT
HELICOPTERS – PROPS

(305) 689-3444

Palm Beach International Airport
P.O. Box 15012
West Palm Beach, FL 33406

# DO YOU NEED TO KNOW *NOW?*

If your business is buying or selling new or used turboprop or jet aircraft, wouldn't you like to receive timely information on daily transactions?

- *BILLS OF SALE*
  - *LEASE AGREEMENTS*
    - *CHATTEL MORTGAGES*
      - *SECURITY AGREEMENTS*
        - *CERTIFICATES OF REPOSSESSION*

This information is monitored and mailed daily to our subscribers. For further information, please mail your business card to Vicki Grissom.

*aviation* *Research*

POST OFFICE BOX 881 ● BETHANY, OK 73008 ● (405) 721-1566

# WORLD TURBO

Same format as Biz-Jet covering executive turboprops Kingairs, Mu 2's, Cheyennes, etc.

Available from:-
"Executive Aircraft Historians"
7, Arkley Court,
Holyport,
Berks,
SL6 2YR

Price: £3.85 UK,
£4.50/$7.50 Overseas

*Executive Aircraft Historians*

## JET AIRCRAFT SALES
### WORLD WIDE

Contact
GENE KINSELLA

P.O. BOX 548
PALM BEACH, FLORIDA 33480
PHONE 305/655-8259   TELEX 803446

# THANK YOU FOR BUYING BIZ-JET 1983

**Are you aware of our other Publications?**

**WORLD AIRLINE FLEETS 1983 NOW PUBLISHED** (592 Pages)
Giving you all the Worlds Airline Companies, Con. Numbers and Reg. Numbers.

**AIRLINE PRODUCTION LIST 1983** (To be published Jan 1983)
A complete list of all Turbo prop Airlines from Beech 99 to Boeing 747's with individual dates.

**AIRLINE DATA NEWS MONTHLY**
A complete listing of Airline news with colour photographs from the Airline World.
All published by Aviation Data Centre Ltd.
Unit 4 Browells Lane, Feltham Middlesex. England.
Tel:01-890 8933
Shop open Mon-Fri 8 am.-8 pm. Callers Welcome
(Send for details of all our other books)
We accept Visa, American Express, Access, Eurocard, Mastercharge.

**P.S. Remember our books are for the Industry and the Enthusiast.**

---

*Altissima Petimus*

## EXECUTIVE JET SALES LIMITED

**WORLD WIDE SUPPLIERS OF EXECUTIVE JET AIRCRAFT**

Lion House, 70 High Street, Newport Pagnell, Buckinghamshire, MK16 8AQ   Telephone: (0908) 612301/61436   Telex: 826800 JETAIR G

# INTRODUCING THE ONLY
# AVIATION MICROFICHE LIBRARY
# BY INSURED AIRCRAFT TITLE SERVICE
## A NEW PRODUCT
## A NEW DIRECTION    A NEW COMMITMENT

With each advancement in the availability of aviation data, an Insured Aircraft Title Service product has been there to meet the need. Today the latest Insured Aircraft Title Service product to follow in this tradition of quality, performance, dependability, and price is the new Aviation Microfiche Library. In fact, we are so convinced and pleased with our product we are offering a money back guarantee if you are not completely satisfied.

Here are the highlights of our library:

I. Our Manufacturer, Model, Serial Number Directory is **pure alphabetical.** The amateur and home-builts are alphabetical by model under "H" for homebuilt. With our system it's as easy as A B C!

II. In addition to listing all manufacturers alphabetically, we have listed all aircraft that have been manufactured by different companies under their most **commonly known manufacturer.** Over 500 references have been inserted to help you locate particular models of aircraft easier. For example:

- Aero Commanders 500, 520, 560 - See Rockwell 500, 520, 560
- Aero Commander 1121 Commodore Jet - See Israel 1121 Commodore
- Butler Aerostar 600, 601 - See Piper Aerostar 600, 601
- Hawker Siddley DH, HS 125 - See Brittish HS 125
- Hansa Jet HFB 320 - See MBB 320 Hansa Jet
- Grumman G159 GI - See Gulfstream G159 GI
- North American NA265 Saberliner - See Rockwell Saber NA265
- Sud Aviation except Falcon Jet - See Aerospat
- Smith 600, 601, 620 Aerostar - See Piper 600, 601, 620 Aerostar

III. We provide a Type, Make Model, Zip Code Directory. This arranges all aircraft by Type:

1. Turbine Fixed Wing
2. Reciprocating Fixed Wing
3. Rotocraft
4. Gliders
5. Blimps, balloons & dirigibles
6. Unknown

The aircraft are then listed alphabetically by manufacturer, by model, and in zip code sequence within the model. References have also been inserted in this directory.

IV. We provide a **Monthly Activity Report** in which we compare the past months file to the current months file. Any activity affecting an aircraft will be indicated on this report. It is alphabetical by manufacturer and by model within the manufacturer.

A "*" indicates something has changed concerning that particular aircraft - either a change of ownership, an address change, an N-Number change, etc. The first line indicates how the information appeared on the previous months files and directly underneath it is how the new information appears. If it has been a change of ownership the first line shows the previous owner and directly underneath it is the new owners information. On an address or N-Number change the second line will only indicate the N-Number or the new address. Therefore, making it easy to differentiate an address or N-Number change from a complete change in ownership.

A new aircraft added to the file is indicated by a "+" and an aircraft taken off of the file will be indicated by a "-". This report is essential in keeping track of who's buying and selling aircraft as well as what particular models of aircraft are moving. Also, to update your own system on address and N-Number changes.

V. We have **decoded** all 7 digit codes on all of the directories. Plus we have added the model names as well as the model numbers.

VI. All of our directories contain the same information and are arranged in the same format. The following information is provided:

- Registration Number
- Year of the aircraft
- Make, model and model name
- Serial Number
- Aircraft Type
- Engine Type
- Number of Engines
- Engine code
- Owners name, address, city, state and zip
- Registration Date

The new Aviation Microfiche Library is the wave of the future, for the needs of today. Not only does it deliver the **highest standards** of quality and performance achievable by any aviation microfiche on the market, it delivers these standards with true economy.

So please call our **Toll Free Number 800-654-4882** or write to the address below. We'll show you that the simplest way to manage the registry is to subscribe to the Aviation Microfiche Library. There's no need to have 20 years of aviation experience in order to use it to its fullest!

 Insured Aircraft Title Service Inc.

Will Rogers World Airport
P.O. BOX 19527 • OKLAHOMA CITY, OKLA 73144
**CALL TOLL FREE 800/654-4882 or 405/681-6663**

# We'll take more care of YOUR Heathrow operation, too!

Whatever kind of executive aircraft you operate, YOU could use the expertise of the British Airways Executive Aircraft Service – which includes, naturally, the resources of the largest international airline in the world – at London's major and most accessible airport.

We offer:

* A staff of specialists familiar with any kind of operation
* VIP passenger service second to none
* Hotel reservations and car hire   * Aircraft catering
* Fuelling company liaison   * Flight clearance
* Flight operations   * Ground power   * Toilet service
* Interior and exterior cleaning   * De-icing
* Licensed engineering for HS125 and BAC 1-11
* Flight clearance and Ground handling overseas
* Business aircraft charter

For more details:
Telephone 01-750 7862/7434 Telex 934703
Sita LHRPEBA Aftn EGLLBAPE Coy freq. 123.65

## British airways

### EXECUTIVE AIRCRAFT SERVICE
At LHR, nobody can take more care of you!